PRENTICE-HALL ECONOMICS SERIES
E. A. J. JOHNSON, *editor*

Other Books by the Authors

The Origins and Development of the American Economy. Also Serbo-Croation translation

By E. A. J. JOHNSON:

American Economic Thought in the Seventeenth Century

Pioneers of American Economic Thought by Ernest Teilhac, translation by Johnson

Some Origins of the Modern Economic World

Predecessors of Adam Smith: The Growth of British Economic Thought

An Economic History of Modern England

The Integration of Europe: Problems and Prospects, editor

By HERMAN KROOSS:

Financial History of the United States, with Paul Studenski

American Economic Development

Twenty-Five Years of Security Credit Control, with Jules I. Bogen

The Federal Reserve System, with others, edited by H. V. Prochnow

New York—America's Front Office

Current printing (last digit):
13 12 11 10 9 8 7 6 5 4

LIBRARY OF CONGRESS CATALOG CARD NO.: 60–5132

PRINTED IN THE UNITED STATES OF AMERICA
02507–C

THE
AMERICAN ECONOMY

Its Origins,
Development,
and
Transformation

An Introduction to Economics
by

E. A. J. Johnson

School of Advanced
International Studies
The Johns Hopkins University

Herman E. Kroos

Graduate Schoo
Business Administra
New York Univ

Prentice-Hall, Inc.

Preface

The cordial and enthusiastic reception of the first edition of this book, entitled *The Origins and Development of the American Economy*, has strengthened our conviction that a short, clear, historical introduction is an indispensable part of the introductory course in economics. In this new edition, which bears a modified title, we have made organizational changes and a great many textual changes to adapt our book better to this important pedagogical task.

Organizationally, we have thought it useful to divide the chapters into major divisions dealing respectively with the European origins of our basic economic institutions, the transplantation and adaptation of these institutions in the new-world environment, and the growth of further-modified or new economic institutions in 19th- and 20th-century America. It should not be overlooked, however, that, as a consequence of this historical development, a progressive transformation of the whole American economy occurred, changing both the structure and the functioning of our economic system. We have tried to indicate the nature of this transforming process not only within the several major sectors but, more particularly, in a fourth part, where we have briefly described how the operation of the whole economy has changed, during times of peace and war, and is being further changed under the impact of better technology, more intelligent planning, wiser management, better labor relations, and sounder and more imaginative methods of governmental intervention. We have not carried this over-all appraisal of the contemporary American economy very far, however, because we believe that until students have familiarized themselves with the elements of economic theory (which presumably will be supplied by some other text used in conjunction with this historical book) they cannot begin to appreciate the complex problems that are involved in explaining the aggregative economic performance of a huge, dynamic economy such as that of present-day America.

We have not merely "revised" this book; we have re-written so much of it that it is virtually a new book. Only the first five chapters, which have stood the test of criticism for years, remain essentially unaltered, but even these chapters have been so meticulously scrutinized for minor errors that not a page remains unchanged; moreover, Chapter 1 has been considerably enlarged. Chapter 6, on the Colonial Period, is new, as is almost all of Chapter 7. In other chapters, the amount of new writing ranges from 25 to 50 per cent. Moreover, wholly new emphasis is provided by building the argument around modern concepts of "economic development" and "transformation."

We have tried to wrestle honestly with the awkward methodological problem that most writers on the history of our economy have either misunderstood or consciously evaded. American economic development cannot be understood unless one recognizes that a complex multi-linear historical process has provided the basic elements of our present economy. Institutional borrowings were not confined to the Colonial Period; they bulk very large in the early Nationalist Period and continue intermittently throughout the latter half of the 19th century and during the 20th century. But whereas they came in blocks in the 17th century and again in the early factory age, they became progressively more selective as the American economy itself became more dynamic and innovative.

As contrasted with an over-simplified neo-Marxist determinist methodology, unwittingly adopted by so many uncritical writers, we have tried to show the complex influence of a multi-linear process. We have tried to evaluate the effect of changes in science and technology, progress in management and finance, and altered attitudes toward the role of government. We have repeatedly emphasized the influence of geography, the changing resource base, and the circumstantially variable combinations of the factors of production. Nor have we neglected the influence of ideas; indeed, throughout the entire treatment we have shown the constant interaction between institutions and economic thinking, whether it was reflected in a theory of just price in the medieval world, in the postulates of classical political economy in the 18th century, in humanitarianism or agrarian attitudes in the 19th century, or in institutionalism in the 20th century. We have tried to indicate those instances where economic ideas represented intellectual trail-blazing as contrasted with the more frequent situations where they merely mirrored, in the intellectual realm, the existing contemporaneous institutions.

It must be recognized that if one attempts to explain economic development in terms of multi-linear shaping and molding forces, one can adopt neither a simple chronological exposition (dealing with the whole economy in convenient time-period chunks) nor the equally unsatisfactory topical-strand description. What really happens is that growth and development proceed from one tentative synthesis of elements to another. Hence one must attempt to do several different things in order to present a realistic account of the complex process of development. One must, from time to time, show the major forces and influences that bring into existence a temporary historical synthesis (as we have done for the Colonial Period, for example). Next, one must try to explain the factors—political, economic, intellectual, or sociological—that tend to alter and modify an existing over-all configuration. These changes are, of course, more precisely traceable within sectors of the economy (for example in agriculture or industry) or within functional areas (for example, in management, technology, or governmental activities). Consequently, the whole story cannot be understood without some back-tracking; thus, the synthesis described in Chapter 7 cannot be fully appreciated until the appropriate earlier sections of the chapters that make up Part Three have been read. In short, the multilinear approach imposes certain responsibilities on the reader and even more duties on the teacher. For whereas, across the whole economy, some degree of synthesis is achieved from time to time, concurrently within the sectors and within the functional areas, such a tentative synthesis is constantly being modified and altered, setting in motion transforming effects upon the whole economy.

We have had to be content with describing only a few of such major syntheses: one in England as of about 1700, one in America during the Colonial Period; another in the early Nationalist Period, and finally the present-day synthesis described in Chapter 15. For the rest, our task has been to trace the multi-linear processes within separate chains of events, and to show how random changes were creating imbalances, thereby destroying an old synthesis or creating a new one. It must be recognized, however, that forward-moving trends were often retarded by countervailing influences of an obstructive and arresting nature, and that economic ideas for the most part were laggard rather than anticipatory. Yet, despite obstacles, the process of transformation was a progressive and cumulative one. It was never architectonically complete, for the simple reason that dynamic forces were constantly transforming sectors of the economy, and the interplay of these changes within sectors, or functional areas, in turn, made any tentative over-all synthesis essentially transitional to a further transformation of the whole economy.

We want to take this occasion to thank the many college teachers throughout the United States and Canada who have offered helpful suggestions and constructive criticism. We cannot particularize these debts, however, because we specifically asked our publisher not to divulge to us the names of our critics. We did this in order to solicit rigorous and frank criticism, preferring to leave the critics anonymous lest we might unwittingly appraise proffered criticism in terms of the age, the college connection, or the personality of the commentator. Nor did we wish to have our critics temper their views from a fear that we might resent blunt remarks or unfavorable comments. We recommend this technique to other writers. For a textbook, if it is to be worth using, must fulfill a genuine pedagogical function, and must, therefore, be adapted to the needs of a wide range of institutions and many teachers. This does not mean that a book should be "written down" to the requirements of the marginal teacher or the marginal student; and prospective users of this book will be able to satisfy themselves within a few moments that we have not indulged in this tawdry business. If anything, we have pitched the level higher in this new edition because we believe quite sincerely that the whole apparatus of teaching needs to set progressively higher bench marks of student performances. Yet in our small niches of the educational world, none of us is wise enough to know just what is needed in a general textbook which must find its sphere of usefulness in hundreds of college and university courses. Our anonymous critics have helped us immeasurably to attune this book to national needs, and we most gratefully acknowledge our indebtedness to all our many professional colleagues who have helped us to plan this new edition.

Much more than before, this is a collaborative work, for although Johnson has written the first seven chapters and Krooss the remaining eight, so much editorial emendation has occurred from one draft to another that the entire book is permeated with shared ideas and joint contributions. Differences still remain, as they should, since complete agreement would scarcely be in the economists' tradition. What we hope we have attained, however, is a fair degree of unity despite diversity.

E. A. J. JOHNSON
HERMAN E. KROOSS

Contents

I   HOW OUR BASIC ECONOMIC INSTITUTIONS ORIGINATED IN EUROPE

1   Introductory explanations and concepts **3**

The Importance of Studying American Economic Development, 3   Scope and Method, 5   Human Wants, 8   The Tyranny of Scarce Means, 8   Ways of Increasing Want-Satisfying Means, 9   The Role of Markets, 11   Influence of Political and Cultural Forces, 11   Saving and Investment, 12   Economic Progress, Growth and Development, 14   Economic Transformation, 16   Need for Understanding Historical Roots, 18

2   The late-medieval background **20**

General Pattern of Economic Life, 20   The Agricultural Village Community, 20   Obligations of Tenants, 23   Manorial Administration, 25   "Ancient Customs" of the Agricultural Community, 25   Relative Freedom of the Towns, 28   The Town as a Production Unit, 29   Protective Purposes of Town Regulations, 30   Social Justice in the Market Place, 32   The Function of Fairs, 34   Development of Export Industries, 35

3   The emergence of capitalism **38**

The Process of Change—Some General Contrasts, 38   Rural Economic Life About 1700, 40   Large Farms and Small, 41   New Farming Practices, 42   Widening

*Markets for Farm Produce, 43   The Rural Wage
Earner, 44   Governmental Policy and Regulations, 45
Changes in Industry and Trade, 47   Changes in
Wants, Purchases and Markets, 48   New Types of
Business Organization, 49   The Rise of the Livery
Companies, 50   Formation of Regulated Companies,
51   Origins of the Joint-Stock Company, 54   Early
Uses of the Joint-Stock Company, 55   The Individual
Proprietorship, 57   Organization of the Putting-Out
System, 59   Life and Labor under the Putting-Out
System, 60   The Spirit of "Capitalism," 61   Sources of
Capital, 62   Commercial Credit, 63   Beginnings of
Commercial Banking, 63   Use of Bank Checks and
Banknotes, 64   Establishment of the Bank of England,
66   Four Basic Institutions that Would Influence the
Future, 66*

4 The beginning of scientific technology 68

*The Dynamism of the British Economy, 68   Recipro-
cal Influences of Technology and Trade, 69   Changed
Attitudes toward Enclosures, 70   Effect of Enclosure
on the Small Landholder, 71   Effect of Enclosure
upon Agricultural Practices, 73   Pioneers of Scientific
Agriculture, 73   Farming Becomes Fashionable, 75
Commercial Preparation for the Industrial Revolution,
76   How Protection for the Wool Industry Unintentionally Built up a Domestic Cotton Industry, 77   The
Synthetic Nature of Invention, 78   Basic Inventions
in the Textile Industry, 79   Arkwrights's Example
Leads to the Adoption of the Factory System, 82   Factories and a New Industrial Discipline, 85   Importance of Iron and Steel in Industry, 86   New Techniques in Ferrous Metallurgy, 87   Application of
Scientific Criteria to Technology, 90   Boulton and
Watt Extend the Use of Steam Power, 91   Impact of
Science on Business Enterprise, 92   Growing Pressures
for Business Freedom, 93*

5 The formulation of capitalist
theory 95

*Deeds and Thoughts, 95 Central Ideas of Medieval
Economic Theory, 96 Mercantilism, the Economic
Ideas of Nationalism, 97 Adam Smith's Wealth of
Nations, 99 Smith's Glorification of Competition, 101
Smith's Recommendations on Economic Policy, 102
Contrast between Appearances and Actuality, 103
Need for Labor Legislation, 105 Malthus' Theory of
Population, 106 Beginning of Labor Legislation, 107
Economic Consequences of the Napoleonic Wars, 108
Influence of the Napoleonic Wars on Economic
Thought, 109 Genesis of the Free-Trade Movement,
111 England Adopts Free Trade by Abolishing the
Corn Laws, 112 Coexistence of Free Trade and Inter-
vention, 113*

II HOW FACTORS OF PRODUCTION AND ECO-NOMIC INSTITUTIONS WERE TRANS-PLANTED AND ADAPTED TO AN AMERICAN ENVIRONMENT

6 Transference and diffusion of economic
institutions in the Colonial Period 117

*Experimental Nature of the Era, 117 Basic Problems
of Settlement—Mobilizing Capital and Recruiting
Labor, 118 Group Settlement, 119 The Indentured-
Servant System, 121 The Headright System, 124
The Transportation of Criminals and Debtors, 125
Negro Slavery, 127 Efforts to Revive Feudal Institutions, 131 Experiments with Theocratic Economic Institutions, 133 Private Property, 135 Types of Agricultural Enterprise, 137 Types of Industrial Enterprise, 141 Types of Commercial Enterprise, 146 The
Heritage from the Colonial Era, 151*

7 Public policy, economic development and the beginnings of transformation **154**

Need for National Economic Policies, 154 Hamilton's Recommendation, 156 Business Demands for Protection, 157 First Experiments with Protective Tariffs, 158 Clay's "American System," 159 Formulation of a Theory of Protection, 160 The Role of Exogenous Factors in Economic Development, 161 The Meaning of Economic Development, 162 Critical Needs of the 19th-Century American Economy, 163 The Importance of Capital Formation, 164 British Efforts to Prevent American Industrialization, 165 International Capital Movements, 166 British Capital Exports to the United States, 167 Spacial Dynamics of Mature Industrial Countries, 169 Factors that Influenced the Flow of Capital to the United States, 170 Ways of Attracting Capital, 171 Some Contrasts Between Capital and Labor Migration, 174 The Influence of European Public Policy on Emigration, 175 Influence of Market Forces on Labor Migration, 177 The Special Importance of Railways as an Energizing Factor, 178 Development Effects of a Linear Railway Axis, 180 Effect of Railway Building on Employment and Business Activity, 182 Governmental Responsibility for Public Improvements, 184 Governmental Participation in Economic Development: The Example of the Southern Railways, 186 Basic Elements in American Developmental Policy, 190 The Beginning of a Process of Economic Transformation, 192 The Interplay of Public Policy and Market Forces, 194

III | HOW MORE EFFICIENT ECONOMIC INSTITUTIONS AND PRODUCTIVE METHODS WERE DEVELOPED AND PERFECTED IN THE 19TH AND 20TH CENTURIES

8 The improvement and extension of
technology 199

*How the Character of the American People Influenced
Technological Progress, 199 Early Efforts to Improve
Technology, 202 The Pioneers in Textile Manufacture, 203 Pioneer Work in the Use of Interchangeable Parts, 205 The Arrival of the "American System"
of Manufacturing, 208 Progress in Machine Tool
Building, 209 Delayed Development of Agricultural
Technology, 212 The Age of Iron and Steel, 215
The "Revolution" in the Use of Power, 216 Education and Changes in the Inventive Process, 218 Scientific Management, 220 Technological Achievements
by the Middle of the 20th Century, 221 The Effects
of Technological Change, 222 Technology and the
Farmer, 224 The Machine and Business Enterprise,
225 Technology and Government, 226 The Automobile as a Factor in Economic Transformation, 227
The Transforming Effects of the Automobile on the
Economy, 232*

9 The evolution of business enterprise and
corporate management 234

*Importance of "Success" in the "Business Game," 234
America's First Big Businessmen, 236 Thomas Hancock—Merchant, 237 The Appearance of Big Business in Manufacturing, 238 The Corporate Form of
Business Organization, 239 Business Policies in the
Age of the Industrialist, 241 The Problem of Competition, 242 The "Heroic" Businessman and the Modal
Businessman, 245 Andrew Carnegie—The Great Industrialist of the "Heroic Age," 246 The Investment
Banker in Industry, 250 John D. Rockefeller—Combination is the Life of Trade, 252 Standard Oil:
Pioneer in Management, 254 Further Consolidation
and Combination, 258 The Ascendancy of Professional Management, 260 The Corporation Problem,
261 Economic Effects of the Separation of Ownership from Control, 263 Further Weakening of Price
Competition, 267*

10 Adapting financial institutions to American environment 268

Factors Influencing Capital Accumulation, 268   Who Did the Saving? 270   Foreign Contributions to Capital Accumulation, 271   The Nature of Financial Institutions, 273   The Conflict between "Sound" and "Easy" Money, 275   American Money Before the Civil War, 276   Early American Commercial Banking, 279   Two Early Experiments with Central Banking, 280   Early Attempts to Regulate Banking, 283   Investment Banking Before the Civil War, 284   Greenbacks and Free Silver, 286   The National Banking System, 289   Investment Banking after the Civil War, 292   The Founding of the Federal Reserve System, 292   Changes in the Reserve System, 294   Commercial Banking in the 20th Century, 296   Breakdown of the Gold Standard, 297   Investment Banking since 1900, 298   Rising Importance of Insurance Companies, 300

11 Formation and development of labor organizations 302

Influence of Economic Environment on Trade-Union Tactics, 302   Labor's Attitudes and Problems before 1840, 306   Labor Unionism Before the Civil War, 307   Wages, Hours, and Living Conditions in the Early 19th Century, 310   Improvement in Labor's Position between 1865 and 1890, 313   The Twilight of Welfare Unionism, 315   How the Worker Fared between 1890 and World War I, 317   The Emergence of the American Federation of Labor, 319   The Changing Composition of the Labor Force, 321   The Worker During the Hectic 'Twenties, 323   Decline of Unionism in the 'Twenties, 324   Growing Opposition of Employers, 325   Effect of the Depression of the 'Thirties on Unions, 327   Dramatic Growth of Unions After the Great Depression, 329

12 Expansion of agriculture and emergence of a chronic farm problem 334

*The Business Motivation of American Farmers, 334
Land as a Factor in American Economic Development,
335 Government Land Policy, 336 The Effects of
the Government's Land Policy, 339 The Westward
Movement and the Influence of the Frontier, 341 The
Economic Organization of Early Agriculture, 343
Southern Agriculture Before the Civil War, 345 From
Self-Sufficiency to Commercial Farming, 347 Agricul-
tural Exports, 348 Agricultural Developments in the
Late 19th Century, 349 Farm Population and the
Farmer's Share of the National Income, 350 The
Tendency to Overproduce, 352 More Machines on
the Farm, 353 The Problem of Farm Prices, 354
The Problem of Raising Capital, 356 The Farmer's
Attempted Solution to His Problems, 358*

13 The changing economic functions of government 362

*Historical Factors that Shaped the Role of Govern-
ment, 362 Government as a Policeman, 365 Government Labor Regulation, 366 How Government Tried
to Sustain Competition in Business, 369 Government
as a Redistributor of Wealth, 373 Assistance to Industry by Means of Tariffs, 374 Government Support
of the Merchant Marine, 376 How Government
Helped the Farmer, 377 Government and Social Welfare, 379 Government as a Conservator, 380 Government as an Entrepreneur, 381 Government as an
Economic Stabilizer, 383 Fiscal and Monetary Affairs
before 1900, 384 The Expansion of Government's
Role as an Economic Stabilizer, 385*

IV | HOW OUR ECONOMIC SYSTEM HAS WORKED IN PEACE AND WAR AND HOW IT HAS INFLUENCED ECONOMIC THINKING

14 How wars changed the American economy **391**

The Diffuse Economic Effect of Wars, 391 The Rising Costs of War and How They Were Met, 392 Money Expansion and Price Inflation During Three Wars, 394 How War Finance Affected Income Distribution, 396 The Effect of War on Industrial Progress, 397 Industry During the Civil War, 398 Industry During World War I, 400 Industrial Progress During World War II, 402 Government Planning for War, 405 Government Controls in World War I, 405 Government Planning During World War II, 406 The Effect of War on Population and the Occupational Mix, 409 Summary Remarks on the Effects of War on Economic Development, 412

15 The adaptation of economic thought to economic change **413**

Ideas and Institutions, 413 The Transformation of the American Economy in the Early 19th Century, 416 American Economic Thought in the Early 1800's, 418 The Emergence of a Laissez Faire Ideology, 419 Basic Changes in the American Economy During the Latter Half of the 19th Century, 421 The Performance of the Economy in the Late 19th Century, 423 Trends in Economic Thought in the Late 19th Century, 425 The Belated Reaction Against Classical Theory Among the Professional Economists, 428 Social Reform Comes into Its Own, 432 The Marshallian Synthesis, 433 Further Transformation of the American Economy in the Early 20th Century, 434 Specialization Among Economists and the Rise of Institutionalism, 438 How the Great Depression Influenced Economic Thought, 440 The American Economy in the 1950's, 444 Major Trends in Economic Thought at Mid-Century, 448

Part I   HOW OUR BASIC

ECONOMIC INSTITUTIONS

ORIGINATED IN EUROPE

1 Introductory explanations and concepts

The Importance of Studying American Economic Development

Within our lifetime, the United States has been compelled by world events to assume new and staggering responsibilities. More by destiny than by choice, the United States has become the leader of those nations of the world engaged in the gigantic task of extending and protecting the fabric of political, economic, and intellectual freedom. This position of world leadership is very largely the result of our tremendous productive capacity, because it is our vast output of goods and services that has enabled us to provide capital equipment and technical assistance to underdeveloped countries and to help other countries rebuild their war-damaged economies and rearm against potential aggression. Despite fears that the United States may have lost its technical preeminence, the fact remains that the vast and complex American pro-

ductive apparatus is beyond question the most remarkable manifestation of economic ingenuity in the history of man for the simple reason
that it makes it possible for the 6 per cent of the world's population
who live in the United States to produce about 30 to 40 per cent of the
world's goods and services.

It is not easy to trace the history of the complicated, massive, versatile,
and ever-expanding productive force that we call the American economic system. Made up of machines, mines, factories, stores, offices,
ships, roads, railroads, airplanes, farms, forests, laboratories, and countless other inanimate parts, the whole apparatus is animated and co-
ordinated by a host of private business enterprises, by hundreds of
public organizations, and by scores of public or private research institutions. Yet all these thousands of specialized business enterprises and
the hundreds of governmental or quasi-governmental organizations
operate within rules that are either voluntarily agreed upon or are
prescribed and revised by democratically elected legislators; hence behind all the decisions that are made within our economic system lies
a climate of opinion, and a pattern of thinking, which it has become
perhaps more fashionable than accurate to call the "ideology" of our
way of life.

This book is designed to give readers an understanding of where our
complex system came from, how it was progressively adapted to new
problems, and why this unique form of economic organization has made
it possible for the United States to have a higher standard of living than
that of any other nation. The analysis can be readily followed because
the "history" has a clear and direct relation to the contemporary environment. It deals with "institutions" with which we are all familiar
since we live in an economy of corporations, banks, factories, and labor
unions; one in which government plays a very important role; one in
which economic policy is crystallizing continuously out of new (or old)
economic ideas. But we live also, unfortunately, in a world in which
war or the threat of war prevents our remarkable productive apparatus
from diffusing all its potential benefit. Were this terrible scourge of the
human race eliminated, we could look forward to a far higher level of
well-being than mankind has ever known; not only for the American
people, but for the entire world community. Whether that blessed day
will ever come is uncertain; and therefore until the prospects of universal disarmament improve, the ominous threat of war can best be met
by ensuring that the American economy continues to grow in pro-
ductiveness and vigor. This can come about in the future, as it has in

the past, only if our economic institutions are flexible and resilient, and capable of adapting themselves to new circumstances. Hence the importance of studying the origins and development of our economy! We believe there is an eagerness to know how this great, benevolent potential of the American economic system came into being. Yet this is only one purpose of this book; another and perhaps more important object is to stimulate active minds to think about how the American economy can become a still more efficient mechanism for augmenting national and international well-being.

Scope and Method

Where did the components of our remarkable system of production come from? How were they put together into an integrated whole? Why did economic organization reach its most effective development in the United States rather than in some other country? These are some of the major questions this book will try to answer. Part I very briefly sketches the European origins of some of our basic economic institutions and their historical development up to the beginning of the 19th century. In order to keep this part of the book as compact and simple as possible, no attempt has been made to write a continuous survey of economic history. The method is rather that of making successive observations at selected time periods for the purpose of ascertaining how and why certain new economic institutions came into being; and to show the process whereby they became integrated within a developing, productive apparatus of interrelated parts, once the component parts had been tested and found useful. The analysis begins with a very brief examination of certain late-medieval institutions. From this point of departure, a jump is made with seven-league boots to about the year 1700 so that the general character of European economic organization at the time when America was being colonized will be understood. Accordingly, the new elements in the economic sphere that had crystallized by 1700 are isolated, described, and related to their respective beginnings. Wherever necessary the path is followed backward in time as far as is necessary to find adequate explanations for the origins of important new elements. Following this method of arbitrary advance and occasional backtracing, another advance is made, this time to about 1800, so that the European economic system contemporaneous with our Constitutional era can be appreciated. Interwoven with the description of the economic institutions which were destined to become the basic components of our American economic system, will be found a modest attempt to appraise the influence of changing economic institutions upon the whole pattern of behavior in the Western world.

Part II surveys the process whereby certain European economic institutions were transplanted into the New World, both in the Colonial Period and later. The treatment of the Colonial Period is rather unorthodox, because we have not attempted to describe the process of settlement or economic expansion in historical terms. Our concern has been primarily with the kinds of European economic institutions that were transferred and diffused, and with the ways in which these random elements were adapted to a new physical environment and slowly integrated into a regional economic system, similar in some ways to European counterparts, yet quite different in other characteristics. But it was not only such impersonal forces as land-man ratios or capital deficiencies that affected the inherited institutions; from the early Colonial Period, a changed pattern of cultural values began to emerge in America, and some attention has accordingly been given to these sociological and psychological factors.

As the over-all configuration of the American economy changed, other economic institutions of later European origin were presently transferred to America either by centrifugal or centripetal forces, and we have indicated how these elements were also progressively woven into emergent new structures by a further process of adjustment and adaptation. Quite unintentionally Europe was hastening the growth of the American economy; at any rate, the immigration of labor and the inflow of capital were making it possible for the American people to exploit their rich natural resources more efficiently. The process whereby productive factors were transferred to the new country was gradual and circumstantial, and many impatient Americans thought the pace was not fast enough. In order to hasten the transplantation of desirable economic institutions, certain encouraging policies were therefore adopted by the several levels of American government, and considerable attention has therefore been given to these developmental experiments. Thus by a process of diffusion, transplantation, and attraction, paralleled by continuous adaptation and modification of borrowed institutions, the United States, by about 1850, had knit certain instrumentalities together into a quite efficient productive and distributive mechanism, one which was even then quite distinguishable both in structure and operation from its European counterparts. It was already a "mixed economy," mostly private, to be sure, but never-

theless depending for its satisfactory functioning upon a very considerable amount of governmental assistance.

Whereas Part II deals with the American economy as a whole, Part
III centers attention on the progress made in six separate, major segments of the economy: technology, business enterprise, finance, labor
organizations, agriculture, and governmental economic activity. Since
in this part an effort is made to trace the major changes that have occurred in each of these sectors for the whole sweep of American history
from the adoption of our Federal type of government to the present,
there must perforce be some backtracking into the time period covered
by Part II. Moreover, it must be noted that the great achievements
in one particular sector not only had profound consequences on other
sectors, but the cumulative development within the several sectors
presently produced a transforming effect upon the whole economy. Such
transformations take considerable time to materialize, and can only
be visualized by comparing the workings of the whole economy at one
time period with its operation at a later time period. Accordingly we
have attempted to describe a few such cross-sectional transforming
effects.

An economic system, however, does not exist in a vacuum. It is not
something split apart from a nation's political and social life, or from
the intellectual life of people who work in factories and mines, on farms
or in professional activities. Formal and informal educational processes
influence the labor force and the management of thousands of our
enterprises, while cultural forces, themselves the product of the past,
condition our habits, and influence the rate of capital accumulation
and the forms of investment. Nor is the operation of an economic system
insulated against economic or political events that occur in other parts
of the world. Wars and revolutions have exerted profound influences
on the whole texture of our economic institutions and on the way they
affect employment and income distribution. But we can, unfortunately,
deal only very sketchily with cultural or political problems, for this
book is precisely what the subtitle indicates; it is an introduction to
economics, not a survey of American history nor even of American
economic history. Our main object is to show the historical origins of
major components of our economic system; to explain how these instrumentalities have helped transform our whole economy; and how
in this process they have made it possible for that minor fraction of
the world's population living in the United States to produce such a
major fraction of the world community's output of want-satisfying goods
and services.

Human Wants

In the modern economic world, millions of people are busily engaged in trying to satisfy their wants. Some work in mines or factories, others in offices or on farms; some do manual work, many do not; some produce physical products, others provide intangible services; some teach, sing, or act, others buy and sell. Some do not work at all, being able to satisfy their wants without onerous exertion. For the most part, those who do work do not bend their efforts directly toward want satisfaction. Instead they seek money incomes which they subsequently (or previously) convert into want-satisfying means. To an extent, moreover, money incomes by themselves seem to satisfy some wants, although ordinarily they constitute only an intermediate goal of human effort. Nor should it be overlooked that most people have a desire for purposeful activity, and the very means whereby they earn their living satisfies a want. By one method or another, therefore, millions of people are constantly trying to satisfy their wants, and this ceaseless effort constitutes one basic aspect of what we call economic activity.

The wants which induce this manifold activity are varied in nature and origin; they comprise, as Aristotle observed long ago, desires for things which delight the body, the mind, and the soul. From a moral point of view, these wants may be good or bad; from a physiological point of view, they may be harmful or beneficial. Regardless of their moral or physiological aspects, they are real and insistent; collectively they arise from the complex nature of man in society. Some wants have an indisputable biological origin, for example, the need for a minimum of food, clothing, or shelter. Other wants such as desire for ornament, travel, or music, for elegant homes or exotic food, have a less obvious biological basis; such wants result from refinements in taste which may perhaps be called psychological. A great many wants, however, are the consequences of certain imitative, competitive, or ostentatious propensities, arising out of group habits or social customs, and are essentially cultural in origin.

The Tyranny of Scarce Means

The number of these multitudinous wants that can be satisfied depends on the availability of want-satisfying means. If all wants of all members of society could be satisfied, there would be no economic problems whatever because there would be no need to economize. In that case we would not have an "economy" but a state of abundance. This fortunate situation can probably never be reached for two reasons: because the supply of some want-satisfying means is absolutely limited, and because the supply of others is relatively limited. Want-satisfying means of the first type comprise unique and non-reproducible goods— the paintings of Botticelli or Raphael, for example. Since they are inadequate in number to satisfy all existing wants, they must be apportioned by some method or other to a fortunate few. The relatively-limited, want-satisfying means differ from the absolutely-limited only in degree. Although they are reproducible, their supply is nevertheless restricted by physical, technical, or economic difficulties which interfere with their increase. If more coal, copper, or zinc is wanted, for example, mines must be deeper or more numerous. Greater cost must therefore be incurred, because labor and capital must be attracted to these industries in larger amounts, and taken away absolutely or relatively from other productive activities.

Since scarcity is characteristic of both the reproducible and the non-reproducible means of want satisfaction, both types must be economized and apportioned among the many persons who desire their want-satisfying services. In non-Communist areas of the modern economic world, this apportioning process is accomplished almost entirely by prices which attach themselves to want-satisfying means in markets.[1] Consequently, the immediate obstacle which prevents people from satisfying all their wants in the modern economic world is the relation between their personal incomes and the prices of things they desire. But this price phenomenon is merely intermediate; the ultimate reason why the wants of all persons cannot be satisfied is to be found in the persisting scarcity of want-satisfying means in relation to total wants.

Ways of Increasing Want-Satisfying Means

People, however, do not submit willingly to the tyranny of scarce means; constant and ceaseless effort is made to overcome or to circumvent its limitations. The great bulk of activities in which the members of the modern economic world are so busily engaged represent society's attempt to make want-satisfying means more abundant. The simplest of these activities is physical work, whereby the gifts of nature are

[1] Even Communist-organized countries have found it necessary to use prices for allocating a great many scarce goods and services.

transformed into want-satisfying means; thus, coal is mined and transported to consumers to serve as fuel, forests are cut to provide lumber for furniture, and metals are converted by labor into tools. By work, therefore, man can appropriate nature's raw materials, and alter, combine, and fashion them so that they will better serve his needs.

Effective work calls for thought and comes to depend upon knowledge. An elementary knowledge of life processes, for example, makes it possible for man to raise field crops, increase the supply of vegetables, or breed and propagate useful animals. Similarly, knowledge of rudimentary principles of physics makes it possible for man to perform tasks otherwise impossible: to move heavy objects, construct buildings, pump water out of deep wells, or build ships and aircraft. The use of intermediate goods, which do not themselves directly satisfy wants, but which create a greater abundance of things that do, is a result of knowledge. Here a roundabout process is involved, whereby assisting goods are first created. But in order to acquire these intermediate goods, primitive impatience must be tempered by an understanding that if immediate satisfaction is temporarily sacrificed, a larger measure of enjoyment may be obtained in the future. This use of intermediate goods, and especially the complex process of tool making and tool using, is generically denoted by the world "technology."

A technological system of production, however, requires a certain amount of organization, and this also is a product of knowledge. Efficient production of want-satisfying means by unassisted, individual work is often difficult or impossible. Many tasks require more strength, more varied ability, more ingenuity than any one person possesses. An adequately organized group of producers, on the other hand, can divide the tasks which must be performed, and the directors of such organizations can assign tasks to different persons in terms of their varying abilities. Greater skill and dexterity, as well as a greater degree of exact knowledge, usually results, especially if specialized tools have also been devised. Hence technology is normally something conjoined with organization. It is closely related to the existing body of scientific knowledge, since its processes must implicitly conform to the laws of the physical or the natural world. At any given time, therefore, technology reveals, in terms of existing knowledge, the degree to which man is able to avail himself of the benefit of natural forces for increasing the supply of want-satisfying means. Yet basically it is human knowledge which is the real prerequisite for the development of organization and of technology, and these in turn, together with adequate markets, make possible a co-operative, tool- or machine-using method of production.

The Role of Markets

Any elaborate form of cooperative production depends fundamentally upon markets, since these agencies, by facilitating buying and selling, permit productive functions to be divided, thereby allowing tasks to be specialized. If adequate marketing facilities exist, one person may confine his productive activities to the making of but one kind of product, and out of the income derived from this occupation he may purchase in markets the other goods and services which his wants demand and his income permits. Consequently, even small local markets permit some occupational specialization, while markets which transcend the boundaries of local areas may make possible a more effective spatial division of labor, allowing whole communities to devote themselves to specialized occupations. Still larger markets allow the tasks peculiar to a given occupation to be much further subdivided, with resulting greater efficiency and lower costs of production. Our modern economic system is based upon occupational, spatial, and intra-occupational division of labor, a socially advantageous situation which has gradually come into being as a consequence of work, knowledge, organization, technology, and the growth of markets.

Influence of Political and Cultural Forces

It should not be overlooked, however, that economic activity takes place within political confines and is tempered by an enveloping set of cultural forces. Consequently, forms of government as well as the body of social traditions and cultural habits exert a profound influence on economic activity. The kind of an economic system we now possess is therefore the outgrowth not merely of economic history, but of political and cultural history as well. These non-economic forces may limit or canalize economic activity. Thus is societies which are socially stratified, either as a consequence of political power or of cultural tradition, wants usually tend to be defined in terms of things which are appropriate to one's station in life. Moreover, in such societies, economic activity is often controlled by patrician, military, or sacerdotal classes, which define the duties of subservient classes. In more democratic societies, in contrast, the limitations imposed upon wants, and on the control of economic activity, are fewer and weaker; for although emulative and customary standards are not lacking, each person has greater power to decide for himself what items of consumption he desires and which things he can afford. Markets will normally reflect this demand, and there emerge, as a consequence, larger possibilities for expanding the size of productive organizations as well as more opportunities for the division of labor, and greater chances of business profits. This results in a larger total amount of economic activity, and a more insistent effort to increase the supply of want-satisfying means. On the other hand, a caste-controlled system may conceivably offer more economic security to its stratified groups than that which emerges in a society marked by a high degree of individual economic initiative; indeed abundant illustrations are available to show that, in democratic societies, the progress of organization and technology has often had harmful as well as beneficent results. For the most part, however, a weakening of those political and cultural forces which formerly restrained consumption and controlled economic activity has resulted in a more efficient, albeit a more complex, economic system. Wants hitherto restricted have been unleashed, leading to greater efforts on the part of individuals to increase their incomes so that they can satisfy a larger number of wants. Wholly new types of organization, as well as revolutionary technology, have come into being. Markets more extensive, more highly organized, and more delicate, have likewise evolved.

Saving and Investment

Greater productive efficiency is always needed if more human wants are to be satisfied, and this in turn calls for the use of more intermediate goods: more tools, implements, machines and non-human energy. All this mass of intermediate productive agents can be subsumed under the word "capital." How does this assisting productive factor come into existence? A very small amount may be found ready made in nature's bounty: diamonds with which to cut hard objects, or cup-shaped stones to serve as primitive grinding mills. Most capital goods, however, are man-made, and are therefore themselves the product of work, organization, knowledge, and technology. The only difference that should be noted is that while capital goods are being made, human productive power must be temporarily withdrawn from the making of consumer goods that are directly capable of satisfying human wants. Thus, an isolated farmer who chooses to build a fanning mill (to clean his grain) will have to forego other directly-productive activities while he provides himself with this capital equipment. Presumably this sacrifice of consumer goods is worthwhile, or else he would not have decided in favor of the fanning mill.

An organized, differentiated community does not make its decisions to produce capital goods in this interrupted way. It normally produces both consumer goods and capital goods at the same time, and hence some people are regularly producing consumer goods (bread, cheese, cotton cloth) while others are regularly building capital goods (sewing machines, trucks, steamships). This concurrent production can occur because of two interrelated activities which we call "saving and investment." Some members of society do not spend all their current incomes on consumer goods; they save a part of their incomes either because their wants are modest, their incomes are very large, or because they place a higher value on goods to be enjoyed in the future than on the enjoyment to be derived from immediate want satisfaction. But whatever may be the motivation, they do save a part of their current incomes. This saving emerges in the form of money funds which they can either "invest" themselves by commissioning the construction of capital goods (as a farmer might do by contracting for the building of a barn or a silo) or they can lend their savings to other members of society who wish to invest in machinery, tools or equipment but who have inadequate funds of their own. In either case, part of the community's income stream is used to finance the capital-goods-producing sector of the economy, thus permitting the concurrent production of capital and consumer goods.

Clearly it is the volume of saving which will limit the amount of investment; although it is the amount of investment which will in turn determine the quantity of capital goods which an economy will possess. "Developing" countries normally channel a sizable amount of national income to the capital-goods-producing industries, while, conversely, "underdeveloped" countries have not in the past emphasized the production of capital goods, or are not doing so at present. Whether this situation has been caused by pervading poverty, by lack of foresight, or by peculiar cultural reasons does not alter the consequence. Underdeveloped countries have a low per capita output, and hence a very limited capacity to save. As a result, investment is relatively small, labor-saving tools and equipment are primitive and scarce, and productivity is low. Thus poverty begets and perpetuates poverty. In contrast, dynamic, developing countries reveal just the reverse tendencies; saving is an habitual propensity, and the personal saving of the economy is constantly seeking the most profitable investment opportunities through capital markets.

It should be recognized, however, that communities (or nations) that possess good natural resources—fertile land, good forests, rich mineral deposits—are in a better position to save and invest than are communities (or nations) with poor resources—eroded lands, little timber, few or low-quality minerals. But resources are not all-governing. Countries like Holland or Denmark have been able to save and invest even though their natural resources were relatively poor. Indeed, these countries have actually improved or enlarged their resources remarkably (by reclamation and soil improvement) because there existed a will to save and invest. Clearly, then, cultural and intellectual forces are also a prerequisite to a vigorous process of saving and investment. Moreover, a really progressive economy must go beyond a routine process of saving and investment; it must invoke the aid of technology to ensure that the accumulated saving will be invested in the most efficient forms of capital that scientific and technical knowledge will permit. Herein lies the distinction between economic growth and development on the one hand, and economic transformation on the other.

Economic Progress, Growth and Development

The word *progress* implies a forward movement, an advancement or improvement. Hence when we speak of *economic progress*, we mean an improvement over a period of time in the capacity of a community[2] to provide its people with want-satisfying means. But the question immediately arises of how one can measure the capacity of an economy to make progress; and to this question there are at least three answers. There can be, through time, an increase in a community's total output of goods and services; an increase in average per capita output; or a

2 It is probably best here to refer to a *community* rather than to a nation since an *economy* can be something other than a nation. It might be, for example, a dependent colony, an independent nation, or a region made up of several contiguous colonies or nations. Thus we can speak of the Virginian economy in 1780, the American economy in 1850, or the West European economy of 1950.

qualitative improvement in the kinds of goods and services which are produced. It is important that we examine these three possible situations a little more closely to see which of them represents real economic progress.

It is by no means certain that a mere increase in a community's total output constitutes genuine economic progress. If, for example, a community possesses reserves of natural resources in the form of unused land, it is possible for population to grow; and, as more land is brought under cultivation, the total output of the community will then increase. The wants of more people admittedly would now be satisfied, but there might be no advancement in the standard of living. There might be just enough saving and investment in the community to provide every producer, on the average, with enough capital goods to maintain a uniform rate of output; but not enough saving and investment to bring about any increase in the average per capita rate of output. Perhaps we might say that in such a situation there would be *growth* but no *development*. Or we might say that there would be an increase in total welfare, since more people could share in the enlarged output; but there would be no improvement in the average welfare of persons or families.

If, on the other hand, a community can, by increased saving and investment, provide itself with additional capital goods so that each producer becomes, on the average, more efficient, then it may be possible to step up production faster than the increase in needs caused by population growth so that average per capita consumption can be increased. Here growth and development would apparently go hand in hand, and it would seem quite appropriate to call this situation one of real economic progress. For not only would the wants of more people be satisfied, but, by reason of the greater per capita output, the average standard of living would rise. Whether all members of the community would share proportionately in this increased productivity of the community would depend upon a whole host of circumstances. Conceivably some people might receive no part of the increased output or only very little, while others might get far more than their proportionate share. This would depend upon the complex interrelations of wages, prices, profits and all other factors that influence personal incomes. But there would be progress, and very clearly this progress would be the result of a more efficient method of production largely ascribable to a more ample supply of capital goods.

A third situation which we can envisage is one where the quality of want-satisfying means changes over a period of time. It is possible to conceive of a type of economic progress wherein the average per capita physical production of certain goods does not increase, but one wherein the want-satisfying power of each unit of such goods becomes so much greater than before that a constant output of improved goods would be tantamount to an increased quantity of older-type goods. Thus if the octane rating of gasoline is increased from 65 to 100, the power-generating capacity of a gallon of gasoline is more than doubled; or if certain rare metals (such as tungsten) are used to harden steel, the tools made from the superior grade of steel may last five times as long as before. Clearly these qualitative improvements, resulting from improved technology, are equivalent to an increase in the supply of want-satisfying means.

Genuine economic progress therefore has at least three aspects: increases in total output, improvements in per capita output, and changes in the qualitative character of want-satisfying means. Thus progress may result partly from an increase in a community's supply of labor, whether from natural increase or immigration; partly from an augmentation of its supply of capital, resulting from saving and investment; and partly from an improvement in technology, as a consequence of scientific progress, research, improved levels of education, and better varieties of business management. By reason of the interaction of all these factors, a really progressive economy does not merely grow and develop; it is essentially *transformed,* and to the nature of this process we must now very briefly turn our attention.

Economic Transformation

It is not enough that an economy should merely grow and develop if it hopes to be genuinely progressive. For even if output were to increase, through time, not only as a total, but as a per capita quantity, this would merely mean the production of more wheat, candles, cotton or other traditional consumer goods; and more wagons, grindstones, hand looms or other time-sanctioned capital goods. It would not supply a community with such things as automobiles, electric power, vacuum cleaners, machine tools, television, or frozen vegetables. Real progress therefore implies something more than growth; it involves a much more far-reaching concept of change, yet one in which growth is nevertheless a basic characteristic.

What, then, is involved in the idea of transformation? It comprehends first of all an improvement in production methods, normally in the direction of using relatively more capital and relatively less labor. At the same time, it brings about changes in input-output relations, so that larger amounts of better quality end products will result from the incorporated raw materials. Thus the same amount of iron will have greater strength in the form of steel than in the form of wrought iron, or the same amount of timber when converted into plywood will cover a larger area of a wall or ceiling. Meanwhile the development of new end products may drastically change patterns of consumption and production. The availability of electric appliances, for example, can largely obviate the need for domestic servants and thereby release a portion of a community's labor supply for other productive purposes.

The use of hitherto unused natural resources such as petroleum (for lighting purposes) may obviate the import of certain non-indigenous resources (whale oil), although it is possible that other new end products (automobiles) may, conversely, necessitate the import of other non-indigenous products (crude rubber for tires). Far-reaching changes are set in motion by this transforming process, not least of which is a redistribution of manpower among various sectors of the economy. As agriculture, for example, is progressively mechanized, fewer and fewer people will be needed to produce food and fibers, and hence relatively more manpower can be devoted to other occupations, such as manufacturing and the service industries.

The essential difference between growth and development, on the one hand, and transformation on the other, may be made clearer by considering two economies, A and B. Let us assume that A produces only two major products, copper and cotton. Conceivably A could be saving at a rate fast enough to increase its capital supply by say 2 per cent a year. A could therefore expand both total and per capita output. Yet it is entirely conceivable that as a result of technological advances in B, aluminum might increasingly replace copper for industrial uses and synthetic fibres might displace cotton as a raw material for making textiles; and were this to occur, then incomes might fall in A despite the economy's commendable rate of growth. It is evident, then, that a really dynamic economy must be based on a combination of growth, development, and transformation. But whereas growth and development can result simply from increases in manpower and capital, transformation must come essentially from exogenous sources: from experimentation, scientific advances, research, and business innovations.

If in one community, cultural, political, or psychological factors tend to retard a change-making process, that community (or nation) will fall behind the rate of progress in other countries. Oppositely, if new technico-economic opportunities, which the growth of knowledge has revealed, call for relatively more mechanics, engineers, chemists, and risk-taking businessmen, and if the (formal or informal) educational system and the cultural and political climate of a community tend to encourage an occupational re-orientation, then the entire process of transformation can be hastened and expanded. Transformation will consequently occur faster in a community where there is freedom to change one's occupation, willingness to take financial risks, and above all a readiness to experiment not only with new products but with new tools, new machinery, and novel forms of business enterprise. But there will be little transformation without a flexible and imaginative variety of new investment; indeed, it is the manufacture of the new kinds of capital equipment, which transformation requires, that partly explains why it can become such an energizing force. The advent of the automobile, for example, brought at first only a small increase in the demand for steel, brass, canvas, and rubber. But when thousands and presently millions of people gave priority to the automobile over their other wants, the whole picture changed. New factories had to be built in which to manufacture cars, new machine tools were needed to press out frames or bodies or for molding tires. Improved roads had to be built, which called for vast quantities of cement and reinforcing steel as well as for earth-moving and road-building machinery. Filling stations, roadside stands, and country motels had to be built; moreover, as the automobile increased personal mobility, vast new suburban areas had to be constructed, comprising not only dwellings but garages, shops, theatres, and schools. All this increased business activity meant greater employment and more business profits; and, as incomes increased, a greater demand for more and more varied consumer goods developed, thus creating the possibilities for a still further transformation of the entire economy.

Need for Understanding Historical Roots

Our present economic system is a product of economic, political, and social history, and is a mechanism so complex that it is virtually impossible for any one person to envisage all its parts. An elaborate price mechanism, a network of business organizations and a great collection of technical devices have come into being as a consequence of increased knowledge and as a result of political and social evolution. The roots of every part of our modern economic system reach deep back into history; each component has its own history and can be understood only in the light of the particular circumstances which brought it into its present form. For this reason, the whole combination of parts, which is a heritage from the past, can only be understood by centering attention on the most significant elements and by sketching in the historical situation which nurtured the growth of these elements.

Yet our 20th century economic system is so complex and bewildering that its basic elements are obscured by the very profusion of its parts. In societies simpler than ours, on the other hand, the fundamental nature of economic organization may more easily be discerned. Before the 19th century the economic world expanded slowly, hence the majority of economic problems, although changing, were not so radically different from one century to another. The 19th century, on the contrary, was really revolutionary; it not only witnessed a doubling of the world's population, but saw this remarkable event coupled with an amazing growth of political democracy. These new forces drastically altered the whole economic picture. In response to these changes the whole economic system of the Western world did not merely *grow,* in the sense that it simply produced more goods to satisfy known wants; it was progressively *transformed.* Methods of producing goods changed drastically; new relations between the input of raw materials and the output of end products occurred; completely new products were made available,[3] leading to important changes in the patterns of consumption. And in the process of transformation a remarkable redistribution of manpower among different occupations occurred. If we are even to begin to understand the huge, powerful, complex economic system in which we live, we must see how it developed historically out of simpler preceding economic systems. But we must visualize not only the reasons why it became more complex and intricate, but how and why it was transformed; because it was this process of transformation that has altered the whole structure of the economy, and thereby changed not only the productive mechanism but to a large extent altered the pattern of human wants and the daily activities of millions of people, thus changing our whole way of life.

[3] It is estimated that over 25 per cent of the kinds of manufactured goods that entered into foreign trade in 1950 did not exist in 1900.

2 The late-medieval background

General Pattern of Economic Life

Although a vast number of changes have occurred in the economic organization of the Western world since medieval times, there are two major ones that deserve special attention: the breakdown of the manorial system of agriculture and the rise of the factory system of industrial production. These two historical events have been the outstanding manifestations of economic change in modern times. Yet change can be measured only by reference to a position of rest, and because the late-medieval world fulfills this condition of rest fairly well, it will be useful to begin with a survey of late-medieval economic life. The analysis will be restricted to the English scene, not because England typifies medieval economic culture better than the Continent, but because the rigid peasant organization of rural society disappeared earlier in England than on the Continent, and because the fundamental changes in the conduct of trade and industry, rather infelicitously called the "Industrial Revolution,"[1] also emerged earlier in England's "green and pleasant land." Moreover, it was Britain rather than the Continent that supplied most of the institutions which were to be the basic components of the American economy.

England in the first half of the 14th century affords an illuminating picture of late-medieval life. On the eve of the Black Death, in 1348–1349, the population included probably 3.5 to 4 million persons. That goods were scarce can hardly be doubted; life for the majority of people was difficult and painful; methods of production were primitive; famines were frequent. Hovels sheltered the agricultural serfs in villages where disease and malnutrition were as widespread as ignorance and superstition. The want scales of most persons were relatively inflexible, for two main reasons: because the Church taught its adherents that the pursuit of the things of this world was fraught with moral dangers; and, secondly, because the mode of life for most people was determined almost entirely by the force of customs. Probably a third factor also helped make wants inelastic: the danger of confiscation, necessarily present in a social organization in which certain servile members of society were regarded as legal chattels of an upper caste.

Production was divided between town and country, with rural economic activity probably more than ten times as important as urban. Yet town production was steadily increasing, competing and cooperating with country production at one and the same time. Local and interregional markets existed, and were already highly organized. Except for a large number of vagrants, individual economic activity was rare; and forms of cooperative production were practiced in both town and country. Economic society was stratified, and the division into social classes was partly confirmed by law and definitely approved by the Church. Control over economic life was largely political, representing to a large extent the ambitions of nobles and churchmen.

The Agricultural Village Community

The economic activity of the great majority of people centered in agricultural village communities, reasonably similar to each other

[1] See Chap. 4.

in many respects but differing considerably in the details of organization. Each rural community was subservient to a resident or non-resident lord, the latter term including not only nobles but also officials of ecclesiastical institutions: cathedrals, abbeys, or monasteries. From lay or ecclesiastical lords, some members of the village community derived rights to use land. But not all members were so fortunate; a large number were landless, and stood in a more precarious economic condition. England's first census (for that is what the Domesday survey of 1086 actually was) revealed three dependent classes of people in the agricultural village communities: villeins, bordars, and slaves. Three centuries later, slavery had almost disappeared, and the dependent classes then included freemen, villeins, and cotters. The cotters of the 14th century were, in relative status, essentially comparable to the bordars of the 11th; the freemen, by and large, occupied a privileged legal position. The actual way in which these three agricultural classes satisfied their wants in the 14th century may be illustrated by explaining the customs which were followed in the Cambridgeshire village of Oakington. It should not be inferred, however, that the customs of this community were necessarily representative of all the village communities in England.

Oakington was one of the many possessions of Crowland Abbey, the ancient foundation of St. Guthlac.[2] In 1344, the village community consisted of 51 landholding tenants, plus an unknown number of their landless relatives. Altogether these 51 landholders had rights to cultivate 570 acres of land. In addition to peasant holdings, the records indicate the existence of "demesne" land used for the exclusive benefit of Crowland Abbey, comprising almost 200 acres of arable and 20 acres of meadow land. This demesne was cultivated partly by a group of hired laborers (*famuli*) who worked for wages, partly by labor services exacted from the members of the village community according to the customs of the manor. The amount of this compulsory labor (*opera*) depended upon the respective status of the members of the village community, but within each social stratum the amount of labor was approximately the same.

Of the 51 members of the village community who cultivated the 570 acres for their own benefit, 12 were freemen, 33 may be designated as villeins, the remaining 6 as cotters. The 12 freemen had the use of

[2] The manorial records of Oakington, preserved at Queens' College, Cambridge, have been edited by Frances Page and published in *The Estates of Crowland Abbey* (Cambridge: The University Press, 1934).

122 acres of land, the villeins of about 428 acres, the 6 cotters of about 20, making the average landholding of the freemen around 10 acres each, of the villeins 13 acres, and of the cotters a little over 3. But these figures are deceptive. The arable lands of Oakington, like those of other English manors, were laid out in three unfenced fields and divided into long narrow strips. Consequently the holdings of any one peasant consisted of scattered strips of land distributed about equally among the three fields. Since it was the general practice to let one of the three fields lie fallow each year, the amount of land cultivated annually would be approximately two-thirds of a peasant's entire holding. Correcting the average holdings by this deduction for fallow, the amount of land actually available for cultivation each year would be: freemen, $6\frac{2}{3}$;[3] villeins, $8\frac{2}{3}$; cotters, 2. This, then, represents the real power which the Oakington tenants possessed for satisfying their wants from arable land. They did, however, have certain additional "common rights," for example (in terms of their status) the right to pasture so many animals (cattle, sheep, pigs, or geese) in the common pasture; the right to cut so much hay in the common meadows; or the right to gather so much firewood in the lord's woods.

Obligations of Tenants

For the right to use these small parcels of land, the unfree Cambridgeshire tenants paid dearly. The 12 freemen apparently performed little if any, labor service, deriving the use of their holdings from money rent. In contrast, the villeins and cotters were not only subject to labor services but also paid a sizeable money rent. Most of the villeins performed 51 "works" each year. A "work" is never explicitly defined in the Cambridgeshire records; its meaning was apparently so well understood that no clarification was needed. From other manorial records, however, we learn that a "work" might be defined in nature (reaping half an acre, shearing a certain number of sheep) or in time (one day's labor at the lord's discretion).[4] The labor comprehended did not need to be performed personally by the landholder; it was his responsibility either to perform the labor himself or to find someone to do it. Such were

[3] Freehold land in many manors lay apart from the open fields, and hence might not be subject to manorial crop rotation.

[4] See N. S. B. Gras, *The Economic and Social History of an English Village* (Cambridge: the University Press, 1930), pp. 66–67; Page, *Estates of Crowland Abbey*, pp. 99–105.

the obligations of the villeins in weekday labor services; in addition each was required to perform special work at certain seasons of the year, and also to pay a money rent which varied between 3 and 6 shillings. Thus, for the annual use of 8⅔ acres of cultivable land, the villeins of Oakington gave in rent more than one day's work each week, plus a money payment equal to the value of 7 to 8 bushels of wheat. Since crop yields were small in medieval England, if this rent money was derived wholly from the sale of wheat, almost the whole produce of one of the precious acres would have to be sold in order to obtain the required rent money.

There were 26 villeins in Oakington known as *fullondidmen*. They were the "15-acre men," who constituted a virtual aristocracy among the unfree tenants. Below them stood seven "five-acre men." Still lower were three "three-acre men"; two holders of three rods; and one person who held only one rod; the last six were cotters who paid varying amounts of labor services and money rents. We need not here go into the details of their servitude, but their condition certainly was not a happy one. With rights to very small areas of land, they and their dependents were compelled to eke out an existence partly from their minute fields, and partly from household industries or from the sale of their services to more prosperous tenants or to the bailiff of the Abbot of Crowland. Yet the 51 landholders of Oakington, although their holdings were patently inadequate, were nevertheless a very fortunate segment of the manor's population. An unknown number of persons had no rights to land whatever. This was because until the breakup of the manor, an unfree tenant holding was inalienable; unchanged in size it passed from father to son. Hence only one son could obtain the use of land, and upon his shoulders fell the responsibility of caring for his aged parents and for his landless brothers and sisters. In Cambridgeshire this problem of "poor relations" was systematically dealt with. Each landholder was required to grant to his landless brothers and sisters (as a group, not to each) the use of half an acre of land in each of the three arable fields. Having done this, his legal responsibility for poor relief ended; migration, misery, and death probably did the rest. The manorial system of control, it is true, was designed to hold this landless element to a minimum; none could marry without the lord's approval[5] and then only by the payment of a marriage fine (*merchet*). Like the landholders, the landless could not

---

[5] This customary regulation applied to landholders as well and was bitterly resented.

leave the manor without the payment of a fine (*chevage*). In the 14th century, however, there was not much more chance of employment outside the manor than within, and flight was not a common event until the latter part of the century, when the disorganizing influence of the Black Death created labor shortages in those manors where a large proportion of people had died, or in cities and towns.

Manorial Administration

The 14th-century manor was to a very large extent socially self-contained. This is quite a different matter, however, from the commonly-made statement that it was economically self-sufficient. As a possession of a lay-lord or an ecclesiastical institution, the manor was an "estate" and, as such, a source of revenue. If it was a part of a group of estates (as Oakington was), consisting, for example, of manors, mills, ferries, markets, or fairs, the whole group was administered to yield income. The "steward" was normally the general manager for a group of estates, while a "bailiff" usually directed the activities of a smaller number or those of a single agricultural community. The chief resident manorial officer was the "reeve," most frequently chosen from the ablest villeins. He supervised the enforced labor of the unfree tenants and collected the money rents. As manager of the demesne farm, he kept the records; and much of the actual knowledge we have about medieval farming is derived from reeves' account books. The manor as a business institution both bought and sold. Most of the goods sold were the property of the lord, and most of the purchases were for the demesne. Thus grain, wool, and hides were the usual products sold, while iron, veterinary supplies, rope, harness, plows, millstones, and other agricultural tools were found among the list of purchases. But villeins also bought and sold; indeed, without something to sell, the Cambridgeshire tenants obviously could not have paid their money rents. And it was this very process which hastened the breakup of the manor: the progressive substitution of money payments for labor services. This process depended necessarily upon an increased quantity of buying and selling, which, in turn, depended upon markets and other agencies facilitating sales.

"Ancient Customs" of the Agricultural Community

Before turning to a description of the towns, wherein most local markets of the medieval world were to be found, a few legal aspects of

the village community need elaboration because they throw light on how agricultural economic activity was controlled. In legal theory, the subservient elements in the village consisted of two strictly separable legal classes: the freemen and the villeins (including cotters). The freeman's relation to his lord was essentially contractual. His right to land was protected in the king's court; his land was alienable. Moreover, the position of the freeman was a privileged one, not only legally, but economically. If labor services were demanded of him, they were usually small, and ordinarily consisted only of "boon-day" work (*precariae*), normally the performance of special tasks at harvest time. Frequently such services were nominal, more a confession of fealty than a labor service. Money rents were by far the usual obligations of the free tenant.

The legal status of the villein was wholly different. In strict theory he was the property of his lord, and being himself property, he could possess none. Having no legal personality, the villein was denied access to the king's courts, although he could seek legal redress against other villeins in the manorial court. Since he was a chattel he could not leave the manor; he was bound to the soil (*adscriptus glebae*) and could, therefore, be captured and brought back should he flee. He held land at the will of the lord and hence the security of his tenure was wholly derived from custom, not from law. He was liable for labor services which, in legal theory, were limited only by the lord's discretion. Custom, however, had come to the aid of the villeins; as a consequence, the labor services of each class of villeins were fairly clearly defined and limited.[6]

This harsh legal theory provided unquestionable authorization for the control of one caste by another, and the manorial court was the institution whereby control was affected. Presided over by the lord's official, the court allotted tenant land (when the death of a villein created a vacant holding) and punished villeins convicted of failing either to perform their labor services or to pay their money-rents. Although the manorial court could, by its prerogative, control every detail of the economic life of the villeins, actually this privilege had been materially restricted by custom. Landholdings were assigned not with newly devised labor services or money rents at each devolution, but according to the "ancient customs." Yet until the Black Death, the

---

6 The rights and obligations of groups of tenants were, sometimes, very simply stated in manorial records, as, for example, "John at the Well shall hold six acres and shall perform 51 works each year."

"ancient customs" represented enough control to comprehend the destiny of every member of an agricultural village community.

The villein, therefore, cultivated his dispersed acres in the time which custom had made his own, followed the rotation of crops which custom dictated, pastured the number of sheep on the common pasture which custom had made appropriate to his status, performed the traditional labor services, and paid the customary obligations (*heriot, merchet, tallage*).[7] Money rents, however, were in the process of change; they were increasing and for two main reasons. Very frequently all the labor services owed to a lord were not needed. When this condition existed, unneeded and unwanted services were replaced by a money payment ("works sold"). Sometimes "commutation" of labor services by money payments had taken place so regularly, year after year, that money payments had become customary. In the second place, ambitious tenants who sold enough products (and thereby had money incomes) were already in the 14th century seeking to rid themselves permanently of labor services, in order to devote all their time to their acres. Since money income was often more attractive to lords than labor services, such a contractual process of commutation gathered momentum, and ultimately became one of the most important reasons for the dissolution of the manor as an authoritarian economic institution.

The tools and implements which the agriculture village community used were limited. Plows represented the most elaborate implements; they were owned either individually, by the lord of a manor, or collectively, by the villeins. Usually both conditions prevailed, the records mentioning the number of plows belonging to the demesne and the number owned by the villeins. Aside from plows, which were indispensable, and aside from the equipment of blacksmiths and millers, which usually belonged to the lord, only primitive carts and hand tools are recorded. Investment in implements by unfree tenants was neither customary nor wise; a society which regarded the subservient elements as legal chattels could not be expected to emphasize investment in tools. The little saving which was possible took the form of hoarding, and surviving peasant communities reflect this propensity even in modern times. Scarcity of tools in medieval economic society necessarily put a premium on physical labor; thus the medieval peasants worked in the

---

7 On taking possession of a holding, a tenant normally paid *heriot* by delivering to the lord his best animal; the marriage fine (*merchet*) was also customary. As contrasted with these obligations, *tallage* was a tax, theoretically discretionary but normalized by custom. These three payments were by no means the only ones for which villeins were liable, but they were the most representative.

ways of their fathers. Only in the church[8] and in rustic festivals did they find relief from their struggle for life's necessities.

Relative Freedom of the Towns

As a community of specialized traders and manufacturers, the medieval town was organized and controlled in ways very different from those which prevailed in the agricultural village community. A larger measure of freedom was evident among medieval town workers, giving rise to the proverb that "town air makes men free." A greater conflict of economic interests required many solutions in the nature of compromise, so that whereas, in the agricultural communities, controls came to be stereotyped, in contrast, the economic rules of the town were progressively changing. Very seldom did the town represent a homogeneous authoritarian economic institution, for, with growth of specialized skill in mercantile or manufacturing activities, authority came to be more and more divided. Thus control by occupational groups existed simultaneously with the political control of the municipality and the surveillance of the Church; this situation, taken in conjunction with the range of occupations which were practiced, converted the medieval town into a far more complex economic aggregation than the manor.

The economic life of the agricultural village community was only partially related to markets; that of the town was directly dependent upon agencies for exchange. Although the towns very frequently had their fields and their commons, and were therefore partly agricultural, an increasing proportion of food, fuel, raw materials, and beasts of burden had to be purchased from the manorial farms. The town's output of manufactured goods was sold in local markets or through merchants in foreign markets. This increasing dependence on buying and selling as an integral part of town life made control over transactions extremely important, and town officials were not modest in assuming such surveillance. For the benefit of the townsmen, the local markets were carefully regulated, but because these regulations were devised in the interest of the town dwellers, the economic classes living within town walls must be described before any proper analysis of markets and other exchange agencies can be attempted.

Because trade had come to be a normal economic activity of towns,

[8] In Oakington today, the church is the only surviving building that dates from the 14th century.

and because trade was driven by money, townsmen had been able to commute any labor services that they may earlier have owed to king, lay-lords, or churchmen. Only in small, backward towns were townsmen still subject to boon-day services. In larger and more flourishing towns, the burgesses not only had achieved freedom from servile obligations, but as a consequence of this freedom, they had obtained complete personal mobility. There had developed also in the towns a different concept of property, involving the right to sell, pledge, or exchange real estate without restriction of manorial or ecclesiastical authority. Freed from *tallage, merchet,* and labor services, the townsmen largely were masters of their personal destinies. Yet, as the external control over their economic life had diminished, the townsmen themselves had created new forms of municipal control, and groups of artisans restrained the liberty of other groups and of their own members by elaborate regulations designed to prevent encroachment upon their respective freedom.

The Town as a Production Unit

The composition of town population in the 14th century included two important and usually dominant elements: the traders and the artisans. Corporative organizations of merchants normally occurred earlier than those of artisans, because trade was usually older than specialized production, and because artisans frequently required the services of merchants to obtain markets wide enough to permit the occupational specialization which necessarily had to precede the corporative organization of a single craft. Once they were formed, merchant and craft gilds became social, fraternal, and religious associations, as well as economic organizations. They held banquets, produced mystery plays, and provided their members with sickness and burial benefits; they dedicated themselves to patron saints, and frequently maintained altars or chapels. Yet first and foremost they were groups of merchants or artisans banded together for economic benefit, for the autonomous control of their respective occupations, and for the exclusion of "foreigners" from their markets. Conceived in a spirit of intense protectionism, the economic philosophy underlying gild organization was narrow and conservative.[10]

Since our immediate concern is with the town as a center of produc-

[10] Eli Hecksher in his excellent *Mercantilism* (London: George Unwin, 1935), explains in detail the goals and purposes of medieval protection.

tion, chief attention should be centered on the craft gilds. Like the manor, the craft gild was stratified, but, unlike the manor, status in the lower segments of the industrial fraternity was not permanent. Usually three classes of members made up the craft fellowship: apprentices, journeymen, and master craftsmen, with the apprentices on the way to becoming journeymen, the journeymen aspiring to become masters. The master craftsman was an independent manufacturer: a business man who bought raw materials, fabricated them, and sold his finished product. If, for example, he was a shoemaker of Coventry, he and all other master shoemakers of that town controlled the internal operation of the shoemakers' gild. In ceremonial meeting the master shoemakers would foregather, elect their "warden" and their "aldermen." As a manufacturer, each master shoemaker was an independent producer who worked in his combined house and shop with the help of his hired journeymen (French *journé,* "paid by the day") and his apprentices (who were his legal children). As a member of the shoemakers' gild, he was nevertheless subject to gild rules, designed to guarantee fair play for all and equal economic opportunity for all the shoemakers of Coventry.

Where complete autonomy had been attained by a craft gild, the control which a warden exercised over his gild was a consequence of delegated power; where wardens were appointed by a territorial prince or by a bishop, control was still essentially political. But the balancing of relative power between various gilds within the same town always involved compromise, and the town governments came to represent a complex process whereby the mayor was compelled to adjudicate disputes between corporative economic groups. Hence two chief problems of control emerged in the medieval town: the internal control of separate craft gilds, and the external control of all the craft gilds which made up the productive economic structure of a medieval town.

Protective Purposes of Town Regulations

The internal control was designed to provide equal opportunities for all full-fledged members of an economic fraternity. The methods were essentially negative, centering on the prevention of overreaching by outlawing ruinous competition, advertising, unfair practices, unlawful tools, unjust wages, or poor workmanship. It became the duty of the warden to guard against these evils, to make diligent search and scrutiny, to punish offenders against the gild rules. Meantime, the process of production adjusted itself institutionally to these rules and prohibitions. Workshops came to be located in the ground-floor apartments of the gildsman's house. By the street window, where all could see, the master craftsman and his journeymen and apprentices worked. The hours of work were limited lest one gildsman take advantage of his fellows; the kinds of tools were defined and all others forbidden, the number of apprentices was restricted, as was also the number of journeymen. The quality of workmanship was carefully scrutinized to guarantee that no adulterating craftsman should cast discredit on his brethren. Thus fidelity and honesty were not left to emerge automatically, but were compelled by the jealousy and suspicion which demanded minute supervision over the methods of production.

The master craftsman was more than a manufacturer—he was at once a custodian of his legal children, an employer of his journeymen, and a merchant as well; and in all these activities he was subject to surveillance. His apprentices were bound by "indentures," bilateral agreements which required faithful application on the part of the apprentices for a period of years,[11] dutiful instruction in craftsmanship on the part of the master, together with suitable food, clothing, and shelter. Should the master fail to perform these parental functions, any aggrieved apprentice might appeal to the warden of the gild for redress.

When the apprentice had duly completed his period of industrial training, he normally became a journeyman. Ordinarily he was expected to remain with his master for another year, working for wages. Sometimes the completion of a "masterpiece" was required of him before he was admitted to the privileges of a master craftsman, although this requirement seems to have been more frequently ignored in England than observed. The whole scheme of probation was designed to guarantee competence as one goal, limitation of members in the industrial fellowship as another.

By the compulsion involved in paternal and representative control, both of which characterized the craft gild, strong emphasis was placed upon honest workmanship. It would be an error, however, to conclude that this emphasis proved that medieval business morality was exemplary. The medieval craftsman "had no more conscience than a plumber;"[12] he worked within a system which was characterized by

11 Usually seven years in England; frequently less in France and Germany.
12 L. F. Salzman, *English Industries of the Middle Ages* (Oxford: The Clarendon Press, 1923), p. 309.

intense local jealousy, a system which so minutely regulated personal activity that only by the wiliest tricks could the individual producer hoodwink his fellow craftsmen.

Nor should it be forgotten that the policy of the craft gild organization was designed not only to protect a group of artisans against competition from other cities but also to safeguard each producer against the competition of his fellow producers. The goal of the group was local monopoly; the goal of the individual craftsman was a proportional share of the benefits of this monopoly. The consequence of this quest for privilege was an emphasis upon quality arising from development of personal skill, and a repression of technical progress which might have emerged as a result of untrammeled initiative. Technical progress, as Pirenne has said,[13] was equivalent to disloyalty: "the ideal was stability of conditions in a stable industrial organization."

Although the craft gilds represent an elaborate early example of controls emerging from conflict of economic interests, these organizations were by no means exempt from outside regulation. The authority of the municipality over the craft gilds was invariably recognized, and the records of Norwich, Bristol, Coventry, Exeter, Oxford, and London provide evidence of the extent to which it was enforced.[14] Some of the town supervision of gild action was undertaken on behalf of consumers, as, for example, the regulation of butchers, bakers, and fishmongers; while other forms of control, notably the licensing of gilds, probably originated either in efforts to repress the growing political independence of the craftsmen or in fiscal ambitions of the towns. In England many craft gilds paid annual dues, either to municipalities or to the Crown, in return for the privilege of industrial monopoly. Such a contractual relation provided a means whereby external control was in part relinquished for a money compensation.

Social Justice in the Market Place

The economic connection between town and country was provided by markets which tied together the stratified agricultural population and the quasi-stratified urban communities. By the 14th century, Eng-

---

[13] In his account of European gilds in the *Encyclopaedia of the Social Sciences*, Vol. VII, p. 213.

[14] For details, see E. Lipson, *The Economic History of England* (London: A. & C. Black, 1929), Vol. I, pp. 328–339.

land had an extensive network of exchange agencies.[15] Most towns maintained continuous markets for the sale of town-made products. In addition, on designated days, a market was held primarily for the sale of agricultural produce brought to the town by country people. Under the supervision of town authorities, these markets were closely regulated, primarily in the interests of the town dwellers who were concerned with ensuring adequate food supplies at the lowest possible prices.

To the town markets came the country folk bringing their grain, flour, beans, peas, chickens, fish, eggs, and lambs; or their flax, wool, and yarn. When held within the close of a cathedral[16] or on Church property, medieval markets sometimes came under the direct surveillance of both ecclesiastical and town authorities. Throughout Christendom, the Church laid down rules of business conduct which were designed to guarantee justice for both buyers and sellers. These rules were practical applications of the ecclesiastical doctrine of just price (justum pretium), a concept which dates back to the writings of the Church Fathers of the 3rd and 4th centuries A.D., and which had been codified by the great theologian, St. Thomas Aquinas, in the 13th century. Based on a social theory which viewed with approval the division of society into classes, the medieval theory of just price sought to permit the members of each class to sell commodities at prices which would appropriately cover their respective costs of production; and since compensation for labor expended in production represented the most important element in the cost of production, the just price was largely derived from the doctrine of fair wages. A reward sufficient to maintain each producer in the social class to which he belonged was interpreted as fair, and the sale of commodities at prices which reflected such fair wages was therefore conceived to answer the demands of justice.

The theory of just price is easier to describe than the actual methods whereby town authorities tried to put this precept into practice. Some prices were arbitrarily fixed, notably those of bread and ale. Efforts

15 Markets were ordinarily located within the walls of the towns, whereas fairs were held at religious shrines or at places calculated to attract the largest possible number of town dwellers, as well as the peasantry.

16 Fairs and markets were even held on the Sabbath day, although this custom was often condemned by the Church. The attitude of the Church toward holding markets on Church property was varied; some churchmen bitterly condemned the use of churches for mercantile purposes, while other ecclesiastical institutions drew desired revenues from fairs and markets. On this subject, see L. F. Salzman, *English Trade in the Middle Ages* (Oxford: The Clarendon Press, 1931), Chap. VII, and Lipson, *The Economic History of England*, Vol. I, pp. 204–208.

to corner the supply of goods (engrossing) were specifically forbidden; purchase of goods en route to market by speculators (forestalling) was likewise outlawed; forbidden also was the purchase of goods within a market with the intention of reselling them in the same market at higher prices (regrating). The modern reliance on competition as a self-regulating force for the determination of prices found but limited acceptance in the medieval world. Hence faults were to be revealed, measures were required to be true and just; in short, markets were to facilitate all legitimate exchange but were not to be perverted into agencies for sheer money-making. It would be a serious error, however, to assume that all these laudable ideals were accomplished.

The Function of Fairs

The hundreds of markets under the supervision of town authority were not the only agencies for trade in medieval England. Another very important agency was the fair. Whereas markets were intended to facilitate exchange within definite neighborhoods and were accordingly located from six to ten miles from each other,[17] the medieval fair served an essentially different purpose. It was, as Salzman has said, a "glorified market," both in duration and in the variety of goods bought and sold. To it came not only people from neighboring towns and manors but merchants from distant towns and from foreign countries. Held usually but once a year on the occasion of a Church festival, the fair was both an outstanding religious gathering and an important economic event. Booths and temporary shops were erected, streets laid out, merchants' chests opened, goods displayed; meantime money changers and bankers set up their tables or stalls where all kinds of money could be converted and where credit arrangements could be negotiated.

Thus the fair provided a much wider range of goods than the local markets. While the fair was in existence, the ordinary mercantile activities of the nearby towns were usually suspended. Local jealousy, which normally excluded competing merchants from other towns and from foreign countries, was powerless to exclude them from the fair. As a result, at famous fairs like Stourbridge in Cambridgeshire there was available an amazing assortment of merchandise: iron and hardware, silks and tapestries, books and parchment, horses and carts, medi-

---

[17] According to Bracton's rule, a new market within 6⅔ miles of an existing market ought to be suppressed.

cines and drugs, to say nothing of the usual staple raw materials and the products of ordinary craftsmanship.

The fair was opened by proclamation; its duration came to be regularized,[18] and its conduct gradually was systematized under the "Law Merchant." This body of "private" international law was common to all European merchants of the medieval world. It was unwritten law, sanctioned by custom, and came to be administered by "Piepowder Courts," juridical bodies composed largely of merchants, which resolved legal problems in the fair transactions. Thus the Law Merchant provided a simple means for the settlement of disputes concerning contracts; its remedies were available to all persons who came to the fair. The Piepowder Courts were informal and prompt in their decisions. Although presided over by a mayor of a corporate town, or by a lord's steward, the verdicts were given by jurors drawn from the ranks of merchants who regularly visited the fair in which the merchants' court was set up. These jurors were concerned with the content of legal pleading rather than the form. If competent witnesses corroborated the making of an agreement between two merchants, such an agreement was considered to be a binding contract. The simplicity, the promptness, and the reasonableness of the Law Merchant extended its employment, and its wide use facilitated peaceful exchange in the medieval fairs. The great fairs were not mere aggregations of petty hucksters; they brought together wholesale merchants from distant places, retailers, and consumers. Large transactions demanded credit accommodation; bills of exchange, letters of credit, and promissory notes were employed, and these negotiable instruments required the legal sanction of the Piepowder Courts to guarantee their fulfilment.

Development of Export Industries

Town and country in medieval England were mutually dependent but, to some extent, the prosperity of each was dependent upon foreign trade. In the early-medieval period England's foreign trade had been largely in the hands of foreign merchants, especially the Italians and merchants belonging to the Hanseatic League. Gradually, English merchants had entered this trade, and, by the 14th century, an increasing proportion of imports and exports were bought and sold by English merchants.

18 Varying, according to the volume of business, from one, two, or three days up to several weeks.

Britain's exports consisted largely of raw materials, such as wool, fleeces, hides, leather, and tin. Wool had long been England's "golden fleece," not only to the growers, but to the government, which collected handsome export duties from the wool merchants. Most of the exported English wool found markets in Flanders, Brabant, and Northern France, the most flourishing cloth-manufacturing centers of medieval Europe. Buyers who traveled throughout the country purchased wool from the growers, and carried it on pack animals to the staple towns, where they sold it for export. Because of its capacity for yielding customs revenue, the wool trade had long been supervised by the government; special pains had been taken to see that all exports were properly assembled at designated ports (staple towns) where the bags were sealed by the collectors of customs.

Long before the 14th century, however, a domestic cloth industry had gradually grown up. Weaving and spinning were carried on in many shires of England during the 12th and the 13th centuries. Indeed, the industry never wholly adjusted itself to a craft-gild organization; and for this reason, industrial rivalry grew up between town and country, a rivalry which was to become acute in the 15th and 16th centuries, and which ultimately contributed abundantly to a weakening of the craft gilds. In the reign of Edward III (1327–1377) the English cloth-making industry had received definite encouragement from the Crown. Flemish artisans were encouraged to migrate to England, while the importation of foreign cloth was forbidden to all but a privileged few. The effect of Edward's industrial policy was salutary. The cloth industry grew, whereas the export of raw wool declined from around 30,000 sacks in the middle of the 14th century to about 7,000 sacks at the beginning of the 16th century. Meantime, however, wool growing had spread over large areas of England, and concurrently a new manufacturing class had rapidly increased its numbers and its power.

This dispersed cloth industry differed from the more usual type of craft-gild production in two respects: it came to be controlled to a large extent by the royal government rather than by town gilds, and it tended, more and more, to be organized by businessmen whose methods of production were based on a wage system rather than upon craft-gild organization. From the point of view of the Crown it was desirable that cloth should gradually take the place of raw wool as a major export since cloth making could provide an increasing source of revenue. For this reason the sale of cloth was concentrated in London at Blackwell

Hall, and into this emporium came the broadcloths, serges, and bays from the weaving districts.

Although the wage system had long existed in the tin-mining industry, it was the woolen industry which really spread this type of industrial organization. With widening domestic and foreign markets for cloth, the craft-gild organization was incapable of satisfying all these markets; and by the end of the 14th century a large part of the cloth industry was already organized by great clothiers, who bought raw wool and had it carded, scoured, spun, and woven by a wage-earning proletariat. Many of the cloth workers were country people who were underemployed in agriculture, and who readily seized any opportunity to find supplemental work; hence, gradually the cloth industry became widely dispersed over the west and the north of England. The exact method whereby this far-flung industry was organized will be described in the next chapter. Here it need only be pointed out that an industrial organization wholly different from the corporative idea of the craft gild was expanding rapidly, a type of organization whose future development was to usher in a very different kind of economic world from that of 14th-century England.

3

The emergence
of capitalism[1]

The Process of Change—Some General Contrasts

The institutions which directed economic life in 14th-century England have either disappeared or have been so materially changed that modern survivals bear little resemblance to their originals. Rural life is no longer organized on a manorial basis, although only in the past generation have a large number of East European manors been superseded by new types of agrarian organization. The craft gild survives only in modified form, and its modern counterpart is perhaps best illustrated by the American Medical Association. Fairs, in the process of history, have been largely specialized. Large industrial fairs are today places

[1] If it were possible to avoid using this ambiguous word, we should all rejoice. But its usage has permeated so much of our economic literature that we cannot now hope to abolish the word. All we can try to do is to make its meaning, in a given context, as clear and precise as possible.

where manufacturers can exhibit their products to prospective buyers; local fairs, in contrast, have lost their importance as agencies for the purchase and sale of merchandise and have, to a large extent, continued as familiar institutions by emphasizing amusement and magic, two elements of medieval origin. Open-stall markets still exist in Europe and in some American cities, although the growth of retail stores has progressively diminished their importance.

Vestiges of medieval economic institutions may thus be found, but our modern way of economic life has changed so completely that the surviving institutions are incongruous. Serfdom, which was the political counterpart of the manor, slowly melted away under the warmth of political democracy; local exclusiveness, which formed the political atmosphere in which the craft gild flourished, was broken down by nationalism which has, in turn, gradually weakened in a 20th-century trend toward internationalism. Apprenticeship, which played such an important part in craft-gild operation, has been largely superseded by more efficient methods of industrial education. As a result of changed methods of transportation, markets have extended far beyond their territorial limits in the medieval world, while money, which played a modest rôle in medieval times, has so widely extended its influence that the whole business of living is now intimately connected with the receipt and expenditure of money and credit. Most important of all, the wage system, which was in its infancy in the 14th century, has spread over almost the entire world, causing vast numbers of people to depend on money wages in order to obtain the goods and services which they need. In the meantime, huge and impersonal agencies of production and exchange, organized by means of business corporations, have come into being, complex institutions which hold the destinies of millions of people in their invisible but powerful hands. Ownership of tools has been divorced from personal skill, leading to definite productive advantages but creating at the same time unrest on the part of industrial workers, and varying degrees of insecurity for great masses of people.

Different economic institutions, different ways of life, different scales of values are therefore the heritage of people born in the 20th century, as contrasted with that of their medieval ancestors. Because modern economic life is at once a set of institutions and a way of life, it cannot be understood unless the historical processes which produced both are comprehended. Very obviously, the complex details of economic history cannot be described in this introductory book, but a part of the process of change can be explained by emphasizing outstanding differences between one period of time and another. This chapter will, therefore, describe briefly the economic life of England about the year 1700 and show how economic institutions and ways of making a living had changed between the middle of the 14th century and the beginning of the 18th.

Rural Economic Life About 1700

Although England and Wales had a population of more than 5 million in 1700, about three-fourths of this number lived in the country.[2] Agriculture was still the most important occupation, although not all country people, by any means, were farmers. The woollen and worsted industries provided either entire or partial employment for thousands of people in country villages, so that the statistical division of the population between town and country gives an erroneous picture of the relative importance of agriculture and industry.

The tillers of the soil were no longer serfs. By commutation of labor services into money payments and by virtue of a changed legal status, the humble villeins of the 14th century had either become agricultural laborers or joined the ranks of the independent "yeomen" who were the pride of England's poets and the mainstay of England's armies. Landholding at the will of lay or ecclesiastical lord had been replaced partly by land ownership but mostly by leaseholding, a practice which was relatively unimportant in the age of Chaucer, but which had grown so extensively by the age of Milton that tenant farmers constituted one of the largest segments of the agrarian population.

Among the forces which had produced this significant change in agrarian structure, one had already revealed itself in the 14th century— the substitution of money rents for labor services—a change made possible by the increased money incomes of the peasants and by the landlords' preference for money rents, rather than for labor services or produce rents. The growth of private property in land and the rearrangement of the open-field strips into compact parcels, however, was a more complex process, one that began in the 15th and 16th centuries as a result of the weakening of feudalism, an increasing supply of money, the growth of the woollen industry, and the increase in town population.

[2] Gregory King in 1696 estimated the total population at 5,500,000, of which 1,400,000 were urban dwellers. London was the only large city, with a population of about 500,000. Next came Norwich and Bristol, although the contrast with London was remarkable, since neither had over 30,000 people.

Public opinion, however, did not view the agrarian changes with favor, and English preachers and social reformers[3] forcefully called attention to a change in farming which they considered undesirable. Landlords were enclosing previously open fields, meadows, common pastures, or waste lands, converting them into sheepwalks. Although the loudness of popular complaint would seem to indicate that this change was threatening the lives of all members of the agricultural village communities, careful statistical computation[4] has revealed that less than 3 per cent of English manorial land was actually enclosed during the period from 1455 to 1607, and that the largest proportion of land enclosed in any county was under 9 per cent. The Tudor enclosures, however, did dramatically call attention to the changes which were slowly transforming medieval agriculture into new patterns. The enclosure of open fields by landlords ushered a commercial spirit into agriculture, while the loud and bitter complaints of the peasants revealed the very important fact that they were no longer serfs.

Large Farms and Small

Careful study of many agricultural communities in the 16th century[5] has thrown a flood of light on the internal changes which took place on many English manors. A miniature land market had actually grown up as prosperous tenants engaged in a busy process of rearranging their dispersed acres into compact bundles. The old distinctions among freeholders, customary tenants (villeins) and cotters still survived but had lost most of their meaning. The only real distinctions were between small farmers and large. The large farmers, with sizeable surpluses to sell in town and city markets, had correspondingly greater money incomes, allowing them to acquire large bundles of land strips by trading, buying, or leasing. Often these consolidated acres had been enclosed into separate farms, a type of peasant enclosure which must be distinguished carefully from landlord enclosure. The former type seldom involved any diminution of arable cultivation; merely a spatial re-

---

[3] Bishop Latimer bitterly assailed the Tudor enclosures in his sermons, as Sir Thomas More had done before him in his *Utopia*.

[4] E. F. Gay, "Inclosures in England," *Quarterly Journal of Economics*, Vol. XVII, pp. 576–79; Arthur H. Johnson, *The Disappearance of the Small Landowner* (Oxford: The Clarendon Press, 1909), pp. 48, 58.

[5] See R. H. Tawney, *The Agrarian Problem in the Sixteenth Century* (London; P. S. King and Son, Ltd., 1912).

arrangement of holdings, and an increased control over larger land areas by the more energetic and more capable peasants.

The new pattern of agriculture may be illustrated by the manor of Horstead with Staninghall, in Norfolk.[6] At the beginning of the 17th century, this manor consisted of 2746 acres, of which about 1700 acres were held by 29 tenants. Among these tenants, however, a striking inequality in holding had come into existence. Three tenants held 265, 270, and 280 acres respectively; three others over 100 acres each; four had 60 acres each; two held 40 acres each; while 17 tenants held acreages varying from one to 20 acres. Here, then, the structure of the agricultural village community had been entirely changed; an aristocracy of large farmers had arisen; the six with holdings of over 100 acres, for example, accounted for 1,225 acres, leaving less than 475 acres for the remaining 23 small farmers. This single illustration indicates the far-reaching internal changes which had taken place on many English manors. An energetic, ambitious group of large farmers was rapidly forging ahead, cultivating large acreages and hiring varying numbers of agricultural laborers. These enterprising farmers had built up their large holdings by outbidding the small farmers in rents, by renting former demesne land, and by purchasing freehold land.[7] Successful in their ventures, they had sufficient capital to stock their pastures with better sheep, cattle, and hogs; they also possessed money to invest in the improvement of the soil. Moreover, they were able to bargain with landlords for long leases, necessary prerequisites for investments in land improvements.

New Farming Practices

During the 17th century, the methods of English agriculture steadily became more efficient. Because population increased, and because prices rose as a result of the inflow of precious metals from Spanish America, adequate profits were available for farmers who were able to transport products to the best markets and who were intelligent enough to make the best use of their soils. New crop rotations came into use; clover and

[6] W. H. R. Curtler, *A Short History of English Agriculture* (Oxford: The Clarendon Press, 1909), pp. 97–98.
[7] During the Commonwealth, large quantities of land which had been confiscated by Parliament were also thrown on the market.

turnips,[8] which had long been cultivated in Holland, were popularized; flax and saffron also appeared on the list of new crops; meantime the cultivation of potatoes yielded a new food crop which was slowly acquiring favor even though extensive planting of this now important article of diet did not occur until a century and a half later. Elizabeth's reign also saw a noticeable increase in the cultivation of hops, fruits, and garden produce in manors near commercial or industrial towns. These important changes in tillage were partly a result of increased botanical knowledge, partly a consequence of the freedom of individual enterprise which the breakup of the rigid status of the medieval manor had made possible. More and more, agriculture was becoming commercialized. Although many rural communities were still largely self-sufficient, an ever-increasing number of large farmers had become skillful businessmen, carrying on extensive buying and selling in the enlarged produce markets.

Widening Markets for Farm Produce

The growth of large leasehold farms was, therefore, correlated with wider markets for agricultural produce. No longer were corn growers[9] dependent upon local markets for the disposal of their surpluses, for the grain trade was now well organized. Some farmers, especially the poorer ones, sold their grain on their farms, although, for the most part, grain was either sold in town markets or disposed of in large lots on the basis of samples. Millers, bakers, commission dealers, and merchants accounted for the bulk of the grain purchases, the millers and bakers buying primarily for local needs, while the merchants carried on wholesale operations in England and also supplied foreign markets with English grain whenever prices warranted and the corn laws permitted.

The marketing of wool was even more efficiently organized than the grain trade. Wool dealers travelled through the country regions buying wool from the graziers, transporting their purchases on pack animals. Since wool manufacturing was dispersed throughout rural England, most of the locally-produced wool was bought up by clothiers, whose operations were confined to particular regions. As wool manufacturing

---

[8] The use of root crops and legumes hastened nitrogen fixation and made it unnecessary to let a third of the arable land lie fallow each year.

[9] The word "corn" in England refers to the small grains: wheat, barley, rye, and oats.

came to serve more discriminating markets, however, choice staple wool became more and more important, and wool buyers accordingly found it profitable to go farther afield. Actually three types of wool buyers can be distinguished: local clothiers who bought their raw materials from nearby farms; regional woolmen who served as middlemen between large numbers of graziers and clothiers; and wool dealers who gathered up raw wool for city-dwelling spinners and weavers or for exporters. The last type was probably the oldest form of wool buying. All through the medieval period, England had been an exporter of wool, and 15th-century records indicate an elaborate organization of collecting and marketing agencies,[10] implemented by credit and closely controlled by the Crown because of the fiscal importance of export duties on England's "golden fleece." But by 1600, the export of cloth was far more important than the export of wool.

The Rural Wage Earner

English argriculture in 1700 was not only attuned to wider markets and implemented by money, it had also adopted the wage system. A large proportion of the agricultural population now consisted of laborers whose economic condition was none too satisfactory. This lowly class comprised persons hired by the year and others who sold their services by the day. Wages varied widely between regions, so that it is difficult to draw dependable conclusions about the level of agricultural wages. There is available, however, enough statistical evidence (together with a sufficient number of contemporaneous observations) to justify the conclusion that agricultural wages were in general so low that the bulk of agricultural laborers "had to rely upon other resources to make both ends meet."[11] Actual farm wages were seldom more than half the cost of providing the simplest necessities for a family of four. Two mitigating tendencies saved the agricultural laborers and their families from starvation: the supplementary wages obtained from the work of women and children in the woollen and worsted industries, and the system of parish poor relief which helped to relieve rural destitution.

The woollen and worsted industries had penetrated into the countryside almost in direct proportion to the reorganization of the agrarian

[10] E. Power and M. M. Postan, eds., *Studies in English Trade in the Fifteenth Century* (London: G. Routledge and Sons, Ltd., 1933), pp. 48–58.
[11] Lipson, *Economic History of England*, Vol. II, pp. 392–93.

structure. Cotters and small landholders had suffered from the agricultural changes. Where land had been enclosed, many cotters had been evicted, and many small landholders had been deprived of pasture rights. Where large farmers had leased the possessions of small holders, the situation was only one step removed. Divorced from the land, this lower stratum of the agricultural village community was ripe for exploitation; as families, they became wage earners, the male members in agriculture, the females and the children as employees of the clothiers. Cheap labor consequently became characteristic not only of English farming but of English manufacturing, a factor contributing abundantly to the conquest of world markets by English merchants.

Governmental Policy and Regulations

For the feudal controls which had regimented agricultural production in the 14th century, a different type of discipline had slowly been substituted. By the beginning of the 18th century, the control over agriculture can be described as divided between the Royal government, the large farmers, and the landlords, so that farming was subject to a rather odd combination of political and economic control. National authority manifested itself in the corn laws and in the regulation of agricultural wages, while the power of landlords and large farmers was exercised by means of the expanding wage system. A word should be said about each type of control.

The Corn Laws date from the 14th century and played an extremely important role in the history of English agriculture from that time until their ultimate repeal in the middle of the 19th century. The earliest legislation (1361) prohibited the export of grain, but this simple type of legislation soon gave way to a conditional prohibition which became the prototype of the 17th-, 18th-, and early 19th-century Corn Laws. Export was permitted provided the domestic price of corn did not exceed stipulated maxima, thus, in theory, assuring an adequate supply of cereals for English consumers at low prices. This type of legislation began in 1437 and was employed, with a great many variations, for over four hundred years. By 1700 the Corn Laws were an integral part of national agricultural policy,[12] as was also the use of bounties granted to exporters of grain when markets were glutted. The purpose of this combination of restraint and encouragement was to promote stability

[12] See Donald G. Barnes, *A History of the English Corn Laws* (New York: F. S. Crofts and Co., 1930).

of grain prices, ensure an adequate amount of tillage, and thereby guarantee an annual grain supply appropriate to national needs.

A second variety of governmental control over agriculture consisted in the regulation of agricultural wages. Like the corn legislation, this policy also had its origin in the late-medieval period. The Black Death of 1348–1349 (which carried off at least a third of England's population) led to severe competition for agricultural laborers and produced a pronounced rise in wages. In the interest of landlords, Parliament unsuccessfully attempted to prevent this unprecedented tendency. Laborers were forbidden to demand wages higher than those prevailing before the epidemic, but although the Statute of Laborers was reenacted several times, it was ineffectual in accomplishing its purpose. To the extent that Parliament again hoped that agriculture could be stabilized by means of legislation, the Elizabethan wage legislation was a continuation of the 14th-century theory. By that time, however, many new problems had arisen which it was also hoped that the Statute of Apprentices (1563) would solve.[13] Land consolidation and the increase in sheep raising were decreasing the rural demand for labor; in the meantime, the growing towns offered to young men opportunities far superior to those available in the country. One policy of the Tudors was to check the townward movement of population, and to compel persons not engaged in other pursuits to devote themselves to farming. Accordingly, all persons between the ages of 12 and 60 not engaged in manufacturing, commerce, or maritime pursuits, or not provided with independent means were required to engage in agriculture. Local justices of the peace were authorized to determine appropriate wages, and the official wages were to be observed by all employers of agricultural labor. The whole policy contemplated in the law of 1563 was designed to reinstitute a thorough control over the agricultural proletariat, and has been described by one authority on the history of English agriculture as the beginning of a conspiracy between the government and other interested groups "to cheat the English workman of his wages, to tie him to the soil, to deprive him of hope, and to degrade him into irremediable poverty."[14]

The wage system which the employers of agricultural labor used was,

---

[13] The effect of this legislation on the British economy has been studied in detail by Margaret Gay Davis in *The Enforcement of English Apprenticeship, 1563–1640* (Cambridge, Mass.: Harvard University Press, 1956).

[14] Thorold Rogers, *Six Centuries of Work and Wages*, Vol. II (London 1884), p. 398.

therefore, a part of a governmental plan, although its administration by local justices of the peace provided a fairly high degree of flexibility, so that striking variations in wages may be found. Chosen from the landlord class, the justices, however, were not unmindful of landlords' interests, and it seems likely that the sanction of the Royal government was a distinct advantage to the agricultural employers. Free bargaining would have given low enough wages in terms of any modern standard of comfort. Without this privilege, agricultural wages were still lower, and their inadequacy contributed to the child and female labor which was widespread in the English woollen and worsted industries long before the advent of the factory system. Low wages also explain why thousands of British subjects were willing to migrate to the new world in the 17th century even if they had to go as indentured servants.

Changes in Industry and Trade

England's urban population had grown absolutely and relatively in the period from 1500 to 1700. London was now a city of over a half million, while England's total urban population was probably three times the number in this one huge city. Yet more important than the increased size of the town and city population were the changes which had taken place in the organization of manufacturing and commerce. The differentiation between town and country, which had been reasonably clear in the 14th century, was now to a large extent obliterated; especially had the spread of the cloth-making industry into the country districts weakened the textile crafts in the towns. Other forces had also dealt most damaging blows to the autonomy of the craft gilds and, as a consequence, throughout British industry there had emerged a new class of businessmen who refused to be bound by the fraternal rules of the craft gilds. Markets for industrial products had widened with unprecedented rapidity during the 16th and 17th centuries. A new continent was being colonized and exploited; trade channels had been opened with Russia, Turkey, India, and the East Indies; foreign trade had revealed to English producers a world so large that contact with its many parts required the services of great trading companies employing huge quantities of capital for their elaborate and expensive projects. In the new companies, the corporative idea of the medieval gild, to a large extent, had been retained, but in the new soil of commercial expansion it produced quite different results. In the process of accumulating enough capital to carry on their extensive operations, some of the business promoters of the 16th and 17th centuries grafted on to the corporative idea of the gild two other medieval scions and produced the joint-stock company which, in turn, became the parent of the modern business corporation. Indeed, long before the rise of the joint-stock companies, the inadequacy of craft-gild organization in manufacturing had progressively been appreciated, and a period of amalgamation occurred which transformed many of these composite organizations into companies that reflected a strong tendency toward integration of productive operations.

Changes in Wants, Purchases, and Markets

In 1699, England's foreign trade had a value of over £10,000,000. Yet this huge sum represented only a small portion of the nation's total trade. Want scales had increased rapidly as an accompaniment of a succession of agrarian changes that broke down the rigidity of peasant life. To the luxury demands of an aristocracy, which comprised but a small segment of the population, there was progressively added a new and increasingly important variety of bourgeois demand.

The expansion of markets and fairs[15] whetted both the desires of the peasantry and of the humble town and city workers. Dazzled by the array of new, unusual goods offered for sale, the great mass of ordinary people slowly abandoned their traditional dress as well as many customary items of diet. The growth of a wage system both in agriculture and in industry supplied money incomes with which new consumer goods could be purchased. In spite of the complaints registered by clergy and nobility, so-called plebeian "excess" and "ostentation" could not be curbed. The quaint regional peasant costumes disappeared, as a new demand grew up within the nation for the tempting varieties of cloth which were sold in every market town. Actually, a new element in demand emerged as a consequence of improved marketing facilities. New fashions and new commodities induced more industry; the indifference of the medieval culture gave way to an eager quest for novel means of want satisfaction.

Thus the markets for industrial products expanded not only territorially but intra-territorially. Spatially widening export markets, which were the fruit of exploration and discovery, combined with

---

[15] In 1676, 1,194 important fairs were held in England and Wales.

socially enlarged domestic markets to give English businessmen a larger arena of operations. To serve these new markets, the medieval craft gilds were patently inadequate, and from the 14th century onward a continuous transmutation occurred in gild structure. The trading function became increasingly important. As larger and more distant markets replaced the local markets of the medieval town, different methods of selling necessarily had to be devised. Those craft gilds which put the finishing touches on a commodity (produced by several crafts) were obviously in a strategic position, since they alone were able to provide the merchants or the exporters with finished products. As a consequence, those gilds which sold semi-manufactured goods (e.g. bladesmiths, spinners, tanners) presently found themselves subservient to gilds that sold completed products (handle-makers, dyers, shoe-makers). In the meantime, throughout the 15th and 16th centuries, a strong tendency toward exclusiveness had also occurred in many craft gilds. A prosperous group of masters frequently dominated gild assemblies, often restricting the promotion of journeymen to mastership by excessive entrance fees or by requiring the completion of a costly masterpiece. In time this process was self-defeating; the excluded journeymen formed themselves into journeymen gilds, organizations of trained workmen whose members abandoned the hope of gild mastership, and who now offered their services for sale to the new types of businessmen which were emerging.

New Types of Business Organization

By 1700 these processes had largely run their courses. Some gilds had been amalgamated into companies[16] manned by a skilled trading element and a wage-earning class of journeymen; other gilds, which had not united with related crafts, either disappeared completely or encountered such vigorous market competition that they sank into impotence. Meanwhile, the national government had usurped the most powerful regulative functions of the craft gilds by assuming control over ap-

[16] Gild amalgamation occurred frequently in the 15th century and became much more common in the 16th. Thus at Norwich, the bladesmiths, locksmiths, and lorimers combined with the smiths, in 1449. At London the pursers and glovers united in 1498; four years later this organization joined the leathersellers; while, in 1517, the pouchmakers were absorbed by the integrated gild. For further details about the process of amalgamation, see Lipson, *Economic History of England*, Vol. II, pp. 375–378.

prenticeship under the Statute of 1563. Thus many economic functions of the craft gilds were taken over by new business organizations, while important juridical powers were assumed by the Crown.

By 1700 four chief forms of business organization largely controlled the industrial and the commercial activities of England: livery companies which had emerged out of the process of gild amalgamation, regulated companies which supervised certain branches of foreign trade, joint-stock companies which were operative both in foreign trade and in domestic industry, and organizations of private businessmen, as for example those of the clothiers in the woollen and worsted industries. Alongside these major types there survived a few craft gilds of the medieval variety, as well as many individual gild masters who attempted to carry on their trades in competition with the "capitalist" organizations which were now dominating commerce and industry. For the most part, however, the skilled craftsmen had become wage earners who no longer controlled the business enterprises to which they belonged.

The Rise of the Livery Companies

Some of the companies which emerged out of gild amalgamation engaged in industry; others were primarily commercial. Although the transformation of the craft gilds was a long, gradual process, the 15th and the 16th centuries witnessed the emergence of many consolidated companies. The impossibility of direct contact with wide markets had slowly forced some craftsmen to relinquish their previous trading functions. Increasingly a trading element grew up which provided systematic outlets for industrial products. Thus the London handle makers obtained control over the bladesmiths and the sheath-makers; the burellers (cloth finishers) came to govern other stages of cloth making; while the haberdashers absorbed the hatters and the cappers.[17] The history of these companies is a record of persistent conflict between industrial and mercantile interests, which ultimately resulted in the triumph of the latter, and the corresponding submergence of the skilled artisan to the level of a wage earner. Gradually shorn of his control over production, the industrial wage earner presently was incapable of owning the tools with which he worked, although the completion of this process had to await the introduction of expensive and elaborate machinery in the 18th and 19th centuries.

17 For details see George Unwin, *Industrial Organization in the Sixteenth and Seventeenth Centuries* (Oxford: The Clarendon Press, 1904).

Expansion of England's trade preceded the expansion of her industry, and the growth of companies out of the craft gilds represented the necessary adjustment of business organizations to impersonal and more distant markets. An oligarchy of wealthy businessmen came to dominate various branches of industry and commerce; their power was consolidated in the formation of the great "livery" companies. Livery implied the wearing of special clothing as a symbol of prestige, and the right to wear livery was an indication of royal approval of liverymen's rights to control trade and industry. The twelve great livery companies included the Mercers, Grocers, Drapers, Fishmongers, Goldsmiths, Skinners, Tailors, Haberdashers, Salters, Ironmongers, Vintners, and Clothworkers. Some, like the Grocers, were primarily commercial. This organization of merchants engaged mostly in wholesale trade,[18] dealt chiefly in wool, cloth, foodstuffs, wine, timber, metals, and dyes; but also in many other commodities such as spices, soap, wax, oil, and fish. Dominated by men of means, the Grocers provided an elaborate and effective distributive system in which artisans could share only by relinquishing their business autonomy.

The livery companies reflected a high degree of continuity between themselves and the craft gilds of the 14th century. Like their predecessors, they were business fraternities, but, unlike the gilds, they no longer were inclusive and democratic. Controlling many stages of production, those livery companies which were chiefly industrial (as, for example, the Clothworkers company) provided the materials upon which groups of skilled artisans worked. In such cases, there had grown up not a dominance by owners of trading capital (money funds available for investment in trading goods) as was the case of the Grocers, but a dominance of industrial capital (money funds invested in raw materials, semi-finished goods, or in tools). By both processes, however, possession of capital had given to a minority considerable power over the life and labor of artisans less prosperous or less enterprising.

Formation of Regulated Companies

As contrasted with the livery companies, the "regulated companies" usually confined their activities to foreign trade. They embodied the

---

[18] See Sylvia Thrupp, "The Grocers of London, a Study of Distributive Trade," in Power and Postan, *Studies in English Trade in the Fifteenth Century.*

corporative idea of the medieval merchant gild and retained in part the gild emphasis on apprenticeship, on the good quality of the products sold, and on the gild idea of individual enterprise conditioned by group restraint. On the other hand, by deliberately excluding artisans, the regulated companies represented a triumph of trading capital interests to the complete exclusion of industrial capital. The halcyon days of the regulated companies covered the latter half of the 16th century and the first part of the 17th. Chartered by the Crown and possessing monopoly trading rights over prescribed territorial areas, they were perforce compelled to ingratiate themselves with the government. Yet with the rise of a vigorous group of private foreign merchants (known then as "interlopers" because they invaded the monopolized trade areas) the regulated companies were presently confronted not only with business competition but also with political difficulties. As a result, even the greatest of the regulated companies, the Merchant Adventurers Company, was shorn of its privileges in 1689, although it still continued to carry on trade down to the 19th century.

The great expansion in England's foreign trade which helped to produce the industrial and agrarian changes which have already been described, can, to a large degree, be attributed to the regulated companies. Foremost among these were the Merchant Adventurers, the Eastland, and the Levant companies. Each was chartered by the Crown;[19] each had a territorial market assigned for the exclusive use of its members; and each was composed of a fellowship of merchants trading as individuals though regulated in their activities both by the Crown and by their fellow members. Assisted by the government (whose ambassadors obtained trading privileges for them from foreign powers) the regulated companies opened up and assiduously cultivated markets for English manufacturers and became the exciters of increased domestic manufacturing and production. At the same time, they protested against the privileges of foreign merchants, who since medieval times had carried out English exports, and they persuaded the government to cancel the trading rights of the Venetians and the Hanseatic League.[20] Colonization and discovery went hand-in-hand with the mercantile operations of the regulated companies and of the joint-stock companies.

[19] Though sanctioned by earlier kings, the Merchant Adventurers derived their authority from a charter granted by Henry VII in 1505; the Eastland Company was incorporated in 1579; the Levant Company in 1581.

[20] The privileges of the Venetians were withdrawn in 1534; the Hanseats were expelled in 1597.

A word should be said about the ways by which the regulated companies carried on their new and difficult varieties of foreign trade; for this purpose, the operations of the Merchant Adventurers will provide adequate illustration. Dominated by an autocratic governor, the organization included 3,500 merchants[21] in 1600, and probably 6,000 in 1650.[22] Membership was obtained in three ways: by inheritance, by apprenticeship, or by purchase.[23] Each method was designed to hold down membership: thus only one son could inherit his father's membership; apprentices served at least eight years' probation; entrance fees were exorbitant, with apprentices, paying at least £50 on entering their novitiate.[24] Although each merchant was a private businessman, he was rigidly limited in his activities. Since the Merchant Adventurers were primarily cloth exporters, control over members was exercised by the simple expedient of assigning quotas; a sliding scale of permissible exports was arranged for members according to seniority, with 1,000 cloths[25] as the maximum which any could ship. Thus by limiting membership and by enforcing the "stint," the Merchant Adventurers regularized the flow of cloth to the European markets. Glutted markets were prevented by allotting to each merchant-member his share of the estimated demand for cloth in each of the markets in which the Merchant Adventurers were represented.

By adhering to the idea of private enterprise limited by group restraint, the regulated companies were similar to the gilds. By insisting on quality workmanship in goods exported, they were also similar. But in their exclusion of artisans, in their restrictive selection of members, and in the scale of their operations, they were strikingly dissimilar. For a long time the Merchant Adventurers were able to keep a whip hand over the English cloth trade and to exercise monopoly power both as buyers of cloth in England and as sellers in the "mart towns" of Europe. This privileged position could not be maintained without political assistance, and the 17th century saw the rise of rivals who were not only equipped with adequate capital but who were also able to find Parliamentary champions. Notable among these rivals were the joint-stock companies, the interlopers, and the clothiers.

21 This estimate was made by John Wheeler who was secretary of the company in 1601.
22 The estimate of another official (Parker) in 1648.
23 For details see Lipson, *Economic History of England,* Vol. II, p. 216.
24 This had risen to £200 in the early part of 17th century.
25 A cloth was ordinarily 24 yards long and 1¾ yards wide.

Origins of the Joint-Stock Company

Though relatively unimportant before 1700 by any strict quantitative test,[26] joint-stock companies were to become the most important instrumentalities for the development of modern business. What then were their origins? From the gilds, the joint-stock companies inherited the idea of "perpetual succession"; hence the new organizations of the 16th century came to be immortal entities in law, separate from the mortal men who created them.[27] From the gilds also came the germs of the joint-stock principle. Religious gilds had held funds (a chest or *camera*) for the benefit of their members; merchant gilds had often used a "joint-stock" of money with which to make group purchases of merchandise subsequently to be partitioned. On the other hand, the methods of organization of the early joint-stock companies were patterned after those of the regulated companies; for the governors and assistants of those trading associations, there emerged counterparts in the treasurers and directors of the joint-stock companies. Moreover, a jointly-owned mass of wealth was not unknown to the regulated companies. Some corporate property came into existence as a result of fines, some was directly accumulated by special levies made by companies on their members.[28]

Elements of the joint-stock company corporative structure were therefore borrowed from the gilds and the regulated companies. Still other elements were derived from the business practices of two types of medieval partnerships, the *commenda* and the *societas*. Careful to prescribe rules of business conduct which would conform with principles of justice and with the Christian duty of charity, the medieval Church forebade the receipt of interest (usury). In spite of this prohibition, businessmen found it profitable to borrow money for the conduct of their affairs, but they discovered that funds were not forthcoming without compensation. Many evasions were accordingly employed to

[26] By 1695, the combined capital of English, Scottish, and Irish joint-stock companies constituted 1.3 per cent of the estimated total national wealth. W. R. Scott, *The Constitution and Finance of English, Scottish and Irish Joint-stock Companies to 1720* (Cambridge: The University Press, 1912), Vol. I, pp. 335–337.

[27] This idea of perpetual succession, explicitly recognized in 14th century religious gilds, found expression in the use of a gild seal, and gave the artificial family the right to own property.

[28] Financially hard-pressed sovereigns often compelled privileged regulated companies to lend them money. Such funds were usually assembled by levies upon the merchant members.

circumvent ecclesiastical prohibitions. The *commenda* was one of these devices, and came to be employed extensively, especially in Italian foreign trade. Money funds were turned over to a ship's master or to travelling agent (*commendatarius*) who employed the funds in trade. For this service he received a share of the profits. Thus the principal[29] (*commendator*) actually became a partner of his agent, supplying him with funds but delegating management of these funds for a particular venture. This separation between capital contribution and management came subsequently to be characteristic of the joint-stock company, and has become an essential element of the modern corporation which grew out of the early joint-stock company.

The *societas* was both an extension and a modification of the *commenda*. If the *commendatarius* also contributed a portion of the money funds for a venture, there came into being a common fund, a "stock" owned jointly by the two members of the organization. Both parties shared risks, and both benefited from gain; each had shares in a joint-stock, and each possessed claims on profits. By this process the *commenda* was transformed into the *societas*. For simple mercantile ventures this alteration made no substantial difference, but, when the *societas* came to be employed in long-term ventures requiring large quantities of capital, a more complex organization came into being. Enough partners were added so that adequate money funds could be accumulated. Thus varying amounts of investment were contributed by the several partners, while corresponding degrees of risk were assumed. Cornwall lead mines came to be organized in this way by large partnerships, which were predecessors of the later joint-stock companies.

The early joint-stock companies wove together, therefore, elements from several origins: the idea of perpetual succession from the gilds, forms of government from the regulated companies, separation of ownership and management from the *commenda,* and the idea of a joint stock partially from the gilds and the regulated companies, but more particularly from the *societas*.

Early Uses of the Joint-Stock Company

By 1700 there were in existence at least one hundred and forty British joint-stock companies controlling capital amounting to four and a

[29] Sir William Ashley aptly called the principal "the home-staying merchant." See his *Introduction to English Economic History and Theory* (London: G. P. Putnam's Sons, 1920), Part II, p. 413.

quarter million pounds. Not all were equally important; indeed, six large companies accounted for over three-fourths of the total joint-stock wealth. More striking than the absolute amount of investment in this relatively new type of business organization were the kinds of enterprise invaded by the joint-stock capital. The companies in existence in 1700 included some organized for purposes of foreign trade (e.g., the East India, African, and Hudsons' Bay Companies); others for fishing, manufacturing, mining, and banking; as well as others owning waterworks, soap factories, and many other industrial properties. Throughout the 17th century, the growth of joint-stock companies had been vigorous; in the closing years of that century and in the first two decades of the next the growth was phenomenal. From 1695 to 1717 the investment in British joint-stock companies quadrupled. This remarkable change in investment habits brought a feverish wave of speculation which led to a disastrous financial collapse in 1720. Thus from the early days of the joint-stock company, benefits and dangers have gone hand in hand.

Although the adoption of the joint-stock principle was gradual, the Russia and African Companies, both founded in 1553, may properly be regarded as the first English joint-stock companies. The former evolved from a regulated company, the latter from a *societas*. From this time onward, varying methods of organization and finance were employed, although, in general, the practices were reasonably similar. The members who formed a company were given "shares"; next the elected officers (governor or treasurer, and his assistants) determined the amount of capital needed. This sum was then divided by the number of shares, after which an assessment (call) was made upon each shareholder. The accumulated funds (the "joint-stock") were then employed, and profits arising from the venture were distributed among the shareholders as dividends. Companies engaging in foreign trade could in this way accumulate a "joint-stock," and employ it by sending out ships and cargo. When the ships returned, both the imported merchandise and the ships could be sold and the enlarged or diminished joint-stock proportionally partitioned. For mining, munitions works, or manufacturing companies, this simple procedure could not be followed. Permanent investments were necessary, which could only be recouped over long periods of time in the form of earnings from successful business operations. Most foreign-trade companies also had some need for permanent capital: for ships, warehouses, foreign trading posts, and fortifications. Little-by-little, the typical methods of the joint-stock companies were changed. The idea of an unimpaired capital (chief sum) investment was adopted. Because of the burdensome assessments, shares were presently divided into salable fractional shares, thereby making possible the distribution of risks among investors with varying rights and responsibilities. Finally came the use of paid-up shares, no longer subject to assessment, and hence the idea of "limited liability" which is today an almost universal corporation practice. By 1700 all kinds of investors were turning over savings to joint-stock companies. Stock-exchange dealings were developed, making it possible for speculators to profit from the changes in the value of joint-stock company shares. The age when business corporations were to dominate economic activity had not yet arrived by any means, but the basic principles for financing large-scale business enterprise had been devised and popularized by the beginning of the 18th century.

The Individual Proprietorship

As important as the livery, regulated, and joint-stock companies were in 1700, a fourth type of business organization, the simple business proprietorship, was probably as significant as all three combined. Contrasted with the companies, which in one form or another continued the corporative principle of the medieval world, the proprietorship reflected the strong tendency toward individualism which had manifested itself, especially since the Reformation. Men of capital and business ability rapidly expanded the scale of their operations by reinvesting their earnings and employing increasing numbers of laborers under a wage system. In small mining operations, in metal working, in linen and silk manufacturing, and especially in the woollen and worsted industries, monied individual businessmen introduced new methods for conducting large-scale enterprise. Because the woollen industries[30] were the largest branches of manufacturing that came to be organized in this way, a brief description of these industries will illustrate adequately the vigor of the individual proprietorship.

Under gild organization the various processes of cloth making: spinning, weaving, fulling (shrinking), dyeing, and shearing had each been performed by separate, independent crafts. With the growth of wider foreign markets for cloth (cultivated assiduously by the regulated com-

[30] The fascinating history of these great industries has been vividly described by E. Lipson in his *History of the English Woollen and Worsted Industries* (London: A. & C. Black, Ltd., 1921).

panies), the craft gilds slowly lost their autonomy, because competing types of business organizations were better fitted to serve the merchant exporters. In London, textile-making gilds amalgamated, while in the rural areas, into which the woollen industry spread as an accompaniment of agrarian change, independent businessmen known as *clothiers* obtained control over the differentiated process of cloth making. A clothier was a capitalist, an employer of labor, and a merchant combined. He bought raw wool, either from growers or from wool dealers, which he "put out," which is to say he turned over to wage-earning artisans for manufacture. Thus carders, spinners, and weavers were provided with materials which they processed in their homes. In the west of England, the scales of operations of some enterprising industrialists were very large: in 1614, for example, a clothier who was a member of Parliament testified that he and his partner employed 3,000 workmen. By his power to deny materials to any employee, the clothier controlled his labor force, thus penalizing bad workmanship, delay in finishing work, or petty larceny. Against this industrial insecurity the artisans in turn tried to protect themselves by working concurrently for several clothiers. As a result, it is difficult to determine accurately how many artisans were employed on a full-time basis by a single clothier.

It is clear enough, however, that many clothiers carried on extensive operations. A careful student of the English woollen and worsted industries has concluded that "a wealthy clothier might employ altogether as many as 800 persons and even more."[31] The clothier's investment consisted primarily of inventories of semi-finished goods; durable equipment was the exception rather than the rule.[32] Members of the wage-earning proletariat, therefore, still retained their tools, although the business independence which the artisan had once possessed in the craft gild was almost completely gone,[33] since the business of buying and selling had been usurped by clothiers who now hired the services of cloth workers on a piece-work basis.

[31] E. Lipson, *History of the English Woollen and Worsted Industries,* p. 15.

[32] Some clothiers owned pack animals for transporting cloth to Blackwell Hall in London; many also owned looms. A few clothiers carried on several manufacturing operations under a single roof, although most early 18th-century large-scale workshops were charitable institutions. Weaving sheds, however, were quite common, and constituted one of the beginnings of a factory system in the woollen and worsted industries.

[33] This was not true in the north of England, where many clothiers were themselves really manufacturers, employing only a few wage-compensated journeymen. See, Herbert Heaton, *The Yorkshire Woollen and Worsted Industries, from the Earliest Times up to the Industrial Revolution* (Oxford: The University Press, 1920).

Organization of the Putting-Out System

The *putting-out system*[34] of manufacture was, therefore, thoroughly "capitalistic." Industrial policies were dictated by the possessors of capital; hence a clear differentiation had arisen between making goods and making money. An industrial organization had emerged which was tied together almost entirely by a wage and profit system, one which relied upon a scheme of production carried on within the homes of the workers; a system quite analogous to that method of production which is designated today as the sweatshop system. A few details about the actual operation of the putting-out system in the woollen and worsted industries will make this comparison clear.

From some convenient center, materials were "put-out" to the wage earners. To this center came spinners for wool and weavers for yarn. To this center the artisans carried back their respective semi-finished products, and here they also received their (piece-work) wages. Technical supervision over the process of manufacture did not exist as it does today in factories; the industrial discipline involved in the putting-out system consisted in a variety of controls accomplished by ruthless inspection before the payment of wages. Herein lay both the strength and the weakness of the system. Rural poverty produced competition among the cloth workers, such keen competition, in fact, that slow or careless workmen could easily and adequately be disciplined by temporary unemployment. On the other hand, the parcelling out of materials to many spinners led to lack of uniformity in yarn, which made the texture of cloth uneven and lowered its sales value. Nor could a wage-system type of control obviate this difficulty; continuous technical supervision was needed, an element which was presently to be provided in the factory system which gradually replaced the putting-out system in the second half of the 18th century.

Women and children did most of the spinning for the clothiers. Since their wages were supplementary to those of husband or father, they were distressingly low. Unmarried females wholly dependent on their wages were wretchedly poor, scarcely able to subsist on the three or four pence a day which were normal wages for spinners. Weaving, on the other hand, was mostly performed by men, although female weaving increased rapidly with the decline of apprenticeship. Resisted by

34 The more familiar older term *domestic system* has been discarded by modern economic historians because it does not accurately describe the basic idea involved.

wage earners and employers alike, the seven-year training period pre-scribed by the Statute of Apprentices[35] could not be enforced since for wage earners it would have delayed their entering remunerative employment, and for employers it would have restricted the number of workers. More and more the home had become an industrial school so that children who grew up in cloth-making households were com-petent to carry on one or more processes at an early age. Many master weavers, however, still took apprentices, especially pauper children; and some also hired journeymen. These vestiges of gild organization, however, became increasingly obsolete, and there emerged, as a result, a disorganized labor supply on which the factory system was subse-quently to feed. Only one branch of the woollen and worsted industries was really immune from immediate reorganization. Contrasted with spinning and weaving, the finishing trades were not ordinarily house-hold occupations. Master cloth dressers, with their own corps of em-ployees, sheared, fulled, and dyed cloth for several clothiers. Their work was sufficiently specialized so that they could escape the competition of country artisans.

Life and Labor Under the Putting-Out System

The large degree of industrial freedom, which romantic admirers have attributed to the putting-out system, was largely a fiction. Long hours of labor were self-imposed because wages were pathetically low; fourteen hours at the loom and two or three more devoted to fetching materials were common. Child labor was not only widespread but inescapable, and therefore cannot be said to begin with the factory age. Nor should it be forgotten that children may be exploited by poverty-stricken parents just as viciously as by factory officials. Unemployment constituted still another discouraging aspect of the putting-out system. The seasonal and irregular character of the cloth markets produced one variety of insecurity, while the deliberate withholding of materials by employers for disciplinary reasons created an even more dreaded contingency.

By this loosely-knit industrial system, manufacture and business enter-prise in the woollen and worsted industries were separated. The clothier sold his finished cloth at Blackwell Hall or other city markets through

35 See p. 31.

commission men. The chief buyers at these centralized markets were wholesale cloth dealers (drapers) and merchant exporters, who respectively supplied the domestic and foreign markets. Conquest of world markets by exporters and increased cultivation of domestic markets by the drapers hinged both upon the price and upon the quality of English cloth. A system of production which utilized cheap labor was admirably suited to accomplish wider sales. In the meantime, the tradition of quality workmanship derived from the craft gilds was, within limitations,[36] continued. Thus the new world of capitalism, which was rapidly adapting and changing economic institutions, prossessed devices both for making money and for making cheap and desirable goods. Out of this combination has come the survival power of capitalism, although out of the separation of business enterprise and industrial production has come disharmony and a great deal of discontent.

The Spirit of "Capitalism"

At the opening of the 18th century, England was enjoying a great commercial and industrial expansion and was preparing for an even greater expansion. Technical and economic forces had conspired to give impetus to the consolidation of some of her agricultural land; the next fifty years were to see unreserved political approval given to land enclosure, and, as a result, technical, economic, and political forces were to bring about a wholesale elimination of small landowners.[37] In industry, the limitations of craft-gild organization had, by 1700, been overcome through corporate organization in some branches and by means of vigorous expansion of proprietorship in others. Both the agrarian and the industrial changes had been facilitated by the extraordinary increase in England's trade, resulting from the skillful cultivation of foreign markets by the regulated and joint-stock companies. Collectively viewed, these agricultural, industrial, and commercial changes have been called "capitalistic." Purposes and motives had become frankly acquisitive, and the gains from this acquisitive process had come to be measured primarily in money units. By the beginning of the 18th century, sale of products for money was usual and normal, and mercantile agencies for the continuous disposal of products had become indispensable to the functioning of the whole business structure. The

[36] See p. 31.
[37] See Chap. 4, following.

productive processes, geared up by the agencies which had taken charge of selling, had been slowly modified, although the second half of the 18th century was to witness a far more profound change in industrial technology. The bulk of capital employed in business projects was as yet largely in circulating form, consisting of money funds, and inventories, rather than machinery. But large amounts of money were needed in the conduct of most forms of business, and the institutions which were pushing to the front in 1700 were those which had devised effective ways for accumulating adequate amounts of capital.

Sources of Capital

From what sources came the ever-increasing quantities of capital which assisted the transformation of economic institutions? Trade had been one rich source of capital since medieval times, and became continually more productive in the 16th and 17th centuries. Since England had no mines, foreign trade provided the only means by which her share of the world's supply of precious metals could be obtained; for this reason, an inordinate amount of attention was paid to the course of foreign trade; for this reason also, many economic writers come to regard the balance of trade as the touchstone of the nation's prosperity. Trade, however, was not the only source of England's money supply. A very large amount was obtained by violence. The Spanish treasure fleets were too great a temptation for Englishmen to resist; even the Crown had its hand in the dirty business of plundering. After the phenomenal success of Drake's expedition[38] (1577), English privateers grew bolder, and their combined efforts brought millions of pounds worth of bullion to England's ports. A third source of capital whereby England's industry was equipped, consisted in loans from European financial centers. Holland had profited richly from foreign trade in the 16th century; and, with increased demand for money funds in England, Dutch capitalists seized the opportunity to lend in England, thereby availing themselves of interest rates much higher than those at home. Amsterdam, however, was not the only capital-exporting city; her neighbor, Antwerp, was no less interested in making foreign loans.

---

[38] The actual amount of bullion seized by Drake is not definitely known. Conservative estimates place the loot at better than £600,000, of which Queen Elizabeth is known to have received £263,790. For various computations, see Scott, *The Constitution and Finance* . . . , Vol. I, pp. 78–82.

Commercial Credit

Thus profits of foreign trade, combined with confiscated Spanish treasure and foreign borrowings, had supplied England with some of the money funds with which her expanding volume of business was conducted. Meanwhile extended use of commercial credit and the development of commercial banking were two other means which hastened England's economic progress. Credit had been regularly given in certain wholesale transactions[39] in the medieval world. By 1700, however, trading on credit had become customary in practically all important branches of trade and industry. Clothiers, for example, gave credit to drapers or to merchants for long periods of time, thus increasing the amount of capital which they needed in their oddly-organized business of wool manufacture. Extension of credit by manufacturers increased the number of merchants, since young men of ability could begin trade with but small personal investments. Open-book accounts and negotiable drafts provided the commonest methods whereby credit was granted; by their use a substantially larger volume of business was conducted than would have occurred had all payments been made in cash.

Beginnings of Commercial Banking

Commercial credit, however, was nothing new. The ancient world from Babylon to Rome had used it; in fact credit transactions can be traced throughout the history of trade. Bank credit, on the other hand is relatively modern,[40] and its systematic employment in England during the latter half of the 17th century had a thoroughly stimulating effect on trade and industry. By 1600, some English businessmen of standing were acting as bankers by receiving deposits and lending money;[41] by 1650

[39] In the fairs, for example, the credit period was frequently the weeks intervening between the close of one fair and the beginning of another in the same regular cycle.

[40] In many nations, bank credit did not come into common use much before the 19th century. Italy and the Low Countries, however, developed effective banking institutions long before England made similar progress.

[41] The medieval agitation concerning usury indicates that money lending was common. What was new in the operations of the "bankers" was that they loaned not their own money but money which had been deposited with them, or, as we shall see, they loaned more funds than they actually possessed.

the goldsmiths in Lombard Street were carrying on genuine banking operations; while, by 1700, a joint-stock bank chartered by the Crown had become an established institution. These rapid changes in banking practices contributed abundantly to the emergence of modern capitalism.

Because money, unlike an animal or a bushel of wheat could not physically reproduce itself, the medieval churchmen said it was "barren." They therefore argued that the lending of money at interest violated Christian principles of morality and was socially unjust. The word and the deed, however, were frequently at variance; money lending was not only practiced, but came gradually to be approved by the Church under certain circumstances.[42] During the 16th century, the medieval prohibition of usury crumbled under the combined pressure of new business opportunities and the waning authority of the Catholic Church. In England both these forces were operative,[43] and, as a consequence, private bankers began their useful work in that country much more extensively than in most countries on the Continent. Contrasted with money lenders, who loaned their own funds, the bankers gathered up other people's money, by paying interest on deposits, and then loaned the collected funds to businessmen. They were, therefore, both borrowers and lenders, with legal responsibilities to their depositors and legal rights against borrowers. But presently, at the hands of the Lombard Street goldsmiths, banking advanced nearer to its modern denotation; both bank checks and bank notes were developed in primitive forms, laying the foundations for the mass of bank credit which later came to play such an indispensable part in sustaining the vitality of the capitalist sectors of the world.

Use of Bank Checks and Banknotes

To depositors, the goldsmiths of Lombard Street issued receipts attesting the amount of money (or bullion) deposited, enabling the holders to withdraw money by presenting these receipts. Gradually the personal appearance of depositors was made unnecessary by the development of the equivalent of modern bank checks. The depositors now merely

[42] In general, money lending which did not exact usury from the poor and which did not involve the receipt of income without risk came to be condoned.

[43] In England, the Usury Laws were repealed in 1545, thus making the receipt of interest legitimate and legal.

ordered the goldsmith-banker to pay to the presenter of a written state-ment (a check) a stipulated amount.[44] The unexampled convenience of check payments recommended the new method, and, from the late 17th century onward, transfer of deposit credit constantly grew more important. The full future importance of this Restoration device can really be appreciated in 20th-century America where over 90 per cent of all transactions are facilitated by bank checks. The check, however, was not the only bank credit instrument which the goldsmiths em-ployed. To depositors who preferred not to use checks, they issued promissory notes which were transferable. Thus the goldsmiths devel-oped both bank checks and banknotes, instruments which are indis-pensable to modern banking practice. But what of their loans? To whom did they lend the money funds represented by their deposit liabilities? Their best customer was the British Government. Faced with recurring deficits arising partly because of the rise in prices (which resulted from the inflow of American treasure) British rulers were compelled to bor-row money in anticipation of taxes. More and more the goldsmith bankers became creditors of the government. By the time of the Com-monwealth, the custom of turning to the goldsmiths in moments of financial need was well established, and Oliver Cromwell was only too content to follow this custom. Charles II adopted the same plan. Such intimate connection between banking and public finance, however, was not without disadvantages. When the government failed to repay its loans (as it did in 1671) the goldsmiths were unable to meet the current demands of their depositors for cash. Fortunately the government was by no means the only borrower of bank credit, although it was the most important. But the difficulties produced by governmental inability to repay were accentuated by the goldsmiths' discovery that they could ordinarily lend more than the actual sums deposited with them, since all their creditors would not demand cash at the same time. The com-bination of such an "uncovered issue" practice with the remissness of the government in repaying its loans produced one of the first banking crises, one that brought all the hardships that normally result when depositors find themselves unable to withdraw their deposits, and resulted in inconveniences to hundreds of businessmen who had come to conduct business on the assumption that the goldsmith banks would continue their useful activities.

44 By 1675 checks were in use. For details concerning the history of English bank-ing see R. D. Richards, *The Early History of Banking in England* (London: P. S. King and Son, Ltd., 1929).

Establishment of the Bank of England

Yet, while one set of governmental financial problems had the effect of creating difficulties for the goldsmiths and their depositors, another somewhat later set of fiscal problems, strangely enough, brought into existence a new banking institution which superseded the goldsmiths. William III, confronted with a desperate financial emergency in 1694, had exhausted every source of revenue. At this juncture a proposal was made by William Paterson that a group of financiers would lend the government £1,200,000 at 8 per cent in perpetuity in exchange for the right to create a joint-stock bank. Thus the dire financial need of the government was the occasion for the introduction of the joint-stock principle into banking and the establishment of the Bank of England, an institution which has had more to do with guiding the monetary policies of the modern world than any other single corporation.[45] Empowered to issue notes, to buy and sell bullion, to discount commercial paper, and to deal in foreign exchange, the Bank of England both cheapened bank credit[46] and made it more secure. Although beset with constant adversities during the early years (not least among which were the deliberate efforts of the goldsmiths to wreck their competitor) the Bank succeeded in establishing itself as the nation's foremost banking institution. It loaned extensively to businessmen. Its strength lay in its skillful management and in its very size. Thirteen hundred persons subscribed to its capital; the day of large things in the realm of finance had definitely begun.

Four Basic Institutions That Would Influence the Future

Four outstanding components of the modern economic world were beyond the experimental stage by about 1700: the wage system, the corporation, the capitalist proprietorship, and the commercial bank. All four reflected the initiative which characterized the 16th and 17th centuries; all four indicated as well the increasing availability of capital. All had profound effects upon the nature of markets, upon

---

[45] Fifteen years after its creation, the Bank of England was granted a monopoly of English joint-stock banking.

[46] Whereas the goldsmiths paid 6 per cent on deposits and charged their borrowers 12 per cent, the Bank of England paid 4 per cent and charged the government 8 per cent. Later these rates were more than cut in half.

business efficiency, and upon business practices conceived in terms of profit-seeking rationality rather than in conformity with custom. In comparison with the immense development which the future was to witness, each of these four institutions was as yet minute. But the relatively stagnant waters of the old order of things had now definitely begun to move, and presently the latent energy contained in new institutions was to be released.

4

The beginning of

scientific technology

The Dynamism of the British Economy

The major cause for England's economic progress before 1700 had been the efficiency of her business organizations; the secret of her still greater progress by 1800 can be attributed to the adoption by these organizations of improved industrial technology. Revolutionary methods in the metallurgical industries, semi-automatic machinery in textile manufacturing, and the use of water and steam power, produced a wholly different apparatus of production. Meanwhile agriculture underwent a complementary development. Commercial changes in the 16th and 17th centuries had hastened the growth of population. The resulting pressure on the food supply set in motion a new tendency toward land enclosure, a process which rapidly gathered momentum in the last four decades of the 18th century and changed rural England from a nation of open fields to one of enclosed separate farms. The physical changes involved in this enclosure movement were more visible but probably less important than the social alterations which accompanied the rearrangement of the land. In the course of seventy-five years, the small landowners practically disappeared; and the places of these sturdy yeomen were taken by wage-earning agricultural laborers hired by business or gentlemen farmers who administered large—often huge —estates. Boldly defying tradition, a few of these business-like farmers experimented with new crops, new techniques, and new machinery. Their example slowly convinced others, so that the 19th century brought to British agriculture a new era, one that relied upon the cooperation of science and business techniques.

Reciprocal Influences of Technology and Trade

These same elements were combined by a new race of industrial leaders who revolutionized the technology of the textile and metal industries. By harnessing fire and water through the use of machinery, they produced a system of production which involved heavy investments in fixed form; and the new scheme required concentrations of laborers in large workshops. Like the putting-out system, this new mode of industrial organization employed the wage system, but it added a new discipline of factory hours and the supervision of foremen and superintendents. The new technology and the new discipline geared up production to unprecedented speed; for the fallible skill of the artisan there was substituted the automatic regularity of the machine. Speed and mechanical precision became indeed the chief productive virtues of the new industrial process; a new, impersonal kind of efficiency was thereby created which made possible the mass-production which has become typical in the modern world.

Hand-in-hand with agricultural and industrial metamorphosis went a more remarkable commercial expansion than the world had ever seen before. Tireless textile machinery fed out millions of bolts of cloth for merchants to sell. To America, Asia, Europe, and Africa flowed inexpensive cottons, light comfortable cloth which rapidly replaced coarse, homespun, flax or woollen textiles, and catered to the wants of very ordinary people. To remote parts of the world went also English hardware, cutlery, and other manufactures which new methods had made less costly. England saw visions of becoming the "workshop of the world," her products sold in every important foreign market!

In all major aspects of her economic organization, England was by 1800 far ahead of other nations. In agriculture she had definitely abandoned medieval organization; in industry, her factory system and machine methods had shown their technical advantages; in commerce, her markets had grown larger both territorially and quantitatively.

Changed Attitudes Toward Enclosures

During the hundred years from 1700 to 1800, England's population had grown by more than three millions.[1] This natural increase could be fed because English agriculture became far more efficient in the 18th century than ever before. Large quantities of capital were invested in drainage, in soil improvement, and in better livestock. The wasteful medieval system of fallowing ground was gradually abandoned; indeed, it could be abandoned because superior ways of enriching the soil were discovered experimentally. These new agricultural methods were definitely hastened also by land enclosure. By itself, enclosure did not make land more productive; it did, however, create a legal framework within which new experiments could be conducted, and it thereby released the initiative and enterprise which characterized the 18th century.

The condemned and lamented enclosure movement of Elizabethan and Jacobean days had practically spent itself by the end of the first quarter of the 17th century. Quantitatively, this early tendency toward agricultural reorganization had not been extremely important; moreover, the majority of fields enclosed had been carved out of demesne or common waste land. Except for continued exchange of strips and the resulting accumulation of compact bundles, arable fields had remained practically undisturbed. The government, moreover, definitely disapproved the earlier enclosure movement. Eager to achieve stability in a changing political and economic milieu, the Tudors staunchly resisted any and all forces which threatened to produce violent change; consequently, commissioners of enclosure were appointed (first under Edward VI) to investigate complaints about the conversion of arable fields into "sheepwalks." By the 18th century, all this was changed. Parliament was now dominated by landlords, whose economic interests were un-

[1] The population of England and Wales in 1801 has been estimated at 8,893,000 persons.

towardly affected by the disparity between rising prices and fixed rents. Their solution for this problem lay in increasing their revenues from land, and with the approval of Parliament they set about to enclose the time-sanctioned open fields and common pastures. Enclosure within a specific village began with a petition addressed to Parliament by the leading landowners requesting the passage of a Bill of Enclosure. Although such a petition required the assent of the owners of four-fifths of the land, enough concentration of ownership already existed in many areas to make only a few signatures necessary. In theory, Parliament was next required to investigate the probable effect of enclosure upon the rights of all members of the particular agricultural community in which enclosure was proposed. Actually, the small landholders found it too expensive to present their objections, and it seems clear that in hundreds of instances the interests of this group were cavalierly disregarded. When enclosure had been authorized, the lands of the village community were surveyed, parcelled out, and fenced at the recipient's cost. Loss of common pasture rights or common-waste privileges were theoretically compensated by individual areas of land now held in severalty. But, in practice, the entire process of reorganization fell into the hands of the lords, the large landholders, and the local rector. In the interests of this group, the whole structure of landholding was recast; in their interest, the traditional common privileges of thousands of small farmers were abruptly and ruthlessly cancelled.

Effect of Enclosure on the Small Landholder

The importance of 18th century enclosures can be appreciated both from the extent and the rapidity of the process. From 1702 to 1797, Parliament passed 1,776 enclosure acts which authorized the creation of fenced fields out of 3,142,374 acres which had hitherto lain common.[2]

	No. of Acts	Acres Involved
1702–1714	2	1,439
1714–1727	16	17,960
1727–1760	226	318,778
1760–1797	1,532	2,804,197

The small landholder, as Mantoux[3] had so accurately said, "could but

[2] The gathering momentum may be seen from the increase in enclosure acts during the course of the century:
[3] *The Industrial Revolution in the Eighteenth Century*, (London; J. Cape, 1934), p. 174.

look on helplessly while these changes took place. . . . He could not prevent the commissioners reserving the best lands for richer men. He was constrained to accept the lot assigned for him, even though he might not consider it an equivalent of his former property." Before enclosure, the small farmers' activities in arable and pasture farming had been spatially distinct; on their lands in the open fields they raised their grain; while on the common pastures, they grazed their animals. After enclosure, the small farmers had but single plots of land for both arable and pasture uses. Except for differences in the soil, the poorer yeomen were not unfavorably affected in the amounts of arable land; in pasture, however, they were infinitely poorer. If a small landowner's share of partitioned common pasture proved to be one acre, private ownership of this additional acre was by no means equivalent to a former privilege of pasturing, for example, several sheep, a cow, and a flock of geese on the commons. Left poorer by enclosure, the small farmers did not long survive, and their exodus from the agricultural villages constituted a veritable social revolution in the closing years of the 18th century.

The new status of the cotters was even more precarious than that of the small yeomen. Although cotters had previously possessed no legal right to common land whatever, they had used the commons. Deprived of these extra-legal privileges, they were actually pauperized by enclosure. So long as the woollen industry flourished in the countryside, some of the impoverished cotters could find employment; but presently parallel developments in industry rapidly weakened the old domestic cloth industry. Caught between the upper millstone of land enclosure and the lower millstone of rural industrial decay, the cotters and small landholders had usually but three alternatives: to leave their ancestral homes, to find local employment as agricultural wage earners, or to become dependent on parish poor relief.

Thus, by undermining the economic security of small landholders and cotters, the 18th-century English enclosure movement precipitated two much-decried results: depopulation of the countryside[4] and concentration of landowning. After a few years of bitter struggle, many small landowners were glad enough to sell their small plots to their more prosperous neighbors. A stream of small yeomen and cotters tore up their long-established roots and trekked away from the ancient villages to seek their fortunes in the rising industrial towns or abroad. Mobility, which could be achieved in the medieval world only by flight or by pay-

---

[4] Goldsmith's "Deserted Village" voiced the concern of many Englishmen over depopulation of the countryside.

ment of *chevage,* was now an indirect consequence of Parliamentary action. Unforeseen and unintended, the development of capitalistic agriculture helped to produce that strong tendency toward personal mobility which not only hastened migration to America but, by many other manifestations, became characteristic of the modern economic world.

Effect of Enclosure upon Agricultural Practices

Although the redistribution of the land involved untold hardship, the effect upon agricultural efficiency was salutary. Technical progress had been virtually impossible in the open fields and common pastures. Methods of crop rotation had necessarily been uniform, inhibiting experiment, while systematic stock breeding was out of the question. Lean, scrawny, half-starved cattle, weighing less than half as much as modern cattle, roamed the close-cropped common pastures. To every farmer intelligent enough to experiment, enclosure provided a laboratory wherein he could embark on new crop rotations, and wherein he could improve his livestock by systematic inbreeding. Not very many 18th-century farmers availed themselves of these opportunities. The crust of custom had, indeed, been broken by the enclosure movement, but many a year was to pass before the hard understructure of customary agricultural methods could be dissolved by the example of a few pioneers of scientific agriculture.

Yet one must not underestimate the influence of these pioneers. In spite of criticism, adverse fortune, and unpopularity, they continued their experiments. Converts to new methods at first were few, but they did increase, and gradually knowledge of the new techniques spread. Science became more and more the handmaiden of the farmer. Out of this union were to come innumerable blessings in the form of better crops; larger, fatter, and more nutritive animals; and a progressive reduction of the proportion of the nation's labor supply devoted to farming. Modern agriculture can properly be said to have originated in England during the 18th century.

Pioneers of Scientific Agriculture

The most effective popularizer of new methods of cultivation and crop rotation was indisputably Jethro Tull. He combined in rare degree theoretical knowledge and practical realism. His writings[5] were based on years of careful research and painstaking experiment. Deep ploughing, persistent cultivation, and continuous rotation, he regarded as the three recipes for abundant harvests. Old fashioned farmers held the new methods in contempt, but fortunately Tull found a devoted disciple in Charles, second Viscount Townshend,[6] who retired from political life in 1730 and devoted himself to agriculture. Following Tull's advice, he experimented with clover and turnips, drilled in his seed instead of sowing it broadcast, and devised a standard four-crop rotation. By these methods Townshend converted his previously barren, sandy wastes into rich productive land, increased his rents, and prospered.

Meantime another agricultural pioneer had achieved results in stock-breeding fully as important as those of Jethro Tull in arable farming. Robert Bakewell, the popularizer of scientific stock-breeding was a yeoman farmer; as a consequence, his new methods were more quickly adopted than those of Tull and Townshend. By careful in-breeding, Bakewell developed compact, small-boned sheep, which were easy to fatten and which could be quickly prepared for market. Moreover, Bakewell's sheep possessed high value not merely as butcher meat but as producers of wool. Although his greatest success was with sheep, Bakewell, also produced wholly new types of cattle by systematic breeding and by close attention to feeding. Other breeders followed his example— with amazing results. Whereas the average weight of cattle at Smithfield market was only 370 pounds in 1710, after the new experiments of Bakewell and his followers were adopted, the average rose to 800 pounds in 1795.[7] Yet, although Tull, Townshend, and Bakewell had laid the groundwork for better arable and pasture farming, the diffusion of these other new methods can largely be attributed to Arthur Young. In his voluminous writings, Young assembled a great fund of information about agricultural methods, systems of land tenure, condition of roads, and kindred subjects. A militant crusader for better farming, Young travelled extensively, observing agricultural practices, and lecturing to thousands of farmers on the advantages of enclosure and

---

[5] *The New Horse-Houghing Husbandry* (London, 1731); *Horse-Hoing Husbandry* (London, 1733).

[6] For a brief account of Townshend's agricultural experiments, see E. P. Rowland (Lord Ernle) *English Farming, Past and Present* (London: Longmans, Green and Co., 1936), pp. 173–175.

[7] Ernle, *English Farming, Past and Present*, p. 188.

systematic farming. The government recognized the importance of his educational work by choosing him as secretary for the Board of Agriculture when that organization was created in 1793.

Farming Becomes Fashionable

By the beginning of the 19th century, many of the principles upon which modern agriculture is based were already established in England. Agricultural pioneers had revealed the advantages of enclosed fields, of scientific experiment, and of investment of capital in land improvement. Farming had been changed from the servile occupation of medieval times; it was now a calling appropriate to nobility or king.[8] Indeed, farming became fashionable with rather peculiar benefits since the fashion brought into agriculture persons of ability and wealth, able to understand the importance of science, and financially competent to assume the risks of experiment. As a consequence, capital was invested in better breeding stock, in better implements, in sub-surface drainage, and in fertilizers. Meanwhile chemistry had emerged as a most useful science. As early as 1757, Francis Home had pointed out the importance of chemistry in agriculture. By the turn of the century, the Board of Agriculture had appointed as its Professor of Chemistry, Humphrey Davy, who for a decade lectured on agricultural chemistry.

England had, therefore, provided a laboratory wherein these important experiments in agriculture were conducted. A small but extremely influential group of educated farmers had emerged, who transformed farming from a tradition-hampered occupation to a far more scientific business. Financial costs of experiments confined the new ways of agriculture to persons with means; the new methods came therefore to be associated with large farmers whose interests in agriculture were primarily pecuniary. In their hands, as Lord Ernle has said, "farms ceased to be self-sufficing industries, and became factories of beef and mutton."[9] Making money in agriculture depended very largely upon producing more and better farm products; and the agricultural pioneers gave an initial impetus to the feverish quest for new ways of increasing agricultural production which has created an awkward dilemma for some countries in the modern world.

[8] George III had a model farm at Windsor and took great pride in his nickname, "Farmer George."

[9] *English Farming, Past and Present*, p. 214.

Commercial Preparation for the Industrial Revolution

The dramatic changes in agriculture, which the 18th century had witnessed, were paralleled by even more far-reaching transformations in English commerce and industry. Markets widened with unprecedented rapidity, and the increase in demand generated boldness of business policy. In the meantime, a great burst of invention revolutionized the technology of the textile and the metallurgical industries. The combined result was an epoch-making change which historians since 1837 have called the "Industrial Revolution."[10] Actually, the forces which had slowly been developing were now rapidly producing effect; the so-called "revolution" was really the fruition of a long series of preparatory changes. Reorganization of agriculture provided one of the most important domestic events of a preparatory nature. At the same time, domestic and overseas commercial development opened up larger outlets for English manufactured products, as well as sources of new imports. Increased demand soon brought pressure on the apparatus of production, and a set of most remarkable technical changes occurred as a result.

The growth of England's foreign trade during the 18th century may be roughly measured by the increase in the tons of shipping leaving English ports. Fully six times the tonnage cleared the customs in 1800 as in 1700.[11] Although the joint-stock companies and the regulated companies had opened up world markets, they were unable to keep these areas monopolized. Harassed on the sea by privateers, and hampered at home by jealous competitors who were able to enlist Parliamentary aid, the exclusive trading companies lost their commercial advantages. London, which had been the center of 17th-century foreign trade, encountered increasing competition from ports in the west and the north of England. India, America, and Africa became lucrative areas of foreign trade, and the latter two continents proved especially profitable areas of exploitation for the merchants of Bristol and Liverpool. The East India Company still continued to be the greatest single company, bringing spices, silks, and cotton textiles from the vast, densely-populated land that Clive had conquered. Meanwhile, England's expansion into the Caribbean and commercial privileges obtained under the

10 The term was first used by Jerome Blanqui. For a succinct criticism of this terminology, see Herbert Heaton's article on the Industrial Revolution in the *Encyclopaedia of the Social Sciences*, Vol. VIII, pp. 3–12.
11 1,924,000 tons as contrasted with 317,000 in 1700.

Treaty of Utrecht had created a large market for slaves. Sugar, fish, grain, lumber, and tobacco made up the major commodities which the British colonies in America yielded. With what were all these commodities from Asia and America purchased? The answer to this question reveals the wide variety of industrial occupations already flourishing in England. Woollens and worsteds, hardware, coal, earthenware, pewter, brass—these were England's chief exports; but to this list must be added a host of unimpressive commodities, ranging from buttons to snuff boxes. With such prosaic goods, English merchants purchased the rare textiles of the Orient, the slaves of Africa (for re-export), and the raw materials of America.

How Protection for the Wool Industry Unintentionally Built up a Domestic Cotton Industry

The ancient woollen and worsted industries found the new trend of English trade distinctly disadvantageous. Tropical and sub-tropical areas provided no export markets. At the same time, the imported Indian silks and calicos proved far more comfortable than English woollens. As a result, the domestic demand for woollen and worsted cloth declined, causing the clothiers to make bitter war on the India Company. For a time Parliament could not decide whether to favor the cotton-cloth importers or the wool manufacturers, but although the India Company was strongly entrenched, the complaints of the woollen industry could not be disregarded. The beginnings of a policy of protection for England's ancient industry may be discerned from such hesitant legislation as that of 1665 which required that every person who died in England be buried in a woollen shroud, or from that of 1697 requiring judges, students, and professors to wear woollen gowns. The woollen manufacturers, however, demanded something more than these cumbersome gestures; they pressed for vigorous legislation and succeeded in obtaining a prohibition against Indian fabrics in 1700, and, in 1721, the passage of a law which forbade the wearing of printed or painted calicos.

Although this "Calico Act" was expressly intended to protect the English woollen, worsted, and silk industries against the competition of imported cotton textiles, there are, as Professor Usher has said, "few instances in history of so great a discrepancy between expectations and results."[12] In spite of the threat of a £20 fine which hung over the head of every wearer of calico, and in spite of the £5 reward offered to informers, the wearing of cotton cloth apparently could not be curbed. As a concession to popular demand for lighter textiles, the Manchester Act of 1735 legalized the wearing of cloth made from an admixture of cotton and linen. Actually, Parliament in attempting to succor the woollen industry had succeeded in protecting England's feeble domestic cotton-textile industry from East Indian competition. Growing slowly but soundly, the English cotton-textile industry practically doubled its output during the first half of the 18th century.[13] Meantime the cotton-textile industry was experimenting with a number of mechanical devices which promised to lower production costs.[14]

Not until 1774 was the Calico Act repealed. Almost immediately came more inventions[15] which made the English cotton industry not merely as efficient as that of the Orient but more so! Thus commerce had provided wage-earning consumers with textiles more attractive than woollens; and an effort to protect the English wool manufacturers against the competition of Oriental cloth actually helped to build up England's domestic cotton industry. This unintended protection created an industry which was in turn compelled to resort to the use of machinery in order to compete with cheap Oriental cotton textiles in world markets. Finally, by the use of machinery, such an advantage was gained that England became the foremost cotton manufacturing nation in the entire world. The history of the English cotton industry is therefore an episode of great importance. It clearly revealed (as did also the iron industry) the importance of machinery in industrial production.

The Synthetic Nature of Invention

To refer to the 18th century in England as an "age of invention" is accurate enough if one does not imply by that phrase any singular or mysterious manifestation of mental activity. Modern biology and

[12] A. P. Usher, *An Introduction to the Industrial History of England* (Boston: Houghton Mifflin Co., 1920), p. 285.

[13] Imports of raw cotton rose from 1,985,868 pounds in 1700 to 2,976,610 pounds in 1751, while the official value of exported cotton goods increased from £23,253 in 1700 to £45,986 in 1751. See Edward Baines Jr., *History of the Cotton Manufacture* (London: H. Fisher, R. Fisher, and P. Jackson, 1835), pp. 346–350.

[14] See pp. 79–85.

[15] Notably Crompton's spinning mule.

psychology have revealed that latent inventive capacity is widely distributed, while the history of science has clearly demonstrated that a single invention is not an isolated occurrence but, in reality, the synthesis of a previous set of unintegrated innovations and discoveries.[16] Yet the actual exercise of such latent inventive capacity is forcefully stimulated by environmental conditions; only in this sense is "necessity the mother of invention." Educational forces and economic circumstances in 18th-century England cooperated in inducing a wholly unprecedented release of hitherto unused inventive capacity, and succeeded in producing a very remarkable set of mechanical and chemical innovations. But far more important than the single episode of new inventions was the heritage which was passed on to the modern economic world. New insights into mechanical possibilities resulted, and the very use of machines generated educational forces which have made invention a normal and regularly expected course of events. Professor Whitehead once said that the greatest invention was really the "invention of invention!"[17] Substantially this is what the 18th century, more than any preceding century, accomplished.

Basic Inventions in the Textile Industry

Textile machinery began in the woollen industry but found its first real area of usefulness in cotton manufacturing. Two questions immediately arise. How could machinery emerge in an industry so highly organized under the putting-out system as woollen manufacturing? Why was it adopted faster and faster in a new industry rather than in an old one? The answer to the first question centers around certain obvious shortcomings of the clothiers' productive organization and around increasing insistence on quality cloth by cloth buyers. The answer to the second illustrates clearly the amount of control which dispersed cloth workers actually possessed over the woollen and worsted industries. By terrorism they delayed the use of machinery in these older industries.

So successful had the facilities for marketing English cloth become by the first quarter of the 18th century that the network of clothier-

---

[16] The process of invention, its psychological basis, and its essentially synthetic nature, has been described accurately by A. P. Usher in his *History of Mechanical Inventions*, Revised Edition (Cambridge: Harvard University Press, 1954). See especially, Chaps. II, III and IV.

[17] *Science and the Modern World* (New York: The Macmillan Co., 1925), p. 136.

organized cloth workers could scarcely keep pace. Relative scarcity of weavers, together with an insistent demand for wider cloth, provided the occasion which called forth the inventive power of John Kay. A combination of skilled weaver and good mechanic, Kay had a total experience large enough to appreciate the limitations of the traditional looms. Cloths over thirty inches wide required two weavers to pass the shuttle back and forth. By combining simple, long-familiar, mechanical principles, Kay made it possible for one person to weave wide cloth. His "fly shuttle," which was shot back and forth by means of a traverse raceway, was driven by the alternate impact of suspended hammers. The invention proved doubly important: its use increased the speed of weaving at the same time that it reduced the manpower needed; and its extended use made yarn relatively scarce, so that now spinning came to be the bottleneck which obstructed the expansion of the textile industry.

Although experiments with spinning machinery had been made before the middle of the 18th century,[18] no successful machine was produced. Meantime the extended use of the fly shuttle had, by 1760, thrown the textile industry out of balance. This widely appreciated situation proved to be the environmental basis for another manifestation of inventive capacity. The first practical spinning machine which resulted may be said to be similar to the fly shuttle in one respect—it was a mechanical, hand-operated device. The inventor, James Hargreaves, a weaver and carpenter, realized, as did every other weaver, that relative scarcity of yarn was an important cause for weavers' unemployment. He found a practical solution for a problem which mechanics and millwrights were trying to solve. His spinning "jenny,"[19] a multiple spinning wheel, operating several spindles and provided with a mechanical carriage for drawing the threads, involved no change in the organization of the spinning industry. No special workshops were needed; neither was the cost of a machine prohibitive for well-circumstanced spinners.

The fly shuttle and the spinning jenny were, therefore, complemen-

---

[18] Lewis Paul and John Wyatt obtained a patent for a spinning machine in 1738. Although the machine was not commercially successful, it was based upon the identical principle (the use of rollers moving at proportionally greater speeds) which later made machine spinning practicable.

[19] Patented in 1767. Especially efficient models could spin as many as 80 threads at once. See, Charles Zilson, "The Entrepreneur in the Industrial Revolution in Britain," in *Entrepreneurship and Economic Growth* (Cambridge, Mass: Harvard University Research Center in Entrepreneurial History, 1954), p. 5.

tary, one improving the quality and increasing the output of cloth, the other accomplishing like results in the production of yarn. But mechanical spinning made slow headway in the woollen industry. Spinners, who had experienced a small wave of prosperity after the introduction of the fly shuttle, bitterly opposed the new machines, and there began a long period of industrial terrorism and sabotage which persisted for almost a half century. The woollen industry was England's "ancient trade." Its very antiquity had rendered its personnel resistant to change. As a consequence, it was in the cotton industry, unhampered by tradition and circumstantially protected, that the new machines found an area of real usefulness.

The technical innovations in weaving and spinning generated a tremendous interest on the part of the public. Meantime, throughout the 18th century, scientific inquiry had increased rapidly. Scientific bodies had collected (as the Royal Society did in its *Philosophical Transactions*)[20] all kinds of ingenious proposals for practical application of mechanical principles, while organizations such as the Society of Arts offered prizes for successful spinning machines. Popular interest and scientific information therefore combined to create a most hospitable atmosphere for the work of inventors. Unlike Kay and Hargreaves, both of whom were engaged in cloth making, the next outstanding figure in the history of textile machinery was a rank outsider. Barber and wig maker though he was by trade, Richard Arkwright not only patented a remarkable spinning machine,[21] but established factories in which his machinery was used, accumulating a huge fortune as a successful cotton manufacturer. Arkwright may, therefore, be regarded as the founder of the factory system, since it was he, more than anyone else, who had the entrepreneurial boldness to break away from the traditional practices which previously governed the organization of the textile trades. It was he who combined vigorous managerial ability with scientific technology, and thereby helped lay the foundations for a type of industrial production which has become characteristic in the modern economic world.

[20] Founded in 1662, this institution became an intellectual center which brought together outstanding thinkers and experimenters. For a succinct account of the early history of the Royal Society, see Martha Ornstein, *The Rôle of Scientific Societies in the Seventeenth Century* (Chicago: The University of Chicago Press, 1928), Chap. IV. For a listing of 18th century proposals for economic improvement advanced in the "Transactions" of the Royal Society, see the check list in the appendixes to E. A. J. Johnson's *Predecessors of Adam Smith* (Englewood Cliffs, N.J. Prentice-Hall, 1937).

[21] In 1769.

Arkwright's "water frame," although not original with him,[22] was based on the principle which underlies one of the methods employed in modern spinning: twisting by means of grooved rollers, and drawing by differentially faster rotation of a series of rollers. This principle had been discovered as early as 1738 by Lewis Paul and John Wyatt and had apparently been used by Thomas Highs[23] in 1767, the same year that Hargreaves patented the jenny. The appearance of Arkwright's machine nevertheless marked a turning point in the textile industry. Whereas the fly shuttle and the spinning jenny were more complex machines than any previously employed, they were still hand-operated tools, designed to be used in the old scheme of organization. Arkwright's machine required power[24] as well as relatively heavy fixed investments. Yet large and permanent investment as a requisite for industrial production was not a new thing; ocean shipping, mining, and iron-making had for a long time required large investments. But the combination of machinery, power, permanent investment, and regimentation of industrial laborers, was substantially new. In this sense, the factory system, involving a divorce of ownership of tools[25] from artisanship, can with propriety be dated from the establishment of Arkwright's water-power cotton mill in 1771.

Arkwright's Example Leads to the Adoption of the Factory System

Arkwright's amazing business career cannot be described here, but one or two episodes are so important that a few words of explanation are necessary. Roller spinning produced precision twisting and drawing, yielding finer thread. This technical advantage made it possible to spin large amounts of fine, cotton yarn by means of the water frame,

22 After Arkwright had brought suits against alleged infringers of his patent (one lost, the other won) his competitors in turn brought suit against him for fraudulently patenting Thomas Highs' invention. A jury found Arkwright guilty in 1785, and the Crown accordingly cancelled his patent. For details of this early patent trial, see Mantoux, *Industrial Revolution*, pp. 232–235; and G. W. Daniels, *The Early English Cotton Manufacture* (Cambridge: The University Press, 1920), pp. 110 ff.

23 Who apparently accomplished something quite frequent in the history of invention: a rediscovery of a device previously invented.

24 First operated by horse power; after 1771 by water, hence the name "water frame."

25 Arkwright's first water-power mill cost some £12,000, a sum obviously too large for any cloth worker or for any group of artisans to provide.

and thereby to produce, in England, increasing quantities of high-grade, pure cotton cloth at low prices. Arkwright's competitors, unable to make use of the new invention because of his patent rights, protested to Parliament that the production of pure cotton cloth violated the Manchester Act, which, it will be recalled, had only legalized cloth produced from an admixture of linen and cotton. Undaunted, Arkwright appealed to Parliament, pointing out the national importance of developing the cotton industry, and, single-handed, persuaded Parliament, in 1774, to repeal the legislation which obstructed his business. The next year this erstwhile barber obtained another patent which covered a series of integrated textile machinery, including devices for carding, roving,[26] and feeding raw cotton into the carding machines. These inventions,[27] together with the water frame, converted cotton manufacture into a machine system of interdependent processes, driven by water power, a system which embraced all the steps in cotton-cloth manufacture except weaving. Hence the production of thread was technically in advance, and once again weaving became the bottleneck of cloth making.

Technical apparatus, however, does not by itself constitute a factory system, but Arkwright's genius soon provided the missing ingredients. He was able to obtain the capital that he lacked from partners whom he persuaded to relinquish managerial duties.[28] Nor did he find difficulty in attracting laborers, employing as many as six hundred in a single mill at Manchester in 1780. Skillfully combining large quantities of capital and large aggregates of labor, he rose to a position of industrial pre-eminence and was knighted, an episode which in itself indicated the increasing social importance of the businessman. Although his cotton industry expanded rapidly from one factory to several, this remarkable businessman retained control and exercised supervision over all. With money making his primary goal, he did not hesitate to employ any method calculated to attain his end; if chicanery or even dishonesty seemed necessary, he did not disdain to employ either; if laws barred his path, he lobbied for legislative revision, and his phenomenal success marked him as a person to be imitated. As a

26 The process of forming carded cotton into coarse ropes preparatory to the making of threads by twisting and drawing these "rovings."

27 Subsequently proven to be the inventions respectively of Daniel Bourne, Thomas Highs, and John Lees.

28 This method of capital accumulation for new textile ventures became typical and remained so until such large amounts of capital were needed that the joint-stock company, which had proved its usefulness in commerce, was introduced.

consequence, Richard Arkwright became, for better or for worse, the model for thousands of businessmen both in his own and subsequent generations. A new world of machinery and world markets emerged, providing ample exercise for the energy, the business acumen, and even the ruthlessness of a new breed of businessmen. The rapid emergence of a great number of gifted entrepreneurs in the 18th century is, in fact, another chapter in the history of invention. Occupational mobility, which had been hastened by the decay of the craft gilds and by agricultural reorganization,[29] released countless persons of genuine ability from conventional restraints, and the resulting atmosphere of business freedom elicited powers of conducting business enterprise hitherto unperceived and unknown! The art of factory administration may indeed be considered one of the most important inventions that the 18th century produced.

This new group of businessmen really put the inter-linked textile inventions to practical tests, and by that very process indicated the next technical problem to be solved. Thus, it was not merely the water frame that made yarn abundant and spinners scarce; it was also Arkwright's business ability which adapted technology to business organization and thereby released the latent productive power of roller spinning. By converting spinning into a factory process, appropriate machinery for mechanical weaving became the imperative next step, and the solution for this problem was found by an English clergyman. But although Edmund Cartwright patented a crude power loom in 1785, years were required to make the machine a commercial success and to overcome opposition. Weavers, who had prospered from the increased production of yarn, bitterly opposed the new invention and destroyed the huge weaving factory which Cartwright and some Manchester spinners had erected in 1789. Moreover, the clergyman-inventor proved to be a poor businessman;[30] more practical ability than his was required to adapt the power loom to factory use. By the turn of the century, however, power weaving had succeeded both at Glasgow and Manchester, al-

[29] Many former yeomen became successful industrialists during the last quarter of the 18th century; Mantoux (*Industrial Revolution,* p. 382) has said that these displaced farmers "provided building materials, so to speak, for the construction of a new class."

[30] The profound difference between technical pioneers and businessmen has been effectively depicted by F. W. Taussig in his Brown University lectures on *Inventors and Money Makers* (New York: The Macmillan Co., 1915); and by Eric Roll, *An Early Experiment in Industrial Organization* (London: Longmans, Green and Co., 1930).

though almost another half century passed before the new method really superseded the traditional hand-loom weaving.

Other minds, meantime, had progressively improved the several processes of cloth making. Samuel Crompton, son of a Lancashire yeoman, succeeded in building a spinning machine (1779) which combined the best features of both Hargreaves' jenny and the water frame, a compound machine which by use of rollers made possible precision twisting, while at the same time, by employing a movable carriage, produced exceedingly strong, fine thread. This machine completed the technical triumph of English machine spinners over East Indian hand spinners. No longer did the English spinners need to fear any competition. Cheapness and quality, the mainspring of modern machine production, had been achieved. Printing of cloth by means of the calico cylinder carried the technical advance still farther, while improved knowledge of chemistry made it possible to adapt the bleaching trades to a scientific process. The whole scheme of textile manufacture was now revolutionized, and in the wake of technical advance came a resulting conquest of world markets.

Factories and a New Industrial Discipline

It should be reiterated, however, that it was cotton manufacture rather than England's ancient woollen industry which became the real area of technical change. Until 1800, the woollen industry "remained essentially provincial and local."[31] Some introduction of machinery did occur, but it met with bitter resistance on the part of skilled craftsmen who saw in the new methods a monstrous competitive force which threatened them with ruin. This artisan protest, widespread and, for a time, thoroughly effective, was at once a manifestation of surviving craft-gild principles and a forewarning of a new type of resistance against insecurity which crystallized during the 19th century in trade-union philosopohy. Thus, fear of exploitation and of unemployment produced riots and destruction of machinery in the 18th century, while the same fear of insecurity produced jurisdictional disputes, restriction of output, and sabotage in the next century. Either form of resistance was symptomatic of a fundamental change in the organization of industry which mechanization was creating.

31 Mantoux, *Industrial Revolution*, p. 268. No student should fail to become familiar with this excellent book, which describes in delightful detail the history of the industrial changes in 18th-century England.

Indeed, an alteration in business methods was probably one of the most important consequences of the adoption of scientific technology. Complex machines, integrated manufacturing processes, and the use of power required that production be concentrated in factories where supervision could be provided constantly. Machines, buildings, and equipment for generating water or steam power required large investments in fixed form. As contrasted with the investment of the 17th-century clothiers, which was primarily tied up in inventories of semi-finished goods, the factory owners of 1800 were compelled to sink huge sums in permanent equipment. Profits depended upon successful and constant utilization of this mass of capital. Proper administration of this new form of equipment presented a complex managerial problem, one which has, in fact, grown more and more difficult to cope with as the amount of permanent investment has progressively increased.

Much of the sordidness of English factory life in the first half of the 19th century can be attributed to the inexperience of factory owners in dealing with this problem of heavy "sunk" costs, of profitably utilizing equipment which can give off its usefulness only over long periods of time. The early English factory owners saw no other solution than to employ their machinery as continuously as possible. Drawing their labor supply from persons already habituated to long hours of work, they were able to compel their employees to submit to fourteen or even six-teen hours of labor a day under the close supervision of factory officials. Moreover, the machines themselves were taskmasters, setting an invariable pace which the wearied hands of factory workers were compelled to follow. The new discipline mercilessly dictated what operators must do, almost reducing laborers to automatons in an impersonal rhythm of industrial regularity. Karl Marx caught the imagination of all critics of modern production when he designated labor under the factory system as "wage-slavery." So it was and so it is: a servitude fully as exacting as any type of slavery, but with this difference, that wages presumably supply the reward which induces persons to accept the monotony, the irksomeness, and the restraint which modern industrial discipline involves.

Importance of Iron and Steel in Industry

Mass production, an indispensable element of the modern economic world, was first successfully achieved, therefore, in the English cotton industry as a consequence of the combination of scientific technology with the vigor of the capitalist proprietorship. Contemporaneous with these experiments in cloth making, innovations fully as important were introduced in the metallurgical trades; fully as important because they completely revolutionized the metal trades, thereby making possible an abundance of iron and steel for structural purposes, for vehicles, and for constructing the new machinery in the mass-production factories. The cotton industry may be said to have provided an object lesson which demonstrated beyond doubt the importance of elaborate power-driven machines; the development of the iron and steel industry made efficient, durable machinery possible.

"Iron, especially in the form of steel," it has cogently been said, "provides the structural basis of industrial civilization."[32] It forms this structural basis, because of its strength, malleability, abundance, and relative cheapness. All of these qualities were profoundly influenced by new methods of smelting, forging, and fabricating iron which were discovered in the 18th century. The use of iron, or of steel for that matter, was nothing new; ancient[33] and medieval[34] societies employed these materials for tools and weapons, and the 16th century had witnessed new uses for iron, especially in the manufacture of cannon. Since a long chain of technical improvements in iron making can be traced which reach back many centuries, why should 18th-century England be singled out as especially important in the history of iron and steel? The answer is simple: English ironmasters discovered a new fuel for smelting iron ore, thereby removing the chief obstacle to the production of cheap pig iron; they also were able to avail themselves of new chemical processes and of steam power, thereby producing superior qualities of iron and steel. Thus, by making better and cheaper iron and steel, the ironmasters of England laid the structural foundations for a type of civilization wholly different from the one into which they were themselves born.

New Techniques in Ferrous Metallurgy

Until the 18th century, iron ore was smelted in England, as elsewhere, by means of charcoal. But over centuries, charcoal production had

[32] Meredith Givens, "History of the Iron and Steel Industry," *Encyclopaedia of Social Sciences,* Vol. VIII, p. 296.

[33] Military needs of the Roman Empire, for example, had led to great development in the technique of forging and tempering.

[34] Belgium was probably the leading medieval iron-producing area, although Spain, Sweden, and Germany were also contributing considerable amounts.

decimated English forests, and, with the growing scarcity of fuel, costs had risen in the iron industry. Faced with sharp competition from Sweden and Germany, the English iron-mining and smelting industry declined so seriously during the 17th century[35] that the handwriting was on the wall; unless a new fuel could be found, England would become almost entirely dependent upon foreign sources of pig iron. This situation was particularly aggravating in view of the patent fact that Great Britain possessed an abundance of both iron and coal. The problem was therefore strictly technical.

For a century, repeated efforts had been made to find a solution, but with no real success. Then came, sometime between 1709 and 1719, a great discovery by Abraham Darby, who, by coking the coal and by using powerful bellows, succeeded in smelting iron by means of coke. As in the case of textile machinery, lack of balance between interdependent segments of an industry had apparently hastened the process of invention. Expansion of markets had greatly stimulated those industries which used pig iron as raw material; increased demand called forth more intense efforts on the part of English iron smelters to solve a problem which had long baffled them. Production of cheap pig iron, however, was only a beginning; there still remained the task of converting pig iron into malleable iron cheaply and efficiently. Experiments begun in 1762 by John Roebuck and by Thomas and George Cranage in 1766 were carried to completion by Peter Onions, in 1783, and even more successfully by Henry Cort, in 1784. Cort's "puddling process" of purifying iron, together with the use of rolling mills, completely altered the iron industry.[36] Meanwhile steel making underwent corresponding improvement; by smelting prepared iron at high temperatures in sealed crucibles, and by the use of charcoal and ground glass, Benjamin Huntsman was able to produce steel of excellent quality.[37] All these metallurgical processes, discovered by practical men, represented chemical innovations which proved eminently useful although they were quite imperfectly understood. Indeed, this very obscurity exerted a profound influence upon pure science, which, because it sought complete explanations, soon became a useful ally of the practical world of industry.

The chemical and metallurgical discoveries made by Darby, Onions,

[35] The total output of English blast furnaces in 1720 has been estimated at only 17,000 tons. See Mantoux, *Industrial Revolution*, p. 278.

[36] As contrasted with hammering, the use of rolling mills increased the speed of malleable iron manufacture at least fifteenfold.

[37] Huntsman was a clockmaker who needed fine-quality steel for watch springs. For details, see Mantoux, *Industrial Revolution*, p. 303.

Cort, and Huntsman could not by themselves, however, have revolutionized the iron and steel industry. A series of mechanical inventions also contributed abundantly to metallurgical progress. Conversion of pig iron into malleable iron required more powerful blowing machinery, and this gap was filled by a water-powered blowing machine invented by John Smeaton in 1760. Nine years later, James Watt succeeded in building a workable steam engine.[38] With Matthew Boulton as his partner, Watt next embarked upon the commercial manufacture of stationary steam engines. As a result, power of definite and predictable amount became available for blowing, hammering, and rolling. Chemical and mechanical inventions could thereafter be integrated into a complete technology, making possible the manufacture of iron and steel by factory methods.

Cheap and efficient iron found an important new market in factory machinery. Iron equipment replaced the early wooden textile machinery, a process made possible largely by Henry Maudsley's improved metal lathe which facilitated the construction of mechanically-precise, power-driven machines. John Wilkinson, in the meantime, had constructed a metal boring machine which made the drilling of accurate pump and engine cylinders possible,[39] an invention which played no small part in making the steam engine a practical success, and, consequently, an indispensable aid to the metal and textile industries.

The economic effects of the new metallurgical processes may be seen easily from the statistics of output. Whereas England produced only 68,000 tons of pig iron in 1788, eighteen years later, in 1806, she produced 250,400 tons. Foreign iron was no longer imported. It did not in fact need to be imported since England now produced nearly half of the total world supply. Not only did pig-iron production provide ample raw materials for subsequent stages of metal manufacturing, but its accelerated rate of production actually threw the iron industry out of equilibrium and thereby hastened the process of complementary invention. John Wilkinson, by perfecting the manufacture of cast iron, astonished his contemporaries by making huge iron castings for bridges, while by the use of close-set rollers he produced sheet iron out of which he constructed the first iron canal boat. Wilkinson was among the few persons who seemed to sense the potential importance of iron and steel;

---

[38] Watt obtained his first patent in 1769. His "steam fire engine," however, was not technically perfected until 1774. See Roll, *An Early Experiment in Industrial Organization,* pp. 13 ff.

[39] *Ibid.,* p. 25.

he predicted that iron would ultimately play a dominant part in industrial civilization. Boldly experimenting, he found a host of new uses for iron, constructing iron chairs, iron pipes, iron vats for breweries, iron bridge girders, iron ship plates, and, finally, for himself, an iron coffin!

Application of Scientific Criteria to Technology

It is, perhaps, inaccurate to classify all the foregoing innovations in the textile and metal industries as "scientific." Almost all of the important inventions were conceived by practical men, who had precious little knowledge either of mechanics or of chemistry. A large portion of scientific knowledge, however, is always derived from practical experience; indeed, pure science constantly finds an important area of usefulness in explaining more accurately why certain empirically-discovered techniques are successful. In 18th-century England, this task of examination, explanation, and improvement was promptly attacked by men with scientific training, and in the history of the steam engine is found an example of the practical benefits which can arise from scientific revision. For James Watt invented the steam engine, not by originating the idea of such a contrivance, but by applying a well-known physical phenomenon (the capacity of steam to expand) to an existing machine (Newcomen's atmospheric pumping engine). Yet this work of "critical revision"[40] proved to be of great importance; it really introduced a new era, one in which science became the indispensable servant of modern industry.[41]

Two quite different steam pumps, one patented in 1698 by Thomas Savery (a Devonshire engineer), the other in 1705 by Thomas Newcomen, represented the progress which had been made in the application of steam power fifty years before Watt's work began. Both devices were useful and workable, especially Newcomen's engine which was extensively used for pumping mines, filling water-wheel reservoirs, and for operating city waterworks. Technically, Savery's engine was closer to the modern steam engine than Newcomen's, since it forced water, which had risen into a partial vacuum by atmospheric pressure, upward

40 Cf. Usher, *A History of Mechanical Inventions,* Chapter II.

41 For a complete story of the development of the steam engine, students are referred to Chapter I of Eric Roll's book whose title is *An Early Experiment in Industrial Organization, being a History of the Firm of Boulton & Watt, 1775–1805.* This splendid book, written when the author was 22 years old, should be a challenge to every young scholar.

by employing the expansive power of steam. Newcomen's engine, on the other hand, merely made use of the vacuum created by condensing steam. Alternate infusion and condensation of steam in a cylinder fitted with a piston which was connected with the counterpoised beam provided up-and-down motion. Yet this clumsy "fire engine," although very wasteful of energy in the alternate heating and cooling process, was a thoroughly practical device which satisfied all but the critical. To this category of critical thinkers, James Watt belonged. His scientific training did not allow him to regard a machine which relied upon the alternate heating and cooling of a steam cylinder as satisfactory, and in 1761 he commenced a series of laboratory experiments on steam pressure. Out of these experiments came Watt's basic contribution: the idea of a separate condensing chamber. At the same time, he concluded that Savery had followed a sound plan by employing the expansive power of steam. By re-adopting this idea, and by making use of a condenser, Watt transformed Newcomen's atmospheric engine into a real steam engine.[42] Later he devised a method for converting steam power into rotary motion,[43] and with this invention his improved engine became capable of generating motive power for an infinite number of uses.

Boulton and Watt Extend the Use of Steam Power

Watt's place in technical history should not, however, be measured either by his invention of the condenser or by his conversion of mechanical pulsation into rotary motion. By systematically investigating the scientific facts which physicists had discovered concerning heat and steam pressure, and by applying underlying principles to an empirically-developed machine, James Watt, more than any other person, deserves to be honored as the founder of truly scientific industrial technology. He bridged the gap between pure science and empirical discovery at exactly the place where connection would provide greatest immediate practical benefit. Moreover, by his subsequent partnership with one of the outstanding businessmen of all England, he was able to introduce steam engines into all kinds of industrial uses. Watt was, therefore, instrumental in weaving together the empirical discoveries of his predecessors with theoretical physics, and at the same time, able to prove the worth of this synthesis to businessmen.

[42] For further details see Mantoux, *Industrial Revolution,* pp. 326–329; Usher, *A History of Mechanical Inventions,* pp. 314–318.
[43] See Roll, *An Early Experiment in Industrial Organization,* pp. 107 ff.

Nor did it take long for businessmen to realize the importance of the steam engine. Instead of selling engines for a fixed price, the firm of Boulton and Watt required their customers to remunerate them for the cost of building and installing a steam engine and to pay a royalty of one-third the saving in coal consumption which the new engine (as contrasted with a Newcomen engine of the same power) actually provided.[44] Thus technical superiority became both the selling argument and the basis of reward. Although this direct appeal to the money-making motive led to frequent disharmony between the engine manufacturers and the engine users, it perforce led to a rapid adoption of steam in mining operations. Meanwhile, in 1781, Watt had perfected his device for converting the power generated by steam into rotary motion. The province of the steam engine was immediately enlarged, first in metal working (blowing, hammering, and rolling) next in flour mills, stone crushers, and sugar-cane mills, while in 1785 steam power was first applied in a spinning factory. By 1800, steam was everywhere replacing water power with extremely important results. No longer did factories need to be located near rapidly flowing streams;[45] the location of industry came now to be determined by nearness of raw materials in some cases, nearness to markets in others, or availability of labor in still other cases. Steam power had created a new form of industrial mobility destined to be of great importance. For it was steam power more than any other factor which permitted the concentration of industry in cities and thus facilitated that strong trend toward urbanization and industrial compactness which has become both a blessing and a curse in the modern economic world!

Impact of Science on Business Enterprise

Centuries of scientific inquiry had yielded a body of scientific principles which were available for industrial utilization.[46] The elementary mechanical and chemical applications of science which have been sketched in the preceding pages were only a prelude to the extensive employment of scientific knowledge in industry which could now be undertaken. The initial steps had been taken under the pressure of the

44 Roll ascribes this shrewd idea "to Watt's initiative." See Roll, *An Early Experiment in Industrial Organization*, p. 27.

45 The early cotton factories were of necessity located where waterpower was available, hence often in country villages rather than cities.

46 Cf. Usher, *A History of Mechanical Inventions*.

peculiar economic circumstances which confronted England in the 18th century. From the time of Watt, business enterprise formed an indissoluble partnership with physical science, and out of this union has come the complex technology of the modern world. This alliance has roots which are primarily economic, although it has had consequences which are not merely economic, but also sociological and political.

The appeal of the new technology to the businessmen of the 18th century was strictly pecuniary. Machine spinning lowered costs at the same time that it produced finer, stronger, and better thread; smelting of iron by coke similarly reduced the cost of pig iron, while the manufacture of malleable iron by the puddling process likewise made manufactured iron not only cheaper but better. The steam engine was adopted for comparable reasons; it reduced the cost of producing energy, while at the same time it permitted factories to be located where all other costs of production would be lower. Scientific technology revealed its potential ability to further the making of business profits, and for this reason it was adopted as an integral part of modern capitalism.

The eagerness with which businessmen sought the advantages of the new cost-reducing technology revealed itself both in a quest for patent privileges and in an effort of the underprivileged to evade patent rights. The 17th-century war between the exclusive trading companies and the interlopers was reenacted in a new setting. Arkwright made a fortune by patenting a machine he did not invent; it was understandable, therefore, why a petition was circulated by steam engine-users asking Parliament to cancel Watt's patent. Inventors armed with patents often found their privileges of small value, since unscrupulous competitors unblushingly copied their machines. More and more, businessmen divided into two categories: those who made money because they had technological advantages arising from legal privileges, and those who were prevented from making money because of the existence of these legal privileges. Clearly the latter were in the majority, and the logical consequence was the rising opposition of businessmen to the engrossing of technical advantages.

Growing Pressures for Business Freedom

Nor did this single form of monopoly exhaust the category of privileges which the new race of businessmen condemned. There was money to be made in industry and in commerce, provided no restraints of a political nature were imposed. Freedom to hire whomsoever they wished, freedom to make whatever they thought advisable, freedom to sell wherever they pleased became the tripartite demand of most industrialists. The corporative spirit of the medieval businessman was dead and buried; a feverish era of ruthless competition became the order of the age.

One basic reason for this aggressive tendency in business enterprise was really sociological. No longer did the maker of goods need to be passive. If only costs could be lowered, the very process would create new demand. An uprooted peasantry, freed from the restraint of tradition by virtue of agrarian reorganization and with want scales made more flexible by the demolition of the customs of the old village communities, provided an enlargement of this new variety of proletarian demand. Moreover the spread of the wage system had made each wage earner the sole judge of how his own wants should be satisfied. Skillful appeal, by cheapness or by chicanery, might divert a portion of thousands of these wage incomes to the advantage of particular manufacturers. Tempting buyers has always been an important element in business, but clearly wh?n there are more buyers and when an increasing proportion are ignorant or ill-informed, this field of endeavor necessarily becomes more important. Moreover, the domestic market represented merely one market for the manufacturers of textiles, hardware, clothing, pottery, or jewelry. English mercantile agencies had by 1800 spread throughout the entire world. Almost every handicraft village in Europe, Asia, Africa, or America became a potential market for the factory-made articles which scientific technology made possible; everywhere in the entire world demand could be stimulated if only cheapness and attractiveness could be combined. In this vast world market, which transcended distance and social stratification, lay potential profits unpredictably large, and English businessmen seem to have promptly and clearly realized this combination of economic fact and sociological peculiarity. One by one, other nations came to appreciate the importance of an artificially-stimulated demand. When this occurred, political significance was subjoined to technological consideration, and presently the capacity of advanced industrial nations to dominate markets in under-developed areas ushered in new opportunities, even though this new variety of "colonialism" led ultimately to a host of aggravating problems.

5

The formulation

of capitalist theory

Deeds and Thoughts

Philosophers, like vegetables, are profoundly influenced by their environment. Although they may protest that their thoughts are strictly objective, time usually proves that their teachings reflect the aspirations, the hopes, and the economic and political ambitions of the age in which they live. Looking back over the past century and more, one can realize that this is what the English economic philosophers of the early factory era also did. The theories which they advanced were in large measure influenced by contemporaneous industrial changes; the commercial policies which they advocated proved nicely suited to accommodate the expansion of England's markets. What they succeeded in formulating came to be a body of capitalist economic theory, although they remained happily unaware of this unintended result of their intellectual labors. Yet economic science, like all science, is largely descriptive, and, to the extent that economic thought during the Industrial Revolution was scientific, it necessarily reflected emerging economic institutions. Its chief fault arose from the fact that it was too British; for a time it explained only those economic phenomena peculiar to England although presently the same theory partially explained what occurred in some other countries whose industrial development was patterned after an English model. In brief, classical political economy, formulated in the latter part of the 18th century and the first part of the 19th, was to a very considerable extent an explanation of a developing capitalistic system. This body of economic theory, passed down as an intellectual heritage, has exerted a profound and pervasive influence upon legislation, political institutions, and modes of thought, and has therefore been an important molding force of many of our institutions. Deeds and thoughts are never far removed from each other; both must be understood.

Central Ideas of Medieval Economic Theory

The content of medieval economic thought had been predominantly ethical, a logical consequence of the dominant position of the Christian Church. Following an ancient Oriental tradition, the Church sanctioned the social stratification of the medieval world and pronounced the result pleasing to God and socially good. Within this stratified world, the Church insisted that economic life should be conducted fairly and justly. Around justice, defined as a set of conditions which would allow each person to live appropriately in his respective class, and around Christian charity (a duty of all), the medieval clergy gradually built up a code of economic behavior which, had it been completely applied, would have stabilized medieval economic life. The doctrine of just price (which in practice was really based on the idea of fair wages[1]) provided the cornerstone of medieval economic teachings, and upon this ethical base the theologians built an elaborate logical structure which comprehended, among its many parts, a theory of property, a doctrine condoning slavery, and a body of argument which condemned the taking of interest. Yet this *corpus* of economic teaching clearly reflected the economic

[1] *Fair* is defined as sufficient to maintain oneself in one's appointed class. See pp. 33–34.

institutions of the medieval world: the theory of property justified feudal tenure; the doctrine of slavery sanctioned serfdom; the concept of a fair wage lent approval to craft-gild organization, while the condemnation of usury revealed the significant fact that the capital market was not yet extremely important.

Mercantilism, the Economic Ideas of Nationalism

In the late 16th century and, more especially, in the 17th century, distinct changes in the content of economic thought are discernible. As contrasted with the penchant of the medieval age for the idea of brotherhood in a world community, 17th-century England, as well as other European nations, ardently embraced the idea of nationalism.[2] This change in emphasis arose, as far as economic causes are concerned, from the increased size of business enterprises and from expansion of markets. As nation-states came into existence as a result of political unification, businessmen attempted to reserve the expanding domestic markets for themselves by persuading the government to enact legislation which would discriminate against foreign competitors. Tariffs and prohibitions which had been used in the medieval period to protect local markets now became approved devices of national commercial policy, and for such market-reserving laws and regulations economic writers built up elaborate, though frequently specious, justification. At the same time, there appeared in contemporary economic literature a labored, though often veiled, insistence that it should be the duty of government to increase the opportunities for money making (especially in foreign trade, which allegedly was especially advantageous to a nation) and to stimulate by every possible method the increase of national production. Nationalism also brought a greater fiscal demand for metallic money as the functions of national governments multiplied. This need for cash, which was intensified by the progressive commutation of labor services, led to an inordinate worship of all commercial policies which favored the exportation of manufactured goods, since finished commodities were obviously capable of obtaining from foreigners the largest amount of gold and silver in exchange for a minimum of incorporated raw materials.

Out of these interlocking, nationally-determined ambitions grew slowly a body of economic theory which emphasized production, ex-

---

2 An idea by no means unimportant in the medieval world, but one which did not exert great influence upon the central body of medieval economic thought.

portation, and money,[3] and which glorified statesmanship as a main-spring of economic prosperity. Usually designated today as "mercantil-ism," this economic philosophy was never thoroughly systematized, and its fragmentary nature still defies accurate generalization. But viewed as an entity, its dominant quality consisted of an ebullient desire for marshalling all human and physical resources capable of enriching a nation. It combined a passionate enthusiasm for generating productive power with a thoroughly naive belief in the efficacy of government to achieve by legislation any and all desired ends. At the same time, the literature of mercantilism was filled with ill-concealed special pleading: merchants emphasized alleged national benefits which they promised would arise from the granting of mercantile privileges; business pro-moters, asking for subsidies, forecast great advantages which would result from their schemes; manufacturers, desiring a monopoly of the home market, assured their readers that tariffs would make everyone more prosperous. All had axes to grind and all explained carefully why the government should turn the crank! Yet, in spite of the pervasive selfishness woven into contemporary economic literature, mercantilism was thoroughly symptomatic of the vital changes which were occurring. Business, then as now, found certain types of government action useful for promoting its profit-making ends, and the special pleading found in mercantilism gives us an early illustration of the intensity with which businessmen set about achieving their pecuniary goals. There was woven into this "primitive political economy," for example, a theory of wages well calculated to subserve the interest of money-making employers. The working classes, said the mercantilist writers, are naturally lazy, dis-solute, and prodigal; hence high wages, instead of stimulating industry, always foster idleness, vice, and unrest. Poverty is therefore a necessary condition for laborers, one which the state ought not only to recognize but to cherish.[4] The guardians of plebeian morality, however, carefully avoided undue mention of the contribution which low wages might make to business profits.

In spite of the chicanery that found its way into the body of mercan-

---

[3] See Eli Heckscher, *Mercantilism*, 2 vols. (London: G. Allen and Unwin, Ltd., 1935), for an analysis of mercantilism as a chapter in economic history; and E. A. J. Johnson, *Predecessors of Adam Smith*, for a critical appraisal of mercantilism as a convergence point for economic ideas.

[4] The contemporary endorsement of this policy has been illustrated vividly by E. S. Furniss in his *Position of the Laborer in a System of Nationalism* (Boston: Houghton Mifflin Co., 1920), Chap. VI; republished, 1957 (New York: Kelley and Millman).

tilist theory, English economic literature of the 17th and early 18th century had an important influence on England's rapid economic progress. It forcefully guided public opinion, whetted individual initiative, and set the stage for technological progress. In bright colors it painted a picture of England's enviable future if lands could be improved, roads made more efficient, inland waterways canalized, inventions stimulated, and the best foreign methods of production acclimatized.[5] It approved all scientific inquiry calculated to have practical uses; it praised the merchant, the businessman, and the inventor. In short, mercantilism to a great extent gave literary expression to business hopes, and hastened materially Britain's transition from a feudal to a capitalistic economy.

Adam Smith's *Wealth of Nations*

Alongside of this emotional and pragmatic economic literature, there had slowly grown up a much smaller, more rational, body of economic theory. Although strongly influenced by natural science, this intellectual current had deep roots in moral philosophy. Like natural science, it was essentially descriptive and critical but, like moral philosophy, it was inherently ethical. Raising more questions than it answered, this new skeleton of economic theory sought to discover how people act in their economic relations, and to ascertain whether these ways were socially desirable. Although Bishop Berkeley and David Hume in England, as well as Richard Cantillon, François Quesnay, and Anne Robert Jacques Turgot in France, had made definite progress in laying the foundations for the new economic science, it was Dr. Adam Smith, Professor of Moral Philosophy at Glasgow University, who first succeeded in building up a system of political economy in his famous *Inquiry into the Nature and Causes of the Wealth of Nations* (London, 1776).

Although objective and judicious, Smith could not wholly escape the dominant trend of his age. No really major changes in the conduct or in the technique of British industry had occurred when he wrote his famous book, but enough of the preparatory change had been completed to allow him to appreciate the vitality which freedom from the restraints of custom was imparting to economic life. Rejecting vigorously, sometimes almost unfairly, the partly-planned economy of his mercantilist

5 Andrew Yarranton's *England's Improvement by Sea and Land* (London: R. Everingham, 1677), is a good sample of 17th-century English mercantilist literature. See also E. A. J. Johnson, "Nehemiah Grew: A Forgotten Mercantilist," *American Economic Review*, Vol. XXI, pp. 463–481, reprinted in his *Predecessors of Adam Smith.*

predecessors, and dismissing apologetically the contemporary French doctrine which insisted that land is the sole cause of all wealth, Smith found the origin of wealth in labor. In his opinion, the incentive to exert this wealth-producing labor lay in the primitive urge of self-interest. Compared with this elemental force, altruism, though not unimportant, was weak. Smith's recipe for increasing wealth did not rely upon benevolence; neither did it require the services of "that insidious and crafty animal, vulgarly called a statesman"; it proposed to minimize government action, and thereby to unleash the powerful force of private initiative. Let obstacles to the exercise of business ability be removed, was his advice; let trade be freed from the shackles of tariffs; let each country produce whatever it is best suited to produce and sell it wherever it can; let all forms of monopoly be destroyed, and the existence of underlying "natural laws" will quickly be revealed. These laws, manifesting a "natural order" in the economic world, were, in fact, Smith's chief concern!

In "rude and primitive" societies, said he, wealth is always a result of human labor, assisted, of course, by natural forces. As societies grow and develop, there arises a natural tendency to exchange commodities, which permits specialization. More efficient methods of production necessarily result, because specialization allows the work of production to be divided into tasks. As a consequence of this division of labor, producers become more skillful, and time is also saved; moreover, concentration upon small, particularized tasks whets the imagination and stimulates invention. The degree to which the work of production can be subdivided depends, however, upon the "extent of the market," and hence the larger the market, the more minutely particularized can the work of production become.

But specialized production requires capital, the supply of which depends upon parsimony and thrift. Thus labor and capital, together with land, create an annual flow of wealth which is divided, according to natural principles, between the suppliers of labor, the owners of capital, and the possessors of land. If unrestrained by tariffs, monopoly, or legal privilege, these natural forces will by themselves bring into existence a maximum quantity of goods and services, thus tending by "natural benevolence" to create the largest possible amount of well-being. The basic explanation of this gladsome conclusion was primarily psychological: each person naturally seeks to gratify his own desires, and hence if everyone is given the liberty to do so, the largest total of human industry will be applied to wealth creation. Nor will such unfettered exercise of personal energy cause social chaos. Facilities for exchange will emerge, providing a mechanism for distributing the products of increased industry to all members of society. Self-interest becomes, therefore, the incentive for economic activity, and, at the same time, the cement which binds the body economic together, so that by the pursuit of private gain everyone will be "led by an invisible hand to promote an end which was no part of his intention."[6]

Smith's Glorification of Competition

In Smith's opinion, legislation which restrained the operation of these natural laws constituted the greatest enemy of economic progress. Bitterly assailing the Statute of Apprentices, the English poor laws, the tangle of tariff legislation, and the legal privileges of joint-stock companies, he rebuked, in no uncertain terms, the political ignorance which he alleged had inspired these restraints upon economic well-being. Yet, in spite of this bold assault, he was not hopeful that the "folly and presumption" of governmental interference within the economic order could be removed. His idealism compelled him to portray the latent benefits of free enterprise, although his political realism caused him to doubt that the salubrious air of freedom would ever envelop the business world.

Any elementary sketch of Smith's economic teaching would be inadequate if it did not emphasize the pivotal position which the businessman occupied in the "natural" economic world. For the entrepreneur, in seeking business profits, was forced to consider carefully the wants of his customers. His reward arose partly from his thrift and parsimony (whereby he accumulated capital) and partly from his ability to combine labor, land, and capital in a manner calculated to produce cheap and desirable commodities which would satisfy the wants of other members of society. It was the businessman, therefore, who subdivided tasks, with resulting social advantages; it was he also who, by frugality, brought into being most of the indispensable capital which made an effective system of production possible. Unlike the landlords, who "love to reap where they never sowed," the entrepreneur, by virtue of his business acumen, combined productive agents, thereby creating an income not only sufficient to pay laborers their wages and landlords their rent, but large enough to leave something over and above wages

[6] Adam Smith, *Wealth of Nations,* Cannon edition (London: Methuen and Co., 1904), Vol. I, p. 421.

and rent in the form of profits. No portion of Smith's economic theory could have been more pleasing to the new race of businessmen who were contemporaneously altering the structure of English industry unless it was his fulsome praise of free trade (which promised to widen the markets of British businessmen) that became the epitome of Smith's program for economic reform.

Yet the capitalist proprietor, although he occupied a dominant place in the economic world, was not regarded as a paragon of virtue. Indeed, it was Smith's distrust of businessmen which led him to place so much emphasis on the desirability of competition. Because businessmen were always conspiring against the public, he said, laws and regulation would not protect the public from exploitation. The best way to restrain the social evils arising from business unscrupulousness, Smith felt, lay in vigorous business competition whereby over-reaching by one ambitious entrepreneur would be nullified by the lower prices or better commodities offered to the public by his competitors.

Smith's Recommendations on Economic Policy

Although he emphasized the productive work of the capitalist pro· prietor, it would be unfair to imply that Adam Smith remained unmindful of the fundamental productive rôle of the laborer. Sensitively aware of the human hardships that existed among workers, he repudiated vigorously the specious assumptions of the mercantilist doctrine justifying the social desirability of low wages. In his opinion, high, not low, wages provided the best device for calling forth the largest amount of laborers' effort and, at the same time, operated as the most effective inducement to sobriety and economy. Yet, distrustful of paternalism, he proposed no scheme for compelling high wages. If economic liberty were provided by a destruction of group privilege, no further machinery would be necessary. Let free choice of occupations be established, especially by abolishing apprenticeship regulations, was Smith's advice, and the status of labor will gradually improve.[7]

Smith's main argument rested, therefore, on the libertarian thesis which postulated that self-interest would provide automatic control over economic behavior if only the stage were set for the free and un-

---

[7] Smith, however, recognized that wage earners are always at a disadvantage in bargaining with employers since the latter "are always and everywhere in a sort of tacit, but constant and uniform, combination not to raise wages."

restrained functioning of natural tendencies. For exactly this kind of economic liberty the rising industrialists of the later part of the 18th century were longing; they and their parliamentary champions found in the *Wealth of Nations* a philosophical rationalization of their quite unphilosophical desires. Within fifteen years after its publication, William Pitt advised the House of Commons that this "celebrated treatise" would "furnish the best solution of every question connected with the history of commerce," while exactly seventy years after the appearance of Smith's book, Sir Robert Peel (the grandson of a yeoman who, following the example of Richard Arkwright, had become a textile manufacturer) finally persuaded Parliament to adopt unilaterally the program of international free trade which the Scottish philosopher had promised would help release the beneficent forces of the natural order.

Contrast Between Appearances and Actuality

Adam Smith died in 1790. Five editions of his book had already appeared and his influence on public opinion was spreading rapidly. Parliament weighed the proposals for legislative reform advocated by this professor who had lectured in the same university where James Watt had carried on his experiments; indeed, between 1783 and 1800, 37 references to the *Wealth of Nations* appear in the records of Parliament. Meanwhile economic reality seemed to vindicate Smith's insight. Merchants in Glasgow,[8] as well as other commercial cities, became staunch advocates of free trade, while leading manufacturers organized the "General Chamber of Manufacturers" for lobbying in support of legislative reform which promised to cheapen the cost of raw materials and widen markets for manufactured goods. Yet it would be erroneous to count these industrialists as genuine disciples of Adam Smith, even though they advocated freer trade, opposed all burdensome regulation, and urged the use of the majesty of law to prevent laborers from forming trade unions. For each part of their program, the manufacturers could, indeed, find some support in Smith's economic theory, but their demands for the suppression of privilege were really motivated by their own desires for new privileges. As a matter of fact, the self-interest of manu-

---

[8] Smith was no desk-chair professor. He often addressed groups of merchants and businessmen in Glasgow. See W. R. Scott, *Adam Smith as Student and Professor* (Glasgow: Jackson Son and Co.), 1937.

facturers, who stood to profit from the adoption of Smith's proposals, proved in a very short space of time to be one basic cause for the hardship and sorrows of laborers in factories and mines. Competition did not provide a self-regulating mechanism which by itself would ensure well-being for wage earners; neither did the growing freedom of laborers to choose their occupations tend to correct the low wages which Smith had partly attributed to unwise regulation. And before the Smithian doctrine of *laissez faire* had been sanctioned either by tariff abolition or by the repeal of the Elizabethan Statute of Apprentices, the government had found it absolutely necessary to intervene on behalf of exploited laborers. Thus, the contradictions involved in Adam Smith's program had revealed themselves before his scheme had been legally adopted!

Introduction of machinery into the textile industry struck fear in the hearts of cloth workers. There followed a wave of violence engineered by artisans who saw in the adoption of machinery an inevitable cause of unemployment and wage reduction. Small armies of frantic laborers undertook to root out this enemy, while factory owners, among them Richard Arkwright, protected their machines with cannon, powder, and grape shot. Industrial warfare cannot be said to have begun with this mutiny against machinery in 18th-century England.[9] But the hardening into trade-union philosophy of the conviction that employers and workers have little or nothing in common was a result of this rebellion of the English artisans, and this heritage of the modern economic world from the early factory age may properly be regarded as one of the most significant. The British government, however, dealt quickly and harshly with the mutineers who tried to hold back the progress of machine industry, first by trial and punishment of machine breakers, next by forbidding workers to form associations of any kind (the Combination Act of 1800) thus indicating that the businessmen although essentially individualistic, would not hesitate to invoke the aid of the state to promote their profit-making ends. But the outlawing of workers' associations really represented a perversion of Adam Smith's proposal that all agencies which restrained competition should be eliminated. He had advocated withdrawing the force of law from any group action designed to interfere with freedom of business enterprise, which was quite a different thing from creating new legislation to prevent groups of workers from doing what their self-interest prompted them to do.

[9] There were, for example, many outbreaks of violence in the Belgian cloth-making industry several centuries before.

Need for Labor Legislation

There was, in fact, genuine necessity for protective group action on the part of factory employees. The shocking and brutal exploitation of women and children in many early factories must remain forever one of the most shameful chapters in English history. Parish paupers of tender years provided the first large supply of docile minors who came under the despotic control of factory foremen. Under the guise of serving an apprenticeship, these unfortunate creatures were herded into industrial cities and entrusted to employers who had, until the passage of the Health and Morals Act of 1802, complete control over their services, their food, and their lodging. The upshot was industrial slavery! By designating pauper children as apprentices, a pretext was available for paying them low wages, since presumably these apprentices, like their medieval predecessors, were learning a trade. Actually this subterfuge permitted factory owners to hire poor children (bound as apprentices until they became of age) at four or five shillings a week to do practically as much work as adult males performed for twenty-five. Opposition to machinery and to the discipline of the factory had mate-rially obstructed the recruiting of factory workers from the ranks of English adult male laborers; in consequence, Ireland and Scotland be-came important sources of male labor. Women and children, however, provided the most docile, as well as the cheapest factory workers, especially in the textile mills where dexterity rather than strength was needed.

The importation of gangs of pauper children from southern counties was facilitated by parish authorities, who sought thereby to hold down local costs of poor relief, and reflects the harsh attitude toward poverty which still survived from the age of mercantilism. Unlike the medieval writers, who accepted poverty as inevitable, and who enjoined everyone to practice Christian charity to the poor, the lawgivers of Elizabethan England proposed to liquidate the beggars, and to this end, workhouses and other provisions were made for compulsory employment of all who obtained parish poor relief. The parish, however, soon proved an unsatisfactory unit for administering the poor law, since each parish sought to reduce its relief expenses by excluding persons likely to become public charges; hence the beggar became a man without a parish, dis-owned by all. Parliament had sought to correct this anomalous situation by the Act of Settlement of 1662 which required that each pauper must be legally "settled" either in the parish of his birth or in another parish where he had lived uninterruptedly; and to this designated "settlement" he could be deported. The burden of poor relief thereafter fell squarely on each parish which, theoretically, could not avoid caring for its own paupers although it was protected against the necessity of relieving destitution in other parishes. With land enclosure, pauperism increased rapidly throughout England, and parish authorities grasped at any opportunity to lighten their burden of relief. At just this juncture, the factory owners in the north of England offered to relieve the poor-law authorities of their redundant charges. Bargains were made with parish officers to turn over children, in lots of 50 or 100, to factory owners who assumed the care (if it may be called care) of these hapless creatures in exchange for their labor. Cheap labor meant cheap cloth, and England's industrial advantage over other nations in 1800 can be attributed partly to the merciless exploitation of helpless parish paupers.

The English poor law was also responsible for still another evil of the early factory age. As the cost of poor relief mounted, parishes often gave small relief allowances to people whose wages were inadequate for the support of their families. Parliament approved this policy in 1782 with the intention of ameliorating the harsh regulations of the workhouses. The real effect of the new system of allowances, however, proved to be quite different from what had been intended. Parish contributions to the livelihood of the poor had a depressing effect on wages, tending often to force them actually below a subsistence rate. Many early factories were consequently able to hire men and, more often, women, for less than it cost them to live, leaving it to the taxpayers to make up the difference. Thus, factory owners found in the English poor law a most useful ally that made the exploitation of labor convenient, relatively easy, and profitable.

Malthus' Theory of Population

Meanwhile, a most well-meaning clergyman, distressed by certain optimistic philosophical ideas then fashionable,[10] enunciated a very pessimistic theory of population which apparently offered a complete explanation for poverty and low wages. There is a natural tendency, said Thomas Malthus in his famous *Essay on the Principle of Population* (1798), for human beings to increase in numbers much more rapidly

[10] Especially those of William Godwin, which postulated that if political institutions were reconstructed, all members of society could live happily with a very small expenditure of labor.

than the means of their subsistence can be augmented. This tendency arises from the intensity of the "passion between the sexes" and from the difficulties encountered in increasing the supply of food. Vice and misery constantly keep this natural tendency in check; pestilence, famine, and war being Nature's brutal correctives for her prodigality in producing people and her niggardliness in providing food. Only by "moral restraint" (by which Malthus meant celibacy and the postponement of marriage) could these unhappy events be prevented.

The Malthusian theory of population fell like manna from heaven into the hands of English businessmen and landlords. Here was a convenient explanation of poverty and low wages, a body of social theory supported by an imposing parade of facts[11] which proved the universality of a "natural" principle of population. Here then was a philosophical font in which factory owners could wash their unclean hands. Low wages had their origin in the "passion between sexes," which resulted in a "natural tendency" for population to outstrip the food supply. For these conditions surely the employer of labor could not be held responsible; in fact, he was really a social benefactor who gave employment to large numbers of these super-abundant poor. The real culprits were the parents who, by failing to curb their reproductive propensities, had brought into existence those unfortunate children whom the factories employed. Thus, by vulgarizing Malthus' thoughtful and penetrating inquiry into the principles underlying population, a further step had been taken toward the formulation of capitalist theory!

Beginning of Labor Legislation

Not everyone in England, fortunately, accepted this simple explanation; nor did Parliament feel that it could be wholly indifferent to the shocking conditions which prevailed in British factories. Humanitarian ideas grew steadily in the 18th and early 19th centuries: Jeremy Bentham urged a complete revision of the savage criminal law; William Wilberforce led the movement for abolishing Negro slavery; David Dale and Robert Owen tried to combine factory management with social reconstruction; while Dr. Percival worked valiantly to improve the sanitary conditions of Manchester. This current of humanitarian ideas had a noticeable effect on Parliament, and bore its first fruit in

---

[11] In his second edition, Malthus compressed the population theory into a few pages and devoted the remainder of the two volumes to marshalling evidence to support it.

the passage of the Health and Morals Act of 1802. This early piece of factory legislation, occasioned by revelations of the bargains which factory owners were making with parish authorities, marks the beginning of a new form of government intervention which the rise of the factory system had made necessary. Because the enforcement of the Act of 1802 was left to local authorities, it failed to accomplish the meritorious ends for which it was designed. It did, however, attempt to help the underprivileged by prescribing sanitary measures and minimum standards of decent comfort for factory "apprentices," by forbidding the employment of children longer than twelve hours a day, by requiring that some provision be made for educating young factory workers, and by providing for the appointment of factory inspectors. In this initial effort to regulate conditions of factory employment is found the beginning of a new element in the modern economic world: humanitarian intervention by the government to prevent ruthless exploitation. Although this ill-enforced law only limited slightly the despotic power of employers, its real importance was, as Mantoux has cogently said, that it "marked the first step on the road which begins at complete laissez-faire and ends at State Socialism."[12] It does not follow, however, that a nation's policy must necessarily traverse the whole length of this "road!"

Economic Consequences of the Napoleonic Wars

The new industrial methods, based upon scientific technology, factory discipline, and regimented cheap labor, were still in their infancy when the Napoleonic wars created a host of new economic problems for England to solve. The whole new apparatus of production, geared to large markets, quickly felt the effects of the interruption of foreign trade. The long wars, however, brought prosperity to British agriculture, leading to more land enclosure and consolidation. Grain imports could no longer come from the Baltic, or from Southern Europe, as they had done before the war, and fewer food supplies could safely arrive from America. As grain prices rose, English farmers converted pasture land into arable, and they also cultivated their pre-war arable land more intensively. An increasing amount of capital was spent on land improvement, a process facilitated by generous lending on the part of country banks. In the meantime, the government purchased huge quantities of foodstuffs for British soldiers, as well as all manner of manufactured goods for prosecuting the war. In the belief that the

12 Mantoux, *Industrial Revolution*, p. 484.

war would be of short duration, no adequate provision had been made for financing these additional government expenditures, and, as a consequence, the Bank of England was called upon to make huge loans to the government. Agricultural prosperity and governmental deficits thus combined to cause a very large increase in banknote circulation, both of country banks and of the Bank of England. These combined forces produced a drastic rise in prices. Wages, however, did not participate in this upward surge; agricultural wages were still largely determined by the Justices of the Peace, while wages among factory workers could not rise in the face of dwindling foreign markets. British wage earners, therefore, found themselves confronted with low wages and high food prices, a distressing situation which produced a new wave of violence, representing once again the instinctive resistence of wage earners against their immediate employers, however blameless they might or might not have been.

Violent changes in prices had occurred countless times before the Napoleonic wars. There was, however, this important difference between the Napoleonic episode and earlier experiences—land enclosure and industrialization had rendered a much larger proportion of agricultural and industrial workers wholly dependent on money wages. When wages failed to rise in proportion to the increase in living costs, wage earners very promptly discovered that they were daily growing poorer. Price changes whittled down incomes already pathetically low, incomes which had previously been barely adequate to provide decent subsistence. The rise in prices during the Napoleonic wars made it abundantly clear that instability of prices constituted not only one of the most serious, but one of the most dangerous problems for an economic system which relies extensively upon a wage system. Even if there had been no Justices to regulate, and no Poor Law to depress them artificially, wages would in all probability have lagged behind the movement of prices, so that workers would have received fewer commodities in exchange for their labor. At any rate, this proved to be the case in subsequent periods of violent price changes.

Influence of the Napoleonic Wars on Economic Thought

Thus, the twenty years of almost continuous warfare brought more hardship to the working classes. Suffering led to violence, which, in turn, caused an apprehensive Parliament to outlaw all workers' associations by passing the Combination Act of 1800. But workers' associations could not be so easily suppressed; secret societies united the bolder wage earners, while some emergent trade unions were disguised as Friendly Societies[13] or Benefit Clubs.[14] Twenty years of warfare also had its effect on contemporaneous thought. Recourse to poorer grades of land, which cessation of grain imports compelled, led to a sharp rise in land rents. Although accentuated by the war, this rise in rents, said the political economists, represented a natural tendency in the economic world, resulting from the pressure on food supply caused by a growing population. The theoretical implications of this natural tendency were carefully worked out by David Ricardo in his *Principles of Political Economy and Taxation,*[15] a book that gave Adam Smith's recommendation of international free trade new theoretical support. Indeed, Ricardo's rent theory became one of the strongest arguments for adopting the "system of no tariffs," which Adam Smith had promised would bring greater economic well-being. Food was dear, said Ricardo, not because rents were high, but because of the increased cost involved in providing enough food for the growing English population. This increase in cost arose from the necessity of using poorer grades of land for cereal growing, or from working hitherto-employed grain land more intensively. The path of wisdom, therefore, lay in allowing free importation of grain from countries with lower agricultural costs. Let England exchange her low-priced manufactured goods, for the low-priced grain of more efficient agricultural countries was Ricardo's advice; by this simple method, the tendency of English rents to rise might be held in check. This argument proved to be as pleasing to British manufacturers as it was distasteful to British landlords.

On the return of peace after Waterloo, fearing that English agriculture (which had been over-extended during the war) would be demoralized unless foreign grain was prevented from coming in, a Tory Parliament, at the behest of the landowners, passed the Corn Law of 1815. This law stipulated that whenever wheat sold for less than 10 shillings per bushel all foreign wheat should be excluded, thus giving English farmers a complete monopoly of the domestic grain market except when grain prices were extremely high. Immediately there came a storm of protest from the new industrial cities. Manufacturers and

---

13 Mutual aid organizations providing sickness or burial benefits.

14 Similar to Friendly Societies but ordinarily drawing their membership from persons engaged in the same occupation. On the early history of British Trade Unionism, see Sidney and Beatrice Webb, *History of Trade Unionism* (London: Longmans, Green and Co., 1920), pp. 56 ff.

15 London, 1817.

merchants had borne the greatest load of war taxes and had subscribed to the lion's share of war loans. Was this legislation, which definitely favored the landed classes, which raised the price of food, and led laborers to demand higher wages, to be their reward? The Corn Law of 1815 thus accentuated the antagonism which industrialization had created, and more sharply divided England into two political camps: landlords on one side, merchants and manufacturers on the other. And the immediate issue was "whether the power of the state should be used to maintain the high incomes of the farmers and landlords, or whether import duties should be reduced to safeguard the incomes of manufacturers and merchants."[16]

Genesis of the Free-Trade Movement

British manufacturers had found themselves in serious difficulties during the war period. Domestic markets, it is true, had increased rapidly, and the government had also proved to be an extremely important customer. But trade with the Continental countries declined as a result of Napoleon's blockade, while American markets had virtually disappeared five years before the United States declared war on Great Britain.[17] Scarcity of shipping, together with the danger from enemy vessels and privateers, materially reduced English trade with Africa and the Orient. Moreover, the return of peace in 1815 brought no great revival of trade since Continental countries obstructed the entry of British goods, while in 1816 a protective American tariff reduced a market that had just begun to revive. The immediate problem confronting British manufacturers was that of finding enough markets for their industrial products, thereby permitting them to recover the heavy investments which had been made in buildings and machinery. By 1820, the manufacturers had begun to lobby for tariff reductions, hoping that if Parliament could be induced to relax the Corn Laws, foreign nations would reciprocate by lowering duties on English manufactures. Free trade was no longer a mere recommendation of philosophers; it had become a practical political issue. A petition to Parliament from London merchants put the matter succinctly: "freedom from restraint is calculated to give the utmost extension to foreign trade."

At the same time, free trade as a program of economic reform made

16 W. C. Mitchell, "The Prospect of Economies," in *The Trend of Economics,* (New York: Alfred A. Knopf, 1924), pp. 5–6.

17 See p. 158.

a strong appeal to a host of liberal-thinking Englishmen. It was consistent with rationalism and humanitarianism. Here, apparently, lay a path that all nations might take with benefits to each and all. If tariffs were removed, each nation might specialize in producing those commodities which it could make most efficiently, and purchase from other countries all commodities which could more cheaply be produced elsewhere. Thus, all nations would presumably gain. Moreover, economic benefits represented only one of the potential blessings of free trade; the political possibilities included greater international understanding and less danger of war, since all nations would be mutually interdependent.

England Adopts Free Trade by Abolishing the Corn Laws

For all that, it was the merchants and the manufacturers, bitter critics of the Corn Law of 1815, who became the leaders in the fight for free trade; to them, tariff reduction meant wider markets and more profits. Accordingly, for their onslaught on the citadel of agricultural protection, they turned to political economy for ammunition. For thirty years after the passage of the Corn Law they kept firing; then in the thirty-first year (1846) they won a great victory, when English commercial policy was revised to their benefit; and industry rather than agriculture became the foremost concern of political leaders in England. When that event occurred, the 19th-century economic system may be said to have arrived. Let us see how this victory was won.

The tactics followed were to demonstrate that the Corn Laws operated to the disadvantage of the great bulk of English people, and it was here that political economy showed its usefulness. Population was increasing with amazing rapidity during the first half of the 19th century,[18] and even though British agriculture continued to become more efficient, feeding these enlarged numbers nevertheless constituted a real problem. Relief of the poor called for higher taxes which were bitterly opposed. A general feeling prevailed that too generous poor relief had bred the increase in numbers; accordingly Parliament revised the Poor Law in 1834. The new legislation compelled applicants for relief to declare themselves paupers; "all or nothing" became the guiding principle, thus ending the unfortunate confusion between wages and poor relief. This

18 The population of England and Wales increased from approximately 11,082,000 when the Corn Law of 1815 was passed to 16,921,000 when the Corn Laws were repealed in 1846, an increase of over 50 per cent in thirty years.

bold cutting of a Gordian knot was undoubtedly a good thing. By revealing clearly the extent of pauperism, it showed the need for a larger volume of employment, a problem complicated by the drift to the industrial centers of people whose pride deterred them from declaring themselves paupers.

The plight of the English poor could therefore be used effectively to further the ambitions of English manufacturers. The Anti-Corn Law League, formed in 1839 by high-minded idealists but financed by manufacturers, set about convincing the laboring classes that their only salvation lay in free trade. Dominated by Richard Cobden, who fervently believed that a policy of *laissez faire* would make everyone prosperous, the League sent a corps of lecturers into every part of England, showered the land with pamphlets, and skillfully lobbied in Whitehall. Plenty of food would be available for the English lower classes was the argument, if only grain were admitted without duty. Repeal of the Corn Laws would thus solve England's industrial problems by widening her foreign markets and thereby increase factory employment. Parliament bowed before the resulting wave of public opinion and, under the leadership of Sir Robert Peel, the Corn Laws were repealed in 1846. Within the next two decades, practically every vestige of protection was swept away. English industrial leaders had molded commercial policy to their wishes.

Coexistence of Free Trade and Intervention

The victory of the manufacturers and merchants, however, was not as complete as is commonly imagined. Although repeal of the Corn Laws did inaugurate an eighty-five-year period of free trade for England,[19] it cannot properly be said to have marked the adoption of *laissez faire*. For state intervention, begun in the Health and Morals Act of 1802, had been shown absolutely necessary to curb the evils of industrialism; and by the legislation of 1833 (which delegated factory regulation to Home Office inspectors) and that of 1844 (which systematized the restriction of working hours and conditions) the force of government had been marshalled to ameliorate the unhappy lot of workers in factories and mines. Profit seeking had occasioned such a ruthless disregard of human suffering that even an unemotional nation realized that regulation of factory employment was imperative. The demand for government control over labor in mines and factories had

[19] In 1931, England abandoned free trade and again put her hope in protection!

come primarily from two sources: from humanitarian leaders and from trade unions. Workers' organizations had not been eliminated by the Combination Act of 1800, but merely driven underground. For twenty-four years, unions, actually invigorated by being outlawed, had knit together the wage earners by fearsome oaths. Then, in 1824–1825, by skillful Parliamentary tactics, the odious Combination Laws were repealed. Though not yet declared legal, trade unions could now function more effectively to curb, in part at least, the exploitative power of British industrialism.

Thus, by the middle of the 19th century, English industrial leaders had found a convenient rationalization in political economy for their policies and had forced Parliament to accede to their demands for a commercial policy which would permit further business growth. They had failed, however, to persuade Parliament to restrict the rôle of government to the limited tasks which Adam Smith's theory of natural liberty had postulated.[20] Certain conspicuous evils connected with industrialism, Parliament could not ignore, and, concurrent with the demands of merchants and manufacturers for freedom from governmental restraint, there had grown up a realization that intervention on behalf of wage earners was a necessary task of government. The union of capitalist enterprise and scientific technology had produced a productive mechanism which was economically desirable, although the ruthlessness arising from the pursuit of business profits regardless of social costs had proved to be a grave social danger.

[20] To protect society from violence or invasion, administer justice, provide certain institutions (e.g., lighthouses) which would not be forthcoming from the motive of private profit.

Part II   HOW FACTORS OF

PRODUCTION

AND ECONOMIC INSTITUTIONS

WERE TRANSPLANTED AND

ADAPTED TO

AN AMERICAN ENVIRONMENT

6 Transference and diffusion of economic institutions in the Colonial Period

Experimental Nature of the Era

Although the settlement of North America was a dramatic and heroic episode, it is not difficult to understand why this historic event occurred. Once explorers had made known the existence of a vast extent of unused land, located in a temperate area, much of it covered with magnificent coniferous or hardwood forests teeming with fur-bearing animals; once the knowledge spread that, in contrast to the agronomically-depleted soils of Europe, there lay in America millions of acres of rich virgin land beneath which a wealth of metals and minerals might also be found, it was not remarkable that the American continent would attract settlers.

The settlement of the Atlantic seaboard proved, however, to be a slow and difficult process. It called for personal courage, hard physical work, and a great deal of business acumen. It required a sizable amount of capital; not merely to cover the costs of transporting settlers and for equipping farms and workshops, but for developing and exploiting the resources of the new world. Since the claims to the new territory were hotly disputed, settlement called for considerable governmental action to provide defense and to supply some of the urgently-needed "social capital" in the form of docks, warehouses, bridges and roads. Consequently the process of settlement became both a governmental and a private affair, complex in its diplomatic, administrative and business aspects.

Our main interest is with the types of institutions which the age of settlement transferred from Europe to America, and which, by a process of adaptation, were to become the basic components of the American economy. Some of these transferred institutions were old and archaic, but these semi-feudal revivals for the most part proved quite unsuitable to the new world. Other relatively new institutions such as joint-stock companies showed themselves to be very useful for initial ventures but of limited utility as continuing mechanisms for administering colonial enterprises. Others were untried new schemes, conceived with the very best of intentions only to prove unworkable in the remote and isolated frontier, where life was difficult and the likelihood of human discord greatly intensified by the immediate problems of survival. Other, more modern institutions that had emerged in Europe during the 15th and 16th centuries, were tested. Altogether the list of experiments is legion, ranging from semi-feudal land systems in New Holland or the Carolinas, communal experiments in Plymouth Plantation, corporate ventures in Virginia, or attempts at ecclesiastical control over public policy in the Puritan colonies. Some settlements relied chiefly on free labor, others on a system of temporary servitude, while still others came to depend heavily upon human slavery. But steadily all these varied and different institutions were altered and adapted to the American environment, and out of this amazing colonial laboratory was to emerge a varied pattern of borrowed and modified institutions which proved to be workable and reasonably efficient.

Basic Problems of Settlement—Mobilizing Capital and Recruiting Labor

Sparsely populated by Indian tribes, few of whom were engaged in agriculture on fixed locations, North America with its vast areas of potential agricultural land and its huge timber resources seemed to offer tremendous opportunities for profitable exploitation. But the actual utilization of these resources, which were granted to joint-stock companies[1] and proprietors,[2] depended upon the accumulation of enough capital to finance colonial ventures and upon the ability to recruit emigrants willing to settle in the new world. Because England had already developed such financial instrumentalities as the joint-stock company, and because the lending and borrowing of sizable amounts of money was already a familiar practice, promoters of colonial ventures were able to induce comparatively large numbers of people to invest money in colonization projects. But the quick returns which so many investors expected did not often materialize because large developmental expenditures had to be made before any staple products, such as sawed lumber, could be made available for export to Europe. The production of basic cash crops, like wheat, tobacco, indigo or rice, could not occur until land had been cleared and an adequate labor supply provided. This labor supply had to be brought to the colonies, since it was soon learned that the American Indians, as contrasted with the inhabitants of Malaya or India, were nomadic, unregimented and unskilled, and therefore almost useless as producers of fabricated or processed exports.[3]

Hence one of the most difficult problems proved to be the working out of ways and means for transferring farmers, artisans and laborers from Europe to America. For this problem five main solutions were found: authorizing settlement by organized groups of people who wished to establish overseas communities; the use of indentured servant contracts; the "headright" system; the "transportation" of criminals; and the resort to Negro slavery. Since all these means had profound historical influences on the kinds of economic institutions which developed in the British-American colonies, and upon the character of the American people, each must be briefly described.

Group Settlement

We cannot here attempt to explain the host of political, religious, cultural, and economic motivations that lay behind the desires of certain groups to leave their ancestral European homes and migrate to the remote and primitive wilderness of a colonial frontier. For the most

[1] Such as the Virginia Company or the Massachusetts Bay Company.

[2] Such as Lord Baltimore, William Penn, or James Oglethorpe.

[3] They did, however, make available for export large quantities of furs, skins, feathers and other animal products.

part, religious motives were governing considerations; thus the Separatists who came to Plymouth, the Puritans who migrated *en masse* to the Massachusetts Bay area, and the German and Moravian groups who settled in Pennsylvania or North Carolina all sought to establish communities wherein they would have greater freedom to worship in ways of their choosing and to organize social and economic life by methods consistent with their ethical beliefs and theories. Since they were already integrated communities, they could organize and plan group migrations, provided adequate capital could be accumulated and provided arrangements could be made for permission to settle in the new world. In some cases, particularly the Puritans who settled Massachusetts Bay Colony, the members of a group were themselves able to finance their migration. In other cases, arrangements had to be made with European businessmen whereunder the migrating groups promised to repay the costs of transportation or other initial costs of settlement. In still other cases, arrangements were made with "proprietors" who had been given colonial land grants, and who were willing to advance transportation costs to responsible groups of settlers in order to obtain a resident labor supply capable of developing their overseas possessions. In a few cases, benevolent proprietors, like James Oglethorpe, made it possible for debtor groups, mercilessly confined in British prisons, to make a new start in the new world.

But group settlements did not fit well into the plans of British businessmen or proprietors who hoped to make direct and fairly prompt profits out of their land grants. The dissenting groups wanted to cut themselves off from Europe, and to create new communities overseas that would be as self-sufficient as possible. Consequently, these neo-autarkic communities proved to be a thorn in the flesh of the British government,[4] which hoped for some clear-cut economic benefits from colonies to compensate for the governmental investments made in defense, public works, and other forms of social capital. By reason of their separatistic tendencies, the religious groups were equally unserviceable to the joint-stock companies that hoped to make money by generating valuable exports, or to proprietors who aspired to administer their overseas estates as business ventures. Consequently, both the English-based joint-stock companies (for example, the Virginia Company) and the proprietors were compelled to resort to other methods for recruiting a labor supply for their colonial possessions.

[4] See E. A. J. Johnson, "Some Evidence of Mercantilism in the Massachusetts Bay," *New England Quarterly,* Vol. I, No. 3.

The Indentured-Servant System

Very few artisans, farmers, or laborers were prepared to finance their own transportation to the new world. Hence contracts (*indentures*) were entered into between the promoters of colonial ventures and prospective emigrants, whereunder the emigrant agreed to a period of temporary servitude in exchange for transportation, maintenance during servitude, and an end-of-servitude compensation, usually in the form of a specified amount of money, tools or land. An indenture was normally prepared in two copies, specifying the rights and obligations of the contracting parties.[5] and hence the scheme, which brought thousands of settlers to America, has come to be known as the *indentured-servant* system. The arrangement had much to recommend it. To the British promoters of colonial ventures it provided a labor force, subject to discipline and, therefore, usable for advancing the economic interests of the employers. Conversely, the system made it possible for strong, able-bodied people with limited economic prospects in Europe to become independent farmers or artisans in the new world once the period of their temporary servitude had ended.

It would be incorrect, however, to believe that this system always brought energetic, industrious and ambitious people to the underpopulated colonies. For whereas thousands of "free willers" or "redemptioners" did voluntarily and deliberately sell their labor services for a number of years[6] in order to obtain ocean passage, and whereas a really excellent labor force was obtained by this means from England, Ireland, Scotland and Germany, a great many indentured servants were probably tricked into emigrating by one scurvy device or another, and these "kidnapped" people often included boys and girls rounded up in city slums or "spirited" out of country villages.[7] One kidnapper admitted, in 1671, that he had sent at least five hundred persons to the colonies each year over a twelve-year period, while another said he had

---

[5] The text of typical contracts can be found in Richard B. Morris's splendid book, *Government and Labor in Early America* (New York: Columbia University Press, 1946), pp. 317–18.

[6] Usually for an average of four years, although the servitude varied from colony to colony and from one time period to another. See Morris, *Government and Labor*, p. 316.

[7] For a graphic picture of the techniques used to gather up "servant" emigrants, see Abbot Emerson Smith, "Indentured Servants; New Light on some of America's 'First Families,' " *Journal of Economic History*, Vol. II, No. 1, pp. 40–54.

sent over eight hundred in a single year.[8] Although the British government was aware of this tawdry business, it was not certain that the labor exporters were really engaged in forcibly abducting people.

In many cases the so-called "kidnappers" were really labor recruiters who hired drummers or pipers to attract attention, extolled the advantages of overseas colonies, and, in general, used every means to persuade young people to come to British port towns and sign contracts. As labor recruiting became more competitive, the recruiters had to offer food, shelter and clothing in order to get the prospective emigrants to sign contracts. But wily rascals soon discovered that it was profitable to sign and then disappear with a new suit of clothes. Consequently, the recruiters literally did incarcerate "servants" they had signed up until they could deliver them to a ship master for transportation to the colonies. Some of the alleged "kidnapping" consisted, therefore, of protective measures taken by the recruiters to insure that the "servants" actually did migrate, since the recruiters' commissions were only paid when the servants actually embarked. No doubt there was some actual, forcible abduction, but for the most part the evils of the system consisted in the misrepresentation of the conditions of servitude and the blandishments used to tempt ignorant and illiterate people to sign indentures.

It was not always the honest, capable, ambitious and virtuous who chose to avail themselves of these apparently generous offers of free transportation to the colonies. Before the age of divorce, the indentured-servant system allowed husbands to abandon unwanted wives; for apprentices unhappy in their seven-year domestic servitude to escape to some new brand of servitude overseas; or for petty thieves and criminals to get aboard a ship before the sheriff reached the dock. The labor recruiter's job was to deliver bodies aboard a ship. He was probably not very scrupulous about the methods he used nor much concerned about the moral character of the men and women he recruited. Consequently the indentured-servant system, which probably financed more than half[9] of the colonial-era immigrants to America, brought a varied and heterogeneous initial labor force.

[8] Edward Channing, *A History of the United States,* Vol. II (New York: The Macmillan Co., 1926), p. 369.

[9] The proportion was lower in New England, and probably much higher in Virginia. See Philip A. Bruce, *Economic History of Virginia in the Seventeenth Century* (New York: P. Smith, 1935), Vol. II, pp. 51 ff. Even as late as 1773–1775, 89 per cent of the port of London emigrants went as indentured servants. See Morris, *Government and Labor,* p. 315.

The great bulk of immigrants signed indentures voluntarily, thus indicating an adventurous spirit. Many, like the sturdy Scotch-Irish or the German redemptioners, were definitely ambitious, energetic and resilient; willing to endure temporary hardship in exchange for an opportunity to make a new start in a new world. Here immigration proved to be a selective process which weeded out the listless, the timid, the over-conservative, or unadaptable. Ambitious immigrants imparted to the American character a willingness to endure difficulties, a belief in progress, and a deep conviction that an individual can make his way in life despite lowly origins. This race of settlers became the self-reliant farmers, pioneers, small businessmen, and artisans of Colonial America.

But intermixed with these hardy, dependable immigrants were escapees from family responsibility, criminals and men of chequered careers, and the misguided, duped, or really kidnapped. These were the men who often resorted to violence in their servant-master relations; who escaped from Maryland, Pennsylvania or Virginia farms and moved out on to the frontiers as squatters, trappers, hunters, and squawmen; who infused a degree of lawlessness, chicanery and deceit into the American culture. Looking for easy ways to make a living, some of them became tricky and unscrupulous horse traders, cattle thieves, or bandits. Yet they too imparted drive and dynamism to the economy. They became masters at risk taking, and in competition with them, the instinctively more conservative were compelled to become more venturesome in their business activities.

Both groups of immigrants, the good and the bad (and there were, of course, all manner of shadings between the two extremes) had one thing in common: they had their hearts and minds set on dreams of "success." This obsession has given a materialistic bent to American culture and has probably made life here more competitive, restless, and unstable than in other countries. But it also resulted in more occupational mobility, and this ceaseless redistribution of talents among occupations, professions, trade and productive enterprises has led to more rapid economic growth and transformation. These peculiarly American characteristics are a result of the insecurity with which every immigrant was faced. In an underdeveloped country there was no institutional security for the individual such as had existed in a manorial or gild economy. It was up to each person to create his own security by hard work, shrewdness in business, saving as much as possible, investing wisely, and by building up reserves in the form of money and property.

The Headright System

Alongside the indentured-servant system there developed the so-called "headright" system which took three forms, all designed to facilitate the immigration of a work force. In the first place there were grants of land made by joint-stock companies or proprietors to people of means who were prepared to bring colonists to America or to finance their transportation. For each person, or "head" so transported (or financed), payment would be made by a parcel of land of so many acres.[10] By consolidating these headrights, sizable estates could be acquired, and by this method British men of means came into possession of large land holdings in America.

In some cases headrights were directly linked with the indentured-servant system. In order to recruit immigrants, it was often necessary to promise "servants" small tracts of land once their period of servitude had ended, so they could make their own living as small farmers when they became free. Since better grades of land were rapidly engrossed, all too often these end-of-servitude land grants proved to be marginal land, or land located farther inland or more remote from navigable streams.[11] Thus, the system brought into the agrarian structure a group of small farmers who tried to make a living in competition with larger farms that had better resources and superior locations in terms of transportation facilities. An unbalanced system of landholding resulted, one which was to have a profound effect not only upon the future pattern of American agriculture but upon the differential prosperity of American farmers.

A third group that came into possession of headrights were those people who could finance their own transportation, and who were induced to migrate to the colonies by the offer of free land, which they could, by their labor and that of their servants, convert into arable fields. The object of the promoters in making these grants was to hasten settlement, hoping that a general regional development would lead to a rise in the value of the land they retained for future sale.

The headright system worked only fairly well. It did bring many independent small farmers, especially to the middle colonies. It induced British people of means to finance the migration of thousands of inden-

[10] As the slave trade developed, masters of slave ships sometimes had the privilege of claiming a "headright" for every African imported.

[11] See Frederick J. Turner, *The Frontier in American History* (New York: Henry Holt and Co., 1921), Chap. III.

tured servants; and, despite its unfairness, it often did provide servants who had fulfilled their labor obligations with plots of land and thereby helped develop an owner-occupier pattern of agriculture. But unfortunately, the system was honeycombed with corruption. Wily ship masters outwitted and deceived proprietors by claiming headrights for crew members who had no intention of staying in America. Fictitious lists of immigrants were also prepared, and headrights were asked for these imaginary settlers. The headright claims to land were then sold to land speculators, who by this process often obtained title to thousands of acres of land. Meantime shrewd jobbers bought up the headrights of people who considered cash at the moment more desirable than land in the future. Thus the system turned out to be a training school for land speculators, and in this way had a deep and lasting effect on American economic behavior. Speculation in land by rich and poor became an American infatuation, with some good results no doubt but with many grave disadvantages. It did hasten the opening up of new territories, but it often led to the reckless wastage of savings which might better have been employed in more prosaic but less venturesome ways. Sometimes speculation forced pioneer farmers to begin operations on poorer and ill-located land since they could not pay the prices asked by the land speculators for better grades of land.

The Transportation of Criminals and Debtors

Only a modest share of the immigrant flow to the American colonies in the 17th and 18th centuries consisted of criminals released from British prisons on the condition that they be "transported" to overseas possessions.[12] The expedient was used, however, on many occasions for two reasons. In the first place there was the constant difficulty of finding enough people willing to migrate, and hence "every now and then the doors of English prisons were opened and batches of convicted felons . . . were handed over" for transportation to the colonies.[13] It is difficult to ascertain whether these hapless individuals were really dangerous or depraved characters. So many "crimes" called for punishment under the savage British criminal laws that the danger of prosecution was

[12] Richard Morris, who has made a very careful study of the colonial labor supply, accepts the estimate that about 50,000 convicts were sent to America, of whom about 20,000 went to Maryland. See his chapter on "Colonial Production" in Harold Williamson, ed., *The Growth of the American Economy* (Englewood Cliffs, N.J.: Prentice-Hall, 1951), p. 68.

[13] Channing, *History of U.S.*, Vol. I, p. 212.

omnipresent. Vagabonds, beggars, or persons with no fixed abode were subject to arrest and were whipped, branded, and imprisoned. Unlicensed peddlers or city waifs might find themselves incarcerated in foul and noisome jails together with thieves, murderers and other actual criminals. Moreover, some of the transported "convicts" were political prisoners who had participated in the various rebellions that occurred in the 17th and 18th centuries.[14]

Deportation of prisoners reduced the cost of caring for them in English jails and at the same time increased the colonial labor supply. Both Cromwell and Charles II sent captive enemies to the colonies, and by the 1660's involuntary transpcrtation of persons had become a well-established procedure not only for criminals in the usual sense, but also for religious dissenters like the Quakers. Although some colonies attempted to prohibit the immigration of felons,[15] the British government vetoed such colonial legislation, and legalized and systematized the procedure by Acts of Parliament.[16] In Pennsylvania and Virginia vigorous opposition developed, although in Maryland, where perhaps the largest number of convicts were sent, the opposition seems to have been much less.[17] Many convicts were educated people who could be used in clerical or professional capacities; in Maryland, for example, on the eve of the Revolution, most of the schoolmasters were transported convicts. It is, therefore, difficult to generalize about the effects of the system on the American economy and upon future American characteristics. Some convicts were undoubtedly very undesirable people who increased lawlessness; others were victims of misfortune who were able to escape from an unwholesome British environment and make a new start in Delaware, Pennsylvania, Maryland or Virginia. Whatever their character, they increased the supply of labor and thereby made a real contribution toward the economic development of the American colonies.

Imprisonment for failure or inability to pay debts made available for emigration a particular group of British "felons" whose unhappy condition stirred the compassion of James Oglethorpe and other British philanthropists, and led to a project for colonizing these unfortunate

14 But Morris, after careful study of court records, has shown that the bulk of these involuntary immigrants were not political prisoners but real criminals, many of whom were guilty of serious offenses. See *Government and Labor,* pp. 328–29.

15 As Virginia did in 1670.

16 By legislation in 1668, 1718 and 1768.

17 There was, however, considerable apprehension, and evidence of increasing crime. See Morris. *Government and Labor,* pp. 330–31.

persons in lands lying between the Savannah and Altamaha rivers.[18] But this commendable, humanitarian plan failed to accomplish its admirable purpose. Relatively few debtors were brought to Georgia[19] and those who were labored under two disadvantages: the land granted to each settler was limited, and the debtor-colonists were forbidden to own slaves. The consequence was that the small owner occupiers attempted to compete with richer landowners who did own slaves. Discouraged by the apparent failure of their experiment, Oglethorpe and his associates first allowed their settlers to hire Negro slaves for long periods (sometimes for life), but this concession helped little because the former debtors had no capital with which to enlarge the scale of their operations. All over the South the plantation system progressively encroached on the small farmers.[20] Yet, in Maryland, Delaware, Virginia, and Carolina, as well as in Georgia, a great many small owners did survive the competition with the plantation, thus establishing alongside the large plantations a system of agriculture which became far more typical of the South than the over-dramatized, large, slave-operated estates.[21] In this parallel system, the units were small farms, operated by white families with the help of a small group of slaves. That this latter type of organization became increasingly important is proven by the fact that plantation owners with between ten and fifty slaves each constituted at the outbreak of the Civil War only 7 per cent of the southern free population, but owned about half of all the slaves in the South.

Negro Slavery

We cannot therefore appreciate the importance of the institution of Negro slavery as a factor in American economic history unless we recognize that it took two major agricultural forms with many intervening variants. At one extreme were the large estates operated by scores of

---

[18] These released debtors were not sold as indentured servants, as were the criminals who were "transported."

[19] Thirty years after the establishment of the colony there were only five to six thousand white people in Georgia.

[20] Even a group of Austrians from the Tyrol had to abandon their group settlement on the Savannah river because they could not compete with the plantation system.

[21] In 1860, only 26 per cent of free southern families owned slaves, and those with fifty or more slaves owned 25 per cent of all the slaves. The best book on agriculture in the ante-bellum South is Lewis Cecil Gray, *History of Agriculture in the Southern United States to 1860* (New York: Peter Smith, 1941).

slaves working under the direction of overseers. At the other extreme were the small farms cultivated by white men assisted by one or two slaves or perhaps a slave family. In between were the medium-sized farms with perhaps five, six, or seven slaves. But it is not correct to assume that slavery was either an essentially southern-colony institution or one entirely related to agriculture. Every colony had slaves; they worked in cities as well as in the country; in warehouses, shops and mills, not merely in fields.

Brought originally to Virginia to provide a labor supply (when other means had proven too slow or inefficient to suit the wishes of land owners who were impatient to obtain returns on their initial investments), they came in increasing numbers[22] to most of the colonies, as the organized slave trade expanded at the hands of both European and American shipowners, and as slave catching became a business along the coast of Africa. Altogether Negro slavery was a sorry, brutal chapter in history, but it must be admitted that it played an important rôle in American economic development. For slaves supplied a very considerable part of the manpower needed to convert natural resources into valuable export commodities or into capital goods. They built roads, houses, barns, levies, and converted forests into fields; they operated mills, ferries, and blast furnaces. They raised enough rice, tobacco, indigo and grain to provide exportable surpluses, thereby giving the colonies claims on much-needed imports.

Tobacco, indigo and rice were the main 17th-century crops largely produced by slave labor, to which list cotton and sugar were added in the 18th century. Because these staple crops were produced in Maryland, Virginia, and the Carolinas and Georgia, it was here that agricultural slavery was most extensively adopted. Dependable statistics are lacking, but estimates of the number of slaves in Virginia indicate how the slave population increased. Thus, Governor Berkeley estimated that there were two thousand slaves in Virginia in 1670, whereas a generation later (1708) the President of the Virginia Council thought the number was about twelve thousand, a six-fold expansion from importation and natural increase in less than forty years.[23] Fifty years later (1760) prob-

22 Between 1619, when the first slaves were brought to Virginia, and the end of legal importation of slaves into the United States in the early 19th century, some 370,000 to 400,000 Africans were brought into the American economy. See, U.S. Bureau of the Census book by W. S. Rossiter, *A Century of Population Growth in the United States, 1790–1900*, (Washington, D.C.: Government Printing Office, 1909), p. 36.

23 See Bruce, *Economic History of Virginia*, Vol. II, p. 108.

ably half of the population of Virginia consisted of slaves. In South Carolina, the growth of the slave population was even more rapid. Already by 1730 they outnumbered the whites, and by 1760 at least two-thirds of the population was black.

In regions such as Virginia and the Carolinas, where slavery became a dominant rather than a marginal institution, slavery quite early had noticeable effects upon the habits of the white population. Shrewd observers, such as William Byrd, saw the deleterious effects; the presence of so many slaves, he said, was filling the white people with pride, and destroying their will to work lest it should make them look like slaves. This disdain of manual work had a permanent debilitating effect not only on the plantation owner and his family but upon the southern small farmers and shop owners as well, and accounts in no small measure for the relatively greater dynamism in those areas where the institution of slavery was of less importance or where it withered away and disappeared.

In Maryland slavery spread more slowly than in Virginia primarily because the farms were smaller and the farmers had less capital. Moreover, aside from tidewater, tobacco-growing areas, Maryland became a grain-growing region, using white labor more frequently than black. In the commercial centers, such as Baltimore or Annapolis, however, a great number of slaves were used for dock laborers, as they also were in Philadelphia and other ports on the Delaware. Indeed, except for the fairly extensive use of slaves on the large New York estates along the Hudson, slavery in the region north of Maryland was essentially a city phenomenon. Thus, in Philadelphia there was a rapid growth of the slave population. This may seem odd in view of the vigorous Quaker condemnation of the enslavement of human beings. The answer, of course, is that some Quakers were opposed to slavery and others were not.[24] Actually the first protests against slavery seem to have come not from Quakers but from the German settlers in Pennsylvania, and it was only gradually that some of the Quakers became leaders in the anti-slavery movement. By 1755, the opposition to slavery apparently had won over a majority of them, since, in that year, a rule was made at the "yearly meeting" that all Quakers who imported slaves should be disavowed by the religious communities. There were still many slaves in Pennsylvania and evidently a large number in the possession of Quakers because three years later (1758) the yearly meeting strongly urged all Quakers to set their slaves free. But businessmen are usually

[24] William Penn, for example, owned Negro slaves.

businessmen whatever their religious persuasions, and it seems likely that many Quakers sold their slaves instead of freeing them.

North of Pennsylvania, slavery took three forms; agricultural slavery on the large New York estates, a limited amount of Indian slavery in New England, and urban slavery in the port towns, especially in Rhode Island and in New York City. Dutch land owners had owned slaves, and the institution was only slightly modified by the British conquest. In Massachusetts the situation was very different. Under the "Body of Liberties" adopted by the Great and General Court (colonial legislature), in 1641, slavery was prohibited except for lawful captives. This exception justified the enslavement of Indian men, women, and children of the Pequot tribe after their fierce uprising. The experiment with Indian slavery, however, proved to be a failure from the economic point of view; very few males were captured while the enslaved women and children required more supervision than their work contribution justified.

Despite the Body of Liberties, it is certain that there were Negro slaves in Boston long after 1641,[25] as there were in all the other large New England ports, although it was in Rhode Island where slavery probably had its strongest hold in the northern colonies. In 1748, for example, 27 per cent of the population of South Kingston was black, and it is fair to assume that a large proportion of these Africans were slaves. For New York City the data are most specific; out of a total population of about 40,000 people in 1700, at least 6,000 were slaves, which is to say 15 per cent. In addition there were many free blacks. It is therefore wrong to suppose that a Negro district (such as Harlem is today) was a post-Civil War phenomenon; it is much more accurate to say that many of New York City's "first families" were black!

There were a great number of freed slaves in the middle-colony cities and in New England. Some had been given their freedom by benevolent owners, some were escapees from the southern colonies. A considerable number, however, were blacks in the higher-age bracket freed by former owners to avoid the cost of maintaining them. The resulting system of labor, under which freed slaves worked alongside free white laborers and both groups faced the competition of slave labor, created extremely difficult labor problems in the colonial ports.[26] It should be remembered also that some of the white workers were indentured servants. What

25 Newspapers as late as 1742 and 1756 offered Negroes for sale.
26 This subject has been explored in detail by Richard Morris in his *Government and Labor in Early America*, pp. 182 ff.

resulted, therefore, was inequality in the competitive process between three basic systems of labor: slavery, temporary servitude, and free wage earners. But since the latter were of two shades of pigmentation, even further difficulties arose. This inharmonious labor market, however, was only a microcosm of what the 19th century was to produce, when indigenous free labor was to find itself in competition with various immigrant groups and also, until 1865, with Negro slaves.

Although slavery existed in varying forms from Massachusetts to Georgia, it was gradually squeezed out in the colonies north of Maryland, and for two main reasons. There was, in the first place, the moral objection of Puritans, Pennsylvania Germans, and Quakers. But the high moralistic argumentation of these anti-slavery groups probably had less to do with the withering away of slavery as an institution north of the Mason-Dixon line than the far less vocal free white laborers and artisans. It was they who had to compete directly with slaves as blacksmiths, coopers, stevedores and general laborers. Moreover, because slave owners, unless they resorted to evasive manumission, had to feed and maintain their slaves whether they worked or not, it became less clear that slavery was really profitable in northern cities, where work might be irregular and where the productivity of free labor was normally much higher. It took however, a long time for this question to be finally settled; and it had not been completely resolved when the Declaration of Independence was signed.[27]

Efforts to Revive Feudal Institutions

When the original British settlements were being made in North America, manorial organization of British agriculture was gradually disintegrating.[28] The great surge of enclosures was yet to come,[29] but steadily, throughout the 16th century, English farmers had been "commuting" their labor services, renting land for money payments, and acquiring legal title to their farms. It is understandable, therefore, why British settlers in America were unwilling to accept, in a region of relatively abundant land, a return to feudal tenure; and it was this resistance that made unworkable the schemes for semi-feudal land tenure that were attempted in some of the American colonies.

[27] Not, as we have been taught to believe, on July 4 when the Declaration was "adopted," but on Aug. 2, 1776. See Edmund C. Burnett, *The Continental Congress* (New York: The Macmillan Co., 1941), pp. 188, 191.

[28] See p. 40.

[29] See p. 71.

Ambitious attempts to reinstitute varieties of feudal control were made in Maryland and the Carolinas. Indeed the settlement of Maryland stems from the desire of Sir George Calvert to establish a great family estate in America.[30] But whereas the original plan was to encourage members of the British aristocracy to develop large manorial estates, Lord Baltimore soon authorized his brother, who was the first governor, to alter these grandiose plans in order to hasten the settlement of the colony. As a result, land was granted to persons in varying amounts depending on the number of settlers the grantees brought to Maryland; it was also given to people who advanced money to Lord Baltimore but did not actually migrate to America. Since either type of grantee found it profitable to sell off his land grants, it was not long before the large landholdings were split up and consequently Maryland, which had been planned as a colony of great estates, became a region of small and medium-sized farms.

The story in the Carolinas is somewhat different, since the ultimate pattern of land holding came to be influenced by the institution of Negro slavery. As in Maryland, the original plan of the Carolina promoters was to create manorial estates. Indeed, it went further than that: an elaborate, although utterly archaic, feudal government was envisaged, with titles of nobility for the governing hierarchy. These paper plans were largely superseded by the march of events. In Carolina there was not one proprietor (as in Maryland) but eight, each with his deputy in the colony. Disagreements developed among these resident deputies; in addition the rank and file of colonists were, in a comparatively short time, opposed to all proprietors and their agents. The outcome was chronic commotion that often bordered on outright insurrection. Meantime the colony was threatened by Indian raids, by Spanish naval forces, and, worst of all, by pirates, who preyed upon the colony's trade with Europe and the West Indies. Conflicts between the British government and the proprietors led to the appointment of a royal governor, and the upshot was that the proprietors surrendered their right to rule the colony and sold their land grants. Presently two Carolina colonies emerged, different in nature both politically and economically. Thus in this hectic period from 1670 to about 1725, the proprietors' dreams of creating a formally-organized feudal colony were completely shattered. What developed instead was a system of small and medium-sized farms using only ancillary slave labor in North Carolina; and, by contrast, a plantation system worked by Negro slaves in South Carolina. As in Maryland, the only lingering effects of the feudal experiment were the

[30] For a brief, vivid account, see Channing, *History of the U.S.*, Vol. I, Chap. IX.

quit rents, originally owed to proprietors and after the surrender of the charter payable to the British government; but to the payment of these charges there was not only bitter but often violent opposition.

Experiments with Theocratic Economic Institutions

In the group settlements of Protestants a number of attempts were made to create institutions that would shape economic life and social conduct in conformity with particular moral and religious goals and purposes. These experiments ranged from the attempts made in Plymouth Plantation (and later in the Moravian communities) to institute common ownership of property, to legislative efforts designed to materialize a regime of "just price" and "fair wages." In some of these experiments the object was not merely to return to certain medieval principles of economic organization[31] but to go back beyond the medieval doctrines to the teachings of the early Christians of the 3rd, 4th, or 5th centuries. The thesis was that a real purification of economic life called for a return to the customs of the Church Fathers, since their original ethical rules for the conduct of social and economic affairs had been compromised when the Church became a temporal and political power. These sincere hopes proved to be as illusory as those of the proprietors who tried to revive feudal institutions.

The Plymouth experiment with common ownership was very short-lived. It was based ideologically on the tradition that averred that the early Christians lived together "and had all things in common except their wives." More practically it was the result of an arrangement made with certain British merchants who had financed the transportation of the Mayflower Pilgrims to America. Under this arrangement, the entire immigrant group agreed to be fed and clothed collectively for seven years, and for the same period all the product of their labor was to go into a common stock out of which the merchants would be reimbursed. But this more or less circumstantial communal economic organization simply would not work.[32] Single men objected to working to support other men's wives and children; industrious people felt that the lazy

---

[31] See pp. 33, ff.

[32] Governor Bradford, who had the unpleasant task of trying to make the system work, ascribes the idea to "the vanity of that conceit of Plato and other ancients . . . that the taking away of [private] property . . . would make them happy and flourishing." But there is evidence to show that other members of the colony drew their justification from the customs of the early Christians. See E. A. J. Johnson (*American Economic Thought in the 17th Century* (London: P. S. King, 1932), Chap. XII.

and indifferent ought not receive equal shares of food and clothing; married men were angry because their wives had to wash clothes and prepare food for other people. After marching the work force to the fields, to building projects, or other work centers for over two years, Governor Bradford, in 1623, abandoned the whole scheme and assigned parcels of land to each family. The effect was immediate: output increased, making it possible for the colonists to repay their collective debts and to buy out those non-resident shareholders in the colonial venture who had contributed funds but had not migrated overseas.

The unhappy experience in Plymouth may well have influenced the policies of the larger Massachusetts Bay Colony, established a decade later. Aside from the common pastures and aside from a few collective municipal institutions (wells, wharfs, markets, or animal pounds) there were no further experiments with communal ownership in New England. On the other hand, the Moravian groups,[33] who came to Bethlehem, Pennsylvania, a hundred years later, and who established other settlements in North Carolina, based their communities on principles of collective ownership and for some time they actually practised what they preached.[34] Other similar experiments were to follow later in the 18th and in the 19th centuries, but from the time that Bradford wrote his scathing criticism of communal ownership, in his remarkable history of Plymouth Plantation, private property became a fundamental cornerstone of the American economy.

This did not mean however, that the beliefs of the Christian groups—Puritans, German pietists, Quakers[35] and many others—had no influence in the shaping of American economic institutions, or that ethical criteria were unimportant. On the contrary, the religious groups left an indelible mark on the American economy. Stressing man's personal responsibility to God and to his fellow man, they did much to develop American individualism by insisting that each person must think constantly about both sacred and material questions. They charged their members with idealism by emphasizing Christian duties; and these personal responsibilities included the building of a better economic society, developing more literate communities, and training more public-spirited citizens. Very often, to be sure, the high hopes of the preachers

---

[33] Although the sect was originally Moravian, the immigrants to America were mostly Germans who had accepted the religious beliefs of the Moravians.

[34] The deep devotion to their principles of Christian collective life is made vividly clear in Adelaide L. Fries, *The Road to Salem* (Chapel Hill: University of North Carolina Press, 1944).

[35] More correctly, members of the Society of Friends.

and theologians were not realized. The Massachusetts Puritans, for example, conscientiously attempted to revive the medieval concepts of "just price" and "fair wages" as a central core of their economic policy. But even though they went so far as to impose a huge, really confiscatory, fine on a hapless hardware merchant for overcharging his customers,[36] they gradually learned that in an expanding economy, where demand was great and supply chronically limited, it was virtually impossible to regulate prices or wages by decrees.[37] Greater production and more competition between producers ultimately proved to be a better recipe for ensuring reasonable prices than criminal prosecution of businessmen temporarily able to make windfall profits.

But the belief that there must be ethical criteria for economic conduct did not disappear. Every church became a school wherein the lessons of right economic conduct were regularly taught, and the sermon became the most important part of the service. Moreover, in frontier communities, the preacher, rector or priest became the arbiter of many community problems. In hundreds of villages and towns, the church infused a set of values and an idealism which has had a permanent effect upon the American character. For despite differences between religious denominations, there was agreement on certain basic rules of economic conduct. It was honorable to work; it was not wrong to save and accumulate wealth. But it was wrong to take advantage of the unwary, or to carry on business that had socially deleterious results. It was the duty of everyone to contribute his proper share to community activities— schools, libraries, churches, hospitals. Aggressive pursuit of wealth was condoned within these prescriptions, and one test of Christian character was what a man did with the wealth he accumulated.[38]

Private Property

The failure of the attempts to revive medieval land tenure in America,[39] the unworkability of communal ownership, and the aliena-

---

[36] For the details see E. A. J. Johnson, *American Economic Thought in the 17th century*, pp. 123–128. See also Bernard Bailyn, *The New England Merchants in the Seventeeth Century* (Cambridge, Mass.: Harvard University Press, 1955), pp. 41–44.

[37] Colonial communities, however, clung persistently to certain regulatory measures, chiefly the control of bread prices, throughout the 18th century and deep into the 19th.

[38] Out of this doctrine of social responsibility came the American custom of returning to society some of the wealth one had acquired. This idea received an extreme interpretation in Andrew Carnegie's remark that "the man who dies rich dies disgraced."

[39] Medieval three-field land systems were instituted in America but this was merely a structural borrowing. The ownership of the strips was almost always private.

tion of land to induce immigration—all these factors led to a general acceptance in Colonial America of the institution of private property in land. This was not really a radical event for English-speaking people, since throughout England in the 16th century the purchase and sale of land had become increasingly common[40] as a monetary economy developed, making it possible for peasants first to rent land for money payments and then to buy the land they cultivated. In America, however, the trend toward private ownership of land could be much more rapid, because immigrants tended to settle in those colonies where "freehold" grants of land were made. Thus, whereas immigration into New York (where a modified manorial system had been inherited from the Dutch) was slow, immigration into Pennsylvania, where freehold grants were generously made, was rapid. Steadily, in all the colonies, private property in land became typical, and land renting was generally regarded as a transitional step to land ownership.

Meantime in England, as private ownership of land became more common, a philosophical justification was formulated known as the "labor theory of property." Although this doctrine was not formally worked out until the end of the 17th century in the writings of John Locke, the basic ideas underlying it were current much earlier and influenced colonial thinking throughout the 17th century. The argument was that it was both reasonable and just that individuals should have complete and undisputed property in parcels of land because land by itself was merely a passive factor of production which had become useful to society because human labor had been invested in it. Since this process of "mixing labor with land" was socially desirable, government should encourage it; and the best way to insure that the process would continue would be to guarantee to the land improver that he would not be deprived of his incorporated labor.[41]

We can readily understand why this labor theory of property made a profound impression in America. There were no arable fields ready for cultivation in the colonial frontier; they had to be created by felling trees, grubbing out shrubs, removing stones, digging drainage ditches, and by many other forms of incorporated labor. For the first settlers therefore, farm making had to precede agriculture; and this process repeated itself in thousands of contexts as the population moved north,

[40] A process vividly described by Richard H. Tawney in his *Agrarian Problem in the 16th Century* (London: Longmans Green and Co., 1912).

[41] On the Lockean theory of property, see Paschal Larkin, *Property in the Eighteenth Century, with Special Reference to England and Locke* (London: Longmans, Green & Co., 1930).

west, and southwest (and even east) in the settlement of a half continent. Thus, in America the labor theory of property was something more than the musings of philosophers; it was a visible reality. If an indentured servant, having worked out his servitude faithfully, were to clear a tract of land, build a cabin and a cattle shed, only to find that he had no title to the land, it would be manifestly unjust to allow him to be deprived of the untold amount of invested labor. He had to be fairly certain, therefore, that he would own the land before he was willing to undergo the hardships that were involved in "making" a farm.[42]

From the very beginning of settlement, therefore, it was recognized that private property in land was indispensable if any genuine economic development were to occur; and the law of real property, as it developed in America, wisely reflected this understanding. The lawyer, consequently, became a most important person in every village and town. It was he who drew up the deeds, searched the titles, and saw to it that the property rights of individuals were properly recorded in the courthouse registers. Meantime the protection of property came to be regarded as one of the main functions of government.

Private property in movable goods (in tools, animals, ships, or inventories) was an accepted institution that called for no special justification. Like private property in land, however, personal property also had to be protected, and consequently each colony had to devise a body of law to punish theft, ensure the fulfillment of contracts, and permit the bequeathing of property to one's heirs or assignees.

Types of Agricultural Enterprise

The great bulk of colonists whether they came as planters, free farmers, indentured servants, convicts or slaves, devoted themselves to agriculture.[43] A wide variety of forms of agricultural enterprise developed, and most of these colonial types of agriculture were reproduced as the frontier moved westward.[44] In a very real sense, then, the Colonial

[42] As population moved westward, however, pioneers did proceed to clear land without the assurance of a title. Out of this ultimately came Federal recognition of the invested labor in the form of a "pre-emption" right of the actual settler, giving him the first option to buy the land he had improved.

[43] The first American census, taken in 1790, defined 95 per cent of the population as rural. Whereas not all of the rural population was engaged in agriculture, it is safe to assume that at least nine-tenths were engaged in some kind of farming.

[44] New types were, of course, added as different soils and different isothermic belts were reached, and as plant breeding became more scientific.

period nurtured and developed the major kinds of farming operations that were to become characteristic.

At least five kinds of agricultural enterprises had become rooted in the colonies by the end of the 17th century; the highly self-sufficient subsistence farms; the general-purpose farms oriented more toward local than foreign markets; the limited-crop farms dependent chiefly on foreign markets; the tenant-operated large estates; and the slave-operated plantations definitely oriented toward foreign markets. This classification greatly oversimplifies the picture because some farming was only incidental to other occupations, such as timber production, fishing, trapping, or trading with the Indians.[45] In general, however, these five major types were distinguishable.

The self-sufficient subsistence farm. A frontier phenomenon that appeared briefly on the seaboard (before any colonial manufacturing had developed), the self-sufficient, subsistence farm moved north into Vermont and New Hampshire, east into Maine, west into upper New York, and southwest into the Appalachian valleys, as the frontier moved outward. It was self-sufficient less from choice than from the absence of adequate transportation facilities. Because crops could not be marketed, or could only be marketed in small quantities, cash incomes were very small. Crops, therefore, had to be diversified so that the basic needs of a pioneer family could be provided. Such a farm family had to produce bread grains (corn, wheat, rye, barley, oats) fibers (flax, wool) meat supplies (cattle, hogs, poultry) dairy products (milk, cheese) and a rather wide range of other household supplies (tallow, wax, leather, lye, vinegar, furniture). In one form or another, this primitive type of agricultural enterprise, inefficient from lack of tools and by reason of the large variety of crops that had to be produced for man and beast, constituted the outer fringe of the frontier. It perhaps made some American farmers resourceful and versatile, but it created at the same time an agrarian group whose life was hard, and who could be easily persuaded that their troubles were caused by the machinations of land speculators, bankers, politicians, or merchants rather than their own low productivity.

The general-purpose farm. The great majority of colonial farms in the more quickly-developed part of the seaboard were quite different

---

[45] The beginnings of the cattle industry developed another quite distinct type of agricultural enterprise in the "ranch." But even this form of agricultural enterprise had colonial roots. See E. E. Dale, *History of the Ranch Cattle Industry*, American Historical Report 1920 (Washington, D.C., 1925).

from the subsistence farms. Chiefly oriented toward villages and towns, these general-purpose farms were linked economically with the village or urban artisans, the port-town merchants, and with lumbering, fishing and food-processing industries. Although self-sufficient in food and partly in fibers, these farms were dependent upon markets in which to sell agricultural produce (as well as timber, tan bark, or pearl ashes) and in which to buy tools, furniture, hardware, glass, kitchen utensils, shoes, spices, and many other consumer goods. Scaled in size to the amount of land that a family could cultivate, these small farms became typical in the Pennsylvania–New Jersey area, and in New England, where the whole plan of settlement was designed to create a high degree of regional self-sufficiency and economic diversification by concurrently developing agriculture, manufacturing, forest exploitation, fishing, and commerce. They called for a village economy as their market counterpart, since mercantile-artisan centers were needed within convenient (five-to-ten-mile) travel radii. Indirectly, these village-oriented farms came to be linked with overseas markets, but this was the consequence of a network of grain or livestock buyers who could assemble or process for export the products purchased in small lots from farmers in the village markets.

Limited-crop farms. The third type of agricultural enterprise by contrast, was rather clearly oriented toward foreign markets. Here we find the large grain farms of Pennsylvania, Western Maryland and the Valley of Virginia, and the large and small tobacco farms in tidewater Maryland, Virginia, North Carolina, and Georgia. The distinguishing feature of these farms was the concentration on one crop (or perhaps two crops) primarily for export. Such agricultural specialization obviously called for a trade network not only capable of marketing the cash crop but also flexible enough to permit the one-crop or few-crop farmers to buy a very wide range of other commodities. The degree of specialization varied considerably; the large grain farms in Western Maryland, for example, were wholly self-sufficient in food (grains, meats, dairy products) whereas tobacco farmers might have to buy corn for their slaves and meat and cheese for their families. Nor can we easily generalize about the amounts of investment that were required for this more specialized type of farming. Large tobacco growers might have considerable investment in drying sheds, as large grain farmers did in granaries and threshing floors. The important distinction was rather that this type of agricultural enterprise was linked with large bulk markets, which in the colonial period were only to be found overseas.[46] In one form or another these one-crop or few-crop farms were to become one basic American type, represented today by the corn-hog farms in Iowa, the large cotton farms of Louisiana or Texas, or the apple orchards of Washington and Oregon. But as the American economy has industrialized and urbanized, these specialized farms have become progressively less oriented toward overseas markets.

Tenant-operated large estates. Originally established in New York, and, to a lesser extent, in New Jersey and Maryland, this type of farm did not move westward[47] or become a typical form of American agricultural enterprise. Some of these farms have survived along the Hudson, although even here they have been partly broken up and reduced in size. They had limited reproduction or survival capacity because of the difficulty involved in keeping a permanent class of tenants who were willing to rent land. In short, because so many Americans had the opportunity of becoming landowners and, despite frequent failures, persistently attempted to do so, estate farming has played an insignificant rôle in the history of American life. As a consequence, the Dutch-English type of agriculture of New York became largely an historical relic, with perhaps only one other parallel and equally static counterpart, represented by the large haciendas established in California in the Spanish era.

The slave-operated plantation. It was slavery, however that allowed an estate form of agriculture to develop and expand southwestward. For whereas the New York variety of estate farming had to attract a hired or tenant labor supply, the southern planter could purchase his work force provided he had the necessary capital. The spread of the plantation system was, therefore, dependent on the cost of slaves (which was for a time kept reasonable by the expansion of the slave trade) and on the capital of the planters (which in turn was partly dependent upon the funds that British merchants were prepared to advance). The whole system came to be intimately related to overseas markets (for tobacco, rice and indigo in the 17th and 18th century; for cotton in the 19th century). It was not really an institution that was "transferred" from Europe to America, for although slavery is as old as man's iniquity, the kind of plantation system that spread on the American continent was

---

[46] It should be remembered that in 1776 Boston and New York were small cities with no more than 20,000 people; that Charleston, the largest city in the South, had less than 15,000; and that only Philadelphia had as many as 35,000.

[47] Expect for some isolated instances as, for example, in upper New York.

originally developed in the British West Indies and was copied in Virginia and Carolina. It relied not on worker incentives, as the other four types of agricultural enterprise did, but upon a discipline enforced upon a servile work force. It required a far larger amount of initial investment because the workers had to be purchased. It had to face one special problem, the likelihood of low productivity per worker; hence a slave owner had to estimate whether the interest and depreciation on his investment per slave plus the cost of food and maintenance when calculated in relation to the slave's low productivity would give a lower cost per unit of product than the wages that would have had to be paid to a free worker. Until the latter part of the 18th century the calculation apparently gave an advantage to the slave system, although the margin of profit was declining. Then in 1793 came the invention of Whitney's cotton gin opening up great new opportunities for the profitable production of short-staple cotton under a plantation system. Negro slavery spread rapidly as cotton cultivation increased and continued as an institution inherited from the colonial era until it was "abolished" by the Emancipation Proclamation. Yet Lincoln's proclamation did not liquidate the plantation. It merely changed it into a subsistence sharecrop system, which another ninety-five years has not really succeeded in rooting out of the American economy.

Types of Industrial Enterprise

Whereas there was a great deal of experimentation in colonial America with agricultural enterprises, there was far less novelty in the forms of industrial enterprise. Indeed, even such fairly well-developed British institutions as the joint-stock company were seldom used, because most colonial industries were small, mainly adapted to limited market areas, and could therefore be administered by single owners or by partnerships. Even ship building or iron making were small enterprises, the former depending more upon the personal skill of shipwrights than on capital equipment, the latter requiring little capital equipment that could not be provided out of local resources. Yet, notwithstanding the essentially imitative character of the colonial industrial enterprises, some adaptation and adjustment to the American environment did occur, and in order to see these modifications we shall examine briefly the five major varieties: the urban crafts, the agricultural market-town industries, the export-oriented industries, the regionally-oriented industries, and the plantation industries.

The urban crafts. Thanks to the diligent research of that indefatigable group of people interested in American antiques, we know a great deal about the urban craftsmen who made the furniture, clocks, mirrors, pewter, silver, and glass which are now the treasured property of private collectors and museums.[48] For the most part these artisans carried on the traditions of the highly-skilled British craftsmen, and for this reason some of their work compares well in design and workmanship with that of their British contemporaries. Much in the medieval fashion, these urban craftsmen used an apprenticeship system for training young men and drew some of their labor supply from these trainees. But their efforts to reproduce a gild system in America encountered many obstacles. The demand for labor was so great that only a limited number of young men, who really wanted to learn a skilled trade, chose to become apprentices for the traditional seven-year period. Efforts by groups of Massachusetts artisans to obtain a legal monopoly of certain crafts met with temporary success in 1644,[49] but after a three-year trial these "charters" were not renewed. Since the object of the charters was to give master craftsmen the power to prevent non-gildsmen from practicing a skilled trade, it seems evident that the competition from artisans who were not certified master craftsmen was becoming more and more acute. Nevertheless, some form of gild organization continued, although progressively the power to exercise control over apprenticeship, standards of workmanship, or prices and wages declined; and by the middle of the 18th century only the remnants of a gild system[50] were to be found except in very highly skilled crafts as represented for example by silversmiths, goldsmiths or wig makers.

The market for the products of the urban artisans was small and essentially aristocratic. Only wealthy merchants, shipowners and members of the landed gentry could afford fine silver, china, furniture, or costumes. Boston, New York, Philadelphia, and Charleston, therefore,

---

[48] There is a vast literature on this subject. See, for example, Wallace Nutting, *A Furniture Treasury* (Framingham, Mass.: Old America Co., 1933); and his *The Clock Book* (Framingham Mass.: Old America Co., 1924); J. B. Kerfoot, *American Pewter* (Boston: Houghton Mifflin Co., 1924).

[49] See Richard Morris, *Government and Labor*, p. 139.

[50] Some of the ceremonial functions of the urban crafts reminiscent of similar activities of the medieval gilds continued well beyond the Colonial Period. On July 23, 1788, for example, when nine American states had approved the New Constitution for a Federal Government, a colorful parade was held in New York. Participating, with floats symbolically indicating approval of the new Constitution by the craftsmen of New York, were the sail makers, coopers, block and pump makers, tailors, furriers, brewers, printers, and blacksmiths. Probably other crafts also participated.

became the chief centers of these skilled trades, although clock making seems to have been far more dispersed. Certain other skilled trades, like china and glass making, were necessarily located near supplies of high-quality clay or silica sand, and hence were not ordinarily located in the large seaboard cities.

Since it was fashionable, even in Puritan colonies, to own British-made furniture, silver or china, and since British craftsmen usually had not only more skill and experience but lower labor costs, the colonial urban craftsmen were constantly faced with foreign competition. Moreover, as the American public became more willing to buy colonial products, the urban craftsmen presently encountered competition from the developing regional industries,[51] and, as more skill was acquired by country artisans, from the agricultural market-town industries. As a consequence, the relative importance of the urban crafts declined, and by the middle of the 19th century their rôle in American industry had become a very modest one. Here, then, was a borrowed institution which was too much linked with an aristocratic structure of society to have a capacity for survival in a society that became more and more democratic.

The agricultural market–town industries. Emerging in response to insistent and immediate needs, there developed in practically every agricultural market–town or village a limited number of multiple-product workshops. Wood-working shops made simple furniture, spinning wheels, flax reels, wooden bowls, mortars for grinding grain, barrels, casks, tubs, and a wide range of other things ranging from the window sash to coffins. Blacksmiths made horseshoes, door latches, scythes, axes, long-handled frying pans, fire-place cranes, harrow pins, in fact all manner of household and farm hardware. Wheelwrights built carts and wagons; leather workers made harness, gloves, shoes, or bellows; tinsmiths produced pots, pans, candlemolds, and sconces; while potters fashioned and glazed jugs, crocks, platters and churns. In addition to these fabricating industries, villages developed processing industries: small flour and grain mills, sawmills and tanneries.

The number of such local industries and the scale of their operations depended upon the agricultural market area they served, which was itself a function of road or water transportation facilities. For the most part, the emphasis was placed on utility, not on fine workmanship. Hence little use was made of apprenticeship; helpers were merely hired to perform simple tasks, and as they acquired more skill they could

51 See p. 145.

demand higher wages or set up their own shops. The range of things which farmers needed, however, compelled the artisans to become versatile, resourceful, and inventive; and consequently there developed a remarkable capacity to devise different kinds of tools and equipment. These market-town workshops became the training centers for American mechanics, laying the foundations for America's industrial development that was to occur when markets widened, as a result of better transportation. Consequently, while the urban crafts gradually atrophied and declined, the market-town industries increased in vitality, because they were resilient enough to adapt themselves constantly to changing demand.

The export-oriented industries. Whereas the urban crafts and the market-town industries catered to domestic demand, another set of industries were dependent upon foreign markets. Their function was to process colonial animal and vegetable products so that bulk could be reduced and value increased. Consequently seaboard flour mills ground, cleaned, bolted, and barrelled flour for export; tobacco warehouses dried, sorted, graded and packed tobacco or ground snuff; lumber mills sawed and planed timber for export, or cut flooring, shingles, and moldings; packing plants barrelled salt pork; distilleries concentrated grain into exportable whiskey and molasses into rum; fur companies scraped, trimmed, and graded deer skins and pelts; naval-stores processors prepared pitch or tar for export and distilled slash-pine gum into turpentine; and forges hammered out bar iron for sale in England.

Since these industries added only relatively little value by processing, their operations had to be on a considerable scale to be profitable. Sometimes their business consisted merely in assembling goods for export; thus shingles were split by farmers in their spare time to specifications dictated by exporters. Usually, however, a certain amount of more precise processing was required, which called for specialized equipment and close supervision over workmen. The export-oriented flour mills became sizable plants; some of them developed advanced mechanical aids, and their managers were pioneers in working out new techniques of mill design, mechanization, and efficient industrial management. Ship building, although carried on essentially as a skilled craft, was also export oriented since a large proportion of the ships were sold abroad. To the list of export industries belongs also the packing of salted fish, the manufacture of whale oil, and the making of pearl ashes (potash) even though the actual production was carried on by thousands of widely-dispersed farmers. In all these varied industries Americans acquired valuable experience in manufacturing and management problems, an experience which was to prove very useful after the Revolutionary War, when mass markets in the expanding frontier area were gradually to become more important than foreign markets.

The regional-oriented industries. Almost from the beginning of American settlement, there grew up a number of industries that attuned themselves to regional domestic markets and can therefore be differentiated from the urban crafts, the market-town industries or the export-oriented industries. These regional industries produced easily transportable commodities that were sold in country stores, by travelling peddlers, or could be used for trading with the Indians. Their wide range of merchandise included all manner of useful things ranging from needles, buttons, or knives, to brass powder horns, spices, thread, clockworks, paint, and corset stays; prosaic commodities the whole American community urgently needed.

By producing inexpensive, standardized commodities, these industries catered to the needs of a large number of people, rich and poor, and since they took away some of the market for British manufactures, they drew upon themselves the bitter criticism of their British competitors and of the British government. Despite this they persisted, and more than one proud American manufacturing enterprise can trace its history back to some small factory in Connecticut, Rhode Island or Pennsylvania.

These manufacturers had the great advantage of selling in an expanding market, and as they made money they ploughed back earnings and increased the scale of their operations. These were the industries that stood to profit from the blunders which the British Government made in the 18th century, and from the resulting "non-importation" tactics which the colonies adopted in retaliation. These industries were to flourish and become typically American as the settlement of the West and the improvement of transportation widened the market areas toward which they were oriented.

Technically and organizationally, they varied widely. Some were small workshops that increased their output by the simple expedient of hiring more labor. Others were small factories that used water power and a good deal of machinery; still others operated on a putting-out basis much as the British woollen and worsted industries had done for centuries.[52] Thus the manufacture of inexpensive boots and shoes in New England came to be organized largely on a putting-out system.

[52] See p. 58.

Boston merchants bought leather (for "uppers" and for soles) and distributed it to country-dwelling cobblers who cut and sewed the uppers, and "pegged" on the soles, and who were paid for their work on a piecework basis. From them the managers of the enterprise received supplies of finished boots and shoes which they sold in local or city markets, or exported to the West Indies and elsewhere.[53] Gradually, however the factory system (which had its modest American origins in some of the regionally-oriented industries) encroached on the putting-out system because, by use of water power[54] and machinery, it could lower the labor costs of production, thus giving it an important advantage in a country where labor was chronically scarce and wages were persistently high.

The plantation industries. Before the rapid extension of short-staple cotton growing, which came after the invention of Whitney's cotton gin in 1793, southern plantations were far less specialized than they later became. Some did concentrate on tobacco, indigo or rice, but most of them were multiple-product enterprises. Slaves were used not only to cultivate fields but to manufacture wood, metal, fibre, or leather products. Thus on George Washington's plantation some 2,000 yards of linen, woollen, and cotton cloth were manufactured. Thousands of barrels were made on plantations, and some planters had iron forges that produced large quantities of nails, tools and hardware, while in other cases Negroes operated flour mills, packing plants, and distilleries. Indeed, during the 18th century there was emerging in the South a type of multiple-product enterprise that contrasted sharply with the one-crop, essentially agricultural, plantation of the forty or fifty years preceding the Civil War.[55] We can only conjecture what might have happened if the cotton gin had never been invented. Perhaps a type of slave-operated industry would have developed that might have given the South an entirely different pattern of economic development.

Types of Commercial Enterprise

In modern America the overwhelming volume of trade is domestic, and only a small fraction is foreign, whereas in the Colonial period the

[53] See Blanche E. Hazard, *The Organization of the Boot and Shoe Industry in Massachusetts before 1875* (Cambridge, Mass.: Harvard University Press, 1921).

[54] Later, by the use of steam power.

[55] A great number of plantation records have been assembled in the Library of the University of North Carolina. When these have been carefully studied we shall know much more than we now do about the variety of activities on the 18th-century plantations.

bulk of trade was foreign, either by origin or destination. Nor is this difficult to understand. In the first place, the colonies "belonged" to a mother country, whose commercial policy was designed to utilize them as markets and as sources of raw materials. Most, though not all, colonial manufacturing was therefore discouraged, restricted and hampered. In the second place, the colonies were "underdeveloped"; they had few tools, little equipment, and limited numbers of skilled artisans capable of making the things so urgently needed; hence it was usually easier and cheaper to import finished consumer (and capital) goods than to try to make them, paying for them by exports of raw materials, furs or semi-processed goods. Yet various types of manufacturing did emerge, challenging progressively the import-export relations of colony and metropolis, and slowly the pattern of trade changed, so that domestic trade began to gain relatively on foreign trade.

Both foreign and domestic trade required mercantile organizations which could adapt themselves to changing political and economic circumstances. Initially these enterprises overlapped considerably, since merchants engaged in foreign trade might also carry on domestic trade. As new marketing problems arose, however, a greater degree of specialization developed and despite overlaps and in-between varieties, we can distinguish five major types of mercantile enterprises: importers and exporters of goods; importers and exporters of goods and slaves; seaboard wholesalers; produce commission-merchants; and retailers.[56]

Exporters and importers of goods. This category of merchants included two rather distinct groups: the sedentary merchants who carried on operations in their countinghouses in seaboard cities, and the masters of sailing vessels who traded from port to port. The first group followed practices that had been traditional in Europe since the 14th century.[57] These shrewd merchants estimated market demand at home and abroad, risked their own capital in the purchase of goods, engaged space on ocean-going vessels, and then dispatched exports to agents abroad (or entrusted them to masters of vessels) authorizing them to buy return cargo. Some merchants specialized in certain kinds of exports (for example, fish, furs, lumber, meat, grain, or tobacco) and to a

56 The degree to which real functional distinctions emerged differed widely from time to time and from region to region. One of the best studies of the gradual emergence of a professional merchant class is Bernard Bailyn's *The New England Merchants in the Seventeenth Century* (Cambridge, Mass.: Harvard University Press, 1955).

57 See N. S. B. Gras, *Business and Capitalism* (New York: F. S. Crofts and Co., 1939), Chap. 3.

lesser extent in particular varieties of imports. Others constantly experimented, and stood ready to export anything that promised to yield
a profit and to import unusual and presumably more profitable items.[58]

The second group, the itinerant merchants, were usually masters
of vessels. They seldom owned ships but more commonly were only
part owners; consequently they had to share the profits of a voyage not
only with the other owners of shipshares, but, on a hierarchical basis,
with the members of their crews.[59] Some masters did own their vessels,
and had their own working capital, but far more frequently a master
was the agent of a group of risk takers. And the risks they took were
many: the risk of losses by shipwreck, damage to cargo, the uncertainty
of prices in foreign ports, to say nothing of the risk that the master
might make bad decisions not merely in navigation but in selling and
buying. But foreign trade, with its adventure and challenge, produced a
remarkably shrewd race of mariner merchants who ranged the seven
seas, selling fish in Spain, buying coffee in Aden, or bringing silks and
spices to Newburyport or Baltimore. They and their sons stood the
new republic in good stead when, after the Revolution, Americans were
excluded from British markets, and American vessels had to find new
export outlets and new sources of necessary imports in other parts of the
world.

Exporters and importers of goods and slaves. The main difference
between this group of merchants and the foregoing was that one group
had no scruples about selling human beings and the other did. But the
fact that one group did traffic in slaves affected the whole pattern of
their trade. They had to convert colonial exports (grain, fish, lumber,
tobacco) into trading goods with which they could purchase slaves from
chieftains on the African coast. Out of this necessity came many varying
polygons of trade. Thus, fish from Massachusetts might be bartered for
sugar in Barbadoes, which in turn was exchanged for bright-colored
cloth in England with which to purchase strong, young slaves from
Ashanti chieftains in the region which is now the republic of Ghana. Because it was uneconomic for the slave ships to return from America in
ballast, in the eastbound traffic the slave ships were general cargo car-

[58] For a description of the operations of Thomas Hancock, an outstanding Colonial
merchant, see p. 237.

[59] The master and crew might, for example, receive one third of the profits. If the
master were himself a part owner he would also share in the remaining two-thirds.
Among the crew, the fractions would depend on the relative importance of each
man's job. An apprentice seaman might receive only 1/200 of the profits, whereas the
master might receive 1/10.

riers, and the peculiar trade triangles, polygons, or other configurations represented efforts to integrate in most profitable patterns the westbound carriage of slaves and the eastbound movement of colonial exports. This widened the geographic range of colonial commerce and increased the business skill of the American merchants or their shipmaster agents by tempting them to break out of a limited colony, mother-country pattern, and carry on trade with other European countries and their overseas possessions.

The combined slave and goods trade also had stimulating effects upon colonial manufacturing. When it was learned that slaves could be purchased in Africa in exchange for rum, distilling became an important New England business. But rum required molasses as a raw material; hence fish (with which to feed slaves) became an export to the West Indies, where is was exchanged for molasses. Blankets, hardware, trinkets, and many other kinds of trading goods were also needed in the slave trade, and, in Massachusetts, Rhode Island, and Connecticut, artisans presently began to manufacture suitable trading goods.

The seaboard wholesalers. Wholesale trade is an essential part of any efficient economic organization because it assembles the output of many small producers and makes this random mass of goods more saleable by grading and classifying commodities. Wholesalers also reduce the transport costs of goods because they purchase, or sell, in quantities large enough to load wagons or ships with goods of uniform quality. They also provide purchasing centers where retailers or distributors can buy the kind of goods their customers want and in amounts consistent with current demand. Since Colonial production was smallscale, dispersed, and the result of varying skills, wholesalers were especially important; they purchased, graded, packed, or baled tobacco, cotton, lumber, hides, wool, and many other products for export. Sometimes their work was interlocked with that of the export-oriented industries,[60] since they supplied to these industries the raw materials which were then processed to meet overseas-market specifications.

Commission men. Whereas the sedentary merchants and the more specialized wholesalers bought and sold on their own account, another group of businessmen acted as agents for sellers (or buyers) of goods, receiving their compensation by percentage commissions. Thus British firms bought colonial products through seaboard agents; while, conversely, tobacco, indigo, rice and cotton planters usually sold their produce through commission men. Out of this experience emerged an

60 See p. 144.

important and characteristic business institution: the large commission firm, dealing normally in only one or a few products. As grain production increased in western Maryland and the valley of Virginia, for example, intermediaries were needed to facilitate the sale of wheat, corn or barley, whether destined for export or for domestic urban consumption. In the same way, tobacco brokerage firms developed, as did cotton brokerage firms in a later period.

Meantime the development of the livestock industry opened opportunities for both livestock buyers and livestock brokers. Indeed, this branch of colonial trade became rather complicated in organization. Both cattle and hogs, were generally driven to market by drovers, the predecessors of the cowboys of a later era in the West. These drovers either acted on behalf of merchants who had purchased the animals, or for farmers who elected to consign their animals to drovers who, as agents, sold the animals at slaughter houses in seaboard cities. On their long trek to market, the animals had to be watered, fed and rested; and a chain of feeding yards grew up along the main droving routes. But neither the drovers nor the feeders were merchants; they received a commission for their services. In all their functions, the commission men became extremely important as the American population moved westward. Far removed from markets, farmers could not make personal contact with the ultimate buyers of their products. Most farmers sold their animals or produce to local livestock, grain, wool, cotton, or tobacco buyers; and these local businessmen, in turn, consigned their newly-purchased animals or produce to commission men who, acting as agents, sold the farm products to processors or exporters.

Retailers. In cities and large towns a fair degree of specialization emerged in retail trade. Grocers, hardware merchants, dry goods stores, pharmacists, stationery shops, ship chandlers, and other specialist retailers, were to be found in large cities such as Boston, Charleston, Baltimore or Philadelphia.[61] In smaller towns and in villages retailers sold a larger range of merchandise and there emerged presently one of the most typical institutions of 17th-, 18th- and 19th-century America, the general store. It sold practically all the things that a local area needed: sugar, salt, spices, kitchenware, drugs, needles, thread, buttons, harness, gloves, caps, hardware, shoes for man and beast, herbs, lamps,

---

[61] It should be recalled in this connection that the urban craftsmen were retailers of their products as well as manufacturers, and this tended to hold down the number of specialized retail shops. Moreover, wholesale importers very often had shops in which odd lots of imported goods were offered for sale at retail. See Bernard Bailyn, *The New England Merchants,* p. 100.

whale oil, and dozens of other equally necessary things. Some of the things it stocked were imported goods (silk, china, or worsted cloth, for example). Other things were made by the regionally-oriented domestic industries (boots, shoes, sugar, lamps, buggy whips, linen or coarse woollen cloth). Still other things in the general store were produced in the local area (cheese, vinegar, honey, crocks, churns, and simple kitchenware). It was indeed an amazing emporium. Fortunately a few have been revived[62] or preserved as historical museums[63] and restocked as far as possible with the wide range of goods which they sold in the pre-department store and pre-supermarket age.

The general store was not merely a place where local residents purchased things, but also a place where they sold agricultural or handicraft products. The local storekeeper soon discovered that he could make money by bartering his wares for grain, hides, timber products, pearl ashes, or even for horses, steers and hogs. He became a local assembler of a community's surplus production, which he, in turn, sent to market through commission men. In this way he obtained funds with which to re-stock the shelves of his general store. In an age when specie money was inadequate to meet business needs, this rather cumbersome system of trade allowed the economy to grow and develop by providing a workable over-all market mechanism. In it the storekeeper[64] became an important local factotum, who not only bought and sold goods, but often provided a post office and a stagecoach depot, and sometimes loaned money, thus performing some of the functions of a local banker. Again and again it was the local storekeeper who accumulated the funds needed to finance new manufacturing ventures, when population had grown and when demand became great enough to justify more specialized capital formation.

The Heritage from the Colonial Era

The energetic, ambitious, courageous, and mostly poor colonists brought to the new world a variety of economic institutions, some archaic, others more modern. Sometimes, fired with idealism, they attempted to create completely novel institutions, only to discover that

---

62 The "Country Store" at Weston, Vermont is an example.

63 A fine one is to be found in the Shelburne Museum, in Shelburne, Vermont.

64 See Thomas D. Clark, *Pills, Petticoats and Plows* (Indianapolis: Bobbs Merrill, Inc., 1944); Lewis E. Atherton, *The Southern Country Store, 1800–1860* (Baton Rouge: Louisiana University Press, 1949).

they had to abandon, change, modify, or adapt institutions if a tolerably efficient economy was to be established. Attempts to revive feudal institutions failed, whereas more flexible forms of organization succeeded in creating thousands of privately-owned farms, plantations, workshops, and commercial enterprises.

The influence of the colonial environment was profound, pervasive, and continuous. Extensive rather than intensive application of labor became typical by reason of the relative abundance of natural resources and the relative scarcity of labor. Where intensive agriculture was attempted (for example, in the production of indigo or rice) little progress could be made without resort to a servile labor force, which the notorious slave trade provided. Meantime the amplitude of resources resulted in a mobile, dispersed population. Plans to maintain compact settlements were, therefore, quite difficult to enforce, and the lure of the frontier constantly drew settlers farther afield. Yet since the chief markets for colonial produce were overseas, cash-crop–producing settlements hugged the watercourses. Frontier farms necessarily had to be highly self-sufficient, and only as population increased, were these frontier farms gradually drawn into a market orbit, first by resourceful merchants who devised simple but workable schemes for buying and selling goods with the least possible use of specie money, later by the development of better transportation facilities and the slow urbanization of the country.

Scarcity of capital goods in an economy which needed tools and equipment to overcome the handicap of labor scarcity created a propensity to save and to invest, and a quickening of the rate of capital formation. But perhaps more important was the emergence of rather different kinds of capital formation than had been characteristic in European countries. Drawn mostly from the ranks of plain and ordinary people, the settlers stood in need of personally-owned productive equipment. In America capital formation was not decided upon by an aristocratic minority. Consequently the bulk of savings were not expended on castles, palaces, or churches; but on tools, barns, ships, iron forges, or other productive facilities capable of increasing the supplies of goods needed by the generality of the population. To some extent this preoccupation with one's personal capital equipment led to the creation of relatively less social capital in the form of roads, bridges, schools, hospitals and other necessary parts of a good economy. This social task, though by no means wholly neglected during the Colonial period, was not really systematically approached until later, when independence and a growing sense of national unity made possible an expansion of the economic rôle of government. Meanwhile the Colonial era, by providing thousands of persons with the freedom to experiment in the business of capital formation, had developed a race of men who were prepared to tackle the larger problems of a national economy. The ways in which they did this will be pointed out in the chapters that follow.

7 Public policy, economic development and the beginnings of transformation

Need for National Economic Policies

Whereas it had been blandly assumed by many advocates of revolution that independence, by relieving American farmers, merchants and manufacturers from British restrictions, would automatically increase American prosperity, the critical 1780's showed that the American economy was extremely fragile, ill-balanced, highly dependent on foreign markets, short on capital equipment, and worst of all, unintegrated and Balkanized. Indeed it really was not an organic economy, but a cluster of former British economic satellites. The painful realization of this situation led ultimately, under the wise leadership of a remarkable group of profound thinkers, to the abandonment of the loose confederation and the adoption of a new Constitution which made possible a constructive national approach to the basic problems of economic development.

It must be remembered, however, that the new nation that came into being thirteen years after the fateful Declaration of Independence was primarily agricultural[1] although commerce provided a livelihood for a fairly large minority, and manufacturing and professions accounted for minor elements. American agriculture, however, was still primitive. Few of the technical innovations that had been introduced into English farming during the 18th century had been transplanted;[2] the bulk of American farmers still resembled 17th-century English yeomen in their simple virtues, the relatively small scale of their operations, and in their reluctance to change traditional methods of tillage. Yet, in some respects they were quite different because a new country, constantly growing in population and possessing abundant supplies of frontier land, provided an environment which stimulated enterprise. Among other things it held before everyone the possibility of profit from appreciation of land values. As a result, all Americans, not merely farmers, tended to become venturesome and optimistic. Moreover, the selective force of emigration had peopled America with persons more energetic and independent than those who hesitated to leave their ancestral homes. Since a vigorous economy requires both personal and financial daring, in this regard the United States in 1789 seemed well prepared for economic development.

Even so, the United States, for several reasons, experienced no industrial development in the last quarter of the 18th century in any way comparable to that which was transforming England. The foreign markets, cultivated by enterprising merchants, wanted agricultural and forest products, not manufactures, while the expanding domestic markets were still largely served by English manufacturers.[3] Moreover, agriculture rather than industry attracted ambitious young men, making industrial labor scarce and expensive. Yet the richness and abundance of American natural resources indicated that if domestic markets could be opened up by adequate means of transportation,

1 By arbitrarily defining "urban population" as people resident in cities of over 8,000 persons, the census of 1790 reported that only 3.3 per cent of the total population was "urban."

2 A few gentlemen farmers in the southern states were beginning to employ some of the methods of progressive English farmers. In general, however, the plantation system resembled feudal rather than 18th-century British agriculture.

3 During the Revolution there was a temporary burgeoning of domestic manufacturing, but with the return of peace, these industries had great difficulty in competing with the far more mature and efficient British firms.

capital accumulated, the supply of industrial labor increased, and the severity of foreign competition mitigated, the United States might become a flourishing manufacturing nation. Although the Federal Union had laid the political and legal basis for a common market, this was not enough; the interior free-trade zone would become an economic reality only as a consequence of economic development.

Hamilton's Recommendation

What special advantage might a nation gain from fostering manufactures when the pursuit of private gain turned a majority of the people to agriculture, lumbering, or commerce? The first succinct American answer was proffered by Alexander Hamilton in his *Report on Manufactures,* which, as Secretary of the Treasury, he submitted to Congress in 1791.[4] This thoughtful document marshalled a series of arguments to show both the political and the economic desirability of stimulating manufactures. Beginning with political considerations, Hamilton asserted that every nation which hopes to remain independent must produce within its frontiers adequate "means of subsistence, habitation, clothing and defence." Without these essentials, no nation can guarantee either the safety or the welfare of its citizens. But new countries cannot expect these requisite commodities to be forthcoming automatically from the pursuit of self-interest for two reasons: because "adventitious barriers" are raised by older countries who are already industrialized; and these competing countries are in a position to undersell manufactures in new countries because they had themselves deliberately stimulated manufactures by artificial methods. And yet, although Hamilton repudiated Adam Smith's thesis, which postulated that freedom from government interference would always permit the most beneficial employment of a nation's productive power, he completely agreed with Smith in asserting that manufacturing permits greater division of labor than agriculture does. Hamilton also pointed

[4] Hamilton played a very important role in pointing out the weaknesses of the loosely-knit government under the Articles of Confederation, in shaping the new Constitution, and in persuading his countrymen to adopt the new Federal plan of government. Of the 85 famous *Federalist* papers, Hamilton may have written as many as 53. Moreover, he was largely responsible for obtaining the acceptance of the Constitution by the State of New York, thereby ensuring that the new government would become a truly national government. For a clear account of Hamilton's great contribution to national unity, see Broadus Mitchell's excellent book *Alexander Hamilton, Youth to Maturity, 1755–1788* (New York: The Macmillan Co., 1957), especially Chaps. 22–26.

out the greater tendency of manufacturers to employ scientific technology, designating the use of machinery as "an artificial force" which is added to man's "natural force." Thus, by the division of labor and by harnessing natural power, manufactures increase a nation's productive capacity. They also attract foreign artisans, thereby enlarging the productive skill within a nation, and they offer opportunities for people with "a diversity of talents" to exercise their varied abilities.

Because Hamilton felt compelled to demonstrate that artificial stimulation of manufacturing would not injure agriculture, he wove into his *Report* another argument designed to prove that home markets for agricultural produce are preferable to foreign markets. The latter, he insisted, are uncertain and unreliable, whereas home markets are always dependable; hence the establishment of a sizable non-agricultural consuming class would stabilize agricultural prosperity by facilitating convenient exchange of surplus agricultural products for domestically-produced manufactures. Yet what advantage would farmers reap if American manufactures were higher priced than foreign goods? Hamilton forestalled this question by asserting that, in a nation well supplied with raw materials, any increase in prices resulting from protection would be temporary. Freed from foreign competition, domestic manufacturers would rapidly enlarge the scale of their operations, thereby achieving economies comparable to those enjoyed by foreign competitors; the "infant industries" would quickly attain maturity, and would then be able to produce at least as cheaply as foreign manufacturers.

Business Demands for Protection

Hamilton's skillful demonstration of the political and economic desirability of protection coincided with a persistent demand for tariffs which originated with groups of American businessmen. Versatile and ambitious profit seekers realized that there was money to be made in manufacturing if the government could be induced to shield them against foreign competition; hence promoters of new ventures exposed to English competition quite naturally endorsed protection, although they were, as yet, unable to enlist any strong Congressional support. Despite this pressure from some business groups, Hamilton's *Report* bore no immediate fruit. A series of laws from 1789 to 1816 did levy new customs duties or modified existing duties, but the main object in practically every case was to provide revenue for the Federal govern-

ment. Meanwhile, the Napoleonic wars were creating acute political
and economic difficulties which ultimately involved the United States
in a second war with England. It was the return of peace that rapidly
crystallized the demand for protection into legislative action.[5]

First Experiments with Protective Tariffs

The fears of manufacturers that the United States would be
inundated with cheap imports promptly became a reality; imports rose
from a value of $13,000,000 in 1814 to $113,000,000 in 1815 and to
$147,000,000 in 1816. Congress acted swiftly by passing the Tariff Act of
1816, which levied duties that averaged about 25 per cent on cotton and
woollen cloth, and about 20 per cent on pig iron; it also imposed specific
duties[6] on a large number of other commodities. The combination of *ad
valorem* and specific duties makes it difficult to state exactly how much
protection the tariff actually afforded, but the average was probably
near 20 per cent.[7] This degree of protection, however, quickly proved
to be inadequate because of the advantages which England possessed
by virtue of cheap labor and more advanced technology. Over the
American tariff barriers, English bar iron was imported in large
quantities,[8] as were also better-grade textiles, leading to severe competition and falling prices. Yet the country at large exhibited no great
concern over the adverse fortune of the American manufacturers. The
southern states looked upon protection with grave misgiving, since
Europe provided them with markets for their tobacco and cotton;
shipowners could scarcely be expected to approve a program which
might bring a decline in the volume of both exports and imports; and
northern farmers did not see any important advantage that they might
gain from a protective tariff. Yet this indifference on the part of a
majority of the voters suddenly ended.

[5] For detailed accounts of American tariff history, see: F. W. Taussig, *Tariff History of the United States,* 8th edition (New York: G. P. Putnam's Sons, 1931); and
Percy Ashley, *Modern Tariff History,* 3rd edition (New York: Dutton and Co.,
1926).
[6] Assessed not according to value, but upon some unit of measurement, e.g., pound,
hundredweight, dozen.
[7] Taussig, *Tariff History of the United States,* p. 19.
[8] Even though the duties on hammered bar iron were 45 cents a hundredweight;
those on rolled bar iron $1.50.

Clay's "American System"[9]

In 1819 the whole business structure of the United States was convulsed by a severe crisis. As prices of agricultural commodities fell disastrously, the idea of a home market for agricultural commodities quickly became a genuine issue. Might not a protective tariff obviate the recurrence of agricultural depressions by building up a stable domestic demand for raw materials, and by creating a sizable urban-dwelling class that would provide a steady market for foodstuffs? Might not protection become a device which would render the United States economically independent, and make it impossible for England to injure American agriculture by her Corn Laws[10] or to jeopardize American industry by cut-throat competition? These hitherto theoretical ideas suddenly became very immediate practical questions.

Henry Clay seized the opportunity to enunciate his "American System," based essentially on Alexander Hamilton's *Report*. A home market, said Clay, is permanent, and cannot suddenly be closed by vindictive action of foreign politicians. Hence a protective tariff, by building up such a home market, brings advantage to the industrial and agricultural classes alike; it exempts the former from ruinous competition, and provides the latter with a superior kind of market. By this appeal, a majority of the members of Congress from western states were induced to support the demands of New England and middle-Atlantic manufacturers for higher tariff duties. The Act of 1824, passed against the wishes of the South (which was finding a growing market for cotton in England) and against the wishes of the commercial interests in New England, raised the duties on cotton and woollen cloth from 25 to 33⅓ per cent, doubled the specific duties on hammered iron, and levied higher duties on hemp, wool, and flax, the latter imposts representing agriculture's share in the new legislation. Yet the attempt to grant real protection to manufacturers and, at the same time, to benefit the western farmers proved to be difficult. Wool manufacturers soon discovered that the duties on raw wool increased the cost of their imported raw materials and thereby whittled away the real protection afforded by the duties on imported woollen cloth.

9 The phrase *American System* was also used later to designate a type of factory organization. See pp. 209–11.
10 See pp. 110–11

Formulation of a Theory of Protection

Skillfully combining their lobbying strength by calling a convention[11] of all persons interested in higher tariffs, the wool manufacturers proceeded to agitate for still higher duties on manufactured goods. And just as English manufacturers who were advocating free trade[12] found justification for their proposed policy in the teachings of English political economy, American businessmen sought to prove that their demands for increased protection could also be justified by economic theory. In Matthew Carey they found their theoretical defender. Never profound but always effective, this gifted Philadelphia newspaper publisher emphasized in his *Essays on Political Economy*[13] the virtues of a protective tariff for developing American manufacturing, and extolled its usefulness in creating a domestic market for agricultural products. Like Clay, he also advocated a program of internal improvement, insisting that a combination of tariffs and government-assisted transportation agencies would create a "harmony of interests" which would ensure permanent prosperity. Carey's work on behalf of protection was not confined to literary efforts; he organized, in 1819, the Philadelphia Society for the Promotion of National Industry which spread tariff propaganda throughout the United States.

Yet the first legislative fruit of this evangelical protectionist movement proved to be rather bitter. The insistent demand of farmers and manufacturers for higher tariffs incensed the representatives of the southern states. Political strategy seemed to indicate that if a grotesquely protective bill were introduced, one that threatened to saddle the New England manufacturers with very high duties on raw materials, it was possible that the northern Representatives would join southern members of Congress in defeating the bill. Unfortunately, the plan miscarried, and, in 1828, Congress passed a weird piece of tariff legislation which proved to be a hodgepodge of protective duties unsystematically scrambled together. It levied higher duties both on manufactured goods and on raw materials, and consequently it pleased no one; to the South it became the "Tariff of Abominations;" to the wool manufacturers, who had engineered its introduction, it brought little advantage because of the higher duties on raw wool.

[11] At Harrisburg, in 1827.
[12] See p. 111.
[13] Philadelphia, H. C. Carey and J. Lea, 1822.

This "Tariff of Abominations" proved to be the high-water mark of American protection in the pre-Civil War period. The cotton-exporting southern states did not merely protest; they threatened to secede, a tactic which brought a downward revision of tariff rates after 1832. This sectional reprisal gave clear evidence of the wide gulf that now separated the nascent industrial enterprises of the northern states from the lingering feudal ideology of the slave-implemented plantation system of the South.[14] By threatening vindictive political action, the southern states were able for the next thirty years to keep American protectionism in check.

Meantime American manufacturing establishments were growing in numbers, size, and prosperity, although it is difficult to prove that protection was the most important cause for this progress.[15] What then did facilitate the transfer of industrial technology from Europe to America? What made possible the remarkable rate of economic development which the United States experienced? The answer is that market forces had more to do with economic transformation than Federal stimulation did. But, as we shall see, this does not mean that the process was entirely set in motion by private enterprise.

The Role of Exogenous Factors in Economic Development

National vanity always tempts one to ascribe a country's economic progress to endogenous factors. We like to think that our farmers were responsible for our agricultural progress, our merchants for our commercial enterprise, and our manufacturers for our remarkable industrial expansion. Yet it often happens that a nation's economic development is determined not only by its own people but by processes at work in other parts of the world. These fortuitous circumstances may be the result of market forces, or they can be the unintentional results of certain governmental policies abroad. Let us see how and why such things can occur.

14 Although slaveowners were a minority among Southern agriculturists, and large slaveowners (those owning over 50 Negroes) a small minority, they nevertheless were able to impose their opinions and their political views upon the majority. See U. B. Phillips, *American Negro Slavery* (New York: D. Appleton & Co., 1918).

15 Taussig concluded: that the high duties on iron actually retarded technical progress in the iron industry (by exempting American charcoal-smelted iron from English competition); that the cotton industry was sufficiently established "probably as early as 1824, and most certainly by 1832" to compete with English mills; and that the woollen industry gave no clear indication that protection had been the cause for its growth. *Tariff History of the United States*, pp. 134–154.

Throughout the 19th century, European funds seeking profitable investment flowed to the United States, largely as a result of quasi-automatic market forces, thus making it possible for Americans to exploit natural resources more efficiently, increase productivity and augment national output. Concurrently, a second type of exogenous assistance to the American economy was occurring: a stream of able-bodied Europeans migrated to the United States, providing the new country with a much-needed labor supply. To some extent this transfer of man power was a response to market forces (differences in wages) but much of the migration was the consequence of governmental policies (or lack of policies) in Britain, Germany, and other European countries. We shall see, then, that the transfer of urgently-needed capital and labor was not wholly an exogenous process. In both instances two interacting forces were at work: one essentially centrifugal, tended to expel productive factors from Europe or elsewhere;[16] the other basically centripetal, tended to attract the self-same factors to the United States. In one sense both forces were responses to market factors (higher earnings for capital or for labor) yet both forces were influenced by governmental policies both abroad and in the United States. This complex interaction of market influences and economic policy we must now try to explain.

The Meaning of Economic Development

In recent years there has been a great deal of talking and writing about "economic development" and about "underdeveloped areas." What do these terms mean? In some contexts the phrase "under-developed areas" apparently refers to "poor" regions where personal in-comes are pathetically low, or to "primitive" economies where there is limited knowledge of technology or systematic agriculture. In other cases the expression refers to "backward" countries that have not kept pace with more "advanced" countries in applied science. Practically always the term refers to "capital-poor" regions. Sometimes the under-developed countries are "overpopulated"; sometimes "underpop-ulated" (with either good or poor natural resources). Yet, despite these seeming differences, the term "underdeveloped areas" has acquired a general and quite consistent meaning. "Underdeveloped" portions of the earth have lower per capita output than "more developed" areas;

---

[16] A considerable amount of textile mill labor, for example, came into New England from French Canada.

and consequently "economic development" refers to some process that can bring about, through time, an increase in per capita productivity. Since the total output of a country is the product of per capita output multiplied by the number of people in the "active population," it is axiomatic that an increase in per capita output of the active population will increase national output; and it follows that if the per capita output and the size of the active population both increase concurrently, then total national output will perforce grow more rapidly.

But very obviously the means that can be employed to increase output will differ markedly between overpopulated and underpopulated areas, between primitive and advanced cultures, between countries with poor resources and good resources. Moreover, it should be noted that certain underdeveloped areas are capable of attracting factors of production (from more developed areas) by the normal workings of prices, wages, or interest rates; whereas in other underdeveloped countries these market forces may fail to bring about any comparable results. In general, it is only those areas which are underpopulated and which possess abundant and good natural resources that can expect to experience much automatic, market-inspired, and business-directed economic development. Other less fortunate regions must make a far more conscious and policy-guided effort to set in motion a process of economic development.

Critical Needs of the 19th-Century American Economy

By remarkable historical circumstances, the less than four million American people, in 1789, had possession of some of the best, and most varied, natural resources that were ever found anywhere. And presently these resources were to be further enlarged by the addition of still more territory west of the Mississippi river. In this huge national domain lay vast stretches of fertile land capable of producing untold bushels of grain, tons of meat, or bales of cotton. In it stood millions of acres of virgin forests; while under the soil lay tremendous deposits of coal, iron, lead, zinc, silver, and copper. Indeed, almost all metals and minerals necessary for industrial growth were included in the legacy which Britain had so unwittingly yielded up to the American revolutionists, or in the added territory which the new republic was to acquire. Here then was an "underdeveloped" country but of a truly unusual kind. It was mostly empty of population, since, in 1789, the great bulk of the people lived east of the Allegheny mountains. Per capita real output in agriculture was low because only the colder, shallower, sandier soils of the eastern seaboard were used, and because tools, machinery, and transport equipment were chronically scarce. Per capita real output in mining or manufacturing was correspondingly low because capital was not available for sinking shafts, harnessing waterpower, or buying steam engines or machinery. Lack of roads and other means of transport prevented the exploitation of the best land and the richest deposits of coal, iron, or non-ferrous metals. Tools and equipment were needed to make it possible for every able-bodied man to produce more. But social capital was fully as necessary to open up better grades of land, more remote forests, and superior mineral deposits; more particularly roads, wharfs, bridges and, presently, steamships and railways, were essential if these fabulous resources were to be purposefully exploited.

More people were needed also, simply because the resources were so extensive that the less than four million people could not possibly utilize effectively the huge natural resources. Moreover, for a time at least, "increasing returns" could be obtained from applying more labor to resources.[17] Hence, immigrants, able-bodied and industrious, would make a net addition to national output, and by increasing the number of domestic consumers would also widen the demand for American products. If they became city dwellers they would buy food from the farmers; if they became farmers they would buy clothes, shoes, hardware and other goods from American manufacturers. Meantime those land-owners, who, in the speculative American tradition, held more land than they could properly cultivate, saw in the immigrant a prospective landbuyer, and hence they too welcomed the incoming Irish, Germans, Swedes, and Norwegians.

The Importance of Capital Formation

But more labor, whether from natural reproduction or from immigration, would make capital (tools, wagons, machines or mechanical equipment) even more essential. Where was it to come from if the nation was to develop? Some of it, of course, could be fashioned out of natural resources, and indeed a tremendous amount of capital was provided by this direct process; thousands of miles of rail fences, or hundreds of barns and sheds represented merely the conversion (by hand labor generally) of standing timber into serviceable agricultural

---

[17] Two men working together would produce more than twice the product of one; three more than thrice the product of one, and so on.

capital. This heroic chapter of frontier life is so familiar that it needs no elaboration. Yet a democratic nation can only go so far with this direct technique of capital formation. For whereas a totalitarian nation can, by one means or another, literally round up a supply of workers and put them to work building roads or factories, a democratic society cannot. A small amount of capital formation may result from voluntary collective labor; and in America social capital represented by roads, bridges, schoolhouses, or churches was often so constructed. But when it came to building factories, railways, or iron foundries, these techniques were not workable; some person or some group of persons had to plan the venture, accumulate the money funds needed to buy the equipment, and hire workers to build the installations.

In this context, then, money funds were the keys to development. Where were they to come from? Some could come from the saving of successful American professional people or businessmen. But with a whole nation in constant need of more capital goods, such saving was either invested directly by the savers, or very promptly loaned at profitable interest rates to people who expected to "trade on the equity," which is to say, entrepreneurs who hoped to earn more from the revenues generated by the capital goods (in which they "invested" the borrowed funds) than they would have to pay out as interest and amortization. As a result, domestic loanable funds were both limited in amount, and eagerly sought after; endogenous market forces, in short, could not supply an adequate amount of loanable funds to satisfy American needs. It was this general capital shortage which set in motion a cross-Atlantic migration of capital from the older or more developed countries of Europe, and which presently supplied America with some of the capital which the American people so urgently needed to increase their per capita output and thereby the entire national output.

British Efforts to Prevent American Industrialization

It was, however, no part of British intention to hasten the industrialization of the United States. Indeed, if the British manufacturers could have controlled the course of 19th-century history, neither the United States, nor Germany, to say nothing of Canada, Australia, or India would have been industrialized. England would have become and remained the "workshop of the world," supplying mass-produced manufactured goods in exchange for raw materials, foodstuffs, and a few products of handicraft skill. Quite frankly the British manufacturers hoped to obtain a world monopoly of mechanized manufacturing by underselling foreign competitors and by refusing to supply them with machinery.

As every one knows, however, the British manufacturers did not control the course of 19th-century industrial history. Machines, methods, and techniques could not be confined to the British Isles. Like outgoing ripples, the factory system spread to Belgium, France, Switzerland, and the United States. Protective tariffs were designed to attract manufacturing industries by making it profitable for manufacturing to be carried on behind tariff walls, although it is difficult to evaluate how successful such efforts actually were.[18] But whereas protection presumably acted as a magnet, drawing industrialization into underdeveloped countries, there were other forces at work which acted like catapults, throwing the new system of production outward into new areas. It is the nature of these exogenous, centrifugal forces that we must examine briefly.

International Capital Movements

It will be recalled that the beginnings of British capitalism were partly made possible by borrowed Dutch capital.[19] Dutch merchants had amassed a great deal of wealth in the 16th and 17th centuries; as a consequence, Amsterdam became a great source of loanable funds, with a well-developed money market, an efficient banking system, and a large number of skilled financiers. Throughout the 18th century, Amsterdam shared the business of finance with her rich neighbor, Antwerp. The great disorganization which came in the wake of Napoleon's campaigns, however, cut heavily into the prosperity of these Low-Country cities, and, more and more, London assumed the position of the foremost European money market. Until 1850, therefore, England provided the bulk of the funds which fertilized economic progress in other countries.

The history of British capital exports in the first half of the 19th century[20] is a story of hope, disillusion, and returning hope. Seeking higher returns than were available at home, capital funds flowed out

18 See pp. 97, ff.
19 See p. 62.
20 See Leland H. Jenks, *The Migration of British Capital to 1875* (New York: Alfred A. Knopf, Inc., 1927); and C. K. Hobson, *The Export of Capital* (London: G. Allen and Unwin, Ltd., 1914).

in every direction, not regularly and continuously, but intermittently. Neither did these funds always seek investment in business enterprises; a very large proportion was lent to foreign governments, frequently with most unhappy results. Indeed, the export of capital can scarcely be regarded as a coldly rational process; unjustified enthusiasm often released great quantities of funds for extravagant and unsound ventures, and consequently losses were frequent and often great. Meanwhile, however, there were profits for the promoters who preyed upon the gullibility of greedy British investors; since it was by the purchase of securities that Britishers provided capital for export.

England's ability to carry on foreign wars from 1793 to 1815 had proved conclusively that her capital was abundant; meantime the huge government borrowings needed to finance the wars had habituated a large part of the British population to investment in securities. With the return of peace, after Waterloo, foreign governments began borrowing. Loans were made to Prussia, Spain, Colombia, Chile, Peru, Mexico, Guatemala, and other countries by inexperienced English investors who purchased foreign government securities from "merchant bankers", whose main interest in the matter arose from the profits they made from floating the loans. Yet even substantial losses did not dampen the rising enthusiasm for foreign investment. The first fifteen years of this exhilarating new experience witnessed an outflow of £50 million to the Continent, £20 million to Latin America, and perhaps as much as £5 or 6 million to the United States.[21]

British Capital Exports to the United States

Although Holland had been the primary source of American borrowings for the Revolutionary War, for funding the American debt in 1791, and for financing the purchase of Louisiana in 1803, many American securities were held in England before Waterloo. After the War of 1812, British funds were invested in American land schemes, as well as in banking ventures. When a number of foreign governments proved unable to meet interest payments on their loans, British investors turned toward business enterprises or to particular kinds of governmental projects which promised to generate income. The Erie Canal conformed nicely to this theory, and most of the bonds issued by the State of New York to finance this highly successful project found their way into the

21 Jenks, *The Migration of British Capital to 1875,* p. 64.

portfolios of British investors. By 1836, at least $90 million had been invested in American canals, and most of the capital for these ambitious public improvements had come from England.

The effect of these British-financed means of transportation on American economic development proved salutary. Farms and villages in the northern portion of the Middle West now became markets for manufactured goods, and, at the same time, cheaper transportation increased the money incomes of the older farm areas in Ohio and New York State. Hence, although British loans to America did increase British exports,[22] they concurrently stimulated American manufacturing, especially by building up transportation systems which carried the products of American factories to the inland markets. British investments in American public improvements, however, led to a land boom in the areas affected by the new canals, a factor that contributed abundantly to the wave of false prosperity which preceded the crisis of 1837. That unfortunate event, which led to heavy British losses, brought a quick end to the first large stream of British investments flowing to the United States. After a decade, however, so many new investment opportunities were to be found in the United States that the reverses of 1837 were forgotten, and British capital once again began flowing in volume to America, especially for railway building in the mid-western states.

These railroads, as well as those which Britain had financed in other parts of the globe, hastened the world process of industrialization, and as manufacturing increased, still more outlets for surplus British capital emerged. European and American factories now borrowed British funds, although until the corporate form of organization became more typical, such ventures could not appeal to a wide range of investors. Nevertheless, British funds financed lace and linen factories in France, machine shops in Belgium, textile mills in Russia, and a whole range of manufacturing enterprises in the United States. With wanton disregard for those business groups in Great Britain who still hoped that England would always remain the foremost industrial

---

[22] A foreign loan is ordinarily the cause of increased goods exports. Thus, when an American loan is floated in England, the British investors buy the securities with British currency. In order to transfer the proceeds, American borrowers will draw sterling drafts on London, offering them for sale in the United States. If the amount of the loan to be transferred is large, the dollar price of sterling will fall. This fall in price will encourage American importers to increase their British purchases, since the means of payment are now more cheaply available.

nation of the world, British investors were rapidly providing foreign countries with competing industrial equipment.

Spatial Dynamics of Mature Industrial Countries

Two quite different processes, each primarily with a British origin, were, therefore, gradually transforming the economic life of the entire world: to countries which interposed no barriers, flowed cheap, attractive, factory-made goods; to countries, like the United States, less willing to accept British merchandise, flowed a stream of capital funds. Critics of modern capitalism have usually interpreted these events as proof of the sinister exploitive power which capitalism unleashes.[23] The dangers involved in such easy generalization are always great.

In the first place, the two processes: exporting goods and exporting capital, had different origins, and were more frequently separate than associated. Merchants and manufacturers exported goods, and, except for granting credit to foreign buyers,[24] had nothing to do with the export of capital. A heterogeneous class of investors and promoters, on the other hand, exported capital, and they, conversely, had little or nothing to do with the export of goods. Nevertheless, the two processes of exporting goods and exporting capital were complementary because, for a time, lending abroad increased the demand of foreigners for British merchandise. Building railroads with British capital, for example, created an immediate increase in the demand for British iron and steel. On the other hand, to the extent that capital exports provided foreign nations with their own industrial equipment, British foreign investment set in motion forces which tended ultimately to decrease the foreign demand for British merchandise. Hence only for a relatively short time would there be an identity of interest between the exporters of goods and the exporters of capital; because only as long as a borrowing country was a "net borrower" (which is to say as long as annual new capital imports exceeded the annual interest and repayments) would there be a resulting "import surplus" of goods.

[23] This thesis was suggested by Karl Marx, amplified by Karl Kautsky, and systematically developed by Rosa Luxemburg. See Marx, *Capital* (London: Allen and Unwin, 1938); Kautsky, *The Class Struggle* (Chicago: C. H. Kerr, 1934); and Luxemburg, *Die Akkumulation des Kapital* (Berlin: Singer, 1913).

[24] Generous granting of commercial credit had an effect similar to that resulting from the direct export of capital: it made it possible for foreigners to buy British goods. It created, however, only the ability to buy British goods, whereas the export of capital gave the recipient the ability to buy goods from any chosen source.

Factors that Influenced the Flow of Capital to the United States

Whereas it might seem that capital would flow readily and continually to an underdeveloped country such as the United States, actually capital imports occurred not steadily and evenly, but in periodic and fitful movements. Profitable opportunities for investment by foreigners were correlated with "surges in westward development,"[25] and these westward thrusts were largely the results of "favorable movements of the prices of key commodities" such as cotton, wheat, or pork.

Despite the steady growth of manufacturing establishments in the United States from the 1820's to the 1860's and the attendant gradual American urbanization, the major markets for American agricultural products were still overseas, in western Europe, and chiefly in Great Britain. British factories were gobbling up huge quantities of raw cotton, while the growing number of British and Belgian factory workers were becoming increasingly dependent upon American wheat, flour, and meat. As exports of raw cotton from the southern states increased, southern farmers (both large and small) concentrated more and more on cotton growing, and bought a larger share of their pork, lard, bacon, cornmeal, flour (and even whiskey) from the north central states, thus partially tying the prosperity of those midwestern states to the variations in the price of raw cotton. When European demand for cotton was brisk, the Southern demand for wheat, flour, cornmeal, and pork increased; and this general prosperity, in turn, led to greater sales of land both in the southern states and in the midwestern states. But to link the newly-purchased lands to the market system called for more public improvements, which meant that more canal and railroad securities would be offered to British investors. Periods of general prosperity also led to increased imports of consumer goods, despite American tariffs, and some of the proceeds from these enlarged sales of consumer goods in America were invested in promising American ventures.[26]

The interlocking of the fortunes of the grain-growing West with the cotton-growing South and the reliance of the South on European (espe-

[25] See Douglass C. North, "International Capital Flows and the Development of the American West," *Journal of Economic History*, Vol. XVI, No. 4 (1956) p. 494.

[26] Not usually by the British exporters; normally they disposed of their dollar balances to their investing fellow-countrymen.

cially British) demand for cotton indicates how dependent the American economy still was on exogenous market forces, on powerful and often capricious forces over which Americans had very limited control. In boom times foreign investors were not only buying canal and railroad shares, but also investing in western lands and lending money to American borrowers, whether factory owners or planters. When business was good, imports of consumer goods, of railway iron, or other forms of capital equipment increased, thus making possible a transfer of real resources to the United States. Conversely when prices fell, westward expansion would slow down, canal and railway building would taper off or come to a halt, and capital imports would decline.

Ways of Attracting Capital

Although capital movements are the consequences of market forces, it should be recognized that these market forces are not wholly impersonal mechanisms. Buyers, sellers, borrowers, and lenders all respond to stimuli. Sellers persuade buyers to buy, and borrowers persuade lenders to lend. Moreover, capital markets resemble commodity markets in that skilled intermediaries actually *sell* the securities (which have been *issued* by borrowers) to investors who are seeking profitable placement for their savings. Consequently, when it became evident that promising outlets for savings could be found in the United States, an energetic group of security salesmen made their appearance in London and other European money markets. Some were honest brokers who advised their clients as conscientiously as they could about the probable earnings of new American enterprises. Others were "high-pressure" salesmen who assured their customers that the projects they recommended were safe, certain, and would be richly rewarding. Still others were down-right swindlers, preying on the gullibility, the cupidity, and the inexperience of unseasoned investors.

Most of the public-improvement bonds of American states, and the bulk of canal-company shares and railway securities were sold through reputable investment houses (usually called *merchant bankers*). Industrial shares and mining stocks, in contrast, were more frequently marketed by a motley group of colorful promoters and fast talkers. The vast scope of their attempted operations is indicated by the number of British companies formed to engage in the mining and milling of metals in the United States.[27] By advertising investment opportunities, by personal salesmanship, and by the use of elaborate displays of ores, maps, and pictures, clever and sometimes unscrupulous promoters and security salesmen lured large amounts of European capital to America. Shuttling back and forth between the United States and the European money markets, these professional and amateur security salesmen and promoters laid before prospective investors all manner of tempting opportunities for investment or, more frequently, "long-shot" speculations. Frequently, to lend respectability to dubious ventures, important people (American or European) were given shares of stock in new companies on the condition that their names could be listed among the directors.[28] Suiting the descriptive literature to prospective investors, every conceivable sales argument was used: to the cautious, safety of investment was emphasized; to the greedy, the probability of fabulous returns; while the wary were supplied with extracts from reports by mining engineers, lawyers, and other technical experts.

The great bulk of capital movements, however, were not attracted by such flamboyant or unprincipled tactics. For the most part the European investors surveyed investment opportunities in America and compared them in terms of risk, yield, and growth factors with alternative investments at home or in other parts of the world. For a time European investors seemed to prefer government (state or local) securities issued to finance public improvements, but after the severe crisis of 1837 (when a number of American states defaulted on interest payments) the European investors became more cautious and discriminatory. Picking and choosing, they selected their investments with greater care, giving preference to the issues of American railways which had dependable traffic or to main-line railroads that stretched deeper into the West.

This investment trend was stimulated by the application to railways of a Federal system of subvention in the form of land grants, a scheme

27 Especially after 1860. Thus, Clark G. Spence mentions 518 British joint-stock companies incorporated between 1860 and 1901 with a total nominal capital of over £77 million to "engage in mining and milling operations in the intermountain west, exclusive of the Pacific Coast." Of these, however, "probably no more than 274 . . . with an aggregate registered capital of £43,127,881, ever became operations." See "When the Pound Sterling went West: British Investments and the American Mineral Frontier," *Journal of Economic History,* Vol. XVI, No. 4 (1956) pp. 482–492.

28 For example, the eminent British economist, James E. Thorold Rogers was a member of the Board of Directors of Crooke's Mining and Smelting Company, but as Spence points out, "time soon proved him much better versed in the history of prices than in Colorado mines and mining companies."

that had been extensively employed in the '20s and '30s to hasten canal building.[29] The method followed was to make free grants of alternate sections (640 acres) along the route of a canal (or railway) to a certain depth on either side of the right of way. Thus, it was as if a railway grant traversed a portion of a checkerboard, and in this swath (say six miles wide) all the black squares were granted to the railway company, while the white squares were retained by the Federal government. The idea underlaying the plan was that the railways, by making it possible for farmers to market their crops, would increase the value of the adjoining land. Profits from the sale of land would, therefore, compensate the railway company for temporarily inadequate revenues from railway traffic. In theory also the government gift conceivably could be cancelled out if the reserved lands (the white squares) were to double in value. There were, however, all manner of complications. Many of the sections had already been sold, making compensatory adjustments necessary; moreover, the scheme failed to provide the railway (or canal) companies with funds at the time when they were most needed, namely during the construction period.

The application of the Federal land-grant subsidy system to railways, which began with the Illinois Central Railroad in 1850,[30] had a stimulating effect on capital imports, and thereby hastened railway construction.[31] For the investor was purchasing not merely shares in a transportation business but an equity in a land company, the value of whose property would presumably increase when the railway was opened to traffic. Unfortunately, the way the system worked did not always conform to the beautiful logic of the plan, since actually it made possible a fantastic amount of inside deals and peculation. But this experiment in using a large part of the nation's natural resources to hasten total national development did constitute one of the boldest

[29] See John B. Rae, "Federal Land Grants in Aid of Canals," *Journal of Economic History*, Vol. IV, No. 2 (1944) pp. 167–178. Altogether some four and a half million acres of land were given away by the Federal government to assist in the building of canals. Although thirty times as much land was ultimately given to encourage railway construction, this ratio ought not to be interpreted to minimize the canal land grants. Many of the railway land grants were of poor quality in the semi-arid great plains, whereas the canal grants were, for the most part, excellent midwest farm land.

[30] For an excellent account of this initial experiment in subsidizing railway building by Federal land grants, see Paul W. Gates, *History of the Illinois Central and Its Colonization Work* (Cambridge, Mass.: Harvard University Press, 1934).

[31] Especially after the Civil War when the transcontinental and other long western railways were built.

attempts ever made to induce foreign capital to migrate to an under-developed area.

Some Contrasts between Capital and Labor Migration

Although European capital moved to the United States largely be-cause of the pervasive influence of market forces, public policy also exerted an influence. Temporary tax exemption of railroads, for ex-ample, might make investment in such enterprises more attractive. On the other hand, when some of the American states defaulted on their public-improvement bonds in the late '30s and early '40s these fiscal policies had a dampening effect on capital movements. Conversely, a decade later, adoption of land-grant aid to railways tended to stimulate the migration of European capital to the United States. It is, therefore, difficult to say just how much influence should be ascribed to public policies and how much to the workings of market forces, but, decade by decade, it would appear that market forces were more influential in luring European capital to America than were the conscious efforts of the framers of public policy.

Can the same be said of immigration? Was it chiefly the differences between European and American wage rates that brought more than 25,000,000 immigrants to the United States during the 19th century? Was it just because able-bodied young men thought they could earn more that they left their homes in Ireland, Germany, Sweden, or Italy and came to Massachusetts, Wisconsin, Minnesota, or California? Or was it the whole pattern of American economic policy—involving such features as the privilege of every person to choose his own occupation, to migrate freely in search of employment, to be exempt from military service, or to acquire property—that was governing? Oppositely, what can one say of the centrifugal forces in Europe? Were they, as was the case for capital, essentially market forces? If relative abundance of capi-tal in Europe lowered interest rates and thereby induced investors to look overseas for higher yields, was it the relative abundance of labor in Europe that lowered (or at least held down) wages and thereby set up corresponding forces stimulating emigration?

Although there are certainly many similarities in the motivation behind capital exports and emigration, there are a number of very important differences. In the case of capital movements two considera-tions are really governing: relative safety of one's investment and the adequacy of the yield. In the case of labor a host of other considerations are involved. The emigrant must leave his ancestral home, his friends, even his family. He must physically relocate himself in a strange environment where customs, language, food, housing, and all other aspects of daily life are different.[32] He must work for unknown employers, at undetermined wages (even if allegedly higher), at unknown tasks, in unfamiliar surroundings. He is, in short, confronted with a whole range of risks and uncertainties. Against these, however, may be set some reasonable probabilities. There is the likelihood that in a country where land is abundant and labor is scarce wages will be higher, annual income greater, and the opportunity to acquire property will be better. Moreover, there was the example of others who had already migrated, who had succeeded in adapting themselves to a new environment, and who wrote glowing letters about the advantage of coming to a dynamic and developing economy.

The Influence of European Public Policy on Emigration

It would be quite inaccurate to assume, however, that all of the Europeans who migrated to the United States did so after making a careful calculation of relative advantages and disadvantages of emigration. Thousands and even millions migrated because of unsatisfactory economic or political circumstances in Europe. To this extent, European public policy acted as a centrifugal force. Take Ireland as just one example. A woeful policy of absentee landlordism and its shameful neglect of intelligent economic development led to conditions of abject poverty. The great bulk of the eight million Irish people in the 1840's literally lived on potatoes alone, largely because a ruthless land-leasing system allowed rapacious landlords (and their resident bailiffs) to deprive their tenants of anything over and above bare subsistence.[33] Virtually no effort was made to diversify agriculture, or to develop fisheries or manufactures. Large areas of the best land were reserved for hunting–preserves for the non-resident landlords. So precarious was the existence of the great mass of people that when a blight attacked

[32] For a graphic account of the psychological and economic hardship that immigrants faced, see Oscar Handlin, *The Uprooted, the Epic Story of the Great Migrations that Made the American People* (Boston: Little Brown & Co., 1951).

[33] The most vivid picture of the hopeless condition of the Irish people in the 1840's is to be found in a novel based squarely on careful historical research. See Cecil Woodham-Smith, *The Reason Why* (London: Constable, 1953), Chap. VI.

the potato fields in 1845 and again in 1846,[34] many hundreds of thousands of people starved to death. In the face of this catastrophe, as many Irish as could crowd on ships migrated to the United States. At least a hundred thousand left for America in 1846 and not until the '90's did the outflow fall below 50,000 a year. Or take the case of the South Germans who fled their homes because they were confronted by an encroachment on their political and economic freedoms. Here again was a centrifugal force originating in short-sighted public policy. Sweden and Denmark could also be cited as illustrating similar expelling policies. Heavy semi-feudal obligations on the peasantry and failure to develop new industries (even though, in Sweden, resources in the form of timber and metals were available) led to a chronic condition of distress which made the decision to migrate a relatively easy one for many Scandinavians.[35]

The short-sightedness of such public policy (or the utter lack of public policy) becomes clearer when one considers what a labor-receiving nation gains from immigration. It is normally the young and able bodied who migrate; "from the earliest records through the eighties of the nineteenth century two-thirds of all immigrants were in the central productive age from 15 to 39."[36] Not a tenth of the immigrants were over 40 years old; thus, people immediately capable of productive effort came, leaving the unproductive children, the aged and the infirm as the responsibility of the labor-releasing country. It is axiomatic that the output of a nation depends on the ratio between the "active population" and the total population. If emigration transfers to an underdeveloped country a labor supply ready to join the active work force, the labor-receiving country is getting a most valuable economic gift from the labor-releasing country. Moreover, emigration is generally a very selective process; the more industrious, energetic and resourceful migrate, whereas the timid, listless, and indifferent remain behind. In consequence, the per-man productivity in an immigrant-receiving country is normally higher than in an emigrant-releasing economy.

34 Actually there were several previous poor crops but the great famine of 1846 was incomparably the worst.

35 "During the half century prior to World War I about a million Swedes emigrated to America. In the 1880s, a decade of agricultural failure, no less than 347,000 left the old country, with a peak of some 100,000 in 1887–88. In most cases it was sheer desperation which drove the Swedes to America and the great Swedish sculptor Carl Milles symbolically depicted this in a monument showing poor Swedes emigrating on the back of a whale." See article entitled "Sweden" in *The Atlantic Monthly*, April, 1957, p. 20.

36 Conrad and Irene B. Tauber, *The Changing Population of the United States* (New York: John Wiley and Sons, 1958), p. 67.

Influence of Market Forces on Labor Migration

Even though there are a host of non-economic factors and an indeterminate number of public-policy considerations that affect human
migration, market forces are probably the most influential. Thus, it was
the prospect of higher wages that brought French Canadians to the
New England textile mills, Italians to the Boston shoe shops, Swedes to
the Jamestown furniture factories, or Germans to the Milwaukee or
Cincinnati machine shops. It was the strong probability that farm
incomes would be greater in Iowa, Wisconsin or Illinois that brought
German, Danish, Swedish or Norwegian immigrants willing to work
as farm hands until they could save enough money to rent or buy farms
of their own. It is said that church bells were rung in villages all over
Germany when news came that Congress had passed the Homestead Act,
making it possible for citizens, whether native or foreign born, to obtain
a quarter section of land (160 acres) at no cost, provided they would
live on the land and improve it. Admittedly this represented a response
to an American public policy which had reduced the price of some land
from $1.25 an acre (which was the pre-Homestead Act selling price) to
zero. Yet the reaction of the prospective homesteaders was a response to
a new market situation; to some persons the difference between a free
quarter section and a farm of equal size costing $200 was apparently
enough to induce them to migrate.

There is, of course, no accurate way whereby historians can evaluate
the motives that lay behind the very personal decisions that millions
of immigrants made. Certain general conclusions can, however, be
reached. Some immigrants were recruited by contractors building canals
or railways, and by mining companies. Here immediate wage differentials rather clearly provided the direct incentive to migration. Many
of these contract laborers did not intend to remain in the United States;
they expected merely to take advantage of short-run employment opportunities, and then decide whether to remain in America or return to
their European (or Asian) homes. In contrast, immigrants who painfully
saved enough money to pay their ocean passage, or who borrowed travel
money from friends or relatives, and who arrived in the United States
without previous employment arrangements constituted a different
category. They were less influenced by immediate wage differentials
than by the long-run opportunities. They did not expect an easy life
in their new homeland, but they did confidently believe that America

had a future, and that they could and would share in this general advance of national prosperity. They looked beyond the immediate market forces, gambling, one might say, on the market forces of the future. A third group consisted of the expellees and refugees, who fled from economic distress (as the Irish did) or from political harassment (as did so many Germans after the ill-fated Revolution of 1848). They came to America not from choice but from necessity; hence, market forces in America had less to do with their migration than circumstantial political and economic factors in Europe. And yet, one may ask, why did they seek refuge in the United States rather than somewhere else in the world? The answer is, of course, that in terms of market forces, our new, developing, increasingly dynamic country seemed to be the best bet!

The immigrants' belief that wages would be higher, or that opportunities in the long run would be better, proved to be not sheer fantasy or wishful thinking but a reality, because the evidence that wages and real earnings were higher in the United States than in Europe (or French Canada) has been clearly established. To some extent, to be sure, these differentials existed because enough labor did not migrate to drive down American wages toward the European levels. It must be recognized, however, that it was not merely the relative scarcity of labor that sustained the comparatively higher level of wages; nor was it the relative abundance of natural resources[37] that automatically influenced the earnings of labor. It was the rate of investment, especially in "social-overhead" or "general-purpose" capital (particularly railways) that brought these resources into the market structure of the economy. Moreover the construction of this widely-dispersed capital equipment created an ever-growing volume of employment capable of absorbing a large share of the domestic and immigrant labor supply. The process was by no means a smooth one; it occurred within a succession of booms and depressions.

The Special Importance of Railways as an Energizing Factor

Yet, despite these cyclical fluctuations, which social capital-building tended to accentuate, it seems likely, as Jenks has so ably pointed out,[38]

---

[37] For generations Canada had vast natural resources in the northern part of the country that had little or no effect on the level of wages.

[38] "Britain and American Railway Development," *Journal of Economic History,* Vol. XI, No. 4 (1951) pp. 375–388; and "Railroads as an Economic Force," *Journal of Economic History,* Vol. IV, No. 1, 1944, pp. 1–21.

that railways more than any other form of investment stimulated and helped transform the American economy. Railways attracted about three-fourths of the total British capital that came to the United States in the seventy-five years before World War I. Admittedly this investment represented only 15 per cent of total American railway capitalization in 1914. It should be noted, however, that American railway promoters (who consistently prevented the British investors from gaining control) ruthlessly and skillfully bloated the total capitalization of railway companies so that the British investors' contributions to the actual cost of railways was far higher than the percentage of total capitalization would indicate. At any rate, foreign investors supplied a sizable share of the funds that went into the American railway system, and without this large volume of capital imports, there would have been, as Jenks has said, "strains upon our international means of payment and upon the internal disposal of our resources, which might have modified in a tangible way the historical contours of our growth." The transfer of those funds, which in some years amounted to half the cost of railway construction, brought real capital into the United States, either in the form of rails or railway iron (some four to five million tons altogether) or in the form of an infinite variety of things that the country could not produce (rubber or tin, for example) or other things that were needed and which the American economy was thereby released from producing.

Yet, it was not merely because railways attracted so predominant a share of capital imports that they exerted such a profound influence on economic development. It was because railways speeded up the rate of exploitation of natural resources, hastened the commercialization of agriculture, augmented the volume of employment, stimulated immigration, extended domestic markets, cheapened the price of outflowing exports (thus increasing foreign demand), raised the value of lands, facilitated regional specialization, increased urbanization, and finally, because they had such a pervasive effect on American business psychology that they, more than any other 19th-century institution, profoundly influenced the economic development of the United States.

Why did the railway have a relatively greater impact on the United States than on Europe? After all it was essentially a British invention and therefore merely one exogenous technical factor transferred to America as a consequence of centrifugal and centripetal market forces. The answer to this question is that a railway in a new country proved to be a somewhat different economic institution from what it was in Great Britain. In an older, more mature industrial country a railway was chiefly a provider of transportation service, connecting deposits of raw materials (such as coal or iron ore) with manufacturing centers, or linking manufacturing centers with import or export points. In America a railway was far more than this. Only a limited number of railways were built to handle existing traffic; most of them were built to generate traffic in the future.

The superiority of the railway as a means of transport, especially over canals, lay in its capacity to overcome (by grades or tunnels) irregularities of terrain. It could link the huge, rich agricultural lands of the combined Ohio and Mississippi river valley system with the eastern seaboard or the Gulf ports. But because American railway builders built their lines in advance of traffic, the whole gigantic business represented something more venturesome and imaginative than contemporaneous railway building in Britain. It was based upon a confident faith that railways would convert empty prairies into "a countryside filled with nodding grain, settlements of industrious families, and other evidences of progress and civilization."[39] More immediately, every railway company reflected the mercenary hopes of promoters who expected to profit from real-estate speculation, from stock market appreciation in the value of railway securities, and from the operating profits of the road as a seller of transportation services. But the total impact of the railway proved to be something far more pervasive and cumulative than a means of increasing the personal incomes of successful promoters or shrewd investors.

Development Effects of a Linear Railway Axis

Unlike a wagon road that can be extended mile by mile, and can be improved gradually as traffic requires (by ballasting, grading, or better bridging), a railroad must be built complete in sizable chunks. In an underdeveloped region, it must be extended far enough to reach some point (such as the confluence of rivers) where there will ultimately be a prospect of attracting enough terminal traffic (or stimulating enough terminal distribution) to justify its construction. As contrasted with a wagon-road system which creates a network of transportation agencies, a railway establishes a linear axis[40] which tends to have polarizing

[39] Jenks, "Railroads as an Economic Force," *Journal of Economic History*, Vol. IV, No. 1 (1944) p. 3.

[40] This subject has been analyzed with rare insight by J. Edwin Holmstrom in his *Railways and Roads in Pioneer Development Overseas* (London: P. S. King and Son, 1934).

economic effects at the extremities (or to a lesser extent at railway-junction points on its axis). The presence of a railway will define, therefore, a spatial configuration more or less in the shape of a dumbbell, within which land values will rise, and business opportunities increase.

The benefits will tend to be greater at the bulbous extremities of this dumbbell configuration. Why will this occur? Assume that a five-hundred-mile railroad has been built between an export-import point (A) and an inland river confluence (B). What can be expected to happen at A and B, respectively? The merchants at A will have a market all along the five-hundred-mile axis plus a terminal market at B (where river, and, presently, road transport lines will radiate still farther afield). Merchants at A can now increase the scale of their operations, becoming regional wholesalers and selling goods (probably in car-load lots) to distributors at junction points or at the railway terminal. They can also buy (again probably in car-load lots) from the whole area served by the railway. Hence, their processing and exporting activities will increase in volume. The effect on manufacturers at A will tend to be of the same nature. Since they now have access to a much larger market, they can increase the scale of their operations, and invest in semi-automatic machinery. The burgeoning of both mercantile and manufacturing operations at A will mean more employment, and the population of A will increase, thus concentrating more consumers in a growing urban center.

At B, the other pole of the railway axis, the effects will be partly the same but somewhat different. Whereas A is a receiving point for primary commodities (grain, meat, hides, furs, timbers or cotton) coming from the area served by the railway, B will tend to be an assembling point for these commodities from the radiating (at first, non-railway) transportation agencies. Stockyards, grain silos, fur companies and similar enterprises will be established at B, and wholesale buyers will enlarge their scale of operations. But soon it will become profitable, in order to minimize shipping costs, to process primary commodities at B in order to reduce the weight of the commodities shipped. Flour mills will, therefore, develop at B, as will slaughterhouses, tanneries, saw mills and other processing industries. Banks will be established because the widening group of enterprises will need bank loans and discounting facilities. Meantime as a terminal distribution point, B will require the services of distributors of commodities it receives from the more developed regions with which it is now connected by rail. B will also develop railway maintenance and repair shops, wagon factories, general purpose machine shops, and a range of other industries. From this genetic process it can be seen how and why the railway stimulated the growth of "cities in the wilderness," in marked contrast to a wagon-road system of transport, which merely tended to proliferate the village economy of the Colonial Period variety.

The transforming effect of railways will not be confined to the poles of a linear axis; at every important junction point (where rivers, canals or other railways feed in traffic to the longer railway axis) a differentiation of economic activity, and a tendency to enlarge the scale of mercantile, processing, and manufacturing activities will occur. At each such junction point will emerge greater opportunities for investments in specialized plant and equipment. Yet by reason of the swift and cheap transportation which the railway provides, these urban centers can be further apart and better situated; and can avail themselves of better locational advantages derived from water power, superior resources, or better marketing facilities. Inland manufacturing centers can, therefore, develop, progressively challenging the previous quasi-monopoly of seaboard cities. It can be seen, then, that a railway can have concentrating effects on some industries (e.g. meat packing or flour milling) and a dispersing effect on others (e.g. furniture making, metalworking, or brewing). Meantime, by providing efficient, swift, transportation services to areas that could not before, because of topography, be served by rivers or canals, the railway increases the value of adjacent land in relation to its nearness to the transportation axis or to the emerging urban centers, which the railroad has brought into existence.

It was, therefore, the polarizing influence of railways that expanded seaboard cities such as Boston, New York, Philadelphia, Charleston, Savannah, or Mobile (the *A* type cities) and inland urban centers such as Buffalo, Cleveland, Chicago, Peoria, Cincinnati, or St. Louis (the *B* type cities) while the stimulating influence of railways on junction points may be illustrated by the growth of Harrisburg, Akron, South Bend, or Kewanee. The whole pattern of American development changed within thirty years after the building of America's first railway.

Effect of Railway Building on Employment and Business Activity

The construction of these ever-lengthening lines of railways created a strong, persistent demand for lumber, stone, rails, and iron products; for land, not merely as right of way but for subsurface coal deposits;

for manpower to build the railways; and for horses, mules, scrapers, and tools. These factors of production had to be combined; this meant that a whole new area of activity opened up for railway promoters, contractors, and a large group of specialists, ranging from surveyors or lawyers, to butchers, bakers, cooks or interpreters. It was railway building that created jobs for thousands of immigrants, and which "disciplined migratory or local labor power to cooperative industrial effort."[41]

Where did all the money come from if not more than half in any year and if only a sixth or a seventh of the total investment came from overseas? Some of it was obtained from *bona fide* savings of Americans, but a much larger share came, directly or indirectly, from bank loans. Armed with money funds, however acquired, the railway builders could then buy rails, lumber, or other structural materials; purchase any land they did not receive free from municipalities, counties, states, or the Federal government; and hire the mule skinners and laborers who formed the construction gangs. By competing for building materials, tools, animals, and labor, the railway builders bid up the prices for all these factors of production, and to the extent that other buyers had to reduce their purchases (as a consequence of higher prices) railway building resulted in an indeterminate amount of involuntary saving. Thus, by market processes, the necessary[42] amount of real resources were channeled into social capital formation. Meantime, a whole range of incomes were enlarged. The immediate effects of railway construction were an increase in wage payments to construction workers, and an enlargement of profits to lumber merchants or iron manufacturers. Next came secondary effects as a growing demand for construction materials increased the demand for manpower for felling timber, quarrying stone, or mining iron ore or coal. In the process, the whole national economy was vitalized; total employment increased, and more spending for consumer goods and capital goods occurred.

Railways had further effects. They led to a succession of derivative innovations. New financial techniques came into use, designed to adapt railway securities to many types of investors, at home or abroad; stock-exchange facilities expanded, simplifying and facilitating the pooling of money funds; new and highly specialized investment banking firms

---

[41] Jenks, "Railroads as an Economic Force" p. 6

[42] "Necessary" has a rather unprecise meaning in this context. For the amount of resources devoted to railway building was not determined by any over-all social plan but decided upon by railway promoters acting in conjunction with self-appointed civic groups whose activities are described on p. 189.

were established to act as intermediaries between lenders and borrowers. The example of the railway led also to emulative mechanical progress. Coal mine owners devised new types of bunkers and elevators to speed up the loading of railway cars; grain elevators rose up on the flat midwest horizon, capable of filling grain cars swiftly by gravity flow. Heavier railway locomotives called for sturdier bridges, and led to drastic changes in the design and structure of trusses and piers. Tunnel cutting required more and better explosives; while the safe movement of increasing traffic on single lines led to the devising of better signalling equipment. Presently, it was the railway system that adopted and spread the influence of the telegraph. Meantime, the enlarged scale of manufacturing operations, which railways steadily stimulated, required more factory equipment, and led to a search for better plant layout and to the adoption of more semi-automatic machinery. Railways demonstrated that initially heavy fixed costs can bring about low unit prices provided plant and equipment are well utilized. The example did not go unnoticed by other businessmen; they too were realizing that output was a function of the productivity of each worker, and that the output of each man depended upon the amount of tools and equipment with which he worked!

Governmental Responsibility for Public Improvements

As the American frontier moved westward, there emerged an amorphous general theory of economic development which, although never formally systematized or expounded, had a profound effect upon the American economy. Unlike a body of abstract theory that often has no influence, this was sometimes discussed in state legislatures, explained in newspapers, debated in lecture halls, and, in varying ways put into practice. One is tempted to say that it was not the great thinkers but the small politicians who rounded out this early 19th-century American theory by experimenting with actual programs of regional and national economic development. For the loosely knit set of ideas which lay behind these programs never hardened into dogmatic theory, nor was a unified national plan ever laid before Congress. Yet for all that, a concept of economic development slowly took form, and gradually became an article of faith. It was a curious blend of Hamiltonian protectionism,[43] the Carey-Clay emphasis on the need for developing national pro-

---

[43] This ingredient varied sectionally. Thus it was an essential part in New England, an important one in the Midwest, but almost uniformly rejected in the South.

ductive powers, and an insistence that one of the basic responsibilities of government (local, state, or Federal) was to increase the nation's social capital. Because it was never formally systematized, this constellation of ideas is hard to describe, even though its influence on the economic history of America was pervasive, cumulative, and lasting. We must, therefore, try to explain the essential elements of this rather nebulous body of political and economic thought.

It sprang out of the American environment, originating not in one man's mind but in many men's minds; not in one place but in thousands of places. Every frontier farmer realized that his income could increase and the value of his land would rise if transportation facilities were made available; every furniture maker, toolmaker or coal mine owner recognized the advantage of more consumers for his furniture, hardware or coal; every artisan, doctor, lawyer or merchant understood that his wages, fees, or profits would increase if his community became more prosperous. But there was general agreement that really prosperous communities cannot be expected to exist as oases in underdeveloped regions; that development must be something essentially organic because community prosperity is a function of regional development, and regional progress inseparable from national economic progress.

By a long, historical process, older, long-populated countries had provided themselves with roads, canals, hospitals, schools, and other forms of social capital—with banks and credit-supplying institutions. In a new country, such as the United States (blessed though it was with wide stretches of rich land, great stands of valuable timber and vast mineral wealth) these essential elements were lacking. How were they to be provided? Although a few toll roads might be built between large cities, no one could expect private businessmen to build roads from the Atlantic seaboard to the headwaters of the Ohio River. But since everyone would gain if roads, canals, railways, bridges, or docks were constructed, was it not logical that everyone should help create this necessary social capital? Governments should, therefore, set in motion programs of public improvements because only governments would have the ability to borrow the large amounts of money which these regional improvements would involve.

But government, being no wiser than the elected representatives who compose it, ought not attempt to assume the total responsibility for such an important task. Judicious businessmen and other men of knowledge and experience should be called upon to contribute managerial direction and capital. Indeed, wherever possible, private men of affairs should plan the desired improvements and should be assisted, to whatever extent necessary, by local, state and Federal governments. A proper development program, therefore, called not for socialistic provision of public works, but for a "mixed" scheme of things comprising government subsidies, land grants and loans, conjoined with private capital contributions and, ultimately, private management.

Internal improvements were regarded as the essential keys to total, national, economic development, since only by roads, canals, and (after the 1830's) by railways could dependable markets for the products of farms, forests and mines be ensured; only thereby could factories achieve economies of scale (even given the benefits of tariff protection); and only after a minimally necessary amount of social capital had come into being would there emerge a "favorable climate" for investments in American enterprise by foreigners. Following this set of principles, most public improvements were planned and built before there was enough traffic to justify their construction,[44] it being the basic premise that these transportation facilities would result in enough economic growth in the areas into which they were extended that the canals, roads, or railways would themselves create a volume of traffic, and thereby generate the revenues necessary to amortize their cost. As a general rule the thesis was a sound one, more so for railways than canals (even though some railways gravely disappointed the hopes of their promoters). But it is easy to understand why there would be some mistakes in building transportation facilities into underdeveloped regions; the remarkable thing is that this experiment in "constructive liberalism"[45] worked as well as it did. New roads, canals, and especially railways spearheaded the movement of population into the West, and thereby increased land values, widened markets for factory products, and opened up new opportunities for local merchants, manufacturers, craftsmen, lawyers, doctors, commissionhouses, and a host of minor specialists ranging from auctioneers or veterinarians to livery stable operators and hotel keepers.

Governmental Participation in Economic Development: The Example of the Southern Railways

For rather inscrutable reasons every culture develops a set of myths. Some are deliberately invented to intensify national confidence and

[44] Except for a limited number of seaboard canals and railways.
[45] See Milton Health's splendid book by this title cited on p. 187.

solidarity; others emerge without such artificial stimulus. Of the latter variety perhaps the most cherished myth of the American people is the widespread belief that once upon a time there existed an "age of *laissez faire*," when economic progress depended almost entirely on private enterprise; and when the economic role of government was limited to maintaining law and order, insuring the faithful fulfillment of contracts, interfering only very modestly through the taxing power with the distribution of income. There is a good deal of half-truth in these cherished beliefs, for it was private enterprise that gave vitality and drive to American economic development. But it is quite incorrect to allege that government did little more than oversee and police the workings of a private enterprise system. Careful studies of the relations between government and private enterprise in Massachusetts,[46] Pennsylvania,[47] Georgia,[48] and Missouri[49] during the period from 1800 to 1860 reveal an astonishing range and variety of governmental economic intervention. Some of this state action was restrictive, forbidding or limiting certain business activities. Thus, for the most part, only persons who obtained charters could engage in banking, and only those who were duly licensed could carry on certain types of business. Conversely, government gave assistance to particular businessmen, groups of businessmen, farmers, merchants, and manufacturers, by means of land grants, loans, grants of money, tax exemptions, or subsidies. Indeed, the range and variety of government assistance was so great that despite the indefatigable labor of historians we will probably never be able to measure the contributions which were made to American economic progress by the combined assistance of Federal, state, and local governments. The important thing to appreciate is that the dramatic economic development that did occur was the consequence of a pragmatic and highly flexible interlocking of private enterprise and governmental assistance.

Some idea of the extent of this cooperation between government and private enterprise can be obtained from the careful research of Professor

[46] Oscar Handlin, *Commonwealth: A Study of the Role of Government in the American Economy, Massachusetts, 1774–1861* (New York: New York University Press, 1947).

[47] Louis Hartz, *Economic Policy and Democratic Thought, Pennsylvania, 1776–1860* (Cambridge, Mass.: Harvard University Press, 1948).

[48] Milton Heath, *Constructive Liberalism, The Role of the State in Economic Development in Georgia to 1860* (Cambridge, Mass.: Harvard University Press, 1954).

[49] James Neal Primm, *Economic Policy in the Development of a Western State, Missouri, 1820–1860* (Cambridge, Mass.: Harvard University Press, 1954).

Milton Heath on the history of railroads in the South.[50] He has shown that at least 55 per cent of the cost of all the railroads built before 1861 (in Georgia, North Carolina, South Carolina, Virginia, Alabama, Arkansas, Florida, Louisiana, Mississippi, Kentucky and Tennessee) was defrayed by the combined contributions of Federal, state, municipal and county governments. Indeed, he believes that if adequate consideration were given to the failure of private investors to pay the full amount of their stock subscriptions, if the value of the services of governmental officials and civil engineers were included as cost factors, and if money values were assigned to tax exemption and to the reinvestment of earnings arising from initial governmental investments, the total contribution of government would be much higher than 55 per cent. In short, as far as the southern railways are concerned (and it is only for these that we have any trustworthy figures) it was government rather than private enterprise which provided the major part of the total investment.

Which branch of government contributed the most? Federal, state or local? Of the $144,000,000 of public expenditures on railway construction in the South before 1861, over 56 per cent was contributed by state governments, 26 per cent by municipalities, almost 13 per cent by county governments, and less than 5 per cent by the Federal government.[51] The outstanding feature of this public effort at capital formation was, as Heath has said, "the all-pervasiveness of the movement, not only among the individual states, but also among the various levels of government." The Federal government's contribution chiefly took the form of land grants;[52] state, municipal, and county governments, on the other hand, purchased railway securities outright and thus provided the railway companies with money funds. In addition they also gave many other forms of assistance ranging from right-of-way grants of land to tax exemptions. Meantime the Federal government remitted tariff duties on imported rails, and other railway iron; assigned army engineers to make the railway surveys; and, in some instances,

50 See his "Public Railway Construction and the Development of Private Enterprise in the South Before 1861" in *The Tasks of Economic History*, (Supplemental issue of *The Journal of Economic History*, Vol. X, 1950) pp. 40–53.

51 The percentages varied widely. Thus, in the southeast states, the Federal contribution was less than 1 per cent whereas in some of the Gulf states it exceeded 30 per cent. In Kentucky, municipal plus county governments accounted for over 95 per cent of public investment; whereas in North Carolina, state contributions were 89 per cent of the total governmental investments.

52 In the post-Civil War period Federal land grants became far more important than they were before the war. See pp. 338–39.

allowed army officers to supervise the actual construction of railways.[53]

What becomes of the myth of *laissez faire* if studies such as Heath's show that perhaps as much as two-thirds of the cost of building the nation's general-purpose capital equipment was borne by government? Should we conclude that it was the foresight of public officials that led to social capital formation and that businessmen constituted only an acquiescing minority? Heath's study shows that the pressure for public investment in railways came chiefly from towns and cities that hoped to benefit from an extension of transport facilities. In such cities and towns was normally to be found "a common leadership," consisting of a group of men who were at the same time the leading businessmen, the heads of civic organizations, and the elected local officials. They did not constitute an oligarchy; instead they "followed strictly democratic processes" by holding public discussions of their quasi-public, quasi-private projects. By such methods, then, was the support of municipal and county governments obtained. The next step was for the leaders of such community groups to consolidate their lobbying strength in state capitals in order to persuade the state legislators (most of whom belonged to the "common leadership") to authorize state contributions to the railway projects. In the same manner, the requests for Federal assistance were carried to Washington by those members of the "common leadership" who were elected Senators and Representatives.

In such a context it is rather difficult to draw sharp lines between the private and the public sectors of the economy. Economic development definitely required public improvements. Businessmen, farmers, lawyers, or doctors could supply some of the funds. But government, by reason of its credit and taxing power, could borrow (mostly from foreign lenders) at lower interest rates than private railway companies could. Moreover, government could exercise the right of eminent domain to compel landowners to sell land for railway right of ways, and it could exempt the railway companies temporarily from taxation, and give many other forms of assistance. Nor did it seem unfair that the taxing power of government should be used to hasten economic development. Everyone would benefit in some way from better transportation; and taxation seemed the fair way to compel "those who would benefit in common with others but who would not subscribe privately"[54] to make some contribution to the stock of social capital.

[53] This aspect of governmental assistance has been described by Forrest G. Hill. See his "Government Engineering Aid to Railways before the Civil War" in *The Journal of Economic History*, Vol. XI, No. 3 (1951), pp. 235–246.

[54] Heath, p. 45.

Yet even though government may have paid for a major part of America's canals, railways or port facilities, there seems to have been very little support for public ownership of such public utilities. Instead the American scheme of things favored the "mixed corporation" in which private management tended to predominate even though government investment might overshadow private investment. Public assistance was viewed as something temporary and developmental. Once a railway could operate profitably, it was argued that the whole enterprise should be turned over to private business. This should not be construed as a reflection of governmental solicitude for private business. Business groups, who had persuaded governments to help them finance speculative but promising ventures, hoped to seize control over the railways should they prove profitable, whereas if the projects proved unprofitable, they were quite content to let government bear the risk of loss. It must also be recognized that neither local, state, nor Federal government was capable of administering such complex business organizations as railways. Local government (and, indeed, state government) was only a part-time task of its personnel. Bureaucracy, for better or worse, was in its infancy. As a result, governments exerted very little influence on the management of railways even in those cases where they had supplied a predominant share of the initial investment. Only when a canal or railway venture proved to be unprofitable did government find itself the hapless manager of an enterprise which the business promoters had deserted.[55]

Basic Elements in American Developmental Policy

One of the remarkable achievements of the Constitutional Convention was the agreement reached whereby the constituent states of the Federal union ceded[56] their claims to western land to the central government, thus providing it with a public domain which it could dispose of for fiscal purposes, or which it could use to hasten the economic development of the nation. This public domain was dramatically increased by the purchase of Louisiana, further enlarged by Mexican cessions following the Mexican war, and still further increased by subsequent cessions

55 As railways superseded canals, and proved themselves a more efficient and more profitable means of transportation, private investors often abandoned their canal management rights and responsibilities, leaving government to operate and maintain the unprofitable canals.

56 Except for some reserved acreages.

and purchases. In Congress a long and often bitter dispute arose over the question of how the public domain should be used. Gradually the idea that the government should only sell its land lost favor in Congress, and presently there emerged, as a basic American policy, the idea that some of the public domain should be alienated by the Federal government to hasten economic development.[57]

Protection of nascent industries from foreign competition by tariffs constitutes a second basic element in American developmental policy. Hotly debated because of the contrasting views of North and South, this policy could not be consistently or emphatically put into operation. But, despite southern opposition, protection did become an integral part of public policy, and it is the mature judgment of economic historians that tariffs did stimulate some capital formation and hasten industrialization. Protection, however, was not an unmixed blessing to the American people; in some instances it meant that costs of consumer goods were considerably higher than they otherwise would have been. Duties which should have been reduced, once "infant industries" had become mature, often became semi-permanent, thus giving some American industries a quasi-monopolistic power over domestic markets.

Public assistance to private business ventures and actual public investment in some ventures represents a third basic element in American development policy. Like protection, this form of governmental subvention was viewed as a necessary but temporary expedient. Yet, although it was short-lived in particular ventures, public assistance became a permanent part of American policy. In one form or another it was used throughout the seventy-five years that witnessed the building of the American railway network. Meantime shipping subsidies, land-reclamation projects, and, presently, vast governmental expenditures for road building continued the idea of government investment in the nation's social capital.

Yet despite these persistent manifestations of public participation in economic development, the predilection of the American people has consistently been for leaving the planning of economic development largely to private initiative; consequently, as Carter Goodrich has said,[58] "the United States achieved its massive economic development without over-all economic planning, without five-year plans of explicit national targets of income and output." How then was it achieved? Part

[57] For a further explanation of American land policy, see pp. 337–38.
[58] "American Development Policy: The Case of Internal Improvements," *Journal of Economic History,* Vol. XVI, No. 4 (1956) p. 449.

of the answer has been given in this chapter which has tried to describe various measures which government employed to promote economic growth. This, however, is only part of the whole picture. In some of the chapters in Part III we will examine the private sectors of the economy, and appraise the more important market mechanisms which were concurrently responsible for the persistent growth and the progressive transformation of the American economy.

The Beginning of a Process of Economic Transformation

By the middle of the 19th century at least five major changes in the American economy were setting in motion a process of economic transformation so far-reaching that the fundamental pattern of the economy which had taken shape in the pre-1790 era was being basically altered. Sociologically, this transformation was made possible because Americans were resourceful, energetic, venturesome, self-confident, and, above all, extremely ambitious. But since all these personal qualities had been fostered in the Colonial period, we must try to ascertain what new factors began to affect the workings of the economy in the 1830's, 40's and 50's, and which led to the beginnings of a genuine transformation of the whole economy. What were these emergent factors?

The first was indisputably the improvement of technology and the extended use of mechanical equipment.[59] The steady increase in the amount and the variety of tools and equipment used both in industry and agriculture was a consequence of an accelerated rate of American invention and innovation, the relative scarcity of labor, and the greater availability of capital, whether from capital imports or domestic saving. At any rate, after a late start, technological progress advanced so rapidly in a number of branches of American manufacturing that competent British visitors not only readily admitted that some American techniques of factory production were superior to European methods, but also went so far as to warn their countrymen that they would have to copy these more efficient methods if they hoped to keep pace with the Americans.

A second main change was a partial reorientation of the pattern of trade. The "home-market" proposal, advanced by Hamilton, Clay and Carey, was no longer a theory but an emerging reality. Admittedly exports of raw cotton, wheat, flour, lard, meat, hides, timber products, and many other primary goods still constituted a very large share of the nation's total trade. But American cotton mills, wool mills, shoe

[59] This subject will be analyzed in detail in Chap. 8.

factories, and furniture factories were consuming a steadily rising volume of raw materials; while steel mills, copper and brass foundries, and machine shops were processing a growing quantity of ferrous and nonferrous metals.

Mass marketing, though not yet typical, was becoming more common for light manufactured products such as clocks, scales, yard goods, or builders' hardware. Even furniture making, long a craft industry, was adopting factory techniques, making it possible for carload lots of standardized chairs and tables to be sold as markets widened when railways commercialized more frontier farms and, concurrently, enlarged the urban population. Retail stores were growing larger and carrying a wider range of commodities, and presently dazzling department stores would tempt more buyers to prefer the precision-made products of factories to the custom-made goods of small manufacturers.

These changes in production and marketing methods could occur because of a third major change, namely the unprecedented increase in population which was a consequence of high domestic birth rates and the increasing inflow of immigrants. Population growth almost always imparts vitality to an economy which possesses varied and ample natural resources, but in new countries the formation of new families tends to have a relatively greater stimulating effect because the new families cannot depend, as they partly can in older countries, on accumulated durable goods such as housing, or on stocks of such semidurable goods as furniture, bedding, kitchen equipment, tools or vehicles. A new country has very limited supplies of such equipment to share with a younger generation, and far less to share with incoming immigrants. Population growth therefore gave a pronounced fillip to a whole group of industries, ranging from stove founding, carpet manufacturing or glass blowing, to buggy building, harness making or tool manufacturing. Moreover, a passion for ultimately owning one's own house came to dominate the minds of both native-born and immigrant young people, intensifying their will to work (thereby increasing national output) and their incentive to save (thereby increasing the nation's stock of capital).

A fourth major change was the redistribution of the nation's manpower among industries and among occupations. More than any other single institution, the railways brought this about by facilitating regional specialization and commercialization of agriculture, making it possible for farmers to invest in labor-saving tools and equipment. Workers released from agriculture could now become factory workers, merchants, lawyers, investment bankers, doctors, or business executives in the rapidly-growing cities. Not every outstanding American business-man was born on a farm, but more of the great entrepreneurs were country born than city born; not because the discipline of doing farm chores made men diligent, or contact with nature made them wise, but simply because there were more young men on farms than in cities, and as new opportunities emerged country boys seized them.

A fifth change, already suggested in our appraisal of the energizing effects of railway building, may be described as a progressive emphasis upon social, or general-purpose, capital formation. This important aspect of economic development had been relatively neglected in the Colonial period for two reasons. In the first place no unified economy existed; the colonies were a cluster of satellites with more ties with the mother country than with one another. Lacking any organic political unity, they could not be expected to devote much of their resources or labor to creating a stock of social capital serviceable to the total colonial economy. In the second place the colonies had been oriented eastward, and hence whatever social capital they did create was primarily designed to facilitate the import-export trade rather than to enlarge the volume of domestic trade. With economic unification came a realization that more emphasis would have to be placed on social capital formation. Yet not until after the War of 1812, and really not until after the delayed and severe post-war crisis of 1819, was there a clear realization that the safety and prosperity of the United States depended upon the systematic development of the resources of the land mass. The Jack-sonian political revolution revealed that the West had become a pow-erful factor in American politics, and warned that the backwoodsmen would insist that their interests be given adequate consideration in the pattern of national economic policy. An era of canal building followed, a buoyant, hopeful episode in social capital formation, blemished, un-fortunately, by the reckless speculative boom it engendered and limited by the technical shortcomings of canals as adequate means for develop-ing the West. Soon, however, in the railroad was found the proper instrumentality for resolving the problem of economic unification and for stepping up the tempo of economic development.

The Interplay of Public Policy and Market Forces

After the Age of Jackson, it took no clairvoyance to appreciate that the United States had a tremendous economic growth potential. Aside from one great political issue, for which unfortunately no peaceful solution could be found, the entire nation was becoming more integrated and economically unified. The problem of the relations between government and private enterprise had been resolved not by some artificial definition of boundaries but by an empirical, flexible program of co-operation that varied from one context to another. The general principle underlying this "mixed system" was that it was the responsibility of a democratic government to use some of its resources, some of its credit, and some of its personnel to hasten the creation of social capital whenever such capital formation promised to improve the well-being of large segments of the population.

But it was no less firmly believed that private enterprise should be given the maximum possible scope and range. For, despite the predisposition to let the government help private enterprise, there was only limited sentiment for governmental restraint on business, or for intervention on behalf of the poor, the aged, the unfortunate or the out-bargained.[60] Market forces were presumed to bring about automatically an adequate measure of economic justice. Yet it was becoming increasingly evident that this presumed distributive justice was often more fanciful than real. Railways had it in their power to jeopardize the incomes of farmers by raising freight rates, and employers could bring distress to hundreds of people by summarily laying off wage earners who sought to bargain collectively for higher wages. Unscrupulous security salesmen could filch the savings of unsuspecting people by selling them worthless stocks or bonds. All these evils and many others were not to be corrected for a long time; not until, by a slow process, organized centers of resistance could develop, and not until a revised view of the rôle of government gradually took form.

Such then was the economic system of the United States that was taking form in the early national era. Unusually dynamic because of the richness and variety of American resources, and because of the drive and ambition of the American people, it was a ruthless and aggressive system. There seemed little doubt but that it would insure further growth of the American economy, although it seemed probable that this growth would come not gradually and smoothly but by periodic booms, separated by periods of "hard times." Nonetheless it was an economic instrumentality which contained within itself the power to transform the economy progressively. Just how it has continued to do

60 There was some; for details see Chap. 13.

this, we must now try to explain by analyzing the major sectors of the American economy one by one. Only after we have done this, can we hazard any opinions about the over-all historical performance of our unique American system of economic organization.

Part III HOW MORE EFFICIENT

ECONOMIC INSTITUTIONS AND

PRODUCTIVE METHODS WERE

DEVELOPED AND PERFECTED

IN THE

19TH AND 20TH CENTURIES

8

The improvement and

extension of technology

How the Character of the American People Influenced Technological Progress

The United States emerged from the Colonial period as an under-developed economy with small-scale agriculture and little manufacturing, dependent for much of its consumer goods and capital equipment on what could be imported from abroad. Less than two centuries later, the American economy had become a vast producer of goods and services, possessing a capital-generating mechanism capable not only of supplying its own investment requirements but also of compensating for many of the capital deficiencies of the rest of the world.[1] This

---

[1] See a recent, superior study by W. Paul Strassman, *Risk and Technological Innovation* (Ithaca, N.Y.: Cornell University Press, 1959).

remarkable transformation was to a great extent the consequence of technological progress, a complicated, many-sided movement that comprehends the substitution of natural energy for human exertion; the mechanization of industry, transportation, and agriculture; the standardization of equipment through the development of machine tools and precision instruments; and the development of mass production by means of specialization, division of labor, and scientific management. In short, technological progress means the application of the analytic methods of science to the industrial arts. We shall explain how these elements of technological progress developed chronologically; but before we do so, it will be necessary to indicate why technological progress took place relatively faster in the United States than in other countries.

The United States today has all the requisites for a thriving economy. With a vast land area, rich natural resources, an efficient labor force, resourceful entrepreneurs, ambitious farmers, and with markets knit together by the marvels of modern transportation and communication, it would be strange indeed if the United States were not a mammoth economy. But it must be remembered that this was not always the case. At the end of the 18th century the United States was just beginning to exploit its land and natural resources; its population was still sparse, its capital scarce, and its transportation facilities primitive. At the time of the Constitutional Convention, all these obstacles to economic growth seemed to portend a slow economic development. Indeed, immediately after the Revolution, Lord Sheffield had written an impressive book, prophesying that the States would have a very gloomy future because of the lack of labor, textile fibres, and machinery. The American character, however, was not attuned to accepting this pessimistic prospect, and it is in the American character that we can find one major explanation for the speed of American technological development.

No doubt the scarcity and high cost of labor would have impelled American producers to resort to machinery at every opportunity, and no doubt European experience would have offered many suggestions on how to acquire the machinery. But this is by no means an adequate or satisfactory explanation of American technological progress. The growth of the American capitalistic system has its peculiar psychological roots. Vigorous economic development always requires that men have within themselves a desire for economic progress, and from the beginning, the American character has reflected this psychological drive.

Unhampered by institutions, such as those of the medieval church or the feudal system, that placed considerable emphasis on non-economic objectives, the American culture tended to emphasize personal success, better standards of living, and the progressive improvement of one's material well-being. To increase production, improve the quality and variety of goods, and encourage consumption of the things desired for man's use and enjoyment were, in many respects, life's most important objectives. Nor were Americans handicapped by self-doubt in following these objectives. Most of the time they exhibited a superb optimism and a sometimes naïve confidence in their ability to control nature and to construct and manipulate machines. In reply to Sheffield, Alexander Hamilton said that there was "in the genius of the people of this country a peculiar aptitude for mechanical improvements." And so there was; in the American environment, businessmen used machines at every opportunity, and, in contrast to European workers, the American labor force was both eager to utilize labor-saving devices and adept in the use of tools.

Thus far, we have been explaining technological progress as though it were nothing more than a state of mind. But it would be a sorry mistake to ascribe the rapid trend toward industrialization that occurred in the United States to psychological factors alone. Technological progress required something more than desire and the right frame of mind. It also required innovative entrepreneurs, a mass market, and an adequate supply of capital. Mass production required mass consumption, and mass consumption required a demanding people and adequate transportation facilities to bring goods from producers to consumers. All these were rapidly forthcoming in the years before the Civil War. A constantly declining mortality rate and a relatively high birth rate, together with waves of immigration from abroad, made it possible for population to double every twenty-three years. Moreover, this was a young population with a high propensity to consume, that is, with an intense desire for things. The voluminous demand which they exerted made it possible for manufacturers to add new capital in the form of tools, machines, and equipment continuously, without scrapping the old. This called for more capital funds to pay the costs of "tooling up" for mass production. These funds came from individual savers, from foreign capitalists, from the transfer of fortunes built up in foreign trade and shipping, and from commercial banks, which began to grow sensationally during and after the War of 1812. Meanwhile transportation facilities were being built as fast as the young nation could build them. Turnpikes and canals appeared in great profusion in the first thirty years of the century and railroads even more spectacularly after

1830. It was against this background that the United States experienced its remarkable technological progress.

Early Efforts to Improve Technology

In 1800 more than four-fifths of the American population was engaged in agriculture or in other rural tasks. A great deal of farming was of the self-sufficient type, and the average farmer used practically the same implements as his British predecessors of the 14th century. The typical plow was crude and awkward, the sickle was of ancient invention, the flail had not been changed since Biblical days, and even the cradle, clumsy as it was, was a rarity. The average farmer paid little attention to proper techniques of animal husbandry, and was either ignorant or contemptuous of scientific farming. The system was typified by the "old oaken bucket that hung in the well," romantic perhaps to look back upon, but to the economist it represented the inefficiency and limited productivity of a system based primarily on human energy and the slow-moving tractive power of oxen.

Industry was not very different. To be sure, there were scattered throughout the colonies fairly sizable flour mills, breweries, distilleries, sugar refineries, and other processing industries, which used somewhat advanced mechanical equipment and division of labor; but aside from wood-working shops, there was no such thing as a factory; that is, a power-driven plant that fabricated material, by the use of machinery, from the raw state to the finished product.

Surprisingly enough, the colonies had produced one-seventh of the world's iron production, but this amounted to only 30,000 tons;[2] and even though the iron industry was the basic heavy industry at that time, it was organized on a small-scale rural basis, the average mill operating for no more than 20 or 30 weeks of the year. Iron ore was smelted in small blast furnaces, using charcoal for fuel. The fires were kept roaring by bellows and blowing cylinders. When a furnace cooled, a small amount of cast iron congealed in hollows scooped out on the sand floor. These "pigs" of crude and impure iron were then refined by innumerable heatings and interminable beatings under a water-driven trip hammer. The resulting product, known as "merchant bar" was sold through country stores to blacksmiths, and to other fabricators of such finished goods as horseshoes, nails, tools, and miscellaneous hardware.

[2] Carl Bridenbaugh, *Cities in Revolt* (New York: Alfred A. Knopf, Inc., 1956), p. 268.

For the most part, then, ironmaking and other types of manufacturing were still conducted as very small-scale industries on a household or handicraft basis. This was not because a considerable portion of the American public was not eager to encourage industry and manufacturing, for they certainly were. The will to manufacture existed long before efficient methods were actually started. Quite early, strenuous efforts were made to stimulate an industrial consciousness, and in these efforts, Americans fully exploited their peculiar gift for forming associations, but mostly to no avail.[3] The difficulty lay in the fact that ambitions far exceeded the means of satisfying them. Many of the things that we take for granted today were unheard of in 1776. This was especially true of machine tools, which constitute the very foundation of industrial technology. Watt's steam engine and Arkwright's water frame were already in existence in England, and, as we have already seen,[4] Crompton was developing his spinning mule. But the only equipment the mechanics who worked on these machines had were such simple hand tools as hammers, chisels, and files. The only measuring devices were simple calipers and wooden rules. Although hand forging was fairly well advanced, metal-cutting appliances were still replicas of the tools of the Middle Ages.

The Pioneers in Textile Manufacture

By the middle of the 19th century, the state of mechanical arts had changed considerably. Even as early as the War of 1812, a good deal of the pioneering work had been done, and the United States was poised for industrial growth. The logical place to start was the textile industry. southern plantations could supply adequate quantities of cheap raw materials; capital requirements were relatively small; and demand was great, because cotton textiles were low-priced necessities that could be standardized. But Americans fully appreciated that, because of an early start, England had a technological superiority in textile manufacture. They understood that this superiority could only be overcome by borrowing Britain's technology. The early American industrial consciousness was, therefore, directed toward transferring the basic technical features of industrialism from Britain to New England, where

[3] See Samuel Reznck, "The Rise and Development of Industrial Consciousness in the United States, 1760–1830," *Journal of Economic and Business History,* Vol. IV, No. 4, 1932.

[4] See pp. 83–85.

Yankee ingenuity, adequate water power, and a soil too poor for really prosperous agriculture promised to provide a favorable environment for manufacturing. To transplant English methods was not, however, a simple task, for Great Britain, from the beginning of the industrial revolution and up to 1845, took great pains to prevent the export of machines, models, or plans, and forbade the emigration of skilled artisans who might transplant technical knowledge. Yet this dam could not hold back the tide of industrialism, and certainly could not prevent the latent inventiveness of Americans from emulating the British technicians. Moreover, English workmen came to America, and with their aid American entrepreneurs constructed and put into operation new kinds of textile machinery. Many of the early attempts were unsuccessful, mostly for lack of skilled labor. Toward the end of the 18th century, however, Samuel Slater, an Englishman who had worked in one of Arkwright's factories, learned that prizes and bounties were being offered in the United States for information concerning the construction of textile machinery. He sailed secretly, and soon after his arrival (helped by a prosperous American merchant, Moses Brown) he built from memory a copy of Arkwright's water frame and set up a small enterprise to spin cotton yarn, an event which Alexander Hamilton announced with great pride in his 1791 *Report on Manufactures*. Soon thereafter, two Yorkshire immigrants, the Scholfield brothers, introduced machine carding in American woollen textile manufacture.

Encouraged by these beginnings, a Bostonian, Francis Cabot Lowell, travelling through Great Britain in 1811, made a painstaking study of English textile manufacturing machinery. Upon his return to the United States, he and other versatile and resourceful New England businessmen determined to shift part of their fortunes (which they had built up from the profits of ocean shipping) into manufacturing. Lowell enlisted the help of Paul Moody, an able mechanic, and together they developed, by 1814, workable textile machinery. Lowell contributed whatever he remembered about British machinery, and Moody elaborated on it from his mechanical knowledge. Thus quite early we can perceive an important characteristic of the American economy: namely that American businessmen were frequently more adaptive and innovative than genuinely inventive. Except in the romances of elementary school books, Americans have been little concerned with invention *per se*. Innovation in productive techniques was the thing to be admired, and hence the way to the much desired goal of success was not necessarily to "invent" a mousetrap, but, in Emerson's phrase, "to build a better mousetrap."

Thus the Americans really acquired most of the mechanical essentials of the factory system from abroad, but they then proceeded to develop this borrowed technology to such an extent that they generally surpassed the old world.

Pioneer Work in the Use of Interchangeable Parts

What we have just said should not be interpreted to mean that Americans did nothing but copy. Their own contribution to technological progress was, even from the beginning, very important. It consisted of improving already existing methods, of adding new machines, tools, and implements, and of producing these things in what were considered great quantities for that day and age. This process, as we have just noted, took place in the early American textile industry. It occurred even more spectacularly in interchangeable parts manufacture and machine tools.

The story of America's activity in the development of interchangeable parts manufacture begins peculiarly enough with Eli Whitney's invention of the cotton gin in 1793. Before Whitney's famous invention, the green-seed cotton that was grown in the South was not a profitable crop. Great quantities of cotton could be raised, but it was uneconomical because the work of separating the fibres from the seeds required too much time and manpower. Whitney's gin solved the whole problem. It eliminated the cleaning bottleneck and made green-seed cotton as useful for textile-making as any other variety, and much cheaper.

Whitney thought he had a bonanza, and after his sojourn in the South he returned to New Haven to manufacture cotton gins. But the gin could be easily copied, and many people did so, without paying Whitney any royalties. Whitney's business soon ran downhill, and by 1798 he was in desperate financial circumstances. Paradoxically, this unfortunate personal event proved to be a lucky thing for the United States, since it caused Whitney to enter the business of manufacturing muskets with interchangeable parts, thereby setting in motion what was to become the "American System" of mass production.[5]

Aside from his considerable mechanical talents, Whitney was a prac-

[5] On machine tools and interchangeable parts, see Joseph W. Roe, *English and American Tool Builders* (New York: McGraw-Hill Book Company, 1926); Jeanette Mirsky and Allan Nevins, *The World of Eli Whitney* (New York: The Macmillan Co., 1952); Constance M. Green, *Eli Whitney and the Birth of American Technology* (Boston: Little Brown and Company, 1956); Felicia Deyrup, *Arms Makers of the Connecticut Valley* (Northampton: Smith College Studies in History, 1948).

tical and shrewd businessman, and finding himself without money and with a broken business, he looked around for some new way to utilize his abilities. Since he was determined to attempt mass-production manufacture, the most logical thing seemed to be to manufacture armaments for the government, because at that time only the government could promptly exert enough demand to provide what we now call mass consumption. "I should like," Whitney wrote the government, "to undertake to manufacture ten or fifteen thousand stand of arms." Faced with possible war with France, the administration readily accepted Whitney's proposal. In a contract signed in June, 1798, Whitney agreed to deliver 4,000 arms by September 30, 1799, and 6,000 more within the next year. For this he was to receive $134,000—$5,000 immediately.

Given the existing state of the industrial arts, Whitney could not possibly have succeeded in fulfilling his part of the bargain. That his proposal was most audacious may be gathered from the fact that the Federal armory at Springfield had produced only 245 stands of arms in its first two years of operations. And when Whitney signed his contract, he did not even have a factory! What he did have was a plan of procedure, and in its general outlines it became the model for all subsequent interchangeable-part, standardized manufacturing. One of his primary objectives was to make machine tools which, as he said, would be "similar to an engraving on a copper plate from which could be taken a great number of impressions perceptibly alike." He kept insisting that a "substitute for European skill must be sought in such an application of mechanism as to give all that regularity, accuracy and finish which is there affected by a skill." Whitney therefore proceeded to build his own jigs and fixtures, and eventually a milling machine. His workmen filed the parts of gunlocks to the hardened jigs or forms in which the parts were held, thus making the gunlock components identical. Like many of his successors in mass production, Whitney preferred to use new and inexperienced workmen rather than to attempt to overcome the prejudices of men who had learned their trade under a different system. But it did not take long to train the new workmen, because the use of jigs and machine tools made the work in the Whitney plant much simpler than in other arms factories.

Not many people thought that Whitney could succeed in his endeavor. The French were especially skeptical, and they spoke from experience since they had attempted interchangeable parts manufacture in 1717 and again in 1785, without success. The British, who had also done something with interchangeable parts in ship building, were equally convinced that Whitney would fail. Even the United States Government was dubious about Whitney's chances, although for somewhat different reasons. Secretary of the Treasury Wolcott, with whom Whitney dealt, had great faith in the inventor, but being a very practical man, he admitted he was skeptical about "theories which have not been sanctioned by experience."

To some extent, the skeptics were right, for Whitney did not meet the requirements of the contract. With typical American optimism, he underestimated the obstacles that he faced, and instead of delivering 4,000 arms in the first year, he delivered only 500; and he required eight years, not two, to fulfill the contract completely. Power did not present any problem, because the New Haven area had ample water power. Procuring a labor supply gave him some trouble, but not a great deal, for the machines eliminated the need for a large force. Capital requirements posed a more difficult problem, but the government continuously advanced him money. Indeed, by the time Whitney finally delivered the last of the 10,000 muskets, the government had advanced him all but $2,450 of the originally agreed-upon $134,000. A still more imposing obstacle, and one to which Whitney had given too little thought, was the procurement of proper materials for the weapons. Most of America's better-grade mineral resources had not yet been discovered, and the quality of American iron and steel was very poor. But the biggest difficulty of all was that Whitney had not allowed nearly enough time for "tooling up." Although he was a most astute businessman, he lacked executive experience, and at that time there existed no precedent for "tooling up," a pre-manufacturing operation which later became a common task in industry. Despite its shortcomings, however, Whitney's experiment was a tremendous success. When, in 1801, he took ten muskets to Washington and demonstrated that the parts were completely interchangeable, his audience was astonished. The performance was so novel that most of the witnesses were unable to believe it.

Although it hardly detracts from their importance, Whitney's ideas on interchangeability were, like almost all "inventions," not completely original with him. We have already commented on the synthetic nature of invention,[6] but it is worthwhile to repeat that an invention is seldom an isolated occurrence, but more frequently a synthesis of a long series of unintegrated inventions and discoveries. Until relatively recently, individual inventors, unknown to each other, worked more or less independently on a given problem. They built on the work of innumerable previous inventors, not in any orderly fashion, but largely by hit-or-

6 See pp. 78–79.

miss methods. Under such circumstances, it was not at all strange that different individuals often produced basically similar inventions simultaneously,[7] making it very difficult to ascertain who actually did "invent" a particular process, machine or device. Thus, in machine tools, the screw auger seems to have been used in the United States as early as 1796, and it was certainly used in England before that, yet no less than five people claimed its invention in the years 1797–99.

Many men before Whitney had made contributions that enabled him to bring his ambitious and extraordinarily valuable ideas to fruition. We have already mentioned the French attempts at interchangeable parts manufacture, and we know that Whitney had some knowledge of them. We also know that Whitney could not have embarked on his venture without considerable knowledge about British technological progress. Smeaton and Wilkinson, for example, had left behind them more advanced techniques for metal working.[8] English toolmakers, like Bramah and Maudsley, who were working at the same time as Whitney, had already made immense contributions to machine-tool technology. Maudsley's slide rest, which made the lathe a more accurate tool, was one of the most important "inventions" in all mechanical history. Even in the United States, Whitney was not the only pioneer. It is quite likely that Simeon North, who began to manufacture pistols with interchangeable parts in 1799, carried specialization and division of labor to even greater lengths than Whitney did. As early as 1808, a worker in the North plant made consecutively 2,000 similar parts. In England, at that time, specialization had progressed to the point of having men work on only one part of a product, but they still performed all the operations on that one part. Hence in England the workers were still finished craftsmen, whereas they never became finished craftsmen in the North plant. Consequently, even at this early date, the American arms worker had gained greater productivity, but he had done so at the expense of losing his identity with the finished product.

The Arrival of the "American System" of Manufacturing

Whitney and North had demonstrated the undoubted feasibility of interchangeable-parts manufacture, but, as is usually the case, it took

---

[7] For an illuminating treatment of the illusions regarding inventions and patents, see S. C. Gilfillan, "Invention as a Factor in Economic History," *The Tasks of Economic History,* Dec., 1945, supplement to Vol. V of the *Journal of Economic History.*
[8] See pp. 89–90.

many years before the innovation was generally accepted. Conservatism among manufacturers and the buying public (in this case, the government), high costs, and honest differences of opinion delayed its widespread adoption. Indeed, it was not until 1813 that the government wrote a contract specifically calling for interchangeable-parts manufacture, an arrangement with Simeon North for the production of 20,-000 pistols. From then on, however, the method spread not only in gunmaking, but in the metal-products industries in general.

About 1830, Chauncey Jerome of Connecticut began to make brass clocks with interchangeable parts, selling them at the unbelievably low price of fifty cents each. In the sewing machine industry (which incidentally had a great influence on the later automobile business) interchangeable-parts manufacture began in 1846. McCormick began making standardized farm machinery in 1847, and Dennison first manufactured watches with interchangeable parts at Waltham in 1848. Meanwhile, the pioneer work of Whitney and North was carried much further by Samuel Colt in the manufacture of revolvers. An ingenious Yankee, Colt raised the capital for developing his revolver from his earnings in his previous career as a lecturer on laughing gas. He used the Whitney plant to fill his first orders, but during the Mexican War, when he first became truly successful, Colt built his own plant and introduced automation long before the word became a part of the American vocabulary. By 1853, Colt's machines were almost completely automatic and could be run by women and children. Hand work was only required in the finishing department, and labor cost had been so reduced that it amounted to only 20 per cent of manufacturing costs.

By 1860, more than twenty American industries were engaged in mass production by means of interchangeable parts, whereas Great Britain was largely still operating on a handicraft basis. Indeed, interchangeable-parts manufacture had become so distinctively American that by the middle of the 19th century, the term "American System" was being used throughout Europe to describe it.

Progress in Machine Tool Building

The remarkable progress that the United States had achieved in mass production would have been completely impossible without the simultaneous and even more rapid progress that was made in designing machine tools and precision instruments. Indeed, the thirty years before the Civil War is a period that probably has not been surpassed for originality and ingenuity in toolbuilding. The adoption of steam power, the existence of a very heavy demand, both domestic and foreign, and the inventive ability of the machine-tool builders brought the industry to a high point of development by 1850. By then, the general principles of machine tools were well established, and since then further progress has been mostly in improvements and refinements.

We can suggest a few of the many contributions that were made to machine-tool building during this period. The first successful milling machine was developed by Whitney in 1818, along lines suggested by French artisans. Meanwhile Blanchard developed wood-working machinery, Christopher Soener introduced the cam control (which made lathe operations automatic) and, somewhat later, F. W. Howe and H. D. Stone introduced the turret lathe while working for the Robbins and Lawrence Company in 1854. The work of Joseph R. Brown, of Brown and Sharpe, was especially important in improving tolerances through better precision instruments. Working on principles developed by the French, Brown made the first inexpensive vernier caliper in 1851. Brown also introduced the micrometer caliper, in 1867; and, when that was adopted, mechanics could achieve tolerances of less than a thousandth of an inch. How important this was may be illustrated by the fact that when Hall made his first hundred rifles at Harper's Ferry Armory in 1824, it was thought that he had achieved an astounding tolerance because "the joint of the breech block was so fitted that a sheet of paper would slide loosely in the joint, but two sheets would stick."

There was a great deal of interrelation among machine-tool builders. Indeed, so closely did these men work together that one can trace an unbroken chain from Bramah and Maudsley through Whitney and North to Leland and Ford and to modern industry in general. There must have been much exchange of information between Whitney and North. Colt used the Whitney plant, and his first superintendent, Elisha K. Root, trained Pratt of Pratt and Whitney. One Hartford arms plant later became the Weed Sewing Machine Company, which later manufactured the Columbia bicycle. William Sellers, who had an important career in machine building in Philadelphia, was trained in New England before the Civil War. Late in his life he became head of the Midvale Steel Company, and it was there, under his encouragement, that Frederick W. Taylor began, in 1880, his work on cutting metals, which resulted in high-speed tools and a general re-design of machine tools. Henry M. Leland, who made the first automobile with interchangeable parts, worked not only for the Springfield Armory, but for Colt and for Brown and Sharpe. These illustrations could be extended much further, but enough has been said to show that the process of invention and innovation is a cooperative, rather than a personal one. The British developed most of the *general* machine tools cooperatively, and the Americans developed *special* machine tools cooperatively. By the time that was accomplished however, the United States was far ahead of Britain in machine building, just as it was ahead in interchangeable-parts manufacture.

When Colt opened his London revolver factory in 1853, he found England so retarded in the machine-tool industry that he was forced to bring both men and tools with him from the United States. How early the British were aware of the American lead we do not know, but very certainly they knew it by 1851.[9] In that year Robbins and Lawrence exhibited guns made with interchangeable parts at the Crystal Palace Exposition in London. These weapons attracted so much attention that a visit was made to American factories in 1853 by a British Commission, whose members were most impressed by the extent of interchangeability and the whole American system of mass production. The commissioners did point out that American goods often appeared crude. They lacked finish and were lightly constructed, but that all these faults were more than balanced by their simplicity, originality, effectiveness, and, above all, their cheapness resulting from the volume of production. As a result of the Commission's visit, the British government, according to the English tool maker, James Nasmyth, "resolved to introduce the American system." The British government ordered 20,000 interchangeable-part rifles and 157 machines for the manufacture of guns. Nor was this all; other governments joined in, and the resulting orders opened up world markets to American gun makers and tool builders.

Why did the United States achieve this superiority in mechanized, mass production? To some extent, it was because of expanding markets, improving transportation, the attitude of a sympathetic government, and a great labor shortage. But this is hardly a complete explanation. As Sawyer has pointed out, "All this" [transformation] had emerged before the 'big' explanations became operative and at a time when principles of comparative advantage might have argued for other lines of growth—

9 See Deyrup, pp. 11, 148; Roe, pp. 5, 104, 138. See also John E. Sawyer, "The American System of Manufacturing," *The Journal of Economic History*, Vol. XIV, No. 4, 1954.

before the transcontinentals [railways] and the open hearths [steel furnaces]; before the ores of the Mesabi or the opening up of oil; before the great capital accumulations associated with later decades; and, most important, before that always-cited bigger American market had come into existence."[10]

English observers seemed to have recognized that much of the explanation for the rapid growth of the "American System" lay in the American environment and the American character. Commenting on what he had seen in the United States, Sir Joseph Whitworth, himself a machine builder of considerable achievement, concluded that the American success resulted from an acute labor shortage, an eagerness to adopt machinery, and the ability to standardize. But this was not all. Over and over, the British commissioners explained the American system in terms of the American character with its restless energy, its rejection of class rigidity, its refusal to be bound by traditional ways of doing things, its goal of economic success, and its optimistic confidence in its ability to handle things mechanical. At times, the commissioners themselves were swept along by the zestful atmosphere of the new world. In their enthusiasm, they often accepted the American dream as a reality, and judged the Horatio Alger tale of rags to riches to be much more universally true than it actually was. "It may be said," the commissioners wrote, "that there is not a working boy of average ability in the New England states, at least, who has not an idea of some mechanical invention or improvement in manufactures, by which, in good time, he hopes to better his position or rise to fortune and social distinction."

Delayed Development of Agricultural Technology

Since well over three-quarters of early Americans were farmers, it seems hard to believe that the nation's first serious ventures were in industrial rather than in agricultural machines. But this is exactly what happened. To be sure, many amateur tinkers, with mechanical aptitudes, did experiment with new types of plows. Charles Newbold patented a cast-iron plow in 1787, but it was clumsy and expensive. Thomas Jefferson devoted some of his varied talents to the mathematics of the plow, and his geometric calculations were later utilized in the construction of a scientific moldboard. On the whole, however, the tools and machinery used in American grain farming were not much

---

[10] *Journal of Economic History,* Vol. XIV, No. 4.

better in 1815 than they had been a century earlier. Yet Europe, especially Britain, was by then using relatively advanced equipment. This
anomaly may seem difficult to understand, especially when it is remembered that the United States had relatively little labor and much
land. A low man-land ratio means high labor costs and will normally
cause businessmen to resort to what economists call the "principle of
substitution," the tendency which in this context would mean the use
of more machinery to offset the cost of scarce and expensive labor. One
would, therefore, have expected that farmers would have adopted labor-
saving machinery as fast as possible, but they did not. Actually, it took
some time for farm machinery to be adopted. There was, however, a
rather simple explanation for what appeared on the surface to be so
illogical. Because of primitive methods of transportation, most American farmers did not have a market in which to dispose of quantity-
produced farm commodities. There was no point in buying machinery
to produce things that could not be marketed.

Yet a technological revolution in agriculture was ready to explode
even at the beginning of the 19th century. It needed only markets and
transportation facilities to set it off, and these were rapidly forthcoming.
Markets sprung up as cities were formed around the incipient industrial
centers. Improved road, water, and especially rail transportation
quickened the tendency toward improvement in farm tools which
relative scarcity of labor already encouraged.[11] Better methods of transportation enabled farmers to bring their crops to market and thus
encouraged them to expand their output. Cheaper and swifter transportation also facilitated the expansion of the factory system and
thereby contributed to the rise in industrial wages. These high urban
wages attracted an increasing number of farm boys and thereby resulted
in a rise in agricultural wages which, in turn, compelled inventive
American farmers to seek technical ways of reducing costs. With the
railroad age, which began around 1840, came a remarkable succession
of agricultural machines which completely outstripped any of the
technology which English 18th-century agricultural progress had produced. The American farm machinery, which was developed during
the two decades preceding the Civil War, may be said to have laid the
permanent foundations for the kind of agriculture which has become

11 The history of agricultural machinery has been adequately described by P. W.
Bidwell and J. I. Falconer, *History of Agriculture in the Northern United States*
(Washington: Carnegie Institution, 1925); and Leo Rogin, *The Introduction of Farm
Machinery* (Berkeley: the University of California Press, 1931).

typical in the modern economic world. The only basic device which does not fall in this period is probably the internal-combustion engine.

By the beginning of the 19th century, many suggestions had already been made for improving the Newbold plow, and progress in the metallurgical trades now made it feasible to adopt these suggestions. Thus in 1819, Jethro Wood patented a cast-iron plow with three interchangeable, standardized parts. Once commercial farming gained a foothold in the East, Wood's plow was widely adopted, but, since heavy soil, rich in humus tends to stick to cast iron, Wood's new-type plow did not scour well in the sticky loam of the Middle West. This was particularly unfortunate because the flat and relatively rockless terrain of the Middle West offered an ideal setting for the extensive use of farm machinery. In 1833 John Deere finally solved the problem by plating a wooden moldboard with high-tempered steel, thereby providing a plow that could break the prairie. By 1847 Deere was manufacturing an all-steel plow. Eventually in 1870, James Oliver succeeded in making a chilled-iron plow, a very efficient tool less expensive than the steel plow, and more versatile than its cast-iron predecessor.

The evolution of the plow was, of course, basic, but it may be argued that the development of harvesting machinery was even more important. Because grain falls out of the sheaves unless it is cut at just the right time, harvesting was the major bottleneck in grain production, a bottleneck which man, since ancient times, had been attempting to break. Many harvesting machines or "reapers" had been patented, but none was really successful until Cyrus McCormick built a comparatively simple but practical machine in 1831. A few years later McCormick moved to Illinois, where he found an expanding market for his machine since the enormous expanse of flat plains offered ideal conditions for using harvesting machines. McCormick took proper advantage of the opportunity and by 1857 he had sold 23,000 machines. Although the early reaper cut manpower needs in half, the machine was still very crude. The history of the harvester, therefore, is a story of constant and progressive improvement and development, until finally, in 1878, a device was evolved (the Appleby twine binder) which not only enabled the harvester to cut the grain, but to bind it as well. Meanwhile, other agricultural processes were rapidly being mechanized. Drills, harrows, corn planters, threshers, corn harvesters, mowing machines, and hay loaders were all conceived before the Civil War. Indeed by then most of them were well beyond the experimental stage.

The Age of Iron and Steel

By the latter part of the 19th century, some branches of American technology were well advanced while others lagged far behind. The basic technological structure in textile machinery and machine tools had been completed, and, in agricultural equipment, a solid foundation had been laid. But a spectacular future was still in store for metallurgy, power, scientific management, and materials handling.[12]

In the early part of the century, mechanization had been, in the main, an extensive process consisting of the replacement of hand labor in basic production. But later, mass production progressed to a point where industry could turn more and more toward intensive mechanization. The process of mechanization, which had always been continuous, now became more complicated as well. Once the primary stages of a productive process had been technically renovated, emphasis turned to improvements in the fabricating machines; to more efficient methods of machine production, such as the utilization of more intricate tools; and to the mechanization of other processes of production, such as conveying, loading, wrapping, and sorting.

As mechanization became more common, as machines came to be made of metal rather than wood, and as the railroad network expanded, the old methods of producing iron no longer sufficed. A mass market had appeared, and improvements had to be made in both the volume and quality of iron and steel. In Great Britain the basic changes in metallurgy were, in order of adoption, the use of coke as fuel, puddling, and rolling. In the United States these innovations occurred in reverse fashion. The old processes of refining by reheating and hammering in open forges gave place to puddling and rolling at about the time of the War of 1812. It was much later, about 1840, that coal and coke replaced charcoal as fuel. The first modern blast furnace was built at Pittsburgh in 1859, but before long there were many more, and their capacity was rapidly increased. The expensive process of making steel by hand, which was in use before the Civil War, surrendered, by the 1870's, to the Bessemer process, which could make much better and much cheaper steel.

American mills soon assumed world leadership in steel production, partly because the Bessemer process required the use of high-grade

12 This uneven rate of development is a common occurrence in economic history. See Simon S. Kuznets, *Secular Movements in Production and Prices* (Boston: Hough ton Mifflin Company, 1930), Chap. 1.

ores, which the United States happened to have in much greater abundance than Europe did. In 1872 the United States produced less than 100,000 tons of steel, and the price was over $150 a ton. Eight years later, we were producing over one million tons, and the price was less than $50 a ton. But presently the Bessemer process, in turn, gave way to better methods. In the 1850's, even before Bessemer had read his famous paper on a new method of producing steel, a German, William Siemens, had demonstrated the advantages of the open-hearth process. Improved by the Martin Brothers in France, this process enabled the steel industry to use inferior ores instead of the high-grade ores required by the Bessemer process.[13] But once again, many years passed before the new process was generally adopted. Open-hearth steel did not surpass Bessemer converter steel until 1895 in Britain, and not until 1910 in the United States.

The "Revolution" in the Use of Power

Concurrently with new techniques in metallurgy, equally important changes were taking place in the use of energy. In the initial period of industrialization, rivers and brooks provided the power to run the nation's factories and machines. Although steam power and the steam engine were well known,[14] water power, on balance, offered greater advantages. Admittedly, the early steam engine, inefficient though it was, could generate four times as much power as a water wheel. Steam also had the advantage of not being limited to the flow of waterways. But so long as New England had an ample supply of water, these advantages were not urgently important. What was important was that water power had distinct cost advantages over steam, both in terms of power-plant construction and operation. A 20-horsepower steam engine cost $13,000, far more than a dam and a water wheel. As late as 1840, it cost only $12 to generate one horsepower by water, but $90 by steam.

13 Here, too, the United States borrowed heavily from Europe. In 1881, Captain Billy Jones, Carnegie's superintendent, told the British Iron and Steel Institute: "While your metallurgists, as well as those of France and Germany, have been devoting their time and talents to the discovery of new processes, we have swallowed the information . . . and have selfishly devoted ourselves to beating you in output." (Burton J. Hendrick, *The Life of Andrew Carnegie* (Garden City: Doubleday and Company, 1932), Vol. I, p. 310.

14 Watt had "invented" the steam engine before Independence, and Oliver Evans, the remarkably versatile and relatively unknown Philadelphia mechanical genius, had, in 1803, built a 24-horsepower steam engine that was a remarkably efficient piece of machinery.

Furthermore, once a dam and a wheel were built, there were, aside from maintenance charges, no energy costs at all.

As industry continued to grow, however, available water-power sites became scarcer, but there was no abject surrender to steam. Attempts were made to make more efficient use of water power. First the "pitch-back" wheel and then the water turbine came into use. By the 1840's, Fall River and Lowell factories were using turbines that were 88 per cent effective. But water-power sites became scarcer and scarcer, and as industries found it advantageous to move nearer their markets, the use of steam power became imperative. By 1850, steam was overtaking water, although as late as 1869, water power still accounted for 50 per cent of industrial power.

Although steam was more efficient and more convenient than water, it had some of the same basic weaknesses. It could not transmit power beyond the range of its belts and shaftings; it often led to excessive industrial centralization because it had to be used fairly near to coal deposits; it could not be used effectively to propel small vehicles; and it was almost completely useless on the farm. Moreover, there were limits to the efficiency of the reciprocating engine, which was the chief means for utilizing steam at the middle of the 19th century. The power that it could generate varied directly with the size of engines, and in most cases it was impractical to build an engine of a size that could generate very large amounts of power. All this was changed by a series of events that occurred in the last quarter of the century. The invention of the steam turbine, the internal-combustion engine, and the application of new devices to the generation of electricity created far more flexible sources of energy than before.

Like most "inventions," the utilization of electricity was a gradual process. Michael Faraday, the British scientist, had discovered the principle of induced current as early as 1831, but not much was done with it until Edison, in 1876, devised a method of using electricity for illumination. As power, however, electricity was very expensive—and not practical for industrial use because it could not be transmitted over long distances from low-cost generating plants. George Westinghouse finally solved this problem by building a transformer that could reduce voltage at the point where current was used, thus permitting electricity to be transmitted at high voltages. As with all inventions, it took time for the transformer to be adopted, but, once it came into use, electricity became feasible as a major power source. In 1900 electricity and the steam engine each supplied about equal percentages of industrial power, but by 1950 seven-eighths of the nation's industrial power came from electric motors. Instead of being chained to water power or to their own steam-power plants, factories could now avail themselves of electric power generated by water power or steam hundreds of miles away. This meant substantial savings in capital, resources, and space, and allowed greater flexibility in the use of power within a factory. It also meant a vast increase in the total amount of power available for production, since coal, water, and fuel oil could be used to generate electricity. But electricity was not too satisfactory for use for vehicles or mobile machines. Here, however, what electricity could not do, the internal-combustion engine could, because its unit size did not limit the total amount of energy it could create. Compact gasoline engines, in automobiles, trucks, and tractors, provided an almost incomprehensible volume of horsepower available for use on the nation's highways and farms.

Education and Changes in the Inventive Process

As mechanization grew more intricate and the use of natural energy more complicated in the latter part of the 19th century, the existing methods for training technicians began to seem inadequate. The typical inventor or technician during the first half of the 19th century was a self-educated artisan with an aptitude for mechanics. He was a past master at trial and error, and many of his accomplishments stemmed from intuition. Yet it is remarkable how much he accomplished without the help of formal education. To some extent, the lack of an education was an advantage, since the early technicians were never dissuaded from attacking a problem that authority insisted was unconquerable.[15] But it was also tremendously disadvantageous because it denied to those who worked in the practical world an adequate knowledge of theoretical fundamentals. When long bridges had to be built and when railroad construction became almost a national mania, better knowledge of engineering became indispensable. When metallurgy evolved into more complicated stages and when electrical research began to tax the imagination, some familiarity with chemistry and physics became

[15] The same year the Wright brothers made their famous flight at Kitty Hawk, a distinguished physicist published a paper proving (?) that sustained flight by a heavier-than-air aeroplane was impossible. Consider also the careers of George Westinghouse and Charles Kettering. Both made tremendous contributions that professional scientists had said were impossible.

a necessity. It was no longer possible to rely solely on the knowledge gained by practical experience. In education, as in other areas of the economy, direct methods were superseded by roundabout methods.

In 1850, when a college founded in 1824 was renamed the Rensselaer Polytechnic Institute and became our first engineering school, only a handful of institutions offered advanced training in the applied sciences. Engineering subjects were taught at the Military Academy at West Point. A considerable mass of scientific fact had been accumulated, but this had not yet been integrated into the instruction given in colleges and universities, all of which still placed chief emphasis on classical studies.[16] As a result, scientific findings had little influence on industry.

During the second half of the century, engineering and mechanical education progressed rapidly. In 1862, under the Morrill Act, the Federal Government began to subsidize colleges for the agricultural and mechanical arts. In 1864, the National Academy of Sciences was founded, and, in the following year, instruction began at the Massachusetts Institute of Technology. By the end of the century there were 147 institutions offering technical education on an advanced level. Of this number, 66 were wholly or partly supported by state or Federal government. With such encouragement, the number of people trained to contribute to technological development increased far faster than did population. Thus, between 1830 and 1930 the number of engineering students increased almost 100 times faster than the population, making the absolute increase almost a thousandfold.[17]

The expansion of educational facilities was merely a symptom of a comprehensive change in the inventive process. Invention was becoming cumulatively more scientific, involving less trial and error, thereby becoming less accidental, more disciplined and more orderly. But it was also becoming less individual, and much more subject to the disadvantage of being fenced in by precedent and bureaucracy. The techniques of mass production were extended to research, which became a business organized on a group basis, so that fewer of the American patents that reached commercial development were the work of inde-

[16] Eli Whitney graduated from Yale, but as a teacher, not as a natural scientist or engineer.

[17] The increase in the number of engineering students was from 50 in 1830 to 47,000 in 1930. S. C. Gilfillan, *The Sociology of Invention* (Chicago: Follett Publishing Company, 1935), p. 79. According to census data, the increase in the number of engineers and technicians between 1870 and 1950 was greater than the increase of any other occupation.

pendent inventors.[18] As it became more of a group business, the inventive process became much more efficient in finding ways to accomplish some predetermined goal. But in the process, as we have begun to learn in the 1950's, basic research suffered.

Scientific Management

The so-called scientific method was not confined to the research laboratory. In the last decade of the 19th century, it began to seep into every aspect of business, including management itself. In fabricating and assembling industrial products the mass-production methods in use under the old organizational business forms had reached a point of diminishing returns. The economies that could be gained by further improvements in machinery, machine tools, and power were not as fruitful as they had been at the beginning of the mechanical age. Industrial engineers, therefore, began to focus their attention on the economies to be gained from improved managerial techniques and better organization of physical facilities. Gradually, during the first decade of the 20th century, a new technique known as scientific management began to catch on.

Scientific management stressed standardization of products and processes; better organization; coordination and control of men, materials, and machines; rigid production planning; time and motion studies; incentive plans; and better selection and training of workers. The various problems of management were approached analytically and studied in detail. In essence, scientific management was, therefore, nonmechanical. But it nevertheless conformed closely to the American character because it sprang from American optimism. It strengthened and accentuated the American penchant for standardization and conformity. Scientific management amended Emerson's dictum by admonishing Americans to build not only better, but greater quantities of mousetraps. And if mass production of mousetraps threatened to exceed the number of mice, little thought was given to cutting production, except to relieve temporary gluts in order to maintain prices. In-

[18] It would be incorrect however, to assume that the research laboratories of large corporations have monopolized invention. In a detailed study of sixty-one 20th-century inventions it was found that thirty-three represented the work of individuals, twenty-one the result of company research laboratories, and the rest were of mixed percentage. See John Jewkes, David Sawers, and Richard Stillerman, *The Sources of Invention* (New York: The Macmillan Co., 1957).

stead, a new branch of the science of management came into existence—
scientific study of how to increase consumption. In addition to innovating to increase the production of goods, businessmen now placed
increased emphasis on innovations to stimulate demand. Advertising,
salesmanship, and instalment credit (despite the great emphasis on
thrift in the American scale of values) became accepted adjuncts of
the American way of life. Thus, business decision making had by the
20th century become recognized as a profession requiring many talents.
Under the impulse of scientific management, business enterprise began
paying greater attention to quality control, statistics, accounting, budg-
etary control, and presently to sales forecasting, personnel administration, and industrial psychology.

Technological Achievements by the Middle of the 20th Century

From the introduction of interchangeable parts to scientific management, technological progress was a long and continuous process, shifting from one line of emphasis to another. Goaded by a drive toward
economic success, spurred by an acute shortage of labor, and fed by
government contracts, American armaments makers had initiated interchangeable-parts manufacturing. This, in turn, required improvisations
in machine tools and precision instruments, the rough outlines of
which were etched into the economy by 1850. Meanwhile, American
farmers, sharing the manufacturer's dreams of economic advancement
(and similarly limited by labor scarcity) began to mechanize agriculture
once transportation facilities had been developed to carry their goods to
broader markets. At the same time, manufacturers made rapid progress
in mechanized mass production of low-priced, standardized consumer
goods like textiles, food products, clocks, and small novelties. By the
middle of the 19th century, the broad growth in mechanization, transportation, and markets had outrun existing power resources and
metallurgical technology. But in the last half of the 19th century, steam,
and later electricity and new methods for mass production of metals,
laid a foundation for a new and even more robust economic growth.

All these developments, constantly improved and elaborated, produced an economy little resembling that of 1775. By the middle of the
20th century, the United States was an industrial complex characterized by mass production, the assembly line, the conveyor belt, and
scientific management. This industrial colossus used heavy machinery

and automatic processes, and derived its energy from gasoline, electric power, fuel oil, and natural gas as well as coke, coal, and water power. The tremendous power which the American people employed in production may be dramatically expressed in the estimate that it would require the labor of 5 billion slaves, which is to say, more than the world's entire population, to do the work now performed by the harnessed natural energy employed in the American economy.

Farmers are using tools and machines powered by gasoline and electricity to do about 60 per cent of their work. An even more dramatic technological change has occurred in manufacturing. The iron industry, to cite one example, has long since become the iron and steel industry. Its modern furnaces are fed not only with iron ore of the best quality, but with scrap metal and iron ore of any quality. Much electronic equipment is used in the productive process, and the use of manpower involves intricate specialization and division of labor. Out of this complex productive process have come new steels for special purposes, such as manganese steel and high-speed carbon steel. Incorporating the research of chemists, physicists and metallurgists, these new steels have given increased durability, cutting power, and speed to machine tools. The modern tool is multiple rather than single, and is about 80 times faster and ten times more accurate than its 19th century counterpart. Meanwhile, non-ferrous and light metals—aluminium, magnesium, tantalium, thorium, platinum, chromium, titanium—have become increasingly popular because of their lightness, resistance to corrosion, and reflexibility or workability. By the 1950's, we had entered an age of triumphant technology, even though the tremendous possibilities of atomic energy had not yet been fully measured, and the fascinatingly uncanny electronic devices—the machines with human attributes— were still novelties, causing the philosopher to muse anew and the economist to dream of a new sprint in the eternal pursuit of economic growth, and the ever-elusive goal of abundance of all desired things.

The Effects of Technological Change

Whether technological change has been more beneficial than harmful depends pretty much upon one's point of view. Some social scientists, although fewer than there once were, are skeptical. They are uneasy about the machine, the assembly line, and the whole complex of mass production. Technology, they contend, has a tendency to dehumanize society; the economic milieu that encourages technological progress is soul-destroying; it tends to corrupt the independence of the individual and it can result in mass technological unemployment.

The majority of economists take a different point of view. To them, technological progress means higher productivity, more goods and services, a higher standard of living and fewer hours of work. Technology more than anything else made it possible to increase man-hour output so much that one manufacturing worker produces in the 1950's the same amount of output that required three workers in the 1890's and six in the 1850's. Again, mainly because of technological progress, one farm worker in the 1950's provides farm commodities for about 20 people, whereas one farm worker in 1820 provided produce for only 4½ people.

But no one knows better than the economist that everything has its price, and that the gains of technological progress were not made without considerable sacrifice. The worker became dependent upon the machine, a fickle master whose whims filled his life with doubt, uncertainty, and insecurity. As the machine replaced human energy, work became more monotonous, and even though the worker might seek escape in day dreaming, the machine created a vast number of sociological problems, such as stunted personality growth, fatigue, and discontent. As the process of mechanization continued, machines became more and more automatic, eliminating some workers altogether.

The elimination of the worker by the machine became a hotly debated issue. According to one variant of economic theory, increased use of machinery did not lead to a net increase in unemployment. It was argued that technological progress, by lowering cost and increasing demand, expanded the quantity of salable goods, thereby increasing the total demand for labor. Moreover, the business of building machines would concurrently increase the demand for labor. The most that these theorists would admit was that workers in an industry that was in the process of mechanization might be temporarily displaced, but they optimistically predicted that these "technologically unemployed" persons would presently be re-absorbed by the over-all expansion of the economy which progressive mechanization would assure. Other social scientists, who believed that man's material wants were not infinite, insisted that technology might bring about a permanent, rather than merely a temporary, displacement of labor. Some condemned the machine itself as the cause of technological unemployment; others held that the economic system rather than the machine was responsible.

The weight of the evidence supports the view that historically technology did not create unemployment, although it did require the worker to make swift adjustments to new tasks and new methods. It placed a special burden on older workers, who were not able to make the necessary adjustments, and who could not maintain the speed or coordination dictated by machine production. Since technological progress resulted in more workers (twice as many in 1929 as in 1900) being employed in machine-producing industries, it increased the vulnerability of the labor force to cyclical unemployment, and thereby increased the worker's insecurity. This lost security he sought to regain by joining unions, by supporting paternalism in government, and by demanding pension and welfare programs.

Technology and the Farmer

The farmer was probably more affected by technology than the manufacturing worker because farm mechanization was a fundamental factor in making farming a business rather than "a way of life." But making farming a business was also one of the chief causes of the so-called farm problem—the problem of making farming pay. Obviously gasoline engines and electric power were technically more efficient than animal and human energy. One gasoline-powered tractor could replace 20 horses on a wheat farm, and gasoline and electric power could perform tasks which horses could never accomplish—pumping or milking, for example. The use of the truck and the auto reduced the time of marketing, widened the market in which the farmer could sell, increased the efficiency of distribution, and made it possible to prolong the actual hours of work by the use of labor shifts.

Yet, in spite of the advantages of power and mechanization, more farmers probably failed from over-mechanization than from under-mechanization. In order for it to pay, mechanization required a larger size farm. But the system of land tenure in the United States was not geared to this. The average American farm in 1900 was less than 150 acres, and even in the 1950's, at over 200 acres,[19] it was still far short of the optimum size for power-driven farm machinery. In agriculture moreover, the scale of business enterprise was too small, since there were two entrepreneurs for every three workers. The whole problem of technology therefore confronted the farmer with a dilemma. Unless he

[19] Much lower, if the enormous acreages of western ranches are not counted.

mechanized he could not produce efficiently or competitively; if he did, he would not be able to use his machinery economically because of his small land holdings. True, he had other possible choices: he could sell out to a large farming corporation, or he could possibly get heavy mechanized work done by contract. But both the idea of selling to a corporation and of renting equipment conflicted with the American folkways' emphasis on economic independence and small business.

Agricultural technology affected the farm problem in other ways. The constant increase in the use of farm machinery raised farm output both directly and indirectly. By bringing more farms within the market radius and by lowering costs, it brought hitherto sub-marginal lands into cultivation. By eliminating animal power, it freed for cultivation many acres previously used for pasture or forage crops and thereby sharply raised total cereal, fibre, and meat production for human consumption. To operate a successful farm required more capital than to start an average non-agricultural business; farm tenancy, therefore, grew at a rapid rate. Moreover, mechanized farming was highly specialized and allowed for little self-sufficiency. Indeed, technology made the farmer entirely dependent on the market, and as such he was forced to become a record-keeping businessman. He had to calculate opportunity costs more carefully and keep in closer touch with markets. And presently, as his problems continued to seem insoluble, he adopted what he considered business tactics: he tried to institute by government legislation the kind of "administered prices" which he contended other businessmen had already created through the devices of monopolistic competition.

The Machine and Business Enterprise

As in the case of agriculture and labor, business enterprise was also profoundly affected by the machine, even though it was the business entrepreneur who made the decisions which determined the extent and rapidity of mechanization and technological development. The boundless energy of the machine, its mechanical efficiency, and its relatively small use of skilled labor fascinated the businessman, for it offered him a method for simultaneously cutting costs, meeting competition, and increasing profits. But it also increased the hazard of faster obsolescence of his capital equipment. Moreover, large quantities of machinery could be used profitably only in large-scale business enterprises, and although the growth of big business could be economically salutary (because it could make possible larger capacity, more efficient operations, and more scientific research) it was, nonetheless, a threat to the traditional American way of life with its time-honored emphasis on individualism, independence, and competition.

The high cost of capital limited free entry into an industry, while among already existing manufacturers, expensive machinery tended in the long run to increase the hazards of competition. To yield maximum returns, a machine had to be run at full capacity, for even if it stood idle, fixed charges in the form of interest, insurance, property taxes, and depreciation would go on. In periods of business depression, therefore, enterprises operating with heavy machinery preferred to cut prices and take losses rather than to close down plants. Weak producers were driven out of the market, and the machine, which had been initially a competitive device, became an instrument tending toward monopoly. Thus the businessman very often ceased to be master of the machine and became its slave.

Technology and Government

From what has been said it should be evident that the great technological changes struck at the very roots of the early 19th-century American way of life. It weakened the independence of the laborer, broke down the self-sufficiency of the farmer, and modified the individualism of the businessman. It also resulted in urban concentration, and subsequently caused the mushroom growth of the satellite suburbs that surrounded every large city. It made distances less important and brought not only the different sections of the nation, but the different areas of the world, into closer proximity. By thus complicating social and economic life, technological change was one of the primary factors in the expansion of the importance of government. So long as the economy was agrarian and relatively primitive in technological development, the average citizen had little to gain from government, and government played only a small rôle in his daily life. But, as technological innovation became more elaborate, the pattern changed. Governments, whether they liked it or not, were forced to take on added responsibilities in a world made smaller and more complicated by technological change.

The Automobile as a Factor in Economic Transformation[20]

We have explained how technological change affected the productivity of particular sectors of the economy (agriculture or iron and steel production, for example) and the impact it had upon certain economic groups (farmers, for example). But technological innovation can exercise a far more extensive and cumulative influence upon the whole economy; it can set in motion far-reaching transforming effects. Such an impact can best be demonstrated by a case study, and no case study offers a better illustration of the sweep, the dynamism, and the effect of technology than does the automobile industry. Started at the turn of the 19th century, this feeble venture developed within the span of a single generation into a colossus of mass production, representing the acme of mechanization, division of labor, and scientific management. Since the dramatic rise of this new industry illustrates the very essence of technological change, we shall briefly describe the factors that made it possible, the long inventive process, the elaboration of machinery, the adoption of a system of mass production, the application of scientific management, and the transforming effects of the end product on everyday social and economic life.

The idea of a self-propelled vehicle was not new. Leonardo da Vinci in the 15th century had the germ of the idea. Roger Bacon before him and Isaac Newton after him both considered the possibility of a steam-propelled vehicle. In 1769 a Frenchman, Joseph Cugnot, actually constructed such a vehicle. So did an American, Oliver Evans, in 1784, and an Englishman, Richard Trevithick, in 1801. By 1860 scientific experiment had gone far enough to allow inventors to turn from steam to gas as a propelling fuel, and in that year a Frenchman, Lenoir, built a gas engine. In 1876, Otto, a German, patented his four-cycle engine, an internal-combustion engine which ultimately made possible the gasoline-driven automobile. Thus, the inventive process which made the automobile possible was a synthesis of the contributions of innumerable

---

[20] There is a vast literature on the automobile industry and on the impact of the automobile upon the American economy. See especially, Allan Nevins *Ford: The Times, the Man, the Company* (New York: Charles Scribner's Sons, 1954); *Ford: Expansion and Contraction* (New York: Charles Scribner's Sons, 1956); Arthur Pound, *The Turning Wheel* (Garden City: Doubleday, Doran and Company, 1934); Ralph C. Epstein, *The Automobile Industry* (Chicago: A. W. Shaw, 1928); Lawrence H. Seltzer, *A Financial History of the American Automobile Industry* (Boston: Houghton Mifflin Company, 1928); Lloyd Morris, *Not So Long Ago* (New York: Random House Inc., 1949).

scientists, technicians, and inventors from all the leading industrial countries. Americans carefully copied the foreign contributions; modified and elaborated them; and then, when the experimental period was over, applied the "American System" of mass production.

The first organization to make automobiles commercially, the French Panhard Company, began operations in 1891, before the first automobile was built in the United States, yet in a short time the United States became the largest producer. There were many reasons for this. The United States had a vast land area well suited for the use of automobiles. It also possessed natural resources usable and available for automobile manufacture. But above all, automobiles proved to be exceptionally well adapted to American cultural values. The American middle class, relatively more numerous and much more *thing*-conscious than their European counterparts, offered a potential mass market. Moreover, scattered among the population were innumerable amateur mechanics with a facility for adapting and improving mechanical devices. In addition, there were already in existence certain mechanical industries, such as bicycle and sewing machine factories, that could contribute directly to the development of the automobile industry.

The technological evolution of the automobile industry may be divided into four periods: the pioneer phase, from 1892 to about 1900; the beginning of mass production, from 1900 to 1908; the expansion of mass production, from 1908 to 1923; and the era of full expansion thereafter. During the pioneer period, the automobile was largely hand-produced for a rather limited local market. The entrepreneurs were mechanics and inventors rather than innovating businessmen, and in time most of these pioneers disappeared from the industry. The chief reason for their lack of success was the difficulty of raising capital. Savings did not readily flow into the automobile business, and capital was not withdrawn rapidly from other businesses and invested in the new industry. The early automobile manufacturers tried to overcome the capital shortage by entering into credit arrangements with body builders and parts manufacturers. Parts and bodies would be purchased on credit and paid for when an automobile was sold. Every automobile was virtually a custom-built job, and the pioneer automobile industry was mostly a small-scale assembly business. Manufacturing by factory methods was not yet possible, and tools and machinery were improvised and "home-made."

Ransom E. Olds, the proprietor of a machine shop, was the first man to attempt to "manufacture" rather than build an automobile. Olds had visions of mass production. He believed that the principles used in manufacturing carriages could be adapted to the automobile. This meant buying parts and assembling them, a scale of operations which in turn required more capital funds than Olds had, but he eventually raised $200,000.

Olds' first factory turned out a complicated car with a pneumatic clutch, cushion tires and an electric starter, a machine too far ahead of its day, and whose price, $1,250, was much too high for mass consumption. A year later he began to produce a $650 Oldsmobile on a mass basis, buying the parts in quantity, and assembling them on an embryonic assembly line. He was the first entrepreneur in the automobile industry to use complex division of labor, the first to use the moving assembly line, and the first to bring the materials to the worker instead of the worker to the materials. By these improved processes, Olds achieved a production of 4,000 cars in 1904, a phenomenal number for that time.

Meanwhile, substantial headway was being made introducing mass production methods in the making of engines, bodies, and parts. Here the pioneer was Henry M. Leland whose Leland-Faulconer Manufacturing Company began laying plans for manufacturing standardized engines with interchangeable parts. As we have already mentioned, Leland had had long experience with interchangeable parts, for he had worked as a machinist in the Colt factory and later with Brown and Sharpe. Leland became so impressed with the idea of manufacturing an automobile with interchangeable parts that he himself now entered the automobile industry and built the Cadillac, the first truly standardized car. In 1906 Leland performed an amazing experiment to prove the worth of a machine-made product with interchangeable parts. He sent three Cadillacs, each with 91 parts, to England, tore them down and threw the parts in a heap. Then Cadillac mechanics, equipped only with wrenches, hammers, screwdrivers, and pliers, proceeded to assemble the parts into three complete automobiles which were driven on a 500-mile test. Leland's test demonstrated, for those who could see, that with the assembly line and interchangeable parts automobile production would be limited only by disposable consumer purchasing power.

To produce interchangeable parts required precision instruments and special machine tools. Leland, therefore, imported a set of "Jo blocks" (steel blocks that were accurate within four-millionths of an inch) so-named after their Swedish producer Carl Johansson. Meanwhile, by 1903, specialized machine tools, such as multiple drill presses for boring cylinder blocks, cylinder grinding machines, and turret lathes to turn fly wheels, had been developed. The preparatory work for mass production had been accomplished. The basic elements were now developed: the assembly line, interchangeable parts, precision instruments, special machine tools, material routing, and machine layout. The automobile industry was ready to expand.

Yet, by 1908, automobile entrepreneurs were tending to produce high-priced cars. The one exception was Henry Ford who, against prevailing opinion, began to manufacture his Model T, a completely standardized product, low-priced, and well within the range of America's middle class. Led by the Ford Motor Company, the automobile business soon embarked upon the greatest development of mass production in history. With a mass market and a standardized product, the Ford Company could and did elaborate the principles laid down by Olds and Leland.[21] Under Walter E. Flanders, who had been hired to step up production to 10,000 cars a year, the Ford Company early in its history applied line-production theory to automobile manufacturing. According to this theory, production should pass continuously from its initial stages to its final form. Machines and tools were arranged by function rather than by kind. Waste motion in a laborer's work and movement was eliminated, so that the job, as well as the parts, became standardized. Working on these principles, the Ford Company split down the job again and again, in order to achieve the goal of having the worker do only one simple routine task with as few motions as possible. By using mechanized overhead conveyors, and automatic equipment, and guided by systematic time and motion studies, Ford engineers reduced the assembly time of a Model T, by January 1914, from the original 12 hours and 28 minutes to 93 minutes.

Meantime, standardization spread throughout the industry. "Inventions" developed by one company were made freely available to other firms after one year. All the components of automobiles were standardized: the 800 different lock washers used in early cars were reduced to 16; the 1,600 types of steel tubing cut to 17; and 230 different kinds of alloy steels standardized at 50. The firm establishment of consumer

[21] It is all too easy to make the error of believing that Henry Ford was the Ford Motor Company. Like other "heroic" personalities in American business, Ford was surrounded with many able men who contributed most importantly to the company's early success. It would be difficult to explain the company's progress without giving some credit to James Couzzens, Childe Harold Wells, Walter Flanders, Charles Sorensen, and many others. On the other hand, it is just as difficult to explain the Ford Company without giving some credit to Henry.

credit in 1916 greatly increased effective demand, and gave further impetus to mass production. New tools and new processes continuously simplified manufacturing procedures. Before the First World War, for example, automobiles had been painted with natural enamels, and so many coats were needed that it took about two weeks for a car to be painted and to dry. After the war, nitrocellulose lacquers were introduced, cutting the drying period, and reducing the painting task from weeks to days. One-piece stamping for bodies was next introduced, eliminating 18 different parts in the underbody alone.

The effects of these improvements in mass production were prodigious. Although the number of firms making cars declined as the scale of operations increased, the number of plants in the automobile business increased from 178 in 1904 to 2,471 in 1923, when the manufacture of automobiles became the largest industry in the country. Man-hour output increased remarkably. In 1912 it took 4,664 man hours to produce a car in one plant; 1,260 in another. By 1923, man hours had been reduced to 813 in the first plant and to 228 in the second. But this increase was obtained at the expense of great wear and tear on the laborer. Turnover was more marked than in other employments; the Ford plant, for example, had to hire 53,000 workers to have a constant corps of 14,000.

Compensating for this, wages in the industry increased, while prices of cars declined as productivity rose. In 1914 Ford adopted the famous 5-dollar, 8-hour day. In 1904 a 2-cylinder Ford cost $1,200 and a 4-cylinder Packard, $7,000. By 1924 a 4-cylinder Ford cost $290 and a 6-cylinder Packard, $2,585. After allowing for changes in the purchasing power of the dollar, the 1924 car cost less than 25 per cent of the price of the 1904 car. Meantime, the quality of the automobile had been very greatly improved. The self-starter replaced the crank; the sedan superseded the touring car. Demountable rims, cord tires, four-wheel brakes, and many other innovations were adopted. All in all, the automobile of 1924 was a much safer, more comfortable and far less nerve-racking vehicle than its predecessors.

After 1924, technological development in the automobile industry became more intensive; innovations consisted mainly in refinements and improvements, since there were few fundamental changes. Meantime the industry became in every way more concentrated. By the late 1950's three companies produced 90 per cent of the nation's automobiles, and 97 per cent of the original assembling companies had disappeared. Management became much more scientific; the individual "great man" disappeared, and was replaced by a massive staff and line organization. At the same time, scientific research became more collective, shifting toward the laboratory of the large corporation. Group research continuously improved the automobile, especially in style; meanwhile the assembly line was made even more efficient. The spectacular days of plant expansion seemed to have passed. Manufacturers were still competing vigorously, but far less in prices and much more in quality, aesthetics and service, much as described in the economic theories of monopolistic and imperfect competition.

The Transforming Effects of the Automobile on the Economy

The influence of automobile technology quickly pervaded the whole of economic life as the nation took to the wheels. By the 'fifties, when production at one time reached 8 million automobiles and trucks, there were 60 million vehicles on the roads of the United States. The effects of the automobile spread to other industries, thus accelerating mass production and technological innovation throughout the whole economy. The automobile industry created wholly new industries and institutions, such as the motel, the gas station, and billboard advertising. The automobile also changed the consumption patterns of the American people. More than one-tenth of consumers' expenditures went into the purchase and maintenance of automobiles. Old moral clichés lost their meaning as the automobile became the distinguishing mark of conspicuous consumption. As car ownership became more widespread, there was a drift toward suburbia. By the close of the heroic age of the automobile business, over 50,000 towns had no direct access to either railroad or waterway. The automobile had become, in many respects, the common denominator of marketing. This was particularly striking in agriculture. Before the advent of the motor truck, the average distance of a middlewestern farmer from his market was eight miles. With the truck, the average distance was extended to eighteen miles— more than doubled; yet in monetary terms, the average ton-mile cost of hauling wheat was cut in half as the truck replaced the horse. With this enlargement of the market area and the reduction in the cost of marketing, new possibilities of geographic division of labor appeared. Freed from part of the costs of marketing, the farmer could devote himself more to those functions for which he had a more natural aptitude.

The automobile also illustrated how technological change tends to change traditional concepts and activities of government. By mid-century, Federal, state, and local governments were collecting about $3 billion from automobile taxes of one sort or another. Expenditures for highways by government were almost equal. The automobile also stimulated the development of inter-municipal authorities, thus helping to break down the traditional separation of municipality, county, and borough. Meantime, in the cultural sphere, the automobile, because it probably influenced the American way of life more than did any other technological development, became the focal point of the whole debate over the merits and demerits of technological progress. The automobile had accelerated the speed of existence, broadened people's horizons, increased the mobility of millions of people at the same time that it contributed to the increase of the national income of the American people. But it was also a peril to life and limb; it tempted people to spend their earnings before they received them, and it disrupted revered social institutions. Newer and bigger automobiles, with consumer credit making possible more conspicuous consumption caused some people to cheer for more, but led others to wonder whether the whole competitive game of pursuing economic success so relentlessly was worth the effort!

9 Evolution of business enterprise and corporate management

Importance of "Success" in the "Business Game"

Over a century ago, a French tourist, fascinated by the hurly-burly of American life, its hustle, energy and drive, wrote in somewhat astonished tones, "apparently trade is more than a source of livelihood, it is a veritable ministry."[1] Many years later, Calvin Coolidge enunciated, "America's business is business," and thereby summed up one of the chief traits of the American character.

From the very beginning, American habits, customs, manners, and folklore were influenced much more by business than by politics, philosophy, or religion. Nor was this strange, for where economic success and rising standards of living were considered to be possible for the

[1] Quoted in Oscar Handlin, *This Was America* (Cambridge: Harvard University Press, 1949), p. 194.

majority, the maker of economic decisions was naturally regarded as one of the most important molders of culture. And it was the businessman (the entrepreneur) more than anyone else who made the decisions that determined the extent and the speed of American economic development. It was he who determined the type and amount of investment, the volume of production, and the measure of technological innovation.

It was business that attracted many of the talents Americans possessed.[2] The "business game" came to be a pervasive factor in American economic and social history, because it was so intimately and inextricably related to our way of life;[3] and the people who practiced it probably best reflected the American character. This was markedly different from the situation in Europe where different cultural patterns existed. There the businessman played no such dominant role; instead the government, the army, and the church attracted much of the talent that in the United States was devoted to business. The resulting diffusion of leadership in Europe led to a relative neglect of economic problems which, in turn, arrested the emergence of vigorous economic growth and development in many European countries. Moreover, European governments never wholly discarded their paternalism; they often surrounded private property, private profit, occupational choice, and other institutions that business cherished, with rules and regulations that impeded businessmen in their pursuit of economic goals. In the United States, by contrast, the "business game" was not only sanctioned but often exalted, and the businessmen who practiced it became leading exponents of American values, extolling the middle-class virtues of self-reliance, hard work, and frugality. Paradoxically, they generally urged conformity to traditional social and economic principles, even though in their business practices they had little reverence for traditional ways of doing things.

Because of its innate and resilient pragmatism, American business enterprise adjusted itself to concrete and tangible changes in the economic framework with greater facility than did labor, the farmer, or government. Priding themselves on their practical outlook, business-

---

[2] It hardly seems necessary to point out that from the middle of the 19th century, the United States produced an army of successful businessmen, but few artists, still fewer great statesmen, and almost no philosophers. Military men who gained fame in the nation's wars ended up, more times than not, as businessmen.

[3] For the development of this theme, see Thomas C. Cochran and William Miller, *The Age of Enterprise* (New York: The Macmillan Company, 1947).

men readily adapted their tactics and institutions to the changes required by population growth, expanding markets, and technological progress. Yet the outstanding businessmen were not successful only because of their psychological characteristics and their native talents. These were undoubtedly important, but what was equally important was the institutional framework within which these entrepreneurs operated. Business success was a result not merely of personal characteristics, but of the opportunity to take advantage of a favorable economic and political environment.

America's First Big Businessmen

For the most part American business operations in the Colonial period were small-scale. Here and there, however, some firms were expanding to meet the community's growing economic needs. Goods had to be imported from abroad and distributed to a market area that was slowly but constantly expanding. Because the local, small business was not equal to these tasks, the gap was filled by the appearance of a race of versatile merchants. Presently there came into existence in the seaboard cities relatively large shipping, brokerage, and wholesale houses, owned, operated, and directed by merchants in countinghouses. By the outbreak of the Revolution, the colonies had developed a merchant aristocracy, including among others the Livingstones, De Lanceys, Beekmans, and Schermerhorns in New York[4]; the Apthorps, the Gardiners, Peter Faneuil, and Thomas Hancock in Boston; Robert Morris and Thomas Wharton in Philadelphia; and Henry Laurens in Charleston. Trade thrived for these 18th-century merchants, and for their successors, men like Astor, Girard, and Derby, who presently reached the top level of the American business class. But their problems were rather different from those of the businessman of today. One student has gone so far as to say that "colonial trade seems to have been nearer the Middle Ages than to our times."[5] There were three principal reasons for this: transportation and communication facilities were ineffably bad; the scale of operations was necessarily restricted because

[4] For a thorough study of these New York merchants, see Virginia D. Harrington, *The New York Merchant on the Eve of the Revolution* (New York: Columbia University Press, 1935).

[5] W. T. Baxter, *The House of Hancock* (Cambridge: Harvard University Press, 1945), p. 295

of the small population and the limited market; and there was no uniform or adequate money system. Yet, on the whole, business was good, and the merchants, demonstrating great ingenuity, thrived and prospered. We may see how this was done by summarizing the career of Thomas Hancock, probably the richest merchant in the American colonies.[6]

Thomas Hancock—Merchant

Thomas Hancock began his business career as an apprentice to a Boston bookbinder. In 1724, he established his own publishing and bookselling business, apparently raising some of his small, but desperately-needed, capital from his father-in-law. He expanded his activities so that presently he was operating a general store. He imported much of his merchandise from Great Britain, and was consequently often hard pressed for foreign exchange. He solved this problem by entering the whale-oil trade, using the oil for export. As his export and import business grew, he began to organize shipping projects. Indeed, he missed no opportunity to turn a shilling or a Spanish dollar, since making money was his primary goal. When King George's War broke out, he became a supplier of the British army and participated in privateering. But he always practiced a nice neutrality, for in the midst of the hostilities he managed to carry on illicit trade with the Caribbean and with Holland. The end of the war temporarily depressed Hancock's business, but he continued as a government supplier, and the resumption of hostilities in the Seven Years War made him immensely rich. He died in 1764, leaving his business to his nephew, John, who spent more time in politics than in business and consequently made less money but achieved more fame than his uncle Thomas.

Hancock's business interests were extremely varied. He was a merchant and a shipper. He provided an informal mail service and did some banking. He was constantly concerned with bills of exchange, and the other complicated trappings of foreign trade. He dabbled in manufacturing and played an important role in the whale-oil industry. All this diversification and lack of specialization was imperative if Hancock was to make money since his volume of business was limited. He considered three sales a day a land-office business. Yet his business affairs were quite complicated. He bought and sold goods on credit, and, in

[6] Baxter, *The House of Hancock*. See also Edward Edelman, "Thomas Hancock, Colonial Merchant," *Journal of Economics and Business History*, Vol. I, 1928–29.

the absence of an adequate money system, handled most transactions by a complicated system of barter known as "country pay." Thus a farmer who bought goods from Hancock might pay a few dozen eggs on account. Hancock might sell these or use them to pay something on an account he ran with his tailor or on the accounts he ran with his suppliers. These arrangements, encompassing barter, running accounts, and occasional cash payments, remained in existence until well into the 19th century because of the general inadequacy of the money system.

The Appearance of "Big Business" in Manufacturing

Hancock had a rare ability for higgling and bargaining and a knack for ferreting out new opportunities for profitable transactions. These special and peculiar talents made him successful as a merchant, but they were of a different order from the skills called for in conducting a manufacturing business. Hancock was similar to many other merchants who had real talents for trade, but not for manufacturing. In time, the economy by-passed these merchants. Growing consumer demand, better marketing facilities, technological progress, and the interruption of international trade, caused by the events leading up to the War of 1812, made possible the appearance of certain branches of domestic manufacturing. This required a different business system. It needed entrepreneurs with more aptitude for innovation, entrepreneurs who could go beyond the techniques of importing and trading that the merchants had developed. The new entrepreneur had to comprehend arrangements for acquiring capital funds to finance large-scale business; for producing goods in mass quantities; for distributing, marketing, and selling them; and for supervising a relatively large labor force.

Small business could not supply such techniques, and unless all prospects of mass production and mass consumption were to be abandoned, much larger business organizations were required. Not that some big business did not already exist. Certainly merchants such as Astor and Girard were big businessmen. The early canal and turnpike companies, were large enterprises, as were some of the banks. In manufacturing, however, a new variety of big business first appeared in the New England textile industry. Here, men like Patrick Tracy Jackson, Francis Cabot Lowell, and Nathan Appleton, all of whom had already made their mark as successful merchants, adapted themselves to changing circumstances and switched their activities from trade to manufacturing. In 1814, with the capital they had amassed as merchants, a group of 15 families, known as the Boston Associates, began to operate the Boston Manufacturing Company, the first American factory in the true sense of the word. From this venture they spread their interests to include all the multifarious manufacturing activities involved in the cotton-textile industry. With the profits from their manufacturing enterprises (which averaged 18.75 per cent annually from 1817 to 1826) they further diversified their holdings, and by 1850 they controlled more than 30 per cent of New England cotton spindles, and dominated Massachusetts railroads, Boston banks, and New England insurance companies.

The business techniques and tactics that had been so successful in the New England textile industry were gradually adopted in many other industries. Large-scale enterprise grew steadily, especially in manufacturing and transportation, but less in the area of trade and service. In the last half of the 19th century, the number of manufacturing wage earners increased fivefold; value added by manufacturing, twelvefold; but the number of manufacturing plants, only fourfold. Thus, the average manufacturing establishment was doing three times as much business at the end of the century as at the middle of the century.

The Corporate Form of Business Organization

Big manufacturing required not only a different type of entrepreneur, but new forms of business organization. Methods and techniques that had been adequate when small-scale operations dominated business were no longer satisfactory in a new age of growing business volume. The sole proprietorship had been adequate for the Yankee peddler, who had no need for a partner (much less for stockholders) in hawking his wares. Similarly, the sole proprietorship or the small partnership was well suited to the business undertakings of the merchants, no matter how far-flung these ventures might be. The corporation or joint-stock company, despite its relative early origin and its use in colonization ventures, was not at all popular in early America. Indeed, it was an oddity, which no merchant house used. Its advantages—limited liability, continuity, and capital-raising ability—were far in advance of the merchant's needs. He was more interested in a more personal type of business organization because of the need for maintaining decision-making power and for preserving the public's faith.

With the appearance of new enterprises that required relatively more capital, the corporation became more appealing.[7] Land companies, turnpikes, canals, banks, and railroads required far more capital than a group of partners could raise in a local area. It cost, for example, about $15 million to build the Baltimore and Ohio Railroad, $30 million for the New York Central, $50 million for the Erie, and $11 million for the Erie Canal. Many of these new business ventures were highly speculative, and would-be investors naturally desired some assurance that their potential losses would be limited. Furthermore, investors were busy with their own projects and could not afford either the time or the energy required to oversee the operations of these new enterprises. The corporation fitted these needs of the investor and the firm better than did either the partnership or the proprietorship. Through the sale of shares of stock, much larger amounts of capital could be raised. The corporation charter protected the investor against excessive risk by limiting his liability, and also relieved him of the burdens of management by providing for a governing board. Moreover, although the corporation had perpetual life, the individual stockholder could sell out at any time without destroying the continuity of operation.

Despite their obvious utility, corporation charters were not easy to obtain. Before the passage of general incorporation laws they were bestowed by special acts of legislatures, a procedure replete with inconvenience, chicanery, and delay. In order to obtain a charter it was necessary to be a favorite of politicians, to engage in lobbying, or to give munificent gifts to those in power. In time this legal obstacle was overcome, and, by 1850, most states had general incorporation laws permitting corporations to be chartered without special legislative acts. Thereafter, corporate business rose steadily. Of all corporation charters issued between 1800 and 1860, half were issued during the 1850's. By 1904 corporations owned one out of every four manufacturing establishments, and produced three-fourths of all manufactured products.[8]

---

[7] See, J. S. Davis, *Essays in the Earlier History of American Corporations* (Cambridge, Mass.: Harvard University Press, 1917); Oscar and Mary F. Handlin, "Origins of the American Business Corporation," *Journal of Economic History*, Vol. V, 1945, pp. 1–23, reprinted in Frederic C. Lane and Jelle C. Riemersma, *Enterprise and Secular Change* (Homewood, Ill.: Richard D. Irwin Inc., 1953), pp. 102–124.

[8] By 1929 the corporate form had spread so much further that corporations owned almost half the establishments, and produced more than 90 per cent of all manufactures. Mining and transportation also made wide use of the corporate form, but it was rare in agriculture, service, finance, and trade. Consequently, in the 1950's only about half the national income was produced under the corporate form.

Business Policies in the Age of the Industrialist

Within the corporate form of business organization, better use could be made of managerial talent than had been possible in the old merchant firms. Mass production in manufacturing involved decision making that exceeded the capacity of the managerial jack-of-all-trades who had made the decisions in the mercantile age. To some extent, therefore, managerial functions by the middle of the 19th century were split up and separated into more categories than had been thought necessary or feasible in the day of the merchant. It must not be thought, however, that this change cut very deeply into the structure of business enterprise. In most cases, only the most rudimentary breakdown of managerial function occurred. Most 19th-century entrepreneurs were still essentially paternalistic and held the reins of managerial control as much as possible in their own hands, so that even the late 19th-century firm was relatively simple as compared with today's massive, complicated, and highly-sophisticated organization.

The 19th-century entrepreneur concentrated his talents on production, not on management, finance, or even marketing. To increase production was the chief goal of his business life, if not of his entire life. That he succeeded remarkably well may be shown by a few figures. By 1890, the United States was the largest manufacturing nation in the world. In less than 50 years, value added by manufacturing had increased sevenfold, and manufacturing production eightfold. Textile mills, which were already humming in 1860, were by 1900 operating one cotton spindle for every four people in the country. The modern steel industry, almost non-existent in 1860, produced in 1910 enough steel to fill 1,250 miles of freight cars.

All this great increase in production clearly emphasized the 19th-century entrepreneur's single-mindedness. He set his sights on plant expansion and increased production; he was much more concerned with supply than with demand. Businessmen really had no public relations policies, since most of them believed that how they ran their business was their private concern; nor could it be said that they had any labor policies, since they considered labor a commodity to be bought in the same way as machinery or raw materials. By absolute standards, wage levels were very low, yet each businessman denied that he had any responsibility for this unhappy situation, always pointing out that he paid what other businessmen were paying, a rationalization that inevitably led to the question of who set the "going wage" in the first place. The truth of the matter is that no wage theory existed. There was a widespread belief in the "wages-fund" doctrine,[9] but wages were really set by a combination of what "George was paying" plus a great deal of market-place haggling.

Businessmen paid somewhat more attention to consumer relations. Here and there were to be found entrepreneurs who devoted part of their imaginative talents to cultivating demand. Cyrus H. McCormick, for example, sold farm equipment on an installment plan, and on a "try-and-buy" basis. A farmer could contract for a $120 reaper by paying a third down, with the balance payable over four months. But McCormick's methods, even though far ahead of his day, were a far cry from today's installment selling techniques. Except for crude and limited advertising, few businessmen made any attempt to whet consumers' propensities to consume. The cliché that Henry Ford later made famous —"you can have any color car provided it's black"—was a typical attitude toward consumer preferences in the 19th century.

The Problem of Competition

Since they paid so little attention to demand and so much attention to production, 19th-century entrepreneurs lived in an atmosphere of price competition which all of them detested, but which most of them practiced diligently and ruthlessly. Some prices were very "sticky" even in the last half of the 19th century, but the prices of miscellaneous manufactured goods, textile products, and metals varied widely. Price difficulties were further complicated by the constant expansion of marketing facilities that brought more areas into competition, and by the almost complete absence of a one-price system. Even in retailing, the policy of one price to all customers was by no means universal. In manufacturing, it was the exception rather than the rule.

Bitter price competition of the kind practiced by uninhibited entrepreneurs may have resulted in considerable social benefits in the form of increased production and lower prices, but it also meant a high rate of business bankruptcy and a high degree of business insecurity. Naturally, therefore, businessmen took steps to eliminate or control price competition. At first these efforts centered around the use of trade associations. Since written contracts designed to fix prices or curtail pro-

9 See p. 305.

duction were illegal under the common law, businessmen often resorted to so-called gentlemen's agreements. One of the earliest of these was entered into in 1818 when the upper Ohio River steamboat operators agreed to regulate rates. But it was not until the 'fifties, when mass production reached a considerable degree of development, that gentlemen's agreements through trade associations really became important. The American Brass Association was formed in 1853 "to meet ruinous competition," and in 1855 the American Iron Association was founded.

Gentlemen's agreements, however, were not very effective because sooner or later one of the parties would sell below the agreed price, and then the whole delicate and carefully-contrived scheme would collapse. In order to correct this difficulty, businessmen formed pools which were really cartel agreements. They either divided the market, fixed quotas, or set up single selling agencies. Pools were usually formed during business depressions after periods of very active competition, and first appeared in numbers during the severe depression of the mid-'seventies. The cordage pool in 1878 was quickly followed by pools in salt, whiskey, coal, and other industries. But, like gentlemen's agreements, pools did not give a satisfactory answer to price competition. They could not maintain a sufficient degree of stability, because their members had too much autonomy and found it easy to evade the self-imposed restrictions. As soon as business declined, price cutting recommenced, and once again many companies were pushed into economic difficulties.

The businessmen's struggle against price competition took a new turn in the last three decades of the 19th century. By then some of the ablest entrepreneurs, men like Rockefeller, Duke, Havemeyer, or McCormick, were trying to solve the problem of price competition by consolidating all or most of the business firms within an entire industry. Between 1879 and 1903 this attempt to achieve monopoly demonstrated itself through the formation of huge trusts and holding companies. The Standard Oil Company, formed in 1879, allegedly was the first "trust." A brilliant lawyer, Samuel C. T. Dodd, formulated the idea from which this colossus grew, but it was not the product of a sudden stroke of genius so much as the result of long experimentation and careful thought on the part of Standard Oil's executives, who were concerned with ways and means of eliminating competition. Under the trust device, stockholders in various enterprises conveyed their shares "in trust" to trustees, receiving "trust certificates" in return. Stockholders continued to receive dividends, but they surrendered their right to vote, thus giving the trustees full control over all the enterprises. The trust device became enormously popular as a method of gaining control over firms within an industry, and soon trusts were formed in whiskey, sugar, cordage, and other industries. But to the public, trusts became synonymous with monopoly, and in the 1880's action was taken to dissolve them by state anti-trust prosecution. By then, however, ingenious lawyers and promoters had invented the "holding company," a new and even more expedient method of exercising control, and one which, it was hoped, the anti-trust laws could not prevent.

New Jersey was the first state to legalize the holding company. In 1888 and 1889, it passed legislation permitting corporations to hold stock in other corporations; then, in 1896, New Jersey companies were granted the privilege of doing business anywhere. These acts permitted entrepreneurs to gain control of a chain of companies at the cost of relatively small amounts of money. Similar laws in other states accelerated this consolidation movement. According to Myron W. Watkins, a careful student of business concentration, no single plant of the early 1800's controlled as much as 10 per cent of the output of a manufactured product. By 1904, in contrast, 318 large combinations, with 5,200 individual plants, controlled about four-fifths of the important industries. They controlled two-fifths of the manufacturing capital of the country, and in many industries they were responsible for more than half the total output.

There are still other ways of illustrating the remarkable growth of business consolidation that occurred in the last years of the 19th century. During the 1880's, the number of iron and steel establishments increased by less then 10 per cent, but output increased by over 100 per cent. Fewer establishments were making farm equipment at the end of the decade than at the beginning, but production had doubled. All this, of course, meant that every year there were more "giants" in business. In 1896, except for railroads, there were not more than a dozen ten-million dollar companies; in 1903, there were 300. One can, therefore, understand why John D. Rockefeller felt impelled to say, "The day of combination is here to stay. Individualism has gone, never to return." But Rockefeller underestimated the persistence of the American belief in competition. Time was to show that many of the early trusts were formed on shaky foundations. Of the mergers that were formed around the turn of the century, some never survived their infancy, and almost half were failures. Those that survived restricted the area of price competition, but did not succeed in reducing the threat of price cutting as much as their creators had wished and hoped.

The "Heroic" Businessman and the Modal Businessman

From the vantage point of today, it seems quite apparent that the main strength of the 19th-century entrepreneur lay in production. In an era when investment demand was huge, and the economy's major need was for more production, the most successful entrepreneurs were those who were bold enough to innovate in plant expansion and to drive ruthlessly forward to ever higher levels of production. Their investment spending was, in the terminology of economics, more "autonomous" than "demand-induced." Indeed they had a blind spot as regards demand. Their forte was to fill a virgin market. They gave little heed to replacement demand. Expanding as fast as possible, their management practices and decision-making processes were seldom well-developed and seldom worked smoothly. Their financial management was weak and often reckless, and they found it difficult to deal with the problem of competition.

We may gain some further insight into the strengths and weaknesses of the big, 19th-century entrepreneurs by examining briefly the business career of one of them: Andrew Carnegie. But before doing so, a word of caution is necessary. To generalize about businessmen is a dangerous pastime. Carnegie was a great entrepreneur in an era when the big business personality was as well known as movie stars, baseball players, and some politicians are today, but he was not, for all that, the really typical American businessman. He represented the big businessman, and although he was immensely successful, and even though his influence was far greater than that of small businessmen, the latter were far more numerous. For every business giant like Carnegie, there were thousands of business midgets. Nor were all businessmen successful; on the contrary, the financial mortality rate among businessmen was always surprisingly high.[10] It would also be a major error to assume, as many have done, that the social characteristics of Carnegie were typical of big businessmen of the late 19th century, or of later ones for that matter.

The most that can be said is that Carnegie represented the American businessman as he has been idealized in legend. According to this

[10] Consider that in the 1950's with 4¼ million businesses, 250 fail every week; and that it is estimated that four of every five enterprises disappear within a decade.

cherished legend, the typical American businessman was a poor farm boy or an immigrant who made good in the best "rags to riches" tradition. With little education and with no financial help from his family, he started at the bottom; and by practicing self-reliance, thrift, diligence, and hard work eventually achieved great economic success. Legend also has it that a "rags-to-riches" career, while very common in the 19th century, has become almost impossible in the 20th century.

Recent research has demonstrated that there is not much truth in any part of this legend. It is a piece of folklore created to glorify the qualities that Americans admire. The average big businessman was not an uneducated farm boy nor an immigrant who spent his early life in poverty. He was (in the 19th century) more likely an American by birth; the son of a New England father; British in ethnic origin; Episcopal, Congregational or Presbyterian in religion; and urban in early environment. Far from being uneducated and poverty-stricken, the typical industrial leader was better educated than most, and was born and bred in a family atmosphere characterized by a relatively high social standing and rather intimate contact with business affairs.[11]

Andrew Carnegie—The Great Industrialist of the "Heroic Age"

Unlike the more typical 19th-century businessman, Andrew Carnegie[12] *was* an immigrant (born in Scotland) who spent his early years in abject poverty. He began to work when he was 13, and through the intercession of a prosperous businessman he began to make a fortune, ulti-

[11] For the legend, see Irvin G. Wylie, *The Self-Made Man in America* (New Brunswick, N.J.: Rutgers University Press, 1954). For studies of the social origins of American business leaders, see F. W. Taussig and C. S. Joslyn, *American Business Leaders* (New York: The Macmillan Company, 1932); Frances W. Gregory and Irene D. Neu, "The American Industrial Elite in the 1870's," in *Men in Business* (Cambridge, Mass.: Harvard University Press, 1952); William Miller, "American Historians and the Business Elite," *Journal of Economic History*, Vol. IX, No. 2, Nov. 1949; Mabel Newcomer, *The Big Business Executive* (New York: Columbia University Press, 1953); W. Lloyd Warner and James C. Abegglen, *Occupational Mobility in American Business and Industry, 1928–1952* (Minneapolis: University of Minnesota Press, 1955).

[12] The best biography of Carnegie is Burton J. Hendrick, *The Life of Andrew Carnegie* (Garden City: Doubleday Doran and Company, 1932), 2 volumes; see especially, Vol. I, Chaps. 3, 11, 15, 19, 20; Vol. II, Chaps. 1–5. The same material has been given an entirely different interpretation in Mathew Josephson, *The Robber Barons* (New York: Harcourt, Brace and Company, 1934), pp. 102–109; 253–260; 389–394; 417–423. For still another interpretation, see James Howard Bridge, *The Inside History of the Carnegie Steel Company* (New York: The Aldine Book Company, 1903).

mately achieving vast material success. Carnegie had great personal charm and abundant ambition, optimism, self-assertiveness, and self-reliance. Some people who knew him went so far as to say that he was "full of brass," vain, boastful, and cocksure. Although he had little formal education, he had an extraordinarily apperceptive and agile mind, and he read more widely than most businessmen. Nevertheless, he relied greatly on intuition, and he was quick to accept responsibility and to make decisions when, as he put it, he "got the flash." Many of his fellow businessmen thought that he was brilliant but flighty. Although he preached the middle-class virtues of hard work and frugality, Carnegie did not work long hours. Every year he spent six months abroad, and between times, he took extended trips away from his headquarters in New York. But he always carried his business with him. Of all that life had to offer (and he lived a far more diversified existence than most entrepreneurs) he seemingly enjoyed most the game of expanding plant and increasing production.

Before entering the steel business, Carnegie spent a varied career as a bobbin boy, a telegraph messenger, secretary to Thomas Scott of the Pennsylvania Railroad, and superintendent of the Pennsylvania's Western Division. By the 1860's, he had already acquired a very lucrative investment portfolio comprising securities in an express company, in an oil speculation, and in companies manufacturing iron, sleeping cars, bridges, locomotives, and rails. What he did for these companies is something of a mystery. He apparently spent most of his time very profitably selling bonds in Europe for American railroads. Certainly he did not then specialize in the iron and steel business.

Meanwhile, Sir Henry Bessemer had invented his "converter" process for making cheap steel. At first, Carnegie was not impressed, for it was one of his axioms that "it don't pay to pioneer." In 1872, however, some 16 years after Bessemer read his historic paper, Carnegie concluded that the day of iron was over, and steel was king. His partners did not share his enthusiasm, but Carnegie nevertheless built a steel plant (which he cannily named after Edgar Thompson, president of the Pennsylvania Railroad). He raised the not inconsiderable capital needed for this venture from his friends and his associates and by liquidating all his own investments. At first Carnegie was a minority partner in the enterprise, but within five years, he owned 58½ per cent of the company.

Carnegie was never an officer in the Carnegie company and he hardly ever attended the weekly meetings of the board of directors. No businessman is worth his salt, he often said, who does not have his affairs so expertly organized that he can drop them at a moment's notice and leave for parts unknown. Despite this disclaimer, there was little doubt that Carnegie was the most influential man in his companies. Unlike Westinghouse or McCormick, Carnegie "had no shadow of claim to rank as inventor, chemist, investigator, or mechanician." He was a production-minded supersalesman with a most unusual aptitude for being able to pick and choose the right men for the right jobs. The list of his associates is long: Captain Bill Jones, his fabulous superintendent; his brother, Thomas, a most able iron master; his long-time partner, Henry Phipps; Charles M. Schwab, who succeeded Jones; Henry Clay Frick, as autocratic and ambitious as Carnegie himself. Carnegie drove these men hard, using financial incentives to spur them on, and setting up intensely competitive rivalries among them to foster ever greater efforts. Of modern management organization there was little, and the boast that the Carnegie associates were one big happy family was mostly a fiction. Some did not speak to each other for years, and the tumultuous quarrel between Carnegie and Frick was one of the most gargantuan in business history. Nor was there much truth about the vaunted independence of the Carnegie officers. Officers and directors were at all times intensely concerned with "what Mr. Carnegie thought," and Mr. Carnegie thought a great deal. He kept himself minutely informed of what was going on and never hesitated to express his opinions.

Keeping informed was not as difficult as it might seem, for the steel business now became his only business interest. From 1873 on, he was a specialist, confining his business activities solely to the Carnegie companies and their allied activities. It was he who supposedly originated the advice: "Put all your eggs in one basket and then watch the basket." From the beginning the basket was a veritable cornucopia. With an up-to-date plant (an unusual phenomenon in 1875), the Carnegie company could sell steel rails for $65 a ton when other producers could not sell for less than $70. Knowing every railroader worth knowing, Carnegie had no difficulty in exerting his magnetic personality to get whatever orders there were to be had. But he was never satisfied, no matter how magnificent the profits or how great the production. He demanded more and more and more. "Whatever I engage in," he once wrote, "I must push inordinately." The acid distillate of competitiveness was in his nature; to fail in any enterprise was for him an unendurable experience, and even in golf or at cards with no stakes involved, he was an extremely hard loser.

Goaded on by his intense ambitions, the Carnegie companies experienced steady and spectacular expansion. According to his chief biographer, Carnegie was the essence of boldness while his partners were often tired and timid.[13] They wanted an occasional breathing spell from the ceaseless effort to increase production. They longed for more dividends and less expansion, but Carnegie always overrode their objections. Year after year the business expanded, until it finally owned three tremendous steel plants, acres of iron-ore mines and coal fields, and miles of railroad. By 1900, this empire produced almost half of American steel, almost as much as did the whole of Great Britain.[14]

Carnegie's goal was technical efficiency, and he did not hesitate to scrap equipment, regardless of how new it was, if it meant lowering production costs. He also worked on the unpopular theory that it was better to expand in periods of depressed rather than prosperous business conditions. As soon as business turned downward, most companies cancelled their plans for expansion and ran for economic shelter. Carnegie, on the other hand, built his original steel works at the beginning of the severe depression of 1873, and all but rebuilt his plants when he converted to the open-hearth process during the 1893 depression. He obtained capital funds by plowing back earnings and by borrowing from banks. Indeed, he made such thorough use of his financial resources that he barely had enough cash to survive extreme downturns in the business cycle. He was in great financial trouble during the 1873 depression; and during the 1893 disaster, he described his lack of cash by saying, "I am in the condition of Mr. Vanderbilt, who once said, 'I am invested up to two years ahead.' "

During these periods of depression, and even during what are now called recessions, Carnegie tried to unload his inventories by ruthlessly slashing prices. More than any other man, he gave the steel business its reputation for being "a prince and a pauper": extremely prosperous in prosperity and desperately depressed in depression. He thrived on competition, especially on price competition, which was the only kind of business competition he recognized. He made no apparent effort to consolidate the steel business, but he certainly did not follow a policy of "live and let live." To him the rule was "dog-eat-dog," and if his com-

13 His associates took a different view, insisting that they had outdone him in economic daring. Said Schwab, "If you look at the record, he (Carnegie) was always nervous about the future, always cautious. It was Bill Jones and I who kept the plant expanding." [Allen Nevins, *John D. Rockefeller* (New York: Charles Scribners Sons, 1940), Vol. II, p. 414].

14 In round figures, the United States produced 10 million tons, Great Britain 5 million, and the Carnegie Co., Ltd., 4 million.

petitive price cutting made things difficult for some weak enterprises, this merely verified the law of Darwin (and of Carnegie's friend Herbert Spencer) that only the fit should survive. He ignored criticism of the social effects of such business policies, because he was utterly paternalistic; since he owned the business, he felt it was only right that he, not the government, not labor unions, not even the public, should call the tune.

Moreover, he knew that judged by almost every economic yardstick, the Carnegie enterprises were among the most successful in history. They had done very well indeed in increasing production and lowering prices. In 1876, they produced 30,000 tons of steel and in 1900 over 4 million tons; but whereas in 1876 steel rails sold for $65 a ton, in 1898 the price was only $17 a ton. If the entrepreneur's goal is profit maximization (as economic theorists claim) Carnegie had succeeded better than any other steelman in achieving it. In 1876, the company made a little less than $200,000; three years later, its profits had passed $1 million, and by the late 1880's, they were over $3 million. But this was just the beginning; in 1890, they passed $5 million, and in 1900, $40 million! The company was originally capitalized, in 1873, at $700,000; 27 years later it was sold for over $400 million. A one per cent share, which cost originally $7,000, was eventually worth over $4 million, and this, of course, did not include the dividends that had been collected over twenty-seven years.

The Investment Banker in Industry

The individualistic "great-man" type of entrepreneur who emphasized production and price competition may have helped raise the American standard of living by increasing the stock of goods. But it was clear by the last quarter of the 19th century that the kind of business system that he favored and fostered could not continue without considerable modification. Very often, his financial policies were too weak to withstand the rigors of business depressions; or his managerial organization was not geared for smooth operation of mass-production enterprise; or his competitors and his associates would not tolerate uninhibited price competition. Either by force of circumstances or by voluntary decision, steps were taken to change or improve the existing structure and overcome some of the weaknesses of the enterprise system. Frequently this change came from outside industry. Thus when a great industrialist's vast enterprises began to totter for want of cash, or when price competition threatened to "demoralize" an industry, it was not uncommon for the investment bankers of Boston's State Street or New York's Wall Street to step in to protect their own interests or those of other creditors or stockholders. This practice of banker intervention became more and more frequent; and, in the last quarter of the 19th century, investment bankers exercised so much influence in non-banking businesses that some writers have used the term "finance capitalism" to characterize this new amalgam of industry and investment banking.[15]

In their business policies, the investment bankers[16] differed quite sharply from the industrialists. Unlike most industrialists, who specialized in a single branch of production, the bankers spread their influence over many different industries. Consequently, their interests were too diversified to permit them to assume a really active entrepreneurial rôle. Within the firm, they delegated most of the actual day-to-day decision-making power to managers. As a result, management began to extend its own influence, and the business system became more and more tinged by the decisions made by a professional managerial class.

As one might expect, investment bankers were more interested in financial policy than in any other aspect of business activity. They preferred the discipline of corporate finance to that of industrial management. Income statements and balance sheets, earnings per share, security prices, capitalization and security flotations interested them much more than the index of industrial production, the output of pig iron, or the volume of car loadings. Because bankers and industrialists were so entirely different, it is not surprising that bankers disliked industrialists and that production men loathed bankers. Morgan thought that Carnegie was a dangerous man who had "demoralized" the steel industry. For his part, Carnegie had little sympathy for newfangled notions of corporate finance. He abhorred speculation and would not tolerate "gamblers" in his organization. Above all, he disliked promoters and boasted, not without reason, that he could operate a steel business much better than a lot of "stock-jobbers" who paid more attention to security manipulation than to steel-making.[17]

Because they were so much concerned with financial matters, the investment bankers were more at home in reorganizing and consolidat-

---

15 See, for example, N. S. B. Gras and Henrietta M. Larson *Casebook in American Business History* (New York: F. S. Crofts and Co., 1939), especially pp. 3–15.

16 The prototype of the investment banker was, of course, J. Pierpont Morgan, and the prototype of the investment banker's industrial manager was Judge Elbert H. Gary.

17 Rockefeller and Ford also had little admiration for bankers.

ing existing businesses than in creating and building new ones. They were not particularly venturesome or bold in expanding production. They were more interested in dividends, stability, and the protection of stockholders' interests than in plowing back earnings and expanding plant. They were opposed to ruthless price competition and favored, instead, a spirit of "live and let live," with stable rather than volatile prices. With such a set of beliefs, it was not surprising that the bankers exerted an important influence in bringing to the fore a concept of "fair prices" vaguely similar to the "just price" of medieval times.[18] Judge Gary of the United States Steel Corporation expressed the idea very well when he said: "I think any of us would rather have the prices of our tailor or our grocer substantially uniform, assuming that they are fair and reasonable, than to have the prices very low in time of panic and depression, and then in other times very high and unreasonable."

John D. Rockefeller—Combination Is the Life of Trade

Wall Street and State Street did not swallow up all the industrial enterprises. Nor did all industrialists follow reckless financial policies. Some met and overcame the problem of competition. A few even put together managerial organizations that continued to operate smoothly long after the retirement of their creators; such, for example, were the Standard Oil enterprises originally put together by John D. Rockefeller and his associates.[19]

Rockefeller's early life followed the Horatio Alger pattern, for unlike the more typical American businessman, he, like Carnegie, made his way from humble origins. He was born in an unpretentious rural home where thrift, diligence, responsibility, business sharpness, and puritanical religion were constantly taught. Very early in life, Rockefeller seems to have known what he wanted. Business success was his goal: "I'm bound to be rich," he said. But business was more than a road to wealth; it was a great game. "Some say," he once told a friend, "that because a man is successful . . . all he is after is to get wealth . . . How blind! . . . That's the thing—accomplishment, playing the game."

To the pursuit of business success, Rockefeller brought imagination, vision, and daring. He thought that careful accountancy was the foun-

[18] See p. 33.
[19] The material on Rockefeller and Standard Oil is voluminous and much of it is excellent. See, especially Allan Nevins, *John D. Rockefeller* (New York: Charles Scribner's Sons, 1940), 2 volumes; Ralph W. and Muriel E. Hidy, *Pioneering in Big Business* (New York: Harper and Brothers, 1955).

dation of stable business, and that the acquisition of large credit facilities was essential to steady expansion. In his own establishment (and in his own life) he practiced faultless order, rigid economy, and a complete mastery of details; but in his dealing with the rest of the business world he followed the boldest and most venturesome policies. He had the precision of a bookkeeper, but he also had imagination and thrust. He disliked hunches and tried to look at every problem with cold logic. Singlemindedly devoted to his business, he did not work hard in the conventional sense of spending long hours at the office, but, like Carnegie, he carried his business problems with him wherever he went.

After a little formal education, Rockefeller got his first job, at 16, as a bookkeeper for a firm of commission merchants. His first week's wages were only $1.20, yet four years later, in 1859, he had accumulated almost $1,000. With this and another $1,000 that he borrowed from his father, Rockefeller and Clark formed a partnership and began business as commission merchants in farm produce. Rockefeller immediately demonstrated the thoroughness and boldness that always characterized his business methods. He paid meticulous attention to every detail of the internal organization, and he expanded the business as fast as possible, borrowing from his father, from the banks, and from anyone else who had lendable dollars. His methods worked very well, and the business was so successful that by 1863, the partnership had a little capital available for outside investment. Together with a man named Andrews, an expert technician, a new partnership for oil refining was formed under the name of Andrews, Clark and Co. Rockefeller, who dominated the firm's business policies, followed the same bold methods that had brought success in the produce business. But friction developed between Clark and Rockefeller, and in 1865, the partnership (which by then owned the largest refinery in Cleveland) was dissolved. Rockefeller bought Clark's interest for $72,500 plus his share of the commission business, and the oil business continued under a new partnership; Rockefeller and Andrews.

In the early 1860's, the oil business was extremely hazardous. Crude oil was being produced in greater quantities than the market could absorb, and sold at prices that producers considered inadequate. A tendency to overproduce also existed in the refining end of the business, for inasmuch as it did not require much capital to erect a refinery, many competitors had entered the business. Severe competition, therefore, characterized both crude oil production and oil refining, and prices were always under pressure, making a "fair rate of return" almost impossible. Most oil men were small businessmen who took a very short-run point of view. They engaged in price cutting, circumvented patent rights, and openly condemned rival products. The industry was engaged more in intrigue than in business, and the bankruptcy rate was very high.

It seems that Rockefeller decided very early in his oil career that horizontal and vertical expansion by means of consolidations offered the best answer to the twin problems of overproduction and competition. Recognizing that he needed more capital funds as well as more business brains and experience, he proceeded as rapidly as possible to acquire associates who had capital or brains, preferably both. In 1865, his brother William joined the company, and a separate organization was set up in New York to handle export sales. Two years later, Rockefeller brought into the business Henry M. Flagler and Stephen V. Harkness, both of whom had money, brains, and business experience. By then, the company was the largest refinery in the world, although its growth had only begun.

One of Flagler's first activities was the negotiation of freight rates. Two railroads and the Erie Canal served Cleveland; and, in the 19th century, when two or more transportation arteries were competing for traffic, it was usual for one or both of them to offer shippers, especially large shippers, rebates from established rates. Traffic agents, in other words, offered shippers discounts in order to obtain business. The cleverest freight solicitor obtained the largest traffic, and the shrewdest shipper secured the lowest rates. Flagler, using the size of his shipments as a weapon, played one railroad against another and the Canal against one or both railroads and thus obtained large rebates. Although similar rebates were given to other refineries, there is little doubt that these discounts were important factors in the company's early success. But they were not the only, or even the most important, factor. Rockefeller and his partners were better organizers, administrators, and technicians than the other refiners; they had better-planned facilities, more capital, and more business sagacity. With the help of rebates, and by using careful methods, the company made money every year, a most amazing record in the post-Civil-War oil business.

Standard Oil: Pioneer in Management

By 1870, the Rockefeller-Andrews-Flagler partnership was a huge affair. Accounting for one-tenth of the country's petroleum business, it owned two refineries, a barrel-making plant, timber lands, a fleet of tank cars, and many sidings and warehouses. The business was now too unwieldy for a partnership form of organization. In order to gain greater flexibility and to provide a better foundation for expansion, the partners incorporated the business as the Standard Oil Company of Ohio, with a $1 million capital. Immediately thereafter, Standard began a concerted drive to eradicate overproduction in the oil industry by eliminating competitors. It used, or at least was accused of using, ruthless methods to drive competitors out of business: boycotts, bribery, strategic price-cutting, railroad rebates, and even sabotage. In its early years, Standard made no particular effort to defend itself against its critics, but gradually it built up a rationale, defending its actions along two lines: first by insisting that competition, instead of being beneficial, really created chaos; and second, by charging that many refiners were not really legitimate businessmen, but blackmailers who had formed companies for the express purpose of selling out to Standard at highly overinflated prices.

In its expansion policy, Standard Oil preferred to buy out rather than fight competitors, but it was certainly not above applying considerable pressure if a seller proved recalcitrant. It usually offered a good, although not a high price, and preferred to pay in stock rather than in cash. When it bought, it acquired everything, including the personnel, together with an agreement that the sellers would stay out of the oil business for a specific time period. In its first few years, Standard bought Clark, Payne and Co., J. A. Bostwick (the largest selling agency in New York), and many other refineries and marketing agencies. In the process, a whole regiment of talented executives (including Payne, Bostwick, Brewster, Pratt, Rogers, and Archbold) were brought into the company. As the company grew, its legal organization underwent some startling changes. The first Standard Oil Trust was formed in 1879, the second in 1882. Ten years later, when the Ohio courts ruled that the trust violated the common law and had to be dissolved, the business was reorganized as a community of interests under Standard Oil (New Jersey). Then in 1899, Jersey Standard became a holding company for the whole enterprise. By 1911, when the Supreme Court ordered its dissolution, Jersey Standard had under its wing seventy directly-held and thirty indirectly-held companies. It was also an operating company with a vast complex of refineries, tankers, and marketing stations.

It is usually thought that Rockefeller was Standard Oil; that he made all the decisions and ruled the organization with a dictator's iron hand. It is true that he did wield more influence than any other Standard executive, but he was never the managerial dictator. Moreover, beginning in 1890, he gradually began to withdraw from the management. By 1895, Archbold had succeeded him as president in everything but the title, and in 1899, Rockefeller withdrew entirely to spend the rest of his life (as did Carnegie after his retirement) supervising his vast investments and his immense charities.

In the Standard Oil Company few men ever made decisions solely on their own responsibility. From the 'seventies on, decision making was a collective responsibility, and a group of executives, not just one individual, formulated policy. The company had a long-range view which necessitated planning and centralized policy formation, and which in turn required collection of information, consultation, and experimentation. All this was done through a committee system that started to function in the early 1870's and was a smooth-working instrument by 1886. An executive committee, consisting of those top managers who were in attendance at 26 Broadway on any given day, laid down general policy, often on recommendations from the field, leaving the vice-presidents and general managers to carry out the ideas. The committee had to approve any new construction costing over $2,500, any appropriation of over $5,000, and any increases in salaries of over $600 a year. Below the executive committee were numerous subordinate committees (manufacturing, export, lubricating oil, etc.) which made recommendations to the top management.

The committee system subjected the process of decision making to all the delays and frustrations inevitably produced by corporate bureaucracy, but on the whole it seems to have worked very satisfactorily. It had the advantage of permitting, as Archbold expressed it, "various individuals to take up the different features of the business as a speciality and accomplish greater efficiency than can be accomplished by an individual who attempts to cover all." If the proof of the pudding is in the eating, the Standard's managerial system needed no apology. Expansion proceeded apace, and profits were breath-taking.[20] The company developed a superb marketing structure and it was unusually efficient in reducing costs. With few exceptions every operation in each sub-

[20] The book value of the Standard Oil combination was $65 million in 1882, $150 million in 1897, and $660 million in 1911. Dividends averaged almost $8 million a year (1882-91) or about 60 per cent of earnings. From 1899 to 1911, dividends varied, from $32 to $47 million ($33 to $48 a share), a little less than half of net earnings.

sidiary company was expected to show a profit. The intricacies of modern cost accounting were of course unknown, but separate accounts were set up to reveal the financial state of the various departments and the various companies, and average costs were carefully computed. The various companies engaged extensively in research, testing, and experiment in order to develop new products, utilize by-products, and lower costs. These cost reductions were to some extent passed on to the consumer, but not in any systematic fashion, for price policy was more or less a hit-and-miss affair with little evidence of any well-formulated theory of price determination. Supply and demand, of course, influenced prices basically, but management had a great deal of discretionary power and could set prices anywhere within a rather broad range. Rockefeller always advocated a large volume of business with a narrow profit margin, but apparently a number of his fellow board-members did not agree with him, since there is some evidence that prices were higher after Archbold succeeded Rockefeller.

Standard Oil executives found it easy to explain the company's extraordinary success. "We had," said Rockefeller, "a group of strong men from the outset. Our general rule was to take no important action till all of us were convinced of its wisdom. We made sure that we were right and had planned for every contingency before we went ahead." Differences of opinion and personality clashes were very prominent among the top executives, but they were always subordinated to the main goal—the achievement of business success.

Standard Oil was the very essence of successful business, and John D. Rockefeller was the quintessence of the successful businessman, who reflected the American character and succeeded remarkably well in achieving the goals and aspirations which Americans so much admire. Logically, therefore, Rockefeller and Standard Oil should have been among the most honored, favored, and famed of all Americans and of all American institutions. But as every one knows, almost the exact opposite was true. Big business was not popular, and Rockefeller and the Standard Oil Company were especially unpopular. Standard Oil did not believe in unbridled competition; it believed in consolidation and combination, and it had been highly successful in achieving it. Controlling 80 to 90 per cent of the petroleum-refining business, it was a practical monopoly. But the American public still believed in competition. It distrusted monopoly and was most antagonistic to any combination which had as much authority over people as it thought the

Standard Oil combination possessed. True enough, the American people also believed in economic efficiency, and Standard Oil was unquestionably efficient. Moreover, it was probably correct to say that price competition had bankrupted more oil refiners than "the trust" ever had. But this was of lesser importance in the American scheme of values than the cherished belief in competition. The American public was caught in an old dilemma; it believed passionately in economic efficiency and material success, but it championed social justice with equal fervor. Economic efficiency and social justice were not wholly compatible, and could not be easily reconciled. This became especially true in the 20th century when public opinion became increasingly convinced that the continuous expansion of big business threatened not only the existence of small enterprises, but of the whole American way of life. A decision had to be made in favor of one of the two opposing values; economic efficiency or social justice. For its part, Standard Oil, following the time-honored business axiom that businessmen should run their businesses as they pleased, maintained its policy of secrecy, and presented no forthright defense of its policies. Whether such a defense would have been of any avail is questionable, but it is certain that public hostility was of more than passing importance in precipitating a public issue, one that was juridically faced in 1911 by the Supreme Court decision which compelled the dissolution of the Standard Oil combination.

Further Consolidation and Combination

The dissolution of Jersey Standard, and other procedures under the Sherman Act, may have slowed down the trend toward business consolidation, but they certainly did not stop it, for with minor interruptions, the combination movement, which had been so evident in the 19th century, continued in the 20th century. Between 1903 and World War I, the rate of business consolidation declined, but it reasserted itself and reached new heights in the 1920's. Once again it fell off during the depression of the 1930's, but after World War II, another resurgence occurred, although the number of mergers did not reach the peak attained in 1929.[21]

21 According to the Federal Trade Commission, there were approximately 1,200 mergers in 1929, 125 in 1949, and 500 in the middle 'fifties. In contrast, the highest estimate for the number of mergers that occurred from 1890 to 1904 is 377.

Mergers were an important cause for the emergence of huge firms; but business giants would have grown even without them. By the middle of the 20th century, there were 67 billion-dollar firms,[22] only a few of which had been created by mergers. Companies with assets of over $10 million accounted for 70 per cent of manufacturers' sales, and companies with assets of $100 million or more accounted for 50 per cent. Between 1899 and 1947 the number of establishments increased by only 20 per cent; the number of employees by 300 per cent; but net output by 1600 per cent!

As the great business giants became ever more gigantic, their legal forms of business organization necessarily became more complicated. The simple, single-stage holding company, that had very satisfactorily controlled late 19th-century big business, no longer sufficed for the far-flung and highly complicated big firm of the 20th century. So, in the 1920's, the holding company device was further elaborated. The multi-stage or pyramided holding company appeared. Layer upon layer of subsidiary companies were added by the parent holding company. Companies borrowed from each other, issued securities, and bought each other's securities. Their relations to each other so far transcended the parent and offspring relation that the most expert corporate genealogist could not unravel them.

The use of non-voting stock very often accompanied the sophisticated holding company pyramid. Prior to World War I, preferred stock usually had voting rights and hence a voice in determining corporate policy. After the war, preferred stock was often issued without voting privileges, and the voting rights of common stock also came to be restricted severely. In order to ensure their control, promoters and financiers of new enterprises sometimes issued two kinds of common stock, voting and non-voting. They sold the non-voting stock to the public and retained the voting stock for themselves. The promoters of the Industrial Rayon Corporation, for example, sold to the public 598,000 shares of non-voting Class A common, and held all of the 2,000 shares of the Class B stock which had sole voting power. Through the use of the holding company and of non-voting common stock, enterprises could be controlled through a fractional investment. It was estimated that in twelve major utility companies the entire equity common stock amounted to only 10 per cent of the $1.5 billion of securities publicly held. In one extreme case, one dollar invested in the voting stock of Insull

---

[22] 22 industrial companies (11 in oil refining), 17 banks, 13 insurance companies, 6 railroads, 5 public utilities, 3 finance companies, and 1 retail establishment.

Utility Investments, Inc., controlled $1,750 of assets in the Georgia Power Company, an operating subsidiary.

In time, steps were taken to limit the use of non-voting common stock, and of the holding company as well. In 1926, the New York Stock Exchange refused to list non-voting common. In the 'thirties, the Federal government, under the Public Utility Holding Company Act, ordered the dissolution of pyramided holding companies in public utilities. But by then corporate business had grown so large that control could be maintained without resorting to artificial mechanisms.

Consolidation had an obviously beneficial effect so long as it enabled a business unit to grow up to the point of maximum economy in a single firm. Intra-plant economies, such as mechanization, mass production, and the use of scientific management techniques, could be accomplished more easily in a large firm. But every individual plant had an optimum size, and once that was reached, further growth frequently failed to yield commensurate benefits. When big business went beyond the point of diminishing returns, it tended to become less efficient than smaller business in cutting costs. In the long run, therefore, there seemed to be no clear-cut evidence that big business could show higher profit rates than medium or small business; nor was there any strong tendency for profits to be equalized among different firms in the same industry.[23]

The Ascendancy of Professional Management

By 1911, when the Supreme Court ordered the dissolution of Jersey Standard, professional managers were operating the company. By then, the old "Standard Oil Crowd," Rockefeller, Flagler, Rogers, et al., (who might be called the self-made pioneers) had been pretty well replaced by a new group of career administrators. By the middle of the 20th century, this trend toward management by a group of specialized professional administrators had spread far beyond Standard Oil and a few other giants, and had become increasingly characteristic of American

[23] The TNEC in 1938 concluded that medium and small businesses had lower costs than large business. [Monograph No. 13, *The Relative Efficiency of Large, Medium Sized and Small Business* (Washington, D.C.: Government Printing Office, 1941).] Another study, made about the same time, concluded that big business fared better than small in depression and not as well in prosperity. Over the course of the whole business cycle, profits were higher in small than in large business. [*How Profitable Is Big Business?* (New York: The Twentieth Century Fund, 1937).] However, more recent studies by the Federal Trade Commission concluded that during the prosperous 1950's, big business showed a better profit picture than did small business.

business.[24] The change toward professional management, like all changes in economic history, had not been revolutionary; it had taken place gradually and continuously. It reflected among other things the government's increasing economic influence, the enhanced importance of labor unions, and a greater concern for public opinion. Above all, however, it represented an organizational adaptation to the continuous growth and the increasing complexity of business enterprise itself. As business organizations grew constantly larger, it became increasingly difficult for the stockholders, (the owners of the business) to control and operate it. The ascendancy of the professional manager, therefore, signalized the so-called "corporation problem," which, in essence, centered around the separation of ownership from control.

The Corporation Problem

Obviously, ownership and control rested in the same person under the sole proprietorship. So long as the proprietor's business was small, the decisions which he made were not complicated and did not require any very extensive knowledge. With the appearance of the great merchants, decision making became a trifle more complicated; but the merchant princes and the partners in shipping and trading enterprises continued to make most of their own decisions and maintained complete control over their enterprises. The administrative organization of business remained simple, and there was no need for a large and departmentalized office. Often a chief clerk and one or two juniors, usually apprentices, comprised the whole office staff. The only typical separation of ownership and control was on the high seas where the ship's captain made decisions, or at trading ports where the supercargo (the trading agent) made them.

Problems of administration, managerial specialization, and departmentalization appeared, however, in the large corporation. The mere existence of the giant corporation meant a separation of ownership from

24 As with all generalizations, there are many exceptions to this one. Henry Ford spent his career operating in the Carnegie style, but the reorganization of the Ford enterprise after his death attested to the all-pervading influence of professional management. The Rockefellers in 1929 succeeded in ousting Col. Robert Stewart, the professional manager of Standard of Indiana, although not without a long and hard struggle. In the 1950's, there were a few highly colorful contests that resulted in the unseating of professional managers, but the very sound and fury that they occasioned demonstrated their increasing rarity.

control, simply because it was physically impossible for all the stockholders to meet together and formulate policy.[25] Even if this difficulty could have been overcome, the stockholders would not have had the necessary familiarity with all the ramifications of the business to make intelligent decisions.

As business became still more complicated and broader in scope, a more sophisticated approach to decision making therefore became necessary. No single individual possessed the required breadth of knowledge or the time and energy to make the thousands of decisions that daily faced a complicated business enterprise. Arthur H. Cole, in describing the increased complexity of business, points out that whereas the House of Hancock consummated about three transactions per working day, a modern department store makes more than 5,000. This increased complexity required specialization. Decisions had to be evaluated more on the basis of their long-run than their short-run effects. A broad knowledge of all phases of the business enterprise, as well as a knowledge of the total business situation throughout the economy, became necessary for intelligent policy formulation. The director of a large enterprise had to use accountancy and statistics. He needed some knowledge of law as well as economics since he worked with a highly sensitive economic machine in an environment of great legal complexity. He also needed some familiarity with psychology and public relations because advertising and service were becoming more important. Moreover, some knowledge of corporate finance was indispensable, because business expansion required a constant flow of capital and, at the same time, the avoidance of as many risks as possible.

Paradoxically, the chief executive of the large professionally-managed enterprise became much more a jack-of-all-trades than his predecessor, the "heroic" business entrepreneur, had been. He was, however, aware of the knowledge that he did not possess[26] and he became more and more appreciative of the repercussions of his business on his competitors, his

[25] Even at an early date, diffused ownership characterized the large corporation. In 1853, for example, there were 2,500 stockholders in the New York Central Railroad.

[26] Crawford Greenewalt, president of Du Pont, has said, "Specific skill in any given field becomes less and less important as the executive advances through successive levels of responsibility. Today, for example, there are thousands of people in the Du Pont Company whose expertness in their special field I can only regard with awe and admiration." Quoted in Herryman Maurer, *Great Enterprise* (New York: the Macmillan Company, 1955), p. 146. This is a very persuasive and sympathetic, if somewhat onesided, study of the professional manager's role in contemporary American life.

customers, and his labor force. Consequently he came more and more to rely on experts in each field: purchasing, production, sales, or personnel. He became also very dependent upon ancillary institutions—on banks, trust companies, insurance companies—and on lawyers, engineers, and consultants for help in various business problems. With all these ramifications, it was necessary to create an appropriate managerial structure. Staffs were departmentalized, and the chief executive had less contact with the actual operation of the business, approaching it indirectly through subordinate officers.[27]

This development had already begun by 1860 in the railroad and canal companies, whose very existence depended on mass administration and mass financing. In that year, for example, the Delaware and Hudson Canal Company required a whole building to house the administrative force that controlled the operations of its 4,200 employees.[28] By the 20th century, infinitely more complicated administrative organizations had been developed. The General Motors Corporation in addition to a board of directors with its chairman and vice-chairman, had a president and two executive vice-presidents, a host of subcommittees, and many divisional managers. It also had service staffs (headed by vice-presidents) for finance, law, engineering, reseach, manufacturing, and personnel. Central management made only the major decisions: it set the general goals and prescribed each division's role in the over-all performance; it determined price ranges, total production, and each division's output quota, capital, and expansion. Thereafter the divisional managers made the administrative decisions, deciding how to produce and sell, allocating their resources as they saw fit; determining the advertising policy; and choosing from whom to buy. Management, like labor, had become completely specialized, illustrating the all-pervasive effects of the division of labor which characterizes our modern complicated economy.

Economic Effects of the Separation of Ownership from Control

In theory, the subdivision of managerial responsibility, and the resulting greater degree of specialization, made business enterprise more

27 Arthur H. Cole has described the evolution of enterprise in terms of empirical entrepreneurship, rational entrepreneurship, and cognitive entrepreneurship. See his "An Approach to the Study of Entrepreneurship," in *The Tasks of Economic History* (supplement to the *Journal of Economic History*, 1946, Vol. VI, No. 4).

28 Thomas C. Cochran, "Business Organization and the Development of An Industrial Discipline," in Harold Williamson, Ed. *Growth of the American Economy* (Englewood Cliffs, N.J.: Prentice Hall, Inc., 1951), p. 286.

rational, thereby improving the efficiency of the business process. Experts made the decisions in each field of business enterprise. Research became more scientific, and innovation more a matter of routine than of vision. But the new system also had great disadvantages. It bred bureaucracy, because the splitting down of complicated decisions, the creation of staff and line organizations, and the departmentalization of management meant more routine and systematized administration, which is the essence of bureaucracy. Although bureaucracy might be the most efficient system for handling day-to-day administration, it tended to reduce initiative, and made business management a dull routine rather than a stimulating adventure; it emphasized stability and security and de-emphasized risk, thereby removing the effectiveness of the old business incentives. In many respects, the problems of managing big business came to resemble the problems of managing big government. Many members of the business managerial group adopted the same psychology and the same working plan as that held by the typical civil service employee. Preservation of one's job became the paramount goal. The ideal was to become an anonymous cog in an enormous machine. Initiative was repressed, because "going out on a limb" might imperil the security of the job holder. Admittedly, the deadening effects of bureaucracy were most evident in the lower echelons of management, but even among top executives there was a tendency to avoid risk and to seek stability. This was especially true in industries dominated by bankers.[28]

Although most of the members of the new managerial class had relatively little share in the ownership of the business for which they made decisions, the business game seemed to hold just as much fascination for them as it had for their predecessors. The general goal, however, was somewhat different. The professional manager, although certainly not indifferent to profits, was more interested in maintaining the business organization than in maximizing short-run profits. Consequently, profits, which had formerly offered by far the greatest business incentive, lost some of their effectiveness in stirring entrepreneurs to ever

[28] In 1927 a General Motors director said "Bankers regard research as most dangerous and a thing that makes banking hazardous, due to the rapid changes it brings about in industry." Cochran and Miller, *The Age of Enterprise*, p. 308. The counsel for a large corporation testified that since it was "responsible for the savings and investment of thousands of shareholders . . . and for the security of thousands of employees" the management "is likely to be cautious and conservative, to take the courses involving the least risk." Quoted by George Stocking, "Steel," House Committee on Judiciary, *Report on Monopoly Power*, p. 966.

greater activity;[29] and financial considerations no longer served as effectively to discourage mistakes, because managers, having little ownership in the business, did not have to pay for mistakes with their own money. In the new context, non-monetary motives, such as prestige, security, morale, and social recognition, although they had always been important, became increasingly important.

The separation of ownership and control also tended to weaken the businessman's position in American society. He began to lose his traditional supremacy. He had never been a hero in the true sense of the word, but he had always been respected and often held in awe. Now society was less impressed with him. It began to take him for granted, an eventuality that had seemed impossible in the 19th century. Americans are personality conscious, but the professional administrator, unlike his predecessor in business, had little to offer to the personality cult. Consequently, most of the leading business executives in the middle of the 20th century were lost in a cloak of anonymity. "Achievement in the executive field," mused one leading executive, "is much less spectacular than comparative success in many of the professions. . . . In fact, the more effective an executive, the more his own identity and personality blend into the background of his organization. Here is a queer paradox. The more able the man, the less he stands out."[30]

As the process of formulating policy and making decisions became more routine, success in business seemed to be accomplished without much of a struggle. It appeared so easy that it lost all its color and came to be accepted as part of ordinary day-to-day existence. Professor Schumpeter recognized this as imperilling the whole structure of capitalist society when he wrote, "Success no longer carries that connotation of individual achievement which would raise not only the man but also his group into a durable position of social leadership . . . . Since capitalist enterprise, by its very achievements, tends to automatize progress, we conclude that it tends to make itself superfluous—to break to pieces under the pressure of its own success."[31]

The separation of ownership and control also emphasized the divergent interest of the different players in the business game, and served

---

[29] Alfred P. Sloan said in 1938, "Making money ceased to interest me years ago. It's the job that counts." *Fortune,* March, 1938.

[30] Quoted by Maurer, p. 81. Mabel Newcomer points out that Charles E. Wilson received about ten times as many notices in the *New York Times* as Secretary of Defense than he had as president of General Motors.

[31] Joseph A. Schumpeter, *Capitalism, Socialism and Democracy* (New York: Harper & Brothers, 1947), pp. 133–4.

thereby to create antagonisms. Conflicts among stockholders, financiers, laborers, and the different members of the managerial hierarchy became more sharply defined. Financiers, attracted by profits from security sales or security speculation, often engaged in freebooting at the expense of a business enterprise. Thus, Drew, Gould, and Fisk milked their railroad empires in the latter part of the 19th century; and Insull, Kreuger, and Hopson were guilty of financial practices which hurt business in the 1920's. Stockholders interested in dividends often thought that management wasted money on meaningless doodads or by rewarding itself overgenerously. But management was more concerned with its own security, and with the stability and continuity of the business enterprise, than in paying large dividends. More and more, enterprises retained earnings in order to finance expansion, to stabilize dividends, and to gain independence from financiers. By the 1950's, corporations were financing about half their total investments from retained earnings and depreciation accruals. At the same time, much to the indignation of stockholders, they were retaining about half the earnings after taxes, paying only half in cash dividends to stockholders. Evidently, the stockholder was no longer the entrepeneur, if he ever had been. Equally certain, the owners of business were no longer reaping all the profits. Because of the new elements that had been introduced, the corporation had taken on an identity and personality of its own. Its managers were as concerned with this intangible personality as they were with any human being.

But the managers themselves had divergent interests that created hostility and open antagonism. Some, exclusively interested in production, had as their goal plant expansion, machinery replacement, advanced techniques, and cost reduction. They were the engineers, the technicians, the scientists, and the production bosses, who had little or no concern with finance and no sympathy with the aims of the financial men. On the other hand, the distribution and financial managers—those interested in sales, public relations, and pure finance—were less concerned with production, and often prevented the production men from accomplishing their goals of expansion. In the average corporation, the financial manager usually received greater money rewards than the production man. But his very existence was dependent upon the private-enterprise profit system, whereas a production man would have status in any society. Consequently, the advertising men, the salesmen and all those whose function was to stimulate demand, had the greatest stake in private capitalism and were its stoutest defenders. Before the separation of ownership and control, every businessman had a stake in capitalism, because every businessman combined in himself an interest in both production and finance.

What has just been said may have conveyed the impression that the modern professional managers were nothing but passive agents, pale by comparison with the individualistic entrepreneurs of the last century. Such an impression would be quite erroneous. Actually the professional managers surpassed the 19th-century entrepreneurs in the two branches of business activity in which the "heroic" businessman seemed to have excelled: in mitigating price competition, and in expanding production.

Further Weakening of Price Competition

Under professional management, the attack against price competition became much more sophisticated. The broadsword tactics of Carnegie and the "Standard Oil Crowd" went out of fashion, and entrepreneurs appeared to have given up their attempts to achieve monopoly. The new type businessmen put greater emphasis on what the economic theorist calls monopolistic or imperfect competition, on such tactics as price leadership, product differentiation, and an emphasis on service. In the search for stable prices, they stressed cooperation and publicity, and frowned upon secrecy and "the old competition." Through trade associations, open-price policy began to gain national standing during the 'twenties; and through price leadership, prices became more stabilized. Businessmen came more and more to believe that price competition, instead of having the advantages so persuasively described in classical economic theory, was disastrous for one and all. In times of economic stress, therefore, they put more reliance on cutting production than on cutting prices. Economic theorists were dubious concerning the long-run effects of the breakdown of price competition, fearing that production and economic growth would suffer as price competition weakened. But the fifty years since 1900 have not conclusively supported these dim forebodings. Economic indexes in that half century progressed substantially. Value added by manufacturing increased tenfold between 1910 and 1956; the index of manufactured production was five times as high in 1956 as in 1910; and in the age of Truman and Eisenhower five times as many tons of steel ingots were produced in comparison with the age of Theodore Roosevelt and Taft. Perhaps this was in spite of the business entrepreneur, but it is much more likely that it took place because of his intelligent action.

10 Adapting financial institutions to American environment

Factors Influencing Capital Accumulation

In the preceding chapter, it was pointed out that attempts by American businessmen to expand production were very often frustrated by chronic insufficiency of capital. Basically, this scarcity of capital was the result of inadequate saving, since, in the last analysis, the volume of capital accumulation depends on the volume of saving. But what determines the amount of saving? It would seem that each individual has the power to decide how much of his income he will spend and how much he will save; he presumably can "abstain," as the classical economist Nassau Senior expressed it, from present consumption, thereby deferring the use of part of his income to the future. Yet in practice we find that human decisions are much less important in determining how much will be saved than a number of economic and social factors over which an individual has little control. His income may be too small to permit any saving, or, conversely, it may be so large that he cannot possibly consume it all. The tradition in which he was reared and the social environment in which he lives may have inculcated habits of thrift or, conversely, a high propensity to consume. Whatever the cause, a large number of individuals habitually or occasionally spend more than they earn; others are either unable or unwilling to do more than balance their budgets; only a third group—the smallest one—finds it possible to save. If this last group saves enough to offset the deficit ("dissaving") caused by those who spend more than they earn, an economy may accumulate capital, which it can use to increase the future national product.

Surprising as it may seem, the statistical evidence we have demonstrates that the American people have not been among the world's leading savers. On the contrary, they have exhibited a very high "propensity to consume." We have been a nation of heavy spenders whose optimism has discounted the possibility of a future rainy day. This phenomenon is somewhat difficult to understand, especially since American folklore has always extolled thrift and frugality. It is doubly hard to understand because, compared with other nations, the United States has had a high national income, not too evenly distributed, and, therefore, should have had a high rate of saving. Economists have long recognized that saving is a function of income, and that the higher the income, the greater, normally, is the rate of saving. Yet, what statistics we have indicate that, although high in dollar terms, American capital formation has been very modest as a percentage of national income. Data are not available for the period before 1869, but the statistics worked out by Kuznets for the years since then show that the percentage of the national income that went into capital formation changed little from decade to decade. Except for the depression years of the 1930's annual capital formation averaged per decade 11 to 14 per cent of the national income. Declines in economic activity during the depression lowered capital formation to an annual average rate of 2 per cent during the decade 1929 to 1938, and in the worst depression years the United States did not replace its used-up capital so that for those years net capital formation became a minus figure. World War II brought a sharp upward trend, and by the end of the war, net capital formation was back to about 10 per cent of the national income.[1]

---

[1] In 1956, total saving (*including government saving and consumers' durable goods*) totalled $114 billion, approximately 25 per cent of gross national product. *Gross* private domestic saving totalled $65 billion, and *net* capital formation about $30 billion.

Who Did the Saving?

Over the whole of American history, saving by individuals, especially by those who have very high personal incomes, has been the chief source of capital accumulation. In most years the majority of Americans were not able to save, and hence made no contribution to the stock of American wealth. Some atypical workers saved part of their incomes, depositing it in savings banks, or using it to purchase a home or set up a business. Farmers, who probably saved more in proportion to their income than urban dwellers, put part of their resources, time, and money into capital investment. They converted standing timber into rail fences and barns, and they purchased tools and machinery out of the money proceeds of their cash crops. But most capital accumulation came from the saving of successful businessmen and professional people.

Much of American saving has resulted from the practice of plowing back earnings. This was done by individual businessmen in the days of the sole proprietorship. Later, when professional administrators took over the management of much of American industry, corporations retained a large share of their profits and thus contributed importantly to total saving. In the years after World War II corporations habitually saved half or more of their net earnings after taxes, and these retained earnings paid for well over half of the huge volume of investment outlays by non-financial companies.

Governments have also contributed to American capital accumulation, although their contributions have never been as important as those of individuals. At first, governments increased the volume of investment by building roads, bridges, schools, and other public works. More recently, they have taken over many of the financial needs that were previously regarded as the individual's own responsibility. With the increased importance of corporations and government as capital accumulators, the saving process changed. A large part of it became involuntary; the individual had less choice over the relative amounts that he might spend or save. If he was a stockholder in a business corporation, the decision was made for him by corporate directors who retained earnings instead of paying them out in dividends. At the same time, as a taxpayer, part of his income was co-opted for capital accumulation.

The extensive corporate practice of using retained business earnings to finance investment spending smoothed the process of capital formation; it simplified the problem of where the money was coming from, and thereby removed many of the obstacles that had stood in the way of economic expansion. It also made business less dependent upon the managers of the money market, on the commercial and investment bankers, whose interests were often not the same as the interest of entrepreneurs directly engaged in industrial production. On the other hand, the practice of retaining earnings reduced the mobility of capital because corporate saving was not available to new enterprises or to would-be entrepreneurs who had ideas but no capital funds. Retained earnings, of course, tended to increase total saving and to reduce income available for consumption; but since corporations did not save because of a desire to take advantage of high interest rates, corporate saving appeared to be based more on institutional factors than on pure economic reasons; and hence the classical theory that the mechanism of the interest rate operating in a free market would automatically create an equilibrium between spending and saving was no longer as applicable as it may once have been.

Foreign Contributions to Capital Accumulation

In the early national era of our history, investment opportunities emerged so rapidly that domestic saving was inadequate to satisfy the demand for funds, and this capital shortage set in motion a capital migration from across the Atlantic.[2] As early as 1815, foreign investors had already invested an estimated $30 million in the United States. Most of this came from British purchases of American securities. In the years after 1815, foreign investors increased their holdings, buying mostly government bonds and the stock of the United States Bank. Although no American railway or manufacturing company entered the foreign money market until 1836, European purchases of government and quasi-government securities released domestic American saving for investment in enterprises requiring more venture capital.

The volume of capital imports varied with the business cycle. During the prosperous 1830's, state governments borrowed extensively from abroad, mostly from Britain. Over half of Pennsylvania's $16 million public debt was owned by overseas investors, and this example shows how eagerly American securities were sought after. These purchases

[2] The general effect of capital inflow on development and transformation has been analysed in Chapter 7. For further information on international capital movements, see Cleona Lewis, *America's Stake in International Investments* (Washington, D.C.: The Brookings Institution, 1938); Leland H. Jenks, *The Migration of British Capital to 1875* (New York: Alfred A. Knopf, Inc., 1927).

of American securities by British investors accelerated American economic development, because the proceeds from the sale of securities were largely used to finance the purchase of urgently-needed, foreign-built capital goods.

During the depression of the late 1830's, capital imports declined, not only because the British, faced with a concurrent depression, had fewer funds to invest, but also because many British investors were embittered because of the losses they had suffered from widespread default and repudiation by American borrowers. Actually, on balance they probably fared better from their American investments than they did from their domestic ones, but this could hardly be expected to mitigate their irritations. As business recovered from depression, however, foreign purchases of American securities increased once again, and by 1853 the United States Treasury estimated that foreigners owned about one-fifth of all American securities. They owned almost half the Federal debt, over half the debt of the states and about one-quarter of local debt and railroad bonds.[3] Their investments in American industry, in contrast, continued to be small, amounting to only about one-tenth of all American industrial stock issues.

The Civil War once again interrupted the flow of foreign funds, but only briefly, for by 1869 total foreign investments in the United States were about $1.5 billion, more than five times as much as in 1850. By the latter part of the 19th century, the pattern changed; the vigorous economic development of the United States had increased domestic saving to such an extent that some American investors now began to invade the international money market. Thus, in the late 1870's, J. P. Morgan and Company participated in a Canadian loan, while two decades later American bankers helped to finance the Boer War. By 1897, Americans had foreign assets of over $680 million. They were still a long way, to be sure, from being net creditors since their international liabilities were $3.4 billion, just five times as great as their international claims. In the first decade of the 20th century, Americans continued to import foreign capital, but not nearly on as large a scale as before. Consequently net liabilities in 1914 were at about the same level as they were in 1897. But this debt was all wiped out as a result of World War I. Indeed the reverse investment process did more than that. American investment

---

[3] In 1850, it was estimated that manufacturing capital was $500 million; government debts, at least $100 million; railroad capital, $318 million; banking capital, $200 million; and at least $600 million was invested in commerce. This made a total of $1.7 billion. *Annual Report of the Secretary of the Treasury*, 1853.

bankers and the United States Government loaned such large sums to the Allied Powers that the United States emerged from the war as an international creditor.

By the 1920's the status of the United States in the international money market had therefore undergone a complete change. Originally the investment problem had been to acquire foreign capital to supplement domestic saving, which was, in most years, inadequate in volume to meet the investment demands of the economy. Gradually domestic saving had increased, and our investment problem became one of finding sound and profitable outlets for American funds. By the 1920's the United States was exporting about $1 billion of capital annually. The depression of the 1930's reduced capital exports sharply, but they increased again during World War II, especially because the Federal government had now emerged as a major supplier of capital. Through Lend-Lease, UNRRA, and ECA (and its successor agencies), the United States Government provided capital for economic recovery and development in Europe and elsewhere. By the 1950's, this had amounted to about $50 billion and was continuing at the rate of about $2 billion a year. Meanwhile, American business enterprise was also acquiring a larger stake in international investment. During the 1940's this type of investment increased 71 per cent (from $7.3 to $12.5 billion) with over 65 per cent of it placed in Latin America and Canada. But although United States foreign investments were increasing, the average annual amount invested abroad was low relative to the national product; or when compared with the relative share of national product that Britain had invested abroad during her economic heyday. For despite the absolute increase in American foreign investments, the net amount was equal to only 6.4 per cent of the gross national product in 1950, a percentage which was less than the 6.8 per cent that had been exported from 1925 to 1929.

The Nature of Financial Institutions

Optimistic and impatient in their pursuit of a higher standard of living, the American people rebelled against the fetters imposed by the shortage of capital. Confident of their power to control things, they refused to resign themselves to scarcity consciousness. Instead, they attempted to increase the capital supply by creating a flexible money and banking system and by molding it to fit their own values and their own goals. But an exchange mechanism and a set of financial institutions cannot by themselves increase the stock of capital goods. No matter how ingeniously operated, a money supply and a banking system cannot by some painless process produce factories, tools, and durable equipment. This is not to say that financial institutions do not perform a productive function. On the contrary, they can encourage saving and they can shift funds from savers to investors thereby increasing the mobility of capital and improving the efficiency of existing capital. Indeed, the transition from an underdeveloped to a developed economy cannot take place without financial institutions any more than it can occur without capital accumulation.

In a really primitive economy, goods and services are traded in much the same way that small boys swap their cherished possessions. There is no monetary system but only barter arrangements; and, in the absence of a medium of exchange, there may not even be a common denominator in which the prices of commodities can be expressed. In that case, there is no price system. Nor is there any banking system nor any substantial debtor-creditor relationships, because surpluses do not exist (except on a very small scale) and without such surpluses there can be no appreciable volume of lending or borrowing.

As an economy progresses, production increases and surpluses appear. As soon as essential consumption needs are satisfied, a community can, if it has the intelligence and the perseverance to do so, devote part of its efforts to the production of primitive tools (capital goods) that can, in turn, make possible more efficient production and lead to the division of labor and specialization. With greater specialization of economic functions and with more diversified production, barter will soon become too awkward and inefficient. The community will, therefore, select a medium of exchange and acquire a money supply to facilitate trade among the producers of different types of goods and services. With the appearance of money, it becomes possible to measure capital goods in terms of the monetary unit. Thus, it is much simpler to say that farmer A's capital is $50 rather than to say that farmer A has two shovels, three hoes, two sickles, and a cart.

The existence of a money supply also makes it possible to utilize surpluses or savings more efficiently. Savings arising from surplus production are scattered among different producers, many of whom may have no intention or ability to use their surpluses directly to increase production. Even if they had such intentions, their individual saving might be too small to be used effectively. On the other hand, many would-be entrepreneurs in the community are anxious to put the community's savings to effective use in some new or better type of productive enterprise. At first, local merchants or storekeepers, by selling goods on long-term credit, may be able to provide some capital funds for indigent but ambitious entrepreneurs. But gradually the community develops such institutions as banks, insurance companies, and security exchanges, which systematically encourage saving (by providing a safe place of deposit), amass capital (by gathering up and consolidating small amounts of saving), and expedite the transfer of funds from savers to those entrepreneurs who can utilize them productively.

The Conflict Between "Sound" and "Easy" Money

A money and banking system has a peculiar propensity for becoming intensely complicated and extraordinarily sophisticated. Thus, money may first be represented by simple commodities (such as cattle, furs, or tobacco) but it rapidly becomes increasingly complex and abstract until it represents nothing but bookkeeping entries in ledgers and journals! Similarly, a banking system may evolve from a primitive stage in which merchants merely advance credit to other businessmen or to farmers, until in more developed form, it consists of a whole galaxy of specialized institutions, each advancing credit in a myriad of subtle ways. Thus today savings banks, insurance companies, investment-banking firms, and trust companies accumulate the savings of numerous individuals and, through the purchase of mortgages or bonds and stocks, transfer these savings to entrepreneurs who will use them to build or expand their business undertakings. Commercial banks, on the other hand, do not ordinarily "transfer" actual money savings from the saver to the entrepreneur. Instead they more often "create" money either in the form of checking accounts or bank notes, and then lend this created money to businessmen, the government, and consumers. Thus commercial bank accounts (demand deposits) usually result from the loans, the discounts, and the investments which commercial banks have made, whereas savings accounts (time deposits) result from actual deposits of money. Because demand deposits represent an increase rather than a transfer of money, they augment total purchasing power, and if this added purchasing power is used in markets, prices will eventually rise. It therefore follows that the activities of commercial banks may be inflationary.

Because money in the form of bank notes and checking accounts is a claim on goods, it has often been easy for a people as optimistic as Americans are to lose sight of the essential difference between money and goods. Instead of recognizing that money is merely a convenient mechanism which improves the exchange process, there was a persistent tendency to consider money and capital as synonymous; and consequently a large part of the population came to believe that the nation's stock of capital goods could be increased simply by increasing the money supply. In like manner, the illusion spread that banks, in the process of creating money, also created capital. Hence, many people believed that "easy" money and loose banking offered an "open sesame" to all the doors of prosperity. On the other hand, another group, usually much smaller in numbers, opposed all attempts to inflate the currency and expand the banking system. Consequently, disputes over the advantages and disadvantages of monetary inflation, over "sound banking," and "sound money" occurred constantly. In this "Perennial Contest for Sound Money," as one of the 19th-century orthodox monetary theorists euphemistically dubbed it,[4] bouts of inflation alternated with periods of sobering deflation. But the odds were usually against the sound money group, and consequently the American money and banking system tended on the whole to tilt more toward easy money and inflation than toward tight money and deflation.[5]

American Money Before the Civil War

Although the American people had tried a variety of ingenious monetary experiments during the Colonial period they had not by the time of the Constitution succeeded in developing a workable coinage or currency system. A sound system of coinage or currency required either an objective standard in the form of specie, or an authority that could effectively regulate the operation of the money and banking system. Neither of these prerequisites was present. A chronic shortage of specie existed, chiefly because Americans in their desire to raise their standard of living and to invest in productive equipment tended to export all available specie in payment for imports of manufactured consumer and capital goods. There was no possibility of regulating the

[4] Alonzo B. Hepburn, *History of Coinage and Currency in the United States and the Perennial Contest for Sound Money* (New York: The Macmillan Company, 1924).

[5] Lest the well-informed reader be immediately appalled by this statement, we hasten to add that there was one great exception: the period from the Civil War to World War I, when, with minor set-backs, the sound money group was in control of the situation.

whole exchange system during the Colonial era because no government had adequate authority to impose restrictions on money and banking.

After the adoption of the Constitution, the Federal government set up a makeshift coinage arrangement in 1791, when it established, on the recommendation of Secretary of the Treasury, Alexander Hamilton, a bimetallic standard. Under this, our first nation-wide monetary system, gold and silver were freely minted into two types of coin: a $10 gold piece containing 247.50 grains, and a silver dollar containing 371.25 grains. Since either metal could be "freely coined," this meant that the government stood ready to buy gold at $19.39 an ounce and silver at $1.29 an ounce. But little gold was coined, because holders of gold could sell it in the international bullion market for over $20 an ounce. One of the best-known principles of economics, Gresham's law, asserts that when two kinds of money are in circulation the less valuable will drive out the more valuable; this principle was therefore operating to change our legal or *de jure* bimetallic standard into a *de facto* monometallic (silver) standard. But even silver coins failed to circulate domestically. Instead, they were exported to the Caribbean area, where they circulated at face value even though they were coined lighter than the Spanish dollars on which they were patterned. The United States, therefore, had a coinage system in name only; in actual practice no American coin higher than five cents really "circulated." Many transactions were still settled on a barter basis; indeed as late as 1832, in answer to a questionnaire, 18 out of 324 manufacturers stated that they disposed of their entire output by barter, and 148 disposed of part by barter. Where a need for metallic money existed, it was satisfied by foreign coins, such as Spanish dollars or Dutch guilders, which were given legal-tender status under American law.

By 1834 some gold deposits had been found in the Appalachian range of North Carolina. Although they did not produce nearly as much as the later-discovered and more-famous California, Alaska, and African gold fields, they did make it possible for the United States to establish a more effective specie standard. Taking advantage of altered circumstances, the administration of Andrew Jackson, whose sympathies were decidedly for hard money, devalued the gold dollar in terms of silver. The weight of the gold dollar was reduced to 23.2 grains (23.22 grains by amendment in 1837) while the silver dollar was kept at its old weight of 371.25 grains. This change made the price of gold at the mint $20.67 an ounce (instead of the former $19.30), and Gresham's law now began to operate in a reverse direction. Since the price of gold in the United

States was now higher than in other places, gold began to flow in while, conversely, silver began to leave the country. The devaluation, therefore, placed the United States on a *de facto* gold standard, although, legally we were still on a bimetallic standard. But the coinage system set up by the United States, even with its later modifications, could not provide nearly enough money to take care of the ever-expanding needs of a growing economy.

Prior to the Civil War, the Federal government did not issue any paper money although some of its short-term securities, issued during the War of 1812 and the depression of 1837, circulated among private citizens as money. In addition, the government and such institutions as the United States Bank, sometimes accepted Federal government securities in payment of public dues or in payment of stock subscriptions. It did happen, then, that government debt was sometimes converted into money even in early American history, but this monetization of the debt occurred on so small a scale that it did not add substantially to the money supply. How then were the money needs of the nation covered, when coined money was patently inadequate? The money famine was overcome, sometimes more than adequately, by paper money issued by commercial banks, and, to a lesser extent, by the notes of an assortment of state-chartered corporations that had the power of issuing paper money.

We have no good statistics on the money supply before the Civil War, but the data we do have show that aggregate money in circulation had

The Money Supply, 1790–1858
(in millions of dollars except per capita figures)

Year	Specie*	State bank note circ.	U.S. Bank note circ.	Per capita money in circ.	Comml. bank dep.	Per capita money, incl. bank dep.
1790	9.0	3	—	3.00	n.a.	n.a.
1800	17.5	16	—	6.22	n.a.	n.a.
1811	30.0	28	—	8.00	n.a.	n.a.
1816	23.0	68	—	12.53	n.a.	n.a.
1820	24.0	41	3.6	7.19	42.5	11.65
1830	32.0	48	12.9	7.26	71.6	12.85
1836	65.0	140	23.7	15.06	120.2	23.00
1843	88.0	59	—	7.87	56.2	10.95
1850	147.0	131	—	12.02	109.6	16.80
1856	230.0	196	—	15.16	212.7	22.70
1858	251.0	155	—	13.78	185.9	20.10

* Did not circulate 1790–1834, 1837–1843, 1857–58.
Source: *Annual Report of the Comptroller of the Currency*, 1876.

an upward secular trend. The money supply also tended to be "elastic," that is, it varied more or less directly with the expansion and contraction of business. This was to be expected, because most of the money in circulation was issued by privately-owned banks in response to the needs of business, and its volume, therefore, depended on the demand for loans, and on the banker's ability and willingness to lend.

Early American Commercial Banking

In the early days of the American money market, there was no sharp line of demarcation between commercial and investment banks. Merchants often engaged in stock brokerage, and importers dealt in foreign exchange. Specialized money markets could not exist until the appearance of highly specialized entrepreneurs. They created a demand for different types of capital institutions, such as investment banks and stock exchanges, which presently arose to meet their needs.

Before the Civil War, commercial banks were easily the most important banks. Although their functions in the economy were almost identical with those of their modern counterpart, their mode of operation was quite different. Making loans, and discounting commercial paper were, of course, their chief business. But whereas in the modern economy, commercial banks create money by issuing credit in the form of demand deposits (checkbook money), before the Civil War they created money by printing their own bank notes which they loaned to borrowers.

Ostensibly, these bank notes were secured by specie (gold and silver) and were redeemable on demand in specie. But in actual practice they often could not be so redeemed. The reasons for this were not too complicated. In times of prosperity, banks increased their note issues up to the limits allowed by law, or to the limit permitted by the existing state of their specie reserves. When prosperity was suddenly succeeded by a business "panic," some of the outstanding paper money supply became redundant, and holders made haste to convert it into specie. Because banks operated on the assumption that only minor calls would be made for specie they could not meet these demands for redemption, and the specie standard had to be abandoned.

On the whole, banking under the widely-differing state regulations led to currency inflation, and state banks were more often distinguished for their high rate of failure than for their record of conservative operations. But this was by no means universal. Banks in the large cities were more consistently solvent than those in rural sections, because a metropolitan area was an industrial and trading economy properly attuned to commercial banking, whereas a rural area was an agricultural economy which needed a kind of financing singularly inappropriate for commercial banks. When a merchant in a large city received a loan from a New York commercial bank, he signed a promissory note. In exchange he received deposit credit, or state bank notes, for the amount of the loan. Normally the borrower's note was payable in specie or in bank notes at the end of 90 days, although it was usually renewable. In rural sections, in contrast, aside from a few small loans to local merchants, such short-term, self-liquidating business loans were practically unknown. The majority of loans were made to farmers who needed credit for much longer periods than the duration of customary urban bank loans. In short, country bank loans were less "liquid," than city-bank loans, that is, they could not be turned into cash as quickly. Consequently, the rate of failure among country banks was inordinately high, particularly whenever prices began to fall in the downswing of the business cycle.

Two Early Experiments with Central Banking

Although state-chartered commercial banks were the most important financial institutions in pre-Civil War America, twice during that period the United States did experiment with central banking. The first such overture occurred in 1791, when the Federal government established the (first) Bank of the United States. So long as it remained in existence, the Bank exercised useful control over the entire banking system; but when its charter expired in 1811 (and was not renewed) state-chartered commercial banks took advantage of the opportunity and expanded very rapidly, partly to meet the needs of business and partly to finance the War of 1812. At any rate, the state banks poured vast amounts of additional money into the economy in the years 1811–1815. Their number doubled and their note circulation quadrupled; the result was price inflation and, presently, the abandonment of specie payments. Indeed, by 1816, money and banking affairs had become so chaotic that in order to restore order, the Jeffersonians, who had always ideologically opposed central banking, reluctantly established the (second) Bank of the United States. Again the charter was limited to 20 years, and again it was not renewed when it expired.

Both of these banks, but especially the second, operated as central banks and therefore exerted a great deal of control over the whole money system. For one thing, each United States Bank issued its own redeemable paper money, and this gave it an obvious means of regulating the money market. In addition, its activities in foreign exchange, its position as government fiscal agent, and its central role in handling the complicated business of intersectional exchange gave it other important means of controlling the state banks and thereby the money supply. Thus, in the process of collecting taxes and in settling foreign and intersectional balances, the Bank was constantly receiving a stream of state-bank notes. It was, therefore, practically always a creditor of the state banks and it could exercise this creditor position to encourage expansion or to compel contraction of the national money market. It could contract the money supply by sending state-bank notes back for redemption, while, conversely, it could encourage money expansion by following a lenient policy in demanding redemption of state-bank notes.

Because of its powers over the money market, central banking was not popular in the expanding economy of the pre-Civil War years when public opinion favored easy money. This was clearly illustrated in the controversy over the proposed rechartering of the second Bank during the administration of Andrew Jackson.[6] In the great debate that culminated in Jackson's veto of the bank-charter bill, the Bank had the support of some economic theorists, and of a few state banks that were strong enough to benefit from a regulated money market. On the other hand, the Bank was strongly opposed by those who believed in hard money, and, paradoxically, also by those who wanted more paper money: debtor farmers, entrepreneurs "on the make," and state bankers whose ambitions were larger than their pocketbooks.

There was still a third group who opposed the Bank—those who were honestly disturbed by the gigantic power which it possessed. Many people branded the Bank a monopoly, but this was an exaggeration, because the Bank never controlled as much as one-quarter of the nation's note circulation. Even so, however, the Bank's president, Nicholas Biddle, who made the vital decisions in the Bank's operations,

[6] The Bank and the Bank controversy have been treated exhaustively. See especially Arthur M. Schlesinger, Jr., *The Age of Jackson* (Boston: Little, Brown and Company, 1945); Ralph C. H. Catterall, *The Second Bank of the United States* (Chicago: University of Chicago Press, 1903); Walter Buckingham Smith, *Economic Aspects of the Second Bank of the United States* (Cambridge, Mass.: Harvard University Press, 1953); Bray Hammond, *Banks and Politics in Early America* (Princeton, N.J.: Princeton University Press, 1958).

was probably not wrong when he said he had the power of life and death over the state commercial banks.

In one sense, then, the refusal of Congress to recharter the Bank constituted an example of successful trust busting: the triumph of small business over big business, and a victory in the eternal war to curtail what Americans thought to be excessive power. In another sense, however, the failure to recharter the Bank represented a victory for irresponsible loose banking over the useful restraints imposed by central banking. At any rate, once the United States Bank was removed as a regulator of commercial banking, state banks again expanded rapidly. Their circulation more than doubled; their loans and discounts more than tripled. Again, specie reserves became badly strained, and, when the economy virtually collapsed, in 1837, specie redemption once again had to be abandoned. By 1843, more than a hundred commercial banks (about 15 per cent of those in existence in 1836) had failed. With business recovery in the '40's, state banking began its third period of great growth, and by 1860, there were more than fifteen hundred such institutions. They constituted a rather feeble financial mechanism for the war years.

The contributions of state commercial banks toward economic development had nevertheless been very important for two reasons: by making loans (to would-be entrepreneurs or to farmers) they encouraged production; by issuing paper money, they facilitated the process of exchange and thereby encouraged business undertakings. But, despite all this, the state banks had grave weaknesses. Scarcity of good commercial loans, inadequate capital and specie reserves, reckless management, and ineffective regulation by government (and by the banks themselves) created a poor foundation for sound banking. As a consequence the state-bank system fulfilled its function in the economy only at the expense of a scourge of bank failures, and of intensified business fluctuations.

The basic weakness of most state commercial banks was that they were attempting to do a commercial banking business largely on the basis of savings-bank assets. It was only in the large cities that banks were able to carry on genuine commercial banking; for it was only where industry was developed that banks could make enough short-term commercial loans to maintain a profitable and sound business turnover. In small towns and country districts, banks made long-term loans against farm mortgages, but issued their own short-term liabilities in the form of bank notes to the borrowers. The borrowers in turn used the bank notes to purchase badly-needed commodities, especially capital goods, from industrial and commercial centers. When the notes were presented for redemption in volume, the average state bank could not turn its assets into cash fast enough, and hence found it difficult to maintain specie payments. For these reasons, bank notes often circulated at a discount, and very frequently became completely valueless. Yet in these areas where capital was scarce and industry and commerce almost nonexistent, popular sentiment favored the establishment of banks in a mistaken belief that they could create capital.

Bad as they may seem in retrospect, these unsound banks were not wholly without advantages. They enabled outlying areas to obtain some of their needed capital from sellers of capital goods in the more developed areas. In short, through state banking, the West developed its economy at the expense of the East, which is to say that they compelled the richer areas of the nation to give assistance to the underdeveloped areas.

Early Attempts to Regulate Banking

The basic weaknesses of state banking would probably have disappeared in the natural course of events, because economic development would ultimately have produced the industrial and commercial environment that is necessary for sound commercial banking. But the process would have been long drawn out, and the American people were impatient. With great faith in the magic power of legislation, they tried to eliminate the weaknesses of commercial banking by passing laws.

These banking laws differed from state to state, and ranged from severe restriction to extreme leniency. Some states formed and owned commercial banks, while others, after especially painful experience with bank failures, prohibited commercial banking altogether. Thus by 1852 there were no incorporated banks in seven southern and western states. But, most commonly, states tried to solve their banking problems by adopting "free banking," a system that incorporated six main features: it permitted banks to obtain charters without special acts of legislature; required some security against bank notes; prescribed certain reserves against deposits; imposed penalties for failure to redeem bank notes in specie on demand; designated specific places for bank note redemption; and provided for periodic bank examinations.

Despite all these attempted safeguards, regulation of commercial banking was impractical in underdeveloped areas, for, no matter how weak the regulations, they could be enforced only if the underlying economic conditions permitted. Where loanable funds were in short supply, the choice was between loose banking and no banking at all: because, if any real attempt were made to regulate banking in these areas, the inevitable result would be to force the banks out of existence. So-called "sound" banking was only possible as industry and commerce developed. But here, as in so many other phases of our economic history, the development proceeded zone by zone. The first effective regulation appeared in the East in the early 1800's. Then, in later years, as each frontier area was transformed into a relatively advanced economy, effective bank regulation spread westward. But, whenever a frontier area prematurely attempted some ambitious project designed to create sound banking by legislation, the result was pitifully ineffective.

Investment Banking Before the Civil War

Although commercial banks provided funds by creating bank credit, they were not the only source of credit for the needs of business. A sizeable amount of credit was extended within the business community itself. Thus a wholesaler or a retailer might obtain credit from a merchant or manufacturer on open-book account by giving a promissory note, or by "accepting" a domestic bill of exchange.[7] In the early 1800's commercial credit was rather sparingly extended, but when it was, the terms were relatively long; rather typically, merchants granted credit to a selected few for terms of six to twelve months. The development of credit agencies (such as Lewis Tappan's Mercantile Agency and Bradstreet's Commercial Agency) in the 1840's presently gave merchants a means of checking on borrowers, thus making it possible for them to extend credit over far wider areas, and to many more buyers. At the same time, improvements in transportation and communication led to a gradual reduction in the credit period. Whereas in 1836 it had been customary to grant six months credit, by the Civil War, 30 to 60 days were the more usual terms.

Aside from those firms specializing in commercial credit, financial institutions which could act as intermediaries between savers and in-

---

[7] The seller of goods would "order" the buyer to pay a stipulated sum of money say 30 days after he received the bill of exchange. The buyer, by "accepting" the bill agreed to these terms, and made the accepted bill a two-name negotiable instrument which could be sold for cash should the manufacturer need money.

vestors were both limited and immature before the Civil War. There were only a few investment bankers, and those who were most successful had to rely heavily on the well-developed London money market. Actually London financed almost all the American export trade and, in addition, bought a large part of the securities issued in the United States.

The American investment market was so important to Britain that a group of houses, known as the Anglo-American merchant bankers, came into existence to facilitate the export of capital.[8] Some of these houses, such as Baring Brothers and, later, Morgan, Peabody and Company, specialized in underwriting American securities. Baring Brothers, especially, played a large part in handling the securities of the Federal government and the Bank of the United States. Other British merchant houses (such as Peach and Pierce, and Lascelles and Maxwell) acted as American bankers by allowing American importers to draw drafts against them. These British credits formed the basis for further extension of credit in the United States; thus, an American dry goods merchant who imported from Britain on the basis of British credit, sold on credit to a jobber, who, in turn, sold on credit to retailers. In time, some importers in the United States with good British connections began to act as intermediaries for other American merchants, and gradually their business in foreign exchange became so important that they dropped their importing business altogether and emerged as full-fledged bankers. Alexander Brown and Son (the predecessor of the present firm of Brown Brothers, Harriman and Company) provides one of the best examples of this evolution from importer to banker.

But the relative unimportance of investment banking in the United States before the Civil War is revealed by the small volume of transactions in the nation's various stock exchanges. Formal stock exchanges had come into being in Philadelphia by 1800, in New York by 1817 (although there had been organized stock transactions in New York as early as 1792), and in Boston in the 1830's. On the New York Stock Exchange, government and bank stock monopolized the early trading; but railroad securities, which did not appear until 1830, became dominant by 1850. Industrial companies, which were usually operated as sole proprietorships or partnerships, lagged far behind. Even as late as 1867

---

8 See N. S. Buck, *The Development of the Organization of Anglo-American Trade, 1800–1860* (New Haven, Conn.: Yale University Press, 1925); Ralph W. Hidy, *The House of Baring in American Trade and Finance* (Cambridge, Mass.: Harvard University Press, 1949).

there were only 15 such stocks traded on the New York Exchange, and many of these were really not industrials by today's definition. In Boston, however, industrials, especially textile and copper mining company shares, were somewhat more prominent than in New York. But, on all exchanges, stock trading was relatively small; before the speculative boom of the 1830's, brokers considered a 100-share day as fair, although in the prosperous years, 1830 to 1834, 1,000-share days were not unusual.

As the economy grew, stock-market activity also increased, and by the mid 'fifties, stock trading had become a big business. By then, the term "call loan" was being commonly used to designate money loaned to stock-market traders, and New York had now achieved a pre-eminent position in the money market.[9] On the New York Stock Exchange, as many as 71,000 shares were traded in one day during the boom of 1857. As stock-market transactions became more profitable, traders expanded their operations. They could do so because bank reserves from all over the country flowed into New York to be loaned to traders who wanted to buy stock on margin. But this pyramiding of bank reserves in New York had the effect of aggravating business "panics," since when money became tight, banks drew down their New York deposits, thus causing multiple credit contractions and thereby greatly intensifying the existing monetary stringency.

Other capital institutions developed as slowly as investment banking in the pre-Civil War period. The trust company hardly existed, and savings banks did not increase significantly until the 1850's, although in that decade their number expanded from 108 to 300, and by 1860 they had 700,000 depositors, with $150 million in deposits. Fire and marine insurance companies, which invested their funds in securities, developed more rapidly than savings banks; but life insurance had such a slow rate of growth that by 1860, when it was estimated that $3 billion of fire and marine insurance was in force, only $180 million in life insurance policies were on the books.

Greenbacks and Free Silver

Before the Civil War, there was a widespread belief in the quantity theory of money, that is, the theory that the level of prices varied directly with the size of the nation's money supply. Most people were

[9] Margaret Myers, *The New York Money Market* (New York: Columbia University Press, 1931).

also convinced that capital could be created by increasing the money supply through the operations of state banks. After the Civil War, prices declined for a long time, and this secular deflation further intensified the faith of the debtor classes in the quantity theory of money. But by then it was no longer possible for state banks to increase the money supply by note issues, because the Federal government had imposed a 10 per cent tax on state-bank notes which drove them out of existence. Advocates of monetary inflation were therefore forced to find some new method for increasing the money supply, and, fortunately, from their point of view, the Federal government had already supplied the method.

During the Civil War, Congress, unwilling to impose taxes heavy enough to meet the costs of war, and unable to borrow enough to cover the margin between receipts and expenditures had authorized the issuance of $450 million of fiat money in the form of United States notes, more familiarly known as "greenbacks." By the end of the war, over $425 million of this first Federal paper money in the nation's history had been actually issued. After the war, easy-money adherents, convinced that more money meant higher prices, not only resisted the retirement of these greenbacks, but urged the government to increase the amount in circulation. The hard-money group, on the other hand, desired a speedy return to specie redemption. They insisted that this could be most easily accomplished by the rapid retirement of the greenbacks, and they urged the government to take such action. The long bitter controversy was finally settled by a compromise: specie payments were resumed in 1879, but the extant greenbacks, approximately $347 million, instead of being retired, were retained as a part of the circulating media.

As a result of this legal limitation, greenbacks no longer offered possibilities for increasing the money supply. Once again, quantity theorists had to seek a new panacea, and this time they found it in silver. It will be remembered[10] that the 1834 devaluation of the gold dollar had caused silver dollars to disappear from circulation. Provision for their minting, had, however, still remained in the law. To make the law conform to reality, Congress, in 1873, officially eliminated the silver dollar from the list of American coins and by doing so placed the country on a *de facto* gold standard. Meanwhile, vast deposits of silver had been discovered in the Rocky Mountain states and the supply increased so

[10] See p. 277.

rapidly, that the market price of silver fell well below $1.29 an ounce. This decline in the price of silver presented a most extraordinary opportunity for the inflationists. All that had to be done, they said, was to restore bimetallism at 16–1, for if the mint again offered $1.29 an ounce, a vast quantity of silver would be brought to the mint and coinage would greatly expand. Of course, this would mean that gold would now be withdrawn from circulation and replaced by silver. But debtor classes were hardly abashed by this prospect; to them the important thing was to increase the money supply in order to increase prices, and silver offered the opportunity. Agitation for the restoration of bimetallism, therefore, immediately began in the silver-mining districts and in the farm states.

From 1876 to the end of the century, free silver was a torrid political issue, with the fire burning most intensely whenever prices declined. At the bottom of the business cycle, many small businessmen, who were ordinarily lukewarm about the efficacy of monetary measures, were desperate enough to support any cause, and they joined the more doctrinaire groups who regarded free silver as a cure-all. The resulting alliance between debtor farmers, economically-harassed businessmen, and silver miners was strong enough to gain some victories over the forces of "sound" money, but not strong enough to obtain Congressional approval for a return to 16–1 bimetallism. Hence two major pieces of compromise silver legislation were passed: the Bland-Allison Act of 1878, and the Sherman Silver Purchase Act of 1890, laws which by varying techniques reintroduced, on a limited scale, the coinage of the silver dollar and the issuance of additional paper currency secured by silver. These monetary experiments were, however, disappointing to the debtor classes because they did not result in an immediate increase in prices. Indeed, they were rather damaging to the easy-money contention that more money would automatically raise prices from depressed levels. Had the experiments been continued and extended, they might have fulfilled the hopes of the quantity theorists. But the gold standard forces never allowed that to happen. In 1893, the Sherman Silver-Purchase Act was repealed, and in the election of 1896, when the issue of bimetallism was presented to the people in an unequivocal way, McKinley, representing monetary conservatism, defeated Bryan, the spokesman for agrarianism and bimetallism. Taking the vote as a mandate, the United States officially adopted the gold standard in 1900, fixing the weight of the gold dollar at 25.8 grains, 9/10 fine (23.22 grains pure).

The National Banking System

While currency issues were being bitterly debated in the post-Civil War period, the continuous growth of the economy, and the accompanying increase in the nation's supply of capital, had brought important, but less spectacular, changes in the structure and operation of American banking. In commercial banking, there were three major developments. First, dual banking was reinstituted by adoption of the "national banking system." Second, the use of checkbook money increased steadily, while the use of bank notes declined. Finally, in the years immediately after the Civil War national banks grew at a rapid rate, while state banks declined; but, conversely, in the late 19th century, state banks were regaining their importance, while national banks were barely holding their own. Why did these changes occur?

During the Civil War, in order to provide a uniform currency, eliminate the overissue of state-bank notes, and create a market for government bonds, the Federal government passed the National Bank Act, which provided for "free banking" on[11] a national scale. Any group of persons who met the specific requirements of the Act could obtain a national bank charter from the United States Comptroller of the Currency. Every national bank was required to deposit, with the Comptroller, United States bonds equal to one-third of its capital, or at least $30,000. Against these bonds, the banks could issue and circulate paper money known as national bank notes. National banks were also required to maintain specified reserves against their deposits, but smaller-city banks and country banks were permitted to deposit part of their reserves in the national banks of the largest cities. National banks were not permitted to own real estate or to make real-estate loans.

But neither a "uniform currency" nor an enlarged market for United States bonds could be achieved unless state-bank notes could be driven out of existence, and for this purpose the national government, by a subsequent amendment to the National Bank Act, levied a 10 per cent tax on state-bank notes. As long as bank notes constituted a chief form of money, the tax discouraged state banking. But presently, as checkbook money became more important in the economy, the tax became meaningless. Consequently many national banks surrendered their Federal charters and once again obtained state charters because the state rules governing banks were more lenient than those stipulated

[11] See p. 283.

in national charters. As checking accounts steadily encroached on bank notes, the business of state banks increased, so that by the 1890's state banks had superseded national banks in importance.

From the point of view of respectable 19th-century monetary theory, the national banking system opened the golden age of money and banking, for under that system bank loans were made against commercial paper that presumably could be liquidated very rapidly in a crisis. Thus depositors and noteholders were better protected than they had previously been; indeed there was little doubt that the national banking system was immeasurably safer for depositors and noteholders than the old state banking system. But the system also had glaring weaknesses. In the first place, national bank currency, secured by Federal bonds, was more inelastic than the state-bank notes which had rested on long and short-term business debt. Then too, by allowing smaller banks to re-deposit their reserves with larger banks, the system encouraged the old evil of pyramiding reserves in New York City. Thereby it reduced the mobility of capital, disrupted the balance between different money markets, and aggravated money-market panics. Thirdly, the national banking system narrowed the farmer's ability to obtain funds because it prohibited loans against real estate. Finally, the system intensified tendencies toward "boom and bust," because it put so much emphasis on commercial loans. The national banks rapidly expanded their loans up to the limit of their legal reserves during prosperity, then stopped credit expansion abruptly when excess reserves were exhausted, and ruthlessly liquidated their loans with equal rapidity during panics. Moreover, there was no central bank which could help stabilize the economy by discouraging expansion during prosperity or soften the impact of deflation during panic and depression. In brief, the national banking system made banking "safer and sounder" but at the expense of greater rigidity and less mobility than had existed under state banking.

The developments in money and banking which we have just described enlarged the Federal government's rôle in currency and coinage, complicated the currency system, and increased the inelasticity of the total money supply. Prior to the Civil War, when the money supply had consisted of specie (gold coins, subsidiary silver, and fractional money) and state-bank notes, the currency, or at least part of it, had tended to be elastic, expanding or contracting with business needs. By the 1880's this was no longer true. State-bank notes had been eliminated from circulation, and the money supply consisted of gold coins and gold certificates, silver dollars and silver certificates, United States notes (greenbacks), national bank notes, subsidiary silver, and fractional money. Although all money was now issued under the regulations of the Federal government, none of it expanded and contracted automatically with changes in business activity. Instead, circulation depended on arbitrary acts of legislation, the amount of gold production, government fiscal policy, and market interest rates. As may be seen from the following table, the circulation of some types of currency increased, others stayed the same, and some actually declined.

Money in Circulation, Selected Years, 1860–1914
(in Millions of Dollars)

Year	Nat'l bank notes	U.S. notes	Silver	Gold	State-bank notes	Other	Bank deposits	Total
1860	—	—	21	207	207	—	310	745
1865	146	328	30	149	143	237	689	1,722
1870	289	325	43	113	2	3	775	1,550
1875	341	350	60	82	1	1	2,009	2,844
1880	337	328	75	233	—	—	2,222	3,195
1890	182	335	408	505	—	—	4,576	6,006
1900	300	318	652	812	—	—	8,513	10,595
1914	715	338	769	1,638	—	—	14,692	18,152

Source: Federal Reserve Board of Governors, *Banking and Monetary Statistics,* Washington, D.C., 1943.

All too frequently instead of being designed to facilitate the operation of the economy, new currencies were introduced in the hope that they would bring about an increase in general prices. Neither the Bland-Allison act nor the Sherman Silver-Purchase Act increased the general price level. Actually, the economy could not digest the added currency, or, to put it in another way, the level of business activity was not high enough to absorb all the currency that was being issued. As the amount of money increased, its velocity (the rate of turnover) declined, for apparently, the currency supply exceeded the needs of the economy. When prices fell, the individual citizen, needing less money to take care of his everyday economic wants, tended to convert his paper and silver money into what he considered the best kind of money, namely gold. Thus, instead of raising prices, as the inflationists had predicted, the new additions to the money system usually resulted in a run on gold.

Investment Banking After the Civil War

The increased use of checkbook money and the greater importance placed on short-term, liquid, commercial paper illustrated the pervasiveness of industrial interests and of monetary orthodoxy in post-Civil War America. Perhaps even more illustrative of the economic evolution that was taking place, however, was the increasing importance of security transactions during the late 19th century. The financing of the Civil War had contributed importantly to this upsurge, for it had, first of all, given the public a greater knowledge and familiarity with both private and governmental securities. Secondly, by reason of large war-time profits, a concentration of funds resulted which could easily be tapped to finance the great business organizations which arose in the post-Civil War period. Then too, toward the end of the century, the national income grew, and with it the volume of dollar saving also expanded. Investment bankers, therefore, found it easier to float large security issues; and the stock exchanges did an ever-increasing volume of business. By 1896, the New York Stock Exchange handled a total of 57 million shares, and by 1901 this had risen to 266 million shares. Bond dealing rose less spectacularly from $394 million to almost $1 billion. The large New York City commercial banks assisted this type of financial activity by soliciting out-of-town bank deposits, which they loaned in the call-money market. At times, half the loans reported by New York national banks were in the call-money market. Meantime the investment bankers, in addition to using the commercial banks, obtained the help of trust companies and insurance companies as auxiliary forces to finance the reorganizations, mergers, and consolidations which they were promoting.

The Founding of the Federal Reserve System

Early 19th-century American money and banking could be characterized as brash and adolescent; it was loose and chaotic, colorful and adventurous, but often very naive. By the end of the century, the system had achieved middle-aged respectability; but it was still characterized by a great deal of self-reliance, individualism, and *laissez-faire*. Government regulation was minimal; the real bills doctrine[12] was firmly entrenched; the gold standard was in its heyday; and the investment

---

[12] The doctrine that a commercial bank's assets should consist almost exclusively of loans against short-term, self-liquidating, commercial paper.

banker had achieved international prestige and importance. Then, soon after the beginning of the 20th century, one could discern a trend in the direction of greater government control over capital markets and over the banking system, greater emphasis on economic stability and less on economic expansion. This trend toward centralized regulation and control occurred largely because of the national banking system's weaknesses, well recognized by 1900. Reserves tended to pyramid and become immobile; currency was inelastic; money-market panics were very severe; and check clearance was costly and inefficient. A belief that these weaknesses could best be corrected by the creation of some form of central banking steadily gained popularity, and culminated in 1913 in the passage of the Federal Reserve Act.

In order to give mobility to bank reserves and to prevent them from pyramiding in New York City, the Act divided the country into twelve districts, each having its own Federal Reserve bank. Each commercial bank belonging to the Reserve System was required to maintain a specific reserve against deposits, either in its own vaults or in the district bank.[13] The Act provided for a more elastic currency by permitting the district banks to issue a new type of paper money—Federal Reserve notes. Since these notes were secured by commercial paper and gold, their volume expanded during periods of prosperity (when business borrowing increased) and contracted in depressions (when business borrowing declined). It was hoped that the severity of money-market panics would be diminished by giving the district banks the power to rediscount commercial paper for its member banks, thus providing them with funds during crises. Finally, the Act replaced the inefficient, costly, and cumbersome system of clearing checks through correspondent banks with a par collection system in which clearing was both rapid and free.

Originally, then, the Federal Reserve System was a quasi-central bank, relatively free from government control. Its central governing body, the Federal Reserve Board, was primarily an administrative agency with little control over the system's operations. Executive power was concentrated in the district banks themselves under the control of the commercial bankers. Even the power to rediscount was not completely centrally controlled, but dispersed throughout the twelve district banks. The system's function appeared to be to improve the nation's commercial-banking machinery, rather than to stabilize the economy.

[13] A 1917 amendment to the Act made it mandatory to deposit all reserves in the district banks.

Changes in the Reserve System

With the passing of time, the original concepts of the Federal Reserve System changed fundamentally.[14] During World War I, the system gave its full support to the Treasury's war-financing program, which meant that it instituted, as far as it was able, an easy money policy. Following the war, when the rediscount rate proved to be less effective than was at first expected, the system began to engage more extensively in open-market operations.[15] Then, in 1923, it formulated a theory of credit control, setting as its goal the encouragement of legitimate business expansion but the discouragement of speculation. Unfortunately, it was largely unsuccessful in achieving these goals either during the stock-market boom of the 'twenties or during the depression of the early 'thirties. During the 'twenties, an easy money policy was more the rule than the exception. But when a tight money policy was occasionally followed, it seems to have had little effect in curbing stock-market speculation. During the depression, on the other hand, easy money policies had little effect in restoring prosperity. These unhappy experiences caused a general loss of faith in the effectiveness of monetary policy, although some authorities still hoped that monetary policies might work if only the Federal Reserve Board were given sufficient power.

Early attempts to centralize power more effectively had failed, but, in the early years of the New Deal, strong central banking became a reality. Most of this was accomplished by the Banking Acts of 1933 and 1935 which greatly expanded the powers of the Board of Governors, by giving it control over the security loans of commercial banks, by centralizing power over open-market operations and the rediscount rate, and by giving the Board the power to vary the reserve requirements of member banks. Thus, the Federal Reserve came to possess many new and powerful tools of monetary control. In prosperity, it could mop up excess reserves by selling government bonds to the member banks and

[14] For a somewhat fuller account of Federal Reserve policy, see Paul Studenski and Herman E. Krooss, *Financial History of the United States* (New York: McGraw-Hill Book Company, 1952). For exhaustive studies, see W. Randolph Burgess, *The Reserve Banks and the Money Market* (New York: Harper and Brothers, 1946); Charles O. Hardy, *Credit Policies of the Federal Reserve System* (Washington D.C.: The Brookings Institution, 1932); Seymour E. Harris, *Twenty Years of Federal Reserve Policy* (Cambridge, Mass.: Harvard University Press, 1933); J. S. Fforde, *The Federal Reserve System*, 1945–1949 (New York: Oxford University Press, 1954).

[15] Pumping money into the economy, when business activity was falling, by buying bonds; withdrawing money from the economy, when business activity seemed to set a boom in motion, by selling bonds.

by raising reserve requirements, and it could discourage banks from expanding their loans by raising the rediscount rate or prohibiting security loans. In depression years it could try to revive the economy by lowering reserve requirements, buying government bonds from the member banks, and reducing the rediscount rate.

Yet, although the Reserve Board now had vast powers over the banking system, it did not always have the freedom to exercise them. Thus, when World War II created very strong inflationary pressures, the Federal Reserve System was not in a position to institute countervailing deflationary measures. Instead, it followed an easy money policy, cooperating with the Treasury which was intent on financing the war at low interest rates. The Federal Reserve Banks pegged interest rates and kept them stabilized throughout the war. They did this by standing ready to buy or sell any quantity of Federal obligations at a fixed price. Thus, they held long-term governments at par and pegged the interest rate on the short-term Treasury bills at $3/8$ of 1 per cent. By placing government interest rates in a strait jacket and keeping them there, the monetary authorities controlled interest rates throughout the money market and largely eliminated the influence of the free market. At the same time, the Federal Reserve's concession in favor of cheap money meant an abandonment of virtually all its powers to check monetary and credit inflation, since cheap money necessarily meant inflation.

At the end of the war, inflationary pressures still overwhelmed the economy, and, as prices rose, belief in the effectiveness of monetary controls again became fashionable. But the Federal Reserve System was in the position of a man who had the well-known bear by the tail. If it continued the practice of supporting the government bond market, it could not take effective action against inflation by selling governments or by utilizing any of its other tools of credit control. On the other hand, if it stopped controlling interest rates, the price of government bonds would plummet downward to the great expense and possible embarrassment of the United States Treasury. The dilemma was resolved in favor of a refurbished faith in monetary controls. The Federal Reserve System gradually withdrew its support of government obligations, and as the peg was withdrawn, interest rates rose gradually. By the 1950's, the Board was able to institute a relatively tight money policy in an effort to control credit and halt the upward trend in prices. Interest rates climbed, but prices also continued to rise, since consumer and investment spending remained high despite the Federal Reserve's tight money policy.

Commercial Banking in the 20th Century

Although the evolution of the Federal Reserve System was the most important development in banking after 1900, there were a number of other significant changes in commercial banking operations. Because of changes in the structure of the economy, in government legislation, and in business financial policy, commercial banking became far less flexible. Its traditional functions were gradually transformed or, in some cases, completely abandoned. By the opening of World War II, it was not an exaggeration to say that commercial banking had become a modified kind of investment banking. The day of the real bills doctrine with its emphasis on self-liquidating, short-term, commercial paper had passed. Business enterprise was less dependent on bank financing, since it was covering a larger portion of its financial needs by reinvesting earnings. Allegiance quietly but steadily shifted from liquidity to "shiftability." As early as 1927, the McFadden Branch Banking Act permitted national banks to purchase investment securities and enlarged their power to make real-estate loans, previously severely restricted. Depression legislation went even further, permitting member banks to borrow against any acceptable assets, and authorizing national banks to make long-term loans on real estate.

Even in the prosperous 'twenties, commercial loans, as bank assets, declined relative to other loans and investments. The dollar volume of commercial loans in member banks remained about the same from 1921 to 1929, but security loans, real-estate loans, and investments increased 121 per cent; 178 per cent, and 67 per cent respectively. The depression accentuated the trend. By 1939, investments by commercial banks in government bonds exceeded their loans, and, by 1950, as a result of the tremendous burden of war finance, commercial banks held $66 billion of government bonds, $11 billion of other investments, and only $45 billion in loans. To a marked degree, the commercial banks had become recipients of deposits, and were now investors in government bonds, instead of lenders of working capital. To some extent this trend was reversed during the 1950's. For as business expanded, the commercial banks sold part of their government bonds to obtain the resources with which to meet the heavy demand for private loans. At the end of 1958, commercial banks held $66 billion of government bonds, about $21 billion of other securities, and almost $100 billion in loans.

Money in Circulation, Selected Years, 1915–1959
(in millions of dollars)

Year	Federal Reserve notes	Government coin and currency	Other	Commercial* bank deposits	Total
1915	71	2,180	782	15,232	18,265
1920	3,065	1,426	690	32,440	37,621
1925	1,636	2,206	682	40,349	44,873
1929	1,693	2,113	653	45,058	49,517
1933	3,061	1,453	920	28,468	33,902
1939	4,484	2,377	186	45,051	52,098
1945	22,867	3,759	120	105,986	132,732
1950	22,760	4,310	86	128,586	155,742
1959**	27,029	4,829	57	177,700	209,615

* Demand and time, but not including interbank or U.S. government deposits.
** June 30.
Source: *Banking and Monetary Statistics, Federal Reserve Bulletin, Statistical Abstract.*

Breakdown of the Gold Standard

As long as the world experienced no major wars and no extreme business fluctuations, the international gold standard operated efficiently. International price movements and gold shipments operated in such a way as to provide a constant tendency toward equilibrium in international trade. But the system never operated as the completely automatic mechanism pictured in theory, because it was always affected by human decisions, such as the manipulation of the rediscount rate in the London money market. But, in the quite rational world of the first fourteen years of the 20th century, the gold standard worked smoothly to facilitate international and domestic trade and payments. When that rational world began to disappear as a result of World War I, the gold standard could not bear the strain, and it also began to disintegrate.

As a result of the major rôle which it played in financing the Allied Powers, the United States emerged from World War I as a major creditor, and Europe came out loaded down with dead-weight debt. The United States, however, could not adjust quickly to its new role as a creditor, which should have been accompanied by a willingness to allow foreign nations to pay the interest and principal on their loans in goods. Instead the United States raised its tariff barriers. To protect their diminished gold and dollar reserves, European nations adopted modified gold-standard arrangements and resorted to exchange controls of one sort or another. Consequently, the importance of the old nexus between international prices and gold shipments was considerably diminished, and the free market was replaced by a manipulated one.

What the war had not accomplished in disrupting the workings of the international gold standard was accomplished by the depression of the 1930's. Nation after nation resorted to monetary techniques in desperate efforts to turn the tide of deflation and to raise domestic prices. The quantity theory of money bloomed afresh in the revival of the notion that increasing the amount of money would immediately raise domestic prices. But manipulating the domestic money supply was incompatible with the gold standard, since artificially-induced price increases would lead to gold exports which would tend to depress prices, neutralizing whatever had been accomplished by money manipulation. The gold standard was, therefore, abandoned, and the 19th-century conviction that money was only a convenience to facilitate trade was replaced by a revived belief in money as a tool that government could use to regulate the economy. Pegged currencies and stabilization funds replaced the free movement of gold across international borders.

The United States was in the forefront of this new movement. In her efforts to raise domestic prices, both coinage and bank credit were manipulated. The Hoover administration attempted to increase the supply of checkbook money by supplying the commercial banks with more bank reserves. The Roosevelt administration went much farther. It abandoned the gold standard, attempted to increase the quantity of pocketbook money by reducing the weight of the gold dollar (from 25.8 grains, $\frac{9}{10}$ fine, to $15\frac{5}{21}$ grains, $\frac{9}{10}$ fine) and by remonetizing silver. On the whole, the results of these monetary measures were disappointing, for, despite a more than 50 per cent increase in the total money supply (currency and bank deposits) between 1934 and 1940, the price level rose by only 3 per cent.

Investment Banking Since 1900

The 19th-century type of investment banking retained its position of importance in the American economy longer than the real bills doctrine and the gold standard. Real bills and the gold standard reached their zenith just before World War I, but the unregulated investment banker reached his peak in the speculative, prosperous decade of the 1920's.

The Liberty Bonds floated during World War I acquainted most Americans with securities. Taking advantage of this situation after the war, business enterprises relied more on security issues than on bank credit to meet their needs for capital funds. The number of firms engaged in selling securities increased even faster than the popularity of securities, and soon almost every whistle stop in the nation had a brokerage office with a stock ticker and stock board. To provide enough securities for this rapidly-expanded investment business, the investment bankers sent their agents all over the world to urge governments and business firms to issue securities. Meantime to keep the demand for securities at a high level, security houses engaged in high-pressure selling and extensive advertising. Insiders rigged the market for specific securities by forming pools or engaging in "wash sales." Some prewar leaders in investment banking were not willing to take part in this new competition, and consequently they lost their position as leaders. Thus J. P. Morgan and Co., who had floated the majority of new issues before the War, placed less than 15 per cent of new issues at the height of the boom of the late '20's.

As the market became more diversified, the nation's fixed debt increased substantially. And it increased in those sectors of the economy least able to handle it. Manufacturing, which was in the best position to tolerate increased debt, did not increase its indebtedness. On the other hand, railroad debt increased rapidly, and by 1929 urban real-estate mortgage debt was more than five times as high as it had been in 1913, although property values had only doubled, and rents had increased by only 50 per cent. Meantime stock prices became tremendously inflated; the Standard and Poor average rose from 80 per cent of the 1935–1939 level in 1919, to 237 per cent in September, 1929; and some stocks which paid no dividends whatever sold as high as $500 a share.

All this came to an end with the collapse of the stock market. In the next two decades, the security business, as measured by the volume of trading and the value of new security issues, failed to recover its previous position, and investment bankers lost much of their importance as mobilizers of capital. There were a number of reasons for this decline. When the market collapsed, the public dropped its naive dreams of quick and easy riches and became concerned with the need for economic security. Government attitudes, legislation, and fiscal policy also contributed to the relative decline of the investment banker and the stock market. In the new era, government, largely because of popular sentiment, laid greater emphasis on security. It passed legislation separating commercial from investment banking, prohibiting pools and "wash sales," restricting margin trading, requiring publicity for new security issues of over $300,000, and requiring competitive bidding for certain types of new security issues. Government fiscal policy, by placing constantly greater emphasis on progressive taxation, seemed to some observers to be discouraging the purchase of securities. And business itself contributed to the declining importance of investment banking since the new independence of business entrepreneurs made them relatively free from the necessity of relying on investment bankers for capital funds. Instead, they made greater use of retained profits to finance their needs.

Rising Importance of Insurance Companies

The greater emphasis placed on safety in mid-20th-century America was reflected in an enormous expansion of life insurance companies and savings and loan associations as collectors of personal savings. Whereas the American public paid only $632 million in life insurance premiums in 1911, they paid $3.4 billion in 1929 and $13.6 billion by 1956. Since personal savings in 1956 were estimated at $25.5 billion, life insurance premiums were equal to more than half of total private savings.[16] This greater emphasis on life insurance as a savings medium illustrated the trend toward security and away from risk. Since life insurance companies have, for the most part, been restricted in their investment policies by state regulations, their portfolios will include only "safe" investments such as government bonds, real estate mortgages, corporate bonds, and triple *A* preferred stock. They have not been able, therefore, to supply capital funds to enterprises entailing a great amount of risk, but, by assuring security (however illusory this may be in the face of steadily rising costs of living) they do encourage saving.

We may therefore conclude that during the 20th century the whole mechanics of savings and investment showed a trend toward ever-greater emphasis on safety and a de-emphasis of risk. Corporations relied less on commercial and investment banks and more on retained earnings. Private savers turned increasingly toward life insurance and savings and loan associations. According to orthodox economc theory, this trend toward security could not help impede economic growth. But

---

[16] Policy reserves increased $4.3 billion in 1956, about 17 per cent of personal savings. Non-fluctuating liquid assets totalled over $250 billion in 1957, of which $80 billion was in life insurance reserves.

in the immediate postwar years the actual performance record demonstrated otherwise, for in those years the nation experienced impressive
economic progress. The vast backlog of demand for consumer durables,
the rehabilitation of the European economy, the expansion of American
plants and, especially, the need for added military equipment and defense requirements—all these forces created enormous investment outlets, so that too little, rather than too much, saving became the problem.
But in the 'fifties, as scarcities became less intense through increased production, the pace of economic growth began to falter. Ironically enough,
it was precisely at that time that stock market activity resurged and took
on some of the feverishness that had characterized it in the 'twenties.

11 Formation and development of labor organizations

Influence of Economic Environment on Trade-Union Tactics

In contrast with European nations where land was more limited and labor relatively plentiful, throughout most of the history of the United States, manpower was the scarce factor of production. This comparative scarcity of labor acted as a stimulus to technological innovation, so that gradually each worker was provided with more tools and was therefore able to produce more per man hour worked. As a consequence, the economic position of the average American laborer was consistently better than that of the European worker.[1] Wages, both in money and in

[1] In the days when many people ascribed the American worker's better circumstance to America's "superior" political system, Thomas Carlyle bluntly exclaimed: "Ye may boast o' yer dimocracy, or any ither 'cracy' or any kind o' political roobish; but the reason why yer laboring folks are so happy is that ye have a vast deal o' land for verra few people." Quoted in David M. Potter, *People of Plenty* (Chicago: University of Chicago Press, 1954), p. 126.

terms of what money could buy, were not only relatively higher than in other nations but showed a consistent upward trend. Although hours of work were initially as long as those of the European worker, little-by-little they declined, and in the course of the past 100 years the average American worker has gained 32 hours of increased leisure per week. Working and living conditions were at first unsatisfactory, but at length factories became safer and more sanitary; housing conditions improved immeasurably, and education and medical facilities were supplied on an ever-increasing scale by private and government agencies. Then too, the worker as a consumer benefited from steady improvements in the quality of products.

The persisting relative scarcity of labor had far-reaching effects on the worker's philosophy, beliefs, and aspirations. It helped make American society one of status, rather than of class. Much more than in other nations, the American worker could move from class to class and achieve an improved status. Like other Americans, he dreamed of economic advancement, and only in rare moments of deep discouragement did he consider himself destined to drag out his years as a permanent member of the laboring class. Because he expected some day to be a landlord, a small businessman, or a substantial entrepreneur, the American worker could not develop a feeling of antipathy toward employers, nor generate an intense devotion to the employee class. His attitude was essentially middle class, not proletarian, and consequently differed from the attitude, beliefs, and outlook of the European worker.

Principally because of this middle-class philosophy, labor unionism grew much more slowly in the United States than in continental Europe or Great Britain. Selig Perlman has pointed out that labor unionism, in essence, represents an attempt to reduce the absolute rights of private property.[2] But American unions could not fight against the rights of private property very aggressively because a belief in the rights of private property was almost as deeply entrenched among the American workers as it was among businessmen and farmers. If they hoped to survive, unions had to proceed cautiously. They had to be conservative rather than radical; hence they sought to maintain stable organizations that could, among other things, keep the opposition of other elements in the community at a minimum. One wing of labor unionism, either rationally or intuitively, quickly recognized the peculiar role of unionism in the American environment. This so-called "business unionism,"

2 Selig Perlman, *A Theory of the Labor Movement* (New York: The Macmillan Company, 1928).

placed more stress on short-run objectives—higher wages and shorter hours—than on long-range, less tangible and more idealistic objectives. Eminently realistic and practical, the spokesmen for business unionism based their strategy, until well into the 20th century, on the proposition that the dynamic American economy with its low man-land ratio, rapid population growth, extensive free-trade area, and a culture devoted to the goal of economic growth, offered the American worker a much more attractive vista than that offered to the European worker. Business unionism recognized that the American labor movement could scarcely pretend to represent a struggle by a down-trodden and economically exploited group against its class enemies. It was, instead, a device for improving labor's bargaining position. For this reason business unionism sought to "control the job," ensure the survival of the union's own organization, and secure for its members the maximum possible improvement of hours, wages, and working conditions.

But business unionism was by no means the only type of American labor unionism. Indeed in the United States there has not been any single or even normal type of labor union, nor any single philosophy of unionism that has maintained a dominant position regardless of changing social and economic circumstances.[3] Consequently in addition to business unionism, there appeared frequently on the American scene variants of "welfare unionism" (which followed long-run, abstract, idealistic objectives) and "political unionism" (which sought to advance the cause of labor by political intervention).

On the whole, American workers tended to favor business unionism. This was especially true during relatively prosperous periods when labor was in a position to press its economic claims most aggressively and successfully. At such times, when the demand for labor was high and the concern for economic advancement was greatest, business unionism was consistently the dominant force in labor unionism. On the other hand, in periods of depression, when the demand for labor fell and the preoccupation with economic advancement palled, welfare unionism increased in popularity. Essentially idealistic and concerned more with the worker's morale and spirit than with higher wages or shorter hours, welfare unionism appealed to the sentimental and idealistic side of the American character that always revealed itself in time of economic travail. But welfare unionism could never maintain a favored position. Its successes were only temporary. As business activity

[3] See Robert F. Hoxie, *Trade Unionism in the United States* (New York: D. A. Appleton and Company, 1921).

revived, the concern was again with direct benefits; and welfare union-ism faded into the background, possibly to re-emerge in the next busi-ness depression.

But regardless of the banner under which it marched, unionism aroused considerable opposition from the community at large; and, until comparatively recent times, legislatures (state and national) and courts took an essentially hostile attitude toward labor organizations. Among occupational groups, farmers were, for the most part, opposed to the aims of the labor unions; but, for obvious reasons, the most implac-able opposition came from employers. Early businessmen took the view that labor organizations not only violated the rights of property but were without point, since wages according to the then-popular "wages fund" doctrine were determined by the ratio between the labor force and available capital funds. Consequently, they argued, "going wages" could not be changed without greatly disturbing the whole economy. Moreover, since the imagined "wages fund" was a fixed amount, it fol-lowed that if wages were raised for some employees the wages of the others would have to go down (or some unemployment would have to correct the imbalance). Strangely enough, labor unions to some extent accepted the arguments underlying the wages-fund doctrine; time and time again labor leaders argued that an increase in the labor supply from increased immigration would reduce the individual's share of total wage payments. This was the same as saying that there was only so much to go around, only so much money in the "wages fund" and this fixed amount divided by the number of workers determined the average wages.

The wages fund theory was either a sham or a delusion, and although remnants of it still exist today, employers slowly discarded it as time passed. Nevertheless, they continued to oppose labor unions, chiefly because of their conviction that unions interfered with the rights of management and the rights of the individual, especially when unions resorted to such devices as the closed shop, the sympathy strike, and the boycott. Entrepreneurs insisted that labor had no "rights in a job" and that wage decisions were a prerogative of management with which labor had no right to interfere. For management to reduce production when goods were in oversupply was good business practice, but for workers to strike when there was an oversupply of labor was not sound! Business-men objected to attempts on the part of laborers to raise or maintain wages on the ground that this constituted dangerous aggression; but they defended action on the part of management to reduce wages as defensive tactics designed to maintain the survival of the firm. Individualistic entrepreneurs were inclined to pay little attention to wages as a factor in demand. Instead, they regarded wages simply as one of the costs of production. Accordingly, with few exceptions, they regarded wage increases as dangerous because they increased the costs of production. What they overlooked was that wage increases also increased the money income of a large group of consumers, and thus resulted in an increase in the demand for products. On the other hand, the spokesmen for labor tended to overemphasize the importance of wage increases in raising purchasing power, and underemphasize wages as factor in the cost of production. As so often happens, both sides were naive and stubborn; although time was to show that the workers were more nearly right than the employers!

Labor's Attitudes and Problems Before 1840

In the era before 1840, before really large-scale immigration began, the supply of American factory labor was especially limited. As manufacturing developed, women and children were employed in large numbers to provide the labor force needed to run the first machines. Because of the prevalent belief that idleness was immoral, and because of the desire (of both employers and employees) to obtain as large an income as possible, hours of work were long, usually 12 to 14 hours a day, or from sunup to sundown. By modern standards, however, the pace of the work was comparatively slow, and relatively little thought was given to what the economist calls "productivity," and raising the output per man hour. Since much of the work was still done by hand, and since working speed was slow, wages were low; although they were, nevertheless, considerably higher than in Europe. Most factory laborers in 1820 earned from 75 cents to $1.25 a day; a few unusual, highly-skilled laborers earned about twice as much; and women were paid about half to three-quarters the rate paid to men. But the demand on the worker's income was much smaller than at a later period. The great majority of expenditures went for food, clothing, and rent; and prices for these things were low. Bread cost about three cents a pound and beef about seven cents. Board in the Chicopee mills was $1.25 a week. In Philadelphia, where workers' wages averaged about $1 a day, it cost about $4 a week to live. To some extent, however, these figures were deceiving. Employers, taking advantage of the shortage of coin and currency, often paid wages in store orders or in depreciated paper currency, and in the process the wage earner was often cheated out of a sizable fraction of his nominal wage.

To augment income, workers hired out their whole families. In one case, a textile worker made a contract with a cotton mill to supply a labor force consisting of himself, his three sons, one daughter, a sister, a nephew, and a niece. The rate of pay per person ranged from 75 cents to $5 a week and the whole family's income was $15.16 a week.[4] Under such circumstances, a family could eke out a precarious existence provided it suffered no unusual vicissitudes. If it was extremely fortunate and avoided sickness (by the grace of Providence) and unemployment (by the shrewdness of the entrepreneur) a working-class family could live comfortably and even save a little money.

Labor Unionism Before the Civil War

Although the American worker was considerably better off than the average European worker, he was far from satisfied with his lot, and attempted to combine with his fellow workers to strengthen his bargaining power. These early efforts at trade unionism, however, were little more than crude gropings. From time to time political and welfare unionism were tried, but there was always a return to pragmatic business unionism, often referred to by labor leaders as "trade unionism of the pure and simple type." Yet, as so often happened with later labor organizations, progress depended almost completely on the vagaries of the business cycle: prosperity meant expansion; depression meant disaster.

The first American labor organizations appeared in the late 18th century among the highly skilled workers—carpenters and shoemakers in Philadelphia, printers in New York, tailors in Baltimore. These early labor organizations were contemporaneous with the merchant capitalist, a bargaining specialist who widened the market area by acting as an intermediary between producers and consumers. Since he was in a strategic position, he played producers off against each other, forcing them into sharp competition. Producers, in turn, were forced to cut prices; consequently they tried to reduce their costs by beating

---

[4] See Caroline F. Ware, *The Early New England Cotton Manufacture* (Boston: Houghton Mifflin Company, 1931); U.S. Department of Labor, Bureau of Labor Statistics, *History of Wages in the United States from Colonial Times to 1928*, Bulletin 604, Washington, D.C., 1934.

down wages. Since more and more goods were now produced for unseen and anonymous buyers, there was less need to place great stress on quality. Quickness and cheapness of manufacture rather than skillful and meticulous workmanship were emphasized. Consequently, producers tried to use unskilled labor in place of skilled whenever they could. It was an attempt to resist this economic situation that led to the early organization of skilled workers. These organizations, however, were not trade unions in the true sense of the term; skilled workers merely banded together to meet specific grievances, and, once their immediate problem had been solved, the organizations disintegrated.

The goals and tactics followed during this era of "dormant unionism," as John R. Commons called it, were similar to those subsequently followed by all "business unions." Workers bargained with employers over wages and hours; they demanded the closed shop; tried to restrict the use of apprentices; engaged in strikes, boycotts, and picketing; and set up benefit funds. They fought an uphill battle against public opinion, meeting great resistance, especially in the courts. Using as a precedent the English common-law interdiction against "conspiracy," the courts held that most labor unions were illegal. This doctrine received its most extreme expression in the famous conspiracy case against the Philadelphia shoemakers in 1806. The court held that "a combination of workmen to raise their wages may be considered from a two-fold point of view; one is, to benefit themselves, the other to injure those who do not join their society. The rule of law condemns both." But this edict never became accepted law in the United States. A milder form of disapprobation prevailed, aptly expressed in an 1821 Pennsylvania decision which held that an act which was legal for an individual became illegal when done by a group if there was a direct intent of inflicting injury or if the act benefited the group to the "prejudice of the public or the oppression of individuals." The case of Commonwealth vs. Hunt, in 1842, modified this doctrine by holding that unions and union tactics were not illegal if not violent, and this still remains the generally-accepted viewpoint toward unions.

In time, labor's grievances broadened, and to redress them local crafts began to coalesce into city trade unions. In 1827, for example, the "trades" (which is to say the skilled crafts) in Philadelphia organized the Mechanics' Union of Trade Associations, and presently similar organizations were formed in other urban areas. These were the first real American trade unions. Initially they turned to politics, since the nature of many of their demands was socio-economic, not purely economic. They were opposed to monopolies, especially in banking; they disliked paper money, and supported Andrew Jackson's hard-money views and his fight to destroy the Bank of the United States; they opposed compulsory service in state militia, and imprisonment for debt; they demanded free public education and mechanics' lien laws.[5] To drive home their demands they formed workingmen's parties in the principal cities. What was probably the first labor party in the world was formed in Philadelphia in 1828. Although they had some early success, the workingmen's parties broke up in 1831 and 1832. They failed, as all American labor parties have failed, primarily because the average American worker was less interested in political objectives than in short-run economic gains. Moreover, the major American political parties, always opportunistic and flexible, quickly adopted the most appealing planks of the labor parties' platforms.

Only the various local labor organizations that survived the disintegration of the early labor parties kept unionism alive. Yet in the speculative boom of the early 1830's these surviving "locals" made progress. By 1836 there were fifty-eight in Philadelphia, fifty-two in New York and lesser numbers in other cities. They now emphasized business unionism and avoided politics; their chief aims were higher wages and the 10-hour day. Stimulated by their local successes, the local unions next proceeded to form, in 1834, a National Trades' Union which, at the height of its career claimed a membership of 300,000. But, in forming this national organization, the trade-union movement was temporarily diverted from business unionism into welfare unionism; it shifted emphasis from its concrete and practical goals toward more grandiose aims. This is evident from the declared purposes of the National Trades' Union, which were "to advance the moral and intellectual condition and pecuniary interests of the laboring classes, promote the establishment of Trades Unions; . . . and . . . publish and disseminate such information as may be useful to mechanics and working men generally."

Employers were disturbed by the success of the trade-union movement. They were particularly bothered by the demand for a 10-hour day, which they opposed on the ground that it would "lead to debauchery" and result in less production. Using the black list as their chief weapon, businessmen began to organize formally to fight against existing or embryonic labor unions. But they might just as well have saved their ammunition, for the whole labor movement quickly collapsed in the de-

[5] Which would give laborers prior claims over other creditors when a business enterprise could not pay all its debts.

pression which began in 1837. Faced with heavy unemployment, trade unionism could not resist employers' wage cuts; nor could the unions offer the worker any other advantages. As a result, labor turned to highly mystical movements dominated by visionary intellectuals. These years of the depression were, in the phrase of Van Wyck Brooks, "the God-Intoxicated Forties," but to the less sophisticated, they were the "hot air" period of American labor history. Idealistic reform philosophies achieved a wide following. A particular form of agrarianism, the Land Reform Movement, which proposed to give every would-be settler a "homestead" free of charge, also aroused enthusiasm among urban workers. Cooperatives, too, had a wide vogue; producers' cooperatives were planned in almost every skilled trade, and consumers' cooperatives were given a trial. Meantime, in the political field, workers expressed their hostility toward immigrant laborers by joining the Native American Party, more familiarly known as the "Know-Nothing Party," whose platform was chiefly based on extreme opposition to foreigners, which is to say, to immigrant workers. On the whole, the reform, cooperative, and political movements of the depression years had little lasting effect. With economic recovery in the 'fifties business unionism came back into a pre-eminent position. Instead of following the pattern of "one big union," each trade union tried to organize the skilled workers in each industry; and instead of experimenting with cooperatives and reform, they emphasized collective bargaining, shorter hours, higher wages, and other short-run objectives.

Wages, Hours, and Living Conditions in the Early 19th Century

By the middle 'fifties in New York City, blacksmiths, building workers, shoemakers, printers, and tailors were making $12 to $20 a week. Among the lesser-skilled and the unskilled, however, there had been less progress. Barbers, for example, earned about $10 a week, and the completely unskilled earned even less. But the cost of living was somewhat lower than in 1820.[6] Consequently, real wages were perhaps 25 per cent higher in 1850 than in 1820. But this increase had occurred erratically. The trend was sharply upward in the 'twenties and early 'thirties, but turned downward in the 1837 depression. Following some recovery, the curve flattened out in the 'forties, and by the mid-'fifties real wages were about at the same level as in 1836.

[6] Horace Greeley, the famous editor, set up a budget, in 1851, of $10.37 a week for a family of five.

Real Wages, 1801–1816: Comparative Estimates
(1820=100)

Year	(1)	(2)	(3)
1801	—	80	60
1814	—	82	56
1820	100	100	100
1829	115	102	120
1834	139	111	145
1837	100	102	111
1844	139	131	152
1849	151	126	168
1857	122	107	164
1860	139	124	188

Sources: (1) Alvin Hansen, "Factors Affecting Trend of Real Wages," *American Economic Review*, March, 1925; (2) Jurgen Kuczinsky, *A Short History of Labor Under Industrial Capitalism* (London: Frederick Muller, Ltd., 1943); (3) Harold G. Moulton, *Controlling Factors in Economic Development* (Washington, D.C.: The Brookings Institution, 1949).

Hours, working conditions, and living conditions did not demonstrate the same degree of progress. As late as the Civil War, hours had hardly been reduced at all. Textile workers still worked 75 hours a week, compared with 69 in Great Britain; and operated 3 or 4 looms, compared with 2 in the 1820's and 2 in Great Britain. But some skilled trades had achieved the 10-hour day, and in government service the 10-hour day was theoretically the rule after 1840. Working conditions were extremely bad. A careful analysis by a physician revealed that not even the model factories at Lowell provided the amount of air necessary for good health. Living conditions in large cities were abominable. As a result of immigration during the late 'forties and the 'fifties and the even greater migration from farm to city, urban population had grown much faster than the over-all population, thus creating a host of new problems. The slums of American metropolitan areas were as foul or fouler than those of Europe; housing was hopelessly inadequate, and medical care was almost unknown.[7]

Many reformers suggested that the workers should move westward into the wide-open spaces of cheap land and unlimited opportunity. But most of the skilled workers were doing well enough where they were, while the unskilled workers, who suffered most from urban concentration, were unable and unwilling to move. In the first place, they did not

[7] In New York, one 10-room house was occupied by 14 families; 18,500 people lived in 8,000 cellars. The average length of life among Boston Irish immigrant families was 14 years. See James Ford, *Slums and Housing* (Cambridge, Mass.: Harvard University Press, 1936). See also, Handlin, *The Uprooted*.

have enough money to pay for the expenses of moving and establishing a homestead. Moreover, as miserable as their lives were, the average workers were constrained by habit, custom, and general inertia to continue to inhabit the hovels of the city.

If the West offered the worker no haven, neither did his employer, since the typical businessman regarded labor as a commodity, and his attitude toward his labor force was usually one of complete indifference. He was unaware of the increases in productivity that might be achieved by scientific study of hours and working conditions, and it never seemed to have occurred to him that labor represented the hard core of the demand for consumer goods. A Fall River entrepreneur said:

> I regard my work-people just as I regard my machinery. So long as they can do my work for what I choose to pay them, I keep them, getting out of them all I can. What they do or how they fare outside my walls I don't know nor do I consider it my business to know.[8]

The skilled workers were just as indifferent to the plight of the unskilled as the employers were. Far from cultivating a sense of labor solidarity, they deliberately formed trade unions whose membership was restricted to the skilled, and whose goal was to raise wages for skilled labor only. During the 1850's the skilled workers began integrating their local trade unions into national organizations. These early "national craft unions" included the Typographical Union founded in 1852, the Hat Finishers' in 1854, and the Iron Molders' in 1859. These unions closely resembled the modern form of restrictive craft union. They tried to institute collective bargaining wherever possible, deemphasized the use of strikes, and sought to obtain "control over the job." They levied initiation fees, usually $1, and membership dues, most commonly 25 cents a month.

Whatever prosperity workers had achieved by 1860 came to an abrupt end during the Civil War. Although money wages rose, they could not keep pace with wartime price inflation, and, as a result, real wages declined sharply, perhaps as much as one-third. Consequently, the war economy, with its heavy demand for labor, extreme price inflation, high profits and general dissatisfaction among workers, created an ideal atmosphere for the expansion of trade unionism; and it was during this period that the national trade unions first demonstrated significant growth. Twenty-one national unions were formed during the 'sixties, and eighteen of these were formed after 1863. But even though they thrived, they were not able to close the gap between wages and prices.

8 N. W. Ware, *The Industrial Worker, 1840–1860* (Boston: Houghton Mifflin and Co., 1924), p. 77.

Improvement in Labor's Position Between 1865 and 1890

The nation's phenomenal economic growth during the thirty years after the Civil War had a mixed effect on the American laborer. By 1890, estimated average wages in manufacturing were 60 per cent higher than they had been in 1860 and about 10 per cent higher than in 1865. But prices had declined substantially so that if we accept Hansen's estimates, real wages had risen almost 70 per cent between 1860 and 1890. But, while earnings rose, there was little improvement in hours or in living conditions.

Year	(1)	(2)	(3)
1860	100	100	100
1861	107	93	100
1865	67	78	69
1873	140	113	124
1879	149	103	115
1890	168	118	182

Real Wages, 1860–1890: Comparative Estimates (1860=100)

Source: (1) Hansen, (2) Kuczinsky, (3) Moulton

Meantime, constant broadening of the market area, increasing intersectional competition, wider use of machinery, larger and more powerful firms, greater development of division of labor, closer-knit employer organizations, and a constant influx of immigrants gave the worker a sense of insecurity, which he attempted to overcome by greater emphasis on trade unionism and closer control over the job. The prewar trend toward national unions of skilled workers continued immediately after the Civil War, the most important new union being the Knights of St. Crispin, which eventually had 50,000 members. Meanwhile, in order to obtain greater bargaining power on a national basis, various local and national trade unions, in 1866, formed a weak federation, the National Labor Union, led by William H. Sylvis of the iron molders.[9] Sylvis, the first really nationally-known labor leader in the country, imprinted his ideas on the National Labor Union, but, since these ideas shifted constantly, the Union's aims and ideology were always in a state of flux. At first, it sought to promote cooperatives, abolish convict labor, restrict immigration, establish a Federal department of labor, and exclude everyone but actual settlers from the public domain. But its chief aim was the 8-hour day which was given an economic rationale by

[9] See Lloyd Ulman, *The Rise of the National Trade Union* (Cambridge, Mass.: Harvard University Press, 1955).

Ira Steward, a Boston machinist, who popularized the drive for shorter hours with the famous couplet: "Whether you work by the piece or work by the day, decreasing the hours increases the pay." Steward supported his basic theory with two principal arguments, one based on costs and the other on demand. He contended that output would automatically be increased by reducing hours, because reducing hours would raise costs and thus encourage technological innovation. In his second argument, Steward denounced the wages fund theory as altogether fallacious, insisting that wages depend on the habits, customs, and standard of living of the workers. He believed that laborers would not work for less than enough to maintain their standard of living. Since shortening the hours of work would increase the wage-earner's leisure, his wants, the volume of his purchases, and, consequently, his standard of living, wages would be automatically raised. Steward was not altogether wrong in his arguments. Higher costs could encourage technological advance, and greater consumption could encourage economic progress, but carried to extremes, Steward's theory, like all purchasing-power theories, would eliminate all profits and in the end defeat its own purposes.

Steward believed that the 8-hour day could be achieved more quickly and more easily by political means than through trade-union activities, and Sylvis shared this view in the last years of his life. The National Labor Union was therefore diverted into the political arena. Although it had a large membership, estimated at 500,000, it had little success in achieving its aims. It did succeed in obtaining the passage of Federal legislation establishing the 8-hour day for government employees, but, in contravention of Steward's theory, the reduction of hours for government employees was not accompanied by an increase in the wage rate, so that total wages actually fell. Meanwhile, the National Labor Union made the mistake of allying itself with the Greenback movement which was not popular among the rank and file of workers who were not in favor of inflation. The Union was further weakened when employers, aroused by frequent strikes, organized a concerted anti-union effort along national lines. Michigan employers started the movement in the early 'seventies with a widely-publicized statement charging that the continuation of unionism and the use of the strike would result in "widespread beggary." Employer organizations spread quickly, using the lockout and the black list. The National Labor Union was, therefore, already in a precarious condition when the depression of 1873 delivered the *coup de grace* to its hopes, aspirations, and continued existence.

The Twilight of Welfare Unionism

During the depression, the trade unions once again suffered severe losses in membership. The mighty Knights of St. Crispin were wiped out altogether, and the unions that did survive saw their membership cut to half or less. Once again labor turned to a type of welfare unionism. Before the depression in 1869, some Philadelphia garment workers had formed a secret society, known as the Noble Order of the Knights of Labor. During the succeeding nine years the organization had a slow growth, but in 1878 after it was reorganized as a permanent, non-secret, labor organization under the leadership of Terence V. Powderly, "Grand Master Workman," it became the most spectacular labor movement of the period.

The Knights emphasized education, legislation, and mutual benefits through cooperation. The Order was extremely idealistic, and its long-range goal was the abolition of the wage system. In the shorter run, it sought "to secure to the workers the full enjoyment of the wealth they create, sufficient leisure in which to develop intellectual, moral, and social faculties." More specifically, it sought the establishment of a bureau of labor statistics, a weekly payday, an 8-hour day, abolition of contract labor, and the prohibition of child labor (below the age of 14). It intended to devote most of its energies to producers' cooperatives and arbitration, and it looked with disfavor on strikes. But it had great difficulty in hewing to its line, and its activities often seemed wildly inconsistent.

The Knights represented the "one big union" type of organization, membership being open to everyone except doctors, lawyers, bankers, and saloonkeepers. The chief authority for guiding the whole union rested ostensibly at the top, in an executive body composed of five members. But in the politics of unionism, the executive body could retain power over the entire organization only by exerting strong leadership. During most of the Knights' history, such strong leadership was lacking, and the rank and file took over control.

Paradoxically, both the spectacular success and the ultimate failure of the Order stemmed from the rebellion of the rank and file. After 15 years of existence, the Knights had a membership of only 60,000. Then, in 1885, despite the Order's well-established antipathy toward strikes it declared one against Jay Gould's Western railroad system. Gould quickly conceded the union's demands, and the prestige gained by the

Knights in this victory partly explained why membership jumped to 700,000 in 1886. But the subsequent decline of the Knights was just as spectacular.

Many causes contributed to the breakdown of the Knights. A second strike against Jay Gould, this time against his Southwestern railway system, was a complete failure; and confidence in the Order tumbled. Meanwhile, the mixed and conflicting interests of the Order's heterogeneous membership disrupted the organization's *esprit de corps*. Moreover, the Order's leaders lacked decisiveness and made many major mistakes. The producers' cooperatives organized by the Knights were financial failures, because most of them were in mining, cooperage, and shoemaking, ventures which required heavy capital investment. The failure of these enterprises to cover costs bled the Order of its resources.

Compounding the Order's difficulties were the sharp controversies between capital and labor in the years after the Civil War. Differences of opinion were rarely settled around the conference table in the give and take of bargaining. More frequently, they resulted in strikes that were much more violent and bloody than contemporaneous strikes in Europe, where labor was supposed to be much more radical than in the United States. Especially violent were: the long coal strike of 1874; the railroad strikes of 1877; and the Haymarket affair of 1886. Respectable opinion was horrified by these events, and even though employers were far from blameless, there was little sympathy for the worker. It was still quite commonly believed that if a man was poor, such was his destiny, and the best he could do was to live frugally and not complain. The Reverend Henry Ward Beecher, for example, looked down from the eminence of his $20,000 a year income and pronounced, "I do not say that a dollar a day is enough to support a working man. But it is enough to support a man! Not enough to support a man and five children if a man insists on smoking and drinking beer . . . But the man who cannot live on bread and water is not fit to live."[10]

Whether the Knights had anything to do with particular strikes or not, public opinion held them responsible, especially for the Haymarket Riot. The conservative press, moreover, exaggerated the Order's importance, and aroused middle-class prejudices against it. The New York *Sun* wrote of the Executive Board: "Five men . . . control the chief interests of five hundred thousand workingmen, and can at any moment take the means of livelihood from two and a half million

---

[10] See Foster Rhea Dulles, *Labor in America* (New York: Thomas Y. Crowell Company, 1949), pp. 114–125.

souls."[11] Finally, and most important, the Order did not adapt itself to the typical American wage earner's desires and interests, which consistently emphasized short- rather than long-term objectives. When the Knights attempted to absorb the independent trade unions, the trade unions in turn took the offensive, and pushed the Knights out of the skilled trades. By 1900, the Knights had only 100,000 members, consisting mostly of farmers, independent mechanics, and small merchants.

How the Worker Fared Between 1890 and World War I

Although the worker's general status had improved by the end of the 19th century, his level of living remained far from utopian. Real wages for the whole labor force had more than doubled during the 19th century, but very few workers in 1900 were paid as much as $18 a week. Average annual earnings in manufacturing were $520, and at least two-thirds of the adult workers made less than $600 a year. Admittedly prices were low: beef could be bought for 18 cents a pound, eggs for 15 cents a dozen, and housing could be had in New York City for $14 a month. Nevertheless, it was estimated that $825 was the minimum necessary for a family of five to maintain a reasonably adequate living standard in New York City. Where the main breadwinner's earnings were insufficient to achieve this standard, family income had to be increased by additional income from children's wages and from lodgers. Apparently this arrangement worked reasonably well, for among 318 working-class families interviewed in New York City, only 86 found it impossible to "make both ends meet" and 116 were able to save some money. In most cases, however, saving was achieved only by practicing extreme frugality in living. After providing for subsistence, there was no substantial surplus available for purchasing any luxury goods or for sustaining mass consumption in other things than necessities.

The plight of the poor did not go unnoticed. In 1904, for example, Robert Hunter, "a man of comfortable means," gave his fellow Americans something to think about when he estimated that if an income of $460 a year was considered essential for people living in cities and $300 essential in the South, then some 10 million people in the United States were poverty stricken. Thus, despite the remarkable economic progress we had achieved, 13 per cent of the population was still living very near the subsistence level.

[11] Quoted by Selig Perlman, *A History of Trade Unionism in the United States* (New York: The Macmillan Co., 1922), p. 88.

Hunter's book was important not so much because of what it said, but because it illustrated that a change was occurring in America's attitude toward poverty and the poor. Well into the 19th century, most people believed that poverty was the result of laziness and profligate living, something that was entirely a man's own fault. By the 20th century, social workers, like Jane Addams and Jacob Riis, scoffed at this explanation. Others, like Hunter, thought that, although some poverty was caused by "dissolute character," a large amount was the result of causes over which the individual had no control. "There is," wrote Hunter, "a poverty which men deserve. . . . There are also a poor which we must not have always with us. The poor of this latter class are . . . the mass of the poor; they are bred of miserable and unjust social conditions."[12]

Hunter claimed that almost all the poor were foreign born, and he argued that "only the very rich and the anarchists favor unrestricted immigration." A majority of labor leaders, many of the sociologists, and some of the economists of the period shared Hunter's belief in the evils of immigration. But, although there may have been some truth in the argument that "the glut of labor" caused by immigration was chiefly responsible for poverty, there were more fundamental economic causes. By the end of the 19th century, the economy did not seem to be operating at the same rapid pace as it had done in the past. National income, manufactured output, and capital accumulation were still increasing, but at a slower rate; and real wages increased hardly at all during the 24 years preceding World War I.[13]

Real Wages, 1890–1920 (Comparative Estimates) (1913–14=100)					
Year	(1)	(2)	(3)	(4)	(5)
1890	96	92	86	100	94
1897	107	93	99	105	85
1905	105	100	95	104	98
1913	100	100	100	100	100
1920	112	125	221	103	99

Sources: (1) Hansen, (2) Kuczinsky, (3) Moulton, (4) Paul Douglas, *Real Wages in the United States* (Boston: Houghton Mifflin Co., 1930). These figures are for weekly real wages; (5) Stanley Lebergott, "Earnings of Non-Farm Employees, 1890–1946," *Journal of the American Statistical Association*, May, 1948. These figures are in terms of all non-farm workers, including unemployed as well as employed.

[12] Robert Hunter, *Poverty* (New York: The Macmillan Company, 1904), p. 63.

[13] The most recent research on real wages comes to sharply different conclusions from those of the earlier studies. Assuming 1909 was equal to 100, it finds that real wages were 77 in 1889, 86 in 1899, and 135 in 1919. See Solomon Fabricant, *Basic Facts on Productivity Change*, National Bureau of Economic Research: Occasional Paper 63, 1959.

On the other hand, working hours had declined from about 60 to 55 a week. The average American worker was obtaining more leisure, but since his real wages remained almost constant, his standard of living was not increasing at the same rate as in the past.

The Emergence of the American Federation of Labor

On the whole there was nothing particularly "gay" about the 'nineties as far as the American worker was concerned. The economy and the individual firm continued to grow, but many workers lost their identity in the plant and on the production line. They gradually had become less optimistic about their chances of moving into the ranks of the employers or of achieving dazzling economic success. All too frequently they were too concerned with the hazards of unemployment to give much thought to the possibilities of moving out of the working class. They, therefore, did not seem to be particularly enthusiastic about any form of unionism, although business unionism, with its promise of short-run, specific, economic gains had more appeal than welfare or political unionism with its long-range objectives.

Thus, by 1890, the conflict between welfare unionism (as symbolized by the Knights of Labor) and business unionism (as represented by the national trade unions), had already been resolved in favor of the business unions typified by such organizations as the iron and steel workers, the cigar makers, the typographers, and other similar groups of organized skilled workers. This pervasive trend in trade unionism was demonstrated most clearly in the history of the American Federation of Labor.[14] The A.F. of L.'s beginnings go back to the formation of the Federation of Organized Trades and Labor Unions in 1881. Using this organization as a base, Samuel Gompers and Adolph Strasser (of the cigar makers) and P. J. McGuire (of the carpenters) founded the A.F. of L. in 1886, and it almost immediately began to grow and prosper.

Formed in an era when consolidation of industry was beginning to be a characteristic feature of American economic development, the A.F. of L. quickly recognized the importance of controlling the job. Its leaders argued that since trusts in industry were inevitable (and could not be controlled by government), the power of such industrial concentrations would have to be counterbalanced through the formation

---

[14] See Lewis L. Lorwin, *The American Federation of Labor* (Washington, D.C.: The Brookings Institution, 1933); Philip Taft, *The A.F. of L. in the Time of Gompers* (New York: Harper & Brothers, 1957).

of equally strong unions which could "control the job" by regulating the supply of skilled labor. The Federation was completely devoted to a policy of business unionism. It was "job and wage conscious," and its individual trade-union components were very often even more so. The Amalgamated Association of Iron and Steel Workers, for example, was so "wage conscious" that it stubbornly resisted attempts by employers in the steel business to institute the 3-shift, 8-hour system, because it would reduce the "take-home pay" of workers.

Although the Federation's chief leaders had been influenced by socialist writings, they quickly abandoned any radical leanings. Concluding that the American worker was interested in immediate gains in wages, hours, and working conditions, and not in the creation of a new society, the leaders of the A.F. of L. emphasized short-run objectives. Their philosophy was pragmatic, not idealistic. As early as 1883, Adolph Strasser said, "We have no ultimate ends. We are going on from day to day. We are fighting only for immediate objects—objects that can be realized in a few years. We are opposed to theories. We are all practical men."

In fighting to win immediate improvements in the status of the skilled laborer, the A.F. of L. opposed political methods for attaining its goals. "Foremost in my mind," said Gompers, "is to tell the politicians to keep their hands off and thus to preserve voluntary institutions and opportunity for individual and group initiative." Even as late as the depression of the 1930's, the A.F. of L. continued to be suspicious of politics; it opposed the whole concept of social welfare through political action, rejecting proposals for social security, minimum wages, and maximum hour legislation. Opposition to political methods, however, did not mean *laissez faire*, for the Federation's platform demanded a great deal of government regulation. The right to organize, and the shorter work week were always chief planks in the A.F. of L. platform; but at times it also included proposals for government ownership of public utilities, limitation of child labor, regulation of corporations, Federal housing, and drastic restriction of immigration.

Confining their attention almost exclusively to skilled laborers, the A.F. of L., and the more specialized railroad brotherhoods, did not include more than a small fraction of the total American labor force. In 1900, only 4 per cent of the workers were organized, and in 1910, but 11 per cent. Only in five industries were as many as one-third of the workers organized. In 1900, only one-quarter of the printers were organized; in 1898, only one-seventh of the brick-layers; and in 1891, less than one-quarter of the steel workers.[15]

Unlike previous periods of union history, union membership in the ascending days of the A.F. of L. did not follow the movement of the business cycle so closely, but seemed to be more correlated with the peculiar conditions of a wartime economy. The Federation, representing the majority of the organized workers, had two great periods of growth: first in the era of the Spanish-American War, and secondly during World War I. The growth between 1898 and 1904 was of a nationwide nature and was not confined to urban areas. Indeed, many small towns experienced a greater increase of unionism than the large cities. But unionism invaded only a small number of occupations. Just before World War I, most trade union members were in the building trades and railroads, with a somewhat lesser representation in the coal, glass, and stone industries. World War I created a labor scarcity which was accentuated by the virtual halt of immigration. As part of its wartime activities, the government encouraged collective bargaining in order to promote smooth industrial relations, and thus gave immense encouragement to union organization and growth. Because of this encouragement and the impetus of the great demand for labor, unionism spread extensively among textile, meat packing, metal, and water-transport workers.

The Changing Composition of the Labor Force

By the end of World War I, the American labor market had become markedly different from that of previous eras. The rate of population growth, which had begun to fall after the Civil War, declined much more sharply from 1900 on, because of a slowing down of the domestic birth rate and, after the 1920's, because of the virtual stoppage of immigration. During the early years of the 20th century, the reduction in the rate of population growth was offset to a great extent by a more intensive use of the available labor force, so that by 1910, 57.9 per cent of the population, fourteen years old or over, were in the labor force, the highest percentage in American history. According to census estimates, child labor reached its peak in 1910, when nearly two million children, between ten and fifteen years old, were employed. In the same year a little more than 25 per cent of females, of fourteen years and over,

15 Leo Wolman, *Ebb and Flow in Trade Unionism* (New York: National Bureau of Economic Research, 1936).

were included in the labor force compared with only 15 per cent in 1880, the all-time low point in female employment.

After 1910, the supply of labor no longer seemed so scarce relative to the demand, and the economy made less intensive use of the labor force. A change seemed to be occurring in the American philosophy and way of life. Americans were placing more emphasis on leisure and on non-economic goals than they had ever done before. The thesis that man was born to work and to die, although by no means passé, no longer seemed dominant. Leisure no longer appeared to be so deadly a sin, and work no longer seemed so purely noble. Moreover, the average American youth was giving more of his time to education, thereby postponing the day when he would go out into the world to seek his fortune. The percentage of young people between the ages of five and twenty attending school increased slowly, from 46 per cent in 1870 to 52 per cent in 1900; but thereafter the increase was accelerated, and reached 73 per cent by 1930. In the face of this thirst for knowledge, child labor almost disappeared. By 1930, less than 10 per cent (400,000) of persons 15 years old or younger were in the labor force. The percentage of older workers also declined. Voluntary retirement became much more common. Moreover, the steady march of industrialization, the constant speedup of production, and the increasingly technological nature of the economic system put an ever greater premium on agility and threw many of the older workers into the industrial scrapheap of involuntary retirement.

Although the family system of hiring that existed in early American industrial history had long since been abandoned, earning an income continued to be a cooperative rather than an individual enterprise. In working-class families during the early part of the 20th century, father's wages were augmented by the earnings of his children, and often by income from boarders. Among 318 New York City working-class families, for example, less than half were supported entirely by the father's income. As the century wore on and as child labor diminished, married women supplied more of the additional income needed to meet the rising standards of living.

Changes were also continually occurring in the occupational composition of the labor force. Farmers and agricultural workers, once the backbone of the American economy, declined steadily in relative numbers. Comprising over half the gainfully occupied in 1870, they declined relatively until 1910 and absolutely thereafter. By 1930, only one-fifth of the gainfully occupied were in agriculture. But at the same time the percentage of the population employed in manufacturing and mechanical industries also declined. Trade, transportation, and especially clerical service accounted for the real expansion in the number of gainfully-occupied people. What was happening to America's occupational pattern can best be expressed in a few figures: in 1870, 77 per cent of employed Americans worked in primary production, 13 per cent were in the service industries, 7 per cent distributed the goods, and 3 per cent were involved in coordinating; by 1940, only 46 per cent were in primary production, 20 per cent supplied services, 23 per cent were concerned with distribution and 11 per cent engaged in coordination.

The Worker During the Hectic 'Twenties

The changes in the size and pattern of the labor force that came with the misnamed "economy of abundance," that was ushered in during the second decade of the 20th century, necessitated far-reaching social readjustment. The problem of economic insecurity became much more acute, and the traditional doctrine of limitless opportunity lost much of its appeal. Large fissures appeared between the ranks of the gainfully occupied, and many echelons of the workers ceased to have any articulate aspirations. The independence so long associated with the ownership of small productive property was weakened steadily, and not replaced with an adequate substitute. In time, the necessity for social readjustment among the changing groups of the gainfully occupied was to be an important factor in the evolution of American thought, economic institutions, and government. It should be noted, however, that none of this was very clear to the worker during the 1920's, for this was an era in which he made great short-run progress, but progress that had the disadvantage of lulling him into unwarranted complacency regarding his future.

General living conditions for the average worker *circa* 1929 were far better than they had been for his predecessor. In 1929, the manufacturing worker's average annual earnings were $1,300. Since the price level had not risen as fast as wages, real wages were much higher—perhaps 20 per cent higher than in 1913—and the average worker was able to buy a larger range of commodities. About two-thirds of his income was now spent for food, clothing, and shelter, compared with three-quarters in the previous generation. More was expended for nonessentials and luxuries, and it is probable that the average wage earner could, and actually did, save more in 1929 than he did in 1900. Not only did real wages increase, but the worker gained another five hours of leisure a week between 1913 and 1929, when the work week was reduced to approximately 50 hours.[16]

Real Wages, 1920–1929 (Comparative Estimates) (1913=100)				
Year	(1)	(2)	(3)	(4)
1923	122	143	118	112
1924	116	149	120	107
1926	122	153	117	113
1929	127	165	—	122

Sources: (1) Kuczinsky, (2) Moulton, (3) Douglas, (4) Lebergott.

The chief reason for the manufacturing wage earner's ability to reduce his hours of work and, at the same time, to raise his money and real wages, lay in the continuous increase in productivity. Mainly because of constant technological progress and the accumulation of capital, over-all productivity for the economy increased about 3 per cent a year between 1920 and 1930. At the pace maintained during the 'twenties, the nation's output would have doubled in 23 years; whereas at the rate of increase prevalent before World War I, it would have taken 63 years to double output. In manufacturing, however, productivity increased even more than it did for the general economy. According to the estimates of Mills, productivity in manufacturing increased 10 per cent a year between 1919 and 1922, probably the highest rate in our history.[17]

Decline of Unionism in the 'Twenties

Paradoxically, prosperity, which in previous history had always nurtured unionism, had just the opposite effect during the 'twenties. With the end of World War I, the decline in the demand for labor and the widespread spirit of anti-radicalism (which at times verged on hysteria) posed great difficulties for trade unions. The unions had, more-

[16] Paul H. Douglas, *Real Wages in the United States, 1890–1926* (Boston: Houghton, Mifflin Company, 1930). The Douglas series, covering 1890 to 1926, differs a great deal from the Bureau of Labor Statistics index which begins with 1909.

[17] Frederick C. Mills, "The Role of Productivity in Economic Growth," *American Economic Review*, Vol. XLII, No. 2, May 1952. Recent studies conclude that physical output per man hour in the private economy increased by about 2.0 per cent annually between 1889 and 1919 and by about 2.6 per cent, 1919–1957. Solomon Fabricant, *Basic Facts on Productivity Change*.

over, come out of the war with an exaggerated sense of power; and in the first years of peace, as employers resisted union attempts to renew collective bargaining agreements and as money wages failed to advance with the cost of living, strikes were frequent. Yet the A.F. of L. could not hold its own, nor could it do so during the remainder of the decade, in some respects the most prosperous decade in the history of American manufacturing. Between 1920 and 1930, total trade-union membership declined from 5 million to 3.4 million; and the Federation's membership fell from 4.1 to 3 million.

Prosperity meant higher wages for the worker, and each increase in wages once again served to accentuate the American laborer's tendency to identify himself with the middle class rather than with the proletariat. Prosperity also meant an increasing rate of mechanization; this, in turn, meant not only a decline in the number of manufacturing workers but an increase in the proportion of semi-skilled laborers. At the same time, the changing composition of the labor force brought a larger number of white-collar workers and women into the employment picture. The trade unions, as they existed in the 'twenties, were not eager to organize the lesser skilled, and were totally unable to cope with the problem of organizing the white-collar workers and the female workers. At this faltering stage of trade-unionism, much to the chagrin and bewilderment of the A.F. of L., the government's friendly and encouraging attitude ended abruptly. The Federation once again found the courts critical of unions if not overtly antagonistic. Even before the war's end, the Supreme Court, in the Hitchman Coal Case, forbade unions from attempting to organize employees who were employed under non-union contracts. In 1922, a district court granted the Attorney General an injunction prohibiting the railroad brotherhoods from picketing or persuading employees to strike. In 1927, the Bedford Stone Case made union boycotts illegal, even where the boycotters were of the same union. Lost in the sea of changing economic conditions and buffeted by the courts, the A.F. of L. suffered strong attacks against it from both the right and the left, from militant employers and from militant radicals. The attack by organized employers was especially devastating.

Growing Opposition of Employers

The early career of the A.F. of L. did not arouse any specific employer opposition. True enough, there were two violent strikes, at Homestead, Pennsylvania, in 1892, and against the Pullman Co. in 1894; but the

Federation remained pretty much aloof from these, even though the steel strike at Homestead involved one of its affiliates, the Amalgamated Association of Iron, Steel, and Tin Workers. Relations between the Federation and management became so harmonious that the period up to 1900 came to be called the "honeymoon period between capital and labor." In 1900, affable relations were formalized when representatives of management and labor cooperated in forming the National Civic Federation, an organization devoted to encouraging collective bargaining, mediation, and arbitration in industrial relations.

Beneath the surface, however, the spectacular growth of unionism caused considerable uneasiness, especially among small businessmen. Entrepreneurs feared that the continued growth of organizations like the A.F. of L. would interfere with their function of making business decisions. They were especially opposed to such union policies as the closed shop, the boycott, limitation on the employer's right to hire and fire, and union restriction of output. Organized opposition to unions first appeared when groups of small businessmen in the Middle West formed local citizens' alliances. The movement quickly became an integrated one. In 1902, the American Anti-boycott Association was organized, and, in 1903, D. M. Parry succeeded in converting the National Association of Manufacturers from a tariff-lobbying trade association to a militant anti-union organization. Under Parry's leadership and the NAM's aegis, anti-union businessmen organized the Citizens' Industrial Association in 1903. By 1904, the nation was studded with anti-union organizations, including the National Founders' Association, the National Metal Trades Association, the National Erectors' Association, and the League for Industrial Rights.

The militant tactics used by these employers' associations included the black list, pledges by members not to enter into closed-shop agreements, financial assistance to employers during strikes, opposition to legislation urged or supported by unions, and campaigns to arouse public opinion in favor of the open shop. In addition, scientific management was used extensively for anti-union purposes as were welfare schemes. On the whole, the anti-union campaign apparently accomplished its purpose, for, as the campaign gathered momentum, membership in unions not only ceased to grow, but actually declined, and, presently, having achieved success, the employers diminished the intensity of their anti-union drive. During World War I, the need for labor, and the government's encouragement of collective bargaining, made anti-unionism temporarily inexpedient. But as soon as the war was over, employers once again organized concerted drives to combat trade unionism.

All through the early postwar period, anti-union employers resisted recognition of the union as the collective bargaining agent. Up and down the nation, they carried on a determined and highly successful crusade to sell the open shop to the American people. Gradually, when it became clear that unionism was not going to extend its membership, anti-union tactics shifted to more positive techniques. The tools of the "tough policy"—the labor spy, the injunction, the black list, and the *agent provocateur*—were still retained, but major emphasis was now placed on "welfare" plans and "industrial democracy," including profit-sharing, stock ownership, wage incentives, scientific management and company unions. Many employers gave wide publicity to the purchasing-power theory, preaching the doctrine of higher production, higher wages, and lower prices, and asserting that it was necessary to pay high wages in order to maintain a high level of demand. For the most part, however, this doctrine was expressed more in words than in action. Many of its loudest exponents actually meant that it would be a grand idea if their competitors paid higher wages. Although trade-union leaders scoffed at "welfare capitalism" and "industrial democracy," their criticism had little influence. They were unable to produce convincing reasons why laborers should join a trade union. On the other hand, the employers' counteroffensive impressed a great many laborers, convincing them that they were receiving more from management than they could receive from organized labor. Under the circumstances, the A.F. of L. floundered during the entire prosperous decade of the 1920's.

Effect of the Depression of the 'Thirties on Unions

The quarter century after 1930 was, in most respects, the most extraordinary period in American labor history. During these years of depression, partial recovery, war, and postwar prosperity, the American worker experienced not only his most tragic economic moments, but also his most phenomenal economic progress. In 1933, the worker was beset by unemployment, low wages, and broken morale; by 1950, the skilled worker had finally achieved the middle-class status for which he had always been striving. But, in achieving it, he had for the most part abandoned his ambitions of becoming wealthy, and now placed greater stress on security and day-to-day well-being than on opportunity.

	Money wages		Real wages	
	hourly	weekly	hourly	weekly
Year	(current dollars)		(1947–1949 dollars)	
1929	.57	25.03	.77	34.15
1933	.44	16.73	.78	30.25
1939	.64	23.86	1.07	40.17
1940	.66	25.20	1.10	42.07
1945	1.02	44.39	1.28	55.63
1950	1.47	59.33	1.43	57.71
1957	2.07	82.39	1.72	68.54

Estimated Manufacturing Earnings, 1929–1957

Source: Bureau of Labor Statistics.

Money wages more than tripled and real wages doubled between 1929 and 1957.[18] But as everybody knows, this remarkable increase did not take place continuously. During the great depression, money wages fell very sharply, although they did not really begin to decline until the last quarter of 1930. Because prices fell more rapidly than hourly money wages, real wages did not fall for those workers who were fortunate enough to have full-time jobs. However, over 25 per cent of the labor force was unemployed, and the majority of those who were employed did not have full-time jobs. Allowing for losses of time caused by unemployment, real wages for the average non-farm employee declined by more than 30 per cent during the depression. But after the depression, money and real wages increased more than at any other time in history. Taking 1933 as a base year and allowing for the reduction in unemployment since then, real earnings have increased almost threefold. In addition, there have been many indirect benefits. Pensions and welfare plans—disability, health, and life insurance—have added immensely to the worker's actual income. All in all, the economic progress that has taken place since the depression, and especially since 1940, has benefited the workers more than any other group in society. Perhaps part of the reason is that the gain in real wages has not been accompanied by any substantial reduction of working hours. The average work week in manufacturing in 1922 was 44 hours; in 1945, 43 hours; and in 1956, 40 hours.[19] As in past periods, the worker had the choice of taking the rewards of greater production in the form of increased wages

[18] Comparisons over a longer period of time are quite unreal, although much more spectacular. City workers in 1948 had a median family income of $3,384 compared with $749 in 1901. Average earnings of factory workers were $2,815 in 1948 compared with $439 in 1901. Corrected for price changes, the $439 becomes approximately $1,350 in 1948 dollars.

[19] Bureau of Labor Statistics. Douglas's estimate for 1926 was 50 hours.

or increased leisure. Before 1900, he tended to place a greater value on higher wages; in the next thirty years he placed greater emphasis on increased leisure; after the depression of the 'thirties he again stressed wages.

Dramatic Growth of Unions After the Great Depression

In the two decades 1930–1950, the general rise in the status of the worker was accompanied by a great growth of trade-union membership. To be sure, the depression years following 1929 accelerated the tendency toward a decline in membership which had already been discernible during the boom years. Having little to offer the laborer during prosperity, trade unions had even less to offer during depression. Membership in the A.F. of L. declined to almost 2 million, and total trade-union membership to less than 3 million. With a floundering policy, the A.F. of L. became vulnerable to "boring from within" by radical groups who gained control of some unions. Yet, considering the malaise of the period, radicalism made astonishingly little progress among labor groups. Indeed, Marxism had more of a vogue among intellectuals than among laborers.

If the depression did not spawn radicalism among the workers, it did prepare the way for the great upsurge in union membership that occurred in the late 'thirties. First of all, it convinced the majority of workers that they would never be anything else but workers, and that their place was in a labor union. Moreover, by the time the depression had run its course, public opinion was much less favorably disposed to the tenets of traditional American conservatism than it had been in previous periods. Poverty was considered to be less the individual's fault than the result of unfavorable social circumstances and poor economic organization. The word "underprivileged" came to be used increasingly in place of the word "poor." Consequently, instead of the 19th-century axiom that aid and assistance should never be carried beyond the barest charity, it came to be quite commonly believed that the underprivileged should be helped through unions and by means of government welfare legislation. Instead of believing that "any one could get a job if he wanted to," the majority of Americans had become much more sympathetic to the worker and to his union, which was regarded as his protector and spokesman.

Reflecting the change in public opinion, government became as friendly to labor unions as it had previously been hostile. There was some evidence of this as early as 1932, when the Norris–La Guardia Act sharply curtailed the use of court injunctions against organized labor, a reform which had been high on the A.F. of L.'s program since 1906. But it was the New Deal that really made government a warm friend of labor. The widely-publicized Section 7 (a) of the National Industrial Recovery Act guaranteed laborers the right to bargain collectively under representatives of their own choosing. The A.F. of L. regarded this legislation as the government's blessing and encouragement of unionism. Labor leaders spread the word, "President Roosevelt wants you to join a union." But the A.F. of L. was not able to take full advantage of its opportunities because it still remained indifferent to the unskilled workers and made no real effort to organize them. But employers did not meekly surrender; they hastily revivified their techniques for organizing company unions, and very quickly seemed to be having the best of it in the struggle with the Federation.

This unsatisfactory course of events was most disturbing to many of the leaders of the A.F. of L., especially to John L. Lewis, who was then a vice-president of the Federation and the head of the largest industrial-type union in the country. At the 1934 convention, Lewis vigorously attacked the Federation's traditional craft-union policies and demanded that a determined effort be made to organize labor along industrial lines. His demands were not met enthusiastically by the other union leaders, but an open rift was temporarily averted by a compromise.

While all this internal strife was going on, the Federal government took action that should have considerably strengthened the position of the labor unions. Immediately after the NRA was declared unconstitutional, Congress moved to replace its Section 7 (a) with a stronger guarantee of the right of collective bargaining. This emerged as the National Labor Relations Act (the Wagner Act) of 1935. The Wagner Act forbade employers to refuse to bargain collectively, to interfere with labor's right to organize, to discriminate against union members, and to dominate a union. Moreover, it set up machinery to supervise elections of bargaining representatives and to enforce the provisions of the Act.

To all intents and purposes, the Wagner Act was a windfall for labor unions, for it eliminated the company union. But it soon became apparent that the A.F. of L. was not going to change its tactics. Lewis therefore came to the 1935 convention with fire in his beetle-browed eyes. He was particularly interested in organizing the steel industry, and when the executive council reported that it did not deem it advisable to launch an organizing campaign in steel, Lewis brought the matter of industrial *versus* craft unionism to a vote. He was opposed by the old-line conservatives—Hutcheson of the Carpenters, Tobin of the teamsters, Woll of the photo-engravers, and Frey of the metal trades—and supported by Murray of the mine workers, Hillman and Dubinsky of the clothing workers, and Howard of the typographers. With all of his not inconsiderable oratorical powers, Lewis lashed out at the craft unionists; he warned the convention that if it did not grasp its opportunity, "high wassail will prevail at the banquet tables of the mighty." Wassail or not, the industrial unionists lost. But instead of meekly ceasing their activities, they met in November, 1935 and formed the Committee for Industrial Organization to work within the A.F. of L. to promote collective bargaining in the mass-production industries. On its part, the A.F. of L. still refused to countenance Lewis's ideas, and demanded that the C.I.O. dissolve. When this was ignored, it suspended the ten dissident unions. Blithely ignoring the A.F. of L., the heretics, in March, 1937, began a drive to organize the steel and automobile industries, and in May, 1938, withdrew completely from the A. F. of L., and renamed their new institution the Congress of Industrial Organization.

Despite violent and temporary setbacks, the C.I.O's early career was a dazzling success. In its first year, its membership was greater than that of the A.F. of L. had ever been. But this was not all; it also had the electrifying effect of dragging the A.F. of L. out of some of its archaic ways. Faced with the new rivalry, the Federation also began to organize the unskilled, and shortly it regained its dominant position. Thus both unions grew amazingly. By 1940, total trade-union membership was over 8.5 million. This increased even further during World War II, and at the war's end, labor unionism was at its peak with 25 per cent of the total labor force enrolled. Eliminating the large groups that were practically unorganized—farmers and white-collar workers—organized labor had within its fold more than one-third of the nation's manufacturing workers. In more than a score of the most important industries, over 80 per cent of the wage earners were members of labor unions. Business unionism had become universal, and, in the process, ideological differences between unions had been largely obliterated, a fact that was well illustrated by the merger of the A.F. of L. and the C.I.O. in 1955. Even radical unionism had become enamored of business unionism; indeed, it followed the tactics of business unionism so faithfully that it often appeared to be more conservative than the traditionally conservative unions themselves. Paradoxically, those labor unions which succeeded best in invading what had always been considered management's exclusive area were the very ones with the strongest sympathy for capitalist institutions.

In the first few post-depression years public opinion was not adverse to the growth of unionism. It was commonly thought at that time that labor had a right to organize and to bargain collectively. But the friendliness toward unions began to cool with the sit-down strikes of 1937. Then during the war, and in the immediate postwar years, more and more people came to believe that unions were achieving too much power. This belief was expressed legislatively in the Taft-Hartley Act of 1947, which sought, as one of its authors expressed it, to make labor as responsible in labor-management relations as the Wagner Act had made capital. Labor denounced the act as "slave legislation." Whether it was or was not, membership continued to grow, but not at the same pace as in previous years.

Obviously union leaders themselves had much to do with union growth. They were essentially pragmatic in their tactics, and were no more given to defending any particular ideology than the labor leaders of the past. Yet they still did not represent labor as a whole; they represented groups of workers—steel workers, miners, garment workers, brewers, and other particular groups. The leaders were still highly opportunistic; and all unions, conservative and radical, continued to emphasize the goals of business unionism and the tactics that had always been used by that type of unionism: the collective bargaining agreement and the closed shop. They did not use the strike more than their predecessors had done. According to available data, in 1945, a year of highly publicized strikes, only 12 per cent of employed wage earners were involved in strikes, whereas, in 1919, at the end of World War I, the comparable figure had been 21 per cent. Data on the percentage of working time lost through strikes have been recorded only since 1927, but no radical increase has occurred since then. In 1945, less than 5 per cent of working time was lost through strikes; this was no more than in 1937, and only slightly more than in 1926.

But although the post-1935 labor leaders used the tactics of their predecessors, they also departed very sharply from the policies of the past. They presented labor's case much more effectively than it had ever been presented before, and they missed no opportunity to employ experts to support labor's arguments. Recognizing that far fewer workers now believed that they would some day leave the ranks of labor, the unions, especially the C.I.O., entered into politics, and broadened labor's legislative goals to include many welfare and pension arrangements, supplementary unemployment benefits, the guaranteed annual wage, and paid vacations. In short, these leaders looked at labor as a way of life, and were therefore philosophically closer to William Sylvis than to Samuel Gompers. Consequently they had much more appeal to the worker than the pre-1935 A.F. of L. had ever had. A change in the attitude of businessmen also contributed to union growth, although naturally in a much more negative way. Employers were not so militantly anti-union as they had been in the 1920's. Nor did they make such valiant attempts (as they had in the "welfare capitalism" of the 'twenties) to outbid the unions for the favor of the worker. Partly because of a change of heart, and partly because of government legislation, most businessmen had come to recognize that unions were here to stay. There were, of course, many spectacular exceptions, such as Ernest Weir and many of the mill owners of the South, but even before the end of the 1930's such rugged individualists as Henry Ford and Tom Girdler had accepted the inevitability of unionization. And, no matter how reluctantly they did so, even these "die-hard" businessmen conceded that a great change had occurred in America's beliefs and attitudes toward unionism. After a century of struggle, and after innumerable ups and downs, trade unionism had become an integral part of American life.

12 Expansion of agriculture and emergence of a chronic farm problem

The Business Motivation of American Farmers

One of the most vexatious political and economic problems in the United States has been the "farm problem," which in one way or another, has always been with us. Essentially, the farm problem is a business problem, centering in the farmer's belief that he does not receive a fair share of the national income.

So long as land was relatively plentiful and labor and capital were scarce, the farm problem was relatively uncomplicated. Then it centered on two questions: how to help the farmer settle the land, and how to assist him to get farm products to market. Although these were not easy to resolve, they were not essentially business problems, for, with occasional and significant exceptions, farming was more a way of life than a business. But as population infiltrated the vast area of the West, the farm problem gradually became much more complex. In the process of settlement, agriculture grew; decade after decade, the story was the same: more farmers plowing more acres, planting more seeds, and reaping larger crops. And as agriculture grew and became more productive, it underwent a striking transformation. Its relative economic importance declined whereas that of the manufacturing and service industries increased. Then too, great changes occurred in the farmer's methods of production. Markets expanded, machinery became more widely used, farming became less self-sufficient and more commercialized. In short, farming became a business.

This was as the farmer wanted it, for he was an American with American values. Unlike his land-bound European counterpart, the American farmer was a mobile person who was "here today and gone tomorrow." Often more interested in land speculation than in land cultivation, he was more of a colonizer than a patron of husbandry. Lacking an intense love of the land, American farmers did not form a peasant class such as existed in Europe. Instead, most American farmers were, or at least wanted to be, agrarian businessmen.

Ironically, the transformation of farming from a way of life to a business, that the farmer desired so ardently, brought something the farmer did not want at all. It produced a new variant of the "farm problem." For as agriculture became a business, the farmer was confronted with many of the problems that harried the industrial entrepreneur. He now faced the headaches of competition, the difficulties of capital raising, the costs of mechanization, and, above all, the problem of getting what he considered to be a fair share of the national income.

Land as a Factor in American Economic Development

Up to 1860 and in many ways until 1890, land exploitation was one of the major activities that conditioned American economic development. Land was the most plentiful productive factor, and, although the American population increased phenomenally, for a time the land area that came under the jurisdiction of the United States increased almost as fast. At the opening of the 19th century, continental United States comprised only about 525 million acres, but by midcentury almost the whole of the present area (about two billion acres) had been acquired. Consequently, although the population doubled every twenty-three years, the land-man ratio did not change greatly. In 1800 the population density was about six persons per square mile; by 1850 it was still less than eight; and in 1860 it was only ten and a half persons per square mile.[1]

After two hundred years of immigration and population growth, there was still plenty of land for the American people. This "land" included not only the great reaches of fertile soil but also rich subsurface resources and bountiful stands of timber, thus providing the indispensable ingredients in the "resource mix" that produced America's amazing economic growth. The existence of this immense, unsettled landmass had inculcated in the American people a spirit of optimism, and provided a psychological cause for their dream of material success. It also encouraged population growth and capital accumulation, because the settlement and cultivation of the land required more people, tools, and equipment. Moreover, the enormous expanse of land and the sheer distance between the Atlantic Coast and the far West made it imperative to develop marketing facilities: turnpikes, canals, and railroads. Their construction required large amounts of capital funds from domestic and foreign saving, and the land offered a means both for attracting and generating saving. Sometimes, for example, land was sold to provide funds for canal or railway construction, or, when it was not sold, it often constituted the security on which credit was granted. Land was sometimes used directly or indirectly to capitalize banks. It strengthened both Federal and state credit, since portions of the public domain were frequently the security which the United States and the individual states pledged when seeking loans in the international money market.

But the abundance of land was not an unmixed blessing; it led to careless methods of agriculture that exhausted the soil,[2] and it made the American farmer a land speculator. Yet, it was the speculative opportunity which land provided that made the settlement of the West so rapid and dramatic, even as it was the succession of American frontiers that supplied dynamic factors in American economic history.

Government Land Policy

Of the two billion acres that comprise the continental United States, the Federal government at one time or another owned 1.4 billion or

---

[1] Even in 1950 population density was only 51 per square mile. Compare this with Belgium (739), United Kingdom (535), The Netherlands (830), and France (200).

[2] A close (British) student of scientific agriculture who visited America in the mid-19th century said that when American farmers were successful it was not because they knew how to farm but because they had "blundered into prosperity."

about 70 per cent. The policies governing the disposal of this public domain were, therefore, of inestimable importance in determining how the land would be settled. At first, government land policy[3] was designed to raise revenue. Consequently, the first land ordinance enacted after the ratification of the Constitution provided for the sale of whole "sections" (areas one mile square containing 640 acres) at land auctions, at which a minimum bid of $2 per acre would be considered, although sales in greater volume were permissible at lower prices. But little land was sold under this arrangement, and presently public land policy became the subject of heated debate in which the arguments mostly reflected sectional economic interests. The westerners on the frontier favored a very liberal land policy, not only because they needed rapid settlement in order to gain political power, but because more settlers would increase the likelihood that urgently-needed transportation facilities would be constructed. Many city wage earners supported this "liberal" land policy because they thought cheap land might offer them a means of escape from the economic difficulties of industrial life. Northern industrialists, in contrast, at first opposed a liberal land policy, fearing that it would drain the East of its labor supply. They dropped their opposition once it became clear that eastern laborers were not emigrating to the West and as it became evident that the opening of the West was widening their market. Meantime, however, the South became increasingly opposed to a liberalized land policy, because free land would very likely increase the number of people supporting a high tariff policy, and, more particularly, because free land would mean more rapid settlement of the West by free labor and consequently a diminution of the South's political power.

By 1820 the western viewpoint was already winning. A series of new land laws had progressively lessened the minimum number of acres that could be purchased, so that by 1820 the minimum parcel had been reduced to 80 acres, and the minimum price per acre to $1.25. By mid-century there was no longer any doubt that the land policy had changed. By general consent and frank congressional admission, its chief purpose was no longer to produce revenue, but to encourage rapid settlement. The liberalization of the land policy reached its fruition in the Homestead Act of 1862, under which a citizen could acquire 160 acres of land simply by fulfilling certain residence requirements and by paying a

[3] For more information on Federal land policy, see B. H. Hibbard, *A History of Public Land Policies* (New York: Peter Smith, 1939); Roy Robbins, *Our Landed Heritage* (Princeton, N.J.: Princeton University Press, 1942).

small filing fee. Subsequent land acts in the 1870's—the Timber Culture Act, the Desert Land Act, and the Timber and Stone Act—made additional acreages available to individuals. Thus, by 1890, one individual, taking advantage of all his opportunities under the various land acts, could obtain 1280 acres of land[4] at a cost of $1,400 plus some filing fees.

In addition to making grants to individuals, the Federal government, by various miscellaneous grants, made land available to states and to corporations. Beginning in 1827, grants to states helped finance internal improvements,[5] and, in 1862, the Morrill Act gave each state 30,000 acres for each of its senators and representatives in Congress, the proceeds to be used to endow colleges for mechanical and agricultural arts. A very large amount of land was also given to encourage the construction of railroads. The first gift of this kind was made in 1850 when the Illinois Central Railroad received 2.5 million acres.[6] The usual railroad grant consisted of a strip 100 feet wide for right of way plus alternate sections to a depth of six miles. In some cases, however, the grant was much larger, running as deep as twenty miles in the states and forty miles in the territories. By 1871, when the government stopped making grants to railroads, it had given them 131 million acres, and the states had granted an additional 49 million.

When it was officially said, in 1890, that the frontier no longer existed, and when a decline in the rate of population increase became apparent, a new trend in public land policy began to appear. The nation at long last began to think seriously about the waste of natural resources that had been an inevitable consequence of a liberal land policy. With a thought to conserving what was left of America's landed heritage, a clause was inserted in the miscellaneous appropriation act of 1890, limiting to 320 acres the total amount of land for which a single individual could file. Some attempts were also made during the ensuing decade to withdraw valuable lands from settlement, but these plans were largely frustrated by western interests still vitally interested in a liberal land policy. Gradually, however, conservation gained favor as a guide to Federal land policy, especially during the Theodore Roosevelt administration at the turn of the century. In a short time almost 150

[4] 160 acres *each* under the Preemption Act of 1841, the Homestead Act, the Timber Culture Act, and the Timber and Stone Act; plus 640 acres under the Desert Land Act.

[5] See p. 172.

[6] See p. 173.

million acres of the public domain (which had hitherto been available virtually free) were withdrawn from patent-right privileges; and at the same time, a forest service was established to supervise the conservation of what remained of America's timber resources. As a result of various types of land reservation, by 1955 the Federal government still owned 400 million acres of land out of an original public domain of 1.4 billion acres. Thus, in a little more than a hundred years, the Federal government had alienated, by sale or gift, approximately one billion acres of land. The four main items in this total were: cash sales of 334 million acres; entries of 285 million acres under the Homestead Act and subsequent land-alienation acts; 224 million acres granted to the states; and 131 million acres given to stimulate railway construction.

The Effects of the Government's Land Policy

The government's land policy influenced the whole pattern of American economic institutions and the social framework within which a large part of American society had its daily existence. It encouraged speculation, thereby accentuating the "boom and bust" character of the American economy. It was a fundamental influence in determining the relatively small size of the average American farm. It played an important role in the development of marketing facilities. It stimulated immigration and profoundly affected the internal dispersion of population.

The government land policy, largely designed to promote the rapid settlement of the West, was ostensibly intended to favor the *bona fide* settler and the lower-income groups whether already on farms or in cities. But, whereas the policy did encourage rapid settlement, it never fulfilled the hopes of some of its idealistic proponents, who visualized a nation of prosperous and happy small-farm owners. Actually it benefited speculators and the middle- and upper-income groups much more than the low-income groups whom land-reform leaders had in mind. To begin with, the low-income groups did not have the financial resources to move and set up a farm even when land was free. Then, too, of those who bought or acquired government land, only a minority intended to cultivate it permanently. All too many hoped to sell and reap a profit in a short while; settle and sell, rather than settle and cultivate, became the principle of western agriculture, as land speculation became a game for a nation of inveterate gamblers. The national consequences of such speculation became apparent quite early. In 1819 and again in the 1830's, frenzied land buying, financed by expanded bank credit, ended, in each case, in a severe panic and a long and deep depression.

To the extent that the government's land policy did succeed in benefiting the small settler; it encouraged an agrarian structural pattern made up of family-sized farms seldom larger than the 160-acre tract of the Homestead Act. But, at the same time, the loose terms and the actual administration of the public land laws made it possible for ingenious speculators to evade the spirit of the law and build up huge land holdings. Under the Homestead Act and other land laws, ambitious land buyers obtained much more than 160 acres by employing "dummies" to file claims which were "pre-empted" at $1.25 an acre in 6 months. As a result, by the 1890's farms and ranches of from 250,000 to over 1 million acres were not uncommon in the West.

Whatever its shortcomings, the government land policy did encourage the building of transportation facilities, first by means of land subsidies to the states and later through direct land grants to the western railroads. These grants were made on the theory that they would help a railway corporation cover a substantial part of its construction costs by providing the railroad promoters with salable land. In actual practice, the effect of the land grants on the railways was somewhat different; their real importance was psychological, for they led promoters to plan new lines and tempted investors to provide the funds with which to construct railways through sparsely-inhibited areas. Reversing the more usual pattern, it was the railroads that brought people to the West; not the people who brought the railroads. Without the land grants (and, of course, the anticipated profit from their sale) it is doubtful whether railroad promoters would have constructed the roads as quickly as they did.

The impact of public land policy on immigration was also mostly psychological. A far greater number of immigrants were attracted to the United States by the prospect of free land than the number who actually became pioneers in the westward movement. Immigrants, especially the Germans and Scandinavians, did their share in settling the West, but their part was not nearly as great as that of the internal migrants. For most immigrants without capital, an operating farm was only a little less unattainable than the pot of gold at the end of the rainbow; and only a minority realized their dream of becoming land owners.

Meantime, however, the acceptance of a liberal land policy had wide ramifications on the Federal government's fiscal policy. By giving the land away, the government sacrificed what might have been an important source of revenue, thereby making Federal revenue dependent almost exclusively on customs duties and excises, and thereby buttressing a highly regressive tax system. The land policy also influenced the ways in which government revenues were spent. Since it encouraged the westward movement, the land policy built up the political importance of western agrarianism, thereby strengthening Congressional groups that favored a policy of governmental assistance for public works. As a result, despite deeply imbedded *laissez-faire* notions, the Federal government not only subsidized railroads and helped finance other types of social capital, but presently it began to spend money for the direct benefit of agriculture. The Morrill Act of 1862 was a case in point. By providing an annual cash subsidy for the support of agricultural education, it raised the farmer's standard of education at government expense, a policy that was of great importance in developing a farm population that was willing to experiment with new crops, new machinery, and new agricultural practices.

The Westward Movement and the Influence of the Frontier

The westward movement was the result of a combination of an enormous land area, an expanding population, the movement of the business cycle, and government land policy. By itself, land would not have caused the westward movement. There had to be a demand for it, and it had to be made easily available. Population growth and waves of prosperity created the demand for land; government policy made the land easy to acquire.

As population increased, the frontier bulged westward, but it moved sporadically, not steadily. Nor should it be assumed that the "westward movement" was always in a westerly direction. It went north from Connecticut, east from New Hampshire, south from Tennessee, and east from California! The first real surge toward the West occurred after the War of 1812 and came to a halt with the depression of 1819. The next great wave of western settlement took place in the 1830's, and by 1840 the frontier had reached the Mississippi River. In the 'fifties, the frontier line took another great jump, and, by the outbreak of the Civil

War, it had reached the 95th meridian. During the prosperity of the 'seventies and 'eighties the Great Plains were settled, and in 1890 the Census Bureau made its famous announcement that there was no longer any American frontier line.

It has been a favorite thesis of some American historians that the frontier acted as a "safety valve" for the steam generated by urban economic and social difficulties. This thesis was vividly stated by a distinguished historian, Frederick Jackson Turner, who said:

> Whenever social conditions tended to crystallize in the East, whenever capital tended to press upon labor or political restraints to impede the freedom of the mass, there was this gate to the free conditions of the frontier. . . . Men would not accept inferior wages, and a permanent position of social subordination, when this promised land of freedom and equality was theirs for the asking.[7]

This idea that the western frontier offered a haven for the oppressed laborers of the East, thereby exerting an upward pressure on wage rates and acting as a healing unguent for the sores of business depression was an old thesis. Turner uncovered a 1634 version of it. Washington and Jefferson, Horace Greeley, and even Karl Marx believed it. Yet, venerable as the theory was and despite its persistence, modern research indicates that it overromanticized the real influence of the frontier and of the West.[8]

It was true that economic life had, as Turner said, a "perennial rebirth" on the frontier. Each frontier area went through a gradual transformation from self-sufficient farming to commercial farming, from household manufacturing to factory manufacturing, from economic infancy to economic adolescence, and from a capital-short subsistence standard of living to a more comfortable level. Nor is there any doubt that the westward movement and the frontier did diffuse population. Of every hundred Americans, 93 lived in the East in 1800 but only 51 lived there in 1860. But the flow of population into the frontier areas did not come from the urban centers. Indeed, city population in the first half of the 19th century increased much faster than rural population. It was, in fact, the city that was a "safety-valve" for the country people, rather than *vice-versa*. Moreover, the frontier offered no haven for the unemployed urban population in periods of depression. The mere wish to go West was not enough; besides desire, the would-be settler needed

---

[7] Frederick Jackson Turner, *The Frontier in American History* (New York: Henry Holt, 1920), p. 259.

[8] See George R. Taylor, ed., *The Turner Thesis* (Boston: D. C. Heath and Co., 1948).

Money and a willingness to break his links with the past. Both of these prerequisites appeared only in years of optimism and plenty. Data on the sales of public land offer clear evidence that the West's drawing power was much more irresistible in periods of prosperity than in periods of depression. The westward movement became a stampede in periods of business boom; it slowed down to a trickle in periods of depression. This was chiefly because of the outlay in money that a settler had to make; it took at least $1,000 to establish a farm in the West in the 1850's, and a surplus of this size was simply not at hand during depressions. Indeed such a sum was very seldom within the grasp of the average city laborer even in good times. The best-paid city worker earned only about $2 a day; from that income he could hardly accumulate sufficient capital to make the long jump to the frontier. And even if he were financially able, he lacked the necessary know-how to be a farmer. Moreover, many people were bound to towns and cities by habit, custom, or pure inertia.

Who, then, did settle the West? For the most part, it was the migrant farmer. Each area was settled by farmers who moved from a contiguous area. For example, Kansas was occupied mainly by people from Missouri, Illinois and Iowa. The typical movement was in short jumps; the long safari from the East to the frontier was exceptional. Few families went from Manhattan Island to Nebraska in one glorious adventure. More typically, great-great-grandfather moved from Connecticut to Ohio in the early 1800's, great-grandfather moved from Ohio to Illinois in the 1830's, grandfather migrated to Iowa in 1860, father pushed on to Nebraska in the 'eighties, and junior made the long jump to California in the 1920's. The migrant to new lands might be an independent farmer who had sold his holdings in the older settlement, or he might be the son of an established farmer who had worked for other farmers, saved part of his income, and, with the aid of father or father-in-law and a mortgage, bought a farm. Occasionally, but less commonly, a tenant or ordinary day laborer might migrate to the West.

The Economic Organization of Early Agriculture[9]

In every frontier area, the pioneer farmer raised his own provisions, made his clothing from the skins of cattle, deer, or raccoons, or from

[9] Still the best study of early northern farming is Percy Wells Bidwell and John J. Falconer, *History of Agriculture in the Northern United States, 1620–1860* (Washington, D.C.: Carnegie Institution, 1925).

home-raised wool or flax; he built his house out of timber or sod, without benefit of glass or iron. Jack-of-all-trades and master of few, he was fortunate if at the end of the year he had a cash income of $100. Thus, although agriculture was of paramount importance in the United States until the end of the 19th century, its organization was not geared to making as large a contribution to the economy as has often been assumed. Without marketing facilities, the frontier farmer was forced to be mostly a self-sufficient producer, rather than a commercial farmer. Consequently, the individual farmer could not institute anything approaching a system of specialization and division of labor on his own farm, nor could farmers as a group do so on an area-wide basis. Moreover, with plenty of land, but little labor and capital, it was necessary to "waste" land and to economize on the use of the other factors. Economically, the farmer could not afford to devote his scarce resources of labor and capital to scientific farming; extensive cultivation was the rule, intensive the exception. Few farmers used even animal fertilizers systematically and most of them were unimaginative in their crop rotation, attempting to restore the fertility of the soil only when it was absolutely necessary. They took what they could from the land and then moved on to greener pastures. Emphasis was on per-man rather than per-acre output. Economically this type of cultivation was for the short-run quite rational, since it gave the farmer a higher income than he would have had if he had devoted part of his resources to ameliorating the soil. In the long-run, however, it wantonly wasted the country's natural resources.

Here and there were some exceptional individuals, and some groups who did experiment with new crops and better animals. Agricultural societies were organized, and farm journals and magazines were published which helped to educate the farmers in the rudiments of soil conservation. As the yield of the soil continued to decline alarmingly, crop rotation and fertilization began to take hold, and by the 1850's, fertilizers were being used to maintain and replenish the fertility of the soil, particularly in the old South. But these were the exceptions rather than the rule. In the 1850's, the "mining" of the American soil was still a commonly-accepted practice. Horace Greeley's *Tribune* editorialized in 1851, "There are whole counties, almost whole states which once yielded 20 bushels of wheat or 40 bushels of corn, yet now average 5 and 20." Among farmers themselves there were some who recognized that land butchery was occurring, but the rank and file were not impressed by these critics. Said one, "To talk of manuring all our farms . . . is simply ridiculous. With the present scarcity and high price of labor, how is the farmer to find time and money or labor to manure his farm of from one hundred and sixty to fifteen thousand acres."[10]

The 19th-century farmer was well aware of the disadvantageous effects of an inadequate labor supply, but he had great obstacles to contend with before he could overcome this difficulty. In the North, where workers were free, the farm owner found his labor problem critical, because the "hired hand" had two, more attractive alternatives: he could possibly stake out his own farm on the frontier, or he could migrate to the city and take advantage of the higher wages offered in manufacturing. Thus the persistent difficulty of obtaining an adequate supply of labor made the family-sized farm characteristic of pre-war northern agriculture.

Southern Agriculture Before the Civil War

In the South, before the Civil War, the problem of a labor supply was in some cases solved by the institution of slavery.[11] But slavery was by no means a universal southern institution. Only 25 per cent of southern families owned slaves, and perhaps only 4 per cent owned enough slaves to reproduce a farm labor supply, and therefore did not need to purchase slaves in the open market. Yet despite the limited extent of the institution, slavery as a form of low-cost labor influenced the entire economic organization of southern agriculture and thereby had a profound effect on the nation's economic development.

Largely because of the existence of slavery, the South never experienced the population growth which characterized the North. In 1830, the density of population in the southern states was 6.4 per square mile, whereas in the central states it was only 3.6 per square mile. But by the end of the century, southern population density was only 27.4 persons per square mile whereas in the central states it was 51.5. While the North was attracting immigrants, most of whom, being in the prime of life, could begin producing as soon as they arrived, the South held no

[10] Quoted in Fred A. Shannon, *The Farmer's Last Frontier* (New York: Farrar and Rinehart, 1945), p. 170. For the last half of the 19th century, this is one of the best studies of American agriculture.

[11] See Lewis C. Gray, *History of Agriculture in the Southern United States to 1860* (New York: Peter Smith, 1941).

lures for immigrants at any time. In 1860 only 3.4 per cent of southern population was foreign-born, and in 1900, only 2.2 per cent. On the other hand, New England's population was 15 per cent foreign-born in 1860 and 25.8 per cent in 1900.

The southern system of agriculture, whether slave or free, also discouraged the widespread use of machinery. Technological progress in northern agriculture was infinitely superior. Because of the westward migration, the demand for land increased; this, coupled with greater technological capabilities for using land, brought about a rise of land values in the North greater than corresponding increases in the South. In 1860, the average per-acre value of farm and improvements was $10.19 in the South, $23.68 in New England, and $20.04 in the central states. By 1900 the disparity was even greater—$8.96 in the South, $25.71 in New England, and $37.52 in the central states.

Whether the institution of slavery caused the relatively poor economic position of the South is a pointless argument. What is more important is the question of whether or not low-cost labor was the culprit. Slavery, in the last analysis, was a system of applying low-priced labor extensively. It could not be used in raising crops which required skill or education. On the other hand, the chief southern crop (cotton) could probably not have been grown except with low-priced labor. The return averaged $15 an acre if the price of cotton was 10 cents a pound, and, relative to man hours, this was not enough to warrant hiring high-priced labor.

Since slaves could not be laid off during the lulls in activity caused by the peculiarities of cotton culture, slave labor was partly utilized in growing corn and other provisions for local consumption. As a result of this diversification, the South grew a substantial part of the nation's total agricultural production, and actually remained more self-sufficient than northern agriculture. In 1860, it raised 43 per cent of the nation's corn, 26 per cent of the wheat, 54 per cent of the hogs, and 36 per cent of the dairy cattle. But cotton, sugar, and rice were the chief cash crops, and hence the raising of grains and animals was seldom as efficient as in the North.

Cotton could not have been grown economically with high-priced labor. But was it grown profitably with slave labor? The price of a Negro (a prime field hand) rose steadily in the ante-bellum South, from about $400 in 1800 to about $1,200 in 1860. If the average price of a slave was $500, and the interest rate were 8 per cent, then the annual cost of a slave, including upkeep and supervision (but not depreciation) was

$84. If cotton sold at 10 cents a pound, it has been estimated that the annual product of a slave was $130, producing a gross profit per slave of $46. However, this method of calculation assumed that slaves replaced themselves, but, for most southerners, this was not the case. And, even when slavery did pay, it had great disadvantages. It increased economic rigidity, because it was not adjustable either to changes in demand or to different methods of production. It also prevented the accumulation of other types of capital, since so much of the southern savings went into slave investment. Thus the South became an essentially agrarian society highly dependent on other regions (or countries) for its manufactured products, its credit, shipping, insurance, and its market. Indeed, it is estimated that, by 1860, 40 cents of every dollar went to the North (mostly to New York) for interest, insurance, and shipping charges.

From Self-Sufficiency to Commercial Farming

As the excesses and lacks in the American economy were partly compensated so that a better balance was achieved in the proportions between the available factors of production, agriculture could contribute more to the social product. Farmers became increasingly commercial, producing more for the market and relatively less for their own consumption. As capital was accumulated, agricultural machinery progressively displaced human and animal labor.

Although commercial farming could not have appeared without better tools and more machinery, above all, it needed marketing facilities. This called for specialized middlemen, for storage facilities, and for the construction of roads, canals, and railroads. All these began to appear on an increasing scale during the first half of the 19th century. Progress in marketing, together with the westward movement of population and the settlement of the land, made possible greater geographic division of labor and increased farm production. Although dependable figures are not available, it has been estimated that gross farm production (as measured in dollars of constant purchasing power) increased about 75 per cent between 1830 and 1850. But better marketing facilities also meant increased agricultural competition. Consequently, farmers in each section restricted their activities more and more to the production of the commodities for which their region was best adapted. Eastern farmers produced perishable crops—vegetables, fruits,

and dairy products—or gave up farming altogether. The South produced cotton; the Northwest grew wheat; the Middle West raised hogs;
and the Great Plains, cattle.

Agricultural Exports

As specialization increased, agriculture became technically more efficient, and this, in itself, contributed more to the economy. But specialization on the farm also led to the abandonment of household manufacturing which, in turn, meant that some persons could now move to
the city and become factory workers. Each such shift from the farm to
industry meant an increase in the national income. Meantime, specialization made it possible for each section of the nation to produce a
surplus, which it could exchange for other commodities, either inter-
sectionally or internationally.

It was the export surplus which American agriculture produced even
in the early years that actually made possible much of the nation's
manufacturing progress, because by exporting farm products the United
States was able to import the capital goods that were indispensable for
the development of American manufacturing. From 1821 until 1870,
exports of farm products averaged well over 60 per cent of total American exports, whereas exports of semi-finished and finished manufactures averaged less than 20 per cent. But as the relative importance of
agriculture declined in the American economy, farm products contributed progressively less to the export total, and by 1890 only slightly
over 50 per cent of America's exports consisted of food and raw materials.

Before the Civil War, cotton was the leading single export of the
United States, constituting in some years considerably more than 50
per cent of the value of total exports. In addition to cotton, the United
States exported tobacco, wheat, flour, and meat products. In 1857, at
the peak of cyclical prosperity, the United States exported 14.6 million
bushels of wheat, 7.5 million bushels of corn, and 3.7 million barrels of
flour. The export of breadstuffs was valued at over $55.5 million, while
the tobacco exports were worth $20.6 million. Without the westward
movement, the extension of marketing facilities, commercial farming,
and division of labor, these exports would not have been possible; and
without these exports the United States would not have been able to
import so many European manufactured and semi-manufactured goods.

Thus commercial farming and specialization raised the nation's whole standard of living. Yet commercial agriculture also had disadvantages: it tended to increase urban concentration; and made farmers more dependent on the market, which is to say, on variable market prices.

Agricultural Developments in the Late 19th Century

The farm problems that we have thus far examined were those of an economic sector suffering from growing pains. By the end of the 19th century, however, it had become apparent that American agriculture had matured; and, because of this, its problems had rather markedly changed. The filling of the land with more people was no longer a primary consideration; the halcyon days of the westward movement were over, and the extensive development of the agricultural economy had been pretty largely accomplished. The problem of agriculture now came to be associated more and more with the individual farmer rather than with agriculture as a whole. The more specific "farm problem"— the riddle of how to enable the farmer to secure an equitable share of the national income, and of how to enable him to solve his personal business problems—had now become one of the nation's most critical political and economic issues.

Between the Civil War and World War II, agriculture experienced two periods of prolonged depression, two periods of great prosperity, and one period which, for want of a better word, may be called normal. Agriculture went through abnormally bad times during most of the years from the end of the Civil War to 1896. Prospects improved at the end of the century, and the years up to World War I were much better for the farmer. The war brought unprecedented prosperity, but agriculture again declined during the 1920's, although other sectors of the economy experienced a much-publicized prosperity. With the depression of the 1930's, the decline became a rout, probably bringing the farmer to the lowest point he had ever experienced in American economic history. Some recovery occurred during the New Deal, but farming was still far from prosperous at the end of the 'thirties. World War II changed this radically; the agricultural trends of the 1920's and 1930's were reversed, and the farmer began to enjoy the greatest prosperity he had ever experienced. But once again peace brought a decline, and by the 1950's the farmer had lost much of his wartime gains, although he was still considerably better off than he had been in the prewar years.

Farm Population and the Farmer's Share of the
National Income

During most of our history we were a nation of farmers rather than of artisans; and hence the small farmer, not the city dweller, was the typical American. In 1800, for example, almost 95 per cent of the population was rural, and, even in 1860, 80 per cent of the population was still rural. It was not until 1890, about 70 years ago, that city population finally exceeded the number of people on farms, and it was not until 1920 that urban population outnumbered rural population. But by then the absolute number of farmers, which had increased with every previous census, had also begun to decline. Rural population declined not because of a fall in the rural birthrate but because the farm population was far more mobile than the city population. Because the demand for the goods and services produced in urban areas was more elastic, town and industry could pay higher wage rates than agriculture, and thus could attract the rural population far more effectively than the country could attract the city dweller. As a result, the flow of population was from the farm to the city.[12]

Despite the fact that 19th-century agriculture employed a majority of the labor force, its share of the national income was proportionately lower than the other segments of the economy. Even as early as 1860, when four-fifths of the population was rural, the shares of the national income received by manufacturing, service, and distribution were larger than agriculture's. Agriculture's share declined even more after the Civil War. Thus in 1860, farmers probably comprised almost 60 per cent of the labor force, but received only slightly more than 30 per cent of the national income. By 1910, farmers constituted only about one-third of the labor force, and their share of income was now less than 15 per cent. Forty years later, the 12 per cent of the labor force who engaged in farming were receiving only 7 per cent of the national income. Farm families therefore represented the vast majority of the one-third of the nation described by President Roosevelt as ill-housed, ill-clothed and ill-fed. Yet many farm families were comfortably well off. The explanation of this paradox lay in the fact that farm income was very unevenly

---

[12] Shannon estimates that for every city laborer who moved to the farm, 20 farmers came to the city. Fred A. Shannon, *The Farmer's Last Frontier* (New York: Farrar and Rinehart, Inc., 1945), p. 357.

distributed. One-tenth of the farmers received half the total farm income, whereas 40 per cent had an income of less than $1,000 a year. It was estimated in the late 1940's that, if 28 per cent of the farmers were eliminated, farm production would decline by only 3 per cent.

				Real private	
	Real farm	Income	Income	productivity	
	wage rate	per worker	per worker	(1947=100)	
Year	(1910–14=100)	(farm)	(non-farm)	Farm	Non-Farm
1910	97	$ 407	$1,078	61.1	51.7
1920	106	786	2,101	60.4	60.0
1930	122	505	1,800	64.4	71.6
1940	108	556	1,547	82.7	94.1
1950	176	2,063	4,508	131.4	114.1
1955	185	2,000	4,508	131.7*	121.7*

Farm and Non-farm Income and Productivity, 1910–1955

* Figures for 1953.

Sources: *Statistical Abstract;* John D. Black, "Agriculture in the Nation's Economy," *American Economic Review,* March 1956; John W. Kendrick, in National Bureau of Economic Research, *Studies in Income and Wealth,* Vol. 16.

The preceding table reveals how the income of farm workers lagged behind that of other workers. In 1910, the average industrial worker's income was about 2½ times that of the average farm worker. By 1930, the disparity had increased, so that the industrial worker was making three and a half times as much as the farm worker. The farmer closed the gap to some extent in the next twenty years, but in the 1950's, the industrial worker's income was still twice as much as that of the farmer's. One of the chief reasons for this was that agriculture had failed to match the improvement in productivity attained by the other sectors of the economy. The table shows that although farm productivity increased considerably from 1920 to 1940, non-farm productivity increased much more. Since farm output per man hour increased only 18 per cent between 1910 and 1940, it is probable that the farmer had not taken advantage of all of agriculture's potentials. Indeed, at the opening of the war, it was estimated that half the then-existing farm population could have taken care of the demand (domestic plus export) if it had utilized all available technological knowledge. As the war progressed and farm labor became scarce, the farmer was practically forced to increase output per man hour, and, for the first time, farm productivity increased faster than non-farm productivity.

The Tendency to Overproduce

Part of the explanation for the farmer's small share of the national income lay in the nature of agriculture, itself, because the economics of farming apparently cannot be shaped to conform to the same pattern as industrial economics. To a very great extent, however, the farmers contributed to their own plight. Not all farmers fared badly, but many who were unsuccessful were so because conservatism, ignorance, or inertia prevented them from making the most of their opportunities. Either because of the inherent nature of agriculture, or because of their own inabilities, farmers were not able to adopt the necessary business policies that would allow them to cope with their business problems.

The very nature of agriculture encouraged a tendency toward overproduction, for, since no single farmer could individually affect the market, each farmer tended to produce as much as he possibly could. The result was that farmers were tempted to increase output both when prices were high and when prices were low. In addition there were other factors that encouraged agriculture's propensity to overproduce. In the 19th century, the Federal land policy, together with continuous increases in farm population, had created more and more farms and caused more and more acreage to be put into crops. When farm population began to decline in the 20th century, acreage in cropland also declined, but farm production did not fall as one might have expected. For by then, with machinery and scientific farming, farmers could produce larger crops with less labor and with less land.

The major wars in which the United States engaged also contributed to agricultural overproduction, for they temporarily required vast increases in farm commodities, and the farmer was encouraged to do all he could to augment production. To encourage greater output during World War I, the Federal government broadened the Department of Agriculture's research and advisory agencies, and ultimately guaranteed the price of basic crops. The farmer rose to the occasion. Cropland was greatly expanded; wheat production soared to over one billion bushels; and corn to over three billion bushels. With the end of the war, much of the demand evaporated, but the farmer found it difficult to curtail production. Two decades later in World War II, the Federal government once again called upon the farmer to produce in order to satisfy the fantastically-increased demand. Again the farmer came through nobly. This time, he did not increase production so much by bringing greater acreage under cultivation but by increasing productivity through the use of more machinery, more fertilizer, and vastly-better farm practices. With 10 per cent fewer workers, farmers produced 50 per cent more than they had during World War I, although they increased cultivated land by only 5 per cent. Each farm worker produced enough in 1945 to support 14 persons, whereas, in 1920, he had supported only 10 and in 1820, about 4. Contour farming came to be widely adopted and better seed was used. Hybrid seed corn, first introduced in 1929, was planted on about 25 per cent of corn acreage in 1945 and increased the yield by at least 15 to 20 per cent. Yet, even though acre yields had increased markedly (about 27 per cent) they were still far less than the yields obtained under the more intensive cultivation practiced in Europe. The average yield of wheat in the United Kingdom, for example, was 19.8 hundredweight per acre, compared to 11 hundredweight per acre in typical areas of the United States. On the other hand, productivity per man-hour was far higher in the United States. It took 12 man-hours to produce an acre of wheat in the United Kingdom; but only 5.5 in the United States.

More Machines on the Farm

The following table shows that the dollar value of farm machinery quadrupled and that the use of fertilizers doubled during World War II. Society benefited vastly from this; it enlarged production and increased

	Farm Production				
Year	Land in farms (millions of acres)	Land in cropland (millions of acres)	No. of farms (millions)	Value of machinery (millions of $)	Use of fertilizer (1,000 short tons)	Index of gross farm prod. (1935–39=100)
1860	—	—	2.0	246	164	—
1880	536	188	4.0	407	753	—
1890	623	248	4.6	494	1,150	—
1900	839	319	5.7	750	2,200	—
1910	879	347	6.4	1,265	5,453	85
1920	956	402	6.5	3,595	7,177	101
1930	987	413	6.5	3,302	8,222	98
1940	1,061	399	6.4	3,135	8,249	108
1950	1,159	409	5.6	12,968	17,984	125
1954	1,158	399	4.8	15,919	20,679	130

Sources: *Historical Statistics; Statistical Abstract.*

productivity, thus making possible a reduction in unit costs and hence lower prices for consumers. But there was room for considerable skepticism regarding the benefits which the farmer as a producer obtained from increased mechanization.

By sound business tests, the decision to use machinery should have been made on a basis of comparing the resulting unit costs with the selling price of the product. For the average farmer, this decision was not at all easy. The typical American farm was family-sized, and, from a strictly economic point of view, such a farm could seldom make enough use of machinery to warrant the required expenditures for cost and upkeep.

The Problem of Farm Prices

Since the demand for agricultural commodities in the aggregate is relatively inelastic, increases in production resulted in much lower prices. On the other hand, stabilized production or abnormal demand (such as occurred during major wars) led to sharp price increases. Thus farm prices tended downward from the end of the Civil War to the late 'nineties as huge acreages were opened up to commercial agriculture by railways. Prices recovered somewhat during the early years of the 20th century when production stabilized, and, consequently, farmers' disposable income rose markedly. Prices jumped rapidly during World War I, but, when demand declined after the war, prices sagged. World War II pushed farm prices to new peaks, but peace again resulted in price declines.

Lower prices of grain and meat benefited urban wage earners and enabled them to increase their real wages. Falling farm prices also had a tremendous impact on the European economy, for when American production of food increased faster than population, the surplus could not be absorbed through increased domestic consumption, and had to be exported to foreign markets at low prices. In the ten years from 1874 to 1883, for example, the United States exported more grain than in the previous fifty years. Wheat exports rose from 91 million bushels in 1873 to a record high of 234 million bushels in 1902. These increased exports caused European agriculture to contract and stimulated further industrialization. But the European governments did not regard the influx of American farm products as an unmixed blessing. Because of a growing dollar shortage, and because their own farmers clamored for protection, France and Germany took steps to restrict American farm imports. Meanwhile other areas (Canada, Argentina, Australia, New Zealand) also began to export farm commodities, and gradually the American farmer encountered severe competition in export markets. As a result, the average fraction of the American wheat crop exported in the ten years before World War I was only 15 per cent, as compared with 41 per cent in 1900.

City dwellers reaped a great economic advantage from falling farm prices, but the American farmer did not gain from the growing total demand for his produce. Since he was a chronic debtor, each decline in the price of his commodity forced him to sell a greater quantity of goods to meet the interest charges on his fixed obligations. What made the situation worse was that farm prices were much more sensitive than industrial prices. Since there were so many sellers, the individual farmer had no influence over the market prices of his own output, nor was it possible for the mass of farmers to cooperate in order to exert any effective control over the total market. The individual farmer's ability to "differentiate" his product was confined to a few producers of milk or eggs who had their own customers. But no amount of advertising could convince a consumer that Farmer Smith's wheat differed from Farmer Brown's. Nor could Farmer Smith, except in a very small way, offer any inducements in the way of service which would lead consumers to prefer his particular farm produce. Consequently, when demand declined, the only strategy that occurred to the average farmer was to increase production, which of course meant lower prices. On the other hand, during those relatively short periods when the demand for farm produce increased, farm prices rose faster than farm production.

		Farm Prices			
Year	Prices of wheat per bushel	Prices received (1910–1914=100)	Prices paid (1910–1914=100)	Parity ratio	Farm debt (billions of $)
1857	.80	—	—	—	—
1864	2.25	—	—	—	—
1870	1.04	—	—	—	—
1890	.84	—	—	—	—
1900	.62	—	—	—	—
1910	.88	102	98	106	4.5
1920	1.43	211	201	104	11.9
1930	.67	125	151	83	12.1
1940	.68	100	124	81	10.2
1950	2.00	258	256	101	12.5
1957	1.94	242	296	82	19.5

Sources: *Historical Statistics; Statistical Abstract.*

As the preceding table reveals, agricultural prices were always more sensitive than industrial prices, and with the passage of time, they seemed to become even more so. In each period of heavily-rising demand, farm prices rose more sharply than industrial prices. Between 1940 and 1950, for example, the parity ratio (prices received by the farmer as a percentage of prices paid for the things he purchased) rose from 81 to 101. On the other hand, in each period of declining demand, farm prices fell more sharply than industrial prices. Thus between 1920 and 1930, the parity ratio fell from 104 to 83, and between 1950 and 1957 from 101 to 82.

The Problem of Raising Capital

Despite the steady decline in farm prices after 1865, the long-run trend in the price of farm land was upward from the Civil War to World War I, because during this period farm population was still increasing, thus intensifying the demand for farm land. In 1860, the average price of an acre of farm land was $16.30. By 1890, it was $21.30. There was some decline in the next decade, but by 1910, it had risen to $39.60. World War I pushed the average price up to $69.38, as farmers, eager to take part in a new bonanza, rushed to buy land. After the war, farm land prices sagged again, finally dropping to $31.71 per acre in 1940, a lower price than in 1910. World War II once again created a farm-land boom, and by the 1950's, the average price was well over $80 an acre.

So long as land prices were rising, farmers had an opportunity to sell out and capture a capital gain even if farming itself did not pay. Hence, rising land prices encouraged the continuance of the "settle and sell" policy that had been so characteristic of the pre-Civil War years. But rising land prices in conjunction with increased mechanization had the disadvantage of requiring a larger fixed investment per dollar of output. Indeed, by this test, farming required a greater outlay of capital than the relative investment required in manufacturing. To set up a farm in 1900 on less than $16,000 or to do so in the 1950's on less than $50,000 was a hazardous economic adventure. But the financial resources of the farmer or would-be farmer were far less than the required capital outlay, and consequently he had to borrow most of his investment, chiefly by mortgaging his land. The money market, however, was not properly geared to the making of farm loans, and hence the raising of necessary funds remained one of the farmer's most bothersome business problems.

The state banks, on which the farmer had relied for much of his credit in the period from 1820 to 1860, declined in number after the Civil War, but the national banks, which replaced them as the nation's most important commercial-banking institutions, were restricted in their ability to make real-estate loans. As a result, the supply of funds available for agriculture in the late 19th century was small compared with the farmer's increasing needs. Nevertheless, by paying high interest rates (7 to 10 per cent ordinarily and often over 12 per cent in the West) and large commission charges, he managed to borrow money, mostly from private lenders. By 1890, when farm debt was about $1,200 per farm (or about one-third the value of land and buildings) half the farms in the country were mortgaged, and in the wheat belt of the Great Plains there were as many mortgages as there were farm families. Farm debt continued to grow until the depression of the 1930's (See table on p. 335.) By then, three-quarters of the nation's farms were mortgaged, and many farmers were apparently able to stay on their farms only by incurring more and more indebtedness. During the depression, changes in farm ownership reached the highest rate in history, and over half of these shifts in ownership occurred as a result of forced sales. This high foreclosure rate cut farm debt, and it dropped even further during World War II, when farmers departed from their previous wartime policy and liquidated rather than increased their debt. But after the war, farm debt once again began to increase at an alarming rate, reaching almost $20 billion in the 1950's.

As the nation's supply of funds increased, and as policy makers came to realize that new solutions for the farmer's financing problem had to be found, the farmer presently found it easier to obtain credit. The growth of life insurance companies added one new source of borrowing, but it was the government which became the chief factor in easing agricultural credit. Under the Federal Reserve Act, national banks were permitted to make farm loans on a very restricted basis. Three years later the Federal Farm Loan Act of 1916 created a government source of long-term farm loans, and in 1923, the Federal Intermediate Credit Act provided for short-term farm credit. The creation of a Federal system of farm-credit agencies not only enabled the farmer to borrow money as easily as the industrialist could, but, in addition, it substantially lowered the interest costs on his indebtedness.

The Farmer's Attempted Solution to
His Problems

Agriculture's ever-recurring economic problems acted as an obstacle to the whole nation's economic progress. But what could society or the farmer do about it? All through the late 19th century and the first half of the 20th century, some critics kept saying that there were just too many farmers who simply produced too much, and that if there were no interference with market forces, the situation would eventually right itself. But the self-adjusting law of supply and demand, although easy to talk about in the abstract, is often difficult to invoke in practice. The farmers, always the most individualistic Americans, would not contract production or move off the farm in sufficiently large numbers to reduce the annual supply of farm products. Furthermore, although it was evident that every switch from agriculture to manufacturing tended to raise the national income, other countries needed American food production, and, without the volume of our agricultural production, it was questionable whether the world community could feed itself. Be that as it may, it became clear that reliance on the automatic operation of supply and demand to alleviate the farmer's difficulties was an extremely dubious solution to the problem. And, in any event, the farmer was having none of it. Instead, as prices declined after the Civil War, he put his faith in the quantity theory of money and called upon the Federal government to increase the money supply in order to raise farm prices.[13] At first, he tried to persuade the government to increase the circulation of greenbacks, and when that failed, he urged the re-establishment of bimetallism and the free coinage of silver. But again he was unsuccessful, because farmers were declining in numbers and consequently their political power was no longer equal to that of other occupational groups.

Meanwhile farmers had begun to form organizations designed to protect their interests and help solve their economic problems. The first really prominent farm organization was the Patrons of Husbandry, better known as the "Grange." It carried on social and educational activities, formed cooperatives, and lobbied for legislation for the benefit of the farmer. Although it had some success in obtaining state legislation regulating railroad rates, its influence declined sharply by

[13] For the farmer's appeal to the government, see Murray R. Benedict's *Farm Policies of the United States, 1790–1950* (New York: The Twentieth Century Fund, 1953); and his *Can We Solve the Farm Problem?* (New York: The Twentieth Century Fund, 1955).

the end of the 19th century. Another organization, the Farmer's Alliance of the 1880's, was chiefly political and was eventually swallowed up by the Populist Party, which became the spokesman for greenbackism and free silver and was eventually absorbed by the Democratic party in the late 'nineties.

When the farmer's prospects improved in the early years of the 20th century, he temporarily lost interest in the causes that he had so enthusiastically espoused in the 1890's. Now that he was living fairly well, his ardor for monetary panaceas waned, and he began to withdraw from the farm organizations. Representing the most optimistic element in the most optimistic nation, the farmer surveyed his future with a firm belief that he would never experience a repetition of his past troubles. But the world was not his oyster, as he painfully discovered when the end of World War I brought a repeat performance of familiar trials and tribulations. Once more the farmer sought a solution, one that would be more effective than the monetary measures he had once supported.

Spokesmen for the farmers argued that other businessmen set their prices in proper relation to costs, and adjusted their production in such a way as to insure adequate business profits. They proposed that farmers should follow this self-same "business game"[14] by modifying the almost purely competitive system under which they operated. Stimulated by these new hopes, farm leaders set about creating new action programs. Organizations, such as the Farmers' Union and the American Farm Bureau Federation, experienced an impressive increase in membership. Farmers began demonstrating their belated abandonment of individualism by forming marketing associations and cooperatives on a grand scale. In 1915, there had been some 5,000 of these farm associations with a membership of 651,000 doing a business of $636 million. But by 1925, there were 11,000 with 2.7 million members and a business of $2.4 billion. Yet despite this growth of farm associations, there was little prospect of combining all the farmers in a disciplined cooperative effort capable of cutting production or regulating prices. An effort was therefore made to persuade the Federal government to pass legislation fixing agricultural prices. Congress enacted such legislation in the McNary-Haugen bills of the 1920's, only to have them vetoed by President Cool-

14 *Wallace's Farmer,* an influential farm periodical, succinctly expressed the farmer's new point of view: "The farmer is getting tired of being the goat. . . . This does not mean that he promises to make a disturbance. . . . It means simply that . . . he sees it is time to study the business game and see how to play it for himself." Russell Lord, *The Wallaces of Iowa* (Boston: Houghton Mifflin Co., 1947), p. 169.

idge, who was convinced that only the inexorable law of supply and demand could solve the farm problem. In 1929, the "Farm Bloc" did, however, succeed in getting legislation which provided loans to farm cooperatives against the pledge of stocks of farm crops. But, since no attempt was made to control the supply of farm products, this law failed to relieve the farmer's difficulties.

The New Deal went much farther in its attempts to help the farmer. In 1933 it passed the Agricultural Adjustment Act, the goal of which was to restore "parity prices," or more particularly, to give the farmer the same purchasing power that he had in the years 1909–1914. It hoped to do this by paying the farmer a subsidy to persuade him to reduce the acreage planted in certain basic crops. The subsidy was financed through a tax on the processors of farm commodities. This processing tax increased the price of food to consumers, and the plan was therefore inconsistent with the New Deal objective of increasing the purchasing power of low-income groups. The dilemma was, however, short-lived, since the AAA was declared unconstitutional in 1936, and the whole set of tactics had to be changed. Hopes were now placed in the Soil Conservation Act, and, in 1938, in the second Agricultural Adjustment Act, the so-called "ever-normal granary" plan. Under the second AAA, the goal was to restore parity prices by reducing the size of crops. Quotas were therefore set by the Secretary of Agriculture, and sales in excess of quotas were taxed; but if the farmer kept his surpluses off the market, he received parity payments in the form of a loan.

While this New Deal legislation was having some effect in reducing crops, nature also was helping to lower farm production. From 1934 to 1936 continued droughts occurred, especially in the Great Plains region. As a result of the combination of government policy and natural disaster, farm production and cropland declined. The decline in production, together with some recovery in national income, raised farm prices and improved the farmer's economic status. By 1935 farm prices averaged 66 per cent above 1932 and 8 per cent above the prewar level. But despite the effects of government policy and widespread drought, they were still far below parity in 1939.

When World War II broke out, the farmer determined that he would not be caught in the same squeeze that had occurred after the Civil War and after World War I. Through the Farm Bloc in Congress, he expressed a reluctance to increase farm production unless the government would guarantee to support farm prices at a figure considerably higher than the rate then in effect. Because effective war operations urgently required increased farm production, the farmer won his point. The government agreed in 1941 to support farm prices at 85 per cent of parity, and in 1942 it not only raised this to 90 per cent but promised that this price-support level would remain in effect for two years after the end of hostilities. The President declared the end of hostilities in 1946, which meant that 90 per cent price supports would presumably end in 1948. When the expiration date came, however, Congress passed compromise legislation continuing until 1950 the rigid price supports at 90 per cent, and also providing for flexible price supports of from 60 to 90 per cent of parity after 1950.

During the war, price supports were of only academic importance, but when farm prices began to decline sharply, in 1948, farmers naturally took advantage of existing legislation and called upon the government for non-interest bearing, non-recourse loans. Very quickly, the Commodity Credit Corporation found itself in possession of a vast quantity of farm commodities[15] on which it had advanced loans, which, in all likelihood, would not be repaid. The difficulty was that despite a decline in cultivated acreage, the farmer, by means of improved technology and better methods, could now produce more per acre. Supply was increasing faster than demand, and the surplus was going into the warehouses of the Commodity Credit Corporation. Something had to be done to reduce the supply of farm products and to reduce the costs of the farm program. The administration's answer, in 1956, was the so-called "soil-bank plan," under which the government agreed to pay an annual rental for withholding land from the production of certain crops. It is still much too early to judge the success of this program, but it seems most unlikely that it will meet the extravagant hopes of its proponents. Moreover, in its early stages at least, the "soil bank" has not materially reduced Federal outlays for the farm program. Indeed, in 1958 the government spent over $5 billion for agricultural assistance, the highest amount in the nation's history. Moreover, farmers were demonstrating at mid-century so remarkable an aptitude for adopting the latest innovations in agricultural technology and scientific methods that production per acre was still increasing faster than population. It seems, therefore, that attempts to reduce the supply of farm commodities by restricting acreage, without regard to increasing the demand intensity for these farm commodities, offer a dubious solution to the farm problem, which in many respects is the oldest and most exasperating problem in the American economy.

[15] Owned stocks had a value of about $5 billion in June 1957.

13

The changing economic

functions of government

Historical Factors that Shaped the Role of Government

Deep in the American character lies a belief that authoritarian control over people is inherently wrong, and hence there is imbedded in American folklore a suspicious hostility toward government, the seat of authority. Yet American governments of one kind or other—Federal, state, county, or municipal—have always exerted some influence over the development of the American economy. In the early years of the 19th century, when the population was predominantly rural, the influence of government was relatively small, but it gradually increased as governments expanded old functions and added new ones, until today governmental economic activities and policies are among the most important factors shaping the economy. A generation ago, businessmen made most of the important decisions that determined whether the economy would expand or contract. Today, in contrast, governmental activities, either through their direct impact or through their indirect effect on the decisions of businessmen, are economic influences that cannot be ignored. For good or evil, the American economy at the middle of the 20th century is, more than ever before, a mixed economy, one in which both private enterprise and government make decisions of vital importance to the course of the economy. It is only the degree of governmental influence that is new, since historically governments have always exerted some economic influence—as policemen protecting life and property, as dispensers of natural resources, as employers of labor, and as owners of business enterprises—but more recently they have also become stabilizers of the economy, and, within limits, redistributors of wealth and income.

Hamiltonian Federalism, which was essentially an American version of mercantilist philosophy, believed in a strong state, and quite frankly argued that the state should favor those economic groups which could contribute most toward building a rich and powerful nation. Under the Federalists, therefore, the Federal government not only endeavored to build the nation's defenses against external and internal enemies, but in order to make the nation economically strong, it proposed to lend assistance to manufacturing, banking, and commerce. Federalism, however, did not truly represent the sentiments of the bulk of individualistic Americans, nor did it adequately attune government to the environmental factors of the early 19th century. A majority of the Founding Fathers—Washington, Adams, Hamilton, and others—were sophisticated gentlemen, more typical of Walpole's England than of Patrick Henry's America. In 1790 the United States was more a nation of farmers than of merchants, manufacturers, or laborers; consequently the citizen in a rural village probably better represented the average American than did a city dweller. Country folk had little to gain from government, especially from the national government which, to a Piedmont farmer or a Kentucky frontiersman, seemed especially remote. For this reason, the philosophy of the Jeffersonian agrarians, who succeeded the Federalists, was much more in harmony with the beliefs of the average American. The Jeffersonian ideal was a weak state, one that would interfere as little as possible with the individual; a state which should have neither debt, nor taxes beyond the simplest; and which should have as its goal a happy, not a powerful nation. Yet despite these preconceptions, the agrarian era from 1800 to the Civil War was not, as has often been suggested, an age of *laissez faire* or a complete triumph of the philosophy that that government is best which governs the least. State and local governments did not hesitate to broaden their activities. In addition to protecting life and property, they advanced credit to private business and sometimes launched and operated business enterprises. True enough, the Federal government was relatively unimportant as a factor in the economic life of the nation during these years, but some in the Federal government who had been ardent exponents of *laissez faire* were losing faith in the doctrine.[1]

The Civil War widened the economic influence of government, and as life became more and more complex in the late 19th and early 20th centuries, this trend continued. State governments further expanded their activities, placing greater emphasis on regulation and less on contributing assistance. Although the Federal government continued to lag somewhat behind the states, by the beginning of the 20th century it was following the trail of regulation originally blazed by the states. There were a number of reasons for this expansion of governmental activity. First of all, the nation was undergoing a continuous social transformation, changing from a rural-agrarian to an urban-industrial life. Secondly, technological changes, especially in transportation and communication, made necessary new types of regulation, which could be enforced only by a much more complex division of authority and responsibility between state and local governments on the one hand, and the Federal government on the other. Thirdly, the United States had now become a major world power. Her bankers were entering the international money market as lenders, and her businessmen were exporting large quantities of manufactured goods. As both business and labor unionism became bigger and bigger, the middle class, caught in between, clamored for protective governmental regulation and control. In answer to this demand, there emerged, in the field of politics, the Progressive Movement of the early 1900's, which reshaped the functions of the Federal government. During the Progressive Era, the Federal government broadened its regulation of business, increased its contributions to agriculture, enlarged its expenditures, and adopted a constructive policy for conserving natural resources. Two world wars and the inter-

[1] For example, Albert Gallatin, one of the most influential of the Jeffersonians: "Gallatin saw that the sweet simplicity of a government which governed as little as possible had been a shallow concept and would not suffice for a government which annexed all of the Louisiana Territory, which fought a sea war and a land war, and which—to his own way of thinking—needed the active planning of internal improvements." Elisabeth Stevenson, *Henry Adams* (New York: The Macmillan Company, 1955), pp. 164–5.

vening catastrophic business depression gave still further impetus to the trend toward greater Federal regulation and control. By the 1950's, the state governments, which had pioneered in opening up new areas for government activity, had largely ceded their position as innovators to the Federal government, and they now played a much smaller rôle in shaping or controlling the economy.

Government as a Policeman

Government's rôle as a policeman, always an important one from an economic point of view, involves two main duties: the protection of life and property, and the regulation of business and labor. State and local governments protect the citizen against crime and fire; they guard his health through sanitary regulations; and, in most cases, provide his water supply. The Federal government serves as a protector against domestic malefactors, but, above all, it gives the nation's citizens protection against external enemies. It is not possible to state precisely how much governments have spent for police and fire protection; for courts of justice, boards of health, food-inspection services, and water commissions; for the state militia, the Army and Navy, and defense assistance to foreign nations; and for all the other forms of protection for life and property. But it seems safe to say that, over the course of American history, the protection of life and property has taken at least 60 cents of every dollar spent by all levels of government.

Not all types of protection were equally important at each stage of our economic development. Some forms of Federal protection did not even exist in the 19th century; and until the 1930's, with the notable exception of war years, total state and local expenditures were much larger than those of the Federal government because state and local police functions concerned themselves with the individual citizen much more, quantitatively, than Federal police activities did. Changes, however, were occurring on the state and local level; expenditures for the most common forms of protection (such as police and fire departments and water supply) declined in relative importance, while the more subtle types of protection (such as sanitary regulations and food inspection) increased relatively.

When, in the 20th century, the Federal government greatly expanded the range of its activities, its national protective measures, especially those involving national defense, began to affect the individual citizen almost as much as state activity. Moreover, many new tasks were assumed: the Federal government began to regulate foods and drugs in 1906; in the same year it inaugurated a serious campaign against plant and animal diseases and pests; and it stepped up its public health program sharply in 1912. Although these were important manifestations of expanding Federal activity, nevertheless at all times it was the Army and Navy which constituted the chief forms of protection provided by the Federal government. Eventually, these military activities dwarfed all other forms of protection, thus becoming, even in peacetime, the Federal government's chief means of influencing the economy.

In 1800, the Army and Navy received 60 cents out of every dollar expended by the Federal government, but this represented a per capita expenditure of only $1.13. In the more peaceful world of the post-Civil War years, Army and Navy expenditures were only 20 per cent of all Federal spending, or about $1 per capita. Before World War I, the Army and Navy took 35 cents of every Federal dollar, or about $2.50 per capita. As the world grew figuratively smaller in the 20th century and far more belligerent, the comfortable days of very modest defense spending passed into ancient history. Even in 1932, at the depth of the great depression, when the illusion of permanent peace was rather firmly entrenched, Army and Navy expenditures nonetheless averaged almost $6 per capita. By the middle 'fifties, in the midst of the Cold War, spending for national security accounted for more than 60 per cent of total Federal expenditures; and national defense, in one form or another, was costing each individual $240.

Government Labor Regulation

Besides providing for the protection of life and property, governments acted as policemen by regulating business and labor. It is often assumed that in exercising these regulatory functions, American governments adopted a policy of encouraging competition. It would be more accurate to say that the aim of a great deal of our regulation has been to protect the weak members of society. Sometimes this has meant encouraging competition; at other times the result has been to limit it. Governmental regulation on behalf of labor, for example, illustrates how limitations were placed on unbridled competition in order to help relatively weaker members of the economy.

Federal regulation of labor did not occur until relatively late in our history, but state governments almost from the beginning undertook some variety of control. At first, their policy was aimed at strengthening competition in the labor market. By court orders, they made labor unions illegal, because it was thought that attempts by unions to organize workers would result in undue control over the supply of labor. But presently public opinion forced both state courts and state governments to alter this outmoded policy. Recognizing that workers were usually weaker than their employers, the states gradually undertook to protect them by strengthening their bargaining power, thereby modifying to some extent the operation of competitive market forces.

The first change in the attitude of state governments came during the reform movement that followed the depression of 1837. In 1842 the Massachusetts Supreme Court held that unions were not illegal in themselves; and, in the same year, the Massachusetts legislature passed a law establishing a maximum ten-hour day for children under twelve. Five years later, New Hampshire established a ten-hour maximum day for women workers. But these pioneer attempts to strengthen the position of labor were mostly ineffective. The Massachusetts law was not enforced, and the intention of the New Hampshire law was largely negated by a clause that permitted workers to contract for a longer day. Nevertheless, government regulation of working conditions steadily expanded. By the 1870's, many states had passed laws regulating the hours of labor, and seventy years later there were 44 such statutes. State minimum wage legislation, inaugurated by Massachusetts in 1912, started much later than regulation of hours, but by 1938 half the states had such laws. Unemployment insurance legislation was adopted still more slowly; Wisconsin passed the first such law in 1932, shortly before the Federal government took over the initiative by adopting a general social security system.

Although it prescribed by law maximum hours for its employees in 1840, and again in 1869, the Federal government did not enter generally into labor regulation until the 20th century. Once having entered the field, however, it broadened its activities fairly rapidly. For the most part, the goal was the same as that of the states: to protect the weaker party to a labor contract. In 1916, Congress, under the urging of President Wilson (and in order to prevent a nation-wide railroad strike) established an eight-hour day for trainmen. During the 1920's Congress passed two Federal laws prohibiting child labor, but both were declared unconstitutional by the Supreme Court. The Federal government made no attempt to regulate hours and wages on a broad national front until the early days of the New Deal, when under the National Industrial Recovery Act it set minimum wages and maximum hours for all workers covered by business codes. When the N.I.R.A. was declared unconstitutional, the Walsh-Healy Act was passed setting minimum standards for workers on government contracts. But it was the Fair Labor Standards Act of 1938 (the Wage and Hour Law) which really provided the first permanent and wide coverage. Including more than 25 per cent of employees, its initial terms set a maximum work week of forty hours (to be achieved by 1940) and a minimum wage of 40 cents an hour (by 1945). Subsequently, because of the inflation that occurred during World War II and the postwar period, the minimum wage was raised to 75 cents an hour and then to $1.00.

The Federal government also attempted to strengthen labor's position as a bargainer by restricting immigration. It excluded Chinese immigrants in 1882; in the same year, it levied a 50-cent head tax on all immigrants and prohibited the admission of certain undersirables. In 1907 Japanese laborers were excluded, and in 1917 Congress further limited immigration by requiring a literacy test and by raising the head tax to $8. But the really important restrictive legislation came in the 1920's when under the pressure of organized labor, postwar nationalism, and a "red scare," Congress passed a series of quota laws, culminating in the Act of 1929 which limited the annual total number of immigrants to 154,000.

The Federal government, like the states, at first opposed labor unions on the theory that unions interfered with free competition in the labor market. But with the great depression of the 1930's it changed its attitude. As the depression worsened, the New Deal leaders actually encouraged the unionization of labor, not merely because workers were the weaker parties to labor contracts but because they believed that recovery would not occur unless spending could increase; and since more spending, in turn, depended on higher wages, it could only materialize if labor could bargain more effectively.

It is not easy to evaluate the effects of government labor legislation on economic development. State regulation of working conditions reduced the accident rate and improved the general health of workers, thereby making the labor force more effective economically. Restrictions against child labor, by improving the general educational level of the population, and by reducing the labor supply, probably improved labor productivity, and quite possibly increased the worker's life span. General wage and hour legislation was relatively ineffectual because, except in rare cases, it followed what the market had already determined. Hence it merely legalized existing situations. Legislation restricting immigration is usually considered to have reduced the American labor supply, thereby giving extra power to labor's bargaining position. But the influence of immigration on population growth was less than is usually supposed, and, in the 1920's, immigration would probably have been small, even without legislative restrictions. Despite these areas of limited influence, it seems that, on the whole, government policy did significantly affect the growth of labor unions. Thus, whereas the Federal government's early antagonism toward labor unions retarded their growth, the sympathetic legislation of the 1930's definitely stimulated their expansion and strengthened labor's bargaining position.

How Government Tried to Sustain Competition in Business

So long as business was conducted by small units operating in a wide market area, price competition was prevalent. Here and there, to be sure, there were local monopolies, but these were the by-products of inadequate market forces. They had no intrinsic powers and were easily destroyed when additional firms entered an area. The appearance of ever-larger business units changed this traditional ebb and flow. People who saw virtue in price competition feared that large-scale enterprise meant the end of that useful process. For the most part, the public regarded large-scale enterprises as actual or potential monopolies that either did or soon would exploit consumers. Consequently, they clamored for government regulation to prevent the real or fanciful threats to their welfare, and governments answered these demands by gradually but steadily increasing their regulation of business. The underlying purpose of regulation was to enforce competition, but governments might have adopted very different purposes. Instead of encouraging competition, they might have encouraged business units to collaborate. Germany, for example, deliberately encouraged cartelization within industries under stringent government regulations. But the United States never cut its public policy to fit any long-range, preconceived pattern; instead, government regulation of business developed pragmatically. It was patchwork, and if there was any underlying theory, it was merely to protect the weaker members from the threats of business consolidation.

When business units were typically small, government regulation was on the state and local level, and even there on a small scale. States regulated banks and insurance companies, and a few states, particularly Massachusetts, regulated railroads. On the whole, these state and local regulations were only partially effective. Banking regulation provided sound banking only in those areas where economic development had proceeded far enough to make it workable. As for the regulations of public carriers, they were openly flouted. When large-scale enterprises became more common, state governments adopted much more elaborate and extensive regulations, and invoked the common law in a serious effort to shore up the competitive system. The so-called "Granger laws" of the 1870's represented a collective effort on the part of farmers to secure relief from what they considered to be the omnipresent monopolistic exploitation by big business, especially by the railroads. Typical Granger laws created state railroad commissions with power to set rates and prevent discrimination. But in 1886, the Supreme Court in effect nullified the Granger laws by deciding that a state could not regulate the intra-state part of interstate commerce. This (Wabash Case) decision re-instilled in shippers, farmers, and consumers a fear of exploitation by railway monopolies. The Federal government attempted to remove this fear by passing, in 1887, the Interstate Commerce Act, thereby inaugurating a new era in the regulation not merely of railways but all big business.

The purpose of the Interstate Commerce Act was to rationalize and nationalize the provisions of the Granger laws. It prohibited discrimination in interstate railroad rates, whether by pools, rebates, or long-and-short-haul discrimination. Soon it became clear, however, that the Act was not fulfilling its purpose; the burden of proof in a controversy between the Interstate Commerce Commission and a railroad was placed on the Commission, not on the railroad; and judicial procedure was so slow that the Commission could not make its policies effective. Furthermore, the law only attacked discrimination. It did not attempt to prescribe "fair" railroad rates, nor did it give the Federal government any control over other interstate carriers, such as steamships or pipe lines. But little by little, Congress passed legislation to close most of these loopholes. The Hepburn Act of 1906 and the Mann-Elkins Act of 1910 gave the Commission power to set rates, and, most important, gave the Commission quasi-judiciary power by shifting the burden of proof from the Commission to the railroads. Under the new system, the Commission was not forced to prove that a railroad had abused its power; instead, the railroad had to prove that the Commission's acts were injudicious.

The hue and cry about monopolistic exploitation was not directed solely against the railroads, but against big business in general. Once the existence of large-scale enterprise came to be generally recognized, the public clamored for governments to break up pools, gentlemen's agreements, and trusts, and to take action to prevent the growth of business combinations. Governments were traditionally sympathetic to such demands. Dating back to medieval England, the common law had denounced monopoly and retraints of trade as actions against the public interest. As business combinations became more frequent, American states invoked the common law to break them up. Thus New York attempted to dissolve the Sugar Trust, Ohio broke up the Standard Oil Trust, Nebraska attacked the Whiskey Trust, and other states took similar action. At the same time, or shortly thereafter, some state legislatures began to adopt positive legislation designed to outlaw trusts. But the efforts were largely unsuccessful, because rival states, in the interests of revenue, enacted legislation which literally invited businessmen to form trusts within their boundaries.

To those who had no particular affection for *laissez faire,* and considerable misgivings concerning the competitive system's ability to maintain itself, it was clear that trusts and combinations could be effectively outlawed or regulated only by the Federal government. Faced with pressure from these critics, Congress somewhat reluctantly adopted the Sherman Anti-trust Act in 1890. Its famous clause declaring "every contract, combination . . . or conspiracy, in restraint of trade . . . to be illegal" seemed forthright enough to be incapable of misinterpretation. But any procedure under the act quickly bogged down in a legal morass. The Supreme Court took a narrow view of the scope and meaning of interstate commerce,[2] thereby vitiating the Sherman Act's effectiveness in breaking up business concentrations. It took more than a score of years before further efforts were made to strengthen the anti-trust legislation. In 1914, Congress established the Federal Trade Commission to prevent unfair business practices, and passed the Clayton Act to strengthen the Sherman Act. But if the purpose of anti-trust legislation was to curb the expansion of big business, neither of these two acts was any more successful than the Sherman Act had been. Business leaders merely changed their tactics to harmonize with the new anti-trust legislation. Around the turn of the century, they dropped the policy of striving

2 Chiefly, in the E. C. Knight Case (1895) which held that manufacturing was not to be construed as interstate commerce.

openly for monopoly and adopted in its stead a policy of "live and let live." The change so impressed the courts that in interpreting anti-trust legislation they began to differentiate between "reasonable" and "unreasonable" restraints of trade and between "good" and "bad" trusts.

The first application of this so-called "rule of reason" occurred in the Standard Oil and American Tobacco Company cases in 1911. Both of these companies were ordered to be dissolved, but the court made it quite clear that they were being dissolved because they had attempted to achieve monopolies and were therefore "bad" trusts. The court made it abundantly clear that it did not intend to condemn "good" trusts, that is, those that did not attempt to acquire a monopoly by engaging in price wars, by endeavoring to prevent the entry of new firms, or by other unsavory policies. The court soon had an opportunity to express the rule of reason positively instead of negatively. In 1920, it refused to order the dissolution of the United States Steel Corporation on the ground that this organization was a "good" trust. During the rest of the 'twenties the Sherman Act and the other anti-trust laws were of legal rather than practical interest.

The failure of anti-trust legislation to restrain business concentration aroused varying reactions among the members of the economic community. The strongest defenders of a restrictive policy proposed that the legislation be tightened and more rigidly enforced; others, insisting that no legislation could stop or even retard the trend toward business consolidation, proposed that the United States drop its emphasis on competition and adopt the German policy of regulating cooperation among business firms. Gradually, the second alternative gained ground. In 1918, the Webb-Pomerene Act permitted cartels in international trade; in 1920, the Transportation Act proposed to pool railroad earnings by taking excess earnings from the stronger roads and giving them to the weaker roads; and in the midst of the depression of the 1930's, the New Deal attempted to reverse the whole traditional American policy of encouraging competition. Through the National Industrial Recovery Act, the Federal government set about to persuade the firms in each major industry to formulate codes setting minimum prices and minimum wages, and establishing production quotas. It was hoped that in this way, that is, by cooperation rather than competition, the economy would be able to recover, and that depression would give way to prosperity. After NIRA was declared unconstitutional, the New Deal reversed its position, and inaugurated the most impressive anti-trust campaign in history. At the same time, however, Congress, in an effort to protect the small businessman against "unfair" competition, passed legislation to permit price-fixing through fair trade laws. Thus, the Federal government's policy toward business became a mixture of inconsistencies. On one hand, the executive branch was attempting to encourage competition on the theory that competition had to be maintained if free enterprise were to retain its dynamic character. Congress, on the other hand, operating on the theory that the weaker small businessman needed protection, was discouraging price competition. Nor was the attitude of the courts more explicit or consistent. In the Alcoa (Aluminum Corporation of America) case a Federal Court attempted to specify just how much control over the market constituted monopoly. Later, in the Cellophane case, a different court held that where a business firm had acted like a competitor, it was a competitor and not a monopolist, even though it controlled a large share of the market for a specific product.

Government as a Redistributor of Wealth

Government's rôle as a giver, or, more accurately, as a redistributor of wealth is almost as old as its activity as a policeman. In early America both the philosophy of government and the nature of the economy created an ideal atmosphere for governmental assistance intended to encourage the growth of trade, industry, and agriculture. Mercantilism, carried over in one form or another from the colonial period and, more fundamentally, from British experience, still underlay the economic philosophy. Moreover, lack of capital and an insatiable desire to raise the standard of living inevitably caused the public to forget its distrust of government, and led people to press for government intervention to assist the process of economic development.[3] It was not strange, therefore, that the Federal government, under the Federalist administrations, tried to embark upon an ambitious program for encouraging industry and commerce. It was equally understandable why state governments with their often greater potentialities gave away land and money on a large scale in order to stimulate economic development. Consequently, the controversy over government intervention never centered around the abstract concept of *laissez faire*, but rather around the question of which type of government—Federal or state—was going to do the

[3] Probably nothing that American governments did was more important economically than the assistance they gave in the development of transportation. This has already been discussed. See pp. 184, ff.

assisting. Occasionally the fires of intervention burned low, and first on one level of government and then on another a quasi-*laissez-faire* philosophy emerged. But public opinion or economic change always provided fresh fuel and, once rekindled, the fires burned more brightly than before.

Assistance to Industry by Means of Tariffs

State governments attempted to encourage the growth of manufacturing by creating a legal atmosphere conducive to the expansion of business, and, sometimes, by contributing financially to specific industries. Under their corporation laws, they granted charters to business organizations; through loans, lotteries, bounties, and privileges of tax exemption, they provided financial assistance. But such financial assistance by states had little long-run influence.

Although the Federal government gave some direct financial assistance to industry, it was through its tariff policy that it most persistently intervened to encourage American business. Initially, the tariff was purely a revenue-raising device. After the War of 1812, however, when war-born industries found it impossible to meet British competition, Congress, responding to insistent business requests, passed the country's first "protective" tariff[4] in 1816. By the 1820's, sectional feeling on the tariff issue had congealed, and tariff-making became a bitter sectional controversy. The East, anxious to protect its industry and to stimulate new industries, became the champion of high protection. The West, believing that high tariffs were necessary to provide a domestic market for its raw materials and so generate funds for internal improvements, gave equally vigorous support to protectionism. Only the South, an essentially agrarian economy exporting cotton and importing manufactured goods, protested strongly against the protectionist trend. But in Congress the southern representatives were out-numbered, and in 1824, and again in 1828, Congress raised the tariff duties. Thereafter a downward trend in tariff rates began as the West lost some of its enthusiasm for the home market argument, and as the opposition of the South became more belligerent. In 1832 and in 1833, the tariff was accordingly reduced. After a slight increase in 1842, the downward course continued, with significant cuts in 1846 and 1857.

The Civil War reversed this trend not only because the South was

4 See pp. 158–160.

(temporarily) not represented in Congress, but because the need for raising revenue during the war had given protectionists an excuse for demanding large increases in tariff rates.[5] Following the war, for some time the South was shorn of almost all its political influence, leaving these free-trade agrarians in a poor position to resist the industrialists. Consequently the high-tariff supporters not only succeeded in preventing any significant reductions in the (presumed temporary) wartime rates, but here and there succeeded in adding tariff duties designed to protect new industries. Meanwhile, they carried on a constant campaign of persuasion for higher tariffs. By 1890 they had convinced large segments of labor that high tariffs meant high wages, and had persuaded many farmers that a high tariff meant greater prosperity for agriculture. So well had they mobilized their forces that they were able to push up the level of tariff rates to new heights in 1890 and in 1897.

As a result of the continuous growth of American manufacturing, however, another reversal in the trend of tariff policy occurred around the beginning of the 20th century. By then it had become quite clear that many infant industries had grown to robust adolescence, and no longer need tariff protection. American manufactured goods were being exported to all parts of the world, and far-sighted industrialists realized that high tariffs might weaken the ability of foreign nations to buy. Moreover, rightly or wrongly, urban populations blamed the high tariff for increases in the cost of living. Under the circumstances, protectionism began to weaken. The first evidence of this appeared, peculiarly enough, in high-tariff laws: both the McKinley Act of 1890, and the Dingley Tariff of 1897 provided for tariff reciprocity. The Payne-Aldrich Tariff of 1909 also indicated that protectionism was no longer as strong as it had been. It contained a statement that the "true principle of protection" meant the "imposition of such duties as will equal the difference between the cost of production at home and abroad." This was certainly a far cry from the earlier contention that high tariffs were directly responsible for America's high scale and America's high standard of living. But, despite its apparent weakening, protectionism prevailed until 1913 when the Underwood Tariff reduced tariff rates to the lowest point since the levels existing before the Civil War.

Protectionism obtained a new lease on life following World War I. The resurgence of nationalism and the appearance of new (war-created) infant industries brought an atmosphere very similar to that which

[5] To maintain the effective prewar level of protection, some increases in rates were needed to offset domestic excise taxes.

followed the War of 1812, and made it possible for protectionists to push through the highest tariffs in American history, the Fordney-McCumber Act of 1922 and the Hawley-Smoot Tariff of 1930. But these were temporary interruptions. In the depressed 'thirties, the New Deal turned away from protection and negotiated reciprocal trade agreements which permitted reductions up to 50 per cent of the rates established by the Hawley-Smoot Act. This program was extended in 1947 to make possible another cut of 50 per cent in existing rates, and was re-extended during the second Eisenhower administration.

The influence of the tariff on economic development was neither as great as protectionists predicated nor as damaging as free traders contended. Even without tariffs, the United States would ultimately have grown to her present position in manufacturing. Her natural resources, entrepreneurs, labor supply, technological potential, and economic philosophy made this inevitable. Nevertheless, some specific tariffs did hasten economic progress by protecting certain American industries in their infant stage, thus enabling them to survive the onslaughts of competition from other, more industrially advanced areas.

Government Support of the Merchant Marine

Although the tariff was the most important type of government encouragement for business, other more direct if less important methods were also used. The Federal government attempted to encourage the expansion of a merchant marine by means of direct subsidies and by enacting navigation acts and discriminatory tonnage duties. Payments for carrying the mail, first granted in 1845, were continued until repealed in the trend toward *laissez faire* that characterized the 1850's. During the first decade after the Civil War, the Federal government again paid mail subsidies to steamship lines. After 1891, the policy of subsidizing the merchant marine achieved permanent status, first, by the traditional method of paying for carrying the mail, and, following World War I, by the more ambitious technique of granting loans or making gifts to assist steamship companies to construct and operate ships.[6]

[6] Judged by today's inflated dollar, subsidies to the merchant marine were not very large: $14.4 million between 1845 and 1858; $6.5 million between 1865 and 1880; and $29.6 million between 1891 and 1928. But the expenditures of the Shipping Board averaged almost $50 million annually during the 1920's and the Maritime Commission spent $122.7 million from 1933 to 1940.

Besides its direct subsidies, the Federal government had very early encouraged American shipping by levying a fifty-cent tonnage duty on foreign-built and foreign-manned ships, as compared with only six cents on American ships. This gave domestic shippers a monopoly on coastwise traffic, a monopoly which Congress formally legalized in 1817 by passing a navigation act prohibiting foreign ships from engaging in American coastal commerce.

The protection which the government offered the American merchant marine served no particular purpose in the period before 1840, because the United States then had so strong a comparative advantage in shipping and shipbuilding that it did not need any government assistance to meet foreign competition. After the Civil War, when the British rapidly shifted from sail to steam, government assistance kept alive an outmoded, wooden, sail-propelled, merchant marine which could not, by itself, compete with foreign operators. The net result was that some resources were channelled into relatively less productive enterprises, with a productivity loss to the whole economy. Of course, the question of building and operating a merchant marine was never wholly a question of economics. In the 19th century it was a matter of national pride, while in the 20th century the decision to build and maintain a merchant marine was made for reasons of survival, especially during the two world wars, and, when such considerations were governing, the economics of the case had to be largely ignored.

How Government Helped the Farmer

Since farmers constituted over ninety per cent of the population of the United States in the early 19th century, it is understandable why government gave them more help and assistance than it gave to other economic sectors. State governments concentrated on helping farmers become better producers. They offered bounties to encourage the growing of special crops, and both states and counties sponsored fairs for the interchange of agricultural information. Out of these fairs grew the state agricultural societies which greatly improved farm practices by disseminating information among farmers on better farming methods. By 1820 it was estimated that there were over a hundred of these societies, most of which received financial aid from state governments. Formal education in agriculture came somewhat later. Michigan founded the first state agricultural college just before the Civil War. During the next decade, agricultural colleges became active centers for farm research. Almost every state, beginning with Connecticut in 1875, added an experiment station to its agricultural college in order to carry on research on plant and animal diseases, develop new seeds and plants, and experiment with new methods of farming.

Until the farm crisis of the post-Civil War era, the Federal government gave the farmer very little direct help. True enough, $1,000 was appropriated to the Patent Office, in 1839, for the importation of foreign plants and seeds, for the distribution of seeds, and for the collection of agricultural statistics. But until the Civil War, the interests of agriculture occupied a small pigeonhole in the multifarious activities of the Patent Office. Then, in 1862, Congress created the Department of Agriculture as a service agency. Its functions expanded continuously, and Congress gave it full cabinet status in 1889.

Like that of the states, the Federal government's initial assistance to agriculture revolved around the question of how to make the farmer a better producer. The Morrill Act provided land grants and small cash appropriations for agricultural colleges. These cash subsidies were increased (by later amendments) until today the Federal government contributes about $10 million a year for the support of the land-grant colleges. Using the state agricultural colleges as operating centers, the Federal government next took steps to encourage scientific agricultural research. Beginning with the Hatch Act of 1887, it gave financial aid to each state to establish an agricultural experiment station. As a direct outgrowth of these stations, the Federal government, in 1902, began an active campaign against plant and animal diseases and pests, especially against the boll weevil. In time, federally supported agricultural education programs were made available to the farmers themselves. By the Smith-Lever Act of 1914, extension courses were established for farmers outside the land-grant colleges. The Act also made provision for a corps of county agents to give advice and help practicing farmers.

From one point of view the governmental efforts to help the farmer to become a better producer were most praiseworthy because it enabled the economy to obtain more output from a given input of labor and capital. But, on the other hand, the program had some unhappy results. It was an important contributing factor to the problem of chronic agricultural surpluses, a problem that the Federal government later attempted to meet by offering price supports as inducements for farmers to reduce production; and presently the Federal government found itself in the illogical position of buying the excess farm production which it had helped farmers to produce.

Government and Social Welfare

Protecting weaker members of society against economic difficulties has always been one of the functions of American government. Cities, towns, and counties normally provided variable amounts of relief for the poor, the aged, and the infirm. As early as 1789 some states established charitable institutions, contributed to the support of private welfare institutions, and adopted public-health measures. The Federal government provided pensions for disabled veterans of the Revolutionary War; and, after the War of 1812, it expanded the pension rolls to include the indigent as well as the disabled veteran. The program was steadily enlarged as wars, large and small, increased the number of claimants; and, by the 1890's, veterans' pensions were the largest single item among Federal expenditures. In addition, the Federal government made some contributions toward augmenting the incomes of another low-income group through its financing of Indian affairs. But expenditures by the Federal government for outright relief purposes were rare before the great depression of the 1930's, although there were occasional exceptions. The first gift of this type occurred in 1827 when $20,000 was appropriated for the relief of victims of a fire in Alexandria, Virginia. Some grants for relief were also made after the Civil War, and in the Progressive Era the practice of assisting the victims of natural disasters became more prominent. The first Federal expenditures for the direct relief of victims of business depression did not come until 1932, although once begun, they were greatly expanded in succeeding years.

From an economic point of view, the most important government programs designed to improve social welfare centered around the Federal government's land policy and state and Federal encouragement of education. With the hope of helping the lower-income groups to obtain a stake in the land, and thereby to improve their economic position, the Federal government adopted a more and more liberal policy. That these hopes and expectations were often disappointed has already been noted.[7] But the liberal land policy undoubtedly succeeded in accomplishing the rapid settlement of the land, and thereby indirectly increased total welfare.

It is generally agreed that government educational programs accelerated American economic progress by improving the quality of the

7 See p. 339.

labor supply, increasing the number of potential entrepreneurs, and hastening technological progress. State governments encouraged education by providing funds for the support of free schools, and by adopting laws making school attendance compulsory. In 1834, Pennsylvania established the first free school system; by 1850, free schools were common, except in the South. Even so, in 1860 the average American had less than three years of formal education.

From the relatively small beginning made during the period from 1830 to 1860, state governments expanded educational facilities after the Civil War along three major lines. They established free secondary schools, especially after 1880, placed greater emphasis on vocational education, and assisted or founded colleges and universities. By 1940, education was mass-consumed. Whereas, in 1890, only one person of every thirty-three between the ages of eighteen and twenty-one was in college, by the 1950's ten out of every thirty-three in this age group were in college. The decline in illiteracy was even more remarkable. In 1870, twenty out of every hundred persons over ten years of age could not read or write, but in 1947 only 2.7 out of every hundred were illiterate.

Government as a Conservator

Conservation of natural resources was a belated correction to the prodigality of the government's rôle as a giver. Rapid alienation of land by the Federal and state governments led to wasteful farm practices and to extravagant use of timber and other bounties of nature. As shortages in some resources appeared or threatened to appear, public interest demanded that the government take steps to conserve what remained. The first conservation programs appeared in the eastern states. New York established a Commission of Fisheries in 1868 and a Forest Reserve Commission in 1885; other eastern states quickly followed suit.

Despite a campaign for a Federal conservation program, the opposition of businessmen interested in exploiting timber and mineral resources delayed any effective Federal action. During the Progressive Era, however, President Roosevelt and President Taft set aside extensive areas of timber, mineral, and oil lands for permanent government reserves. The Forest Service was greatly expanded, and a program of systematic reforestation was instituted. At the same time, the Federal government inaugurated a long-range program of land reclamation through dam and irrigation projects. It was under this program, begun in 1902 and continued to the present, that such colossal projects as the Boulder and Grand Coulee Dams were built. Meantime, the several states expanded their forest preserves and established recreation facilities, such as picnic grounds and beaches. The Federal government, through its river and harbors program, began plans for long-range flood control; and, by its agricultural programs (in cooperation with the states), undertook measures to combat soil erosion and to encourage scientific farming.

Looking back from the vantage point of the 1950's, however, it is quite evident that as a conservator the Federal government was too cautious, too woefully unscientific and unimaginative in its approaches to the conservation problem. This was especially unfortunate because scientists such as John Wesley Powell were pointing out ways in which really constructive resource conservation could be achieved. In his *Report on the Lands of the Arid Regions of the United States* (1875), Powell outlined a resource-development plan which, if it had been adopted, might have had profound effects on the development of the low-rainfall regions. As one of his admirers has said, Powell

would have thrown the 160-acre farm and the existing lands laws out of the window. . . . He would have tied water rights to land titles, to prevent land monopoly based on control of water resources. He would have rewritten the water laws and made them uniform among the western states; he would have organized new western states, not by rigid and unrealistic boundaries of political counties, but by watersheds and river valleys. He would have prevented settlement on lands for which there was not and could not be an adequate water supply. . . . Listened to in time, he might have saved us many things: the dust bowl of the 1930's, the dust bowls of Texas in the 1950's; the acrimonious and snarled lawsuits among states for the water of the great interstate rivers; the erosion and loss of soil, the ruin of watersheds, the floods that in the lower reaches of the great rivers bear testimony to the malpractices on the headwaters.[8]

Government as an Entrepreneur

With economic growth, the government's role as a hirer of labor, and as an owner and operator of business enterprises expanded along with

[8] From Wallace Stegner's "Introduction" to a reprint of Powell's, *The Exploration of the Colorado River,* originally published in 1875 (Chicago: The University of Chicago Press, 1958).

its other activities. Federal, state, and local governments probably employed one out of every fifty workers in 1860, whereas by 1900 they were hiring one out of every twenty-four. Thus, even in the 19th century, when *laissez faire* is presumed to have been at its zenith, government employment grew more rapidly than total employment. After 1900, government employment expanded still more rapidly. By 1920, one out of every fifteen workers was in government service, and by 1957 one out of every seven. The Federal government was by no means exclusively responsible for this phenomenal increase; but, with the 20th-century trend toward greater centralization, the number of Federal employees grew faster than the number of employees in the other two levels of government. In 1900, the Federal government had employed 26 per cent of all public workers; this contrasts with almost 50 per cent in 1957. Excluding the armed forces, Federal employees constituted 15 per cent of all government workers in 1900, 22 per cent in 1940, and 30 per cent in 1957.

One of the reasons why government employment expanded was that government business enterprises were growing. To some extent this meant that government was competing with private business. Quite early some state governments built and operated canals and railways, or created and operated commercial banks. But a much more important reason was that in urban communities governments were taking over more and more functions that in a rural economy had either not been performed at all or had been performed by the citizens themselves.

As early as the 1840's, city governments built waterworks that entailed, for those days, very large financial investments. New York, for example, spent $9 million on the Croton reservoir and aqueduct; and Boston about $5 million on its municipal water supply. At a later date, municipalities built and operated hospitals, electric-light and gas plants, rapid-transit lines, vehicular tunnels and bridges, city markets, auditoriums, and even cemeteries. Under the aegis of state governments, the turnpike was restored to a place of great importance in the 20th century. Meanwhile, the Federal government built and operated the Panama Canal, administered an inland waterways corporation, and finally built and managed, under an independent authority, the vast Tennessee Valley Project.

It would be impossible to place a money value on the contribution to economic development made by government business enterprise. What government normally "produces" is intangible services, and its activity represents very little socialization of the production of goods. Nevertheless, the expansion in the number of services provided by government has greatly helped to increase the standard of living, and, since the benefits have accrued mostly to those in the lower-income groups, expansion of government services has been an important factor in creating a more equal distribution of income.

Government as an Economic Stabilizer

The idea of government responsibility for stabilizing the economy is comparatively new. Admittedly before 1900, the belief that the government could and should use its powers over money and banking to regulate prices was widely held. But the notion that government should shape its expenditure, revenue, and debt policies in such ways as to influence the distribution of wealth, to eliminate unemployment, or to create a balance between inflationary and deflationary forces was too utterly fantastic for most people to accept.

Of course, government controls over money and banking and over its own fiscal policies always affected the economy, whether intended or not. But, before the United States became an industrial, urbanized economy and a world power, two factors tended to obscure this. Government expenditures and revenues constituted but a small part of the national income, and their economic impact was, therefore, not very great.[9] Secondly, governments either tried to divorce themselves from influencing the economy, or they followed, rather than led, changes in business activity. About 1900 some faint signs of skepticism concerning the traditional operation of government fiscal affairs began to appear, and by 1913 the demand for more effective government control over banking through the medium of a central bank had gained enough converts to make possible the creation of the Federal Reserve System. It was the depression of the 1930's, however, that brought a drastic change in the attitude toward governmental responsibility for a more efficiently-operating economic order, and by the outbreak of World War II, the role of government as an economic stabilizer was generally, if not unanimously, accepted.

[9] Except in time of war, government expenditures before 1900 amounted to but 8 per cent of the annual national income. Federal expenditures were about $5 per capita in 1889. The states spent about $1 per capita, and local governments about $8 per capita, amounts much too small to permit effective use of fiscal policy to stabilize the economy.

Fiscal and Monetary Affairs Before 1900

The idea of a "fiscal policy" in the sense of a well-considered and carefully-formulated set of goals to control government fiscal affairs did not exist before 1900. The first rule for governments was to balance their budgets. If they were forced to borrow, by reason of unavoidable circumstances such as depression or war, the recommended procedure was to pay off the debt as rapidly as possible. In practice, however, government expenditures varied directly with fluctuations in business activity. During periods of prosperity, government expenditures increased substantially, and during depressions they were pruned as much as possible. Consequently, government disbursement policy actually intensified booms by adding marginal expenditures to already swollen spending at the height of the cycle, and accentuated depressions by reducing expenditures when spending was most needed as a stabilizing force.

Expenditures by type showed little similarity on the three different levels of government. Federal expenditures in the early 19th century were concentrated on internal and external protection. Investment expenditures, such as river and harbor improvements, and construction of roads and public buildings, were relatively small; and payments to consumers in the lower-income brackets amounted to less than 20 per cent of total Federal spending. On the other hand, state and local expenditures for social welfare were already important as early as 1840.

By 1890, the pattern of Federal expenditures had changed substantially. Veterans' pensions took thirty-three cents of each dollar, another seventeen cents covered the Army and Navy, holders of the government debt received twelve cents in interest payments, and investment spending accounted for about twenty cents. Federal spending was, therefore, tending toward greater emphasis on payments for the benefit of consumers and on direct investment spending. State and local governments exhibited a similar trend, since the bulk of their spending continued to be for social welfare and for capital outlays.

Tax systems at the end of the 19th century were the end result of a long period of improvisation. As they had always done, local governments relied almost exclusively on property taxes. On the state level, inheritance and corporation taxes had been added to the general property tax. Customs duties contributed most to the Federal revenue, but excises, (almost exclusively on alcoholic beverages and tobacco) produced from 35 to 45 per cent.

Because Federal expenditures for the lower-income groups were relatively small, and because the Federal tax system was extremely regressive (taking a larger share out of small incomes than out of large ones) Federal fiscal policy during the 19th century tended to shift income from consumers in the lower-income groups to savers in the upper-income groups. State and local fiscal activities probably benefited middle-income groups the most, for, although their tax systems were also regressive, expenditures benefited upper-income groups less than they helped the middle class or the poor. For the over-all economy, the effect of government fiscal affairs were probably more advantageous than disadvantageous; consumption expenditures were probably lower than they would otherwise have been, but saving was higher; and in a period of capital scarcity, one could argue that there was a greater national need for savings and investment than for consumption spending.

The Expansion of Government's Rôle as an Economic Stabilizer

The expansion of government activity in the 20th century brought in its wake an immense increase in government expenditures, and made fiscal affairs much more important in the total economy. By the outbreak of World War I, the Federal government was spending $735 million a year, state governments almost $400 million, and local governments, $1.5 billion. Total government expenditures, $2.6 billion, were equal to approximately 10 per cent of the national income. World War I greatly accentuated the trend toward higher government expenditures, and at the height of that war Federal spending equalled about 25 per cent of the national income. With the end of World War I, Federal spending (as after each of our major wars) stabilized at about four and a half times the prewar level, but state and local spending soared. Then, during the depression of the 1930's, state and local expenditures dropped sharply, while Federal spending tripled. The composition of Federal spending also changed drastically, because most of the increase in disbursements had to be devoted to social welfare expenditures in the form of relief, public works, and subsidies for agriculture. World War II necessitated still larger expenditures, but immediately after the war Federal spending declined as sharply as after previous wars. State and local government spending, however, especially for education and highways, greatly increased.

By the 1950's government expenditures were equal to one-third of the national income. State governments spent over $10 billion, local governments over $25 billion, and the Federal government, well over $70 billion. Of each dollar spent by the Federal government, sixty cents went for national defense, seven cents for veterans' benefits, three cents for international finance, thirteen cents for interest on the public debt, and eight cents for agriculture.The remaining nine cents covered the cost of all other governmental activities, the social security program, and public works.

As expenditures kept on increasing, neither the tariff nor excise taxes on spirits and tobacco could produce the revenue needed by the Federal government; neither could the property tax be stretched to meet the financial requirements of state and local governments. Under the circumstances, it was inevitable that resort would be made to the vast untapped possibilities of the income tax. Consequently, a trend toward direct and progressive taxation became one of the outstanding characteristics of the 20th century. In the years 1910 to 1916, income taxes accounted for less than 10 per cent of Federal revenue, with the rest divided about equally bteween excises and customs. During the 1920's, in contrast, 55.6 per cent of Federal revenue came from income taxes, and about 30 per cent from excises. By the 1950's direct taxes produced 70 per cent of Federal receipts, with the individual income tax alone contributing over 40 per cent. Excise taxes produced almost 20 per cent, and custom duties, once the leading source of revenue, now brought in less than 1 per cent. Local governments still raised seven-eighths of their revenue from property taxes. As for state governments, direct taxes on incomes and estates produced almost 20 per cent of their total revenue, while the sales tax, an outgrowth of the depression, added another 20 per cent, and motor vehicle and gasoline taxes produced 30 per cent.

Once government expenditures and receipts had grown to the point where they equalled a relatively high proportion of national income, the influence of governmental fiscal policy over the economy assumed new and much greater significance. It became clear that variations in government spending, or shifts in government taxation, would profoundly affect the whole economy. Vague concepts of fiscal and monetary affairs which had been adequate when public finance was a passive economic factor had to be sharpened. New goals had to be formulated, and new policies enunciated to guide public finance now that it had become an active force in determining the course of the economy.

New philosophies do not develop overnight, but, by 1938, a theory of fiscal and monetary policy had been fairly well formulated. The new goals were to vary government spending in order to maintain full employment, to use the government's tax policy to achieve a more equitable distribution of the national income, and to use monetary techniques to assure an even flow of purchasing power throughout the economy. These new goals were based upon the thesis that total spending determined the level of employment, and that government expenditures could be used as a balance wheel to stabilize the economy at a full-employment level. Thus, in periods of declining business activity, "compensatory fiscal policy" called for increased government spending, reduced taxes, and rising public debt to assure that there would be aggregate expenditures great enough to create full employment. On the other hand, when inflationary pressures were rampant, it required reductions in government spending, increased taxes, and repayment of public debt in order to reduce total expenditures and counteract inflation.

But it was extremely difficult to put these new concepts of fiscal policy into practice. It was not easy to persuade Americans that depression and deflation required the therapy of heavy government spending and grossly unbalanced budgets. Such a prescription ran counter to traditional thinking. Allegiance to the balanced budget was deeply ingrained in the American ideology, and could not be sloughed off overnight. Nor was it any easier to sell Americans the idea that periods of inflation required low spending, high taxes, and budget surpluses. It was difficult and sometimes even impossible in boom times (mainly for reasons of national defense) to reduce government spending. Moreover, prosperity accentuated the need for government services, such as schools and highways, and these services cost money. Then too, it was difficult to maintain high tax rates in prosperity when government treasuries were being inundated with money. Americans might tolerate high tax rates in the interests of maintaining a balanced budget, but by the same token the clamor for tax reduction was always loudest in inflationary periods when fiscal theory called for an opposite policy. Yet those who had faith in fiscal policy could gain some encouragement from some of the events that occurred in the years following World War II. True enough, the Federal budget, and those of other governments as well, were at record peace-time levels, but, for the first time in any postwar period, wholesale tax reductions did not occur.[10]

It was now generally understood that government finance, whether determined by sound economic theory or improvised for reasons of expediency or military survival, fundamentally affected the course of the economy. Admittedly, larger government expenditures during the great depression had not eliminated unemployment, but they surely helped to mitigate it. Oppositely, swollen government expenditures in war and postwar periods had contributed heavily to price and money inflation. One thing was very clear: government finance was having an increasing effect on the flow of income. During the 19th century, it had transferred some income from low-income taxpayers to upper-income recipients of government expenditures. In the 20th century, the combination of a relatively progressive tax structure and greater expenditures for the benefit of low-income groups had quite a different incidence; it resulted in a considerable shift of income from the upper- to lower-income groups.[11] Rather paradoxically, it was a capitalistic society that was giving practical application to the Marxist dictum, "from each according to his ability, to each according to his need," proving once more that social solicitude is not the monopoly of any ideology, and that considerations of welfare may be best implemented in societies which emphasize production and business vitality.

[10] Some tax reductions did eventuate. President Truman vetoed two tax reduction bills, but Congress finally succeeded in over-riding his veto. A tax reduction bill was passed during the first Eisenhower administration with the President's approval, but the administration successfully resisted subsequent Congressional attempts—some half-hearted and some determined—to reduce taxes.

[11] Any attempt to measure the shift quantitatively requires more courage than most people possess. Yet, one attempt has been made. John H. Adler estimated that after deducting taxes and adding government benefits, all income groups up to $4,000 gained from government fiscal policy. See Kenyon Poole, *Fiscal Policies and the American Economy* (Englewood Cliffs, N.J.: Prentice-Hall, Inc., 1951), p. 396.

Part IV HOW OUR ECONOMIC

SYSTEM HAS WORKED

IN PEACE AND WAR

AND HOW IT HAS INFLUENCED

ECONOMIC THINKING

14 How wars changed
the American economy

The Diffuse Economic Effect of Wars

Of all the factors that led to the expansion of the Federal government's economic influence, none has been more important than war. Wars have disrupted and changed the whole economy, and each major war has had a greater disruptive effect than the previous one. In all three major wars—the Civil War, World War I, and World War II—the nation's mass-production means were turned to war.[1] Waging war became a business. Industrial facilities were converted from the production of peacetime goods to the production of goods needed in war.

---

[1] Whether he said it or not, the remark attributed to General Nathan Forrest, "Get there fustest with the mostest men," summed up in one sentence the American approach to the economics of war. If Forrest had added to his sentence "and with the mostest machines" his analysis would have been even more accurate.

New industries had to be created. Agricultural production, excessive in peacetime, became inadequate for war needs and had to be expanded. The labor force, reduced by the requirements of the armed forces. nevertheless had to be greatly augmented in order to meet the goals of increased production. To cover the stupendous costs of a war program, government fiscal affairs were reorganized, with enormous effects on the money supply, the cost of living, and the distribution of income. To offset the inflationary influence of war finance, governments resorted to direct controls over prices, wages, and production, thereby increasing their area of activities. Moreover, wars continued to affect the economy long after hostilities had ceased. Some of their influence became permanently embedded in the pattern of economic life, and, although the public wistfully longed to return to the "good old days," it never was possible to restore the *status quo ante bellum* or to return to "normalcy."

The Rising Costs of War and How They Were Met

There seems to be a destiny that plays with the costs of war, for each of America's three major wars cost ten and a half times the previous one. Four and one-quarter years of Civil War cost the Union $3.2 billion, $2\frac{1}{4}$ years of World War I cost $33.4 billion, and 6 years of World War II cost $360 billion.[2]

Each war also entailed very large indirect financial costs that continued long after the war was over, and resulted in multiplied government expenditures. Interest payments on expanded debt were much higher after each war than before, and, in addition, pension payments and veterans' programs required ever greater outlays. The last pension from the War of 1812 was paid in 1945, Civil War pension payments did not reach their peak until 1921 and those for the Spanish-American War not until 1948. With these unavoidable obligations, total Federal expenditures after each war were between four and four and one half times higher than in prewar years. Before the Civil War, Federal expenditures were approximately $65 million annually; by the 1870's they were approximately $260 million. Before World War I the Federal government spent about $700 million; in the 1920's it spent $3¼ billion. Just before World War II, Federal spending was

---

[2] It is estimated that it cost $25,000 to kill a man in the Civil War and over $100,-000 in World War II. Chester W. Wright, *Economic Problems of War and Its Aftermath* (Chicago: University of Chicago Press, 1942), p. 56.

about $9 billion a year; after the war it was well over $40 billion.[3] War, more than anything else, raised the level of government expenditures.

Government can cover the costs of a war by increasing taxes, by borrowing from individuals, corporations, savings banks, and insurance companies; by borrowing from commercial banks; by borrowing from the central banks; or by printing paper money. They can, of course, use any combination of the five different methods. Each method has a different effect on the national income, the distribution of income, the amount of spending, the amount of saving, and the price level.

In general, taxation and borrowing from non-bank investors transfer money from individuals to the government; they do not, therefore, increase the amount of money or the aggregate purchasing power of the economy, and are, therefore, non-inflationary. On the other hand, when a government issues paper money, it increases the money supply and adds to the total amount of purchasing power, thus giving impetus to price inflation. The same thing will result, but in a more subtle or complicated fashion, if the government borrows by selling its securities to commercial banks or to the central bank. When an individual buys government securities, he pays for them in cash, and the transaction represents nothing but a transfer of cash from the buyer to the government; consequently, there is no net increase in the money supply. But when a commercial bank (or the central bank) buys securities or makes a loan to a government, it does not transfer cash. Instead, it creates a deposit for the security seller (in this case the government), enabling it to write checks. This results in a net increase in the money supply and in total purchasing power. Since all this new money will be spent, the net effect will be to increase the demand for goods and resources, thus raising prices, and thereby increasing the cost of the war. Fortunately, inflationary methods of war finance also create deflationary pressures that partially offset the effects of the inflationary pressures. Inflation raises the national income in money terms, and therefore tax revenues rise without any increase in tax rates. Moreover, as the national income rises, money saving tends to increase and hence it becomes easier not only to sell bonds to individuals but to raise tax rates.

It would appear that the interests of economic stability would best be served by levying taxes high enough, and equitably enough, to cover the total cost of war without disturbing income distribution, but this

[3] By the late '50's it had risen to over $70 billion largely because of the great costs of defense occasioned by the Cold War.

has never been accomplished.[4] In covering the costs of its major wars, the United States has resorted to all five methods of financing. Although taxes were increased during each war, loans always provided the major share of the money needed. Taxes paid for only a little more than 20 per cent of the Civil War, 30 per cent of World War I, and 45 per cent of World War II. To make up the remainder, the government borrowed heavily from individuals and commercial banks. Then too, during the Civil War the government issued paper money, and in both World Wars the Treasury borrowed from the Federal Reserve banks.

It will be noted that in each successive war a larger share of war-caused costs was raised by taxation. This represented a decided improvement, but the same cannot be said for the other policies of war financing. If money cannot be raised by taxes, economic stability will best be maintained by borrowing from non-bank investors, because any of the other three methods will result in an enlarged money supply and price inflation. During the Civil War, more than 10 per cent of the total cost was covered by issuing paper money. It is not possible to state how much the government borrowed from the commercial banks, but it must have been at least another 40 per cent. No paper money was issued during World War I, but about 15 per cent of the war's total costs was financed by borrowings from the commercial banks and the Federal Reserve System. In World War II, loans from commercial banks covered approximately 15 per cent of the total war costs, and another 5 per cent was raised by borrowing from the Federal Reserve System. In summary we may therefore say that probably 50 per cent of the Civil War's costs was raised through inflationary methods, compared with about 15 per cent in World War I, and about 20 per cent in World War II.

Money Expansion and Price Inflation During Three Wars

Because of the extensive use of inflationary methods of war financing, the amount of currency and coin (pocketbook money) and the amount of bank deposits (checkbook money) rose sharply during each of America's major wars. In 1860, money in circulation was estimated at about $14 per capita, but by 1865 it was over $30. Data on commercial bank deposits are not available for the Civil-War period, but the de-

---

[4] For a somewhat fuller description of the history of war finance, see Paul Studenski and Herman E. Krooss, *Financial History of the United States* (New York: McGraw-Hill Book Co., 1952).

posits of the war-created National Banking System alone were almost $500 million in 1865, and the deposits of the Associated Banks of New York increased from $80 million to $224 million during the war. Fed by a larger money supply, increased government spending pushed wholesale prices up to more than twice the prewar level, while the cost of living increased by almost 70 per cent.[5]

During World War I, money in circulation rose rather modestly from about $39 per capita in 1917 to $46 in 1919, but commercial bank deposits increased from $250 per capita to $330. Thus, the total money supply expanded by 30 per cent whereas the output of goods and services actually declined between 1917 and 1919. With more money chasing fewer goods, price inflation set in. Wholesale prices rose by 20 per cent between 1917 and 1919, and the consumer price level was 40 per cent higher in 1919 than in 1917.

World War II brought a repetition of the usual wartime pattern of higher spending, money expansion, and price inflation. Per capita money in circulation increased greatly, from $72 in 1941 to $200 in 1946. Commercial bank deposits almost doubled (from $535 to $1,012 per capita). Hence, at the end of the war, there was twice as much money for each man, woman, and child as there had been at the beginning of hostilities. But to offset this, production was relatively high, and consequently wholesale prices increased by only 26 per cent, while the cost of living in 1946 was 21 per cent higher than in 1941.[6]

In only one case did the return of peace bring a decline in prices. Following the Civil War, Federal revenues substantially exceeded expenditures, and the surplus was used to reduce the number of greenbacks in circulation. At the same time, the creation of the National Banking System and the imposition of a prohibitive tax on state-bank notes also cut down the supply of money. This reduction in the money supply, accompanied as it was by a decline in total spending, tended to reduce prices. After both World Wars, however, the expected peacetime developments which should have countervailed wartime monetary and price inflation did not emerge, and the price level continued up-

[5] For an explanation of how reasonably dependable data on the movement of prices have been discovered and assembled, see Ethel D. Hoover, "Wholesale and Retail Prices in the Nineteenth Century," *Journal of Economic History,* Vol. XVIII, No. 3 (September 1958), pp. 298–316.

[6] In both World Wars, inflation started long before the nation declared war. Wholesale prices doubled between 1914 and 1919, and increased by 40 per cent between 1940 and 1946. The cost of living increased 80 per cent between 1914 and 1919, and almost 40 per cent between 1940 and 1946.

ward. In each case, the Treasury had a substantial surplus which it used for debt repayment. But this deflationary influence was more than offset by increases in private, state, and local debt. At the same time, gold, which had flowed out of the country during the war years, began to flow back in, increasing bank reserves and making possible a further expansion in the supply of bank credit. Operating through increased spending by business entrepreneurs and consumers, this enlarged monetary supply pushed prices even higher than they had been during the wars.

How War Finance Affected Income Distribution

The methods used in financing the Civil War made the rich richer and the poor poorer, but the financing of the two World Wars had much the opposite effect. Production during the Civil War did not increase sufficiently to compensate for the amount of goods used up in fighting the war. Consequently, after what was used for war had been deducted, there were less goods and services available for the civilian economy than there had been in the previous peacetime period. In other words, part of the "real costs" of the war were paid for by a decline in the standard of living. Almost all of this burden was borne by the lower-income groups. Excise taxes and customs duties (the backbone of Civil War revenue) were passed on to consumers in the form of higher prices, and fell most heavily on those at the bottom of the income scale. At the same time, lower-income groups received a relatively small share of government expenditures. Thus, Civil War financing shifted wealth from the poor to the wealthy.

World War I also reduced the amount of goods available for the civilian population. Total production of goods and services increased from $60.5 billion to $75.2 billion, but 25 per cent of the latter was used for the war. Moreover, a large part of the apparent increase of production was unreal, since it resulted from price inflation. After subtracting war costs and correcting for changes in the price level, there were less goods and services available for consumers than there had been before the war. As in the Civil War, part of the "real costs" of World War I were consequently paid for by a decline in the standard of living. Unlike the Civil War, however, the burden of taxes in World War I fell most heavily on people in the upper-income brackets, because much higher income-tax rates came into effect after 1917. In addition, individuals in the lower-income groups bought more war bonds during World War I than during the Civil War. The entirely different war-finance policy of World War I, therefore, resulted in a quite different effect on income distribution. Instead of income shifts from the bottom to the top (with the lower-income groups bearing the brunt of war costs) the lower-income groups improved their relative position during World War I, and the major burden of war costs, fell on the wealthy. Business profits were abnormally high in 1916, but, under the impact of heavier taxation, they had declined by the end of the war. On the other hand, real wages remained about the same throughout the war period, and farm income rose spectacularly. In short, industrialists and *rentiers* were worse off at the end of the war than before, wage earners maintained their position, and farmers improved their lot substantially.

The effect of World War II on income distribution was still different. Gross national product more than doubled, rising from a little over $100 billion in 1940 to $213.7 billion in 1944. Government purchases in 1944 amounted to $96.5 billion, leaving goods worth $117.2 billion for the civilian economy. Even after allowing for changes in prices, the civilian economy had approximately the same amount of goods and services as it had had before the war. However, because of government spending and heavier employment, World War II shifted income downward. Even more than in World War I, the poor did relatively better than the wealthy.

The Effect of War on Industrial Progress

When men fought wars in which clubs were the only weapons, manpower at the front was the important thing and technology a minor matter. But economic progress steadily enhanced the importance of weapons and armor, and hence the technology of warfare became relatively more important. War became increasingly a mechanized business, and victory came to depend more on the mobilization and utilization of economic resources than on the amount of manpower in the armed forces. Yet, with the possible exception of World War II, the wars in which the United States has been engaged have not quickened but have more likely discouraged technological progress. Innovation, the heart of technological progress, is probably most stimulated by falling prices and sharp competition. Neither condition exists in time of war. Consequently, wartime increases in production have resulted not so much from technological progress as from the reorganization of industry and from the employment of previously-unemployed resources, because it so happened that each war began in a period of depressed business and unemployment.

Before the era of mechanized warfare, mobilization had little direct effect on industry. The military plan was to throw as much manpower at the enemy as possible, and, except for fortuitous circumstances, manufacturing enterprises continued to function on a "business as usual" basis. Mechanized war, in contrast, has profound effects on industry, and each increase in military mechanization affects industry more sharply, for the goal in this type of war is to throw as much armor and other hardware at the enemy as possible. Since it becomes imperative to dedicate the entire economy to maximizing war production, decisions are not determined so much by economic considerations as by the necessities of survival. Production must be expanded, not in order to provide a higher standard of living for civilians, but to provide the sinews of war. Existing industrial facilities must be "converted" from civilian to military end-product manufacture. New industries, many of which may be economically inefficient, must be created to provide goods which were formerly imported or were not needed in peacetime.

Industry During the Civil War[7]

The Civil War is often called the first "total war" in history, but it was total war only in the sense that it subjected the southern civilian population to the sufferings of war, and was fought by large masses of ordinary citizens and and not by professional soldiers. It was not total war as the term is understood today, for it did not require the whole economy to shift to war production; it emphasized manpower much more than mechanization.

When the war began, pundits who were presumed to know about such things prophesied a quick victory for the North because of its vast economic superiority. But the North never made maximum use of these advantages, and hence it was superior manpower rather than mechanization that finally won the War.[8] In fact, although the Civil War stimulated certain industries, it seems, on the whole, to have re-

[7] The best study of the Civil War economy is still E. D. Fite, *Social and Industrial Conditions in the North during the Civil War* (New York: The Macmillan Co., 1910).

[8] With over 1 million men in the Union Army at the close of the war, the North used only 8,000 cannon and 4 million rifles.

tarded rather than to have accelerated manufacturing progress. Available data, admittedly inadequate, show that, by comparison with the immediate prewar years, the accomplishments of the war in raising production were nothing to boast about. This is especially significant because deep depression had characterized the immediate pre-Civil War era. Entering the war with vast unemployed economic resources, the economy should have been able, merely by the use of available resources, to produce a vastly greater quantity of goods. Actually, the value added by manufacturing (when expressed in constant dollars) was relatively lower during the ten years from 1859 to 1869 than for any other decade. Furthermore, the available index of total production shows an increase of only $13\frac{1}{3}$ per cent from 1863 to 1865, whereas in the first year after the war there was a 34 per cent increase.

Production of certain war commodities increased amazingly, but this was almost entirely offset by declines in civilian-goods production. The annual consumption of wool rose from 85 million pounds in 1860 to 213 million pounds at the height of the war. Wool, as well as munitions, was a staple of the war economy, for the Union's armed forces used 75 million pounds in 1865, and, to satisfy this demand, factory operations were on a 24-hour day, 7-day week basis. Meat packing also demonstrated great progress, the number of hogs packed increasing from 270,000 to 900,000 during the War. On the other hand, railroad construction came to a virtual halt during the war. There was only slight progress in pig-iron production which rose from 800,000 tons in 1860 to 1 million tons in 1864, and there was hardly any increase in coal production (in Pennsylvania, 9.5 million tons were mined in 1860, and only 10 million tons in 1864). The cotton textile industry, cut off from its raw-material supplies, suffered heavily in the first two years of the war, when mills operated at 25 to 50 per cent of capacity. Thereafter, however, production increased as the North's occupation of the South partially restored the supply of raw cotton.

The failure to make a better showing in production resulted from a slowing down in technological progress. To be sure, because of large governmental demand and the shortage of manpower, standardization made great progress in clothing, tents, tools, and munitions. On the other hand, the number of patents (admittedly a poor yard-stick) increased at a much slower rate than before the war. Whereas between 1855 and 1860, the number of patents granted had more than doubled, during the war itself, the increase was less than 50 per cent. Even in armaments, where technological progress should have been most pronounced, the results were appallingly meager. Throughout the war, both sides continued to use the muzzle-loading rifle, although the newly-developed breech loader was demonstrably faster and more effective. Although the Gatling gun, the predecessor of the modern machine gun, was patented as early as 1862, it was not widely used.

There was some extension of the factory system and of mass production, but only in the essential war industries: munitions, clothing, meat packing, and food processing. Here the long-run effects were quite significant, and mass production became a permanent characteristic of these industries, thus providing models for later extensions of the system. Meantime, some conversion of industrial facilities from peace to war production did occur, but this shift was not impressive, and its long-run effects were not very great. Cotton and carpet factories were converted to woollen cloth production; saw factories turned to the manufacture of sabers; and jewelry manufacturers made buttons for army and navy uniforms.

Industry During World War I

The amount of armament, munitions, and war machines used in World War I was fantastically higher than in the Civil War, indeed the weight of metal fired in just one offensive in 1918 equalled the entire amount fired by the North during the whole Civil War. Being far more mechanized, World War I required a greater industrial effort and much more planning. New industries had to be created, old industries expanded and converted, and new facilities built to provide the necessary tools of war. The Federal government for the first time engaged in comprehensive economic planning and set up elaborate controls to regulate the economy.[9] Hence, the whole civilian population was affected to a far greater extent than in any previous war in American history.

Actually, most of the expansion in production that occurred during the World War I era had already been accomplished by the time the United States finally entered the war. When Franz Ferdinand was assassinated at Sarajevo, the United States was entering a period of business depression, and the outbreak of hostilities at first intensified the economic decline. This was short-lived, however, and by 1916 much of the nation's unemployed resources had already been put to work

[9] See, Bernard M. Baruch, *American Industry in the War* (Englewood Cliffs, N.J.: Prentice-Hall, 1941).

manufacturing war supplies for Europe. In 1916 alone the United States exported over $1 billion worth of munitions. Industrial production increased by almost 20 per cent between 1915 and 1916. Steel production jumped from 32 million to 43 million tons, and copper output from 694,000 to 964,000 tons. Capital expenditures for manufacturing plant and equipment increased from $616 million in 1915 to $1.1 billion in 1916, and industrial profits were the most phenomenal in history.

When the United States entered the war in April, 1917, the demand for war supplies became appreciably greater and new problems in economic planning presented themselves. The new variety of semi-mechanized warfare required different types of goods from those which had been found satisfactory in previous wars. There was a far greater demand for coal and petroleum, and for new types of strategic materials such as diamond dies and abrasives, alloy steels, and aluminum sheets and castings. New industries had to be created to build aircraft and to manufacture chemicals which formerly had been imported. Shipbuilding, long a feeble and inefficient American industry, had to be expanded to provide transportation for men and materials to a war being fought 3,000 miles away. Yet, although the production of war goods increased remarkably, there was no similar increase in total production, largely because of declining productivity, and material and manpower bottlenecks. Indeed, industrial production increased less than 1 per cent between 1916 and 1917, and in 1918 and 1919 it was actually lower than in 1916. Value added by manufacturing, when corrected for changes in the price level, was not much greater in 1919 than in 1914, and probably not as high as in 1916. Steel production did not increase substantially, and copper output declined from the peak reached in 1916. But the production of manganese ore, chromite, and aluminum increased quite remarkably.

For the whole economy, technological progress once again failed to maintain a fast enough pace to enable the nation to take war production in its stride. Capital expenditures for new manufacturing plant and equipment were $2.5 billion in 1918 as compared with $1.1 billion in 1916; but since the wholesale price level had increased by over 50 per cent, capital equipment was not growing at a much higher rate at the end of the war than at the beginning. The number of patents granted declined during World War I just as it had during the Civil War. In 1911, 34,000 patents were granted, in 1916, 46,000; but in 1919, only 39,000.

The failure of production to expand sufficiently to take care of the increased demand occasioned by the war necessitated extensive conversion of industrial facilities from civilian to war production. Carpet factories began producing military clothing; horseshoe plants made trench picks; stove founders manufactured grenades and bombs. Standardization was greatly accelerated; the variety of goods available for civilians was cut drastically, and earnest attempts were made to institute economies and to eliminate waste in industrial processes. Shoe styles were cut about two-thirds. The number of planters and drills fell from 784 to 29, and the variety of buggy wheels from 232 to 46. Economies in packing goods were supposed to save 17,000 carloads of freight space, 141 million cartons, and 500,000 packing cases a year. The yardage used in the manufacture of clothing was reduced 15 per cent in men's wear and 25 per cent in women's. The paper used by daily and weekly newspapers was reduced 15 per cent, and that of Sunday newspapers by 20 per cent.

The transition from war to peace was accomplished very quickly after World War I. Industry entered the postwar years with improved plants and equipment, and the nation had a backlog of saving which could be used to finance further capital expenditures. Once the immediate postwar depression was over, industrial production and productivity progressed remarkably through the 1920's. Industry quickly surpassed its wartime performance, in some cases as early as 1921 and in general by 1923, when the index of manufacturing production was 30 per cent higher than in 1919.

Industrial Progress During World War II

In every respect, World War II was more nearly a total war than either the Civil War or World War I, and therefore affected the entire economy and the process of economic development much more fundamentally.[10] Whereas the Civil War had had little effect on civilian life in the North, and World War I resulted in but insignificant changes in the pattern of consumption, World War II had extensive repercussions on everyday life. Moreover, technology, which had been used on a small scale in the Civil War and somewhat more extensively in World War I, was the most striking feature of World War II. In World War

[10] For a general account, see, U.S. Bureau of the Budget, *The United States at War* (Washington D.C.: Government Printing Office, 1946). See also Francis Walton, *Miracle of World War II* (New York: The Macmillan Co., 1956).

I an infantry division required about 3,500 mechanical horsepower to keep it going; in World War II it required 400,000, more than a hundred times as much. As a result of increased dependence on technology, war required not merely far more minerals, but also new materials formerly unknown to the layman; and their introduction had far-reaching economic implications for the future.

In contrast to the experience during World War I and the Civil War, the American economy during World War II made greater progress not only during the prewar defense period, but in the period of actual hostilities. Gross national product (in constant prices) increased 72 per cent between 1939 and 1944. Industrial activity expanded beyond the wildest dreams of the most optimistic, increasing 48 per cent between 1939 and 1941, and another 45 per cent by the end of the war. Steel production jumped from 47 million tons in 1939 to 80 million in 1944; copper, from 713,000 tons to over 1 million; manganese ore, from 33,000 tons to 248,000; chromite, from 4,000 to 143,000 tons; and aluminum, from 327,000 to 1,840,000 tons. American industry produced stupendous amounts of war materials: 300,000 planes, 124,000 ships, 41 billion rounds of ammunitions, 100,000 tanks and armored vehicles, and much else.

The amazing record of production during World War II could not have been achieved without the almost complete mobilization of the entire economy. For industry, this meant the maximum utilization of existing resources, the creation of new facilities, the conversion of industrial plants from peace to war production, and multi-shift operations. But, as in previous wars, most of the increase in production came from the use of resources previously unemployed. The United States entered the defense period with a large number of unemployed workers, and with extensive unused plant and capital equipment. Most of these factors were quickly put to work, and, by the end of the war, existing facilities were operating at capacity. Further expansion of production occurred as a result of the enlargement of industrial plants, the construction of new facilities, and the addition of large amounts of equipment. Expenditures for construction and new equipment between 1940 and 1945 exceeded $60 billion ($10 billion for direct military construction, $13 billion for expansion of non-manufacturing facilities, and $25.5 billion for manufacturing facilities). Of the total war-material expansion, 75 per cent was publicly-financed. Thus the government for the first time became the chief financier of industrial plant for war production.

Although the expansion of production took place at a remarkably rapid rate, it nevertheless took from $1\frac{1}{2}$ to $3\frac{1}{2}$ years to reach maximum output. In the interim, the needs of total war could be satisfied only by converting much of the nation's industrial facilities from civilian production to war production. Many of the gadgets to which civilians had long been accustomed suddenly became scarce, or disappeared altogether. Bobby pins and white shirts, nylon stockings and rubber bands became collector's items. Radios and electric appliances for civilians were not produced at all, since plants had been converted to the production of electronic equipment for war. But the most remarkable example of conversion from peace to war production occurred in the automobile industry. The making of motor cars for civilian use ceased in February, 1942, and the 1,000 plants engaged in automobile production began to manufacture war goods. But still more facilities were needed, hence the existing plants were expanded by the investment of more than $1 billion, 80 per cent government-financed. The automobile industry by itself (or through sub-contracting with small businesses previously producing cash registers, steam shovels, outboard motors, and similar things) turned out more than 10 per cent of all war production, producing all the tanks and combat vehicles and a large share of the air-craft engines and machine guns.

World War II was the first war in which science was really mobilized to develop technology for warfare. It was also "the first war in history to be affected decisively by weapons unknown at the outbreak of hostilities."[11] Although the number of patents granted declined greatly (just as had been the case during the Civil War and during World War I) the number of new devices and processes developed during the war was most impressive. Great strides were made in producing synthetic rubber and synthetic gasoline. Antibiotic drugs changed the whole process of medical care. The war developed radar and other electronic devices. Above all, scientists opened up the whole new field of atomic energy with effects which will not be fathomed for generations in the future. It would be hard to visualize how the "Manhattan Project," which developed the atomic bomb, could have been undertaken except in time of war, when costs were no concern and when government, private enterprise, and human genius could join forces in a magnificent technological endeavor.

[11] Irwin Stewart, *Organizing Scientific Research for War* (Boston: Little, Brown and Co., 1948), p. ix.

Government Planning for War

Modern warfare, involving as it does vast outlays of men and materials, must be intricately planned by some central agency and only government can provide this necessary co-ordination. In wartime, therefore, the government becomes the regulator of the economy, and war creates the atmosphere for a wide extension of governmental power. Ordinarily in a free enterprise economy, goods are allocated through the mechanism of market prices. But total war creates problems in the allocation and pricing of goods that cannot be solved satisfactorily in the market place. The need for specific goods for war, and the necessary curtailment of civilian production create a wide range of scarcities. Meantime, the expansion of the money supply and the great increase in government spending causes inflationary pressures. Were no controls used, more money would be proffered for fewer goods and prices would skyrocket, causing social injustice and a loss of morale. Moreover, if the free market economy were left unchanged, the government would be forced to bid against civilians for commodities necessary to the war effort. None of these things can be permitted. In a war economy, the market mechanism must be temporarily abandoned in the interests of justice and morale, of defense and survival. Consequently, government directives replace free choices by sellers and buyers as means for determining the allocation and pricing of goods. Economic values, here as elsewhere, take a subordinate place to the needs of defense; and, the more total the war, the more complete and pervasive the rule of government decree.

Although the power and importance of the Federal government increased as a result of the Civil War, its influence over the economy was exerted indirectly rather than directly. Scarcities were not a major problem, and there was relatively little centralized planning. The government did not help to finance any private manufacturing enterprises, but it did operate a few establishments under its own auspices: a clothing factory, three laboratories to produce drugs and medicines, and a few meat-packing plants.

Government Controls in World War I

The direct controls exerted by the Federal government over the economy in World War I were probably less important for their influence during the war itself than for their long-run effects. A good part of the war period was spent in developing administrative machinery; and, whereas controls were never imposed widely enough to have a great effect on the war itself, they acted as precedents and models for later attempts at peacetime planning (such as the NIRA) and for the much more ambitious planning program of World War II.

Price control provides a good example of the type of government regulation of the economy utilized during World War I. Price control was not a completely new thing; it had been tried, unsuccessfully, by the states during the American Revolution. The experience in World War I, although much better, was still far from satisfactory. The War Industries Board, which administered the program, always considered price controls as subordinate to priorities and allocations. It therefore fixed prices selectively rather than generally. It attempted to set the prices of certain specific commodities at the source (on a basis of estimated costs plus a reasonable profit) hoping that this would result in "reasonable" retail prices; but it soon learned that price control was a very difficult thing to put into practice. Since many prices were intricately interrelated, fixing the price of one commodity had a reaction on the supply and on the prices of a number of other goods, necessitating further price fixing. Thus, selective price controls led inevitably to an extension of the number of commodities under control, and gradually certain prices were fixed all along the line.

Moreover, price controls without rationing could not be effective, especially when the volume of money was constantly increasing and the supply of goods constantly decreasing. Fortunately, World War I was short, and the supply of goods held up reasonably well; hence the really knotty problems inherent in the administration of price controls did not have to be faced. Nevertheless, the war demand for some materials was so great that serious shortages did occur. Coal production was a case in point. In 1915, the United States produced 532 million tons of bituminous and anthracite coal. By 1918, this had been increased to about 675 million tons, but this fell far short of the needs of the civilian plus the war economy. Consequently, the Fuel Administration had to allocate coal by rationing it among business and residential users.

Government Planning During World War II

When World War II began, no master plan of mobilization existed. At first, the organization of agencies to direct and control the nation's economy followed the model set by World War I; but it was soon realized that World War II, being more nearly a total war than World War I, required much more extensive planning and far wider governmental controls. For a time, however, planning evolved on a piecemeal and opportunistic basis, resulting in a complicated succession of agencies and programs.

In May 1940, the President created the Office for Emergency Management (O.E.M.) and resurrected the Council of National Defense originally established in World War I. But neither of these two agencies could plan effectively for war mobilization, because their powers were too nebulous. The first important unit set up in the O.E.M. for active planning was the Office of Production Management (O.P.M.), created in January, 1941. O.P.M. was responsible for advising, planning, co-ordinating, and stimulating the production of materials necessary for defense. Since it could not change the stated requirements of the War and Navy Departments, and since it had no authority over civilian production, its power rested entirely on its authority to control priorities. This left a gaping hole in the planning machinery, for, although the issuance of priorities in the interests of defense provided the military with basic commodities, it diminished the supply of goods available for the civilian economy, creating extreme scarcities, and causing precipitate price increases. In order to alleviate this difficulty, the administration, in April, 1941, created the Office of Price Administration and Civilian Supply (O.P.A.C.S.) charging it with responsibility for stabilizing prices and maintaining a flow of essential goods to the civilian economy. Like the other initial government agencies, however, O.P.A.C.S. lacked the power to enforce its decisions; it had to rely on persuasion and cooperation to keep prices down, and "jawbone price control," as it was called, was pitifully ineffective.

There were other weaknesses in O.P.M. and O.P.A.C.S. The O.P.M. could not formulate an over-all plan for directing the entire economy. It was also headed by a partnership, not by a single individual; and there was no clear-cut differentiation of powers between it and the O.P.A.C.S. The rivalries which existed all along the line interfered with efficient administration. In an attempt to improve matters, the Supply Priorities and Allocations Board (S.P.A.B.) was superimposed on the O.P.M. in August 1941. This made a bad situation worse, since there were now three, instead of two, organizations vying with each other for top position. Once the nation became an actual belligerent, such division of authority proved intolerable, and, consequently, in

January, 1942, O.P.M. and S.P.A.B. were abolished, and the War Production Board (W.P.B.) was created under a single administrative head. At the same time, the Office of Price Administration (O.P.A.) a subdivision of O.P.A.C.S., was placed on a statutory basis.

The powers over production given to the W.P.B. were the widest ever delegated in the United States. They included general direction of procurement and production, administration of priorities, and allocation of materials and production facilities. The O.P.A.'s powers were also extremely broad; it could fix prices for all non-farm commodities and ration civilian goods. While price controls had many disadvantages (and resulted in the creation of black markets), the O.P.A. had considerable success in restraining price inflation. It resorted to general rather than specific controls, and rationed the civilian supply of meats, fats, gasoline, fuel oil, shoes, and sugar.

The administrative machinery set up under the W.P.B. and O.P.A., although far superior to that of the preceding authorities was still not satisfactory, for, in the course of time, other agencies, such as the War Manpower Commission and the Office of Defense Transportation, became extremely important, and no single agency existed to coordinate all the different plans and activities of the war effort. There was, for example, no single agency which could allocate manpower among the military services, industry, and agriculture. In order to overcome these difficulties and to unify the direction of the entire economy, the President, in May 1943, created the Office of War Mobilization, thereby setting up the wartime administrative machinery in its final form. Thus, by the end of the war, governmental activity had been greatly intensified and expanded to cover the whole economy. Basic commodities and manpower were subject to priorities, and were allocated among the different sectors of the economy according to the urgency of needs. Civilian goods were price-fixed and rationed. The government had complete control over new construction, prohibiting it except where essential, and financing a large portion of it.

With the return of peace, the government could not, even if it had wished, revert to the relatively minor position it had occupied before the war. It was now the largest employer in the world. Its enormous expenditures, constituting 25 per cent of the gross national product, had become the chief single factor in determining the course of the economy. Whatever tax program it adopted would fundamentally affect saving, spending, and the distribution of income. Its debt, greater than the combined debt of all other borrowers, influenced the amount of money in circulation and the ups and downs in the price level. In the interests of national defense, it had to stimulate production, accumulate a vast stockpile of goods, and help maintain the defense of Western Europe. Whatever action it took as policeman, entrepreneur, conservator, or stabilizer, would influence economic development fundamentally.

The Effect of War on Population and on the Occupational Mix

In explaining the effects of major wars on the price level or on expanded functions of government, it is easy to overlook some of the more permanent influences. Thus, wars, by affecting the death rate, the birth rate, or immigration, change the rate of population growth, and thereby affect the supply of labor, not only in the short run but for many years after. Whether wars are mechanized or not, they create an extraordinary demand for manpower, and thereby transform the occupational structure of a nation's labor force.

In the Civil War, the demand for manpower was largely for the armed forces, not for workers to produce war goods. At its peak, the Union Army consisted of about one million men, while the Confederate Army numbered perhaps 666,000. The number of workers needed to supply all the troops with war goods probably totalled about one million. Consequently, the Civil War increased the demand for labor by somewhat over 2½ million. In the North some of this increased demand was met by immigrant labor; for the country as a whole, the remainder was covered by the reemployment of previously unemployed workers, the natural growth of population, and the shifting of workers from peacetime to war production.

But while the demand for labor rose substantially during the Civil War, population growth was not maintained at its previous rapid rate. Total war casualties from battle and disease were about 635,000. Although immigration continued at about the same rate as previously, the birth rate declined, so that the population increase during the decade 1860 to 1870 was estimated to be about 1.3 million less than might normally have been expected.[12] This decline in the rate of population growth had long-run repercussions on the economy, for it

[12] Chester W. Wright, "The More Enduring Economic Consequences of America's Wars," *The Tasks of Economic History,* December, 1943. (Supplement to the *Journal of Economic History,* Vol. V.)

slowed up the enlargement of the nation's productive capacity by making the scarcest factor, labor, scarcer than ever.

World War I had much the same effect on the demand for manpower as did the Civil War, although by 1919 war required relatively less manpower in the armed forces and far more to produce war equipment. By the end of the war, some 4.8 million men had served in the armed forces. This was roughly 5 per cent of the population, compared with 10 per cent in the Civil War. But it was estimated that three to five men were required in industry and transport to produce and ship the equipment and supplies needed by one man at the front. On the basis of this estimate, at least six million workers were needed for war production, making the total demand for manpower about ten million.

The initial demand for war workers was satisfied by reemploying the unemployed. Thereafter the government, through the United States Employment Service and state and local agencies, actively engaged in mobilizing labor for war production. From Puerto Rico and the Virgin Islands, 100,000 laborers were imported; 300,000 boys were recruited for farm work; and nearly a million women added to the gainfully-occupied work force. Yet, there were offsetting factors to this expansion of the labor force; immigration virtually ceased during the war, and the average work week in manufacturing declined from 55 hours to 53.6 hours. Since the supply of labor was not increased sufficiently to take care of the war demand, a reallocation of the existing labor force became necessary. Workers were shifted from peacetime tasks to war production chiefly by the inducement of higher pay, and the composition and functions of the labor force were thereby fundamentally affected. The number of farm workers decreased by more than 10 per cent, while the number of workers in the service industries expanded by $33\frac{1}{3}$ per cent. The relatively few workers in forestry and fishing were further reduced, whereas the number of manufacturing workers increased by more than 10 per cent. Moreover, World War I once again changed the rate of population growth. The increase in population between 1910 and 1920 was 3.3 million less than expected because of the stoppage of immigration and, to a lesser degree, because of war mortality. These changes in the size and composition of the labor force did not disappear with the return of peace, but became part of a new occupational structure which, in turn, projected itself with relatively small changes through the inter-war period.

The demand for manpower in World War II far exceeded that of World War I. Fighting on two fronts, the armed forces required more than three times the personnel needed in World War I. Approximately 14 million individuals served in the armed forces at one time or other. This represented more than 10 per cent of the population, and was therefore a relatively greater mobilization than that of the Civil War.[13] In addition, approximately two million civilians worked for the government in war activities. The greatest demand for manpower resulted from the need to supply the technological equipment for mechanized war. Each man at the front required approximately 12 men in industry and transportation; an armored division used 400,000 mechanical horsepower to keep it going; and eight tons of shipping were needed to send one man to the fighting front together with an additional one ton a month to keep him supplied. Mechanized warfare had really arrived, for even in the combat zones, it required 1½ to 3 men behind the lines for each man at the front.

Normally, the American labor force constitutes about 40 per cent of the population, but this was far from sufficient to meet the extraordinary demands of war, and, consequently, severe economizing and broad allocation of labor were necessary. Unemployed manpower (8 million in 1940) was rapidly put back to work. The labor force grew swiftly, and, at the peak of the war in 1944, it comprised 66 million persons or about 47 per cent of the population. Roughly seven million of these were persons who would not ordinarily have been gainfully employed, but who were in the labor force because of patriotic motives or because they could not resist the high wartime wage rates. About 2.8 million of the seven million were from 14 to 19 years old, and had interrupted their schooling or had taken part-time jobs. Another 1½ million were recruited housewives; 800,000 were persons who had delayed retirement or returned to work although retired; and the remainder were marginal workers. The manpower pool for war production was further increased by shifting workers from peacetime work to war production, and by increasing the length of the average work week. By 1942, eight million workers had shifted to war production, and hours of work had increased from 38 per week in 1940 to 45 in 1944.

Once again the addition of new workers and the shift from peace to war production wrought vast changes, seemingly of a permanent nature, in the composition and functions of the labor force. In 1940, only 14.2 million females were in the labor force, constituting 25 per cent of the total. By 1945, in contrast, there were 19.3 million female workers, 30

---

[13] With the exception of Soviet Russia, the other belligerents in World War II mobilized an even greater proportion of their population.

per cent of the total labor force. "Rosie the Riveter" was as famous a personage in World War II as the "Ship-yard Worker" had been in World War I. As in World War I, farm workers were especially eager to move into war plants, and farm employment declined by almost one million, or approximately 10 per cent between 1940 and 1945. The number of workers in mining, construction, and finance also fell, but only slightly. On the other hand, the number of workers in manufacturing increased by almost 50 per cent, and the number of government workers increased similarly.

Unlike the Civil War and World War I, World War II accelerated, rather than retarded, the rate of population growth. Casualties were relatively smaller than in the previous wars; 201,000 Americans were killed in World War II,[14] four times as many as in World War I (but only two and a half times as many as automobiles kill in a similar period of time). Non-battle deaths, however, were lower for the armed forces than for similar age groups among civilians. Moreover, the crude birth rate during World War II was higher than it had been at any time since the middle 'twenties. From 17.9 (per thousand persons) in 1940, it jumped rapidly to 21.5 in 1943. Since the civilian death rate remained about the same as it was in 1940, the increased birth rate resulted in a much larger growth in population during the war years than in previous years.

Summary Remarks on the Effects of War on Economic Development

On the basis of available evidence, America's major wars, with the possible exception of World War II, appear to have retarded rather than accelerated economic growth. Except in World War II, they interrupted technological innovation, and deterred population growth. Wars also wasted natural resources, reduced output per man hour, reduced the standard of living, and threw the economy off balance by unleashing price inflation and by encouraging high-cost industry and over-expanded agricultural output. Superficially, it might appear that wars made the economy run faster, but whatever improvements appeared were largely the result of employing previously unemployed factors of production. Peace and preparedness has had a much greater effect than war on the remarkable economic development which the United States has experienced.

14 Britain lost 306,000; France, 200,000; Germany, 2.9 million; and Russia, 7 million.

15

The adaptation of economic
thought to economic change

Ideas and Institutions

During the seventeen decades of our national history, important and sometimes truly dramatic changes have occurred in individual sectors of the American economy. An economy, however, is more than a random collection of economic sectors; it is an organic whole. If the entire economy is vigorous and dynamic, it will undergo a comprehensive transformation as a result of the interrelated changes and developments that occur in the several sectors. The process, however, is not merely a consequence of chance inter-sector blendings and interactions; it is one that is profoundly influenced by movements in ideas, by acts of human insight, and by changes in value judgments. We cannot, therefore, attempt to appraise the progressive transformation of the American economy as a whole unless we also explore these changes in economic thinking. It is with this task of showing the interplay of changing ideas and changing institutions, that we are concerned in this final chapter.

When the Constitution was adopted in 1789, the United States was an underdeveloped economy only recently removed politically from a colonial status. Most of the inhabitants were farmers, pursuing a more or less self-sufficient life along the eastern seaboard. Here and there, were clusters of population, but they were more like villages than cities. The typical centers of economic activity were the farm, the home, the small shop, and the countinghouse of the sedentary merchant. Although a considerable number of domestic servants were employed, there was only the feeblest development of "service industries," those "tertiary industries" which play such an influential role in our modern economy. What little manufacturing existed was small-scale, carried on with simple tools and equipment, and serving a market area severely restricted by primitive means of transportation and communication. Consequently, business enterprise was necessarily small-scale, and was conducted almost entirely by sole proprietors or by small groups of partners. Business decisions were based more on intuition, hunch, and flashes of inspiration than on careful market analysis. With few machines (and these few of a crude and primitive type) production relied heavily on hand labor. Consequently, since there was little opportunity for specialization and division of labor, productivity was very low and working hours were necessarily long. Life was uncomplicated and essentially individualistic. Relations between employer and employee were paternalistic; there were no labor unions, and a belief prevailed that there was little need for anything but the most rudimentary form of government.

Gradually, this underdeveloped economy was transformed into the highly complicated economic system that exists today. The market area continuously expanded, and the center of economic activity moved westward. Relatively, agriculture and the extractive industries declined, whereas the manufacturing and service industries expanded; business enterprises became increasingly sophisticated; and, as economic life became ever more complex, government came to play an increasingly important role. High birth rates, low death rates, and immigration quickened population growth. At the same time, capital was steadily accumulated, and, as a result of more tools and equipment, productivity rose, sometimes slowly, at other times spectacularly, but, in the aggregate, faster than population, thus making possible genuine economic growth as measured by real per capita income. With increased per capita income came higher real wages and reductions in working hours. As a consequence, the members of each new generation not only commanded more goods and services than their predecessors, but they also had more leisure in which to enjoy them.

Economic evolution, however, brought new problems, for economic development is never a smooth and uninterrupted story of one long, unbroken journey onward and upward along the path to Utopia. More often it reads like an economic "pilgrim's progress." For every year and a half spent in climbing heights of prosperity, there intervened a year of descent into the pits of depression. Exhilarating waves of prosperity followed by frightening nightmares of depression, the erratic performance, the subtle operation, and the continuous transformation of an intricate economic mechanism called for description and explanation. For every society is under a compulsion to explain itself, and the more introspective the culture, the greater its need to reduce its whole pattern of life to some rational explanation. It is the social scientists who undertake the task of trying to describe and explain how a society operates—philosophers and moralists are concerned with its aspirations; sociologists with its social structure and the pattern of activities; historians with the process of change; and economists with the ways whereby man actually makes a living and the processes through which the whole economic organism really functions.

Like all other social scientists, the economist tries to be objective. Looking for general principles, he aspires to formulate explanations that will hold good for all time and all places. But, no matter how sincerely he tries, he can never achieve complete objectivity. His findings are inevitably tarnished by his own subjective values, and, since these findings are, to a large extent, unwittingly descriptive, they reflect the peculiar and essentially ephemeral social, political, and ethical climate in which he thinks and has his being. Hence, the most representative economic theorist of any particular period is one who, speaking for the majority of his colleagues, presents a discerning description and plausible rationale for an existing economic system. At the same time, however, there usually exists a minority of thinkers who cannot accept the prevailing analysis. Out of step with the majority, these dissenters constitute an "underworld" of economic theorists. With more or less logic, for this too is a relative thing, they question the discovered principles which the majority often construe as irrefutable economic laws.

So long as an existing economic and social pattern remains largely unchanged, the theories of the minority gain few adherents. But, as the economic, political, and social atmosphere is modified, and as the institutional framework begins to change, economic theory also undergoes a gradual transformation. Skepticism regarding many of the economic laws espoused by the majority gains ground, and sometimes the "heresies" of the minority attain such general acceptance that the majority opinion passes into the limbo of historical residue, leaving for posterity only a small part of what had allegedly been a comprehensive economic analysis.

The American culture, less concerned with abstractions and less given to philosophical musings than the European, made relatively small contributions to the building of tight-woven fabrics of theoretical social science. For its explanation of how an economic system worked, it depended, to a large measure, on European theoretical contributions. Thus, in turn, Ricardo and Say, Mill and Bastiat, the German historical school, the Austrian school, Marshall and Keynes—all had a profound influence on American economic thought. But even so, these imported doctrines, as we shall see, were modified, sometimes subtly and at other times drastically, to make them reasonably applicable to the realities of American economic life.

The Transformation of the American Economy in the Early 19th Century

The transformation of American economic life began far back in the Colonial period and continues today, but the process has never been as simple as it seems in retrospect. History recognizes few revolutions, and certainly the profound changes that occurred in American life did not happen suddenly. Change is evolutionary and subtle, and an unpredictable, multi-linear process probably plays a more powerful rôle than the calculated plans of mankind. None of the people who lived during an era of pervasive transformation planned it that way, and only a few of them were aware of what was taking place. Even in retrospect, the sweeping nature of the early transformation becomes recognizable only in the first half of the 19th century.[1] It was during

[1] See above, Chap. 7.

those years that America emerged from the status of a colonial economy, and the United States itself embarked upon the ambitious venture of settling the West. The nation was still overwhelmingly rural, although here and there, larger-scale types of manufacturing were beginning to appear. As manufacturing expanded, many cities experienced a mushroom growth, their population growing much faster than the population of the nation as a whole. Into older and newer cities, there poured from the rural regions, and from across the Atlantic, an army of workers to provide a new, urban, laboring class.

Meanwhile, a fundamental change was also taking place in rural economic life. Commercial agriculture was rapidly displacing self-sufficient farming in the Northeast, and cotton culture and the plantation system were becoming an integral part of the southern way of life. To provide the facilities to get the farmers' products to town markets, and to distribute the manufacturers' products into the rural hinterland, better transportation facilities were rapidly built, and by the end of the early national era, a network of turnpikes and canals existed in the settled portion of the country. But this was only the beginning of the extensive expansion of the market area which was soon to occur.

Yet, even by the Jacksonian Era, the United States had already taken on some of the hallmarks of a business civilization. We had become a nation of "hustlers."[2] Businessmen, land speculators, commercial farmers, state bankers, and even urban laborers were beginning to dream the great American dream of material success. Lush economic opportunity and easy money gave promise of a magnificent future. Wealth and income were rising, and the first millionaires had arrived to dazzle the American scene. Outwardly it seemed that the United States had done phenomenally well. But although aggregate income and wealth had swollen, the enlarging population diluted much of the gain, and there was, if we are to believe the less-than-satisfactory statistics that are available to us, little if any increase in real per capita income during the early years of the 19th century. Moreover, it was during these years that the United States experienced (in 1819) its first really serious business depression, and had its first sad experience with loose and speculative commercial banking. The pattern of "boom and bust," of monetary inflation and deflation, that was to distinguish the American economy for so long, had already appeared.

[2] Carl Russell Fish, *The Rise of the Common Man* (New York: The Macmillan Company, 1939), p. 3.

American Economic Thought in the Early 1800's

The economic evolution with all its social and political implications that we have just sketched greatly stimulated intellectual activity, and especially economic thought.[3] But the transformation that occurred during the first part of the 19th century was so deep, and so complicated, that instead of leading to any easy agreement among economists, it produced severe disagreement. Amateur economists argued heatedly and often impatiently about a vast number of issues, but, basically, controversy centered around two crucial questions: the government's rôle in the economy, especially its tariff and internal improvement policies; and the nature of money and banking. In one corner were arrayed those who favored an industrial, rather than an agrarian, society. They were not, however, mere panderers to the new industrial or business class, although businessmen were, of course, sympathetic to their point of view. Rather, they were followers of the neo-mercantilist tradition of Alexander Hamilton. As such, they urged the Federal government to broaden its powers, and to use them to encourage the growth of manufacturing. As we have noted in a previous context,[4] they presented arguments extolling the economic and social advantages of an industrial society. Arguing logically for tariff protection for infant industries, and for Federal subsidies for internal improvements, they built up an economic rationale which justified the legislative demands of many American businessmen. Yet, despite the large popular following they attracted, their leading spokesmen never succeeded in convincing all their fellow economists, or the country at large, that their doctrines were correct or adequate. The neo-mercantilistic formulae appealed to northern manufacturers and to some western farmers, but they did not satisfy eastern farmers, southern planters, or most of the small businessmen. Nor did they appeal to the majority of academic economic theorists, in whom the classical economics of Adam Smith, David Ricardo, and J. B. Say aroused so much more enthusiasm.

Ricardo[5] first gained admirers and disciples in the United States as a result of his writings during the "bullion controversy" that followed the Napoleonic Wars. He argued that the right way to correct

---

[3] By far the most exhaustive study of American economic thought is Joseph Dorfman's *The Economic Mind in American Civilization*, 5 volumes (New York: The Viking Press, 1946, 1949, 1959).

[4] See pp. 156–58.

[5] See pp. 110–11.

price inflation was to contract the currency and restore a specie standard. Many Americans concerned about the inflation that accompanied the War of 1812 were tremendously impressed by Ricardo's analysis. At about the same time, J. B. Say, the French exponent of Smithian *laissez faire*, also became very influential in the United States, and presently, in an effort to explain American economic society, American economists and publicists blended portions of the theories enunciated by Ricardo, the Physiocrats, and Say into a tentative admixture.[6] As a consequence, for a time, the economics of Ricardo and the far more optimistic doctrines of J. B. Say were expounded in college classrooms, and Say's text was by far the most widely used.[7] Thus classical economics dominated American collegiate instruction, and, among the formally-educated, it permeated American thinking. Yet many American theorists became increasingly adroit in rejecting those portions of European theory that did not fit the American scene and the American way of doing things, so that presently classical economics as taught in American institutions came to be a modified version that at least partly reflected American opportunism and adaptability.

The Emergence of a *Laissez-Faire* Ideology

Ricardian economics was essentially pessimistic, for it was based on the belief that man could never overcome the niggardliness of nature. The cornerstones of Ricardian economics were: *1)* a belief that costs, especially labor costs, determined value; *2)* the principle of comparative costs (or comparative advantage) which held that a nation should produce only those goods for which it had comparatively low costs of production and should import those goods which it found comparatively expensive to produce; *3)* a deeply imbedded belief in *laissez faire; 4)* the idea that rent was a surplus or unearned income; and *5)* the "iron law of wages" which averred that labor was doomed to a wage that could never rise above subsistence.

6 Thomas Jefferson, the elder statesman of agrarianism, had a wide knowledge of contemporary development in economic thought. He corresponded with Say and with Dupont de Nemours (one of the Physiocrats). He was temperamentally sympathetic to their theories, although in practice he often took action counter to the tenets of agrarianism, thus demonstrating the difficulty of reconciling action and philosophy.

7 No less than fourteen editions of Say's *Principles* were published in America. See Ernest Teilhac, *Pioneers of American Economic Thought,* translated from the French by E. A. J. Johnson (New York: The Macmillan Co., 1936), p. 113.

This body of theory was more appropriate to a static than a dynamic economy. Consequently, British industrialists could subscribe enthusiastically to it, for, having the advantage of an early start, they could manufacture more efficiently than other nations. They saw nothing but benefit for themselves from free trade and *laissez faire,* since thereby they would be assured of the widest markets for their manufactured exports and the lowest prices for their imports of food and raw materials. There were a number of reasons why Americans could not accept the whole body of Ricardian principles with equal complacency. With her vast land mass, her varied natural resources, and her chronic labor shortage, America was too lush, too much a land of opportunity, to permit the acceptance of Ricardian pessimism. Moreover, a nation of land speculators could not admit that rent was an unearned increment; nor could agrarians completely and wholeheartedly accept *laissez faire.* Some did, to be sure, share Ricardo's aversion to tariffs, but, in general, they took a friendly interest in certain other forms of governmental intervention. For the western farmer, the vast expanse of land and the dispersion of the population made marketing a more pressing problem than it was in Britain, and inevitably created an insistent demand for government intervention in the building of transportation facilities. Furthermore, the great distances that separated the United States from Europe, as well as the westward movement that absorbed so much of America's energies, made American economic thinking much more nationalistic than England's. Finally, most agrarians, faced with a chronic shortage of capital, were sympathetic to monetary experiments of the kind that Ricardo considered idiotic heresies.

Whereas southern farmers and plantation owners found it easy to agree with Ricardo and classical economics (although even they had certain reservations), western farmers found little comfort in his theories. Industrialists found even less, since they were of the opinion that American manufacturing, suffering from the disadvantage of a late start, could not compete successfully with English industry without some governmental help. As a basis for immediate economic policy, therefore, they rejected *laissez faire,* and supported tariffs and other neo-mercantilistic policies of protection and assistance for business. Most of them, however, did accept the basic Ricardian ideas on money and on the labor-cost theory of value; indeed, they enthusiastically championed the "wages fund theory" that classical economics had formulated. Thus, on the floor of the Senate, Daniel Webster, the able spokesman for New England businessmen, defended the Bank of the

United States as a bulwark against unsound money. Yet he championed the tariff, and described himself as shocked and bewildered when the administration argued that it was not the proper function of the Federal government to take action to alleviate a "business revulsion."[8]

Basic Changes in the American Economy During the Latter Half of the 19th Century

For all their efforts, the spokesmen for industrialism achieved little of immediate importance in their attempt to shape the economic and political policy of their day. Aside from a temporary and indecisive victory in the "Tariff of Abominations" of 1828, protectionism lost ground in the face of southern opposition. Meantime, the end of the Bank of the United States dealt a serious blow to sound banking; and, with the Jacksonian triumph, the Federal government displayed a singularly apathetic attitude toward economic intervention. More and more the philosophy of agrarianism, with its distrust of banks and big business, pervaded American politics. Yet much of this domination was illusory, for, by the 1850's, agrarianism was obviously losing its vigor. It had reached its peak in the Jacksonian Era; by the 1850's it had achieved all its political objectives and had ceased to be an effective economic philosophy. Even though the nation was still predominantly rural, agrarianism had lost its imagination and vision. It lacked new goals and objectives, and by the Civil War it was merely playing out what had become a rather purposeless existence. Meanwhile, industrialism had steadily gained ground, and by the end of the Civil War it had replaced agrarianism as the dominant force in politics.

By the late 19th century, the United States had become an industrial nation. More people now lived in urban areas than on farms, and the value of manufacturing output exceeded that of agricultural production. The extensive development of the American economy had been largely completed, and a new era of intensive development was beginning. Some of the dynamism of a raw society had disappeared, although it should not be assumed that the American economy had become static. Far from it! But its dynamics were different from those of a society struggling to emerge from an underdeveloped condition. The great internal colonization period was over, and the Census Bureau was

8 See Robert L. Carey, *Daniel Webster as an Economist* (New York: Columbia University Press, 1929).

about to announce the momentous news that there was no longer a frontier line in the United States. Crisscrossed by a network of railroads, the nation was well on its way to becoming one vast market area rather than a set of isolated regional markets. By the 1890's, moreover, the business spirit—the emphasis on short-run economic goals, on corporate concentration, and on bigness—permeated all segments of the economy. Even farming had become a business; it was now more a commercial undertaking than a way of life. Labor unions, too, had become business institutions; welfare unionism was waning, while business unionism was entering its halcyon period.

In manufacturing, heavy industry now supplemented the light industry of the early years of the century, making possible a new era—the age of steel. Large-scale manufacturing and big business had come to stay. By the 1870's mass-production leviathans had developed in iron and steel, petroleum refining, railroad equipment, and other basic industries. By the 1890's, one firm produced half the nation's steel output, another refined three-quarters of the fuel oil, and still another produced over 90 per cent of the nation's sugar. Giantism in business had come to be a common rather than a rare feature of American economic life.

The entrepreneurs who organized and operated these large-scale enterprises found it impossible to work by the rule-of-thumb methods that the small businessmen of the preceding era had found satisfactory. Large-scale operations involved heavy capital investment, and created critical problems arising from sunk costs and from joint demand. In order to deal successfully with such problems, businessmen had to be much better informed than the tradition-bound "old timer." Indeed, some of them, men like Carnegie and Rockefeller, were presently experimenting with highly-sophisticated business techniques. Inexorably, the continuous surge of big business was driving the large-scale firms toward collective action and what came to be called "social responsibility." Yet the "heroic" businessmen, as Schumpeter called them, were the very antithesis of groupism. They were still essentially individualistic, aggressive, and ruthless. Striving to achieve a monopoly position in their respective industries, men like Gould in railroads, Carnegie in steel, Rockefeller in oil, Havemeyer in sugar, were apparently little concerned with the social effects of their business methods, and felt little need to explain their success, accepting it as part of their destiny. With supreme self-confidence, they believed that they were successful because the rule of the survival of the fittest applied in economics as much as in biology. In those rare moments when the spirit moved them to offer explanations, they ascribed their success to hard work, self-reliance, thrift, and a competitive spirit. Never had Social Darwinism and the Protestant Ethic been so extolled, and never before had businessmen had so comfortable a rationale for their activities and their achievements.

The Performance of the Economy in the Late 19th Century

The acceleration of mass production and the emergence of an industrial society in the last half of the 19th century had a most invigorating, although somewhat erratic, effect on the American economy. In terms of wealth and total income, the United States was far richer in 1890 than she had been in 1825, but most of the gains were achieved after the Civil War. Aggregate income had continued to increase secularly in the second quarter of the century, and, out of each year's product, a sizeable slice had been saved and invested. With larger and more efficient mills and factories, with better tools and machines, and with more roads, canals, and railways, production increased; but so did population, so that (if we are to believe available data) even though aggregate income rose, real per capita income in 1860 was about the same as it had been in 1825. The Civil War probably had a disastrous effect on the accumulation of wealth, since the cost of the war apparently took not only all the current income over and above what the private economy consumed, but part of previously-accumulated wealth as well.

In the post-Civil War Period, however, the forces unleashed by the accelerated expansion of heavy industry gave a new and greater impetus to the American economy. Between the end of the war and 1900, population continued to increase, although at a slower rate than in the early 1800's. Meanwhile, capital accumulation and investment in capital goods continued at a brisk rate, and productivity rose. Using more land and relying heavily on machinery, American agriculture greatly increased aggregate production as well as output per man. Wheat farmers were producing ten times as much in 1890 as in 1800, but meantime the man hours required to produce a bushel of wheat had fallen from four hours in 1800 to less than one hour in 1890. But if American agriculture had done well in increasing output, American manufacturing industry had done even better. Between 1850 and 1890, manufacturing production increased at least ten-fold. By 1890, American steel mills were producing more steel than England and Germany combined. As production soared, so did aggregate income. Meanwhile prices declined, giving the urban consumer an economic windfall in the form of higher real wages. The decline in food prices was most marked. They were so low in the 1890's that the fashionable Waldorf-Astoria hotel in New York could serve a roast-beef dinner for sixty cents.

So great was the rise in production that by 1890 we could, for the first time, be sure that real per capita income had increased. Economic statisticians tell us that the per capita real income in 1890 was almost double what it had been at the end of the Civil War. This was a superb performance, but the color of the economic picture was not one deep tinge of rose. There were large patches of gloomy gray, and, here and there, even some splotches of dismal black. Periodically, the economy was rocked by severe and prolonged depressions. Such depressions occurred in 1837–42 after an abnormal burst of land speculation; in 1857–61 when the first great railroad building era came to an end; in 1873–78 when railroad building again ground to a halt; and in 1893–97 after a period of heavy investment in manufacturing. Depressions, of course affected the whole nation, but they were essentially industrial phenomena, for no matter how bad conditions might become, farmers kept on producing. They did not starve, and, heartless as it may sound, they at least kept busy. But in the cities depressions produced unemployment and extreme privation, and resulted in a great waste of resources. Thus, as industrialism became more prevalent, the tragic results of depression become more wide-spread; and by the late 19th century, unemployment was a chronic rather than an abnormal or occasional by-product of economic life.

Even when the economy was performing well, everybody did not share alike in its progress. Although average income rose magnificently, some people got much more than the average and some considerably less. It also seemed that as industry expanded, income distribution became increasingly unequal. To be sure, most members of American society went up the ladder as their incomes rose. Moreover, as industry grew, so did the middle class, for industry enlarged it with the jobs it was creating; hence there emerged an increasing number of managers, junior executives, whitecollar workers, agents, and members of the ancillary professionals—a host of lawyers, and, in the late 19th century, of accountants and advertising men. But if we are to judge income distribution on the basis of the difference between the very poor and the very rich, then in the late 19th century the gap was getting wider.

In the rural areas, "tobacco-road" dogpatches had always marred the serene bucolic environment, but they were less obtrusive than the poverty-stricken neighborhoods that existed in the urban centers. In every town and city, overcrowded, blighted, and squalid slums existed almost next door to the mansions of the rich. The only solace for the urban worker was the fact that he had cheap food prices. But for the nation as a whole this was not an unmixed blessing. Although cheap food raised urban real wages, it was a source of immense irritation to the farmer. All during the last portion of the 19th century the farmer fretted about his wretched plight. He complained that farm prices were too low and that he was not receiving a fair share of the national income, and he blamed his misfortunes on faulty governmental policy, on national banking and tight money, on regressive taxation, and a general political bias in favor of industrialism.

Trends in American Economic Thought in the Late 19th Century

The fundamental changes that were occurring in the post-Civil War American economy at first eluded most of the economists. The nation had become an industrial society; the government, as a result of the Civil War, was playing a larger rôle in the economy; the protective tariff had become a tenet of political faith; and labor unions were on the rise. Yet, none of these basic changes seems to have impressed the majority of the economists. Nor did they seem particularly concerned with the problems of declining prices, income distribution, or the business cycle, even in the midst of the depression of 1873. Almost all were devotees of the classical school who still championed *laissez-faire* ideology and who were surprisingly dependent on English and French economic thinkers for their basic theory. To be sure, John Stuart Mill had replaced Ricardo as the leading authority; the optimism of the *laissez-faire* French economist Bastiat had supplanted Ricardian pessimism; and a text by an American, Francis Wayland, written in the best "wages fund" tradition, had superseded Say's book in collegiate popularity. But these changes were trivial and insignificant. American economists still wrote as though a *laissez-faire* economy actually existed, and they still thought in terms of inexorable economic forces which would determine what would happen despite all efforts by any individual or of any group to control them.

Except for their general predilection in favor of free trade, the tenets of the majority of economists, especially their dim views about government intervention, were enthusiastically received by businessmen. At first glance, this might seem a sharp about-face from the attitude that businessmen had taken in the early 19th century, when they had been so eager for government assistance and intervention. The inconsistency was, however, more apparent than real. Businessmen had always welcomed government intervention if it favored business. They had always opposed intervention if it meant the regulation of business. In the early 19th century, government intervention for the most part had been designed to help business, and businessmen had therefore favored it. After the Civil War, most proposals for government intervention were focused on regulation, and to these overtures businessmen were hostile. Indeed, nothing irked the business community more than attempts by government to fence it in. Oppositely, nothing sounded sweeter to business ears than the voices that were raised in opposition to government regulation. Consequently, no social theory had more influence among businessmen than that of Herbert Spencer (1820–1903) the extreme *laissez-faire*, English, social philosopher. Spencer preached a determinism as dogmatic as that enunciated by Karl Marx, but he reached entirely different conclusions. Believing in natural selection and the survival of the fittest, he insisted that anything that interfered with the law of natural selection would necessarily have evil results. Thus, he was sharply critical of government in general and of governmental economic activity in particular. There should be, said Spencer, no mint, no postal service, no public education, no regulation of industry, no poor relief, no social legislation.

Spencer first expressed his views in his *Social Statics* (1850), and by the latter part of the century these ideas were being approvingly quoted by many American businessmen, intellectuals, and academicians. But the Spencerian notions never commanded a wide following among the amateur economists who were then, as usual, very plentiful, very articulate, and very influential among laymen. These amateurs either rejected classical *laissez-faire* economics altogether, or gave it a new twist that led to conclusions sharply divergent from those arrived at by the orthodox economists. In either case, the net result was a departure from the strict tenets of *laissez faire* and a recognition of the need for stronger and more positive government intervention.

Henry C. Carey (1793–1879) was perhaps the foremost opponent of classicism in the United States. Retiring from the printing business at the age of 42, he spent the rest of his life writing about economics. Essentially optimistic, he centered most of his criticism on the Ricardian theory of rent, averring that the whole history of America proved how utterly wrong Ricardo was. But Carey was no mere destructive critic. He argued positively for systematic protectionism, and for treating land as a special type of capital. Although he had little influence on the professional economists of his day, he had considerable influence abroad and on American economists of the next generation. In his own day, he helped to bridge the gap between the anti-Ricardian agrarians and the influential American businessmen. In doing so, he rather unintentionally kept alive the interventionist doctrines pioneered by Alexander Hamilton, Daniel Raymond, Matthew Carey, and Friedrick List.

Printing apparently had a capacity for breeding amateur economists. First came Matthew Carey.[9] Then came his son, Henry C. Finally, Henry George (1839–1897), the most influential of those Americans who accepted the whole doctrine of classicism and then proceeded to reinterpret it, was also associated with the printing business, but as a newspaper reporter and itinerant printer, not as an entrepreneur. Self-educated, highly emotional, extremely sensitive to the sufferings of humanity, and possessed with apostolic zeal, George, in the words of one scholar, "questioned the world rather than its thinkers."[10] Distressed by the widespread poverty of the post-Civil War era, George sought a solution to the paradox of poverty in the midst of evident progress.

Living in California, George could not help but observe the extraordinarily active speculation in land that was taking place, and he concluded that the explanation of the paradox of progress and poverty lay in land rent. He came to the conclusion that since land was God-given and not produced by man, income from land was an "unearned increment." He agreed with Ricardo that land rent absorbed all surpluses; whereas wages, interest, and profits, under the force of competition, would be held down to modest levels. As more resources were brought into use, only rent would increase. Hence George concluded that, under existing institutional arrangements, progress inevitably created poverty, for as land became relatively scarcer, the share of national income going to landlords increased, while the shares of the other productive factors—labor and capital—declined relatively. More-

9 See p. 160.
10 R. G. Tugwell, "Henry George," *Encyclopaedia of the Social Sciences* (New York: The Macmillan Co., 1933).

over, when land was held out of production by speculators, in anticipation of greater unearned increments, depressions resulted, because labor and capital were forced to stop producing. As a solution to the problems caused by rising land values and increasing rents, George proposed to "appropriate all rent by taxation . . . to abolish all taxation except that upon land values." It is important to note that George's proposal had a double edge. On the one hand, he was proposing to put an end to land speculation and to stop the private appropriation of unearned increments through a 100 per cent tax on rent; while, on the other hand, he was proposing that the government should encourage the fullest application of labor and capital in the productive process by abolishing all taxes on them.

George published his *Progress and Poverty* in 1879 shortly after the depression of the '70's. Written with passionate eloquence and in an inspired style, the book sold widely. In characteristically crusading fashion, George traveled up and down the country making speeches. On the platform of the "single tax," he ran for mayor of New York City in 1886 and was defeated in a very close election. But even though he had a very large popular following, he convinced very few academic economists that his theory was correct. He was much more successful in converting businessmen, and the substantial funds they contributed for the dissemination of "single-tax" theory helped to establish a foundation to teach George's economic principles. Although that foundation still exists, the "single tax" is farther from adoption than ever. The constant expansion of industrialism has dulled the once-burning issue of land speculation. Moreover, with the rise of large-scale business, it seemed to many people that there was more than one reason for "unearned increments."

The Belated Reaction Against Classical Theory Among the Professional Economists

During the last years of the 19th century and the first years of the 20th century, classical economics began to give way to newer concepts even among academic economists. The classical analysis had never really fitted the American scene, and presently its premises, methodology, philosophy, and internal logic were subjected to broad and effective critiscism. New theories and new research in psychology (especially William McDougall's work on instincts) raised skepticism regarding the basic classical assumptions about the nature of man. The hedonistic calculus—the theory advanced by Jeremy Bentham and other classical thinkers that economic behavior was motivated exclusively by an inherent tendency to maximize pleasures and minimize pains—was beginning to be regarded as a fairy tale. Sociologists such as Charles Cooley questioned the usefulness of all economic theory, observing that the theorist was like a man who watched "only the second hand of a watch; he counts the seconds with care, but is hardly in a position to tell what time it is." Meanwhile, economists of the German historical school were levelling telling criticism against the classical method and philosophy; while economists of the Austrian school were questioning the essential content of classical economic analysis.

Insisting that there were no universal economic laws appropriate for all times and all places, the members of the historical school advocated an inductive or historical approach as a more realistic approach to economic problems than the deductive method used by Smith and Ricardo. They were also sharply critical of the *laissez-faire* bent of the classicists, and like almost all German economists they urged that government should play a major role in economic life. In contrast to the historical school, the adherents of the Austrian school were convinced that there really were universal economic laws, but they criticized the classical school on the ground that it over-emphasized costs and virtually ignored demand. This criticism was undoubtedly justified. The classicists, living in a world where scarcity had been everywhere apparent, naturally emphasized the problems of production, which is to say the nature of supply; consequently, they tended to think more in terms of cost than of demand. With the accelerated economic progress of the late 19th century, however, problems of production, although by no means solved, seemed less crucial, while problems of distribution, in contrast, began to loom larger and larger. More stress came therefore to be placed on demand, previously the stepchild of value theory. The pioneers in this new departure were the mathematical subjectivists (Gossen and Jevons) and the Austrians (Menger, von Wieser, and Böhm-Bawerk). But going to the other extreme, these economists virtually ignored supply in favor of demand, which they explained in terms of "marginal utility," defined as the enjoyment derived from the consumption of the last unit of a series of goods.

This international maelstrom of conflicting ideas had a profound effect on American economic thought, especially in the 1880's when a new crop of economists was beginning to achieve some prominence.

Many of them were trained in continental Europe, and having no necessary predilection for *laissez faire,* they created a cleavage in academic economic thought by taking issue with the older economists who, with few exceptions, maintained their allegiance to classical theory and *laissez faire.* It would be a mistake, however, to think that the older economists were mere apologists for the *status quo.* They very honestly believed that an economy run by market forces (an economy guided, directed, and planned by the relatively insignificant individual decisions of millions of producers and consumers) was superior to any other kind. Such a market economy might admittedly be imperfect; but they argued that, where planning was diffused, many mistakes could be made without any calamitous results, since no single decision would be big enough to be earth-shaking. On the other hand, they feared that if government were given broad powers over the economy, each of its decisions would be momentous, and, if a mistake were made (which was inevitable considering the frailties of human beings), the results would be disastrous. Thus, it would be better to suffer the irritations of an imperfect market economy than to risk the tragedies that might result from giving the government the power to make far-reaching decisions. No one expressed this point of view more forcefully than William Graham Sumner (1840–1910), who for years was the spokesman for the most extreme, old-guard philosophy. A follower of Herbert Spencer, Sumner could see no good whatever in government intervention. A drastic Social Darwinian, he condemned not only socialism, but trade unionism, protectionism, and all social legislation as well.

The younger rebels found it impossible to take the same austere, hands-off attitude that their elders displayed. Eager to grapple with the problems of the emergent American industrial society, they reacted in one way or another against classical thought, some even going so far as to regard competition with misgivings. They itched to analyze such aspects of the new society as the expansion of big business, the growth of labor unions, and the new importance of public finance; or to tackle the problems of falling prices and depressed agriculture. They did not in any sense advocate revolution or an abrupt break with the past. They wanted only general reform and improvement, and they thought that this could be easily achieved through increased government intervention. The more ardent members of the group founded the American Economic Association in 1885, and its first declaration of policy said that "The doctrine of *laissez faire* is unsafe in politics and unsound in morals," a statement that was later modified to read: "We regard the state as an agency whose positive assistance is one of the indispensable conditions of human progress."

The Association represented a protest against narrow, conventional European economics; and its statement of policy was construed as a declaration of emancipation from economic dogmatism. It represented the considered thought of such younger economists as Francis A. Walker (1840–1897), Simon N. Patten (1852–1922), John Bates Clark (1847–1938) and Richard T. Ely (1854–1953). It was fitting that Walker was the first president of the Association. A partisan of the historical school, he favored more government economic intervention. He himself played an active part in government activities, being superintendent of the 1870 census. As a writer and teacher, he effectively attacked conservatism in general, and did more than anyone else to refute the wages-fund theory. Sympathetic to the underdog and always interested in current problems, he supported legislation to help labor, and he was one of the few economists who championed the cause of free silver in the bitter monetary debate of the '80's and '90's. Yet he was no radical. He vehemently attacked George's single tax, did not wholly approve of trade unions, and regarded the "heroic" entrepreneur as the chief agent of production and the motivator of economic progress. Walker's influence within the field was tremendous, and his textbook, *Political Economy,* was for many years the most widely used in the United States.

Of all the younger economists, however, none made a greater contribution to economic theory than John Bates Clark. Primarily interested in value and distribution, Clark considered the classical analysis incomplete. Unaware of what Jevons was doing in England, he arrived independently at many of the same conclusions, including a concept of marginal utility. Building on marginal analysis, he then developed a theory of distribution in which the cardinal thesis was that under conditions of competition each factor of production tended to receive an amount equal to its marginal product. In this "marginal productivity theory of distribution," the wages of labor, for example, were determined by the amount produced by the least efficient (the marginal) worker. Clark later expanded his theory to show that under a system of really free competition each factor would tend to receive the wealth it produced. Thus expanded, Clark's theory of "specific productivity," as it was called, still remains a cornerstone in the theory of distribution. It obviously had most important implications for the every-day problems of economic life. If, as Clark suggested, each factor tended to receive what it produced, then any action on the part of any seller of resources to get more for a given factor than that factor could add to production would disrupt the smooth operation of the entire economy. The whole theory assumed the existence of free competition, since without free competition some factors would be exploited. But, as critics were quick to point out, free competition was not as universal as some thinkers had assumed it to be. Clark was well aware of this, and the growth of large, quasi-monopolistic, business enterprise disturbed him. He sensed that, with the passage of time, the problem of monopoly would become evermore serious. For him, therefore, the central economic problem became the control of trusts; and toward the end of the century, he was actively proposing legislation to deal with the problem of monopoly.

Social Reform Comes into Its Own

Despite the insight which their theoretical refinements provided, it was not the professional economists who made the major recommendations for changes in American economic policy. For the most part, the chief and most effective revolt against *laissez faire* came from social workers and intellectuals outside the gild of professional economists. This group was concerned more with poverty, the distribution of wealth, and the quest for social justice than with abstract problems of value and distribution, public finance, or the nature of economic theory. It should be recalled that classical economics had explained poverty as an effect of nature's niggardliness on the one hand, and irrational population growth, on the other.[11] It was, therefore, something that could not be overcome by governmental intervention. But great differences in wealth and income were now developing in the United States, and this contrast between poverty and plenty became too conspicuous to be ignored. Social scientists, clergymen, journalists, social workers, and miscellaneous intellectuals demanded that something be done about it. Henry George had had his answer in the single tax, but that seemed too impractical, bland, and slow for those who wanted hasty action. What the reformers wanted was a broad program of government action, a program that combined government regulation, differential taxation of incomes, and, above all, social legislation. What they asked for, in other words, was a minuscule version of what we now call the welfare state.[12]

11 See p. 106.
12 See Sidney Fine, *Laissez-Faire and the General-Welfare State* (Ann Arbor: University of Michigan Press, 1956).

Some of the younger economists lent their direct encouragement to the reformers, but the really doctrinaire Old Guard saw little merit in these "unsound" proposals. With the passage of time, however, the gap between the Old Guard and the young rebels gradually narrowed. Each side gave a little and the protruding edges of extreme opinion were slowly worn down. In the process, views changed; thus Clark, who had started off as a Christian socialist, came to the opinion that social reform was not a part of economics, and Richard Ely, once labelled a socialist by the Old Guard, became increasingly conservative; while oppositely some members of the Old Guard shifted their opinions and, admitting that this was not the best of all possible worlds, allowed some scope for government intervention.

The Marshallian Synthesis

Although there was considerable agreement among economists about how an economic system operates, on specific matters of thought they were split into a number of diverse groups, each emphasizing one aspect of the discipline—sometimes to the almost total exclusion of all others. The situation needed some one to pick up the different threads and weave them together in a harmonious whole. What was called for, apparently, was not so much a new theory as a synthesis that could combine the classical emphasis on cost with the newer emphasis on demand, and one that could find a middle road between those extremists who still insisted that *laissez faire* was a reality and those other extremists who believed that the government could, simply by passing laws, solve all social problems.

For a time, it appeared that Alfred Marshall (1842–1924), the great British economist, had provided such a synthesis. Explaining value as synchronously determined by supply and demand, he attempted to give equal weight to cost and utility. He also modified the classical view of competition, for, although agreeing with the traditional contention that competition was the best motivating force for economic growth, he was not sure that competition in the pure state assumed by the classicists ever could exist in the real world. He also recognized that economic drives were restricted by law, custom, and inertia, and, consequently, he could not accept the classical hedonistic calculus. With misgivings about competition and skeptical about the pleasure-pain analysis, Marshall could not unqualifiedly accept *laissez faire*, but considered some government intervention as necessary. Indeed, Marshall, although an equilibrium theorist, saw decided weaknesses in equilibrium theory. No matter how modified, this kind of theory was essentially static, and a static theory could not adequately explain a dynamic economic process. Deeply influenced by the Victorian belief in progress, Marshall was fascinated by the problems associated with the dynamics of economic growth. In countless *obiter dicta* delivered in his lectures, Marshall gave a much wider latitude to his misgivings and skepticism than he did in his written work. It was this aspect of his teaching that was most influential on the future course of economic thought, for in this way he planted seeds that later sprang to life in a lush growth of new theory developed by his students, especially by John Maynard Keynes.

Further Transformation of the American Economy in the Early 20th Century

Marshall's neo-classicism spread rapidly throughout the English-speaking world. It was an ideal rationale for the changing British economy, and, as taught in one form or another on almost every college campus, it was also inestimably influential in the United States. This was quite understandable, because Marshall's economics harmonized well with the early 20th century. This was an era of industrial consolidation and increased concentration, one that continued, with more emphasis and greater acceleration, the trend toward a more intensive type of economic development that had begun around the middle of the 19th century. It was during this period that the economic trends that had first been discerned in the post-Civil War world were ripening into maturity. The decline in the rate of population growth that had begun with the Civil War continued in the early 20th Century. The railroad network had been completed, the motor truck had appeared on the highways and byways, regional boundaries had taken on a certain artificiality, and the nation had become one great consolidated market area. By the 1920's, large-scale business was a well-recognized and generally-accepted fact of life. Even in agriculture a tendency toward concentration was apparent. Year by year, there were larger and fewer farms, and the farm population was declining not only in relation to the over-all population—as it had always done—but absolutely as well. The drift of population was still toward the cities, but by now the cities themselves were spilling people into the suburbs and by the 'twenties, megopolis was beginning to replace metropolis.

The economy performed well in this era of more intensive development, for it possessed genuinely dynamic factors. The most important
of these dynamic factors was the remarkable increase in productivity
that occurred in the early 20th century, especially during the first few
years of the 1920's. The number of man-hours required to produce a
bushel of wheat, a ton of steel, a model-T Ford, and the other goods
that sustained America's high standard of living declined spectacularly.
It is estimated that man-hour output in manufacturing more than
doubled between 1890 and 1929. Unfortunately, agriculture did not
make the same strides, although its productivity did increase about 30
per cent.

The great gains in productivity had, of course, a most exhilarating
effect on the economy. First of all, they made possible substantial reductions in working hours without a decline in the level of wages and
hence in the standard of living. Indeed, because of a greater man-hour
output, the standard of living continued to rise despite marked increases
in leisure time. It is estimated that between 1890 and 1929, working
hours were cut one-third, but real per-capita income increased by 50
per cent. Although much of this increased income went to people in
the upper-income brackets, almost everyone shared to some extent in
the progress. The wages of the burgeoning urban clerical group rose
sharply, and real wages in manufacturing increased impressively. Thus,
if Americans in the middle and at the bottom of the income ladder
were no better off when compared with those at the top, they were,
nevertheless, considerably better off in absolute terms. All this had
a profound if somewhat unnoticed effect on consumption patterns. In
the so-called "good old days" before the 20th century, the vast bulk of
consumer income was spent for the necessities of life. Little was available for the purchase of frills and frivolities, and this little was mostly
consumed by the very rich, the well-to-do, and the comfortable. Since
there was no mass market for the durable consumer goods and household gadgets that are today considered so indispensable, they either
did not exist or were not very commonly used before World War I. But
all this changed drastically in the 20th century, more especially during
the 'twenties. As productivity continued to rise, more and more people
attained incomes that enabled them to live in middle-class style, and for
the first time there existed a foundation for the mass consumption of
durable goods. But increased income alone was not enough to effect a
transition to new consumption patterns. People had to be persuaded to

spend, and presently businessmen, with new concern for the demand side of the demand-supply equation, added the necessary new marketing techniques that whetted the appetites of the multitudes who were to make up the suddenly-recognized middle-class mass market.

Advertising, previously largely localized, emerged as a national industry. Systematic, aggressive salesmanship replaced the good-natured, haphazard methods of the 19th century "drummer." Installment credit, frowned on by the Calvinistic precepts of 19th-century America, grew from less than $1 billion at the end of World War I to $8 billion by 1929. Aided and abetted by these newly-emphasized techniques, Americans spent an increasing share of the income they obtained from their increased productivity on new consumer durable goods. During the 'twenties, mechanical refrigerators, gas stoves, electric toasters, washing machines, and vacuum cleaners became common household goods. The radio and the movies occupied much of America's new-found leisure and introduced a new levelling and conforming influence. But it was the automobile that really symbolized the new consumption era. In 1913, only one of every fourteen families owned an automobile; by 1925, one out of every two families owned one. With increased demand for consumer durables, the service industries mushroomed. Gasoline stations, garages, restaurants, and roadstands sprang up to service the American automobiles and to feed and refresh their passengers. Repair shops and appliance stores dotted the main streets of the small towns and the off-avenues of the larger cities.

Meantime, in order to sell their goods and deliver them, to repair the gadgets, to keep the growing volume of records and accounts, the expanding service industries required more and more labor.[13] They had little trouble in finding it, for productivity, which had done so much to create the service industries, also offered them a solution to their manpower problems. With increased productivity and smaller increases in population, fewer workers were needed on the farms. It was these displaced farm workers who directly or indirectly provided the labor force needed in the booming service industries. Previously, those who left the farm had gone to the city to run the machines and tend the furnaces in the manufacturing industries. But now that outlet for surplus rural manpower was declining relatively. The great increase in productivity, induced by continuous improvements in techniques,

[13] The service industries employed less than 20 per cent of the labor force in 1870, 25 per cent in 1900, over 35 per cent in 1930, and well over 40 per cent in 1950. See George Stigler, *Trends in Employment in the Service Industries* (Princeton, N.J.: Princeton University Press, 1956), p. 6.

enabled manufacturers to turn out a constantly larger product with the same number of workers. Displaced farmers still came to the city, but now they far more frequently found employment in the service industries rather than in the factories.

On balance, the economic effects of the rapid rise of the consumer industries were most salutary. It was wonderful to have an automobile and to have all the indescribable conveniences of countless labor-saving devices. They were the symbols of a comfortable economic life. But the new importance of consumer durables was not without its disadvantages.

Since some appliances and gadgets lasted indefinitely, the market for them could be quickly saturated. Overproduction was, therefore, a constant menace that could only be averted by intense use of marketing techniques and by constant development of newly-improved products. But, unlike life's absolute necessities, the purchase of an automobile or a refrigerator was a type of discretionary spending, one that could be postponed and, if necessary, postponed indefinitely. Like capital goods, consumer durables were, therefore, cyclically elastic. Their producers went through periods of feast and famine. In prosperity, consumer durables sold magnificently; in recession they were a drug on the market. Hence, as more and more of the consumer's dollars were expended for durable goods, a large portion of total demand became much more quixotic and more difficult to forecast. There no longer existed so solid and substantial a base of consumer spending to act as a bulwark against an economic downturn, because, in the new consumption pattern, the demand for consumer durables dried up very rapidly with a downturn in business, and thereby further depressed the economy.

All this, of course, made the business cycle and economic life in general more complicated than it had been a generation earlier. But in the new century, Americans were remodelling their lives and learning to live with the economic structure that they had built with such extraordinary rapidity. In this remodelling process, the government, especially the Federal government, became a much more important economic institution. Government leaders were no longer so certain of the essential beneficence of the policy of ambivalent *laissez faire* that had prevailed in the late 19th century. A few people went so far as to question such solidly entrenched principles as the balanced budget and regressive taxation, and many more were willing to drop the hands-off policy that had limited the government's economic activities. During the so-called "Progressive Era," therefore, a philosophy of neo-mercantilism and a new nationalism emerged as the dominant political creed. Cautiously following its precepts, the Federal government gradually but greatly expanded both its monetary and fiscal activities.

Specialization Among Economists and the Rise of Institutionalism

The early 20th century did not lack spokesmen to provide a rationale for these new political trends. It was a period of great storm and stress in intellectual circles, and from this ferment, social scientists emerged with a rekindled interest in economic factors. More times than not, this new interest in economic factors expressed sympathy for more government intervention. Thus, two of the most influential books of the period —Van Hise's *Concentration and Control* (1912) and Croly's *The Promise of American Life* (1909)—provided justification for more government intervention, and both deeply impressed political leaders.

Spurred by the vigorous criticism of their fellow social scientists, American economists tried to make their studies more practical. For the majority, this meant greater specialization and greater interest in current controversies, even though many continued to approach these realistic problems within the framework of the neo-classical system of economic theory. Thus Frank Fetter attempted to found an American psychological school; F. W. Taussig wrote his classic studies on the tariff; Irving Fisher, Benjamin Anderson, and E. W. Kemmerer became specialists in money; and, in one way or another, almost every prominent economist lent the weight of his opinion to political controversies.

For a minority of economists, however, this specialization was not enough. These dissenters believed it necessary to break away completely from traditional economics. Pursuing the lines laid down by the German historical school, a group of them, the "institutionalists" as they were called, rejected the concept of universal economic law and attempted to analyze conditions as they were. Little interested in causes and effects, they failed to produce a complete and systematized analysis of the economic system, and, therefore, they did not constitute a "school" of economic theory. Theirs were the voices of dissent, and since they disturbed the easy tenor of the mainstream of economic thought, the pioneers in this movement usually were not very cordially welcomed in academic circles. Yet their influence permeated the whole of economic analysis. Few American economists, in fact, have been more influential than such pioneer institutionalists as John R. Commons (1862–1945), Thorstein Veblen (1857–1929), and Wesley C. Mitchell (1874–1948). Of these three, perhaps Veblen left the most indelible imprint.

A caustic critic with a vitriolic, albeit often abstruse, style, Veblen dismissed all the premises of classical economics as untenable. He believed that, although man's behavior was conditioned by instincts, his actual activities were largely determined by certain customs and traditions to which he had become so habituated that they were imbedded in the social order as "institutions." There was nothing natural, he said, about such institutions as private property, business enterprise, the money economy, or capitalism; they had merely developed to fit the peculiar social and economic climate of a given era. In time, as the climate changed, many institutions lost their usefulness; nevertheless, they remained, because man found it difficult, indeed almost impossible, to slough off any part of his inherited institutional framework.

A belief in institutionalism gave the new-type economist a wide latitude. Since he refused to admit the existence of any universal economic laws, the institutionalist had two courses open to him: he could become a rebel against the existing social order by dismissing some or all current institutions as anachronistic; or he could shrug his shoulders, accept the institutional framework, and then devote himself to an exhaustive description of the economic process taking place within that existing framework. Veblen chose the first of these alternatives; he rebelled against the whole social structure, especially against the economic institutions, many of which he considered to be in constant and bitter conflict with each other. In a series of books,[14] Veblen subjected the existing economic system to a withering, but novel and discerning criticism. To him the United States in the 20th century was not an individualistic or even a capitalistic economy, but a "pecuniary" one, in which money accumulation, conspicuous consumption, and other imbecilic values were the guiding lights. In this environment, there were heroes and villains. The engineers and technicians were heroes because they were industrious and constructive. The financiers and the businessmen, on the other hand, were the villains, since they were predatory and destructive. Veblen believed that there was an unavoidable and irreconcilable conflict between business and technology, because business, in order to maintain profits, was under a compulsion to

14 Especially *The Theory of the Leisure Class* (1899), *The Theory of Business Enterprise* (1904) and *The Engineers and the Price System* (1921).

restrict output and therefore tended to obstruct or neutralize advances in technology. Veblen, therefore, concluded that the institution of business enterprise was destroying man's "instinct for workmanship," and was generating repeated business crises which would eventually destroy the system (which was in any event anachronistic).

Wesley Mitchell best exemplified the second approach of institutionalism. Although he agreed with Veblen's ideas on institutions, Mitchell accepted the institutional framework as it existed, and instead of rebelling against the resulting scheme of things, he devoted his career to an attempt to describe exactly how the economic system really operated. He concentrated on investigating the business cycle, and, after years of painstaking study, mostly through the medium of statistics, he presented a detailed description of the cycle. In his opinion each phase of the cycle (revival, prosperity, panic, and depression) contained within itself the germs of the next phase; but the behavior of the price level and the changing expectations of businessmen were the primary causes for the continuous oscillations in the volume of business activity. Unlike most other business-cycle theorists, Mitchell did not propound any general theory of business fluctuations. Instead, he thought that the constantly changing institutional framework would make it imperative for each generation to formulate its own cycle theory. Thus he followed his predecessor and teacher, Veblen, in imbedding in economic thought the idea that economic analysis can never be more than a transitory explanation of economic reality.

How the Great Depression Influenced Economic Thought

There were of course a great many other economists, professional and amateur, in the first quarter of the 20th century. By the 1920's, however, little new was forthcoming from the professionals, and the amateurs were pretty much in agreement that the most perplexing problems in economic life—those associated with production and with the business cycle—had been largely solved. Big business had solved the first, and the Federal Reserve system had cured the second. All that remained were problems of distribution, and only a few economists, such as the Englishman John A. Hobson, and the American (professor-businessman) team of Foster and Catchings, thought that these problems were difficult and critical.

The impact of the depression put an abrupt end to optimism and complacency by bringing the world of economic ideas face to face with stark reality. As it became shockingly clear that the business cycle, far from being a thing of the past, was more calamitous than ever, academicians as well as laymen became increasingly skeptical regarding orthodox economics. The Pollyanna views of businessmen and their spokesmen, who had wielded such great influence in the 'twenties, fell into disrepute. On the other hand, the social scientists outside the economic discipline—the humanitarian liberals, and the social workers whose strength had ebbed during the 'twenties—now emerged with new prestige, and soon reached the peak of their influence. Under the stresses and strains of economic collapse, old principles and old precepts lost their persuasive power. Day by day, under the pressure of public opinion, the government was compelled to expand its economic activity, and it seemed altogether unreal to continue to talk in terms of *laissez faire*. The orthodox explanation of price making also began to appear a bit dubious, or at least oversimplified. Moreover, more and more people were beginning to believe that the economic system could not be explained as the result of the activities of rational, economic beings. It seemed that the institutionalists were right in thinking that the actions of people reflected group habits, customs, and traditions. How groups acted appeared to be more important than how a hypothetical individual might act. Hence it seemed evident that the working of the economy would have to be studied in an aggregate sense, which is to say descriptively, analytically, and statistically, in terms of occupational breakdowns, income brackets, and other meaningful categories. The useful approach needed to be macroscopic rather than microscopic, aggregative rather than atomistic.

The various attempts made during the depression to bring economics more in harmony with the real world followed three major lines: a vast increase in the influence of institutionalism; the formulation of a theory of monopolistic competition; and the emergence of "Keynesian economics." These new developments so infiltrated economic thinking that, by the outbreak of World War II, orthodox economics had become almost entirely outmoded. To a very large extent, what had been the underworld of economic theory in the 'twenties represented by the 'forties the accepted doctrine of the majority of economists.

To many economists, especially to specialists, institutionalism seemed to be as close to reality as economics could get. Nevertheless, during the depression, just as in its early beginnings, institutionalism split down into various shadings; and the only area of agreement seemed to be a lack of faith in the existence of any organic body of economic

law. Some members of the group, following Mitchell's example, devoted themselves to detailed, factual research, attempting to show as
objectively as possible what had happened and what was actually taking
place in the economy. To this group, economic theory was less important than statistics and accounting. Other institutionalists, however, treated with equal skepticism both the existence of economic law
and the expediency of the Mitchell approach. This group became pragmatic planners. Starting with the existing situation and holding the
abstractions of theory and the lessons of empiricism in contempt, they
placed their faith in governmental intervention. It was their belief
that great things could be done through legislation, by government
directives, or as a result of plans of one kind or other. They judged the
value of any given proposal, not on the basis of deductive reasoning, but
in terms of its presumed pragmatic benefits. If it worked, it was good;
if it did not work, it was bad. To this group of pragmatists, many of
whom guided the New Deal in its early days, economics was concerned
with public policy, and its characteristics were expediency and opportunism. The National Industrial Recovery Act, the Agricultural Adjustment Act, and a body of new labor legislation represented some of
the end products that emanated from these institutionalists, and demonstrated their faith in planning and socio-economic legislation.

Meanwhile, neo-classical price theory, long recognized as one of the
weakest parts of economic theory, was both elaborated and critically
revised during the 'thirties by the formulation of a theory of "monopolistic competition" by Edward Chamberlin in the United States, and
by a theory of "imperfect competition" by Joan Robinson in England.
Recognizing the existence of gigantic industrial firms that controlled
a large share of production, and seeing that tremendous amounts of
advertising were capable of giving similar products identities of their
own, Chamberlin concluded that there really existed a market situation
that was neither pure competition nor monopoly but a hybrid of the
two. He called this third type "monopolistic competition," and he considered it much more prevalent than either pure competition or monopoly. Under monopolistic competition, prices could not be explained
in terms of over-all supply and demand, because every firm engaging in
this type of competition established its prices on the basis of the cost of
and the demand for its individualized product, rather than on the basis
of the supply and demand schedules for the industry as a whole. The
price of a Ford automobile, for example, would be set on the basis of its
own cost and in relation to the demand for Fords, not on the basis of

demand and supply for automobiles in the aggregate. Thus, according to the theory of monopolistic competition, most industrial prices were "administered prices"; that is, they were determined by a few individuals, rather than by many. It followed, therefore, that monopolistic competition theory provided an additional rationale for government economic intervention, because, if prices could be set by individual decision, rather than by the market mechanism of supply and demand, why could they not be fixed by government decree and why, under certain circumstances, would not the intervention of government be necessary in order to protect consumers?

Institutionalism and monopolistic competition theory dealt with limited aspects of the economic system, and, although they were important, they were probably less influential in their repercussion on economic thought than the third development of the depression period: the so-called "Keynesian Revolution." Like Ricardo and Marshall, the British economist John Maynard Keynes enunciated a "general theory," building partly on the work of his predecessors. But there the similarity ceased. Ricardo and Marshall were the theorists of a rational, economic world. They developed their systems during eras of relatively buoyant economic growth, and, even though they tended to be basically pessimistic, they nevertheless looked forward to a constantly expanding economy. Keynes, in contrast, was the theorist of the depression era. He and many of his predecessors who had held similar ideas were relatively unknown and uninfluential during the prosperous 'twenties, but with the depression, Keynes moved out of the underworld of economic theory, and his reputation grew and his influence rapidly widened.

Classical economics had assumed a condition of full employment, and had argued that any departure from that enviable state was a temporary matter which would be quickly rectified. Keynes, on the other hand, believed that the western world had reached a state of "economic maturity," a condition of "secular stagnation" in which unemployment had become chronic. His theory, therefore, concentrated on the problem of alleviating unemployment and, since the enterprise system was not solving the problem, Keynes came to be greatly concerned with governmental economic policy. Ricardo and Marshall had emphasized costs. They had thought in terms of individual decisions, and, for this reason, they paid more attention to economic margins than to economic aggregates or averages. In decided contrast, Keynes emphasized aggregate demand and total spending rather than costs. He was a macro-economist, thinking more in terms of the whole economy than in terms of individual actions, and emphasizing aggregates more than margins.[15]

At the risk of considerable oversimplification, it may be said that Keynes believed that, as an economy advances, saving increases. At the same time, profits decline because of the falling "marginal efficiency of capital." There is, consequently, in advanced economies a tendency for investment spending to lag behind saving. This reduces the total volume of spending, diminishes effective demand, and creates unemployment. As a solution, the Keynesian analysis proposed that the government should try to encourage investment by holding down the interest rate. But, if the private economy did not respond to this inducement and maintain a sufficiently high level of investment spending, the government should fill the gap by deficit spending.

Because it was at once a body of theory and a recipe for economic policy, Keynesian economics quickly acquired two different meanings. Some economists considered it an excellent tool of analysis, and went at the business of constructing elaborate mathematical models to explain what would occur or what had already occurred in the economy. Other economists, especially some of the younger Americans, were unduly impressed by Keynes' theory of secular stagnation. Pointing to the declining rate of population growth, the end of the frontier, and the tendency of corporate enterprise to finance itself through retained earnings, they concluded that the United States had arrived at a state of economic maturity, and that further progress could be accomplished only by a heavy rate of government spending. Thus, regardless of which Keynesian variant was followed, the theory led logically to the building of models to serve as guides for the formulation of public policy.

The American Economy in the 1950's

The changes that occurred in American economic life after World War II made a shambles of the secular stagnation thesis.[16] Instead of following a downward drift toward the prewar doldrums, the post-World War II years reinstituted trends that in many ways reproduced

[15] Keynes did, of course, use marginal concepts such as the marginal propensity to consume and the marginal efficiency of capital; but national income, total spending, and total saving were at the heart of the Keynesian system. For a compact summary of Keynes' theories, see Dudley Dillard, *The Economics of John Maynard Keynes* (Englewood Cliffs, N.J.: Prentice-Hall, Inc., 1948).

[16] But this is not necessarily a premanent condition. "Secular stagnation" may be badly damaged, but it is not dead.

the pattern of the 'twenties. Instead of contracting, the economy progressed buoyantly. Productivity increased at the same unusual rate that had prevailed in the 'twenties, so that by the middle 'fifties, output per man hour was more than half again as much as 1929. As a result, real, per capita, disposable income by 1956 was 70 per cent higher than in 1929, more than twice as much as at the bottom of the depression, and 70 per cent higher than in 1935.

But although strikingly similar, there were at least six distinct differences between the 'fifties and the 'twenties. Foremost of these was the fact that for the first time in almost a century, the rate of population growth increased rather than decreased. In an entirely unexpected reversal of a long-standing social pattern, Americans began to use some of their gains from rising productivity to raise larger families instead of to shorten working hours. In the 'fifties, in short, they chose to have more children rather than more leisure. Although the resulting rate of population growth diluted the individual's share of aggregate income, it led to a significant increase in actual and potential aggregate demand. Population growth was, therefore, probably the most important single factor in the reblossoming of optimism that characterized the 'fifties.

A second important difference was that, in the 'fifties, gains in income were distributed much more evenly than they had been in the 'twenties. During and after World War II, the lowest income groups made the greatest gains in income. Thus, between 1935 and the 1950's, the income of those in the bottom tenth of the income ladder rose by about 80 per cent, while the top 5 per cent of income recipients experienced a less than 20 per cent increase. On the basis of the standard used in 1935, 80 per cent of American families could be regarded as being in the middle class in the 1950's. This, of course, meant a broader participation in a higher standard of living. By the 'fifties, so-called "discretionary demand" laid claim to over half of the incomes of American families. Consumer durable goods constituted almost 40 per cent of the nation's total reproducible wealth and many of these commodities, such as television sets, air-conditioning units, and automatic washers, had not been in use before the war. By 1957, about 60 per cent of American families owned their own homes, as contrasted with 41 per cent in 1940. Moreover, a college education was no longer a privilege reserved for the "rich and well-born." By 1957, one out of every three young people of college age was in college, compared with one out of twelve in 1930 and with one out of twenty-five in 1900. Regardless of the optimism generated by this progress the millenium had not yet been reached. As in the 'twenties, farmers as a total group did not share in the greater income as fully as did the urban classes. Even among city dwellers, moreover, there were many who had not done at all well, since it was estimated that at least one-quarter of city workers still did not earn enough to support a modestly satisfactory standard of living.

A third important difference was the general acceptance of a larger economic role for government. Depression-induced legislation—social security, unemployment insurance, and labor legislation—had met with wide public acclaim, and was now firmly imbedded in the American system. Even the philosophy of compensatory fiscal policy, once bitterly assailed, had become respectable. The government was admittedly not using its fiscal tools in the all-out way desired or recommended by the exponents of compensatory fiscal policy, but most political leaders accepted the idea that the government not only could but should use its powers over expenditures, revenues, and the public debt to alleviate recessions and to prevent inflationary booms. A more mixed economy, one which combined private enterprise and a sizable degree of government intervention, had, therefore, become part of the American way of life. Even the business groups who had been its strongest opponents accepted the new concept. Thus, in the 1950's, organizations such as the Committee for Economic Development were offering suggestions on how government intervention could be most efficient.

The fourth major difference between the 'twenties and the 'fifties was the change that had occurred in business enterprise. By the middle 'fifties, the affairs of America's largest firms were being conducted not by owner-managers, but by hired, professional managers. Relying heavily on sophisticated and presumably expert advisers from ancillary institutions and on their own specialized experts, they used complicated staff and line management, together with advanced techniques in cost accounting, advertising, salesmanship, public relations, and the other branches of business administration to maintain and build their business organizations. It was no longer so true, if it had ever been, that the businessman's *sine qua non* was the maximization of profits. By the middle of the 20th century, the maintenance of the organization had become fully as important, and preserving an organization compelled business leaders to pay more attention to all the people affected by an enterprise: workers, owners, customers, and the government.

A fifth significant change had occurred in the status and composition of American labor unions. There was a certain innocuousness about the labor unions of the 'twenties that no longer existed in the 'fifties. By the middle of the century, labor unions were powerful instruments, and much the same changes in outlook and tactics that had taken place among business entrepreneurs were now taking place among labor-union leaders. Sweet reasonableness and intuition still guided some, but many others resembled the so-called "robber barons" of 19th century business. Ruthless, shrewd, and well-informed, they were among the power elite of 20th-century America. So also were the relatively fewer sophisticated labor leaders who, with a fair knowledge of the whole economic system, were assuming a striking resemblance to the sophisticated professional business managers. But sophisticated or not, the labor unions of the 1950's succeeded in maintaining or increasing labor's share of the national income. In this they were, of course, greatly assisted by an extraordinarily heavy demand for labor. It was an era of full employment, one in which the government was committed to maintaining full employment, and one in which business was embarking on a most ambitious program of capital expenditures. Thus, in the 'fifties, aggregate demand was maintained at an extremely high level through the combined efforts of labor, government and business.

The transformation in business enterprise and labor unionism was symptomatic of a sixth important difference between the 'twenties and the 'fifties. In the course of a single generation, Americans had become much more concerned with "security" than they had ever been in the past. To be sure, there was a great deal of surface optimism in the post-World War II period, but the lessons of the great depression of the 1930's were not easy to forget. Fewer people nursed the illusion that they could become magnificently wealthy. Most Americans, young and old, reconciled themselves to a life of genteel poverty or suburban comfort. All this was well illustrated in the changes that had occurred in the American saving pattern. If only cash and other liquid assets were included in one's definition of savings, then Americans were saving at a slower rate than previously. But if one defines saving to include consumer durable goods, the rate of saving was as high as it had ever been. There had, moreover, been a great transformation in the types of saving. Pensions and social security, mortgage repayments and life insurance were much more important. Cash and securities were less important. The propensity to save had become much more rigid, less voluntary, and more contractual.

Major Trends in Economic Thought at Mid-Century

As a result of the forces that have played upon it, contemporary American economic thought is essentially eclectic. Like the elaborate creation of a master confectioner, it contains innumerable ingredients, but the flavor of the last-added ingredient is usually dominant, and the new creation bears little resemblance to any of its original elements. On the whole, economic theory today is strikingly similar to the pattern of thought that emerged at the end of the great depression in the late 1930's. To be sure, the prosperity experienced after World War II created some differences. What is usually called "conservatism" has had something of a renaissance from the low point that it reached during the depression, while, oppositely, "liberalism" has retreated to some extent. The businessman has regained some of the prestige he lost during the great economic debacle, and there is more skepticism about the virtues of economic planning than there was in the 1930's. Then too, the obsession with deflation that naturally characterized the gloomy 'thirties has been replaced in the ebullient 'fifties by worry about inflation. The belief that the economy was suffering from secular stagnation has given way to a revived belief that the business cycle has been conquered, and that the only economic difficulties we shall experience will be temporary, small recessions interrupting continued economic progress. But aside from these psychological and philosophical differences, the economic mixture is much as before. It still contains some elements of classical economics. Indeed, American economic thought has at long last accepted the international point of view of the classicists. Mindful of the important part that it must play in the world economy, the nation has abandoned its early provincial view of economics and adopted a more cosmopolitan attitude.

Marshallian neo-classical theory is still used to explain price making under conditions of pure competition, but most prices are explained by monopolistic-competition theory, although the original statement of that theory has been much qualified and elaborated. The Austrian school continues to exert an influence, since marginal analysis still occupies a very important niche in price theory and in the theory of wages. Yet the whole body of American economic thought is heavily permeated with institutionalism, which provides the normal approach to economic problems, such as those involving agriculture, labor, or monopoly, where great stress is placed on the importance of legislation. Finally,

Keynesian theory, although still new enough to generate controversy, has influenced almost all writers; consequently, increased emphasis is placed on the importance of analyzing the national income and relating the operation of the entire economy to public policy.

Even though each major school of economic thought continues to exert some influence on American economic thinking, it seems clear that it is really the representatives of the economic underworld of a generation ago, the institutionalists and the Keynesians, who are now dominant. Basically, this is because *laissez faire* has faded farther and farther into the limbo of history, and has been replaced by a belief that economic stability and growth call for an enlarging sphere of governmental activity. Once again, therefore, we find that useful economic theory must be adjusted to the economic realities it attempts to explain. In a society as dynamic as the United States, economic thought must keep abreast of this process of change. If it fails to do so, it will not be helpful to those who are trying to understand how the economic system works at present; nor will it influence the destinies of the American people in the future, when, unquestionably, our social, economic, and political responsibilities will be even greater than they are now.

Index

A

Abegglen, James C., 246*n.*
Absentee landlordism, 175
Act of Settlement of 1662, 105
Addams, Jane, 318
Adler, John H., 387*n.*
Adscriptus glebae, 26
Advertising, national, 436
Advertising men, 266
Africa, and slave trade, 128, 149
 trade with, 111, 149
African Company, 56
Agrarianism, 38, 310, 419*n.*, 421
Agricultural Adjustment Act, 360, 442
Agricultural colleges, 219, 377–378
Agricultural experiment stations, 378
Agricultural exports, 348–349
Agricultural machinery, 353
 development of, 213–215
 farmer and, 224–225
Agricultural market towns, industries in, 143–144
Agricultural products and production, 352–353
 and domestic market, 160
 and exports, 348, 354–355
 increase in, 352–353
 in wartime, 392
 widening market for, 43–49
Agricultural societies, 344
Agricultural village communities, in 18th century England, 41, 45

late-medieval, 21–28
 towns and, 32–34
Agricultural workers, competition for, 46
 decrease in, 322, 410–411, 436
 productivity of, 223
 wages of, 44–45, 109
Agriculture:
 American, 124, 127*n.*, 138–141, 157, 202, 375, 434
  commercialization of, 193, 347–348, 417
  diversification of, 175
  early, 343–345, 414
  government assistance to, 359–361, 381
  in late 19th century, 349
  mechanization of, 221, 224–225, 335
  overproduction in, 352–353, 423
  per capita output in, 163–164
  raising capital for, 356–357
  southern, before Civil War, 345–347
  specialization in, 139–140, 193, 348
  technology and, 212–214, 361
 capitalistic, 73
 in England, 41–46, 68–70, 75, 110
 and Industrial Revolution, 76
 medieval, 41
 modern, 73, 354
 scientific, 73–75, 366*n.*, 381
Alexandria, Virginia, 379
Altruism, 100
Aluminum Corporation of America (ALCOA), 373
Amalgamated Association of Iron and Steel Workers, 320, 326

450

America, British imports from, 108 (*See also* United States)
American Anti-boycott Association, 326
American Brass Association, 243
American character, 234
    technological progress and, 199–202, 212
American culture, 416
    immigrants and, 123
American Economic Association, 430–431
American economy, 140
    automobile industry and, 232–233
    developmental policy for, 190–192
    land as factor in, 335–336
    in 19th century, 163–164
    railways and, 178–180
    religious groups and, 134
    stabilizing of, 383–388
    transformation of, 192–194
        in early 19th century, 416–417
        in early 20th century, 434–438
        in last half of 19th century, 421–425
        in the 1950's, 444–447
    wars and, 391–412
American Farm Bureau Federation, 359
American Federation of Labor (A.F. of L.), 325–327, 330–331, 333
    formation of, 319–321
American frontier, end of, 342, 422
    influence of, 341–343
American Iron Association, 243
American Medical Association, 38
"American System," 159, 205, 208–209, 211–212, 228
American Tobacco Company, 372
Amsterdam, 63, 166
Anderson, Benjamin, 438
Andrews, Clark and Co., 253
Annapolis, 129
Antibiotic drugs, 404
Anti-Corn Law League, 113
Anti-slavery movement, 129
Anti-trust legislation, 372
Anti-union organizations, 326
Antwerp, 63, 166
Appleton, Nathan, 238
Apprentices, 30–31
    as indentured servants, 122
    pauper children as, 60
Apprenticeship, 102–105
    in America, 142–143
    decline of, 39
    length of, 31n.
Archbold, Mr., 256–257
Aristocracy, merchant, 236
Aristotle, 8
Arkwright, Richard, 81, 93, 103–104
Arkwright's "water frame," 81, 204
Arms and armaments, 205–211, 399–400 (*See also* Munitions)
Army engineers, 188–189
Articles of Confederation, 156n.
Artisans, 29–30, 58, 104
    in America, 121, 142
Ashley, Percy, 158n.
Ashley, Sir William, 55n.
Associated Banks of New York, 395
Atlantic seaboard, settlement of, 117–118
Atomic bomb, 404
Austrians, 127n., 416, 429, 448
Automobile industry, and the economy, 232–233
    evolution of, 228
    literature on, 227n.
    mass production in, 228, 230–231
    war and, 404
Automobiles, and economic transformation, 227–228, 442–443
    first, 211, 228

B

Bacon, Roger, 227
Bailyn, Bernard, 135n., 147n., 150n.
Baines, Edward, Jr., 78n.
Bakewell, Robert, 74
Baltimore, 129, 150, 307
Baltimore, Lord, 119n., 132
Baltimore & Ohio Railroad, cost of, 240
Bank checks, use of, 64–65
Bank credit, 60–66, 340
Bank deposits, demand, 275
    time, 275
    wars and, 394–395
Bank of England, establishment of, 66
    government loans by, 109
Bank failures, 279–280, 282
Bank notes, 109, 275, 280
    of commercial banks, 279
    of national banks, 289
    of state banks, 281, 287, 395
    use of, 64–65, 283
Bank reserves, 395–396
Bankers, 63
Banking Act of 1933, 294
Banking systems, 275
    national, 289–291, 395
Banks and banking, 64–65, 183, 240, 272, 275, 336, 364
    business domination by, 264
    charters and, 187
    commercial (*see* Commercial banks)
    "free," 283
    investment (*see* Investment banking)
    regulation of, 283–284, 370
    savings (*see* Savings banks)
    state (*see* State banks)
Bargaining by wage earners, 102n. (*See also* Collective bargaining)
Baring Brothers, 285
Barnes, Donald G., 45n.
Barter, 238, 274, 277
Baruch, Bernard M., 400n.
Bastiat, 416, 425
Baxter, W. T., 236n.–237n.
Bedford Stone Case, 325
Beecher, the Rev. Henry Ward, quoted, 316
Beggars, 105
Belgium 87n.
    population density of, 336n.
Benedict, Murray R., 358n.
Benefit Clubs, 110
Bentham, Jeremy, 107, 429
Berkeley, Bishop, 99
Berkeley, Governor, 128
Bessemer, Sir Henry, 247
Bessemer process, 215–216, 247
Bethlehem, Pennsylvania, 134
Biddle, Nicholas, 281
Bidwell, P. W., 213n., 343n.
Big business, 282, 422
    in manufacturing, 238–239
    opposition to, 371
    profits of, 260n.
Bill of Enclosure, 71
Bills of exchange, 284
Bimetallism, 277, 288, 358
Birth rate, 193, 201, 321, 414
    rural, 350
    war and, 409, 412
Black, John D., 351
Black Death, 21, 25–26, 46
Black lists, 314, 326–327
Blackwell Hall, 36–37, 58n., 60
Blanchard, 210
Bland-Allison Act, 288, 291
Blanqui, Jerome, 76n.
Blast furnaces, 215
Body of Liberties, 130

Boer War, 272
Bonds, 167, 292
  government (see Government bonds)
  public-improvement, 171
Booms, 343 (See also Inflation)
  of 1857, 286
Boon-day work, 26, 29
Bordars, 22
Boston, 130, 140n., 142, 147, 150 286, 311
Boston Associates, 239
Boston Manufacturing Company, 239
Bostwick, J. A., 255
Boulder Dam, 381
Boulton, Matthew, 89, 91–92
Bourne, Daniel, 83n.
Boycotts, 325
Brabant, 36
Bracton's rule, 34n.
Bradford, Governor, 133n.–134
Bradstreet's Commercial Agency, 284
Bramah, 208
Bridenbaugh, Carl, 202n.
Bridge, James Howard, 246n
British West Indies, 141
Brokerage firms, 150
Brooks, Van Wyck, quoted, 310
Brown, Alexander, and Son, 285
Brown, Joseph R., 210
Brown, Moses, 204
Bruce, Philip A., 122n., 129n.
Bryan, William Jennings, 288
Buck, N. S., 285n.
Bureaucracy, 190, 264
Burgess, W. Randolph, 294n.
Burnett, Edmund C., 131n.
Business, big (See also Big business; Business
      enterprises; Industry):
  complexity of, 262
  expansion of, 249
  government assistance to, 191
  government regulation of, 365–373, 426, 446
  small, 238, 414
Business conduct, rules of, 33, 54, 135
Business cycles, 307, 321, 437, 440–441
Business enterprises, evolution of, 234–237
  government-operated, 382
  increased size of, 97
  technology and, 225–226
  types of, 49–50, 141–151
Business freedom, 93–95
"Business game," success in, 234–236
Business morality, medieval, 31–32
Business policies of industrialists, 241–242
Business proprietorship, 66
  sole (see Sole proprietorship)
Businessmen, 84n., 97, 101–102
  American, 201, 204, 312, 362, 446
    decision making by, 235
    "heroic," 236 245–267, 422
    tariffs and, 157–160
    typical, 246
    unions and, 309, 325–327
  British, 420
  distrust of, 102
  European, 120, 235
  evolution of, 49, 83–84
  technology and, 93
Byrd, William, 129

C

Cadillac car, 229
Calico Act, 77
  repeal of, 78
California, 140, 343
Call loans, 286
Calvert, Sir George, 132
Cambridgeshire, England, 22–25, 34
Canada, 162n., 177, 273

Canals, 190n., 194, 382, 417
  cost of, 240
  financing of, 167–168, 170, 186, 336
  land grants for, 172–173
Cantillon, Richard, 99
Capital:
  accumulation of, 414, 423
  agricultural 42, 140, 164–165, 356–357
  British, 167–173, 179
  circulating, 62
  definition of, 12
  economic progress and, 16
  export of, 273, 285
  flow of to United States, 170–173
  of joint-stock companies, 55–57
  labor and, 100
  mobility of, 271
  production and, 100
  risking of, 147
  for settlement, 118–120
  shortage of, 165, 268
  social (see Social capital)
  sources of, 62, 101
  transfer of, 162, 166–173, 192
Capital formation, 152–153, 188, 194
  importance of, 164–165
Capital goods, 13, 274
  import of, 147
  scarcity of, 152, 165
Capital investment, 70
  unimpaired, 57
Capital movements, international, 166–167
  labor migration and, 174–175
Capitalism, American, 200, 266–267
  "welfare," 333
  British, 166
    emergence of, 38–67
    spirit of, 61–62
    survival power of, 61
  modern, criticism of, 169
Capitalistic society, 387
Capitalistic theory, formation of, 95–114
Carey, Henry C., 426–427
Carey, Matthew, 160, 427
Carey, Robert L., 421n.
Caribbean, foreign trade and, 76
Carlyle, Thomas, quoted, 302n.
Carnegie, Andrew, 245–252
  quoted, 153n.
Carolinas, the, 118, 128, 132, 141 (See also
      North and South Carolina)
Cartels, 369, 372
Cartwright, Edmund, 84
Cash, need for, 97 (See also Money)
Cash crops, 119, 138
Cast iron, 89
Catholic Church, 64
Catternall, Ralph C. H., 281n.
Cattle, 348
  scientific breeding of, 74
Cattle industry, beginnings of, 138n.
Cellophane case, 373
Census, first American, 137n.
Central banking, 280–283
Chamberlin, Edward, 442
Change, economic progress and, 16–18
Channing, Edward, 122n., 125n., 132n.
Charles II, 65, 126
Charleston, South Carolina, 140n., 142, 150
Charters, bank, 187
  corporation, 240
Check payments, convenience of, 65
Checking accounts, 275, 290, 292, 394
Chemicals, 401
Chemistry, in agriculture, 75
  inventions and, 89
Chevage, 73
Child labor, 45, 47, 59–60, 105, 321, 367–368
Chinese immigrants, 368

Church, the, economic life and, 21, 28, 33, 54, 64, 96, 133, 135
Cities, 382
   railways and growth of, 182
Citizens' Industrial Association, 326
Civil War, 127, 272, 311, 364, 374, 402–403, 405
   and American economy, 391–392
   banking during, 289
   costs of, 392, 394
   income distribution and, 396–397, 423
   industry during, 398–400
   manpower during, 409, 411
   prices after, 395
Clark, John Bates, 431–433
Clark, Payne and Company, 255
Clark, Thomas D., 151n.
Classes, social, late-medieval, 22, 33 (See also Merchant class; Middle class)
Clay, Henry, 159–160
Clayton Act, 372
Clock making, 143
Closed shop, 308, 326, 332
Cloth, export of, 44, 53
   marketing of, 79
Cloth industry, 36–37, 79–80
Clothiers, 43–44, 50, 58, 63
   and putting-out system, 59–61
Coal production, 399, 401, 406
Coal strike of 1874, 316
Cobden, Richard, 113
Cochran, Thomas C., 235n., 263n.
Coinage system, 277
Cold War, 366, 393n.
Cole, Arthur H., 262–263n.
Collective bargaining, 321, 326, 332, 368–369
Collective ownership, 134
Colleges, agricultural, 377–378
   land-grant, 338, 378
   subsidies for, 219, 341, 378
Colonial Period, economic institutions in, 117–151
   heritage from, 151–153
Colonization, American (see Colonial Period)
   mercantile operations and, 52
Colt, Samuel, 209
Combination Act of 1800, 104, 109, 114
Commenda, 54–55
Commerce, in 18th century England, 47–48
   expansion of, 69–70 (See also Exports; Foreign trade)
Commercial banks and banking, 201, 275
   American, 292, 382, 394–395
   assets of, 292n.
   early, 279–280
   in 20th century, 296–297
   beginnings of, 63–66
   influence of, 66–67
Commercial credit, 63, 169n., 284
Commercial entreprises (see Business enterprises)
Commission men, 149–150
Committee for Economic Development, 446
Committee for Industrial Organization, 331
Commodities, 145
Commodity Credit Corporation, 361
Commons, John R., 439
   quoted, 308
Commonwealth, the, public finance during, 65
Communal experiments, settlements as, 118, 134
Communist countries, 9n. (See also Soviet Russia)
Community, 14–15
   economy of, 15n.
Community activities, participation in, 135
Companies, British, 49–50
   joint-stock, 50, 54–57
   livery, 50–51
   regulated, formation of, 51–53

Competition, 34, 102, 104–105, 123
   agricultural, 335, 355
   cut-throat, 159
   foreign, 97, 143, 156–158, 191
   free, 432
   and Industrial Revolution, 76
   for labor, 122, 131, 367–368
   labor regulation and, 366–367, 369–373, 430
   price (see Price competition)
   theories of, 442
Confederate Army, 409
Congress of Industrial Organization (C.I.O.), 331, 333
Connecticut, 145, 149, 378
Conservation, of natural resources, 339, 380–381
   soil, 344
Constitution Convention, 190
Consumer goods, 13, 18, 437
   changes in, 48
   import of, 147, 170
Consumer relations, 242
Consumption, 271, 274
   mass, 238, 435
   war and, 399
Contract laborers, 177
Contracts, 137
Cooley, Charles, 429
Coolidge, Calvin, 359–360
   quoted, 234
Cooperatives, 310, 359
Copper, 401
Corn, English meaning of, 43n.
   hybrid seed, 353
Corn Law of 1815, 110–112
Corn Laws, 45, 159
   abolishing of, 112–113
   relaxation of, 111
Corporate finance, 251
Corporate property, 54
Corporate ventures, settlement and, 118
Corporation charters, 240
Corporation taxes, 384
Corporations, 39, 66, 239–240
   modern, 55, 57
   earnings of, 266, 270, 300
   land grants to, 338
   problem of, 261–267
Corruption in headright system, 125
Cort, Henry, 88–89
Cost of living, 109, 310
   tariffs and, 375
   war and, 395n.
Cost reduction, technology and, 93
Costs, value and, 419
Cotters, 22, 26, 41, 45, 72
Cotton, 171
   export of, 159, 348
   Oriental, 78
   raising of, 128, 140, 146, 346–348, 417
   raw, 78n., 170, 399
Cotton brokerage firms, 150
Cotton cloth, duties on, 159
Cotton gin, 141, 146, 206
Cotton industry, 77–78, 161n., 399
   invention and, 78–85
Council of National Defense, 407
Courts, manorial, 27
Couzzens, James, 230n.
Craft gilds, 29–32, 38–39, 48–49, 61, 97
   amalgamation of, 49.–50
   in America, 142
   livery companies and, 50–51
Crafts, urban, in America, 142–143
Craftsmen, 30–32, 50
   in America, 142–143
Cranage, Thomas and George, 88

Credit, 285
  bank, 60–66, 340
  commercial, 63
  farm, 357
  in medieval times, 35
Credit agencies, 284
Creditors, government, 65
Criminal law, British, 107
Criminals as emigrants, 119, 122
Crompton, Samuel, 85
Crompton's spinning mule, 78n., 85
Cromwell, Oliver, 65, 126
Crop rotation, 42, 74
Crops, cash, 119, 138
  diversification of, 138
  in 18th century England, 42–43
  limited, 139–140
  marketing of, 138
  in the South, 128
Croton reservoir, 382
Crowland Abbey, 22, 24
Cugnot, Joseph, 227
Culture, American, 123, 416
  economic system and, 11–12, 17–18
  medieval, 48
Currency inflation, 279, 387
Curtler, W. H. R., 42n.
Customs duties (see Duties)

D

Dale, David, 107
Dale, E. E., 138n.
Dams, 381
Daniels, G. W., 82n.
Darby, Abraham, 88
Davis, J. S., 240n.
Davis, Margaret Gay, 46n.
Davy, Humphrey, 75
Death rate, 201, 412, 414
Debtors, emigration of, 120, 126–127
Decision making, businessmen and, 235, 241, 262
Declaration of Independence, 131, 155
Deere, John, 214
Delaware, 126
Delaware and Hudson Canal Company, 263
Demand, 95, 429, 447
  discretionary, 445
  income and, 18
  supply and, 11–12, 358, 360
Democratic societies, supply and demand in, 11–12
Denmark, 14, 176
Dennison, 209
Depositors, protection of, 290
Depressions, 243, 249, 293, 307, 340–343, 349, 379, 384, 399–400, 415
  of 1819, 341, 417
  of 1837, 272, 278, 367
  of 1857–61, 424
  of 1869, 315
  of 1873–78, 424
  of 1893–97, 424
  of the 1930's, 258, 269, 273, 294, 296, 298, 320, 357, 365, 372, 383, 402
    and economic thought, 440–444
    and the unions, 327–329
Deyrup, Felicia, 205n., 211n.
Dillard, Dudley, 444n.
Dingley Tariff, 375
Discovery, mercantile operations and, 52
Distilleries, 144, 146
Distribution, problems of, 440
Dividends, 243, 266
Dodd, Samuel C. T., 243
Domesday survey of 1086, 22
Dorfman, Joseph, 418n.

Douglas, Paul, 318, 324
Drake, 63
Drapers, 61
Drovers, 150
Dulles, Foster Rhea, 316n.
DuPont Company, 262
Dupont de Nemours, 419n.
Duties, 161
  ad valorem, 158
  customs, 157, 341, 384–385 396
  remission of, 188
  specific, 158–159
  tonnage, 377

E

Earnings, corporation, 266, 270, 300
  manufacturing, 1929–1957, table, 328
East, the, tariffs and, 374 (See also New England)
East India Company, 56, 76–77
Eastland Company, 52
ECA, 273
Economic development, in America, 161 (See also American economy)
  Europe and, 5–6
  exogenous factors in, 161–163
  government participation in, 186–190
  importance of studying, 3–5
  internal developments and, 186
  culture and, 11–12
  and economic transformation, 16–18
  in Europe, 5–6
  government and, 11–12
  meaning of, 162–163
Economic institutions, changes in, 39–40
  modern, 39
Economic laws, 429
Economic liberty, 103
Economic life, rural, in 18th century England, 40–47
Economic literature, public opinion and, 99
Economic planning, war and, 400–401, 406–409
Economic policies, national, and market forces, 194–196
  need for, 154–156
Economic progress, business organizations and, 68
  definition of, 14
  measuring capacity of, 14–15
  three aspects of, 16
Economic systems, American, complexity of, 18–19
  history of, 19
  late-medieval, 20–37
Economic theory, medieval, 96–97
  modern (see Economic thought)
Economic thought, 414
  American, 418–419, 426–429
    depression of the 1930's and, 440–444
    at mid-century, 448–449
  Napoleonic Wars and, 109–111
  in 17th century, 97
Economic transformation, 16–18
  automobiles and, 227–233
Economics, classical, 420, 426, 428–432, 439, 443
  Keynesian, 441
Economists, amateur, 418, 427
  American, 426–428, 438, 440
    and New Deal, 442
  Austrian, 416, 429, 448
  British, 440
  European, 431
  German, 416, 429, 438
  professional, 415, 426
  specialization among, 438–440

Economy, American (see American economy)
British, 434
changes in, 413
and community, 14–15
European, 354
"Economy of abundance," 323
Edelman, Edward, 237n.
Education, agricultural, 219, 341, 377–378 (See also Colleges; Schools)
encouragement of, 379
increase in, 322, 445
inventive process and, 218–220
state aid for, 380
Edward VI, 70
Edward III, 36
Efficiency, productive, 69
Eisenhower administration, 376, 387n.
Electric motors, 218
Electric power, 217–218, 224
Electronics, 404
Ely, Richard T., 431, 433
Emancipation Proclamation, 141
Emigrants, recruiting of, 119–126 (See also Immigrants)
Emigration, 155 (See also Immigration)
European public policy and, 175–176
wages and, 47
Eminent domain, right of, 189
Employer organizations, 314, 326
Employers, bargaining with, 102n. (See also Collective bargaining; Management)
union opposition from, 305, 325–327
Employment, 18
compulsory, 105
factory, 113, 348
under manorial system, 25
railway building and, 182–184
Enclosure movement, 70
Energy (see Power)
Engineering, 218
Engineering schools, 219
England, 424 (See also Great Britain)
age of invention in, 78
agriculture in, 213
economic life in, history of, 20–37, 41–67
economic progress in, 68
economic theory in, 99
first census in, 22
iron and steel in, 87–90
population of, in 1801, 70n.
before 1700, 42, 46–47
private ownership of land in, 136
technology in, 68–69, 215
Engrossing, 34
Entrepreneurs, 84 (See also Businessmen)
customers and, 101
government as, 187, 403, 408, 441, 446
Epstein, Ralph C., 227n.
Equilibrium theory, 434
Equipment, industrial, 164, 192 (See also Tools)
financing of, 168–169
profits and, 86
Erie Canal, 167, 254
cost of, 240
Erie RR, cost of, 240
Ernle, Lord, 74n.–75
Essay on the Principle of Population, Malthus, 106
Essays on Political Economy, Carey, 160
Estates, American, 124, 127, 132
slaves on, 129–130
tenant-operated, 140–141
British, manors and, 25
Europe, 297, 409
agriculture in, 213, 353
banking in, 64
economic thought in, 47, 109–111, 416, 429, 431, 438, 440, 448

labor unionism in, 303
medieval, economic life in, 20–21
foreign trade in, 35–37
wages in, 306
Evans, Oliver, 216n., 227
"Ever-normal granary" plan, 360
Exchange agencies in medieval England, 33–34
Excise taxes, 341, 386, 396
Exploitation, in America, 119
of labor, 85, 97–98, 104, 106
Explorers, 117
Export industries, in America, 144–145
development of, 35–37, 44
Exporters, of goods, 147–148
of goods and slaves, 148–149
world markets and, 61
Exports, American, 119, 348, 354
English, 52, 69–70
Extension courses, 378

F

Fabricant, Solomon, 318n., 324n.
Factories, employment in, 113, 348 (See also Manufacturing)
first American, 239
small, 145
Factory conditions, American, 311
British, 86, 107–108, 113
Factory employees, group protective action by, 105 (See also Workers)
Factory-made goods, cheap, 169
Factory system, 47, 60
in America, 145–146, 213
founding of, 81
and industrial discipline, 85–86, 108
regulation and, 113
spread of, 166, 193, 400
Fair Labor Standards Act, 368
Fair trade laws, 373
Fairs, 33n.
and commercial credit, 63n.
expansion of, 48
medieval, function of, 34–35
length of, 35n
modern, agricultural, 378
industrial, 38–39
Falconer, J. I., 213n. 343n.
Fall River, Massachusetts, 312
Families, size of, 445
Family labor, 307, 322
Famine of 1846, 176n.
Faraday, Michael, 217
Farm Bloc, 360
Farm credit, 357
Farm debt, 357
Farm journals and magazines, 344
Farm leaders, 359
Farm loans, 357
Farm making, 136–137, 343
Farm mortgages, 282
Farm problem, 225, 334–335, 349
farmers and, 358–361
Farm produce (see Agricultural products)
Farm workers (see Agricultural workers)
Farmers:
American, 121, 124, 137, 221–222, 414
business motivation of, 334–335
decrease in, 322
and farm problem, 358–361
government help for, 377–378
and labor unions, 305
loans to, 380
migrant, 343
and national income, 334, 350–351, 425
political power of, 358
saving by, 270
technology and, 224–225
18th century English, 41–42
Farmers' Alliance, 359

Farmers' organizations, 358–359
Farmers' Union, 359
Farming (see Agriculture; headings under Agricultural)
Farms, American, 128
　frontier, 152
　general-purpose, 138–139
　limited-crop, 139–140
　price of, 356
　self-sufficient subsistence, 138
　size of, 224–225, 345, 354
　types of, 137–141
　in 18th century England, 41–42
Federal Farm Loan Act, 357
Federal Intermediate Credit Act, 357
Federal Reserve Act, 293, 357
Federal Reserve banks, 293, 295
Federal Reserve Board, 293–295
Federal Reserve notes, 293
Federal Reserve System, 296 394
　changes in, 294–295
　founding of, 292–293
Federal Trade Commission, 258n., 372
Federalism, 363, 373
Federalist papers, 156n.
Federation of Organized Trades and Labor Unions, 319
Female labor, 45, 47, 105, 322, 367, 410–411
Ferrous metallurgy (see Metallurgy)
Fertilizer, use of, 344, 353
Fetter, Frank, 438
Feudalism, 40
　in America, 131–133
Fforde, J. S., 294n.
Financial managers, 266
Financiers, 166, 266
Financing, basic principles of, 57
Fine, Sidney, 432n.
Fish, Carl Russell, 417n.
Fisher, Irving, 438
Fite, E. D., 398n.
Flagler, Henry M., 254
Flanders, 36
Flanders, Walter E., 230
Flood control, 381
Flour mills, 144, 146
Fly shuttle, 80, 82
Food, population and, 110
　price of, 109, 424–425
Food supply, agriculture and, 68–69
　population and, 107
Ford, Henry, 230, 251n., 261n., 333
　quoted, 242
Ford, James, 311
Ford Motor Company, 230–231
Fordney-McComber Act, 376
Foreign loans, 168n.
Foreign trade, 97 (See also Exports)
　in American colonial period, 147–148
　in England, in 18th century, 76–77
　expansion of, 35–37
　in medieval times, 35–37
　registered companies and, 51–53
　in 16th and 17th centuries, 48–49, 62
　Napoleonic Wars and, 108–109
Forestalling, 34
Forges, 144, 146, 215
France, 31n., 36, 216, 227–228, 354
　economic theory in, 99–100
　population density of, 336n.
　war casualties of, 412n.
Free choice of occupation, 102–104
Free trade, 102, 111, 160, 420, 426
　abandonment of, 113n.
　international, 110
　intervention and, 113–114
Free-trade movement, genesis of, 111–112
Freedom, business, 93–95
　religious, 120

Freehold land, 23n., 42, 136
Freeman, 22, 26
Freight rates, 254
French Canada, 162n., 177
Frick, Henry Clay, 248
Friendly Societies, 110
Fries, Adelaide L., 134
Fuel Administration, 406
Fullondidmen, 24
Fur companies, 144
Furniss, E. S., 98n.

G

Gallatin, Albert, 364n.
Gary, Elbert H., 251n.–252
Gasoline, synthetic, 404
　tax on, 386
Gasoline engines, 218, 224
Gates, Paul W., 173n.
Gay, E. F., 41n.
General Chamber of Manufacturers, 103
General Motors Corporation, 263–264n.
General stores, 150–151
Gentlemen's agreements, 243, 371
George, Henry, 427–428, 432
George III, 75n.
Georgia, 127–128, 139, 187
German settlers, 120, 129, 131, 134, 176–178, 340
Germany, 31n., 87n.–88, 216n., 354, 369, 412n., 424
Gilds (see Craft gilds)
Gilfillan, S. C., 208n., 219n.
Girdler, Tom, 333
Givens, Meredith, 87n.
Glasgow, 103
Glasgow University, 99
Godwin, William, 106n.
Gold, 277–278, 396
Gold Standard, 278, 287–288, 292
　breakdown of, 297–298
Goldsmith, Oliver, 72n.
Goldsmiths, banking and, 64–66n.
Gompers, Samuel, 319, 333
　quoted, 320
Goodrich, Carter, 191
Goods, creation of, 10
　intermediate, 10
　money and, 276
Gould, Jay, 315–316
Government, British:
　business and 97–99
　and capital accumulation, 270
　economic role of, 187
　economics and, 11–12
　and indentured servants, 122
　and protection of property, 137
　technology and, 226
　United States (see United States government)
Government assistance, 187, 191, 373
Government bonds, 271, 294, 296, 299
Government control of agriculture, 45–47
Government debts, 272n.
Government employment, 382
Government intervention, 156, 426–427, 430, 432–433, 438
　free trade and, 113–114
Government regulation, 426
　increase in, 365
　unions and, 320
Government responsibility, public improvements and, 184–186
Government securities, 278, 393 (See also Government bonds)
Grain, export of, 354
　import of, 108, 110
　raising of, 129, 150

Grand Coulee Dam, 381
Grange, the, 358
"Granger laws," 370
Gras, N. S. B., 23*n*., 147*n*., 251*n*.
Gray, Lewis Cecil, 127*n*., 345*n*.
Great Britain, agriculture in, 353 (*See also* England)
  hours of labor in, 311
  labor unionism in, 303
  loans to, 65
  population density of, 336*n*.
  war casualties of, 412*n*.
Great Plains, drought in, 360
  settlement of, 342, 357
Greeley, Horace, 310*n*., 342, 344
Green, Constance M., 205*n*.
Greenback movement, 314, 359
Greenbacks, 287, 291, 358
Greenewalt, Crawford, 262*n*.
Gregory, Frances W., 246*n*.
Gresham's law, 277

H

Hamilton, Alexander, 156–157, 159, 204, 277, 427
  quoted, 201
Hammond, Bray, 281*n*.
Hancock, John, 237
Hancock, Thomas, 148*n*., 236–238
Handlin, Oscar, 175*n*., 187*n*., 234*n*., 240*n*.
Hanseatic League, 35, 52
Hansen, Alvin, 311, 313, 318
Hardy, Charles O., 294*n*.
Hargreaves, James, 80–82
Harkness, Stephen V., 254
Harrington, Virginia D., 236*n*.
Harris, Seymour E., 294*n*.
Hartz, Louis, 187*n*.
Hat Finishers' Union, 312
Hatch Act, 378
Hawley-Smoot Tariff, 376
Haymarket riot of 1886, 316
Hazard, Blanche E., 146*n*.
Head tax, 368
Headright system, 119, 124–125
Health and Morals Act of 1802, 105, 108, 113
Heath, Milton, 186*n*.–188
Heaton, Herbert, 58*n*., 76*n*.
Heckscher, Eli, 29*n*., 98*n*.
Hendrick, Burton, J., 246*n*.
  quoted, 216*n*.
Henry VII, 62*n*.
Hepburn, Alonzo B., 276*n*.
Hepburn Act, 370
Heriot, 27
Hibbard B. H., 337*n*.
Hidy, Muriel E., 252*n*.
Hidy, Ralph W., 252*n*., 285*n*.
Highs, Thomas, 82–83*n*
Highways, automobiles and, 233 (*See also* Roads)
Hill, Forrest G., 189*n*
Hitchman Coal Case, 325
Hoarding, 27
Hobson, C. K., 166*n*
Hobson, John A., 440
Hog raising, 138, 140, 348
Holding companies, 243–244, 260
Holland (*see* Netherlands)
Holstrom, J. Edwin, 180*n*.
Home, Francis, 75
"Home-market" proposal, 192
Home ownership, 445
Homestead, Pennsylvania, 325–326
Homestead Act, 177, 338–339
Hoover, Ethel D., 395*n*.
Hoover administration, 298
Horstead Manor, 42

Hours of labor, 31, 113, 303, 311–312, 314, 414
  maximum, 368
  reduction in, 319, 328, 415, 435
  self-imposed, 60
  for women, 367
Housing, 311
Howe, F. W., 210
Hoxie, Robert F., 304*n*.
Hudson's Bay Company, 56
Human wants, origin of, 8
  satisfaction of, 8–10, 12, 15–16, 48
Humanitarianism, 107, 112, 114
Hume, David, 99
Hunter, Robert, 317–318
  quoted, 318
Huntsman, Benjamin, 88–89
Hybrid seed corn, 353

I

Illinois, 343
Illinois Central Railroad, 173, 338
Illiteracy, decline in, 380
Immigrants, 164, 177, 193, 310–311*n*., 345
  and American character, 123
  fictitious lists of, 125
  literacy tests for, 368
Immigration, decrease in, 321
  land policies and, 340
  population and, 414
  poverty and, 318
  restriction of, 368–369
  wages and, 174, 178
  war and, 409–410
"Imperfect competition" theory, 442
Implements, 27
Importers, of goods, 147–148
  of goods and slaves, 148–149
Imports, 171
  cheap, 158
  forbidding of, 36
  grain, 108, 110
Incentive, self-interest and, 100
Income, cash, 138
  distribution of, wars and, 396–397
  farm, 397
  of industrial workers, 351
  under manorial system, 27
  national (*see* National income)
  in 19th century, 423
  per capita, 417
  prices and, 9, 109
  profit and, 101–102
  saving and investment of (*see* Saving)
  in 20th century, 435, 445
Income taxes, 386, 396
Indentured servants, 121–123, 130–131, 137
Indentures, 121
  voluntary signing of, 123
Indians, 118, 130, 132, 389
Indigo, raising of, 128, 140, 146
Individual proprietorship (*see* Sole proprietorship)
Individualism, American, 134
Industrial leaders, American (*See also* Businessmen, "heroic"):
  British, 69, 114
Industrial methods, 86, 108
Industrial progress (*see* Technology)
Industrial Rayon Corporation, 259
Industrial relations, arbitration in, 326
Industrial Revolution, 21, 96
  commercial preparation for, 76–77
Industrial shares, 171
Industrial workers (*see* Workers)
Industrialists (*see* Businessmen)
Industrialization, 110, 155, 165–166, 354

Industries, agricultural market-town, 143–144
  export, 35–37, 44, 144–145
  nascent, protection of, 191
  plantation, 146
  regional oriented, 145–146
Industry, American, during Civil War, 398–400 (*See also* Business; Manufacturing)
  foreign investment in, 272
  heavy, 422–423
  in World War I, 400–402
  in World War II, 402–404
  iron and steel in, 86–87
  specialization in, 208
  technology and, 202
  terrorism in, 81, 104
Inflation, 276, 287, 295, 368, 417, 419, 448
  currency, 279, 387
  price, 312, 387, 394–396, 412
Inheritance taxes, 384
Initiative, individual, 99–100, 264
Inland waterways, 382
Insecurity, economic, 323
Installment credit, 242, 436
Institutionalism, 438–443
Insull Utility Investments, Inc., 259–260
Insurance companies, 275, 286, 292, 357
  importance of, 300–301
  regulation of, 370
Intellectuals, 426, 432
Interest, 54, 63n.–64, 96–97
Interest rates, 66n., 165, 174, 271, 295
Interlopers, 54, 93
Interstate commerce, regulation of, 370
Interstate Commerce Commission, 370
Invention, 204–208
  age of, 78
  and cotton industry, 78–85
  education and, 218–220
  research and, 219–220n.
  synthetic nature of, 78–79, 207–208
Investment, 12–15
  in American colonies, 119, 152, 167–169
  international, 273
  under manorial system, 27
  in United States, 183, 186, 300
Investment bankers, 250–252, 285
Investment banking, after Civil War, 292
  before Civil War, 284–286
  since 1900, 298–300
Investment houses, 171, 183
Investors, British, 167–173, 179, 272
Iowa, 140, 343
Ireland, 175
Iron, age of, 215–216
  importance of in industry, 86–87
  new techniques for, 87–90
Iron industry, 161n., 202, 222, 244
"Iron law of wages," 419
Iron Molders' Union, 312
Irrigation projects, 381
Italian settlers, 177
Italy, 63n.

J

Jackson, Andrew, 277, 281
Jackson, Patrick Tracy, 238
Jacksonian Era, 417, 421
Japanese immigrants, 368
Jefferson, Thomas, 212, 342, 419n.
Jenks, Leland H., 166n., 178–180n.
Jerome, Chauncey, 209
Jewkes, John, 220n.
Johansson, Carl, 229
Johnson, Arthur H., 41n.

Johnson, E. A. J., 81n., 98n.–99n., 120n. 133n., 135n.
Joint-stock banking, English, 66n.
Joint-stock companies, 101, 172n.
  in America, 118–120, 124, 141
  early uses of, 55–57
  first, 56
  origins of, 54–55
Jones, Captain Billy, 216n., 248
Jones, Thomas, 248
Josephson, Mathew, 246n.
Joslyn, C. S., 246n.
Journeymen, 30–31, 49
Journeymen gilds, 49
Justices of the peace, 46–47, 109

K

Kansas, 343
Kautsky, Karl, 169n.
Kay, John, 80–81
Kemmerer, E. W., 438
Kendrick, John W., 351
Kentucky, 188n.
Kerfoot, J. B., 142n.
Kettering, Charles, 218n.
Keynes, John Maynard, 434, 443–444
Keynesian economics, 441, 443–444, 449
Kidnapping of emigrants, 121–122
King, Gregory, 40n.
Knight, E. C., Case, 372n.
Knights of St. Crispin, 313, 315
"Know-Nothing Party," 310
Knowledge, production and, 10–11
Krooss, Herman E., 294n., 394n.
Kuczinsky, Jurgen, 311, 313, 318, 324
Kuznets, Simon S., 215n., 269

L

Labor, agricultural (*see also* Agricultural labor; Workers)
  attitudes and problems in before 1840, 306–307
  and capital, 100, 174–175
  cheap, 45, 106, 108
  child (*see* Child labor)
  division of, 156–157
  exploitation of, 104–106
  female (*see* Female labor)
  free, 118, 131
  government regulation of, 365–373
  improved conditions of, 313–314
  industrial, 155–156
  male, 45, 59, 105
  manual, 129
  market forces and migration of, 177–178
  mobility of, 84, 123, 162
  scarcity of, 25, 155–156, 302, 321, 409–412
  supply of (*see* Labor supply)
  unskilled, 308
Labor contracts, 368
Labor force, agriculture and, 350
  changes in composition of, 321–323
  population and, 411
Labor legislation, 330, 442
  beginning of, 107–108
  Federal, 367–369
  need for, 105–106
  state, 367
Labor-management relations, 332
Labor organizations, first, 307–310
  formation and development of, 302–333
Labor party, first, 309
Labor services, 26–27, 29, 40
Labor supply, in the colonies, 119–120
  factories and, 86
  in United States, 162, 302–303, 337, 345, 367–369, 409–412

Labor unions, 422
  early, 307–310, 312–314
  farmers and, 305
  government and, 330, 368–369
  illegality of, 308, 367
  opposition to, 326
  power of, 332, 447
  public opinion and, 308, 330, 367
Laboring class, 303
Laissez-faire, 187–188, 372, 376, 382
  doctrine of, 104, 108, 113, 292, 341, 364, 373–374, 419–421, 425–426, 433, 441
  revolt against, 429–430, 432, 437, 449
Land, in America, and economic development, 335–336
  farm, prices of, 356
  free, 124, 337
  government policy for, 337–341, 379
  speculation in, 335
  "waste," 344
  in England, enclosure of, 41, 70–73, 106
  ownership of, 22–24
  in 1700, 40, 45
  as sole source of wealth, 100
Land auctions, 337
Land booms, 168
Land companies, 173, 240
Land grants, 187
  canal and railway, 172–173, 338, 340–341
  to colleges, 338, 378
  colonial, 120, 124, 136
  to states, 338–339
Land Reform Movement, 310
Land theory of property, 136–137
Landholders, English, 23–24, 40–41, 45, 61, 71–73
Landholdings, in America, 124
  in England, 40–42, 71
  assignment of, 26
Landlords, American, and national income, 427
  English, 41, 70, 110–111
  absentee, 175
Larkin, Paschal, 136n.
Larson, Henrietta M., 251n.
Late-medieval times, 20–37
Lathes, 210
Latimer, Bishop, 41n.
Latin America, 167, 273
Law Merchant, 35
Laws, in colonies, 137 (*See also* legislation)
  under manorial system, 26
Lawyers, importance of, 137
League for Industrial Rights, 326
Leaseholding, 40, 42
Lebergott, Stanley, 319, 324
Lees, John, 83n.
Legislation, anti-trust, 372
  and the economy, 101
  factory, 108
  fair-trade, 373
  labor (*see* Labor legislation)
  minimum-wage, 367
  protective (*see* Protective tariff)
  restricting immigration, 368–369
Leisure, 322, 329, 415
Leland, Henry M., 211, 229
Lend-Lease, 273
Lenoir, 227
Levant Company, 52
Lewis Cleona, 271n.
Lewis, John L., 330
Liberty Bonds, 299
Life, protection of, 365–366
Life span, average, in 19th century, 311n.
Limited liability, 57
Lipson, E., 32n., 44n., 49n., 53n., 57n.–58n.
List, Friedrich, 427

Literacy tests for immigrants, 368
Livery companies, 50–51
Livestock industry, 150 (*See also* Cattle; Hogs)
Living conditions, 303, 311–312
Loans, 63, 183
  commercial, 296
  to farmers, 280, 357
  foreign, 168n.
  to government, 109, 168
  interest on, 54
  real-estate, 289–290, 296
Local government, 187–188, 190, 370
  activities of, 364, 382
  expenditures of, 385
  taxes of, 384, 386
Locke, John, 136
Lockouts, 314
London, 36, 40n., 49n.–50, 166, 285, 297
Lords, late-medieval, 22–23, 26–27
Lorwin, Lewis L., 319n.
Louisiana, 140, 167, 190
Low Countries, 63n.
Lowell, Francis Cabot, 204, 238
Lowell, Massachusetts, 311
Lumber mills, 144
Luxemburg, Rosa, 169n.
Luxury goods, 48

M

McCormick, Cyrus, 209, 214, 242
McDougall, William, 428
McFadden Branch Banking Act, 296
Machine parts, interchangeable, 205–208, 229
Machine tools, 203, 205–212, 222
Machinery, 68–69, 157, 200–201
  agricultural (*see* Agricultural machinery)
  and business enterprises, 225–226
  iron and steel for, 89
  opposition to, 105
  textile, 79–85, 104–105
McKinley, William, 288
McKinley Act, 375
McNary-Haugen bills, 359
Maine, 138
Malthus, Thomas, 106–107
Management, 86, 145, 190
  capital contribution and, 55
  professional, 260–261, 264, 267, 446
  scientific, 220–221, 231
Manchester, England, 107
Manchester Act, 83
Manhattan Project, 404
Mann-Elkins Act, 370
Manorial system, 24–25, 38
  in America, 136
Manors, 22, 25, 27, 42
Manpower (*see* Labor; Workers)
Mantoux, 82n., 85n., 88n., 91n.
  quoted, 71–72, 84n., 108
Manual labor, 129
Manufacturers, 103
  American, 203–233
  British, 155, 165–166, 203–204
  free trade and, 160
  industrial fairs and, 38–39
  taxes and, 110–111
Manufacturing, in America, 145, 155n.–156, 160–161, 267, 414 (*See also* Business enterprises; Industry)
  technology and, 202–233
  in eighteenth century England, 43–45, 47–48
Marginal efficiency of capital, theory of, 444
Marginal utility, 429
Maritime Commission, 376n.

Market forces, 161–162, 165, 430
  agriculture and, 358
  capital movements and. 171, 174–175
  and labor migration, 177–178
  public policy and, 194–196
Marketing, of farm produce, 43–44
  mass, 193
  of wool, 43–44
Marketing associations, 359
Markets, American, agricultural, 213, 347
    expansion of, 112, 422
    free trade and, 111
    transportation and, 39, 145–146, 168, 213, 417
  domestic, 61, 95, 111, 155
  English, 12, 32–34, 39, 48–49
    late-medieval, 28
    role of, 11
  expansion of, 47–49, 97
  foreign, 155
  for luxuries, 142
  world, 61, 95, 97, 108
Marshall, Alfred, 433, 443
  synthesis of, 433–434, 448
Martin brothers, 216
Marx, Karl, 86, 169n., 342, 426
Marxism, 329, 387
Maryland, 123, 125n.–126, 128–129, 132, 139–140, 150
Mass production, 69, 201, 205–206, 209, 211–212, 238, 241, 422–423
  in automobile industry, 228, 230–231
  war and, 400
Massachusetts, 130, 142, 149, 187, 239, 367, 370
Massachusetts Bay Company, 119n., 134
Massachusetts Institute of Technology, 219
Master craftsmen, 30–32, 142
Materialism in America, 123
Maundsley, Henry, 89, 208
Maurer, Herryman, 262n.
Means, scarcity of, 8–9
  ways of increasing, 9–11
Meat products, 348, 399
Mechanics' Union of Trade Associations, 308
Mechanization, 215
  of agriculture, 221, 224–225
Medical care, 311
Mercantile agencies, spread of, 95
Mercantilism, 97–99, 135, 373
Merchant Adventurers Company, 52–53
Merchant bankers, 171
Merchant class, emergence of, 147n.
Merchant gilds, 54
Merchant marine, government support of, 376–377
Merchants, 111, 147–148, 236
Merchet, 27
Mergers, 244, 258–259 (See also Monopoly; Trusts)
Metal industry, 69, 103
Metallurgy, 87–90, 215–216, 218
Metals, 42, 62, 117, 163
Mexican War, 190, 209
Michigan, 314, 377
Middle class, growth of, 424, 435–436, 445
Middle West, 184n., 214
  markets in, 168
  unions in, 326
Mill, John Stuart, 425
Miller, William, 235n., 246n.
Milles, Carl, 176n.
Mills, Frederick C., 324
Minerals, 117, 163, 207, 380
Minimum-wage legislation, 368
  state, 367
Mining, 240n.
Mining stocks, 171
Mirsky, Jeannette, 205n.
Missouri, 187

Mitchell, Broadus, 156n.
Mitchell, Wesley C., 439–440, 442
Money, 39, 98, 274
  before Civil War, 276–279
  "easy," 275–276, 287
  goods and, 276
  hard, 287, 309
  and human wants, 8
  metallic, demand for, 97
  "sound," 275–276
  trade and, 29
  in wartime, 394–396
Money deposits, 63, 394
Money expansion, wars and, 394–396
Money making, 97
Money markets, 166, 285, 297
  central banking and, 281
  international, 272
  specialized, 279
Money supply, 287–288, 290–291, 298
  1790–1858, table, 278
  1860–1914, table, 291
  1915–1959, table, 297
  war and, 395
Money system inadequate, 237–238
Money wages, 39, 48
"Monopolistic competition" theory, 442
Monopoly, 93, 281, 309, 371–373, 432
  by crafts, 142
  of home markets, 98
  in medieval times, 32
  in 19th century, 243–244
Moody, Paul, 204
Moravians, 120, 133–134
More, Sir Thomas, 41n.
Morgan, J. P. and Co., 272, 299
Morgan, J. Pierpont, 251
Morgan, Peabody and Company, 285
Morrill Act, 219, 338, 341, 378
Morris, Lloyd, 227n.
Morris, Richard B., 121n.–122n., 125n.–126n., 130n., 142n.
Mortgages, farm, 282, 357
Motor vehicle taxes, 386
Moulton, Harold G., 311, 313, 318, 324
Municipal institutions, collective, 134
Municipalities, authority of, 32 (See also Cities)
Munitions, 399–401 (See also Arms)
Mutual aid organizations, 110n.
Myers, Margaret, 286n.

N

Napoleonic Wars, economic consequences of, 108–109, 158
  and economic thought, 109–111
Nasmyth, James, 211
Nassau Senior, 268
National Academy of Sciences, 219
National Association of Manufacturers (NAM), 326
National Bank Act, 289
National Banking System, 289–291, 395
National banks, 357
National Civic Federation, 326
National defense, 365–366, 386, 409
National Erectors' Association, 326
National Founders' Association, 326
National income, 183, 306, 328n., 383, 449
  capital formation and, 269
  corporate business and, 240n.
  farm and non-farm, table, 351
  farmer's share of, 334, 350–351, 425, 446
  landlords and, 427
  saving and, 393
National Industrial Recovery Act, 330, 368, 372, 442
National Labor Relations Act (Wagner Act), 330

National Labor Union, 313–314
National Metal Trades Association, 326
National security, 366
National Trades' Union, 309
Nationalism, 375, 420
  economic ideas of, 97–99
Native American Party, 310
Natural resources, 14–15, 17
  of United States, 155, 162–164, 344, 412
Nebraska, 343, 372
Negro slaves, 127–131, 345–347
  cost of, 140, 346
  freed, 130
  ownership of, 127n., 345
Negro slavery, 96–97, 107, 118, 127–131, 140–141, 345–347
  abolition of, 141
  land holding and, 132
  protests against, 129, 131
Netherlands, the, 14, 43, 63, 166–167
  population density of, 336n.
Neu, Irene D., 246n.
Nevins, Allen, 205n., 227n., 249n., 252n.
New Deal, 294, 330, 349, 360, 368, 372, 376
New England, 122n., 130, 134, 139, 149, 159–160, 162n., 184n., 203–204, 216, 239, 346
New Hampshire, 138, 367
New Holland, 118
New Jersey, 139–140, 244
New products, development of, 17
New York Central, 240, 262n.
New York City, 130, 140n., 142, 292–293, 307, 309–310, 322, 428
New York State, 129–130, 136, 138, 140, 156n., 167–168, 372, 380
New York Stock Exchange, 260, 285–286, 292
New York Sun, 316
New York Tribune, 344
Newbold, Charles, 212, 214
Newcomen, Thomas, 90–91
Newcomer, Mabel, 246n., 265n.
Nobility, 75, 132
Noble Order of the Knights of Labor, 315–317
Norfolk, England, 42
Norris-La Guardia Act, 330
North, the, 377, 345–346, 398, 402, 409
North, Douglass C., 170n.
North, Simeon, 208–209
North Carolina, 120, 132, 134, 139, 188n.
Norwich, England, 49n.
Nutting, Wallace, 142n.

O

Occupation, free choice of, 102–104
Office for Emergency Management (O.E.M.), 407
Office of Price Administration (O.P.A.), 408
Office of Price Administration and Civilian Supply (O.P.A.C.S.), 407–308
Office of Production Management (O.P.M.), 407–408
Office of War Mobilization, 408
Oglethorpe, James, 119n.–120, 126–127
Ohio, 168, 343, 372
Okington, England, 22–25, 28n.
Olds, Ransom E., 228–229
Oliver, James, 214
Onions, Peter, 88
Open-book accounts, 63
Oregon, 140
Ornstein, Martha, 81n.
Output (see Production)
"Overpopulated" areas, 162
Overproduction, 352–353, 437
Owen, Robert, 107
Ownership, control and, 261, 263

P

Packard car, 231
Packing plants, 144, 146
Panics, 279, 286, 293, 340
Panhard Company, 228
Paper money, 278, 394
Parliament, 46, 70–71, 105, 109–111, 126
  and factory conditions, 107–108
  and free trade, 103
  land confiscation by, 42n.
Parry, D. M., 326
Partnerships, medieval, 54–55
Patents, 82, 93, 219, 399, 401, 404
Paternalism, 102, 235, 241
Paterson, William, 66
Patrons of Husbandry (Grange), 358
Patten, Simon N., 431
Paul, Lewis, 80n., 82
Pauper children as apprentices, 60, 105
Pauperism, 106, 113 (See also Poverty)
Payne-Aldrich Tariff, 375
Peasants, English, 23, 41–42, 48, 136
Peel, Sir Robert, 103, 113
Penn, William, 119n., 129n.
Pennsylvania, 120, 123, 126, 129, 134, 136, 139, 145, 187, 308, 380, 399
Pennsylvania Railroad, 247
Pensions, 328, 379, 386, 477
Percival, Dr., 107
Perlman, Selig, 303, 317n.
Philadelphia, 129, 140n., 142, 150, 306–307, 309, 315
Philadelphia Society for the Promotion of National Industry, 160
Phillips, U. B., 161n.
Phipps, Henry, 248
Physiocrats, 419
Piece-work, 58
Piepowder Courts, 35
Pig iron, 88–89, 399
Pirenne, quoted, 32
Pitt, William, quoted, 103
Plantation system, 127, 140–141, 146, 155n., 161, 417
Plows, 57, 212, 214
Plymouth, Massachusetts, 120
Plymouth Plantation, 118, 133
Political economy, 96, 160
Political Economy, Walker, 431
Politics, economics and, 11–12, 28
  labor and, 309–310
  unions and, 333
Poole, Kenyon, 387n.
Pools, 243, 371
Poor, the, American attitude toward, 318, 329
  in wartime, 397
Poor laws, English, 101, 106, 112
Poor relief, 24, 105–106, 112
Population, English, commercial changes and, 68
  in 18th century, 70, 112n.
  in late-medieval times, 21
  before 1700, 42, 46–47
  food and, 160
  Malthus' theory of, 106–107
  United States, 163, 193, 321, 335–336, 341, 414, 423, 445
    decline in, 434
    density of, 336n., 345
    flow of, 342
    in 1800, 202
    rural, 342, 350–352, 356, 434
    in 1790, 155n.
    slave, 129–130
    urban, 311
    war and, 409–412
Populist Party, 359
Pound, Arthur, 227n.

Poverty, American attitude toward, 318, 329
  necessity of, 98
  population and, 107, 432
  progress and, 427
  rural, 59
Powderley, Terence V., 315
Powell, John Wesley, quoted, 381
Power, for machinery, 82, 91–92
  revolution in use of, 216–218
  in 20th century, 221–222
Power, E., 44n.
Precariae, 26
Preemption Act of 1841, 338n.
Price competition, 242–243, 267
Price controls, 406, 408
Prices, agricultural, 42, 159, 354–356, 358–361
  cost and, 359
  fair, 252
  fixed, 243, 373
  food, 109, 424–425
  income and, 9
  just, theory of, 33–34, 96, 133, 135, 252
  protection and (*see* Protective tariff)
  rise in, 109, 288
  slashing of, 249
  theories of, 442–443
  wars and, 395, 401
Primm, James Neal, 187n.
Priorities, wartime, 407–408
Prisoners, British, deportation of, 126
Private property, in America, 134–137
  land as, 40
Privateering, 63, 76
Production, 10–15, 69
  agricultural (*see* Agricultural production)
  capital and, 100
  in late-medieval times, 21, 28
  mass (*see* Mass production)
  and Napoleonic Wars, 108
  United States, 3–4, 6–7, 162, 421
    economic progress and, 274
    emphasis on, 241
    improved technique and, 436
    national, 97, 162–163
    prices and, 135
    profits and, 358
    wartime, 395, 399, 402–404
Productivity, 306, 414
  farm, 351, 353
  in the 1950's, 445
  per capita, 141, 163–164, 412, 435
  "specific," theory of, 431
  technology and, 223, 436
  in the 'Twenties, 324
Profit, 18, 55, 114, 183
  incentive and, 264
  income and, 101–102
  production and, 359
  tariffs and, 112
  technology and, 93, 95
  wars and, 397
Progress, definition of, 14
  economic (*see* Economic progress)
  poverty and, 427
  scientific (*see* Technology)
Progress and Poverty, George, 428
Progressive Era, 379–380, 437
Progressive movement, 364
Promoters, 121, 169, 172, 251
Property, 137
  common ownership of, 133–134
  concepts of, 29, 96–97, 136–137
  private (*see* Private property)
  protection of, 137, 365–366
Property taxes, 384, 386
Proprietors, 119–120, 124, 132–133 (*See also* Sole proprietorship)

Prosperity, 154, 160, 170, 276, 341–343, 415
  agricultural, 109, 124, 157, 336n., 348, 375
  bank notes and, 293
  economic, statesmanship and, 98
  and government services, 387
  unionism and, 324
  wages and, 325
  war and, 312
Protective tariffs, 166
  American, 111, 157–159, 191, 374–376, 418, 421
  reduction of, 112
Psychology, 428–429
Public domain, 190–191, 337
Public health, 366
Public improvements, 171, 184–186
Public opinion, 441
  agrarian change and, 41
  and big business, 257, 371–372
  economic literature and, 99
  and government assistance, 374
  and unionism, 308, 330, 367
Public ownership of utilities, 190
Public relations, 442
Public utilities, 190, 260
Public Utility Holding Company Act, 260
Puerto Rico, 410
Pullman Co. strike, 325
Puritans, 118, 120, 131, 134–135
Putting-out system, 59–61
  in America, 145–146

Q

Quakers, 126, 129–131, 134
Quantity theory of money, 286, 298, 358
Quesnay, François, 99
Quit rents, 133
Quotas, agricultural, 360
  for immigrants, 368
  production, 372

R

Radicalism, 329
Rae, John B., 173n.
Railroad brotherhoods, 320
Railroad strikes of 1877, 316
Railroads, 172, 180–181, 254, 299, 382
  building of, 168–170, 182–184, 336, 399
  cost of, 240
  and growth of cities, 182
  importance of, 178–180, 194
  rates of, 370
  regulation of, 370
  southern, 188–190
  tax-exemption of, 174
Railroad commissions, state, 370
Railway grants, 173, 188, 338–341
Railway securities, 170, 183, 188, 385
Rationalism, 112, 114
Raw materials, 10, 36, 147, 160, 193
Raymond, Daniel, 427
Real-estate loans, 289–290, 296
Real wages, 310, 323, 328, 415, 424–425
  1801–1816, table, 311
  1860–1890, table, 313
  1890–1920, table, 318
  1920–1929, table, 324
  war and, 397
Recessions, 249 (*See also* Depressions)
Reciprocal trade agreements, 376
Rediscount rate, 295
Regrating, 34
Regulated companies, 51–53, 56
Religious gilds, 54
Religious groups, settlement by, 119–120, 134
Rensselaer Polytechnic Institute, 219

Rent, 299, 419, 427–428
  in England, 24–26, 40
Report on Manufactures, Hamilton, 156–157, 159, 204
Research, 219–220*n.*, 232, 264*n.*
  agricultural, 352, 378
Retailers, 150–151, 193
Retirement, voluntary, 322
Revolutionary War, 379, 406
Rezneck, Samuel, 203*n.*
Rhode Island, 130, 145, 149
Ricardian economy 418–420, 426
Ricardo, David, 110, 418–420, 427, 443
Rice, growing of, 128, 140, 146
Richards, R. D., 65*n.*
Rights-of-way, railway, 188–189
Riis, Jacob, 318
Risk taking, 123, 147–148
Road building, 191, 240, 417 (*See also* Highways)
Robbins, Roy, 337*n.*
Rockefeller, John D., 244, 251*n.*–257
Rockefeller family, 261*n.*
Roe, Joseph W., 205*n.*
Roebuck, John, 88
Rogers, James E. Thorold, 172*n.*
  quoted, 46
Rogin, Leo, 213*n.*
Roll, Eric, 84*n.*, 89*n.*–92*n.*
Roosevelt, Franklin D., 330, 350
Roosevelt, Theodore, 339, 380
Roosevelt (F.D.) administration, 298
Root, Elisha K., 210
Rossiter, W. S., 129*n.*
Rowland, E. P., 74*n.*
Royalty, 54*n.*, 75
Rubber, synthetic, 404

S

Sabotage, 81, 104
St. Thomas Aquinas, 33
Salesmen, 266
Salesmanship, 436
Salzman, L. F., 33*n.*
  quoted, 31, 34
Sanitary conditions, 107, 311
Savery, Thomas, 90
Saving, 12–15, 135, 165, 192, 317, 447
  domestic, 272–273
  earnings and, 270
  individual, 270
  investment and, 57, 152, 171, 183, 300
  under manorial system, 27
  national income and, 393
  utilization of, 274
Savings banks, 275, 286
Sawers, David, 220*n.*
Sawyer, John E., quoted, 211–212
Say, J. B., 418–419
Schlesinger, Arthur M., 281*n.*
Schofield brothers, 204
Schools, free, 380
Schumpeter, Joseph A, quoted, 265
Schwab, Charles M., 248
  quoted, 249*n.*
Science, 81
  and business enterprise, 92–93
  and technology, 90–92
Scientific management, 220–221, 231
Scott, Thomas, 247
Scott, W. R., 54*n.*, 103*n.*
Secret societies, 110, 315
Secular stagnation, theory of, 444
Securities, canal, 170
  government, 172, 299
  investment in, 167, 271
  railroad, 170, 183, 188

Security, 123, 224, 327, 336, 447
Self-interest, 100–102
Sellers, William, 210
Seltzer, Lawrence H., 227*n.*
Separatists, 120
Service industries, growth of, 414, 436–437
Servitude (*see* Slavery)
Settlement, basic problems of, 118–119
  group, 119–120
  by headright system, 119 124–125
  and indentured servants, 119, 121–124
  land policy and, 338–339
  and Negro slavery, 119, 127–131
  and transportation of criminals, 119, 125–126
Shannon, Fred A., 345*n.*
Sheep raising, 41, 46, 70
Sheffield, Lord, 200–201
Shelburne Museum, Vermont, 151*n.*
Sherman Act, 258, 372
Sherman Silver Purchase Act, 288, 291
Shipping, 76, 111, 191
Siemers, William, 216
Silver, 277–278, 287–288
  free, 288, 358–359
Single tax theory, 427–428, 432
Slater, Samuel, 204
Slave trade, 124*n.*, 128, 140, 148–149
Slavery:
  Indian, 130
  industrial, 105
  Negro (*see* Negro slavery)
  temporary, 118
  wage-, 86
Slaves, 21–22, 40–41, 76–77
  Negro (*see* Negro slaves)
Sloan, Alfred P., 265*n.*
Slums, 311, 425
Smeaton, John, 89, 208
Smith, Abbot Emerson, 121*n.*
Smith, Adam, 99–104, 156, 418
Smith, Walter Buckingham, 281*n.*
Smith-Lever Act, 378
Smithfield market, 74
Social capital, 117, 152, 164–165, 185, 189, 194, 341
Social reform, 432–433
Social responsibility, 135*n.*
Social scientists, 441
Social security system, 367, 386, 447
Social Statics, Spencer, 426
Social welfare, government and, 379–380, 385–386
Social workers, 318, 432
Socialism, 108, 430
Societas, 54–56
Society, 11–12
  primitive, 100
  protection of, 114*n.*
Sociology, 429
Soener, Christopher, 210
Soil, 42
  conservation of, 344, 381
  exhaustion of, 336
"Soil-bank plan," 361
Soil Conservation Act, 360
Sole proprietorship, 57–58, 239, 261, 276, 414
Sorensen, Charles, 230*n.*
South, the, 170, 184*n.*
  agriculture in, 127*n.*, 345–347
  plantation system in, 127, 140–141, 146, 155*n.*, 161, 417
  schools in, 380
  and tariffs, 158, 337, 375
  and unions, 333
South Carolina, 129, 132
South Kingston, Rhode Island, 130
Soviet Russia, 411*n.*–412*n.*
Spain, 87*n.*

Spanish-American War, 321, 392
Spanish navy, 132
Spanish treasure, 62–63
Specie, 277, 280, 291
"Specific productivity" theory, 431
Speculation, 172–773, 194, 251
    land, 125, 335, 339–340, 427–428
Spence, Clark G., 172n.
Spencer, Herbert, 426
Spinning machinery, 80–82
Standard of living, economic progress and, 15
    in United States, 4–5, 234, 273, 276, 314, 319,
        342, 412, 435, 445–446
Standard Oil Company, 243, 252, 255–258, 260–
        261n.
Standard Oil Trust, 255, 371–372
Standardization, 399
State banks, 290, 357
    failure of, 279–280, 282
    notes of, 281, 287, 289, 395
State government, 187–188, 190, 370, 373
    activities of, 364–365, 367, 382
    and conservation, 380
    and education, 380
    expenditures of, 385
    taxes of, 384
States, land grants to, 338–339
Status, 30, 303, 317
Statute of Apprentices, 46, 50, 60, 101, 104
Statute of Laborers, 46
Steam engines, 89–92, 216
Steam power, 91–92, 146n., 216
Steam turbines, 217
Steel, 222, 249, 401
    age of, 215–216, 422
    importance of, 86–87
    new techniques for, 88–90
    for plows, 214
Steel industry, 241, 244, 423–424
Stevenson, Elizabeth, quoted, 364n.
Steward, Ira, 314
Stewart, Irwin, 404n.
Stewart, Col. Robert, 261n.
Stigler, George, 436n.
Stillerman, Richard, 220n.
Stock, common, 259–260
    preferred, 259
Stock exchanges, 183, 285, 299
Stockholders, 243, 262, 266
Stocking, George, 264n.
Stone, H. D., 210
Strasser, Adolph, 319
    quoted, 320
Strassman, W. Paul, 199n.
Strikes, 308, 315–316, 325–326, 332
Studenski, Paul, 294n., 394n.
Subsidies, government, 98, 187, 418
    agricultural, 360
    education, 219
    mail, 376
    shipping, 191, 376–377
Success, American dream of, 417
Sugar, 128
Sugar Trust, 371
Sumner, William Graham, 430
Supply, 9
    and demand, 11–12, 358, 360
Supply Priorities and Allocations Board
        (S.P.A.B.), 407–408
Surpluses, 274
    agricultural, 378
    United States Treasury, 396
Sweden, 87n.–88, 176
Swedish settlers, 177
Swindlers, 171
Sylvis, William H., 313, 333
Synthetics, war and, 404

T

Taft, Philip, 319n.
Taft, William Howard, 380
Taft-Hartley Act, 332
Tallage, 27
Tappan's, Lewis, Mercantile Agency, 284
"Tariff of Abominations," 160–161, 421
Tariff Act of 1816, 158–159
Tariff legislation, 101
Tariff propaganda, 160
Tariffs, 97, 297, 337, 374, 386
    protective (see Protective tariffs)
    reciprocal, 375
    remission of, 188
Tauber, Conrad and Irene B., 176n.
Taussig, F. W., 84n., 158n., 161n., 246n., 438
Tawney, R. H., 41n., 136n.
Tax exemptions, 187–188, 373
    of railways, 174
Taxation, 384–385
    abolishing of, 428
    and costs of war, 394
    progressive, 300, 387
    regressive, 341, 385
Taxes, automobile, 233
    Federal, 384–385
    poor relief and, 112
    reduction of, 387
    single, 427–428
    state and local, 384
    war, 111, 287, 393–396, 408
Taylor, Frederick W., 210
Technology, 32, 222–224
    agricultural, 212–214, 224–225
    beginning of, 68–94
    and business enterprise, 225–226
    definition of, 10
    and economic development, 14, 16–18
    and government, 226
    improvement and extension of, 199–233
    and industrial methods, 108, 157, 192
    science and, 90–91
    and trade, 69–70
    war and, 397–398, 402–404, 412
Teilhac, Ernest, 419n.
Tenant-operated farms, 40, 140
Tenants, 22–25, 41
    rights of, 26n.
Tennessee Valley Project, 382
Texas, 140
Textile industry, 68–69, 239, 241
    Belgian, 104n.
    labor for, 162n., 307, 311
    machinery and, 79–85, 104, 203–204
    pioneers in, 203–205
Thompson, Edgar, 247
Thrift, 100–101, 269
Thrupp, Sylvia, 51n.
Timber, 336, 380
Timber Culture Act, 338
Timber and Stone Act 338
Tobacco, 128, 139–140, 146, 348
Tobacco brokerage firms, 150
Tonnage duties, 377
"Tooling up," 207
Tools, 10–11, 164, 192, 203, 209–212
    machine (see Machine tools)
    in manorial system, 27
    ownership of, 39, 58, 82
Totalitarian nations, 165
Towns, in Colonial Period, 139
    late-medieval, 28–34
Townshend, Viscount Charles, 74
Trade, English, expansion of, 51
    foreign (see Foreign trade)
    late-medieval, 28–29
    restraints of, 372
    technology and, 69–70

Trade associations, 243
Trade unions, 103–104, 114, 308 (*See also* Labor unions)
  membership in, 1940, 331
  tactics of, 302–306
Trading companies, 76, 93
Transportation, 189, 201, 240n., 340, 417 (*See also* type of transportation, as Railroads)
  government assistance for, 373n.
  land values and, 185
  markets and, 39, 145–146, 168, 213, 417
Transportation Act, 372
Treaty of Utrecht, 77
Trevithick, Richard, 227
Truman, Harry S., 387n.
Trust companies, 275, 286, 292
Trusts, 243–244, 255–257, 371–372, 432
Tudor kings, 41, 46, 70
Tugwell, R. G., 427n.
Tull, Jethro, 73–74
Turgot, Anne Robert Jacques, 99
Turner, Frederick Jackson, quoted, 342
Typographical Union, 312

U

Ulman, Lloyd, 313n.
"Underdeveloped areas," 162, 166, 180
Underdeveloped countries, 13
"Underpopulated" areas, 162
Underwood Tariff, 375
Unearned increment, 427–428
Unemployment, 60, 310
  machines and, 85 104, 224
  war and, 398, 411
Unemployment insurance, 367
Union leaders, 330–332, 447
Unionism, business, 304
  after Civil War, 313–314
  before Civil War, 307–310, 312
  decline of in 'Twenties, 324–325
  depression of the 1930's and, 327–329
  growth of, 329–333, 447
  "political," 304
  politics and, 309–310, 333
  welfare, 304–305, 315–317, 422
Unions (*see* Labor unions; Trade unions)
United States, Colonial Period in, 5–6, 117–153
    (*See also* United States government)
  flow of capital to, 170–173
  industrial development in, 155
  manufacturing in, 241
  natural resources of, 155
  population of (*see* Population)
  responsibilties of, 3
  urbanization of, 170
  as world power, 364
United States Army, 366
United States Bank, 271, 280–282, 309, 420–421
United States Bureau of the Budget, 402n.
United States Congress, 287
  and fair trade laws, 372–373
  and shipping, 377
  tariff legislation by 158–160, 374–376
United States Constitution, 154
United States Department of Agriculture, 352, 378
United States Department of Labor, Bureau of Labor Statistics, 307n., 328
United States Employment Service, 410
United States Forest Service, 339, 380
United States government, 6–7, 205–207 (*See also* headings under Federal)
  and agricultural credit, 357
  borrowing by, 393–394
  debt of, 299, 408
  economic functions of, 362–388, 426
  economic planning by, 400–401, 403, 406–409, 441, 446
  and education, 219
  expenditures of, 383–388
    war and, 393–394, 396, 408
  and farm problem, 359–361
  fiscal policy of, 341, 384–385, 446
  foreign loans of, 273
  land policy of, 337–341, 379
  power of, 405, 414, 437–438
  revenue of, 341, 384
  role of, historical factors and, 362–365
United States Navy, 366
United States Navy Department, 407
United States Patent Office, 378
United States Steel Corporation, 252, 372
United States Supreme Court:
  and holding companies, 255
  and interstate commerce, 372
  and labor legislation, 367
  and trusts, 258, 260
  and unions, 325
United States Treasury, 272, 396
United States War Department, 407
UNRRA, 273
Unwin, George, 50n.
Usher, E. P., 78n.–79n, 90n., 92n.
Usury (*see* Interest)
Usury laws, repeal of, 64n.
Utopia, More, 41n.

V

Veblen, Thorstein, 439–440
Venetians, 53
Vermont, 138, 151n.
Veterans' benefits, 379, 386
Villages, farms and, 139
Villeins, 22–23, 25–27, 40–41
Vinci, Leonardo da, 227
Virgin Islands, 410
Virginia, 118, 123, 126, 128–129, 139, 141, 150
Virginia Company, 119n.–120

W

Wage earners, government protection of, 114
    (*see also* Workers)
  rural, 44–45
Wage and Hour Law, 368
Wage reduction, machinery and, 104
Wage system, growth of, 48
  influence of, 66
  in medieval England, 37
Wages, in automobile industry, 231
  economic thought on, 419
  factory system and, 86, 105, 213
  fair, 97, 133, 135
    definition of, 96n.
  farm, 44–45, 109
    regulation of, 46–47
  high, 102, 375
    idleness and, 98
  immigration and, 47, 174, 178
  low, 47, 102, 105, 107, 241, 306
  minimum, 368
  money, 328
  production and, 306
  prosperity and, 325
  real (*see* Real wages)
  theory of, 98
"Wages-fund" doctrine, 242, 303, 420, 425
Wagner Act, 330
Wales, 40, 48n., 70n., 112n.
Walker, Francis A., 431
Wallace's Farmer, 359n.
Walsh-Healy Act, 368
Walton, Francis, 402n.
Wants, changes in, 48

War, 4, 112 (*See also* names of wars, as Civil War)
  agricultural production and, 352, 392
  cost of, 392, 394
  economic effects of, 391–412
  government planning for, 405
  industrial progress and, 397–398, 412
  inflation and, 394–396
  mechanized, 397, 411
War casualties, 409–410, 412
War of 1812, 201, 204, 215, 238, 278, 280, 341, 379, 392
War Industries Board, 406
War Manpower Commission, 408
Ware, Caroline F., 307n.
Ware, N. W., quoted, 312
Warner, W. Lloyd, 246n.
Washington, George, 146, 342
Washington State, 140
Water power, 82, 92n., 207, 216–218
Watkins, Myron W., 244
Watt, James, 89–93, 103, 216n.
Wayland, Francis, 425
Wealth, accumulation of, 135 (*See also* Money)
  land as source of, 100
  redistribution of, 373–374, 396–397, 423, 445
Wealth of Nations, Smith, 99–104
Weaving, 59, 83–84
Webb, Sidney and Beatrice, 110n.
Webb-Pomerene Act, 372
Webster, Daniel, 420
Weir, Ernest, 333
"Welfare capitalism," 333
Welfare plans, 328
Welfare state, 432
Wells, Childe Harold, 230n.
West, the, 312, 342, 357
  development of, 283
  political power of, 194
  settlement of, 145, 163, 170, 186, 334–339, 341, 417
  size of farms in, 340
  tariffs and, 374
West Indies, 141, 147, 149
Western world, economic changes in, 20
Westinghouse, George, 217–218n.
Weston, Vermont, 151n.
Wheat, 348, 353–354, 423
Wheeler, John, 53n.
Whiskey Trust, 372
White population, slavery and, 129
Whitehead, Professor, quoted, 79
Whitney, Eli, 206–208, 210, 219n.
Whitney's cotton gin, 141, 146, 206
Whitworth, Sir Joseph, 212
Wholesalers, 149
Wilberforce, William, 107
Wilkinson, John, 89, 208
William III, 66
Wilson, Charles E., 265n.
Wilson, Woodrow, 367
Wisconsin, 367
Wives, abandoned, as indentured servants, 122
Wolcott, Mr., 207
Wolman, Leo, 321n.
Women, labor by (*see* Female labor)

Wood, Jethro, 214
Woodham-Smith, Cecil, 175n.
Wood-working machinery, 210
Wool, 36, 43–44
  wartime consumption of, 399
Wool buyers, 43–44
Wool manufacturers, 159–160
Woollen cloth, 159, 400
Woollen industry, 44–45, 47, 85
  in America, 161n.
  and individual proprietorship, 57–58
  protection and, 77–78
  putting-out system in, 59–61
  workers in, 79–80
Work, 135
  in late-medieval times, 23, 26–27
  physical, 9–10, 27
Work hours (*see* Hours of labor)
Workers, American, 302–303, 317–319, 322–324 (*See also* Labor)
  income of, 351
  European, 302–303
  farm (*see* Agricultural workers)
  importing of, 410
  industrial, money wages and, 109
  technological progress and, 222–224
Workers' associations, outlawing of, 109
Workhouses, 105–106
Working classes, 98
Working conditions, 113, 303, 367 (*See also* Factory conditions)
Workmanship, 31–32, 61
Workshops, 145
World leadership, United States and, 3, 364
World War I, 272, 294, 297–299, 321, 326, 352, 354, 356, 385, 402–403, 407, 410
  cost of, 392, 394
  government controls in, 405–406
  and income distribution, 396
  industry during, 400–402
  money incirculation in, 395
World War I, 272, 292, 297–299, 321, 326, 354, 356–357, 360–361, 368, 385
  cost of, 392, 394
  government planning during, 406–409
  income distribution during, 397, 445
  industrial progress during, 403–404
  manpower in, 410
  money expansion in, 395
Worsted industry, 44–45, 47, 58
  putting-out system in, 59–61
  workers in, 79–80
Wright, Chester W., 392n., 409n.
Wright brothers, 218n.
Wyatt, John, 80n., 82
Wylie, Irvin G., 246n.

Y

Yankee ingenuity, 204
Yarranton, Andrew, 99n.
Yeomen, 40, 72, 84n.
Young, Arthur, 74–75

Z

Zilson, Charles, 80n.